Hospitality and Catering GNVQ: Advanced Textbook

Hospitality and Catering GNVQ: Advanced Textbook

Series editor: Yvonne Johns

BUTTERWORTH
HEINEMANN

Butterworth-Heinemann Ltd
Linacre House, Jordan Hill, Oxford OX2 8DP

 A member of the Reed Elsevier plc group

OXFORD LONDON BOSTON
MUNICH NEW DELHI SINGAPORE SYDNEY
TOKYO TORONTO WELLINGTON

First published 1995
Reprinted 1995

British Library Cataloguing in Publication Data
Johns, Yvonne
    Hospitality and Catering GNVQ –
    Advanced Textbook –
    (Butterworth-Heinemann GNVQ Series)
    I. Title II. Rimington, Michael
    III. Series
    640.712

ISBN 0 7506 1943 0

Composition by Genesis Typesetting, Laser Quay, Rochester, Kent
Printed in Great Britain by Bath Press, Avon

CONTENTS

INTRODUCTION ix
LIST OF CONTRIBUTORS xi
ACKNOWLEDGEMENTS xiii

1 INVESTIGATE THE HOSPITALITY
AND CATERING INDUSTRY 1

Sectors and scale of the industry 1

What is hospitality and catering? –
The sectors of the industry – The
organizational structure of the
industry – The scale of the
hospitality and catering industry –
Commercial outlets – The catering
services industry – Sources of data –
Employment patterns – Career and
employment opportunities –
Management structure – Conclusion –
Test your knowledge

External factors affecting growth 23

External influences on the industry –
Effects of external influences –
Internal influences – Current trends
and their effects – Test your
knowledge

Evaluating the importance of
influences affecting the operation of
a hospitality and catering outlet 39

Types of organizations – Influences
affecting the operation of a
hospitality and catering outlet – The
Etrop Grange Hotel – The scale and
scope of the outlet – Current trends
and future prospects

Assessment 61

2 HUMAN RESOURCES 64

Teams and how they work in
hospitality and catering 64

The individual – Perception and
motivation – Communications –
Recruitment and appointment –
Teams – Conclusions – Assignment
2.1

Staff achievement and satisfaction 79

Job structure – Training – Incentives –
Staff satisfaction – Conclusions –
Assignment 2.2

Work standards and performance 87

Legislation – Workplace procedures –
Sources of information and advice –
Conclusions – Assignment 2.3 –
Further reading

3 PROVIDING CUSTOMER SERVICE
IN HOSPITALITY AND CATERING 100

Customers 100

External and internal customers – Age
groups of customers – Cultural
background of customers – Customers
with special needs – Special
requirements – Individuals or groups –
Market segmentation – Purpose of
customer service – Customer needs –
Customer expectations – Delivering
customer service – Customer
perceptions – Customers'
requirements – Influences on
customer behaviour – Telephone skills
– Active listening skills – Social skills –
Customers' well-being – Conclusions

Evaluating the operation of customer service   114

The need for a customer service policy – Constraints and limitations in providing customer service – Reasons for evaluating customer service – Standards – Customer service data – Operations of customer service – Quality – Measurement of customer service – Training and development needs

Provision of customer service   124

Customer services – Requirements of good customer service – Hygiene, health, safety and security requirements – Test your knowledge – Assignment – Further reading

4 FOOD PREPARATION AND COOKING   133

Hygiene, health and safety   133

Legislation – Food hygiene – Safety – Describing food

The factors that contribute to food preparation and cooking   156

Cooking systems – Skills in the cooking process

Planning and implementing a food-preparation and cooking system   166

Planning cooking systems – Planning resources and requirements – Planning your work – Monitoring issues

Evaluating the operation of food preparation and cooking   177

The importance of skills – The Larder Chef – Resources, equipment and staff in the preparation of food – Chef de Cuisine – Assignment activity – Assessment activity 1: Plan and organize cooking methods/systems – Assessment activity 2: Implement a plan for preparing and cooking food – Test your knowledge – Assessment brief – Sources of information – Further reading

5 FOOD AND DRINK SERVICES   192

The various systems used in food and drink services   192

Styles of service – Skills in food and drink systems – Skills and training needs

The factors that contribute to food preparation and cooking   201

Customers' expectations – Restaurants

Planning and implementation of a food and drink service   207

Customer satisfaction – Handling complaints – Ensuring quality service – Quality service in function catering – Licensing laws

The planning and delivery of food and drink services   217

Criteria – Themed event: checklist for preparation – Formulating an action plan – Meeting financial targets – Monitoring of events – Internal monitoring – Assembly of evidence: a log book of assessment activities – GNVQ Assessment and Accreditation Profiles

6 PURCHASING, COSTING AND FINANCE   232

Measuring financial performance   232

Introduction – Users of financial information – Reasons for measuring financial performance – Types of financial statement and other data

needed to measure financial
performance – Ways of measuring
financial performance – Conclusion –
Test your knowledge

**Purchasing requirements,
procedures and controls**   263

The products to be purchased –
Sources of supply and methods of
purchasing – The stages in the
purchasing process – Responsibilities
of the purchaser – Controls in the
purchasing system – Conclusion – Test
your knowledge

**Calculating the cost and price of
goods or services**   283

Types of costs – How costs change –
The costs which make up a 'unit' of
goods or service – Calculating costs –
Determining the cost of a unit of
goods or service – Apportioning
indirect costs – Calculating the total
cost of goods and services –
Calculating the selling price – Use of
computers – Conclusion – Test your
knowledge

Assignment   317

7 **ACCOMMODATION OPERATIONS**   320

Types of accommodation   320

Customer requirements – Customer
services – Maintenance – Special
customer needs – Security – Fire
precautions – Lost property – Types of
accommodation

**Physical resources required to
provide accommodation services**   335

Types of cleaning – Cleaning methods
– Cleaning chemicals – The Control of
Substances Hazardous to Health
Regulations 1987 (COSHH) –
Customer supplies – Cleaning routines

– Textiles – Furnishings – Furniture –
Control of physical resources

Staffing accommodation services   357

Administration – Financial control

8 **RECEPTION AND FRONT OFFICE
    OPERATIONS**   370

**Customer requirements for
Reception and Front Office
operations**   370

Goods and services in the hospitality
industry – Customers/guests –
Customer/guest requirements –
In-house services – Reception and
Front Office procedures – Test your
knowledge

**Reservation systems for maximizing
occupancy and rooms revenue**   383

Reservation systems – Room
availability records – Increasing room
sales using improved selling
techniques – Test your knowledge

**Appropriate Reception and Front
Office information systems**   391

Reception and Front Office
information – Types of Front Office
information – Forecasting and
statistical data – Front Office
information systems which assist
customer service – Other advances in
Front Office information systems –
Conclusion – Test your knowledge

**The implications of legal
requirements governing Reception
and Front Office operations**   398

The history of hotel legislation –
Definition of a hotel – Hotels in law –
Inns versus private hotels – Legal
duties of an innkeeper: care of guests'
luggage – Extent of the innkeeper's

liability – Other factors concerning
the care of guests' luggage – The
rights of an innkeeper – Other
legislation governing Reception/Front
Office procedures – Conclusion – Test
your knowledge

Exercise 407

Assignment 408

THE WORK LOG 410

GLOSSARY 417

INDEX 425

INTRODUCTION

Welcome to this Advanced book on hospitality and catering which closely reflects the eight mandatory units for the GNVQ qualification in Hospitality and Catering Advanced Level. The book seeks to encourage student-centred learning by providing the knowledge and skills necessary for the eight units. It provides a framework on which to build further and encourages you to do this by attempting the tasks and self-test questions dispersed throughout the text. We have taken account of the National Council Vocational Qualification (NCVQ) mandatory units and test specifications. In addition, we have followed the recommendations of the pilot colleges and have consulted with industry in order to give you up-to-date knowledge and inform you of current practices.

The book is therefore concerned with building on knowledge and information. While it is self-contained you are still encouraged to use additional sources of relevant information to supplement your learning and gathering of evidence to satisfy the performance criteria for your portfolio. The information found in this Advanced text assumes that no previous knowledge has been taken from the Intermediate text and it is thus self-contained. It covers:

- Investigating the industry
- Working relationships of teams, roles and responsibilities of staff
- Work standards and conditions of employment
- The implementation and evaluation of customer service
- Methods of food preparation, cooking and service

- Food and drink service systems
- Measuring financial performance
- Purchasing requirements, processes and controls
- Types of accommodation, benefits, standards and services
- Methods of maintaining physical resources
- Procedures, documentation, information systems and legal requirements

Supervisory occupations within the hospitality and catering industry will require you to have a wide range of knowledge and skills. This book encourages you to take the necessary steps to acquire that knowledge by building your portfolio with the help of the tasks, test questions and assignments.

While the authors have tried to keep each unit as close to the mandatory units as possible, the nature of the hospitality and catering industry is so diverse that some integration of knowledge and skill is essential. Where appropriate, this is mentioned in the text.

Throughout the book we have tried to avoid the use of sexist or racist terminology. The hospitality and catering industry is known to have job opportunities for both sexes of wide-ranging abilities, including all ethnic groups from a variety of cultural backgrounds. The opportunities for a career in this industry are encouraging and it is hoped that this book will help you to achieve the success you hope for to progress into either employment or further study of the hotel and catering industry.

Y. Johns

CONTRIBUTORS

Series Editor

Yvonne Johns, BTEC Higher Education Centre Manager; BTEC External Verifier; BTEC External Education Adviser; formerly Head of Faculty, Business, Care & Hospitality, Leicester Southfields College

Series Consultant

Michael Rimmington, BTEC Chief Examiner; Principal Lecturer, Sheffield Hallam University

Contributors

Hilary Firth, Deputy Head of Faculty, Business, Care & Hospitality, Leicester Southfields College; Chief Examiner, City and Guilds; BTEC External Education Adviser

Carol Johnson, Lecturer, Sheffield College

Stephen Moore, GNVQ Coordinator, Blackpool & Fylde College; BTEC External Verifier

Patricia Morrell, Lecturer, Macclesfield College

Irene Norman, Llandrillo College

Christine Parry, Lecturer, Wirral Metropolitan College

Peter Trigg, Head of Department, Hotel Management and Leisure Studies, Wirral Metropolitan College; BTEC External Verifier

Margaret Weaver, FCCA, Lecturer, Stockport College

ACKNOWLEDGEMENTS

Unit 1

We are grateful to John and Sue Roebuck for permission to feature their hotel and special thanks go to Andrew Paul, the General Manager, who spent many hours with the author discussing the background details.

Unit 3

Acknowledgements are due to the Holiday Inns, London and Manchester, to the Reception staff at the Kensington Close Hotel, London and to Mount Charlotte Thistle Hotel, Leeds.

Unit 4

The following are thanked for their help in compiling this unit:

Blodgett Catering Equipment Ltd
Christine Parry
Chris Pashley
English Tourist Board
Moorwoods Vulcan Ltd
Socomel UW Ltd
The Electricity Council
The Hotel & Catering Training Company
Victors Catering Equipment Ltd
Wirral Metropolitan College
Enviroclean
The University of Sheffield
The Royal Hallamshire Hospital
The Sheffield College
Tesco Ltd

INVESTIGATE THE HOSPITALITY AND CATERING INDUSTRY

The hospitality and catering industry is a diverse and complex one. It can be likened to a chameleon which constantly changes to meet external and internal demands. Those that do not change will find themselves no longer in business. This makes the industry an exciting and interesting career prospect for those who are prepared to work and progress.

This unit is concerned with understanding the environment you are going to be working in, and appreciating the numerous organizations, outlets, facilities and operations that make up the hospitality and catering industry. Sources of information on how the industry operates will be considered, as well as ways in which it has developed and how it has changed to meet customers' needs.

We will investigate the external influences on the industry – how government policies, the recession, wars, etc. affect our industry. The industry is a major employer in the UK, and the economic contribution it makes to the country will be examined. We will also look at the employment patterns of the industry and the wide range of employment opportunities and educational routes open to you.

This unit is about *investigating* the industry. It will help you to formulate ideas and guide you in the types of evidence you require for your GNVQ portfolio. It is by no means fully comprehensive. You need to start collecting evidence *now*; make contact with your local outlets so that they will help and support you through the whole of your GNVQ course. Keep updating your information constantly by reading relevant literature in your college or school library.

▪ SECTORS AND SCALE OF THE INDUSTRY ▪

What is hospitality and catering?

The hospitality and catering industry is a vast and complex one which covers all the operations involving the provision of accommodation, food and refreshments, alcoholic drinks and other items (such as cigarettes, tobaccos, gaming machines, etc.). The two terms 'hospitality' and 'catering' can be defined in many ways, but the following definitions are acceptable in most circumstances.

Definition

- **Hospitality** means providing the services which make the customer feel welcome – the ambience, the quality of staff service, warmth, the contribution to the 'comfort factor'.
- **Catering** means meeting the basic needs of food, drink and accommodation.

The sectors of the industry

The hospitality and catering industry can be divided into two distinct sectors. These are:

- The commercial sector
- The catering services sector

The commercial sector

This includes those establishments which provide food, drink, refreshments and accommodation in exchange for money. They are run as businesses and their main reason for operating is to provide these products and services to make profit. The outlets included in this sector are:

1 Hotels
2 Restaurants (for the consumption of food and drink etc., mainly *on* the premises)
3 Take-aways, e.g. fish and chip shops, hamburger bars, pizza bars (for the consumption of food and drink etc. mainly *off* the premises)
4 Clubs (excluding gaming clubs)
5 Holiday camps and caravan sites

Other facilities within these outlets (e.g. leisure facilities in a hotel) may also be profit-orientated, but the main reason for the existence of the outlet is to provide hospitality and catering products and services.

The catering services sector

This sector exists to provide hospitality and catering services in a manner similar to the commercial sector, the difference being that these services are *secondary* or *indirect*.

Definition

- **Secondary** or **indirect** services are ones which are not the main activity of the organization but are provided to support the main activity.

These outlets would include:

1 Hospitals
2 Prisons
3 Public institutions, e.g. educational establishments such as schools and colleges
4 Armed forces
5 Residential homes
6 Leisure and tourism outlets
7 Employee feeding

The customers in this sector are not there mainly for the hospitality and catering provision but for other purposes. Can you imagine someone committing a criminal offence just to enjoy the prison food?

The catering services sector, being a secondary or indirect service, does not necessarily have to be profit-led. Most outlets within this sector are *subsidized*, have to *break-even* or need to meet a proportion of their costs (e.g. food costs or wages costs) through their sales.

Definition

- **Subsidized** means that part of the operational costs are met from another source.

For example, hospital catering is funded from monies raised to run the whole hospital, perhaps provided by regional health authorities, trustees and other sources. In other words, the hospital catering service does not make a profit – it more likely makes a loss, and that loss is covered from general funds available to the hospital.

Definition

- **Break-even** means that enough sales must be generated to meet all the costs associated with those sales, e.g. the food, wages of those concerned, heating, lighting and other overheads, etc. No profit (or loss) is made or budgeted.

Using appropriate sources, make a study of your local and surrounding area of hospitality and catering outlets. Categorize your outlets into commercial and catering services sectors. Use graphs and/or charts to illustrate your answer.

The organizational structure of the industry

Earlier in this section the words 'organization', 'outlets' and 'facilities' have been used. What do they mean and where do they fit in as a part of the scale of the industry?

Figure 1.1 illustrates the various parts of an organization. The breakdown of an organization into its various parts in this way should help to clarify your understanding of some of the terms used in this book.

Definition

- An **organization** is the company which owns the various outlets.
- An **outlet** is a unit of management or an establishment found within each sector, usually on one site, (e.g. a hotel, a public house, a restaurant, a hospital), normally comprising of a number of operations.

- **Facilities** are the operations provided by the outlet (e.g. rooms, bars, restaurants) which earn revenue for the organization.

'Facilities' also has a more general meaning in that it describes supporting services such as trouser presses, hair dryers, shampoo and soap supplies, etc. in rooms, or leisure facilities within the hotel. These are also called 'amenities'.

Definition

- **Operations** are activities or groups of activities which may earn revenue for the organization (e.g. accommodation) or which may provide supporting services which do not directly earn revenue (e.g. housekeeping).

A hotel bedroom will be supported by Accommodation Operations which would include room servicing and perhaps laundry operations. Other operations which support the entire outlet would include Administration, Reception and Maintenance. Operations may also be referred to as 'departments'.

The scale of the hospitality and catering industry

The hospitality and catering industry, as we have discussed, is divided into two defined sectors – commercial and catering services. Due to the nature of the industry, the boundaries of

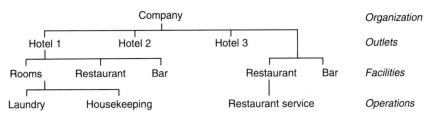

Figure 1.1 Organization chart

these two sectors are constantly changing, resulting in overlaps and mergers. For example, contract catering, which previously supplied catering services to private and commercial organizations, is now being encouraged to supply to the catering services sector (e.g. schools and hospitals).

You may now appreciate the difficulties in defining the scale of the hospitality and catering industry with regards to its structure, the number of businesses, customer markets, etc. Access to information with regard to the scale and size of the industry is led by the commercial sector, as this is the sector where catering demands and markets are constantly being researched, in order to highlight new markets where potential increased profits may be made.

Task 1.2

Take an in-depth look at your college's or school's provision of hospitality and catering services. Identify which areas are commercial and which are part of the catering services sector. Where, if at all, do these sectors overlap or merge?

Numbers employed

Table 1.1 shows the numbers employed in the commercial sector of the industry. This sector employs over one and a quarter million people. Over 60 per cent are employed in restaurants and public house outlets which are largely operated by self-employed or sole proprietors. This correlates closely with Table 1.2, where the public house and restaurant outlets combined represent 37.5 per cent of the total number of outlets in the commercial sector. Public houses account for over one-third of the total catering outlets, with hotels accounting for almost 26 per cent of the commercial sector.

Table 1.1 Employment in the industry 1991–1992

	1991	1992
Commercial sectors		
Hotels	296,000	289,200
Restaurants	291,900	295,500
Pubs and bars	328,300	327,000
Clubs	141,500	138,300
Contract catering	128,800	115,700
Self-employed	160,000	165,000
Total	1,346,500	1,330,700

Table 1.2 Numbers of establishments in Britain, commercial sectors 1984–1991 (thousands)

	1984	1987	1989	1991
Hotels	57.1	62.9	55.6	52.2
Restaurants	87.5	86.3	100.9	99.9
Pubs and bars	73.1	74.8	75.9	77.1
Clubs	17.0	16.5	16.4	16.1
Contract catering	17.4	18.9	23.1	19.2
Total	252.1	259.4	271.9	264.5

Source: Census of Employment/Labour Force Survey

As may be seen from Table 1.2, restaurants have the largest total group of catering outlets and have been the least affected by the latest depression in the economy. However, the growth within pubs and bars has experienced a slow decline due to several factors. For example, government legislation has brought changes in social trends regarding drinking habits, etc., which will be discussed later in this unit.

Table 1.3 shows the numbers employed in the hospitality and catering services industry. Within this sector you may see the three areas that monopolize this sector are industry, education and medical. The sharp decline in the industrial sector of 51,500 employees may be a reflection of the recent trends towards contract catering or possibly due to the then depressed economy with a reduction in the numbers of outlets as a result of cutbacks and/or closures. The slight growth in the largest

Table 1.3 Numbers employed in the hospitality and catering industry

	1991	1992
Recreation/cultural	49,100	57,800
Travel	39,300	34,800
Retail distribution	66,800	61,600
Industrial	313,600	262,100
Education	227,000	247,800
Medical	335,300	342,100
Public administration	73,800	73,100
Total	1,104,900	1,079,300
Total industry	**2,451,400**	**2,410,000**

Source: Census of Employment/Labour Force Survey

section, medical, may be in part due to increases in private medical care. There has also been an increase in the number of older people who require medical care. The increase in the education sector may be due to the expansion in further and higher education.

Commercial outlets

Hotels and other residential outlets

The hotel industry is both complicated and diverse. In the UK market 'hotel' is a word which encompasses a variety of establishments such as:

- Licensed and unlicensed hotels
- Guest houses
- Inns
- Motels
- Boarding houses

Each outlet provides different products and services to meet its customers' demands. Hotel facilities might include:

- À la carte restaurants
- Bar and lounge areas
- Coffee shops
- Cocktail bars
- Banqueting and conference suites

- Additional leisure areas such as pools, gymnasia, aerobics tuition, beauty salons which would be serviced by the food and beverage operations providing leisure bars for the service of food and drink, and vending machines.

Providing an à la carte restaurant or a 24-hour room service facility may not gain much in the way of generating additional profits, but such provision would allow the hotel to achieve a better reputation or a higher grading (e.g. more 'stars'), which in turn would justify a higher accommodation charge and therefore an increase in overall revenue.

Hotel classification schemes

There have been several attempts to standardize the system for classifying hotels. Unfortunately, it still remains somewhat confusing. Initial classification started at the beginning of the twentieth century, introduced by the motoring organizations. The Royal Automobile Club (RAC) and the Automobile Association (AA) are probably the best known. These classifications have been further developed, in trying to assess the quality of service within the outlets. This is done by awarding percentage marks to the star to reflect the facilities offered (catering) and the standard of service (hospitality).

More recently, additional categories have been introduced which indicate consumer needs. These categories do not necessarily reflect the facilities offered but attempt to reflect the 'hospitality' side, based on descriptions such as 'warm and friendly', 'relaxed and personal', as you might expect in establishments such as country houses or nineteenth century inns.

AA classification

The classification relies on a system of inspection, which might result in new outlets being added to the scheme or existing ones being deleted. The classification is personal to the proprietor, not the outlet, and it lapses automatically on a change of ownership.

For *hotels*, an application is made to the AA which is followed by an unannounced overnight visit by an inspector. After the inspector has tested all the services as far as possible, and paid the bill, his or her identity will be made known and the hotelier will then conduct a tour of the premises. At this stage the inspector will discuss any deficiencies and make a recommendation to the AA Hotel Appointment Committee. The hotelier will be informed of their decision, and appeals are possible through the AA or through the British Hotels Restaurants and Caterers Association. Unannounced routine inspections are then carried out to check that the standards are being maintained.

The AA star-grading system is shown in Table 1.4. In addition, the AA awards 'extra' symbols to denote areas where food or service is particularly outstanding compared with other hotels within the same star classification. These include *red stars*, *rosettes* and *merit* symbols (Figure 1.2).

Table 1.4 AA classification system

★	Hotels and inns generally of small scale with acceptable facilities and furnishings. Adequate bath and lavatory arrangements. Meals are provided for residents but their availablity to non-residents may be limited.
★★	Hotels offering a higher standard of accommodation, and some bedrooms containing a private bathroom/shower with lavatory.
★★★	Well-appointed hotels with more spacious accommodation with the majority of bedrooms containing a private bathroom/shower with lavatory. Fuller meal facilities are provided.
★★★★	Exceptionally well-appointed hotels offering a high standard of comfort and service with bedrooms providing a private bathroom/shower with lavatory.
★★★★★	Luxury hotels offering the highest international standards.

Reproduced by courtesy of the AA

Figure 1.2 The stars, rosettes and merit symbols awarded by the AA

Other classifications

Apart from the AA and RAC, in 1987 the British Tourist Board for England, Scotland, Wales and Northern Ireland introduced their own classification system using 'crowns'.

The 'crown' system came under review during early 1994, led by the Minister for Tourism. It was intended to update and clarify the classification, thereby making it easier for the customer to understand. (See the industry press for details.)There are also special symbols which denote gradings for country house hotels, lodges and inns (Figure 1.3).

Figure 1.3 The symbols for country house hotels, lodges and inns

Task 1.3

Research into all the classifications which could be associated with hotels and restaurants. Define each level of classification by its facilities and/or services. Look at the hotels in your locality – how are they classified?

Market size

Many attempts have been made to establish the exact number of hotels in the UK. Different figures have been produced which vary according to the body that has carried out the research. These inconsistencies are partly due to interpretation as to what constitutes a hotel. The English Tourist Board and the government's Standard Industrial Classification includes guest houses as hotels. 'Consensus' is a body which uses the indicator of 'size' for its classification. Other bodies use other definitions to determine the numbers. Therefore published numbers of hotels range from 18,000 to 29,000.

Hotel *room occupancy rates* for 1993 averaged 48 per cent. This is approximately 9 per cent lower than the 1990 figures. The 1994 figures are showing a slight improvement, much to the relief of the sector. The increase is not significant enough to assume that we are out of the recession.

Definition

● **Room occupancy rates** *are used to measure the percentage of rooms let out of the total of rooms available for letting.*

Using the figures of the English Tourist Board, the hotels operated by major companies make up only 5.4 per cent of the total number of outlets, but account for 25 per cent of all bedrooms.

Turnover

Definition

● **Turnover** *is the income which is earned from the sale of products and services. It is sometimes also called* **revenue**.

The official government source uses the VAT (value added tax) system to calculate the number of hotels and their size, but this naturally excludes businesses which are not registered for VAT, i.e. the smaller ones. In 1990, 14,410 hotels and other residential outlets were registered for VAT in the UK. Of these:

● 92.2 per cent fall below the £1 million turnover level
● 77 per cent had a turnover of less than £250,000
● Approximately one-third had a turnover between £23,000 and £50,000

In 1990 the turnover limit for VAT registration was £23,000 so any establishments with a turnover of less than this figure would be excluded from these statistics. This could well include a great number of guest houses and bed-and-breakfast accommodation. As of December 1993, the VAT registration threshold had risen to £45,000. This will affect the number of hotels included in this category. The most recent estimated figures quoted by the Hotel and Catering Training Company indicate that the number of establishments is now nearer 52,200 (see Table 1.2).

Task 1.4

Using trade journals and relevant published data, research into the major hotel chains and find out who owns what.

Apart from the AA and RAC and similar classification schemes, hotels are also classified by the type of consumer market at which the outlet is aimed. The demand for accommodation in the hotel market can be broadly divided into two areas:

1 UK people travelling within the UK for business or pleasure
2 Foreign visitors travelling to the UK for business or pleasure

It is important that where the consumer demand is, so the hotels are situated. An established entrepreneur is quoted as saying there are only three rules for success in the hotel business – location, location and location.

The hotels do not just have to be in the right location, they must also have the right facilities to accommodate the consumer demands in the area. For example:

1 Resort areas such as Blackpool, Scarborough and Brighton, being seaside resorts, all have similar outlets, i.e.:
Large and small hotels
Bed-and-breakfast outlets
Self-catering facilities
Mobile stands, e.g. hot dogs, jacket potatoes, ice cream
Fish restaurants
Leisure activities, e.g. fun fairs, amusement arcades, theme worlds
Caravan and camping parks
2 Country areas would perhaps have the following:
More traditional, older hotels and inns
Country pubs
National Heritage activities
Caravan and camping parks

These two location types would cater predominantly for the visitor away from home for pleasure; some host large conferences, particularly 'out of season', such as annual political party conferences.

Large towns and cities are geared to the business and short-stay pleasure consumer. Types of facilities here cover:

- Larger hotels from national and international chains
- Quality restaurants
- Greater choice of ethnic restaurants

- Fast-food and 'eating on the premises' outlets, with names, such as Pizza Hut, Kentucky Fried Chicken
- Leisure and entertainment facilities

These lists are by no means comprehensive. They are meant to give a broad view which can then be developed on a local basis.

Task 1.5

Using directories, local newspapers, etc., research into the types of outlets and the facilities which are being offered. Analyse your findings and comment on any gaps in the market where demands are not being met.

Hotel types

To meet consumer demands for food, drink and accommodation, different types of hotels have developed which may be classified as follows.

International hotels

These are owned by large chain companies operating around the world. In order to promote a recognized consumer identity, these companies build, renovate and offer services and facilities to exactly the same standards in each hotel, depending on the corporate image. This results in consumers being given consistency, security and dependability. Operating as high-quality hotels, and offering the standard facilities you might expect from such hotels, increasing business and conference demands have caused them to provide a further range of services, such as:

- Secretarial, such as typing, fax, etc.
- Complex telephone linkages, worldwide communications, etc.

- Bedrooms which include better working facilities such as desks, improved lighting, etc.
- Increasing technology for conference presentations, particularly audio and visual aids

Commercial and leisure hotels

Sited in cities and large towns, these types of hotels are predominantly used by the business sector from Mondays to Thursdays and by the short-break sector from Fridays to Sundays. Offering a wide range of facilities to accommodate the needs of both types of consumer, they have an underlying reputation of high standards and efficient service, combined with a relaxed atmosphere and consumer-orientated staff. In-house facilities often include:

- Some form of leisure facilities
- Limited room service
- Tea- and coffee-making facilities in bedrooms, with trouser press, hair dryer, toiletries etc.

Resort hotels

These are predominantly aimed at consumers for pleasure on a long-stay basis (four nights or more). The accommodation ranges from simple, unlicensed bed-and-breakfast establishments to licensed premises offering food and drink throughout the day – although often with time constraints (e.g. dinner served between 6.30 p.m. and 9.30 p.m.). These types of hotels aim to give the customer 'hospitality' rather than a wide range of facilities, the emphasis being on the friendly atmosphere and therefore maintaining repeat business (i.e. the same customers returning year after year).

Transient hotels and motels

These may also be categorized as *budget hotels*. This is a rapidly developing area in which overseas ownership has increased more than any other hotel sector. These hotels may be found at motorway service areas (e.g.

Travelodges) or near motorway exits and on major road routes (e.g. Novotel and Travel Inns – Novotel is owned by a European company which owns several hotels in this sector). All offer a basic standard of accommodation with few facilities, to provide for the needs of the 'on-the-road' business traveller.

Residential hotels

These offer long-stay accommodation, predominantly for the elderly or homeless. Basic facilities of a clean standard are provided, but without perhaps the privacy of individual bathrooms. The food and drink is usually supplied at fixed times, with limited choice. Basic tea- and coffee-making facilities are usually in the bedrooms. Those supplying accommodation for the homeless might have no provision for meals but offer limited cooking facilities in rooms or shared kitchens.

The above definitions are by no means prescriptive. The rich variety of hotels cannot be so easily classified, hence the numerous classification systems which exist and which were described earlier in this section.

Restaurants

As defined by the VAT trade classification No. 8857, these are 'Restaurants, cafés, snack bars and other establishments selling food for consumption on the premises only'. As previously mentioned, boundaries within sectors do overlap. The main purpose is to supply a waiter/waitress table service, but many restaurants provide eating on the premises (EOP) as well as a take-away service.

Some outlets (e.g. Pizzaland and its competitors) who provide a table service and a take-away service actually fall into the category of Fast Food, rather than Restaurants. This section is concerned solely with EOPs.

The *Business Monitor* PA1003 VAT statistics show that in 1990 there were 17,835 restaurants – 5.4

per cent more than in 1989. The operational area would cover food preparation and food and drink services.

As a result of various social and cultural changes, there are now a vast number of different types and styles of restaurants offering ranges from elaborate French 'nouveau cuisine' to ethnic restaurants (e.g. Chinese, Japanese, Indian and Caribbean).

Task 1.6

Using your local and surrounding area, identify the different types of restaurant outlets available to you. Categorize your findings into ethnic, European, British, etc. and illustrate your answer with the use of charts and/or graphs.

Due to a higher level of customer expectation, most restaurants now have a lounge area which is used for pre-meal drinks and coffee service. The area allows the customer to relax and enjoy the atmosphere before and after the meal. It also enables a faster turnover of customers at the restaurant tables.

Take-away and fast-food outlets

Take-away and fast-food outlets offer limited-choice menus, fast service of the entire meal at low cost, no reservation system, with a level of service suitable for customers to eat off the premises.

Types of outlets

These include:

- Fish and chip shops
- Pizza and pasta parlours
- Baked potato places
- Hamburger bars
- Fried chicken outlets
- Ethnic take-aways (e.g. Chinese, Indian, Greek)
- Sandwich bars

As the concept implies, the essence of this type of outlet is *speed*.

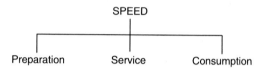

The menu items are limited with no scope for 'tailored' meals, except perhaps for the omission of garnishes. It is bad luck if you are a vegan but wish to participate in one of the famous burger chains. All customers eat to a recognized formula and all items are manufactured off-site with the net result of *standardization* of product.

Definition

- ***Standardization*** *means that wherever you go in the country (and some chains say this applies throughout the world) the product (e.g. a hamburger) will be exactly the same.*

To achieve this standardization, all food items are prepared using advanced technology with regards to the type, quality and weight of ingredients, the heat used, the length of cooking time, etc. Some people regard this process as 'de-skilling' the job.

Outlets are often owned by large chains or *franchised* out to individuals. McDonald's restaurants are a well-known example of franchising.

Definition

- A **franchise** *exists where an individual operator is granted a licence to operate an outlet using the larger organization's name and products.*

The location of the outlet is of great importance with regard to these types of operation. Few people will travel far for this type of meal experience. Most are sited in city or town centres, or on busy main roads where there are facilities to park or even 'drive thru'. The operation is usually 'no frills' where food items are served, eaten and drunk in disposable containers. The price to the customer is of particular importance. Aware of competitors' prices, customers are always looking for 'value for money'.

The innovation of this type of outlet has, in the main, originated in the United States. Major worldwide companies such as McDonald's, Burger King, Pizza Hut, Kentucky Fried Chicken all started there. There are some initiatives, however, which have not succeeded. Taco Bell, the Mexican fast-food outlet, is an example. This franchise was launched several years ago with little success.

Number of outlets

Using government statistics and *Keynote* estimates between 1985 and 1990, it is gauged that there would be a total of 122,016 take-away and fast-food units, representing a growth of just under 5 per cent from the number in 1985.

Public houses and bars

Traditionally, public houses (pubs) were primarily there for the service of alcoholic beverages to predominantly male consumers, providing an area for leisure activities (e.g. darts, cribbage, dominoes, etc.) on the premises. The supply of food was non-existent or limited to the provision of pickled eggs, pickled onions and the occasional packet of nuts.

The characteristics of today's pubs are vastly different. Due to changing customer demands, pubs now have a more social appeal, attracting families with children, more females and the more affluent young 18–24-year-olds with 'theme pubs'.

Food has now become an important part of the business with several breweries incorporating restaurants (e.g. Whitbread's public house empire includes the Beefeater Steak Houses). Apart from increasing sales through food, it also taps into a market normally inaccessible to pubs due to licensing laws – the market which encourages families to eat in pubs.

Turnover

Of the 77,000-plus outlets in 1991, fewer than 0.5 per cent had a turnover of £1 million or more. The majority of 92 per cent had a turnover of less than £250,000 per year, indicating that the most common type of unit in this area is small.

On a regional level, as may be seen from Figure 1.4, the largest number of outlets with a full on-licence falls in the South-east, which represents 25 per cent of the total of 19,275 outlets, according to the *Liquor Licensing*

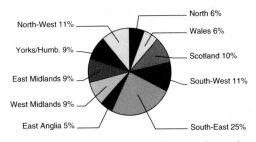

Figure 1.4 Percentages of full on-licences by region, June 1992. (*Source*: HCTB)

Statistics 1993, published by the Home Office. The highest number of outlets per head of the population falls in the area of the South-west, which represents only 11 per cent of the total sector, but which has 1.85 outlets per 1000 of the population. Other areas were Wales (1.73 outlets per 1000), East Anglia (1.71 outlets per 1000), East Midlands (1.69 per 1000) respectively, with the South-east having the least number of outlets per head at only 1.14 per 1000 of the population.

Clubs

Clubs often provide food, drink and, in some cases, accommodation for members or their guests. There are various types of clubs, including working-men's clubs, social clubs, political clubs, and private, elite clubs. Within these, there are two main types:

1 Registered clubs
2 Proprietary clubs

Registered clubs are ones which oversee the management with an elected committee. The members own the club and its contents, including the food and drink, and they pay their membership fees into a common fund. The food and drink is sold at competitive prices, therefore the profit element is lower than it would be in, say, a pub or a restaurant. This profit is put back into the club's common fund. This therefore is a non-profit-making club and, as such, a true member club which does not have to have a Justice's licence. It has only to be registered.

Proprietary clubs are owned by individuals or organizations that are purely profit making. They will therefore require a Justice's licence to operate. A high proportion attract the younger end of the market which would predominantly buy alcoholic drinks, although meals and refreshments have gained ground in recent years.

Holiday camps and caravan sites

The industry has made an enormous effort to improve the image of holiday camps and caravan sites from the 'Hi-di-Hi' customer perception of the 1940s and 1950s. Changes in the customer climate have forced holiday camps and caravan sites to upgrade their facilities by providing more facilities and to a higher standard. For example, holiday camps now supply larger accommodation with en-suite showers, better kitchen equipment and more luxurious lounge areas. The advent of Centre Parcs, which provides all modern leisure facilities under cover and therefore no longer needs to rely on the weather, has brought the more discerning clientele into this sector.

Even touring caravan parks have improved their facilities. The Caravan Club now provides fully tiled, centrally heated toilet and shower blocks with free hair dryers in the majority of its main sites. Hot water, once a problem on many sites, is now expected to be instantly available at all times of the day. The 'roughing-it' attitude which once prevailed is now a thing of the past, with today's modern caravanner having mains electric, full oven, refrigerator, microwave and all 'mod cons' within the caravan, so it follows that the facilities of the site must be of comparable standard.

Facilities which may be offered in holiday camps or caravan sites include:

● Leisure – indoor (e.g. gyms, table tennis, sauna, solarium) and outdoor (e.g. tennis, horse riding, archery, pitch and putt, children's play areas)
● Take-aways
● Bars
● Souvenir shops
● Travel shops for booking excursions, entertainment, etc. (normally on a local basis)
● Room servicing – changing of bed linen, tea towels (holiday camps only)

Task 1.7

Using relevant trade journals, investigate who are the major companies left in the holiday camp sector. Research into the types of facilities each has to offer. What interests, if any, do they have in the European Union?

Contract catering

Contract catering, also known as the food service management industry, services that sector of the Industry where the provision of food and drink is not the main activity – i.e. the catering services sector. The outlets which are serviced by contract catering include the following:

- Employee feeding
- Schools, colleges and universities
- Hospitals and healthcare providers
- Welfare and local authorities

In reality, these are often non-profit making.

This particular sector of contract catering cannot be so succinctly defined. Over the last few years, the fastest growth area is connected with the commercial outlets which are many and varied but which include:

- Employee feeding
- Leisure centres
- Railway stations
- Department stores
- Public events
- Theatres etc.
- Airports – in-flight and land-based

The growth has been around 14 per cent since 1990.

The number of employee feeding outlets has actually declined. In 1990, employee-feeding represented around 80 per cent of the total outlets in this sector. Now it is just over a half. The main reason for this decrease is the closure of businesses due to the economic recession. This has led, however, to investment in new markets, especially in the commercial catering sectors. The total number of outlets operated by food service management companies has increased largely due to the expansion into state education. The number of meals served increased from 804 million in 1992 to 944 million in 1993. Due to the expansion of outlets and meals serviced, this sector now employs a total of 118,418, both part- and full-time staff. As you might imagine, turnover has also increased from £1.58 billion to £2 billion – a significant amount in the light of the hard economic recession. Growth into the overseas markets is reflected by the annual increase in turnover which has doubled over the past two years in this sector.

Task 1.8

Investigate your own college or school employee-feeding provision. Is it managed by contract caterers? If so, who are they? What part does your outlet play with regards to the company's overall size in the education market?

The catering services industry

As already discussed, the diversity of the industry makes it difficult to define exact areas of commercial and catering services sectors. Some catering services operations have, through government legislation, changed enormously over the last ten years. Previously controlled government outlets (e.g. hospitals, schools meals, prisons, residential homes, etc.) are now having to put their catering services to tender.

Definition

- *A **tender** is an offer to complete a certain task or provide goods and services within a certain time and for a fixed amount of money.*

This has opened up the contract catering market, allowing for further opportunities for growth which at one time were inaccessible. As these consumers have little or no alternative to eating elsewhere, they are classed as semi-captive or captive customers.

Characteristics of catering service outlets

There are certain characteristics which affect all catering service outlets. Some of these are as follows:

1 The consumers. These are captive or semi-captive. Therefore the nutritional value of the food they eat is of great importance as it could be their only means of sustenance.
2 The actual customer range will vary due to the demographic nature of the locality, e.g. whether it is of ethnic origin, what age groups it contains, what special dietary needs are to be fulfilled, what race or creed are the customers.
3 Financial constraints imposed by national and/or local governments with regards to expenditure and budgets which directly affect the end-product. This could influence the customer's choice and types of food items available.
4 Menu choice to provide variety is an important aspect, especially when talking about captive customers; often menus run on a cyclical basis which has been carefully costed to meet budget requirements. This means that the menus each week are not the same but vary so that a spread of expensive and economical meals is offered at all times.

Hospitals

Hospital catering has evolved and developed out of government legislation. To see how, we must go back in time, to:

- *Pre-1948* Hospitals were charitable organizations, run by voluntary workers.
- *1946 – the National Health Act 1948* This was introduced by the government at that time, who brought the hospital services under the government and the National Health Service (NHS) was born. This led to a formal structuring of the catering facilities with the introduction of hospital catering managers and supporting staff.
- *1963 – The Platt Report* This highlighted the problem areas in the catering operations in hospitals. These included poor standards of food, lack of nutritional value contained in the food due to poor production methods, lack of choice, and inability to cope with the various customer needs. The unfortunate effect was that customers (i.e. patients) took longer to recover. Lack of hygiene and poor administration added to the inefficiency.
- *1972 – The Salmon Committee* The Salmon Committee concluded their investigation of the NHS which led to its reorganization in 1974 and the basis of the modern-day hospital service. It created sixteen regional health authorities in England. Within each regional health authority were district authorities. This resulted in a more structured and effective administration. It also made its administration extremely top-heavy and its organization chart cumbersome.
- *1979* A Royal Commission on the NHS advised a total reorganization of the administrative structure to make the service more customer-focused, cost effective and more caring in which to work. The Departments of Health and of Social Security then control the forecast for each region. They are also responsible for setting the *cost levels*.

Definition

● **Cost levels** *are the allowances given for the provision of food for one full week.*

Approximate guidelines for cost levels are:

1 Food cost 60 per cent
2 Overheads 40per cent

The average food spend per patient per day in the NHS may range from £1.37 to £1.60, for all meals including five drinks. Financial budgets are allocated annually. The funds are calculated on a regional basis which are then distributed to districts and individual hospitals.

Within the hospitals, there are price variances depending on for whom they are providing the service. Staff employed within the hospital eat at a subsidized rate. However, visitors and the general public are charged a more realistic price.

As hospitals have been put under pressure to meet increasingly higher costs, catering managers have had to consider marketing techniques and the utilization of under-used areas to generate extra finance. The result is that some hospitals organize functions, luncheons, reception events, etc. to boost their income.

Hospital catering managers have three main consumer types within their service area to consider:

● Patients
● Staff
● Visitors

Patients

In a general hospital patients' needs vary according to why they are there. For example, some are there for maternity services, some for surgical procedures, others require geriatric care.

Consideration needs to be given to the fact that the catering service is perhaps their only source of food. The nutritional value, hygiene and presentation must all be of the highest standards to aid the recovery of the patient.

The catering standards have come a long way from the first meals served in hospitals. It is now appreciated that patients are also 'customers' and, as such, more details on meals are available. Most hospitals now offer a choice of menu items for all meal times. Higher standards in crockery, cutlery and the actual overall appearance of the tray and meal are some of the more positive moves made by hospitals in catering for the patients.

Although there are now choice menus, the consideration as to why patients are in hospital must have a direct bearing on the type of food they can eat. The dietary aspects of hospital catering over the years has become more complex. These will be covered in detail in Unit 4.

Staff

Hospital staff will range from senior medical and administrative, who could perhaps have a separate waitress service and dining room, to doctors, nurses and porters with a cafeteria-type service with vending machines that they may share with visitors. Meals are usually based on menu items similar to those supplied for patients. The advent of vending machines has allowed a 24-hour service to be operated, raising revenue without an increase in labour costs. 'Micro-vending' allows staff to have a choice of chilled meals which are then reheated in an adjacent microwave cooker by following simple instructions.

Visitors and the public

This is the area which has the potential to increase the revenue of the hospital. Traditionally, it has never been exploited because of the image conjured up of eating in hospital. The slogan 'Come to ABC General

Hospital for a great meal out!' does not really inspire. However, a number of hospitals have had considerable success, mainly due either to the situation of the hospital or to its catering facilities. For example:

● Guy's Hospital – its 29th-floor Hospitality Suite has exceptional views of London.
● Southampton Hospital – its Pedlars Coffee Shop and Truffles Restaurant have access directly from the street, so that customers do not feel that they are in a hospital at all.
● The first McDonald's has now been established in at least one hospital, with perhaps more to follow.

Tendering

Since 1989 the health authorities have been legally obliged to put out the catering operations to competitive tendering. This competition has opened up the market to contract caterers and in-house management teams. The process of tendering is as follows:

1 An invitation to tender is advertised by the hospital in the press.
2 This is open to 'in-house' management teams and external contractors.
3 Tendered offers are then submitted following the requirements of the tender. These would state:
   Description of the hospital
   Number of beds
   Details of present catering facilities
   Legal requirements
   Quality of food, menu types
   Staff requirements
   Equipment and materials requirements
   Required security and insurance
   A health and hygiene statement
   The contract period
   The price
   The system for monitoring standards
   Details of the termination of the contract.

The contract catering industry in 1994 had 95 outlets producing 39 million meals (British Hospitality Association, *Contract Catering Survey, 1994*)

Educational establishments

In the Education Act 1944, local authorities were required to provide school meals and free milk in all maintained schools. By the mid-1950s these had to be of a certain nutritional value. In 1980 the government decided that the local authority no longer had to provide meals to a specified nutritional standard. They actively encouraged 'fast-food' type meals with a variety of choice and price. More facilities for children to bring packed lunches were provided.

In 1987 the Local Government Act introduced the legal obligation for local authorities to tender competitively. 'In-house' catering now had to compete with contract caterers. Contract caterers expanded into the education market, and now have 2383 outlets, producing 94 million meals, in state schools and further and higher education. This is an increase of a little over 13 per cent for 1993 (British Hospitality Association, *Contract Catering Survey 1994*). Independent schools total 587 outlets and 100 million meals per annum

Prisons

Until recently, prisons have provided their own in-house catering services. They were not subjected to any external or internal influences. Since the government opened up the once-closed markets to competitors in the same way as in hospitals and education, prison catering services can also be provided by contract caterers through tendering. Hospital catering services cater for two main types of customer:

1 Staff
2 'Captive customers'

Senior officers and administrators, wardens, external staff (e.g. consultants, medical, teaching, etc.) require catering facilities to be situated away from the 'captive customer', with similar food on a cafeteria-type service. Some senior staff may have a separate dining room.

Definition

Captive customers are those customers who have no choice of outlet.

The food items with regards to quality, choice and standards of presentation, have improved immensely over the last few years. Menus are run on a cyclical basis with menu-item choices to prevent boredom and lack of interest in the customer.

Consideration needs to be given not only to the nutritional value of the meal but also to the type of customers. There will be a mixture of age groups and social backgrounds. Cultural and ethnic preferences must be considered, as well as dietary ones such as those of vegetarians. The catering services sector can no longer be dictatorial in what, how and to what standards they produce food to the 'captive customer'.

Sources of data

There are numerous sources of data connected with the hospitality and catering industry, from those gathered as a result of public survey to those appearing in trade publications. There have been numerous to classify the industry, the most recent attempt being the Standard Industrial Classification (SIC), updated in 1980. Although this has a broad scope, it still omits parts of the employee-feeding and welfare sectors. The classification starts with broad, similar activity headings, which in turn are broken down into more specific activities, thus being able to gain various types of detail as required. Since the first SIC in 1948 it has been revised four times and published by the government's Central Statistical Office.

In the 1980 SIC there are nine main economic activities which are then subdivided into class activities (e.g. Hotel and Catering). From this class section, the classification breaks down into group and then into industrial activities. The following list illustrates the divisions:

1 *Class*   Hotel and catering (Class 66)
2 *Group*   Restaurants, cafés and snack bars, etc. (Group 66.1)
3 *Activity*   Licensed premises. Unlicensed premises (Activity 66.11)

Other public surveys where information can be sought are:

● *The Family Expenditure Survey*
● *Social Trends*
● Office of Population Census and Survey – Population Projection (OPCS)
● Central Statistical Office (CSO)
● National Income and Expenditure Blue Book
● Department of Trade and Industry – Business Monitoring Service

Trade publications are another source of data, often including sections from the surveys mentioned above. Examples of such publications are:

● *Caterer and Hotelkeeper*
● *Chef*
● *Food and Drink*
● *Hospitality* (the official magazine of the Hotel, Catering and Institutional management Association – HCIMA)
● Publications from the Hospitality and Catering Training Company
● Publications from the tourist boards

Employment patterns

Demands by consumers on the hospitality and catering industry peaks and troughs not only on a seasonal basis (e.g. Christmas, Easter, summer vacations) but also weekly or daily. Controlling labour costs in such a variable market is of prime management importance. Labour is an extremely expensive cost, both directly in the form of actual monies paid to the employees and indirectly in the form of National Insurance and possibly pension and

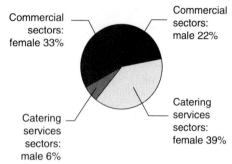

Figure 1.5 Percentage employment in the commercial and catering services sectors by gender, 1992, (Source: *HCTB*)

health-scheme contributions. An imbalance of labour costs to sales can, if gone unnoticed, cause serious losses to an outlet. (In-depth details of costs and their effects on profits can be found in Unit 6.)

In 1992 there were 2.4 million people employed in the whole of the catering and hospitality and related industries, representing approximately 10 per cent of the total UK workforce. This may be broken down into:

1 1,330,700 in the hotel and commercial sector
2 1,079,300 in the catering services sector

In the commercial sector in 1992 over 72 per cent of employees were female, of which 70 per cent were part-time employees. This suits both the employers, to cope with demand fluctuations, and the employees, especially women working while running a home. Over the last ten years there has been an increase in male employees of approximately 8 per cent in the commercial sectors. This is probably due to the reduction of employment in traditional industries (e.g. engineering, mining etc.). This has forced men to re-evaluate their positions and hence look to the hospitality and catering industry, which has seen growth in certain sectors over the last few years (Figure 1.5).

Split shifts

Apart from the part-time employment, fluctuations in daily demands are coped with by full-time employees working split shifts. This

is where an 8-hour working day is broken down into (usually) two set times or shifts to cope with demand. For example, a chef in a hotel kitchen might work from 10 a.m. to 2 p.m., and from 6 p.m. to 10 p.m. to cover the peak lunch and dinner times. Split shifts are very tiring as there is little one can do between shifts and therefore they become long working days.

Straight shifts

A straight shift is where the employees will work through an 8-hour session (a shift). These shifts again are flexible in when they start, to meet the needs of the operation. An employee may be on a set shift. For example:

● A night manager working in a hotel, responsible for the day's audits and late residents could work from 11.00 p.m. to 7.00 a.m.
● A duty manager could have a flexible shift over a period of a week. A week's rota might appear as follows:

Monday	7.00 a.m. to 3.00 p.m.
Tuesday	Day off
Wednesday	7.00 a.m. to 3.00 p.m.
Thursday	Day off
Friday	3.00 p.m. to 11.00 p.m.
Saturday	9.00 a.m. to 5.00 p.m.
Sunday	3.00 p.m. to 11.00 p.m.

Note that weekends are part of a normal working week in most commercial operations, and in a high proportion of catering service operations.

Employees paid on an hourly basis are normally classed as *waged staff*.

Definition

Waged staff are employees paid on a weekly basis, with overtime, normally paid one week after the work has been done.

Managers and supervisors are normally classed as *salaried staff*.

Definition

Salaried staff *are employees paid on a monthly basis, with little or no payment for overtime. Overtime is infrequent and in small amounts, and is usually regarded as 'goodwill' towards the company. Working Bank Holidays and on normal days off is usually repaid 'in lieu', with hours off to be taken as and when required.*

The industry is renowned for high levels of labour turnover, the main reasons for leaving the workplace being:

● Low pay
● Long unsociable hours
● Lack of job satisfaction
● Lack of management recognition

For far too long, managers have looked upon high staff turnover as part of the industry's make-up. Only in the last few years have some organizations realized the value of their employees and have begun to appreciate that reducing staff turnover maintains standards for quality and service. Many now recognize the 'social' skills of employees, especially those who interface with the public. Improved working conditions, incentives and bonuses for high performance at all levels are some of the ways in which the industry is tackling the high turnover problem.

As the hospitality and catering industry responds to regional demands, rather than to national trends, so too does the demand for labour. On a regional and national basis, the catering services sector remains relatively stable as long as the hospitals, schools, etc. remain open. In the commercial sectors there are far more fluctuations. In large towns and cities employment patterns remain, to a great extent, constant, although turnover would be relatively high, especially in the unskilled areas. Rural areas, however, where work is less constant and more open to changes in demand, would result in lower turnover patterns due to less job availability and therefore less security.

Women in the workplace

With the decrease in the numbers of 16–19-year-olds, the industry will have to look to other labour markets. The role of women in the hospitality and catering industry has dominated in some sectors, e.g. school meals, employee feeding – the types of operations which facilitate working women with children. However, an increasing number of women are playing a far greater role in the labour force, and their economic value is growing. The major motivating factors of the last decade for this growth have been:

1 An increase in home ownership and interest rates has forced women back to work to help support the male's salary, against high mortgages and the repossession of homes in 1991.
2 Annual increases in standards of living and expectations have encouraged women to return to work to help pay for them.
3 Rising unemployment and redundancy in the male labour force have also made it essential for women to return to work, in many cases becoming the family provider.

The balance of the workforce between male and female still shows males as the largest sector:

● In 1985 the ratio was 58:42 in favour of men.
● In 1985–1990 there was a general rise in the UK workforce of 7 per cent. By 1990 the ratio of male to female workers was 56:44 – a reduction of 2 per cent in men.
● By 1995 the forecasted rates will be 55:45 with parity by the year 2000

As all occupations are now tapping into this female market, hospitality and catering, renowned for its long hours, low pay with few employee facilities, is improving working conditions in order to compete for this labour market. Some would say 'about time too'.

Task 1.9

Working in pairs or small groups, carry out a survey of commercial and catering services outlets. For each outlet, record the ratio of male to female employees. Monitor the job types held by each sex – i.e. manager, supervisor, operative. How does the information you have gathered on job types compare with the male/female ratio?

Career and employment opportunities

The hospitality and catering industry has extensive employment opportunities that meet the needs of all different types of prospective employee, from women returning to work after family commitments, to adults retraining after redundancy, to those on an academic route doing NVQs or GNVQs. The Training and Enterprise Councils (TECs) are regionally based and respond to regional/local demands from employers in various vocational areas. TECs therefore may provide financial assistance to enable unemployed people to train or retrain.

During your progress at college or school you need to take stock of the type of career path you would want to follow on completion of the course. There are opportunities in employment and in higher education. Some of these are as follows.

Education route

1 The Hotel, Catering and Institutional Management Association (HCIMA) offers the highest specific catering qualification which can be gained through a full- or part-time course or via distance learning programmes.
2 Degree courses in catering and related subjects, or in more general management subjects
3 Higher National Diploma (HND) course, through full-time study.
4 Higher National Certificate (HNC) course, through part-time study.

Task 1.10

Using your college or school facilities, investigate the various types of higher education courses which would be open to you on successful completion of your present course. Choose one local college or university and three other areas in which you might be interested. This will assist you in your career action planning for your National Record of Achievement.

Employment route

During your progress through your course, and by completing your personal statement for your National Record of Achievement, you should have been able to clarify the functional areas best suited to your personality and abilities. An extrovert would be best suited to a busy restaurant or reception area where their personality and social skills could be put to best use, rather than perhaps Accommodation Operations, which has less customer contact.

An example of a career action plan for a successful GNVQ student could be as follows:

Five-year action plan

Career aim:
Assistant food and beverage manager in a luxury hotel

Career plan:
Year 1   First full-time job – trainee management scheme in 2/3-star hotel
Year 2   Trainee specializing in the food and beverage area
Year 3   Assistant food and beverage manager with a different company, 3/4-star hotel (to increase knowledge and show flexibility). Start part-time degree or HCIMA course
Year 4   Food and beverage manager in same hotel. Continue with course
Year 5   Complete degree or HCIMA course. Assistant food and beverage manager in 5-star hotel

---

Task 1.11

Produce a statement of your strengths and weaknesses. Ask your classmates what they think your strengths and weaknesses are. Formulate a realistic five-year career action plan which you would hope to follow. Start to research and collect data with regards to the organization, establishment and operational area which will aid you in meeting your action plan.

Employment opportunities within the hospitality and catering industry are vast even though within your locality the sector may be small or seasonal. For example, holiday resorts such as Blackpool have seasonal employment

opportunities. To meet your action plan, flexibility not only in your attitude to the work but also in where you live will be a major asset.

Although other units in this book will cover in more detail the various management and operational areas open to you in the hospitality and catering industry, to support you in formulating your career plan the following is a brief overview.

Management structure

General manager
Overall responsibility for an outlet.

Main duties may cover:
● Forecasting profits
● Devising budgets
● Establishing appraisal system, grievance procedures, etc.
● Meeting overall organization demands (if outlet is part of a larger organization)
● Oversee internal affairs

Unless a small outlet, a general manager would not normally be involved in the actual operational areas of an outlet

Duty/operational managers
Overall responsibility for an outlet during their working hours, on an operational basis.

Main duties would include:
● Maintaining budget requirements in a particular operational area, e.g. food preparation to make a gross profit of 60 per cent
● Meeting target requirements set, e.g. 80 per cent room occupancy to be met by the reception/accommodation area
● Day-to-day monitoring of an area
● Staff training – awareness of needs, monitoring training programmes
● Maintaining health and safety regulations for employees and customers
● Supporting the general manager as and when required in a variety of managerial roles

Supervisors

Responsibility for a small operational area, e.g. restaurant, bar, reception.

Main duties would include:
- Day-to-day 'hands on' running of the area
- Dealing with staff queries
- Dealing with customer queries and complaints

Operatives
- Responsible to the company for maintaining standards of quality, service, hygiene and safety of themselves and customers.
- Their main role is performing the tasks within an operational area.

Over three-quarters of all employees in the industry are in the operative and craft positions. It is at this level where staff turnover is the highest and where job areas decline in recession. Ten per cent of employees are in managerial/supervisory roles.

Task 1.12

Investigate, by using your local jobcentre or newspaper, three different occupations in the hospitality and catering industry which relate closely to your action plan. Make appropriate enquiries to identify the following:

- Hours of work
- Rate of pay and conditions
- Job description
- Career prospects

The operational areas available depend on the sector in which you decide to work. These can be divided as follows:

- Food and beverage service
- Food preparation
- Reception
- Accommodation
- Portering
- Administration

Administration is an area which usually employs people who have specialized in specific areas (e.g. personnel, accountancy, marketing, etc.). The above is a broad-based list, covering the main areas – the areas you would find in a particular outlet would depend on the outlet itself and the organization to which it belonged.

Task 1.13

Research two hospitality and catering outlets from each of the sectors (commercial and catering services). Identify which operational areas are involved. Have any of them been integrated because of the size or type of outlet?

Conclusion

In this section, we have looked at the sectors and scale of the hospitality and catering industry. You should have discovered the relationships between the different sectors and how the operational areas differ, depending on the styles of outlets and the regional demands. We have also considered how the sectors of the industry classify themselves according to the facilities they offer. You have used key sources of data to find out information about your local demands and employment opportunities. Finally, we have looked at employment patterns and opportunities within the industry itself.

Test your knowledge

1 What are the two main sectors of the industry?
2 List the types of outlets to be found in each sector.

3 Explain the difference between the following terms, giving examples:
   Organization
   Outlet
   Facility
   Operation
4 List the present hotel-classification schemes.
5 Apart from structured hotel-classification schemes, how else is the hotel market classified, and why?
6 In the contract catering sector where has been the main growth area and why? Where has the sector declined and why?
7 What are the characteristics of catering services outlets?
8 The hospitality and catering industry is renowned for its high labour turnover. Why is this? How can management improve the situation?

▪ EXTERNAL FACTORS AFFECTING GROWTH ▪

The hospitality and catering industry plays a vital economic role. As an employer, it ranks the third largest in the UK, with a workforce of approximately 2.5 million people, including those in related industries. The catering allied trades in 1991 had an approximate turnover of

£31.1 million (inclusive of VAT), clearly indicating the importance of the hospitality and catering industry in economic terms.

As the industry is defined as the provider of all food and drink away from home, its operating units are both diverse and complex. Having already discussed the commercial and catering services industries, you should now be more aware of the profit- and non-profit making areas. All outlets, from small ones owned by private individuals to the large *conglomerates*, play an important role in the UK economic and social climate.

Definition

● *A conglomerate* is a group of unrelated firms which have merged together into one company. The original firms may have activities which complement each other, or they may be completely contrasting and unconnected.

Table 1.5 shows the number of outlets in each category in the three years 1989, 1990 and 1991, together with the turnover during 1991.

The catering market responds at a *regional* level. It is affected by the community and local needs, rather than by national trends. These

Table 1.5 Number of outlets in the commercial sector

	1989	1990	1991	1991 turnover (inc. VAT) (£ millions)
Hotels and other residential establishments	13,779	14,444	13,633	6.4
Holiday camps/camping, caravan sites	1,889	2,027	1,949	1.1
Restaurants, cafés, snack bars, EOPs	17,327	17,842	17,288	3.8
Take-aways, fish and chip shops, eating off premises	29,928	30,921	29,319	3.8
Public houses	41,339	40,155	39,169	10.4
Clubs (excluding sports and gaming clubs)	17,342	16,806	16,489	2.8
Catering contractors	2,509	2,704	2,459	2.1

Source: Central Statistical Office

social trends and factors affect the amount of choice in an area, and include:

- Disposable incomes
- Socio-economic groupings
- Standards of living
- Leisure activities
- Cultural influences
- Eating and drinking habits

External influences on the industry

As you can see from Table 1.5, without exception there has been a sudden decline in the number of outlets right across the hospitality and catering industry. This is due to the fact that the industry is extremely price-sensitive. The principal influences upon demand, especially meals eaten outside the home in the commercial sector, are economic and social. By 1991, the economic recession which hit the UK and the world, had an immediate affect.

The current economic climate	
1979–81	Economic decline; UK in recession
1982–mid-89	Rapid economic growth which led to higher inflation. The government attempted control of inflation by increasing interest rates over a period of 18 months.
1990–93	Major economic decline worldwide. Recession more severe than in 1979–81

The impact on the hospitality and catering industry of rising unemployment, the fall in productivity levels and higher interest rates on credit has reduced the amount of money available to spend on leisure activities. This is defined as *real disposable income*.

Definition

- **Real disposable income** is the personal income left after all main expenditures have been removed.

The essential difference between the current recession and the one in 1979 is that it has hit the prosperous South and South-east of the UK, affecting both senior management and supervisors.

Higher interest rates affect not only the customer but also the operations themselves with increased interest rates on borrowed capital.

Government legislation has increased VAT rates in recent years, and has introduced VAT on fuel. Budget tax increases on alcohol, insurance and business rates cause major external pressures both indirectly (having to pay increased prices from suppliers) and directly (having to increase their own prices to meet the new taxes and rates). This has had a negative impact on the hospitality and catering industry.

Disposable incomes

Different regions have different disposable incomes and these are shown in Figure 1.6. As expressed in the figure, the lowest average weekly disposable income was in Northern Ireland at £116, while London and the South-east was the highest, at £156 and £141 respectively. Although taking a drop in 1990, the South-east, East Anglia and the South-west have steadily remained about the UK average.

The average national weekly spend on meals eaten outside the home during 1989 was £8.68. In the same year, Greater London had the highest expenditure of £12.19 – a little over 46 per cent above the national average. The lowest expenditure regions continue to be Wales, the North and both East and West Midlands. This was before the present recession, which saw

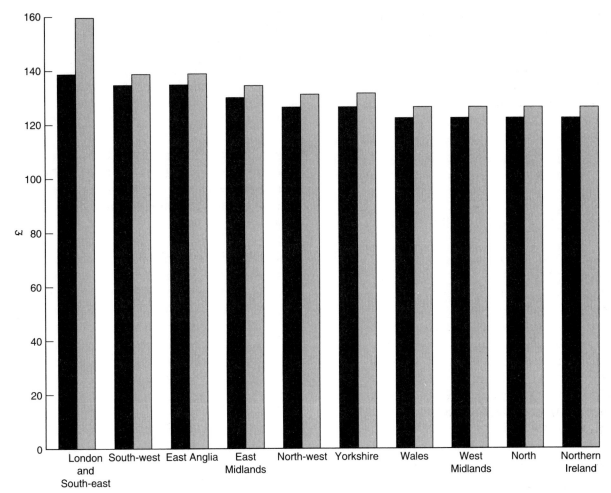

Figure 1.6 Range of average weekly household disposable income per head by region, 1991. (*Source*: Central Statistical Office)

only a small dip between 1989 and 1991. Estimates predict that the recession has bitten hard, consequently a deceleration of eating out has taken place.

As you would appreciate, there is a high *correlation* between the level of income a person has and the amount of disposable income available.

Definition

- **A correlation** *is a relationship which exists between two or more things which causes each one to change in response to changes in the others.*

This correlation is not so accurate at the lower end of the scale. People on incomes of less than £50 per week actually spend more on eating out than those directly above, in the bracket £50 to £75. This is probably due to the fact that the £50 per week income contains the unemployed and single people who turn to the convenience of cheap take-aways/fast-food restaurants which fits readily into their style of living.

Socio-economic factors

The socio-economic classification was devised mainly as a marketing and market research tool to define the UK population. As yet, nothing has been devised to take its place even though

Table 1.6 Social-economic groupings

Groups	Social status	Occupation
A	Upper middle class	Higher management, administrators, professionals
B	Middle class	Intermediate management, administrators, professionals
C	Lower middle class	Supervisory, clerical or junior management, administrators, professionals
C_2	Skilled working class	Skilled manual workers
D	Working class	Semi-and unskilled manual workers
E	Lowest level of subsistence	Pensioners, widows, casual and low-grade workers

Source: Joint Industry Committee for National Readership Surveys

it does have its anomalies. The population is divided by these groupings not by income but by profession – although there is a definite correlation between the two (Table 1.6). The classification takes into account:

- Education level
- Type of employment
- Background
- Lifestyle
- Social aspirations
- Income, to an extent

With this type of classification it is possible to have a person with a low income but with a good education and the potential to improve his or her status classified in a higher socio-economic group than a well-off tradesperson with a poor education. This is because of their differing backgrounds, lifestyle and social aspirations.

Population

Using these groups, the population may now be statistically examined. The ABC groups account for 40 per cent of the population, with C_2, D and E accounting for the other 60 per cent. Increasing pressures to become 'upwardly mobile' has swelled the higher-status groups over the past eighty years. This has been achieved by a three-pronged approach (Figure 1.7).

Under Margaret Thatcher the Conservative government encouraged home ownership, offering tax incentives, and the buying of council houses. Low interest rates also provided an incentive to buy.

Marketing has encouraged better lifestyles through the advertising media in aspects such as holidays, furnishings, kitchen equipment, etc., increasing consumer expectations in all walks of life, especially in the hospitality and catering sectors. Consumers are now more aware of the products and services offered, and will no longer be content with poor-quality provision.

The consequent effect on the hospitality and catering industry has been an increase in eating away from the home. This in turn has increased the variety of eating establishments, with many people becoming more adventurous in choice and style of restaurant which require higher standards of service and value for money. Eating away from the home on a regular basis is costly, and, not surprisingly, is mainly supported by the higher socio-economic groups.

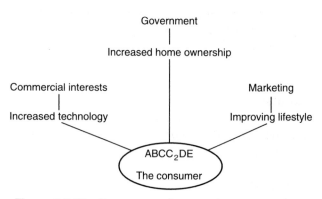

Figure 1.7 The three-pronged approach

On the whole, there has been a general increase except in the E group, especially for mid-day meals in the higher social group, probably due to the business and conference trade.

Cultural influences

Although the UK is a relatively small island it did, during the old Empire/Commonwealth, rule over a large proportion of the world. Acceptance of a wide variety of different culinary foods and styles has been an ongoing process since that time. The influx in the 1950s and 1960s of immigrants from the Caribbean, Asia and Africa greatly influenced the hospitality and catering industry, with rapid acceptance of ethnic restaurants, including Chinese and Indian, with West Indian to a lesser degree. Through the advent of increased travel a large number of European restaurants have also appeared on the market (e.g. French, Italian, Greek and Spanish).

By the late 1960s the US fast-food concept arrived in the UK in the guise of the hamburger. The US influence has been maintained in the take-away/fast-food sector to the extent that it has to be said that the UK is approximately ten years behind the United States in its food concepts. Influenced greatly by the movement of people, not just in the UK but worldwide, the effect of increasing acceptance of different styles is ongoing. Recent trends, especially in the London area, have included sushi, the Japanese tradition of preparing and eating raw fish. There are now sushi bars and even a take-away Sushi Lunch Box counter in Harrods (they even supply the chopsticks).

Settlement of immigrants has a major local cultural influence on the hospitality and catering industry. The most popular region for immigrants is the South-east of England. Five other regions which have a sizeable influx are:

1. East Midlands
2. East Anglia
3. Yorkshire
4. North-west England
5. Scotland

These are obviously exposed to a greater variety of ethnic culinary styles and foods than the other regions.

Task 1.14

Investigate locally the different types and styles of service offered by ethnic outlets. Research into how long these establishments have been in business. Illustrate your answers by using graphs/charts as appropriate.

Demographic trends

Definition

- **Demographics** *is the study of population statistics*

Government population censuses and surveys can produce data showing what is happening to the population now, with regards to the numbers in each age group, and can make reasonably accurate forecasts of what will happen in the future. Between the early 1950s and 1970s the UK population grew steadily. Since then, this increase has slowed down. By the years 2001–2011 there is a projected decrease, especially in Scotland, and a deceleration in England, Wales and Northern Ireland.

You might wonder what this has to do with the hospitality and catering industry. The industry needs to keep abreast of the population age so that we can forecast the types of markets which will be opened to us in the future. A decline in the birth rate from the early 1970s has significantly reduced the proportion of children under the age of 16, which will have a notable effect on fast-food operations. As in the case of 'burgers', this age group is their main marketing target. However, there has been an increase of 16–39-year-olds and the 65+ age group. In reality, the population is growing older and living longer.

Over the next decade the catering industry will need a change in emphasis away from the children's and teenage markets towards the needs of older consumers. Already McDonald's is trying to encourage loyalty to their product with the under-16s so that it is maintained throughout their adult life. This is accomplished in various ways, including Kiddies Parties, hats and balloons, special offers, vouchers, etc.

Tourism

'Tourism' is a word which conjures up a vision of daytrippers, holidays at home or abroad, excursions and travelling. A broad definition of a tourist could be: 'a person who travels and stays away from home for leisure which is pleasure-orientated (e.g. holidays, health clubs, sports, etc.) or for business (e.g. conferences, study breaks, etc. where leisure is a subsidiary activity)'.

This difference between leisure and business has a direct impact on the hospitality and catering industry. Those tourists involved in leisure will want to be indulged, to have a pampered pleasurable experience with perhaps various activities and services to meet their individual needs. (Customers in this group would invariably stay away from home for two or more nights.) A high level of customer care is needed to provide these services to a level which will satisfy the tourist's demands.

Business tourists would perhaps stay away from home only overnight. Primarily there for business purposes, they might welcome the extra addition of leisure activities. Some companies promote this combined 'business and pleasure' opportunity to relieve stress, thereby maintaining a high level of performance in the employees. For example, a business conference for executive managers could be planned at a luxury hotel, after which a workout in the gym, a relaxing swim in the pool, combined with a high level of customer care would rejuvenate them for the following day.

Task 1.15

Look at the hospitality and catering industry facilities associated with tourism in your locality. Categorize the facilities offered into leisure and business. Research into which (leisure or business) has the greatest demand and why.

The hotel tourist industry has its roots in the Victorian railway era. The railways terminated at a hotel and British Rail actually owned many hotel properties, including the Grand Hotel in Manchester and the Grosvenor Hotel in London, which has its own entrance into Victoria Station.

The Development of Tourism bill in 1968 gave a much-needed boost to the hotel sector by helping to create 40,000 new hotel beds in four years, and guaranteed £200 million investment in the industry through government provision of grants and loans. During this period, Trust House Forte Posthouse chain developed, taking advantage of the grants which contributed to 15–20 per cent of the capital cost of a typical 150-bedroom hotel.

UK accommodation has, in general, been criticized for poor standards and high costs, with little or no apparent forward planning, especially with regards to the infrastructure. A prime example here is the onset of the Channel Tunnel opening. The French have developed super-fast, super-efficient trains which will run on existing English tracks but with far less efficiency as the UK has not the *infrastructure* in place to facilitate the trains' needs.

Definition

● **Infrastructure** *means the basic services required to support a major development, (e.g. road, rail, air links, etc.).*

Tourism as part of the UK economy has, largely due to the recession, declined since 1991. British people took an estimated 34 million holidays (four or more nights) away from home in 1991. The numbers in 1992 decreased by 2 million to 32 million. From around 1980 there has been a steady decline in the numbers of British people holidaying in Britain for more than four nights. In 1988 there was an upturn from below 30 million to approximately 33 million, where it has stabilized.

Accommodation

The most popular overall type of accommodation in 1992 was self-catering, representing 53 per cent of all British holidays, with serviced accommodation at 30 per cent. However, the single most popular type of accommodation was hotels, represented as:

● Main holiday 24 per cent
● Additional holiday 26 per cent
● All holidays 25 per cent

A close second overall were caravans at 23 per cent.

As can be seen from Figure 1.8, holidays taken within the UK have only a 2 per cent variance between the groups. Greater differentials occur when analysing holidays taken abroad with (as

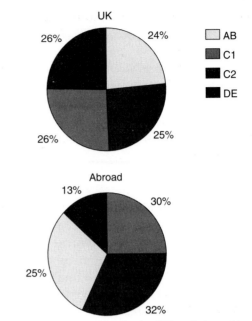

Figure 1.8 Holiday taking in the UK and abroad by social class

you might expect), the smallest groups being DE. A, B and C represent over 60 per cent of the total holidays abroad.

During 1992, an estimated total of 118 million trips of one night or more were taken by UK residents in the UK or abroad. These trips represent 653 million nights away from home and generated a total expenditure of £25,070 million. The most popular English destination for holidays in 1992 by far was the West Country with 21 per cent, Northumbria being the least popular with only 4 per cent. For business purposes, London is the most popular with 19 per cent of all destinations.

Task 1.16

Using your college, school or local library, find the most recent English Hotel Occupancy survey conducted by Horwath. Using the information in this survey, prepare a report on the following:

1 List the locations in England which the survey covers. State how the survey defines each location.
2 Explain what has occurred over the last five years with regards to the annual occupancy rate.
3 How does the room occupancy rate differ at each location, affecting local demands?

There were 18,535,000 visitors to the UK according to the Internal Passenger Survey (IPS) in 1992 – an 8 per cent improvement on the previous year. The spending by these visitors also increased by 7 per cent to a total of £7891 million. The adverse effect on overseas visitors in 1991 was the direct result of the Gulf War, especially to visitors from North America and the rest of the world – a total loss in 1991 of 1,267,000 visits.

The regional pattern of overseas tourism in 1992 still has London as the predominant destination with a total of 9,971,830 (53 per cent) visits, representing £4,153,324 (53.2 per cent) expenditure. The popularity of London has varied little over the last ten years.

The single most popular type of accommodation used by overseas visitors is hotels. Fifty-nine per cent used some type of hotel accommodation (licensed, unlicensed or bed and breakfast), for at least some part of their visit. Nearly half (48 per cent) used them as their main form of accommodation.

Apart from the Gulf War, which seriously affected overseas visitors, other recent external influences which have influenced trade, especially from America, and hence have impacted on the hospitality and catering industry, were the spate of IRA bombs in London and the Lockerbie plane crash in December 1988.

The Americans are now returning to the UK albeit slowly, but to the great relief of the quality hotels. This upturn in tourism has also had a direct effect on recruitment levels, and employment prospects within the industry are again looking promising.

Competition

It might appear a little short-sighted, in a small town with a McDonald's and a Burger King already established, to open an independent burger bar. The majority of the consumer market will have established loyalties to the larger 'image' makers. Being faced with competition is a healthy experience/situation. It ensures that each outlet provides the best possible services to the consumer for the best possible price. The consumer cannot fail to win. But what of the outlets?

Each outlet must look to the provision of the services they offer compared to those of their competitors. By using various marketing tools each must build up an individual or organizational image which potential consumers recognise. Competitive pricing policies are *essential* but not to the extent of creating a 'price war' in which one or more businesses could 'go to the wall' because of insufficient financial reserves. An example of this is Freddie Laker, whose cut-price flights to the USA were countered by British Airways and eventually Laker lost.

Influences of legislation

A whole range of laws impinge on the hospitality and catering industry. These can be broken down into two main types of law:

1 Daily operational laws, i.e. those which need to be complied with and understood every single day of operation (e.g. food hygiene laws, laws on the display of tariffs, weights and measures laws, etc.
2 Business laws, (e.g. those to do with employment such as contracts, pay, etc., VAT regulations, fire precautions, health and safety).

The effects of the laws should be to safeguard the business, the customers and the employees.

The major influence on the industry in recent years has been the Food Safety Act 1990. This has forced managers to improve, monitor and train staff in the handling, storage and preparation of food items for human consumption. This section will provide short key points on legal issues as more detailed aspects will be covered in depth in the appropriate sections of this book.

Types of laws

English law may be classified in a number of different ways. For business purposes the most important are: *Legislation* or *Statutory Instruments*:

- Legislation is derived from Parliamentary Acts
- Statutory Instruments are updates of the original legislation

Civil law concerns dealings with individuals. It is not aimed at punishment but at ensuring that an agreement, damage or injury is made good. For example, under the Health and Safety at Work etc. Act 1974 an employee may bring a civil action against his or her employer if a piece of equipment has not been correctly maintained and an accident occurs which results in an injury.

Criminal law protects society as a whole. Its actions are concerned with the punishment or deterring of individuals guilty of committing an offence.

Data Protection Act 1984

Areas within the hospitality and catering industry need to consider if data are kept on a computer. Examples might include:

- Guest reservation systems
- Guest registration and personal details
- Internal reservations

- Mailing lists
- Credit limits
- 'Black' lists
- Staff records

If records are kept only for accounting purposes, the outlet would be exempt from registering. Organizations now tend to keep customer history files so that they can offer guests individual attention to room preferences, service level requirements, special requests, dietary needs, etc.

Food Safety Act 1990

This required major changes to update and expand existing food laws. A brief overview (as it will be covered in Unit 2 and in depth in Unit 4) of the major changes is as follows:

1 Sections 1–8 define in detail what is meant by 'food and drink fit for human consumption'; the definition of 'sale of food'; the responsibilities of the owner for the business premises; the duties of the Environmental Health Officer (EHO).
2 Sections 9–13 define the powers of the EHO and explain the various Improvement Notices and Prohibition Orders which can be used in premises which break the Act.
3 Sections 14–22 involves consumer protection with regards to the nature and quality of the product (e.g. frozen food sold as fresh). It includes the way in which the written description of a product is used (e.g. on a menu, roast leg of lamb when in fact a shoulder is used). These sections also cover the business of the owner/manager if a genuine mistake has been made and can be justified.
4 Sections 23–26 enable local authorities to run food hygiene courses.
5 Sections 27–31 describe Ministers' powers of food sampling from businesses.
6 Sections 32 and 33 define authority for Powers of Entry.
7 Sections 34–39 define prosecution and penalties.
8 Section 40 refines the codes of practice.

Task 1.17

Working in pairs or small groups, choose ONE each of the above sets of Sections of the Food Safety Act 1990 and examine the Sections in detail. Produce a short report on the contents of those Sections for your colleagues

Food Hygiene (General) Regulations 1970

The law concerning hygiene in all food premises is contained in these regulations. A breach of them could result in the issuing of an Improvement Notice (Food Safety Act 1990, Section 10) (see above). The principal requirements relate to:

- Cleanliness of premises and equipment
- Hygienic food-handling procedures
- Personal hygiene of food handlers
- Maintenance and repair of premises
- Water supply and washing facilities
- Waste disposal
- Temperature and time control of certain foods

The Food Hygiene (Amendment) Regulations 1990 and 1991

The amendment is specifically concerned with chill and hot temperature controls for certain foods. Chilled foods are to be kept between 5°C and 8°C, and hot foods at 63°C.

Emphasis is also placed on monitoring equipment in that it functions correctly. This monitoring should be noted so that it is available for discussion with the enforcement officers as and when appropriate.

The EU (General) Food Hygiene Directive

This is at the consultation stage at present. Following this, regulations will be put before parliament and an enforced Code of Practice will be available by June 1994. The Code will be brought into force by June 1995. A brief summary of the directive is as follows:

1. Set conditions necessary for hygienic production
2. Contains basic rules for food premises
3. Industry in harness with enforcement agencies, consumers and the government to develop voluntary guides of good practice

Fire Precautions (Hotel and Boarding Houses) Order 1972

A fire certificate issued by the local fire authority is required for any premises used for the business of providing sleeping accommodation for staff, or sleeping, dining, lounge areas or other accommodation for guests.

Definition

- A **Guest** *is any member of the public for whom accommodation is provided.*

The order applies to any premises providing:

- Sleeping accommodation for more than six persons, being staff or guests
- Sleeping accommodation on any floor above the first floor of the premises for staff or guests
- Sleeping accommodation below the ground floor of the premises for staff or guests.

Definition

- The **first floor** *is any floor above the ground floor.*

Fire Precautions Act 1971

On application for a fire certificate the fire authorities may require plans of the premises.

After a fire authority inspection a certificate may be issued or an order served on the applicant informing him or her of improvements or alterations which need to be completed before a certificate will be issued. The right of appeal to the magistrates' courts by any person refused a certificate may be made. Notice of appeal must be given 21 days from the date on which the notice was refused or improvements and alterations requested.

Offences against the Act are:

1 Operating without a fire certificate (liable to a fine and/or imprisonment
2 Failure to keep or display a copy of the fire certificate on the premises – liable to a fine
3 Obstructing access to the premises by a fire inspector at any reasonable time:
    To request evidence of existing fire certificate
    To ascertain whether a fire certificate is required (liable to a fine)
    To ensure that fire standards are being maintained

Trade Union Reform and Employment Rights Act 1993

This Act has amended the Employment Protection (Consolidated) Act 1978 and the Employment Acts of 1980 to 1990. The main areas of change include: all new employees working 8 hours or more a week and whose employment lasts for a month of more are entitled to receive a written statement of particulars of employment. The employer must provide the statement not later than 2 months after the employee started.

There is a difference between a Contract of Employment and a Written Statement of Particulars. A Contract of Employment is a legally binding agreement which may be oral or written. A Written Statement of Particulars is intended for information only, containing the more important terms of employment which the employer believes form part of the contract.

This new Act also requires the employer, on request by the employees, to provide written statements to existing employees who were not eligible in previous Acts (for example employees who worked between 8 and 16 hours per week). The Particulars must provide certain details in a single document known as the 'principal statement'.

Definition

● **The principal statement**

The details listed contain all relevant working conditions from the name and address of the employer and employee to stating rates of pay, hours to be worked, holiday entitlements which relate specifically to the employee. It must also contain general terms and conditions of all employees (for example sick pay, length of notice required, disciplinary and grievance procedures, etc.).

Licensing Act 1964/Licensing (Amendment) Act 1980/Licensing Act 1988

The Licensing Act covers all aspects of the control of alcoholic liquor. The principal elements are concerned with:

● Types of licences
● Licensing procedures
● Fees
● Permitted hours
● Regulations with regards to licensed premises
● Young persons
● Clubs
● Weights and measures law
● Displaying of notices
● Price list regulations
● New towns
● Sporting Events (Control of Alcohol, etc.) Act 1985

The major influence which affected the industry came in 1988 when permitted hours were increased from nine per day Monday to

Saturday to opening times between 11 a.m. and 11 p.m.. Sunday hours have remained approximately the same, e.g. 12 noon – 3 p.m. and 7 p.m.–10.30 p.m. The industry, having been given the go-ahead for a 12-hour day, soon realized that in some outlets this was not viable as there were few customers and all the extra staffing and overheads were still needed.

Other recent effects have included the necessity not only to display a current bar price list but also that list now has to include the alcoholic contents of each drink. This includes any dispensed beverage, wines by the glass, etc. Bottled wines do not have to be listed as the alcoholic strength should be shown on the label.

European legislation

Many of the UK's new laws and amendments to existing laws are now affected by the European Union (formerly called the European Community). The laws which are affected can be those of the UK or they may be laws which cover the whole of the EU. There are four types of laws or rules which affect member states:

1 *Regulations* These are binding on all member states, without the need for any further legislation. They are effective in the courts just as UK law is effective.
2 *Directives* These are laws which might already be covered by UK legislation, but if not, the UK laws will need to be amended to comply with the directives.
3 *Decisions* These are decisions made by European courts and which are binding on those to whom the decision is directed, whether this is a member state or an individual.
4 Recommendations As this implies, these do not have any binding effect.

Effects of external influences

We have discussed the external influences which affect the growth, scale and provision of the products and services in the hospitality and catering industry. Here is a brief review of those influences for your reference:

UK economy

Recent economic events has caused:

- Decline in factories, therefore a reduction in employee feeding; contract caterers lost in the region of 540 outlets between 1993 and 1994
- Reduction in the number of hospitality and catering and related trades between 1990 and 1991 totalled a drop of 3.5 per cent
- Recent lower interest rates are starting to contribute towards a slight recovery in the industry
- Decrease in personal tax allowances, increases in National Insurance payments and credit interest rates, changes in allowances for business expenditure, and reduced disposable incomes all impact on outlets
- Decrease in outlets, increased unemployment, decline in work available
- Exchange rates – as these rise, England becomes too expensive a holiday destination and therefore there is a reduction in tourism, especially from America

Table 1.7 shows the number of businesses in each area of the industry, in both 1990 and 1991, with the percentage decline in each area.

UK legislation

Through government Acts:

- The policies of the government in the late 1980s encouraged contract caterers to tender into the catering services sector of hospitals, education, prisons, etc.
- Hygiene regulations
- EU regulations – relaxed regulations on duty-free alcohol has increased drinking in the home and thereby reduced the amount bought in public houses

Table 1.7 Number of businesses

	1990	1991	% decline
Catering trades	124,900	120,305	3.7
Hotels and other residential establishments	14,444	13,633	5.6
Holiday camps, camping and caravan sites	2,027	1,949	3.8
Fish and chip shops, sandwich bars, food for consumption mainly or wholly off the premises	30,921	29,319	5.2
Public houses	40,155	39,169	2.5
Clubs	16,806	16,489	1.9
Catering contractors	2,704	2,459	9.1
Total	231,327	223,323	3.5

Source: Central Statistical Office

Crises

Crises have a direct effect on tourism.

- The Gulf War in 1991 resulted in a decrease in the number of American tourists and a reduction in the occupancy rates in quality hotels and in tourist areas of England.
- The Lockerbie air crash in 1988 had a similar effect
- Internal bombings. Earlier attacks kept tourists away, but these no longer seem to have such an effect

Tourism

Increases in interest rates, taxes, etc. have impacted on the price to the customer. Increased charges in hotels, bed and breakfast outlets etc., have led to an increase in self-catering, caravan holidays, etc. This has resulted in:

- The hotel market remaining depressed
- Some increased satisfaction in self-catering, caravans and self-catering holiday camps
- More people turning to overseas holidays
- Due to decreases in disposable income, slight reductions at traditionally active times of year, (e.g. Christmas and Easter)

Competition

- Most growth and competition has emerged in the fast-food operations
- Fierce competition between city and town holidays have produced cut-price rack rates to try to maintain a reasonable occupancy rate.

Definition

- **Rack rate** is the calculated price of a bedroom which includes direct and indirect costs and a standard profit margin.

Task 1.18

The above lists are by no means complete. Look at your local area. Write a report on how external factors have affected the scale and provision of services in the hospitality and catering sectors. Identify how two of the outlets have adapted to these external influences and the significant changes they have had to make

Internal influences

External factors bring pressures on our industry beyond our control. Internal influences are pressures caused by the industry. Industrial organizations and outlets need to be managed effectively in order for the organization to function and maintain its position in the competitive market place in which we live.

Some of the internal influences which can affect the growth of hospitality and catering outlets are:

1 The labour market
2 Working conditions
3 Facilities offered
4 Availability/use of equipment
5 Control systems
6 Local environments

Labour market

Because of the industry's peaks and troughs, the demand for labour often coincides with these, i.e. a surplus of staff when activities are low, a shortage when sales peak. This produces a labour force which consists of a comparatively small number of full-time staff, usually with key roles, and a large part-time workforce as and when required.

Unfortunately, because of this, there are enormous difficulties in maintaining stability in standards of food production and service, especially in large towns and cities, where the demand for part-time staff is high. Some companies have overcome this by encouraging part-time staff to have loyalties to a company. Contracted part-time staff get all the benefits of full-time members which might include the use of in-house leisure facilities and bonus/ incentive schemes.

The hospitality and catering industry is notorious for its poor working conditions, long hours, low pay and high staff turnover, which have for a long time been inherent in the industry. It has taken progressive management techniques to reverse these trends. Staff who are happily employed not only reflect this in their level of customer care but are also more open to training and development. Staff turnover is reduced, together with absenteeism and sickness.

These innovative management techniques used in the catering industry have created, in part, a higher standard of management teams which reflects down through the lines of responsibility, to a more knowledgeable and efficient workforce.

The location of the outlet also has an important influence as regards staffing levels. Having looked at the demographic situation, you are now aware that the population is gradually getting older. This affects not only customer potential but also staffing. An outlet in a small, rural area would probably have more difficulty in finding suitable staff than one in a large town or city. This lack of staff will directly affect the outlet's growth. An outlet is unable to expand without the staff to support it.

Task 1.19

Working in pairs or small groups, choose three different types of outlet in your locality and discuss what might influence each outlet's labour market and how it might be affected.

Facilities offered

We have already discussed the social trends and factors which affect the amount of choice in an area, e.g. disposable incomes, socio-economic groups, standards of living, etc. These have a direct influence on the internal factors of:

- Type of facilities offered
- Style of operation
- Prices charged

In a resort hotel, the food, beverage and accommodation facilities are of greater importance to the customer who will be staying over a longer period, compared to the guest who is staying only for one night. Short-stay customers would be looking for basic food and beverage service and accommodation to a reasonable standard, without the social aspects which a long-stay customer would require.

It is simpler to relate to the facilities found in a hotel as these can be cross-referenced throughout the hospitality and catering industry in all sectors and outlets. For example, the basic kitchen facilities in a hotel would be similar to those in a hospital. The main difference here would be (in most cases) the scale of operation.

Control systems

A direct influence on the health of an outlet is the control system which exists within it. In isolation, the control system will not maintain the business prosperity unless management constantly support it and use the data it provides to update its operational policies. A control system should monitor not only income but also (perhaps more carefully) the costs associated with earning the income. This is often a far more difficult exercise. A regular monitoring of costs in line with budgets and forecasts, and the current volume of business, is essential for growth.

Current trends and their effects

As you are now aware, the UK recession has hit all aspects of the hospitality and catering industry. Both the business and leisure markets have been affected. It is always difficult to establish in one volatile industry the current trends as they change to meet consumer demands. Present trends and future prospects appear to be as follows.

Demographic trends

This is the change in the structure of the population.

1 A decrease in below 16-year-olds will lead to a reduction in demand for the presently popular younger food market outlets, (e.g. burger bars).
2 Fast-food outlets need to be aware of this shortage now to promote loyalty in their present customers, so as they grow older they will still support this type of food style.
3 Markets solely or mainly reliant on the younger age group need to look to the young adult markets. Market strategies need to consider the 16–24-year-olds and exploit married couples with families.

Employment trends

These are linked closely with the demographic changes.

1 A reduction in the number of school-leavers will affect the younger food market outlets with regard to a fall in the number of suitable employees.
2 A gradual increase in the adult population employed will reduce spending by these people.
3 Employers are recognizing staff potential which has led to an increase in staff training and development.
4 More companies are introducing appraisal systems to encourage staff development and loyalty, which in turn will lead to a reduction in staff turnover.
5 Improvements in conditions of service are taking place.
6 In this competitive time, with fewer customers as a result of the recession, companies are offering incentives and

bonuses for achieving budgets forecasts and sales targets.

7 There are increases in the number of women in the workforce.

Effects on socio-economic groups

● A and B groups appear to be the least affected group of the recession.
● C and C_2 groups have been affected by increased interest rates in the early 1990s, changes in taxation affecting business allowances, recent increases in taxation and National Insurance contributions. All these have greatly reduced the disposable income of people in these groups, hitting the commercial sector with a reduction in business and conference work and the leisure sector with a fall in leisure activities.
● D groups have also been affected by higher interest rates and job insecurity. Higher taxes etc. have increased drinking in the home and therefore the impact on public houses.
● E groups have shown little impact except perhaps in the UK tourism sector where fewer pensioners are going away to resort hotels. The external influences of VAT on fuel bills has led to an insecurity as to how much disposable income they now have.

Demand for the hospitality and catering industry

Some areas which have been affected in recent years with regard to demand are:

1 Expansion of contract caterers into the catering services sector of welfare, i.e. hospitals, education, prisons, etc.
2 Reduction of contract catering outlets in the business and industry sectors
3 Continued recession impacting on the commercial sectors; loss of outlets across all operations (e.g. hotels, restaurants, etc.). There appeared to be a slight improvement at the start of 1994

4 Reduction in UK tourism, again impacting on the commercial sectors
5 Fast-food outlets, an area which has seen growth over the last few years, are easily susceptible to:
  Changes in customer tastes
  Environmental issues (e.g. with regard to disposable packaging)
  The emphasis on healthy eating issues
  Social demands with regards to drinking alcohol – both affecting health and driving capabilities
  Reduction in the consumer and employment market of school leavers
  Decrease in the number of suitable sites on the market
6 Gradual increase in the number of businesswomen travelling alone has led to some hotels giving extra consideration to their security (for example, the Crown Plaza in Manchester). Hotels can also help by increasing staff awareness – it should not be assumed that a female will always be accompanied by a partner.

The commercial sectors have had to look to encourage new markets, for example:

● By introducing short-break holidays, especially those connected with a particular activity, such as Murder Weekends, wine-appreciation weekends, clay pigeon shoots, etc.
● By extending the services of pre- or after-theatre dinners by including 'split dinners' – the Café Royal in London offers a first and main course before the show, with the sweet and coffee courses afterwards. This also encourages the sales of liqueurs etc. which would not have been consumed with a normal pre-theatre meal.

Effects on companies

To cope with the present economic climate, the large companies have had to take measures to protect themselves by:

- Decreasing the number of operations
- Reducing managers in non-revenue-earning operations (e.g. personnel and training, administration)
- A decline in non-essential facilities, such as:
  Doormen
  Porterage
  Concierge desks
- A reduction in other facilities offered, such as:
  Room service
  Night porterage/managers

Smaller companies have suffered more severely than the larger ones, because they are owned by individuals and families with fewer reserves to fall back on when hard times come and remain for a long period. Some commercial outlets with few reserves have gone into receivership. As with the larger companies, there have been reductions in the numbers of operations and facilities offered, etc.

Test your knowledge

1 How has the present UK economy impacted on the hospitality and catering industry?
2 What do you understand by the word 'demographics'?
3 How has the recent UK legislation affected the hospitality and catering industry?
4 What impact has the EU legislation had on the hospitality and catering industry?
5 In what areas can you see the hospitality and catering industry developing, in order to maintain an increase in growth?

▪ EVALUATING THE IMPORTANCE OF INFLUENCES AFFECTING THE OPERATION OF A HOSPITALITY AND CATERING OUTLET ▪

In this section we will look at a particular hospitality and catering outlet and examine the way in which the outlet has developed and the reasons why it has done so. The external and internal influences which affect the operations of the outlet will be considered and their importance evaluated. When you have concluded this section, you should be able to choose an outlet to examine yourself in a similar manner.

Types of organizations

There are several different types of business organization, and an outlet may be part of an organization or it may be autonomous (stand-alone). Before we can look at the outlet of our choice we need to examine the different types of organizations. Business organization may be classified in three ways:

- According to their type of activity
- By sector
- According to their legal classification

Type of activity

This classification is concerned with the level at which the organization or business operates. The three levels are:

1 Primary – the first stages of production (e.g. agriculture, mining); it also includes the production of some raw materials such as iron, as well as items ready for sale such as fresh fruit
2 Secondary – concerned with manufacturing of goods (for example the production of convenience foods, equipment, washing machines, etc.)
3 Tertiary – service industries, i.e. organizations which may not produce actual goods but provide a service (e.g. police, education, catering)

The last classification would include the hospitality and catering industry as it is usually regarded as a service industry. However, our industry also manufactures (in the production of food, for example), therefore it overlaps both the secondary and tertiary levels. For this reason, this type of classification is not often used by the hospitality and catering industry.

Classification by sector

This is a simplistic grouping of businesses according to whether they are privately or publicly owned:

- Public - all organizations controlled by the government, whether by local or national government, or by organizations in which the government has an interest
- Private sector – all organizations controlled by private individuals or groups of individuals, or by companies

It is difficult actually to define public sector organizations as these change along with changes in government policies. Many former public organizations and corporations included the water boards, gas and electricity corporations, etc. Some public corporations still exist, such as British Rail and the Royal Mail, but the ownership of these may change in the future.

Our industry covers both these classifications with its privately owned commercial sector and publicly owned or dominated organizations such as prisons, hospitals, schools, etc.

Classification by legal structure

Unincorporated associations

These are business run by individuals or in partnership with a group of individuals:

1 Sole trader – this is the simplest form of organization, which accounts for a large percentage of all the commercial outlets in the industry, especially in the small hotel and restaurant sectors. The owner has complete control over the business and is personally liable for all debts incurred. This *liability is*

unlimited in respect of the business. The owner is responsible for providing the capital for the business, and is entitled to all the profits (after paying the necessary tax) or suffers all the losses.

Definition

- **Unlimited liability** *means that there is no limit to the amount which the owner can be called upon to pay towards the debts of the organization.*

2 Partnership – this is formed by a group of individuals carrying on a business with a common view to make a profit. Each partner may bring capital or expertise into the business. The liability for the business's debts is still with the partners (i.e. it is unlimited as for a sole trader). It is possible for some partners to have *limited liability*. In these cases, those partners are limited to the amount of capital which they have put into the business. They are called 'sleeping partners' and they must take no part in the running of the business. This is useful where a partner has money to invest but no expertise to offer.

Definition

- **Limited liability** *means that there is a limit to the amount which an owner can be called upon to pay towards the debts of the organization.*

In the absence of any other agreement, all partners are entitled to a share in the running of the business, an equal share in its profits (or its losses), and full liability for all debts.

Neither of these types of organization is suitable for large ventures with heavy capital requirements.

Task 1.20

Explain in your own words, your interpretation of the following terms:

- *Sole trader*
- *Unlimited partnership*
- *Limited partnership*

Registered companies

A company is one which is owned by several 'members'. Each member buys a 'share' or several shares in the company, thereby contributing a portion of the capital which the company requires. These members are also referred to as *shareholders*.

Definition

- A **shareholder** *is a person, or another organization, who owns a share (a part) of the company.*

Shareholders have limited liability for the debts of the company. This is usually limited to the amount they have paid for their shares (or the amount still owing if they have not yet paid in full). Different kinds of shares carry different rights – some carry the right to a fixed amount of profit, or to varying amounts of profit; some entitle the shareholder to vote at meetings; some have other benefits and restrictions.

There are two main types of company, which were redefined to meet European Economic Community standards, in the Companies Act 1985.

Private companies

These are often centred around a family-run business. The shareholders are likely to be part of the same family. Private companies may not offer their shares to the public; they may sell their shares only with the agreement of the other shareholders. The shareholders often work in the company as well as contributing to its management. The average size of a private company is small as the maximum number of shareholders allowed by law is fifty.

Public companies

A public company is one which offers shares to the public. They must include in their name the words 'public limited company' (plc).

The company runs entirely separately from the shareholders, who are rarely involved in the management of the company, although share-ownership by employees is more popular these days. Despite this, many shareholders of large public companies leave the running of the company to its team of directors and senior managers.

Task 1.21

Explain the differences between public and private limited companies. Where possible, give examples of local outlets which fall into these two categories.

Multinational organizations

Some companies are very large and operate in several countries. These are classed as 'multinational organizations'. Prime examples of these types of organization in the industry are:

- Forte
- Holiday Inns
- Compass Catering

Task 1.22

Investigate other multinational organizations connected with the hospitality and catering industry.

Some of the large nationals and multinationals are conglomerates, which means that they have developed by merging together with other firms into one company.

Consortia

Many independent hotels combine together with other similar independents to enable them to remain viable and to compete effectively with the larger national companies. A group of independent hotels which combine together is called a consortium. A consortium normally provides four main advantages to its members:

1 A general marketing and promotion service, usually linked to an internal set-up; this covers brochure design and production
2 A referral booking system, whereby members pass customers on to other member hotels in preference to competing ones
3 Specialized provision of services such as conferences and weekend breaks
4 A group purchasing scheme

In return, a member is expected to:

● Meet certain basic criteria (e.g. standards of service)
● Conform to and participate in the consortium's marketing plans and activities such as brochures
● Pay an annual fee, usually related to size

The UK has over thirty hotel consortia, offering a range of marketing and purchasing services to both independent and group-owned hotels. An example of a national consortium is Best Western, which has 3200 hotels worldwide, 185 hotels in the UK with 8500 bedrooms, the majority being 2- and 3-star outlets.

Task 1.23

Additional to the nationally run consortia, there are many local ones which represent the interests of a particular locality. Using your local tourist board and other sources, investigate:

1 Your local consortia
2 Two national consortia

In each case, find out:

● *How many hotels each consortium covers*
● *How many beds each consortium has available*
● *What publicity materials they produce*
● *How the annual fee is calculated*

Influences affecting the operation of a hospitality and catering outlet

It is extremely difficult to generalize the internal and external effects on an 'outlet'. It does, of course, depend on:

● The outlet
● Where the outlet is located
● Why the outlet is there
● How the outlet operates
● The market segment at which the outlet aims

These factors can only really be assessed on a local basis, by looking at particular outlets.

Previously in this unit we have discussed the effects of the *external* influences on the industry generally, with regards to:

● UK and EU legislation
● The UK economy

- Crises
- Tourism
- Competition

We have also discussed the *internal* influences on the industry, with regards to:

- Management structures
- Working conditions
- Staffing levels
- Facilities available

This information can now be transposed to a local level and used as a basis to investigate outlets within your own locality.

To illustrate how this can be done, a outlet in the author's locality has been selected. One of the reasons for the choice of a hotel is that this type of operation is extremely sensitive to changes in the economic and political environment. Coming from the commercial sector it requires to be profit-orientated and price-sensitive, and therefore more affected by current trends and external and internal influences.

An outlet from the catering services sector would not be so greatly influenced by as many factors as most changes are due to government legislation (e.g. hospitals and education services given out to tenders).

Case study: The Etrop Grange Hotel

History of the building

Since Etrop Grange was built in 1780, the world around it has changed completely. As William Moss, dressed in powdered wig and stockings, stood and admired his fine gardens, could he ever have imagined how dramatic those changes would be? More than 200 years on, Etrop Grange has not only survived, it has been lovingly restored to its former glory, and despite the onslaught of progress, William's home has retained all its elegance and timeless grace (Figure 1.9.).

In fact, Etrop Grange has become unique. Transformed from a private home to a privately owned hotel and restaurant, it now enjoys a fine reputation not only for its superb cuisine, exquisite accommodation and friendly atmosphere but also for the convenience of its location. Within walking distance of Manchester Airport, Etrop Grange is now just a walk away from the world!

Behind the stately Georgian facade, Etrop Grange has also retained its unique ambience. The luxury, character and sheer elegance of the Georgian era is reflected in every detail, and the standard of decoration, antique furnishings and quality of fittings is evident throughout. The magnificent restaurant has an excellent reputation for superb food with a well-balanced mix of traditional and modern English cuisine and an extensive selection of fine wines.

In addition to the obvious advantages of having an airport 'en suite', the location of Etrop Grange is ideal in many other ways. With a comprehensive motorway network and Inter-City stations only minutes away, Etrop Grange is easily accessible from every part of the country, yet the hills and plains of Cheshire offer all the benefits of its rural aspect. Cheshire boasts an abundance of stately homes, museums and historical attractions, and Etrop Grange stands at the gateway to North Wales, the Peak District, the Yorkshire Dales and the Lake District (Figure 1.10).

Development of the building

The building was bought by Sue and John Roebuck in 1985, as a family home. The house itself was derelict, and as they were in the process of rebuilding it they saw the potential for opening part of it as a small restaurant. In 1986 they converted the front part of the house into a 24-cover restaurant. It ran with Sue managing it with the help of two staff. It quickly gained a high reputation. In 1987 three guest bedrooms were furbished, and in 1988 a further five were developed, giving a total of

The Country House Hotel & Restaurant
at
Manchester Airport

ETROP GRANGE
THORLEY LANE, MANCHESTER AIRPORT, M22 5NR
TELEPHONE: 061-499 0500
FACSIMILE: 061-499 0790

Figure 1.9

HOW TO FIND ETROP GRANGE

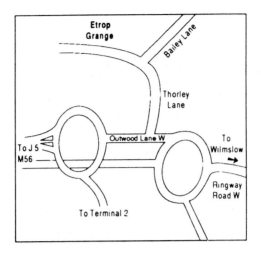

Location By Car	M56/Junction 5	1 min
	M6/Junction 19	15 mins
	Manchester Airport	3 mins
	Manchester City Centre	12 mins
	Wilmslow/Inter-City	10 mins
	Stockport/Inter-City	9 mins
	Gateway to North Wales, Lake District, Yorkshire Dales and Peak District.	

Shopping — Manchester, Stockport, Chester, Wilmslow, Altrincham and Macclesfield all have superb shopping centres and facilities.

Entertainment — Manchester - The Palace Theatre, The Opera House, The Royal Exchange Theatre, The Library Theatre, Granada Studios, Chinatown, museums and art galleries, cinemas and nightclubs, Hallé Orchestra. Stockport - Davenport Theatre.

Local Places of Interest — The Peak National Park, Lyme Park, Styal Country Park and Quarry Bank Mill, Gawsworth Hall, Adlington Hall, Capesthorne Hall, Jodrell Bank, Tatton Park, Arley Hall and Gardens, Dunham Park, Macclesfield Silk Museums, all within half an hour's drive of Etrop Grange.

ETROP GRANGE
THORLEY LANE, MANCHESTER AIRPORT, M22 5NR
TEL: 061 499 0500 FAX: 061 499 0790

Figure 1.10

eight. In 1988 and 1989, with a booming economy, Sue and John produced a business plan for a major extension of the property, to develop a new 30-cover restaurant and 27 bedrooms. The building development cost of this project was in excess of £3 million. Apart from the restaurant and bedrooms, a new kitchen and conference room was also included. The year 1991 saw further development. By September, the 27 bedrooms were opened and a new 80-cover restaurant and bar. By December, the final seven bedrooms were completed, giving a total of 41 bedrooms.

Internal influences on the business

At the start of the business, it was run by Sue, John and a few assistant staff. The input of the owners in the everyday running was substantial. After the first phase of development was completed in 1987, the organizational structure shown in Figure 1.11 existed.

There was a heavy bias towards the restaurant/kitchen brigade due to the fact that the emphasis at that time was still on operating as a restaurant with five bedrooms. By January

1992, with the development finally completed, comprising 41 bedrooms and an 80-cover restaurant, with conference and banqueting facilities, the organization appeared as in Figure 1.12.

On completion of the hotel, the development was slower than was originally expected. There were two reasons for this:

1 It was a new hotel looking for different markets from when it first opened
2 The recession contributed towards a reduced business market

Task 1.24

Look at the organizational chart in Figure 1.12 and write a short report on:

- Which departments are overstaffed?
- What in your opinion would be a more realistic staffing figure and why?

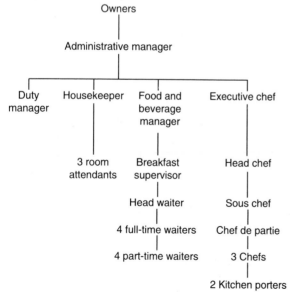

Figure 1.11 Etrop Grange's organizational structure in 1987

By the end of 1992, occupancy levels were up to 62 per cent.

The present organizational structure now includes a General Manager (who was originally the Sales and Marketing Manager) and an Administrative/Financial Manager. The House Manager is now responsible for the housekeeping staff (which includes only five maids and a turndown maid), the reception staff, the porters, the conference and banqueting staff and a part-time maintenance worker. There is a separate small accounts department. There have also been adjustments to the kitchen staffing, with no third chef, only two chefs de partie and two commis chefs, no breakfast chef or junior pastry chef, and only three kitchen porters. There are, however, currently two trainee chefs. Changes in the

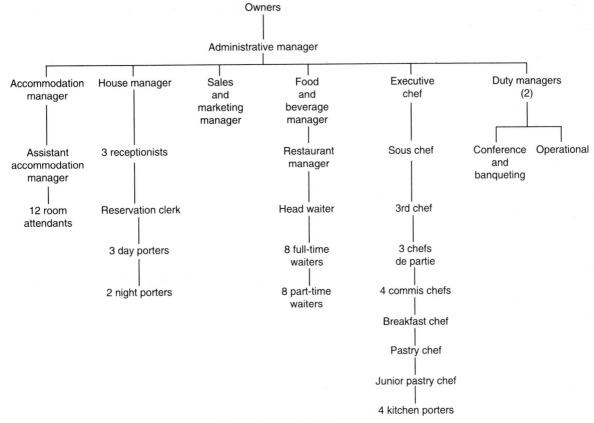

Figure 1.12 The organizational structure of Etrop Grange in 1992

food and beverage area include the addition of a breakfast supervisor and two chefs de rang. The total number of employees is now 45 full-time and ten part-time.

Employment patterns

Non-supervisory staff

This includes administrative, receptionists, porters and maids, who tend to work straight shifts. For example, a maid's hours would be 7 a.m. to 3 p.m. Restaurant and kitchen staff work both straight and split shifts, for example:

Restaurant waiter
  10.30 a.m. to 3.30 p.m.   6.30 p.m until finished
                            (around midnight)
Chef
  10.00 a.m. to 2.30 p.m   6.00 p.m to 10.30 p.m
                            (total 10 hours)

Full-time basic hours are between 40 and 45 over a 5-day period. Although this includes a 10-hour day, this would be averaged over the week. Any member of staff who works overtime is paid at an hourly rate.

Managers and supervisors

These may be required to work straight or split duties, the number of hours being 'as required in the course of their duties'. This might mean a 30-hour week one week, but with another week requiring 60 hours. They are paid a set rate which reflects their responsibilities and the hours required to work.

All staff are paid 4-weekly, directly into their personal bank accounts. There are no cash payments for security and administrative reasons.

Recruitment

Etrop Grange is a local employer and proactively recruits within the close vicinity of the hotel. Jobs are advertised in the local and surrounding jobcentres and the local press. The hotel has no staff accommodation and therefore is restricted to local employment or staff who have their own transport facilities. They also maintain a file of general vacancy applications which come through the post on a regular basis.

Task 1.25

Research your local newspapers for job opportunities in the industry. Which jobs do you think might be difficult to fill and why? Can you suggest any amendments to the advertisements (without telling any untruths) which might highlight the more attractive aspects of the jobs on offer?

Trends

The general response to advertised positions is not always good and the past quality of applicants is variable. In the present economic climate, with high unemployment, there has been a noticeable increase in the number of 'no shows' at interviews – it is now quite common to invite eight applicants for interview and expect only five to turn up.

Certain types of position are difficult to fill – for example, positions for part-time porters. A recent advertisement was placed for a retired/redundant person aged between 45 and 55, with a good personality (as they are required to interface with customers). The work is not particularly heavy. The post took 2 months to fill.

It is felt by the General Manager that the overall general perception of some of the positions in hotels is that they are easy jobs to perform, when in fact they demand dedication, the ability to work under pressure, considerable tact and diplomacy with customers, and the ability to work as part of a team. As an example, a full-time receptionist was appointed, but stayed for only 4 weeks – she stated that she found the position too highly pressured and could not cope.

Working conditions

The hotel provides all uniforms, and maintains them, in the following operational areas:

- Reception
- Housekeeping
- Restaurant
- Kitchen

Where blouses or shirts are required, these are bought and maintained by the staff themselves.

The hotel provides a staff rest room for tea/coffee and lunch breaks (but no meals are provided while on duty). A male and female staff changing room is provided, with lockers. A vending machine serving free hot and cold drinks is available to all staff.

Staff development

There is no formal staff development programme. However, the General Manager actively looks to his staff for potential development. The two chef de rang levels in the restaurant were created in recognition of the standards and quality of work produced by staff, without having to wait for higher or supervisory vacancies to arise. In this way, the hotel maintains highly qualified staff who achieve the hotel's high standards of quality and consistency and are happy to remain with the organization. By recognising the potential of employees, staff turnover has been reduced to a minimum. There is at present an informal appraisal system in operation, on a regular 6-monthly basis.

Staff training

Staff training takes place in three ways:

1 *In-house* Staff are trained on-the-job. Potential is recognized and developed. Promotion is given as a reward to staff for effort and loyalty.
2 *External courses* Individual staff can see the benefits, not only to themselves, but also to the organization of attending external courses. Attendance is supported by the hotel, by allowing time off and, where applicable, financial support for successful outcomes.
3 *NVQ training* Management is currently investigating the advantages of investing in training supervisory and managerial staff to become assessors and internal verifiers, to enable them to operate as a certified training centre for NVQ in all facilities and operations.

Sales and marketing strategy

The external factors affecting the hotel when it opened gave rise to the management's approach to sales and marketing. In their first year they were a new hotel and in order to raise awareness they offered very competitive deals to attract initial business. They opened not just in a depressed UK market but also at a time when hotels, especially large chains, were greatly affected by the Gulf War. At this time there was a substantial drop in international traffic, especially of the US and UK business markets, with reduced monies for conference and business expenditure. Companies were consequently looking for competitive deals.

Andrew Paul, the present General Manager (originally employed on a 42-week contract as Sales and Marketing Manager) responded positively by seeking the business market which the hotel might not otherwise have needed to do had the market been buoyant. He instigated a massive awareness of the hotel with a combination of adverts, editorial features in local, national and international newspapers and magazines.

Definition

● *Editorial features are articles of interest which are put into newspapers and magazines without cost to the subject of the article.*

Task 1.26

Look in your own local newspapers and see if you can recognize any catering outlet which the paper has covered in an editorial feature.

Etrop Grange possessed many points of interest for an editorial feature, including the following:

● It was a derelict Georgian house being refurbished
● It was in sole ownership
● It was opened and extended in a depressed market
● It offers individual and characteristic services
● It is successful in a very competitive location

The *Daily Telegraph* contained a page and a half editorial feature, with pictures. This was exposure which the hotel itself could never have afforded.

Local coverage

Editorial features also appeared in other locations such as:

- *Cheshire Life* magazine
- Local radio, using Etrop Grange to provide a competition prize – for example, a Mother's Day competition offered free lunch or dinner to the mother nominated as Best Mum
- Mail shots specifically aimed at local businesses; these were researched through *Yellow Pages* and the local Chamber of Commerce directory
- ABTA – advertising through travel agents locally and nationally
- Customer history file – using their own data built up since the restaurant opened in 1988

National coverage

- Press advertisements mainly in business newspapers rather than consumer-based newspapers
- Features and competitions in consumer magazines and press (e.g. *Good Housekeeping, Country and Home*)
- Selected advertisements in Brides, which led to a feature on Honeymoon Hideaways
- Editorial visits – promotion by writing to key editors in a 200-mile catchment area aimed at editorial feature which would attract the travel and tourism customer using Manchester Airport, and 'where to stay before and after your flight' slogans. The editors were offered a free weekend and the hotel ran a competition in each of the participating newspapers

Over the past four years, Etrop Grange has gained many national and international awards, as can be seen in Figure 1.13.

International coverage

Great care had to be taken with international advertising due to the distance between the hotel and its potential market and the cost of such advertising. Andrew Paul had to be very specific in when, where and how to advertise. There is great potential in the American market as this type of 'olde-worlde' outlet has great appeal. Few American buildings are as old as Etrop Grange.

An advertisement was placed in the *Hotel and Travel Index*. It consisted of a 1-inch x 3-inch numbered advert, bold typed, with the number corresponding to a map of the local area. There are four editions per year of the *Index*, at a cost of £2500. All travel agents in America use it. In conjunction with the Tourist Board and the British Tourist Association, and to gain familiarity with agents, Etrop Grange play host to their top agents on a regular basis – several visits each year. Taking into account the overall reduction because of the Gulf War, these two ventures have proved to be very successful. Etrop Grange has daily enquiries now for accommodation from the USA. The knock-on effect is that they are now also getting enquiries from Canadian business even though there has been no direct advertising or marketing input in Canada!

European coverage

Here Etrop Grange is tapping into the corporate business area with local offices. Having gained a reputation with locally based businesses, these businesses are now recommending the Etrop Grange to their directors/managers visiting from other offices.

Etrop Grange is also listed in the *European Connection*, which is purely a brochure published once a year listing hotels of distinction in the European Union, and is distributed among travel agents as well as being left *in situ*.

There has been very small interest shown by the Japanese market, which may be worth looking into in the future, but at present the expenditure necessary to gain the small amount of business is not considered a priority.

ETROP GRANGE AWARDS

ENGLAND FOR EXCELLENCE

HORWATH HOTEL OF THE YEAR 1992

SILVER

North West Tourist Board Hotel of the Year, 1992

"Cheshire Life" Magazine - Hotel of the Year, 1991/2

"Which Hotel Guide" - County Hotel of the Year, 1992

"Egon Ronay" - Recommended 1993

"Michelin Guide" - Recommended 1993

"American Express" - Best of Britain Hotel 1991/92

Figure 1.13

Task 1.27

Look at your college or school catering facility. What type of marketing strategy would you use to promote it?

Market targets

Over the years, Etrop Grange has predominantly aimed at and attracted the senior management and professional sector, i.e. the socio-economic groupings of A, B and C. They have two distinct markets – corporate business and overnight travel.

Definition

● **Corporate business** is business with the senior management of companies.

From Monday to Thursday, corporate business, aimed at those of general manager and senior status, forms the major part of Etrop Grange's business. The hotel is used for high-level conferences and accommodation for managers travelling to this area. The companies involved usually have high budget levels for this type of spending. Etrop Grange attracts this type of business due to its location, with excellent transport via Manchester Airport's motorway and rail network. Because of this transport advantage, many companies are relocating into this area and looking for good accommodation and corporate business rates and facilities.

From Friday to Sunday, Etrop Grange is used mainly for overnight travellers. The hotel is included in Golden Rail and British Airways brochures for overnight accommodation, among others. Travellers taking an early-morning flight, particularly those from the USA, enjoy finishing their holiday in a hotel like Etrop Grange.

The hotel does not attract much domestic holiday trade as it is perceived that the area does not offer much in the way of attractions for any reasonable length of stay. This attitude could be disputed as the hotel is on the outskirts of Manchester, with its night life including clubs and theatres, its excellent shopping centre and its superb historic cathedral. It is also on the fringe of Cheshire, where the scientific Jodrell Bank centre is located. Cheshire also boasts traditional cattle markets, the city of Chester with its many Tudor buildings and many delightful public gardens such as Tatton Park and Lyme Park, each with historic houses and deer parks. Other historic buildings abound in the area. The hills of the Peak District are a very short drive away, including caverns and caves, farm life, mountains to climb and country villages to relax in. The spa town of Buxton is also only a short drive away.

Conference business

The sales mix has changed over the last two years. Business looked for smaller events on a more regular basis rather than larger events. Some business has stopped completely while new business has taken its place. During 1994, there was a slow improvement in the economy and a noticeable recovery was felt, both by the hotel itself and to the businesses using it.

Competition

In the immediate locality there are four relatively close hotels. These are:

● The Manchester Airport Hilton
● The Forte Creste
● The Four Seasons
● The Wilmslow Moat House

At least two of these hotels are aiming at the same socio-economic groupings and corporate business. All offer similar core facilities and operations but in totally different styles. The whole of Etrop Grange's philosophy is on personal service and familiarization with individual customer needs. This has been successfully achieved as there is a high level of repeat business.

Competition is looked upon as healthy. It keeps the hotel 'on its toes' in maintaining high levels of standards and social skills. The four hotels in the area meet as an 'association' on a regular basis, looking at ways of increasing business overall. It was generally agreed that Manchester Airport should support the hotels as they do cater for a high proportion of the airport trade.

The hotels have produced a brochure called *Manchester Airport Hotels*. It is endorsed by the Airport and sponsored by British Airways, American Express and Hertz. This brochure is believed to be the first of its kind. The airport agreed to distribute it in all their mailings to associated groups as part of their corporate literature. British Airways have also distributed the brochure in all their aircraft seatbanks, and in all offices worldwide. The British Tourist Authority have also distributed them in their offices.

Influence of legislation

The Health and Safety at Work etc. Act 1974/The Food Act 1990

Due to the very substantial changes which have occurred in recent years, Etrop Grange now has its own Environmental Health Officer-consultant. He makes two final visits per year and three to four spot-checks to make sure that staff are meeting regulation requirements. The administration of maintaining fridge/freezer temperature records, dating and labelling of all products, monitoring cleaning schedules, etc. have all added an extra burden to the physical administration and documentation required.

Control of Substances Hazardous to Health

The General Manager has instigated regular updating through internal memos and staff meetings, and all new developments are considered. These administrative procedures take key people away from the operational issues, although they do see the need for regular checks and monitoring. Details of all COSHH regulations are kept in the Health and Safety file which is available to *all* staff from Reception.

Fire Precautions Act 1971

A valid fire certificate is held and displayed. There are two fire training days and two full hotel evacuations practices per year. The policy of the hotel is that if the fire alarm sounds during the night there is a full evacuation with an automatic visit from the fire brigade.

Employment Protection Consolidation Act 1978

All full-time members of staff are given written contracts of employment. The hotel is now in the process of giving all part-time members written contracts to comply with the new regulations. To comply with the recent Statutory Sick Pay regulations, the hotel is providing its own 'self-certification' form which will have to be completed in front of a senior member of staff by all employees who are sick. Employees will be required to explain their absence from work and the management are hopeful that this procedure will deter the 'non-sick' people from being absent. Refusal to complete a form will be treated as gross misconduct with definite disciplinary action, e.g. stopping of pay when off to being dismissed.

Data Protection Act 1984

This is not applicable at the moment, but the hotel is looking into gaining a certificate to be able to hold a customer listing on computer.

Trades Description Act/Consumer Protection Act/Licensing Act

The hotel meets all the requirements of the above legislation, i.e.:

- Displaying tariffs in the Reception area
- Displaying the notice of the Hotel Proprietors Act
- Displaying bar prices and alcoholic levels
- Accurately describing menu items

The scale and scope of the outlet

Trading since the major development of 1991 has been as follows:

Year 1 – net turnover £1.65 million
Year 2 – net turnover £1.72 million
Year 3 – net turnover £1.8 million (expected budget)

Due to the current depressed market, there has been only minimal growth, which is an indication of how good the products and services are to have achieved this.

The management approach has been to:

1 Offer sensible long-term corporate rates
2 'Sell from the top', i.e. use a rate which is not too far below the rack rate, rather than adopting the approach of massive reductions, as did some of their competitors
3 Maintain rack rate tariffs at the same level as in the previous year, thereby responding to the economic depression and the reduction in disposable incomes and company expense accounts

Definition

- **Rack rate** is the set price for a room, depending on the type of room.

The aim of the hotel is to increase occupancy rates but not by the reduction of rack rates.

During 1994, there appeared to be a small growth in occupancy levels, to 68 per cent, an overall rise of 6 per cent on the first year's trading. There has also been a small growth in all facilities and operational areas within the hotel over the last trading year. This is in spite of furious competition from hotels in closer reach of the Airport with similar basic facilities (for example the Hilton and Forte hotels).

Scope

These are the products and services which comprise the hotel's activities.

Dining facilities

A fine dining restaurant has a fixed-price menu, over a five-course structure which allows the customer to have an *à la carte* style menu, while knowing how much they are paying. It combines choice with food budgets, satisfying both the customers and the business (Figure 1.14).

Opening times are:

Breakfast	7 days a week	7.00–9.00 a.m.
Luncheon	6 days a week (closed Saturdays)	12–2.00 p.m.
Dinner	7 days a week	7.00–10.00 p.m.

Roses Tea Room

This caters for morning coffee, light luncheons and afternoon teas. Offering a wide range of croissants, Danish pastries, etc. and a variety of savoury items, including grilled steaks. Opening times are 10.30 a.m. to 5.30 p.m., 7 days a week.

Private dining rooms

There are six private dining rooms which will accommodate various party sizes of 4, 10, 18, 20, 50 and 80 covers. Parties of 10 covers and under are allowed to choose from the restaurant menu; parties of over this number have a selection of set private dining menus from which to choose. The host may select a set menu for the guests from a very wide

STARTERS

Celery and Apple Soup with Double Gloucester Cheese

Layers of Fresh Fruit topped with a Glazed Cinnamon Sabayon
and a Compote of Warm Berries

Crisp Salad of Onions, Leeks and Tomatoes
topped with a Warm Poached Egg and a Poppy Seed Dressing

SECOND COURSE
(May be taken as a First Course)

A Terrine of Corn Fed Chicken, Baby Leeks and Sweet Corn
set on a Saffron Infused Mayonnaise

Slices of Cured Scotch Salmon layered with Blackberries
around Quenelles of Dill Mousse

Wild Mushroom, Walnuts and Blue Stilton Cheese
topped with a Porridge Oat Crumble

Pan-Fried Lambs Kidneys
with Red Onions, Thyme and a Hot English Mustard

Pressing of Honey and Rosemary Scented Duckling
with a Warm Chutney of Onion and Tomato

Figure 1.14

MAIN COURSES

Baked Fillet of Mullet on a Bed of Pickled Samphire
with a Vermouth and Thyme Sauce

Whole Dover Sole Grilled or Pan-fried
(£5.00 supplement)

Traditional Daily Roast

Pan-Fried Breast of Chicken stuffed with Field Mushrooms
on a Spiced Tomato Coulis

Lamb Stew and Savoury Herb Dumplings

Pan-fried Lamb's Liver with Onion Gravy and Crisp Bacon

Collops of Beef on a Bed of Baby Root Vegetables and Rosemary Gravy

Baked Filo Parcel of Cauliflower and Broccoli
bound with a Cheshire Cheese Hollandaise

PUDDINGS AND DESSERTS

Layers of Puff Pastry and Caramelised Pears with Vanilla Cream

Roly Poly Pudding with Traditional Vanilla Anglaise

A Platter of Winter Fruits glazed with a Kirsch Sabayon
and an Elderflower Ice Cream

Bread and Butter Pudding

or

CHEESE COURSE

A Platter of British Cheeses to include
Appleby Red Cheshire, Pencarreg Brie and Double Gloucester with
Chives and Onions

FRESHLY BREWED COFFEE SERVED WITH HOMEMADE SWEETMEATS
£1.75

TWO COURSES - TWELVE POUNDS AND NINETY FIVE PENCE
THREE COURSES - FOURTEEN POUNDS AND NINETY FIVE PENCE

Guests are politely requested to refrain from smoking
in the Conservatory area of the Restaurant

Figure 1.14 Continued

FISH DISHES

(May be taken as a Fish Course or a Main Course)

A Gathering of Seafood poached in Dry Vermouth and Parsley
on a Bed of Courgette Spaghetti

Whole Dover Sole poached with Queen Scallops and Basmati Rice
topped with a Mild Curried Sauce Mousseline

Fillet of Monkfish with Smoked Salmon and Garlic Butter
Deep Fried set on an Onion and Garlic Sauce

MEAT AND POULTRY DISHES

Beef Olives with Black Pudding and Wild Mushrooms
on a Rich Tomato and Tarragon Gravy

Slices of Calves Liver Pan Fried
with Kumquats and Peaches finished with Cognac

Almond Coated Breast of Pheasant
Pan-Fried in Butter with Roasted Garlic
and a Rich Pheasant Gravy

Fillet of Lamb wrapped with Pistachio Nuts,
Roasted and set onto Redcurrant Pan Juices

Poached Breast of Chicken stuffed with Ripe Avocado
on a Tomato and Basil sauce

VEGETARIAN DISHES

Pan-Fried Onions, Potatoes and Sweet Peppers
with Spinach Linguine and a Savoury Paprika Sauce

Casserole of Asparagus and Mushrooms
between layers of Puff Pastry

A TWO COURSE DINNER MENU
TWENTY TWO POUNDS & FIFTY PENCE

A THREE COURSE DINNER MENU
TWENTY SIX POUNDS & FIFTY PENCE

A FOUR COURSE DINNER MENU
TWENTY NINE POUNDS & FIFTY PENCE

A FIVE COURSE DINNER MENU
THIRTY ONE POUNDS & FIFTY PENCE

Inclusive of Value Added Tax

Figure 1.14 Continued

menu-selector in advance of the event. Prices are in accordance with the number of courses required. An example of a four-course meal is shown in Figure 1.15.

The price also includes exclusive use of an appropriate private dining room, personalized menus, and VAT. The rates were those applying during 1994.

Marquee

There are facilities to have a marquee in the grounds of the hotel, by prior arrangement.

Room service

The hotel provides a 24-hour room service. Between 7.00 a.m. and midnight it is operated mainly by the restaurant and kitchen staff, and is supported late every night by the night porter. A full range of hot and cold items is available. Between midnight and 7.00 a.m. the service is operated by the night porter, with a limited choice of hot and cold items.

Kitchen

This services all operational areas, such as the restaurant, private dining rooms, room service and tea rooms. All menu items in the restaurant and private dining rooms are cooked to order.

The hotel buys locally produced fresh produce when available, taking advantage of seasonal items and favourable buying patterns. The majority of menu items are prepared on the premises (for example, all bread items, pastries, sweets, handmade chocolates served with coffee, etc.). This explains the size of the kitchen brigade.

Thin slices of Fresh Salmon marinated with fresh herbs and dill, set around a light mousse of Cucumber and Fresh Limes

Vintage port sorbet with raisins

Loin of Cheshire Pork stuffed with a forcemeat of Fresh Apricots and Black Cherries, with a marmalade glaze and set on a Cream and Calvados Brandy sauce with Red Apples

An Almond Tulip basket filled with Grand Marnier Ice Cream and Fresh Summer Berries, set on a Light Fruit Coulis

Freshly brewed coffee and homemade sweetmeats

(The last item is not classed as a 'course' but is included in the price)

£27.50 per guest

Figure 1.15

The hotel does not agree with the current trend by larger organizations of standardization. They believe in and encourage the chefs to use their creativity in the preparation and cooking of menu items. The same dish (e.g. a soup) on a menu would have different daily variations depending on the chef who has prepared it. This approach and individualization is expected from the customers and is a reason why many become regular diners, loyal to Etrop Grange. Business people who regularly travel perhaps in a chain organization, where menus are the same or similar in each outlet, eventually suffer from 'menu fatigue', which is one of the main reasons why, when they are in the Cheshire area, a high proportion who have come to know about Etrop Grange choose to stay there in preference to one of the larger chain competitors.

Menu changes

Certain items on the luncheon or dinner menus are changed on a weekly basis.

Accommodation

Etrop Grange's 41-bedroom accommodation comprises the following:

- Two courtyard suites
- Seven four-poster bedrooms
- Four twin rooms
- Three single rooms (one non-smoking)
- Twenty-five standard doubles (nine non-smoking)

Within the last 12 months a decision was made when some rooms were being refurbished to offer a non-smoking bedroom facility. An area in the restaurant also became a non-smoking area.

Each bedroom has its own individual characteristics, as regards:

- Design and shape
- Size
- Decor
- Amenities offered

Suites and four-posters have extra amenities such as additional toiletries, bath robes, baskets of fruit and even a jacuzzi.

There is also a hotel wedding package available for honeymooners (Figure 1.16). In keeping with the hotel, all the reception rooms, private dining rooms, etc. are furnished with antiques and various first-edition books. There has been minimal loss over the last few years. One area of loss which has baffled management and staff is from the bathroom area. All these areas, in keeping with the rest of the hotel, are furnished in old-fashioned style, including the toilets which have a high water closet and chain pull, finished with a distinctive blue and while porcelain handle. Every single one of these handles has been removed from the hotel. All forty-one bedrooms are now handle-less!

Reception

There is no formal reception desk. There is an antique desk used only by customers paying bills. The computerized registration system is situated in a small office to the rear of the room. Emphasis is then on greeting and talking to the customer, making sure that on arrival or departure the receptionist is actually talking to the customer and not hiding behind a computer. On arrival all guests' bags are carried to their rooms. Regular customers are given the room they prefer, which they either request on booking or which is chosen by the receptionist when preparing the room plan using the Guest History facility.

Administrative work connected with the reception area includes:

- Daily reconciliation of income
- Sales and purchasing ledgers
- Calculating the food and beverage gross profit
- Banking
- Payroll calculations
- Trial balance and profit and loss account preparation

ETROP GRANGE
WEDDING NIGHT PACKAGE

(Rates per room. Prices valid until 31 December 1994)

Etrop Grange offers 41 Executive Bedrooms and Suites, all of which have
been individually designed and furnished with a wealth of antique furniture.
Our Four Poster Master Bedrooms benefit from a small seating area and spa baths,
and both Courtyard Suites have a separate living room with direct
access from the courtyard.

	Mon-Thurs	Fri-Sun
Courtyard Suite (with spa bath and separate living room)	£150.00	£125.00
Four Poster Master (with spa bath)	£130.00	£115.00
Executive Double	£120.00	£90.00

The above rates include the following:

* Half bottle of chilled Champagne in your room
* Homemade chocolates in your room
* Full English Breakfast
* Courtesy transport to Manchester Airport

The above rates are per room and are inclusive of Value Added Tax

The Country House Hotel & Restaurant
at
Manchester Airport

ETROP GRANGE
THORLEY LANE, MANCHESTER AIRPORT, M22 5NR
TEL: 061 499 0500 FAX: 061 499 0790

Figure 1.16

This work is carried out by the accounts clerk and Administrative/Finance Manager. A non-executive financial director prepares the monthly accounts using the above-gathered information.

Reception services

Reception services which are available for use by all customers include a full range of secretarial services such as shorthand, word processing, photocopying and fax facilities.

Conference facilities

All customers have access to:

- Overhead projectors
- Audio and visual equipment (e.g. video player and monitor, video role-play kit, carousel projector and screen)
- Flipcharts and pad
- Screens

plus speciality audio and visual equipment on request.

The General Manager also works in the reception area. His responsibilities, apart from overseeing the day-to-day operations of the hotel, include the production of budgets, feasibility studies, sales and marketing duties, etc. The last responsibility perhaps holds the key to the increasing success of the hotel which has survived in a depressed market.

Current trends and future prospects

Overall the hotel is in an positive mood. There were slight indications at the beginning of 1994 that the economy in this locality was slowly improving and the corporate business markets were taking a positive upward turn. Companies are now planning more in advance as they feel more confident in the market and the economy. Due to the style and atmosphere of the hotel an increase of single female visitors has been noticed – approximately 25 per cent of single occupancies are female.

The hotel now has planning permission for a further thirty bedrooms and increased conference facilities although at this time there is no real prospect for development.

It is envisaged that there may be an extension to the restaurant with further private dining rooms and conference facilities with an extra six bedroom suites above, plus an increase in the size of the existing function room from fifty-five covers to an eighty-cover ballroom.

Business diversification

At present Sue and John Roebuck own not only Etrop Grange but also have bases in five restaurants in their own branded chain, the Famous Chop House and Pudding Emporium. These have opened over the last 18 months with options to buy at any point in time. The original outlay for refurbishment, fittings and launch was approximately £10,000–£25,000 per unit. All are performing well even in the current economic climate and against stiff competition. All are situated in village centres. The hope is eventually to own a further hotel and develop the restaurants on a national basis, turning the organization from that of a sole trader to a public limited company in order to raise the necessary capital.

• ASSESSMENT •

An investigation of the hospitality and catering industry with reference to commercial and catering services outlets in general, with specific reference to your locality.

Framework
You will be expected to compile a total of three reports. Your reports will consist of an in-depth study of:

- One commercial outlet
- One catering services outlet
- One outlet of your own choice

Your reports must show evidence of at least one visit to the outlet and contain relevant support material.

Complete the following tasks in the order you find most appropriate.

Task 1

Make a survey of your locality – an area as directed by your tutor. Using as many sources as possible, identify as many catering outlets as you can find.

Task 2

Categorize your outlets into appropriate types of organization, e.g.

- Commercial/catering services
- Sole ownership/public company
- Captive/semi-captive/non-captive customers
- European/ethnic

and any other categories you consider suitable.

A single outlet may be entered into one or more categories where applicable, e.g.:

Chinese restaurant – sole ownership
                     non-captive customers
                     ethnic

Evaluate your findings with regards to past influences and current trends. How has your area changed in respect of the types and number of outlets in recent times. Consider possible reasons for these changes.

Illustrate your findings with suitable graphs and charts.

Task 3

From your findings, choose three outlets you wish to cover in your reports, to contain:

- One commercial sector outlet
- One catering services sector outlet
- One outlet of your own choice

Within your reports, the following should be covered:

1 An explanation of the relationship between the sectors of the industry
2 A description of the operational areas within each outlet
3 A discussion of the products and services offered with regards to the type of outlet
4 Identification of the internal and external influences affecting the outlets
5 A description of the growth and/or decline of the outlets due to the current internal and external influences
6 A description of the employment patterns of the locality and any deficiencies or excesses identified
7 A description of the employment patterns of the outlets
8 Identification of career and employment opportunities in at least three key positions with regard to the skills and qualifications required, the promotional prospects, etc.
9 An investigation into and discussion of the current trends and future prospects
10 An explanation of appropriate classification systems

Task 4

Your evidence must be produced in report format as appropriate.

All supporting materials should be tabulated and cross-referenced in the text.

Task 5

Prepare a fifteen-minute oral presentation of your findings to the remainder of your group, selected tutors and invited members of the Industry. Use any visual aids you feel necessary to enhance your presentation, e.g. OHPs, flipcharts, photographs, etc.

Assessment coverage:
Element 1.1 PCs 2, 3, 4, 6
Element 1.2 PCs 1, 2, 3
Element 1.3 PCs 1, 2, 3, 4

Core skills:

Communication:

    Element 3.2 PCs 1–4

    Element 3.3 PCs 1–3

    Element 3.4 PCs 1–3

Information Technology:

    Element 3.1 PCs 1–7

    Element 3.2 PCs 1–7

    Element 3.3 PCs 1–5

Application of numbers:

    Element 3.1 PCs 1–6

    Element 3.3 PCs 1, 2, 4, 5, 6

Further reading

Automobile Association, *Hotel Guides*

British Hospitality Association, *Contract Catering Survey '94*

Croner Publications:
Catering
Reference for Employers
Europe

Davies, B. and Stone, S., *Food and Beverage Management*

Hotel & Catering Training Company, *Key Facts & Figures*

Key Note Publishing, *Market Review '91*

Royal Automobile Club, *Hotel Guide*

Tourist Board, *'Insight' Social Trends*

HUMAN RESOURCES

Note: Throughout this unit people are referred to generally as male. This does not mean that the role of the female is undervalued but male is used simply as a convenience term and should be taken as referring to both men and women.

Human relations is basically a study of people – the people we work with, the people who are our bosses, the people we are responsible for and, perhaps most importantly, the people who are customers for the hospitality and catering industry. People are very important to all of us. Human behaviour and resources takes these basic requirements and suggests different ways of being able to tackle situations so everyone benefits. Obviously this has to be done within company guidelines, but an awareness of different techniques could help.

In this unit we aim to:

- Study teams and how they work in the industry
- Assess staff achievement and satisfaction
- Look at work standards and performance

▪ TEAMS AND HOW THEY WORK IN HOSPITALITY AND CATERING ▪

The individual

Before we look at how teams work it is important that we know a little about people as individuals and some of the things that influence us in forming our own outlook on life. We all recognize the physical differences between people. These include factors such as height, age, sex, appearance and ethnicity.

Task 2.1

We take in some information about people without even recognizing or registering that we have done so. Think of someone for a few seconds you are close to – parent, brother, sister or friend. Make a few notes on what you remember about them, as if you were describing them to someone else.

Although this is a fairly simple exercise you can see how much information we remember about someone – the colour of their hair or eyes or perhaps their general appearance and shape. All these are important in the communication process and influence how we appear to the world. Taking this a stage further, we also need to be aware of what makes us individuals in terms of our personalities.

People have vastly differing intellectual abilities. We all know people who we think are very clever and others to whom we feel superior. Society measures our intellectual ability in terms of educational achievement – the grades we obtain. Some people have to work very hard to get through their courses, others do not. This does not seem quite fair, but it is the level that prospective employers recognize.

Task 2.2

Study the symbols and terms in Test A below for 2 minutes. Cover up the rest of the page while you do this. Don't cheat!

Test A

1	◯	Wheel	6	(woman symbol)	Woman
2	▭	Container	7	⊤	Tea
3	⋀⋀⋀	Water	8	(cup symbol)	Cup
4	(tree symbol)	Tree	9	+	Plus
5	(man symbol)	Man	10	—	Minus

Accurately reproduce the following symbols:

1 Water
2 Tea
3 Man
4 Cup
5 Plus

Most people do well at this and receive full marks for the exercise.

Now study the symbols in Test B below, again for 2 minutes. Do not look at the questions below.

Test B

1	(symbol) +	Lorry	6	(symbol) —	Library
2	(cloud !!!)	Oasis	7	(symbols)	Nightmare
3	(symbols)	Marriage	8	(symbols)	Bottle of wine
4	(lorry symbol)	Cup of tea	9	(symbols)	Old man
5	(symbol) —	Power cut			

Accurately reproduce the following symbols:

1 Oasis
2 Cup of tea
3 Power cut
4 Nightmare
5 Old man

Why do you think that Test B was more difficult than A? Was it because there were two symbols in Test B? Was it because they were not logical? Could you remember the symbols in Test A and did that affect your results in Test B? This may seem like fun but there is a reason for the exercise. Before you even started to learn the symbols there will have been things you have done today that will affect your memory. You may have got up late – so you had to rush to arrive on time. You will have been set other tasks, you will have talked with friends – all of which affects our memory. Filtering out or cataloguing memories, thoughts and experiences is important and affects our lives.

Task 2.3

1 Which of the following is the penultimate letter in the word

REST?

- *R*
- *E*
- *S*
- *T*

2 Who is third in alphabetical order?
- *Retring*
- *Reynold*
- *Rodgers*
- *Raymond*

3 What is a turbine?
- *Fish*
- *Engine*
- *Tower*
- *String*

4 What does debate mean?
- *Comment*
- *Talk*
- *Argue*
- *Create*

5 Wheels are to a car as runners are to
- *Lorry*
- *Track*
- *Tank*
- *Sledge*

How did you score? Is there a difference between memory and intelligence? Does this show that you are very clever if you did well in this exercise? Or perhaps it is just how your logic works and how your mind allows you to see the world. There is a group called Mensa whose members have an IQ score of 140 or more. IQ or intelligence quotient is a theoretical measurement of intelligence in comparison to a formula. Such tests tend to

measure three areas of ability: spatial, verbal and numerical.

There are many criticisms of this type of testing – for example, this concentrates only on specific skills, it does not allow for individual creativity, musical ability or business skills. Another criticism is that if someone is coached in the skills needed to do well in the tests, they can improve their score.

Another area of intellectual ability is the way in which we solve problems. Some people are best at dealing with problems that only have one solution, while others are better at developing a number of alternative ideas.

The first group are called convergent thinkers, and they tend to use a logical and conservative approach to problem solving. They favour tests such as the standard intelligence tests. The second group are called divergent thinkers, and they tend to have qualities of originality, favour variety and show imagination. Both styles are useful and we may use the different types in different situations: one is not superior to the other.

Task 2.4

Look at the following list of qualities

- *Sociable*
- *Outgoing*
- *Talkative*
- *Careful*
- *Reliable*
- *Calm*
- *Moody*
- *Anxious*
- *Quiet*
- *Touchy*
- *Optimistic*
- *Active*

Pick out three that best describe you. Do not discuss this with anyone else – it is important that it is your view of you.

From this kind of exercise a psychologist called Hans Eysenck suggested that people can be categorized into different personality areas (Figure 2.1). According to Eysenck an extrovert is a person who is outgoing, sociable, impulsive and likes variety, while an introvert is quiet, reserved, plans carefully for the future and generally looks on the bad side of things (a pessimist). He then suggests that people can be further divided into emotionally stable and emotionally unstable groups. Stable people stay

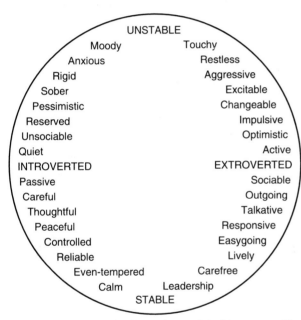

Figure 2.1 Eysenck's dimensions related to personality traits

calm, can cope with stress and remain controlled in most situations. Unstable people are moody, easily upset and suffer from anxiety which may cause illness, such as headache and insomnia. However, this is only one theorist's interpretation of the situation. There are no hard-and-fast rules. Our background and culture as well as society will influence how we react to others and our view of life. The dietary habits of different groups of people are a good example of this.

Task 2.5

Find out the dietary restrictions for the following groups of people:

- *Jewish*
- *Muslim*
- *Hindu*
- *Vegan*

Why do people follow these strict rules?

We should also note that even within this broad area, there will be other influences called subcultures and these will include the family, the neighbourhood, work (or, conversely, unemployment), friends and associates.

Perceptions and motivation

Having already considered people as individuals we now need to explore the areas of perception and motivation. Perception is an attempt to understand and give meaning to the wide range of signals created by our senses. There are five senses: sight, hearing, smell, touch and taste. Research has been carried out by various groups, but generally the pattern shown in Figure 2.2 emerges.

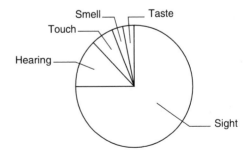

3% through the sense of TASTE
3% through the sense of SMELL
6% through the sense of TOUCH
13% through the sense of HEARING
75% through the sense of SIGHT

Figure 2.2 The ratio of the five senses

Should there be a reason for one of our senses not working, or not functioning properly the others will compensate – e.g. blind people generally have a good sense of hearing and sensitive touch which will help them to deal with the world.

be different from how others interpret that same information.

Perception is selective because we cannot record all the information we receive so we concentrate on some areas and not on others. That is why some people see the young girl in the illustration and others the old woman.

Task 2.6

Look at the following illustration:

What do you see?
The old woman or the young girl?
Can you see the other person?

Task 2.7

Look at the following illustration:

Even though this is really a group of squiggles we still make sense of it and see a man smoking a pipe.

Our brains do not like confusion or things that we do not understand, because that could mean we have something to fear, so we try to rearrange visual information so that it makes sense to us. How you interpret information may

These exercises are useful to show how we as individuals make sense of the world and these are important in the hospitality and catering industry.

Task 2.8

Write down your impressions of:

● *McDonald's*
● *Deep Pan Pizza*
● *A hospital reception desk*
● *A travel lodge*

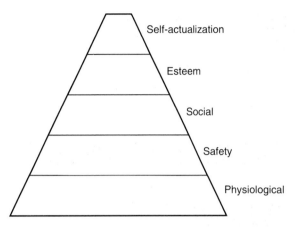

Figure 2.3 Maslow's hierarchy of needs

Try to include information on decor, atmosphere, staff and the product. How do the two compare? What styles have they adopted? You as a customer have perceptions about these businesses. This will affect your purchasing behaviour. If you are influenced, imagine how this will affect other customers.

Let us move on to motivation. Motivation can be explained as the reasons we do things. Again we will all have different reasons for attempting to achieve different goals in life. There have been many theories put together by a group of psychologists called behavioural scientists. They look at what makes us behave in certain ways. The aspect we need to look at is how these theories can be applied to people at work, to encourage them to work more productively. Although there are plenty of theories, we are going to review two that have implications for hospitality and catering. S. A. H. Maslow saw humans as constantly needing to satisfy one need or another and made a list in the priority that those needs would be placed (Figure 2.3):

1 Physiological – the basic requirements for life, food, warmth, shelter, etc.
2 Safety – freedom from threat and danger
3 Social – a sense of belonging, friendship and acceptance of what we are
4 Esteem – a sense of achievement, recognition and respect, of what and who we are, from others
5 Self-actualization – self-fulfilment and personal growth and development. Learning for the sake of learning.

Maslow's hierarchy of needs is often represented as a pyramid. We all start at the bottom and will move upwards as each criteria is fulfilled. However, if you have achieved a certain level and your circumstances change dramatically, according to Maslow you may fall down the pyramid and have to start again.

An example would be when you leave home. Hopefully, at present, you have food, warmth, shelter and security and lots of friends. When you leave home to set up for yourself, although you will still have friends, you will have to provide for yourself the food, warmth, shelter and security, so according to Maslow you are starting again. Many hotel advertisements appeal to Maslow's hierarchy in order to attract customers, for example there are no surprises at a hotel appealing to our sense of security, or no two hotels are the same – appealing to the ego needs of the individual. So if we provide a safe, clean, well-run establishment, with friendly, approachable staff, then Maslow's requirements will have been fulfilled.

D. McGregor put forward a theory that attempts to explain the opposite management styles. This is called theory Theory X and Theory Y. Theory X basically suggests that people are lazy and do not like to work. They have to be bossed, ordered and organized and that, given any excuse, they try to do the minimum possible. This is authoritarian.

Theory Y gives the other view. It says that people like to work, that everyone has ideas that they have a right to put forward and that if good enough, the ideas should be used. This is a democratic view of management.

Task 2.9

Copy out the following statements on a sheet of paper and cut out each statement. Make two lines of statements, one headed Theory X, the other Theory Y.

- *Achievement of a goal is enough reward.*
- *It is natural to work to the best of your ability.*
- *With experience, people look for extra responsibility.*
- *The average human being prefers to be directed, wishes to avoid responsibility and has little ambition.*
- *Under the conditions of modern industrial life, the intellectual abilities of individuals are not developed to their full potential.*
- *A kitchen porter may not be as efficient or thorough if he knows it is pre-decided the time work finishes.*
- *The average person has an aversion to work and will avoid it if they can.*
- *A restaurant that closes at 11 p.m. may try to rush customers because staff cannot leave until the customers have finished. This may give a bad impression.*

How did you do? Did you find this easy? Parts of this theory are used by companies in incentive schemes (used to increase productivity), which we will look at in more detail later.

Communications

We all consider ourselves good communicators. After all, by the time we can start work or move on to more advanced qualifications, we have managed to achieve what we want, or let people know how we feel – or do we? Part of our self-esteem, that part of us that acts as a shock absorber against the hurtful things in the world, requires us to see ourselves as balanced, honest, able and, most importantly, good communicators. Very often there is a difference between what we have said and what we think we have said, and between how we think we have handled people and how they think they have been treated. We often hear that there has been a breakdown in communication, so communication is a two-way process with responsibilities on each side.

Task 2.10

How effective is your communication process? Think about the following situations, then comment honestly on your performance orally in class, as a working member of a class group, in written assignments, interacting with teaching staff and local employers; interpreting the correct body language signals from others.

Rather than imagining communications as a linear process (following along a line in one way) it is best to see them as a circle, because when one person says something, hopefully it will prompt others to reply. The process can be analysed as follows:

1 Intention of sender There must be some information, a set of orders or instructions, an idea that another person or group needs, in other words there must be a message.

2 Transmitting the message When the information has been put together in terms that the receiver can understand, we must then consider the most effective way to communicate. How would you pass on fire drill instructions? Why is that method best?

3 Receiving the message There is no point in sending a message if the receiver is not cooperating. *Here the responsibility changes from the sender to the receiver. This may not seem difficult, but it is a skill that requires concentration, effort and often a great deal of hard work.*

4 Interpretation of the message *This is the test of how successful the sender has been in transmitting the message in an appropriate way and how well the receiver can apply himself to understanding. If culinary French is used in a kitchen, what should and could happen? This illustrates that, although the correct terminology was used in an acceptable form, if the chef de partie's knowledge was not up to the same standard confusion will result.*

5 Feedback *This tests whether the communication is successful. A simple demonstration of whether the communication has been understood or not is the action that results from it (e.g. go and close the door). Generally, the choice of the means of communication will be between written and oral methods. This is because precise meaning is given to the use of language, while the interpretation of non-verbal communication may be open to distortion or the incorrect information being picked up. Written communications include memoranda, letters, newspapers, posters, questionnaires, etc.*

There is another area of communication that gives us a lot of information about others and it does not involve speaking. This is called non-verbal communication and it is the ability to convey information and feelings through the use of body language. It includes:

1 Facial expressions – smiles, frowns, narrowed eyes, transmitting friendliness, anger, etc.
2 Gestures – thumbs-up signs, pointing fingers, head nods, shaking of the head showing disagreement, focus, etc.
3 Movements – pacing up and down, finger drumming, strolling, transmitting anxiety, impatience, boredom, etc.
4 Physical contact – shaking hands, prodding with forefinger, slapping on the back, transmitting greeting or insistence
5 Positioning – keeping a respectful distance, looking over someone's shoulder, sitting close to someone, transmitting awareness of different status, close working relationship, etc.
6 Posture – standing upright, lounging, sitting hunched up, leaning forward, spreading oneself in a chair, transmitting alertness, self-confidence (or over-confidence), nervousness, etc.

Recruitment and appointment

Before we finally start to consider how teams function and operate, we really need to look at the recruitment and appointment of staff. How can you have a team if people are not replaced when they leave or when the company expands?

The selection of new staff falls into three separate activities. First, a job description should be drawn up, stating what a particular job consists of and set in its context. This is followed by a job specification which details the qualities of the ideal person for the job. Finally each applicant should be matched against the ideal to evaluate their suitability for the job.

Task 2.11

Look at the following symbols and note their meaning:

Task 2.12

Find an advertisement from a specialist magazine such as the Caterer & Hotelkeeper. *From the information given, decide the qualities required for the job and draw up job descriptions and specifications that would be appropriate to the job being advertised.*

Many of the advertisements for jobs require staff to be flexible so they can cover for absent colleagues and a range of skills are required. This shows an individual in a number of situations. Multi-skilling is a way of enriching a job and is important to the industry. Following the receipt of application forms, the applicants are viewed against the criteria for the job and the most suitable are asked for interview.

Interviews are a conversation with a purpose – one side to find out about the applicant, the other to find out if they want to work in that job and company. Sometimes four or five people may be involved in interviewing candidates in sequence and then they compare notes. Sometimes they may act as a panel. Sometimes an interview panel will recall an applicant from the waiting room and offer them the job verbally at the end of the interview process. Sometimes a job offer is sent in writing through the post. Whichever way is used, the job offer will be made a short time after the interview. The official contract may also be enclosed with the offer letter. Remember, if accepting, this is a legally binding document on both sides.

Teams

Up to this point we have concentrated on the individual and how he or she may be recruited into the organization. Now it is important that we consider people and how they work as members of a 'team'. Sometimes teams may also be called 'groups'. As we found when looking at Maslow's work, we all need to feel part of a group or team in both social and work situations.

Task 2.13

Try to identify how many different groups or teams you belong to. What are their purposes (e.g. work, social) and how long have you been a member? Are they static or are they constantly changing?

Just as individuals must communicate in the course of their work, it is also likely that they operate as part of a team. The hospitality and catering industry relies heavily on team effort and cooperation in order to provide a service and product that the customer wants.

There are many definitions of teams, but basically they are 'two or more people who have set objectives, who communicate regularly to achieve these objectives and who determine the behaviour that is acceptable'. Teams will also have the following characteristics.

1 A set membership
2 A sense of shared purpose, i.e. a reason for being in existence
3 Interdependence, i.e. people needing each other
4 Communication
5 The ability to act as a unit when necessary.

We can further split them into formal and informal teams. Formal teams will be created by organizations in order to carry out a certain task. You may be familiar with the term 'kitchen brigade' for example, who will have definite responsibilities in the production of food. They will have an imposed structure, membership and procedure. This means that someone in authority will decide who works in that team, what the team is to do and who has responsibility for the standard of the work of that group of people. Informal teams are not set up by management but rely on social interaction. In other words, they are groups of people who have formed together through friendship and common interest. People rely on friendship and if that breaks down or changes, then the team will also change.

There are different stages in the development of any team and someone who has the responsibility of encouraging a group of people to work together should be aware of them.

Stage 1 Forming

When a team is given a task, it is important that individuals are sure what the task is and how best to achieve the end result. They also need to be aware of the resources they need and the additional information they require.

Task 2.14

Working in 'teams' (groups), you have been asked to prepare a menu for a restaurant. What other information are you going to need before you decide what you are going to offer?

Stage 2 Storming

Many teams go through times of disruption and disagreement. This is likely to happen when original ideas are challenged and new ones put forward. If a team does go through this and survives, then a new secure foundation will have been established and there will be more trust.

Stage 3 Norming

This is when the team starts to operate as a unit rather than as a number of individuals trying to impose their own ideas and get their own way.

Stage 4 Performing

Only when the team has been through the other stages will they then achieve the highest levels of performance.

Task 2.15

How could you tell if a group of people working together were truly a team?

Attributes of a team

- *Identity* It can be recognized by its members and usually those outside it.
- *Behaviour* It requires its members to conform to established patterns (norms), attitudes and behaviour.
- *Purpose* It has clearly defined aims and objectives.
- *Hierarchy* It develops, either formally or informally, a leadership and 'pecking order' or hierarchy, which its members accept.
- *Exclusivity* It has the power to allow or reject admission and also to expel anyone from its membership.
- *Solidarity* It demands loyalty from its members and can experience internal disruption while showing an external image.
- *Capacity for change* Its life may be long or short. It may form, disintegrate, and reform, depending on external circumstances and motivation.

Team structures and roles

There are many influences on the structure of teams and the way they operate. This is called the dynamics of the team and shows how people have interlocking roles, rather like pieces of a jigsaw all fitting together.

There will always be an established interaction, which means that behaviour will be adapted depending on the status of the individual being dealt with, e.g. there will be 'in jokes' between team members on the same level or grade but not necessarily the same amount of joking with someone who is in a position of responsibility.

Task 2.16

Think about how you 'interact' with the members of your class or group. How does the group behave when a member of staff is present? Does the behaviour change? How?

The way in which the task that the team has to achieve is organized will affect the structure. For example, a production line will focus around the people in the centre of the line, with those on the ends being isolated, while the kitchen 'partie' system encourages the formation of several small subgroups or 'corners' such as starters, vegetables, main course and dessert within the brigade.

The communication patterns that are used depend on the task of the team. In its simplest form those people who need to communicate with each other to complete a task will tend to form a structural link, e.g. in a fast-food store (Figure 2.4).

One of the problems associated with teams is that members who are perceived as having high status, either because of the force of their personality (informally) or because of their position in the organization (formally), may influence the team and so create a structure centred around themselves.

As well as having a 'position' within a team, each member may also have a 'role' to play. According to K. D. Benne and P. Steats, these roles can be divided into three main types – task, maintenance and self-orientated.

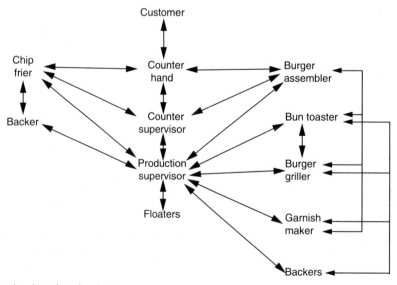

Figure 2.4 Communication in a fast-food store

For a team to function effectively, all the task and maintenance roles must be carried out by some person or persons in the team at some stage. Some members will perform more than one role and it is the leader's responsibility to ensure that task and maintenance roles are completed but individual roles are avoided.

Task 2.17

Look at the following list of roles. Try to put them under the headings of task, maintenance and self-orientated.

- *Initiator*
- *Encourager*
- *Blocker*
- *Compromiser*
- *Comedian*
- *Attention seeker*
- *Decision maker*
- *Commentator*
- *Observer*
- *Coordinator*
- *Peacekeeper*
- *Standard setter*
- *Aggressor*
- *Harmonizer*
- *Information giver*
- *Evaluator*
- *Opinion seeker.*

If you are not sure what any of these terms mean, look them up in a dictionary and make a note of them.

The effective working of teams is also very important and will be influenced by different factors. These include the production of ideas, the commitment, job satisfaction and productivity. Although a team is made up of individuals, a team is likely to produce a greater number of ideas than one person can, given the same amount of time. This is because one idea can develop out of another and discussion can give further inspiration. Second, teams will give a better quality of ideas because they can be refined and discussed before being implemented. Teams also provide shared responsibility for an idea which may be an important support for some individuals.

When trying to encourage commitment, people are more likely to carry out a decision if they have had an input in making it, rather than having it imposed upon them, so it can be important to include teams in the decision-making process.

As individuals, we are social animals who have a need for a social interaction with each other. Teams supply the forum for this interaction, leading to job satisfaction, so reducing absenteeism and labour turnover.

There are certain tasks that cannot be done by one person but must be tackled by a team. Often when jobs are carried out by a team they are achieved more quickly and effectively. Making beds is one example – can you think of any others?

There are other areas called 'environmental variables' which will influence the way in which teams operate. All organizations have an established routine – their own way of doing things – which is bound to affect the way teams develop their own rules, procedures and structure. This is going to vary depending on the organization.

In addition to being affected by the organizational environment, the actual place where meetings are held, the amount of noise, the seating arrangements and the warmth/cold of the venue are going to have an influence. This is called the physical environment. There may also be an interdependence between teams for the whole operation to run smoothly (e.g. chefs and waiting staff) if there is too much competition or too little cooperation the whole system fails to operate properly, resulting in bad service.

We have already discussed teams within the main categories of being either formal or informal. We now need to concentrate on the formal teams in more detail, because it is these within which we are expected to work.

There may be many different types of formal teams and at different times we may be expected to work in more than one at any given moment. However, generally we work within one area or another. Examples of these teams include organized teams, *ad hoc* teams, long- and short-term teams.

When any of us are appointed to a position with a company, we are 'slotted' into a team. The team is already in existence but will have to adapt to include the new person. This is why selecting the correct candidate for a job is so important. If the wrong person is appointed it can cause all sorts of team problems. Nothing remains static and a newcomer will mean that the team will change slightly. Hopefully the overall team performance is not affected.

In this situation we are talking of organized teams. *Ad hoc* is a Latin term which means 'for the purpose of...' So when an *ad hoc* team is put together this will be to achieve a set outcome, e.g. a special one-off function, such as catering and food service for an event like the Grand National. Although this is held on an annual basis, the people providing the hospitality will change and perhaps only the organizers will remain the same.

Communications and responsibilities are important here. People need to know what is expected of them. Individuals may not know each other and the team may not be integrated, so there is a greater scope for problems to arise.

Long-term teams are those that are expected to be working together for some time. These are going to include restaurant and kitchen brigades, as well as reception and housekeeping brigades, which have definite structures and allow for the smooth and efficient running of a facility. A brigade is the total number of staff employed in an area to serve customers. This is the correct term for a 'team' in the restaurant, kitchen reception and housekeeping areas.

Task 2.18

We have mentioned both kitchen and restaurant brigades, but what is meant by a brigade? Write down what you think they are.

Look at the following titles and decide whether they work in a kitchen or a food service capacity. It may be slightly difficult as we are giving their traditional French titles.

- Commis débarrasseur
- Chef de rang
- Chef de partie
- Maître d'hotel
- Chef de reception
- Commis chef
- Sous chef
- Chef de cuisine

To find out if you are correct, look at Figures 2.5–2.8. The organizational chart for kitchens and food service areas, reception and accommodation operations (housekeeping) may appear as in the figures but these are only an overview. Each facility will have its own chain of responsibility.

Some firms require operatives, technicians and technologists, others need craftsmen, supervisors and managers. The hospitality and catering industry is made up of:

1 People with similar craft skills, the craftsmen involved with production
2 The supervisors such as chef de partie, who are in charge of certain elements of food production
3 Those who use management skills and determine policy

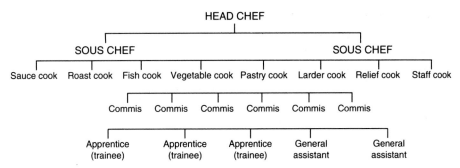

Figure 2.5 A traditional kitchen brigade in a large hotel

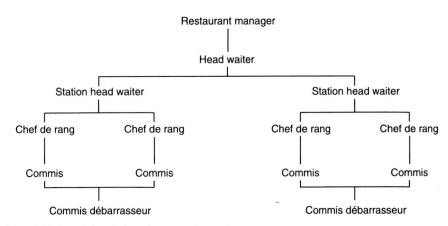

Figure 2.6 A traditional kitchen brigade in a large restaurant

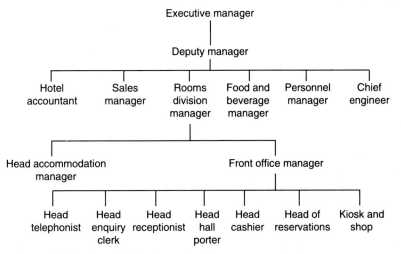

Figure 2.7 Departmental organization in a 600-bedroom hotel

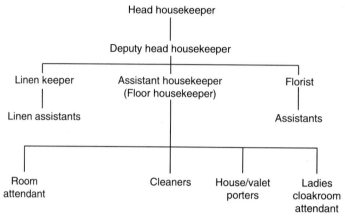

Figure 2.8 Organization chart for the accommodation department in a key large hotel

Task 2.19

Find out the main roles and responsibilities of the following:

- *Food and Beverage Manager*
- *Commis waiter*
- *Head chef*
- *Chef de partie*
- *Senior Receptionist*
- *Concierge*
- *Assistant housekeeper*

As you will have established the main functions of managers, these, particularly in large organizations, will be largely administrative. This includes the maintenance of standards, staff rotas, staff training and appointment of staff in conjunction with the personnel department. Supervisors have areas of responsibility that include forecasting and planning, organizing, directing, coordinating and controlling. Again, depending on the size of the facility, there may not be both managers and supervisors, so there will be areas of duty that overlap. In some smaller units, the supervisor/manager is the same person.

A craftsperson is someone who has specific skills. This will be someone who either prepares the food or who serves customers. A further breakdown of the job responsibilities of different people within a brigade will be given in the next section.

Conclusions

There are very few operations in the hospitality and catering industry that are entirely performed by individuals. Most work is carried out by a group of workers acting as a team. The team aspect of the workers will be emphasized by staff wearing distinctive uniforms which can be used to identify company, department and status of the individual. It is relatively easy to distinguish between one type of employee and another (e.g. Chef and Receptionist). As well as creating 'team spirit', however, such uniforms also establish the status for each team that may detract from the effective operation of the organization as a whole.

Whatever the problems, it is important for managers to understand how teams work, because being put in charge of a team identifies an individual as a manager. At the same time as leading a team, the manager will also be part of a team – the management team of the unit.

• Assignment 2.1 •

Investigation into the operation of teams within the hospitality and catering industry

In order to find out how the hospitality and catering industry operates in practice, and how it makes use of team structure, you are going to be expected to research into different operations. You will need to find out how two different teams work within different aspects of the industry. This means you will have to obtain information about two different organizations and compare and contrast the structure of the brigades. What are the different responsibilities of the people within those teams? What do their jobs entail? Try to construct a chart to show the organization of the team and relate this back to the jobs people have.

The information needs to be produced in report form. Information about writing letters, memos and producing reports can be found in the resource pack that accompanies this text.

• STAFF ACHIEVEMENT AND SATISFACTION •

In this section we are going to move on to look at:

● Job structure and work practices
● Training
● Incentives (methods of encouraging people to work)
● Staff satisfaction

Job structure

Task 2.20

Think of either your part-time job or the responsibilities that you undertook when you were on work placement. Write down what you did, what you were expected to do and how you went about doing it.

What you have produced as a result of this exercise is, in simple terms, a job structure. You have written down what your job entails and the responsibilities involved in it.

We need to look at job structures in the hospitality and catering industries and so we will consider each of the departments in turn.

Task 2.21

Refer back to the organizational structures for each department in the previous section. Write down what you think each individual in the kitchen brigade does. Keep the notes you have just made and compare them with the following information.

The kitchen brigade is responsible for the production of food. This is fairly obvious but it also means that anyone who works in this area may have to work unusual hours or systems, particularly if food has to be available day and night. Some people will work 'straight shifts' – the normal working day – but others will have to work 'split shifts'. The split shifts system is operated so that staff are available to produce foods over peak times – lunch and dinner – with time off in between. In this instance the working hours may be from 9.30 a.m. until 2.30 p.m. and then 6 p.m. to 10 p.m. Some companies may operate a two-shift system to cover lunch and dinner services and their typical day would be 8 a.m. to 4 p.m. and 4 p.m. to 11 p.m. For more information on the operation of the split-shift system see Unit 1.

Most kitchens are run under the 'partie' system. They will all have responsibilities for different aspects of food production such as a fish corner or vegetable corner, but the number of parties and the amount of staff they each have will depend on the size of the establishment.

The two-shift system we mentioned earlier will have a chef de partie in charge of one shift and a demi-chef de partie in charge of the other. We will now look at the kitchen operation in more detail.

Chef de cuisine (Head Chef)

In many large kitchens the functions of the Head Chef tends to be administrative and it will only be the smaller kitchens where the Head Chef is actually involved in food preparation. The Head Chef, no matter what the size of the organization, will be expected to arrange:

1 The organization of the kitchen
2 The development of menus
3 The ordering of commodities (foods)
4 The appointment of staff
5 The supervision of kitchen operatives, particularly at service time.
6 The operation running at a profit

As well as this he or she will have to have a good working knowledge of equipment and its purchase and may also be responsible for the stores, washing up, etc.

Sous chef (Second Chef)

Whenever the Head Chef is off duty, the Second Chef takes over. The function being to run the kitchen as the Chef wants it run and to ensure that it operates smoothly. Again depending on the size of the kitchen, there may be a number of sous chefs who have responsibility for different service areas (e.g. banquets).

Chef de partie

These staff are responsible for work in specific sections or 'corners' of the kitchen, and obviously have specialist knowledge. The chef de partie will organize the work within a section, delegate and make full use of each individual's skills within a section. Here it is very important the people do operate as a team to produce the best possible results.

Commis chefs (assistant cooks)

These people help or assist the chef de partie. The number of assistants in a corner will vary depending on the type of work they do and how many are being catered for. For example, the vegetable partie tends to be larger than the fish partie, because of the quantity of vegetables required compared with the amount of fish dishes. Vegetables are usually served with every main course (and obviously vegetarian ones), so more people with appropriate skills have to be available to work. There may also be a first commis, who will probably be able to take charge of the section if necessary.

There are two other important groups within the kitchen – the kitchen porters and the 'plongeur'. Kitchen porters are responsible for general cleaning duties and again the number employed will vary with the size of the organization. The scullery or 'plongeur' person is responsible for collecting and washing pots and pans and then returning them to their correct place.

This is a very traditional view of the kitchen organization and recent eating trends and foods will give rise to others. In Figure 2.4 we showed, for example, the organization within a fast-food kitchen such as McDonald's.

Again, people have specific responsibilities and certain skill levels, but it could be argued that the amount of technology used, and reliance on that technology, will result in staff being less flexible and having specific skills for a specific area. In a fast-food store the kitchen team is called a 'crew' rather than a 'brigade' and the possibility of being expected to overlap into different areas is much greater, especially at peak times. The general aim for McDonald's service is for people to enter the building, be served and seated, all within 2 minutes. Most do their best to achieve this. There is a similar comparison applicable to restaurant service. Again we will review the traditional structure first.

Task 2.22

Again, refer back to the restaurant organizational structure in Figure 2.6 and write down the duties of each area as you see them. Customers' demands and expectations are constantly changing and there are fashions and trends as with everything.

Maître d'hôtel (Head of restaurant and food service)

In charge of the restaurant and staff during the set-up of the restaurant and food service, the Head waiter is responsible for seating arrangements and table plans; greeting guests; supervising the service and dealing with problems and complaints.

Maître d'hôtel Carée (Station Head waiter)

Responsible for a section of the restaurant, will greet guests, take orders and supervise the service of the station. A station is similar to a partie/corner in the kitchen and will include a certain number of tables.

Chef de rang (Station waiter)

In charge of a group of tables (or rang) of about twenty places (covers), the Station waiter will take orders, serve dishes and is responsible for efficiency and cleanliness.

Commis

This is an assistant who works with the Station waiter by taking food checks to the kitchen, bringing food to the sideboard, helping with the service and cleaning tables and sideboard. You may also have heard the term Wine waiter (Sommelier), who is responsible for service of all alcoholic and non-alcoholic drinks except tea and coffee.

Again, there are definite job requirements in different areas. The fast-food industry is slightly different. Here although people will have responsibility to greet and seat guests, individual waiters may then assume the role of taking orders; delivering them to the kitchen; setting the table with the correct cutlery and serving, then clearing away.

Certain breweries have taken the customer responsibility a stage further. Customers are required to find their own tables, select their food, then go to a central ordering point with their table number and order, where the till records the order, sending it through to the kitchen and producing a bill at the same time. Customers are expected to pay at this stage. When produced the waiter will bring the food and cutlery to the table and then clear away on completion of the meal. They will also be expected to clean the tables once the customers have departed.

Apart from these two important areas, the reception and housekeeping are also an integral part of the hospitality and catering industry. Although their duties vary, the responsibility of both areas will apply whether they are in traditional hotels or travel lodges.

Task 2.23

What do you think a receptionist does? Write down your thoughts. Is there a difference between the job of a hotel receptionist, a car showroom receptionist or a dental receptionist? Write down what you think they do.

The main responsibilities of the receptionist, whether it is a large or small operation, is receiving and welcoming the guest; maintaining all records related to the guest's stay and selling accommodation. Irrespective of the size of the hotel and type of clientele, various records must be kept. The equipment and systems will vary, but the principles remain the same. The functions of the reception office include selling accommodation; receiving and welcoming guests; checking in and registering guests; checking out guests and dealing with their accounts; handling enquiries, complaints and providing information; dealing with advanced reservations; recording of room status; dealing with incoming and outgoing mail and telephone communications and finally the maintenance of good communications with all departments.

All hotels are expected to give 24-hour service. To achieve this in larger hotels, a brigade of receptionists work in shifts to give this level of cover. A senior receptionist (Chef de brigade) would be in charge of each brigade and the reception manager would be responsible for the organization and efficient working of the reception office. In medium-sized hotels there would probably not be a night brigade, but a night cashier, night porter or both, who would deal with late arrivals and departures. In small hotels the receptionist may be required to complete split shifts like the chefs, again morning to lunch-time then off duty until late afternoon and returning to work during the evening.

The housekeeping department again has a range of duties that are not always obvious at first glance. The Head housekeeper will be involved in engaging, dismissing and training staff; making up duty rotas; holiday lists and wage sheets; completing room-occupancy lists; dealing with guests' complaints and requests; checking maintenance work; controlling and supervising the linen room; ordering and issuing stores and checking the work of the staff. The team here will include room attendants, staff assistants, cleaners and porters.

Depending on the market at which the provision is aimed, the responsibilities of people in reception and housekeeping will be expected to be more flexible, the nearer they are to the less expensive market sector.

Training

There is a difference between training and learning. Training is basically concerned with helping people to acquire simple technical skills (such as chopping an onion), whereas learning is much broader and attempts to develop the ability to adapt behaviour to suit the situation within which individuals finds themselves. The role of training in the hospitality and catering industry is usually concerned with taking people with either few or none of the required skills and developing these individuals so that their standards of performance are at the desired level.

The hospitality and catering industry has introduced a system of National Vocational Qualifications (NVQ). This is a system that assesses individuals' practical skills. They are not specifically about training, but they can be used as a standard at which people can aim their skill level.

Rather than seeing poor performance as needing criticism or disciplinary action, in most situations simple training and guidance will be more effective. There are three main types of training programmes:

1 Initial training when an individual starts a job. This is important because it will either give the person the skills or will check the level of their skills, in order to carry out their day-to-day tasks.
2 Refresher training to introduce staff to either new working methods or equipment. This type of training can also be used for assessment purposes to find out how someone is progressing in a job, or possibly to assess their suitability for promotion.

3 Remedial training. This may prove necessary after initial training, particularly if staff do not prove as capable as first thought at completing their tasks, or perhaps they have encountered difficulty in a particular part of the work. It is important that this is regarded as being of help to the individual and not necessarily a disciplinary issue.

Having described the main types or categories of training we are now going to consider how we might achieve the training aims. Again there are three main approaches:

- *Trial and error* In this situation the employer either works alone with very little guidance and learns by his or her mistakes, or he or she will learn the job by working alongside a more experienced member of staff.

Task 2.24

Do you think this method of training will always be successful? What problems could come from this type of training? Having identified some of the problems we now move on to the other approaches.

- On-the-job training *This will be carried out in the work situation by qualified instructors, either in a classroom or in a practical situation. The training programme is planned to provide easy-to-follow guidance in the particular tasks required. This type of training needs periodic evaluation to make sure that it is cost effective and relevant to the needs of the individual and the organization.*
- Off-the-job training *This training takes place away from the work situation, either at an employer's training centre or at a local college on a day release (i.e. one day a week for an academic year) or on a block release basis. (i.e. so many weeks in a block). The length of training will depend on the grade of staff and the company's aims and requirements of the training programme.*

Task 2.25

Draw up a training programme for a new member of staff. You are going to give instructions on a very simple process, such as boiling an egg, answering a telephone and dealing with an enquiry or making a bed. The new employee has no experience to draw on.

Once you have decided your skills training programme, try it out on a colleague. They can only follow your instructions and cannot show any initiative. How did you do?

Most training has a standard approach which can be broken down into five stages.

Planning

This is going to include identifying the people who need the training, what the aims for the training are and where and when the training is to take place.

The next stage is to break down the task into its component parts and to be aware of the perception of each stage of the task to achieve a good performance. This is so that the trainee will be aware of his or her performance in comparison with the standard. For instance, when chopping an onion, the trainee is taught to look for blemishes on the skin, judge how many knife cuts are necessary, etc. The last stage is to put together a total training plan which will include other necessary items, such as tools and equipment and to find a suitable venue for the training session.

Starting

When starting any training programme it is very important that people are in the right frame of mind and are motivated towards doing well. Resentment at being sent and having their skills questioned will mean that individuals may be disruptive and will not be open to the training process, so arousing interest is important. This may be done by displaying the finished product, performing the skill, or perhaps even shock may be appropriate – especially if something like health and safety is being covered. Second, it is important to tell the trainees why they need to be able to complete a task and that it is not a threat to the individual, but part of the process of trying to standardize a procedure.

Giving the instruction

The most effective way of instructing people is a well-planned well-presented demonstration of the skill being learned. In order that the trainees are aware of the 'normal' standards of performance the skill should be demonstrated at the expected speed.

The demonstration should then be broken down into small, achievable chunks of learning, with the trainee being made aware of the perceptual cues. The trainees should be made to feel part of the learning process by asking questions and checking that they understand.

Allowing the trainee to practise

No matter how good the demonstration, the trainee is going to acquire the skills only through supervised practice. We stress 'supervised' because it is very easy for bad habits and skills to appear at this stage. Trainees should be allowed enough time for them to feel confident with the skill and should practise until they show the necessary level of skill.

Once all the steps have been covered, the complete task should then be redemonstrated at half-speed, with questioning of the trainees throughout to check their knowledge. Finally the trainees can practise the complete task with the supervisor monitoring their performance by

correcting, guiding and, most importantly, praising where appropriate, Everyone needs reassurance when they are doing something new.

Many companies have also introduced an 'investors in people' scheme. This tries to recognize the importance of training both to the individual and to the company and looks towards total quality management for customers.

Task 2.26

Using the same information as in the previous task, now put together a different training programme in the light of the theory we have just done. Again, 'teach' a colleague this new skill. Was this easier? More effective?

Evaluation

Having put together a good training programme and passed on the appropriate skills to new employees, it is very important to monitor how they are performing in the workplace. In the workplace trainees will gain from the input of supervisors and more experienced colleagues, the need for assessment of the individual will continue, but hopefully this monitoring will decrease as the trainee reaches the required standard.

Task 2.27

Look at the following stages in the training process:

- *Assess staff's present knowledge and skill*
- *Identify training needs*
- *Prepare training plan*
- *Implement training*
- *Evaluate instructions*
- *Evaluate training programme*

Identify the person responsible for the training and suggest the documentation required.

Draw up a table and complete by adding who and what you think are involved. We have completed the first line as an example.

Stages involved	Person responsible (who)	Document produced (what)
Identify knowledge and skills	Personnel Manager	Job specification Job description

Incentives

According to the *Oxford English Dictionary*, the word 'incentive' means 'something that raises or encourages a person to some action or effort'. This is quite simply what incentive schemes aim to do – to encourage people either as individuals or as teams to work harder to achieve a goal set by the organization and, in return, receive some kind of reward.

Obviously the competitive spirit within individuals is encouraged through such schemes. If incentive schemes are organized on a group basis, all the members of a team work together to achieve a common goal (e.g. the Front Office team).

There is an increasing tendency in the hospitality and catering industry to make extra payments to staff through incentive schemes or bonuses. Seasonal establishments often make end-of-season payments as incentives, in order to encourage the staff to complete the agreed period of work.

Task 2.28

Think either of your part-time work or of someone you know who is employed. How are they encouraged to work more productively? What inducements are offered? How successful is the scheme? How effective do you think incentive schemes will be? What commitment is someone going to have to the quality of service they give? For other practical applications of incentive schemes refer to the section on customer care in Unit 3.

There are many disadvantages to using incentive schemes when the public and customers are involved in the process. We also have to be aware of the effect such schemes may have on our effort; the quality and care of service we give and, most importantly, the safety of ourselves, our colleagues and customers. Too much rushing compromises us in all these areas and could result in an accident. As mentioned earlier, this may foster a competitive spirit. Not all aspects of competition are bad, but when there could be an element of danger this has to be acknowledged and evaluated.

Staff satisfaction

In order for any of us to work to our optimum (best) potential, the environment within which we work is very important. Although we did not mention the work of F. Herzberg when we looked at motivation, it is now reasonable that we consider his theory in relation to the work environment.

Herzberg's theory is often called the two-factor theory. He suggests that the work situation can be divided into elements. The areas that cause dissatisfaction such as conditions of work, pay and physical conditions he calls 'hygiene' or 'maintainance' factors. Those elements of the work which motivate people are responsibility, recognition, achievement and advancement, and these are refered to as 'motivators'. Herzberg found that the workforce can be motivated to achieve certain goals or targets set by management as long as certain minimum requirements regarding the work environment have been met. He referred to 'maintenance' or 'hygiene' factors as affecting our motivation badly, but if these factors are taken by management and used as the minimum standard or expectation of the workforce in relation to job conditions, motivation could be improved. These maintenance factors may include:

1 Implementation of basic legal health and safety requirements
2 The perceived position of the individual in the organization (e.g. whether they feel 'valued' or not)
3 The physical environment – heating, lighting, etc.
4 The provision of adequate leisure or recreational facilities and groups

The environment within which we work and the conditions found there must be of a certain standard if individuals are to reach the objectives set for them. If the conditions in which we work are good, then supervisors and managers may encourage staff to work beyond the minimum level.

Task 2.29

List the maintenance factors that staff may require in the following work areas. One example has been given in each area to help.

- *Hotel kitchen (e.g. regular and consistent supply of hot clean water for pot-wash purposes)*
- *The reception team (changing-room facilities close to the reception area for staff use)*
- *The housekeeping department (access to washing equipment in laundry rooms)*

As we can see from this, a work environment which lacks adequate health, safety, welfare and social conditions will not have a motivating or positive effect upon workers'

performance. Another important area is that of welfare. This can be described as a concern for staff well-being. Applied welfare is the way in which the employer shows his or her concern for staff. Staff welfare is an important part of the job of personnel departments and, depending on the size of the organization, the task is either performed by one person or it is only a part of an individual's job, and there will be other responsibilities in addition to this aspect.

Within the hospitality and catering industry, staff accommodation is often necessary. This should be regarded as a person's home, not just where they live, so it should be comfortable. Rest rooms or dining rooms should also receive attention. Staff should be encouraged to use them, when appropriate, for off-duty activities, because, in addition to 'live-in' staff, there will also be personnel working split shifts. Staff meals are often provided as part of an employee's remuneration (pay), but they are often criticized by staff and sometimes abused by employers. We acknowledge that it is not practical or economic to expect staff to receive the same meals as guests, but it should not be a situation where waste or unsold food should be found. The employer should be concerned with the quality and quantity of food for the staff.

Staff uniforms, when provided by a company, are a remuneration benefit and ensure that the staff do not have to wear their own clothes while at work. The welfare aspect would be shown in the provision of uniforms that are comfortable to wear and not ill-fitting.

In addition to specific welfare requirements such as those we have just reviewed there may also be a need for advisory or counselling facilities for staff. This will help staff to deal with any problems that they may have. If counselling takes place effectively and helps staff with their problems, it will raise staff morale.

Conclusions

In this section we have looked at various factors that affect staff achievement and satisfaction. We have reviewed jobs, their structure and how they fit into the organization's hierarchy. We have also had an overview of their main responsibilities and compared the traditional with more current provision. We then went on to explore training and training programmes and then to decide the best format for a training programme to follow.

Incentive schemes and their implications were then discussed and the important aspect of not compromising existing provision and customers was dealt with.

Finally we analysed what was meant by working conditions, welfare and benefits and placed this in context of the hospitality and catering industry.

▪ Assignment 2.2 ▪

Investigation into staff achievement and satisfaction

In order to evaluate how the industry works in relation to the theory, the next assignment requires that you actually research work situations. You will need to find out information from two different types of work situation, e.g. an hotel and a fast-food restaurant. Give information on the job structures, the work practices that the company uses and any incentive schemes that may be in operation.

Also discuss how effective you think those incentive schemes are for individuals and groups in the work situation you are reviewing. Do they improve productivity?

▪ WORK STANDARDS AND PERFORMANCE ▪

In this final section dealing with human resources we are going to look at:
● Legal requirements in the workplace
● Procedures used to maintain standards and performance
● Sources of information and advice

Legislation

We will consider legislation in relation to the workplace for two reasons:

1 To make sure that you are aware of the legal position when you are appointed to a position within a company
2 You may be involved in some aspect of human resources and it will be important for you to be familiar with some of the aims of legislation

However, before we look at the laws in detail it is important that we have an overview of the British legal system. The system is divided into two different areas: criminal law and civil law.

Task 2.30

What do you think are the differences between the two types of law? Give examples of each.

Criminal law deals with offences that may affect one or more people and which are acts of disobedience against the state. This sounds fairly complicated, but it simply means that someone (or a group of people) have committed a crime which could affect lots of people. The prosecution of individuals is brought by an official representative of the state, such as the police, public standards officers (e.g. Weights and Measures representatives) or Customs and Excise officers (e.g. VAT inspectors) and the cost of bringing the case to court is at the public's expense. Decisions about the case are given by elected officials and the aim is to regulate individual behaviour.

Task 2.31

What sort of punishments do you think this court can impose?

This court can use set punishments which depend on the crime committed, but they include prison, probation, community service and fining.

Civil law is a collection of rules and principles which have been applied since the time of the Norman Conquest, and their main aim is to regulate the behaviour between individuals, public bodies and institutions. There are different aspects of the form of law, but the law of contract deals with and regulates business dealings and the law of tort protects individuals against trespass, negligence and defamation.

There are no set punishments and each case is judged individually but damages (money settlements) or injunctions (legal instructions to keep away from a person, property or not to publish information in the press) can be given, depending on the seriousness of the offence. In the court system the case is at the individual's expense and people or organizations are 'sued'.

Task 2.32

Prosecution is a term used in criminal law. Suing somebody is a term used in civil law.

So is the terminology correct in the following statement?

'Trespassers will be prosecuted.'

If not, why not?

Task 2.33

There are different terms and definitions used in different courts. Find out the meaning of the following terms:

- *Plaintiff*
- *Defendant (civil court)*
- *Defendant (criminal court)*
- *Accused*
- *Injunction*

We are now going to look at the law as it relates to the individual in the work situation. This is under the branch of civil law.

Although you will have to be aware of laws relating to recruitment and selection, such as racial discrimination and equal opportunities, we are first going to review the contract of employment and cover the others later.

Contracts

Contract law determines whether a promise is legally enforceable and the consequences of that promise. There are many different types of contract, but we are going to confine our studies to employment contract.

This legislation governs the individual employment rights of employees and there have been a number of Acts to cover employment. At present the Trades Union Reform and Employment Rights Act 1993 is the major piece of legislation. It states that a written statement of the terms of employment must be given to any new employees who work more than eight hours a week and who have been in employment for more than one month.

Task 2.34

What do you think this statement should include so that it is legal? Does your list agree with the following?

1 The names of employer and employee
2 The date employment began
3 The scale or rate of pay (remuneration), or the way it is worked out
4 The intervals of payment, i.e. weekly, monthly, etc.
5 Hours of work, including normal hours of work
6 Holiday entitlements including information on public holidays and holiday pay
7 Job title or brief job description
8 The place of work or an indication of the requirement to work in various places

After a further two-month period (therefore after three months in total), the employer must also provide:

● Terms and conditions relating to sickness/injury, etc.
● Rules on pension schemes
● Length of notice to be given by both employer and employee
● Disciplinary rules and disciplinary appeals procedure

Having started work and completed your contract it is important to be aware of 'Common Law' rights and responsibilities. As far as the employee is concerned this is going to cover such aspects as:

● Obeying lawful orders
● Giving careful service
● Being loyal to the employer
● Accounting to the employer for any loss or damage caused through negligence

Equally, the employer also has responsibilities under common law and these include:

● Payment of the agreed remuneration
● To provide safe working conditions for the employee
● To observe all laws relating to the maintenance of welfare and safety conditions (statutory sick pay; Health and Safety at Work Act)

Hopefully, there would then follow many years of service with the company, but unfortunately this does not always happen. Reasons for leaving employment may be quite varied.

Task 2.35

Make a list of the reasons people would leave their jobs. It may look something like this:

1 Dismissal due to poor performance; breaking the rules; poor code of conduct
2 Redundancy, due to seasonal business; changes in the organization or economic forces on the business
3 Resignation because of promotion or a move to another company; dissatisfaction or personal reasons
4 Retirement – reaching retirement age; physical ill health; mental ill-health or company schemes for 'shedding' staff.

We can see from this that the contract can be terminated by either the employer or the employee. However, no matter who terminates the contract, notice periods have to be either given or served.

An employee is required to give at least one week's notice in writing to terminate the contract, but this does not increase with the length of service given. In certain circumstances, the employee may have accepted a contract in which notice periods are specified, e.g. two weeks or one month, and in this instance the employee would be expected to serve these periods. The amount of notice which an employer gives an employee will depend on how long the employee has been working for the company. After one month of service, the employer has to give at least one week's notice. This stays the same until the employee has worked for the company for two years continuously. After two years' service the employer has to give two weeks' notice and this continues to rise until, after twelve years' continuous service, the employer has to give twelve weeks' notice. Any service of over twelve years will still receive twelve weeks' notice.

These are the minimum periods of notice. If the contract of employment specifies longer, then it is that period that applies. Redundancy is presumed to happen when the employer:

● Stops, or intends to stop, carrying on business
● Ceases to carry on business where the employee is employed (e.g. closes down one restaurant in a chain)
● Does not require as many employees to do a certain type of work (e.g. hotel changes hands from one company to another and restructuring of the organization takes place)

Redundancy payments vary and the calculation is complicated, generally taken as being one week's pay for each year of service, to a limit of twenty years' service.

Redundancy may be voluntary. This is when an employer asks for volunteers to give up their jobs. It may be an expensive method as there must be an adequate cash incentive.

Task 2.36

Make a list of other aspects that are going to affect employers and employees and the workplace. Then find if there are laws to cover them.

Other statutes

A reasonable amount of legislation has been produced in the UK to safeguard employees' interests and improve their position. Obviously we are not able to cover all of these in this text but the outline of the main Acts is discussed.

Health and Safety at Work etc. Act 1974 (HASAWA)

All people at work except domestic servants in private households are covered by this Act. It imposes a general duty of care on most people associated with work activities.

Equal Pay Act 1970

This provides for equal pay and conditions for men and women doing the same or broadly similar work.

Sex Discrimination Act 1975

This Act makes it illegal to discriminate on the grounds of sex.

Race Relations Act 1976

This Act makes it an offence to discriminate on the grounds of colour, race or national origins. It prevents advertisements for staff from particular countries or the rejection of a guest solely on the grounds of colour, race or national origins.

Employment of Young People

Legally, children are defined as being under the minimum school-leaving age and the regulations governing their employment are very strict. However, regulations which previously governed a young person's hours of work in certain employment situations are no longer in force. It is illegal to employ a person under the age of eighteen in a bar when it is open for the consumption of liquor. They may be employed elsewhere and enter through the bar to pass or receive messages.

The Food Safety Act 1990

This Act seeks to protect the consumer from potential danger, using a variety of powers of control.

- It protects against being offered harmful or unfit food.
- It protects against being offered substandard food.
- It safeguards against the false or misleading labelling of food.
- It requires all food premises to be registered with the local authority.
- It makes provision for food handlers to be trained in food hygiene.
- It allows government ministers to make emergency orders to deal with potentially serious problems relating to food.

This is dealt with in much greater detail in Unit 4, as is other legislation relating to food hygiene.

Workplace procedures

In this section we are going to review the procedures and records that may be in operation in many establishments within the hospitality and catering industry. These fall under the following headings:

- Induction
- Records

- Performance assessment and appraisal
- Disciplinary and grievance procedures, and finally
- Trades unions, professional bodies and industrial tribunals

Depending on the size of the establishment, these functions may be carried out by a personnel department, a small group of people or an individual.

Induction

This is the process of integrating a new person into an organization or team.

Task 2.37

Think about your part-time job or work-placement experience. How did you know what to do through the working day/hours? Was enough/too much information given?

When people have been appointed to a job, new staff need to be given a short training time aimed at making them familiar with:

1 Company policies
2 Company rules and procedures
3 An overview of the company's activities
4 The range of products or services
5 The structure and organizational systems
6 Introductions to the employee's immediate colleagues

There has been a good deal of research into levels of staff turnover. This has revealed that the highest staff turnover happens during the first two months of employment in a new company/job. There may be many reasons for this, but it could perhaps indicate that either the candidate recruited for a position was wrong or that the induction programme was inadequate and people did not feel 'at ease' in the new job. This shows that proper induction procedures are beneficial to both the organization and the individual.

Records

The personnel function of maintaining and updating information for each employee is very important. In small organizations, apart from basic details and wage records (a legal requirement), the employer will probably rely on memory and personal contact for information concerning his or her employees. In larger establishments the information is likely to be held on computerized databases, which can be very useful for their speed and efficiency.

Task 2.38

What information do you think employers would need to keep about their staff? Do you think the files should be confidential or open access for everyone? Why?

The records start with the application form which will give details of the employee and background information about previous employment and experience. This may be verified with references from independent sources about the individual and copies of certificates, examination results, etc. No matter how the records are held (either on paper or on computer), a personnel record card should be developed.

Task 2.39

Why do you think it is important to keep records? Who should be able to see them?

Performance assessment and appraisal

It is very important that the workforce is able to meet the demands and expectations of the organization, and that they achieve the levels of performance the company requires. Therefore it is also important that people know what the company is aiming for, but these aims should be broken into segments and delegated to the appropriate sections or teams. This means that supervisors will be expected to set goals at which individuals should aim. Inherent in this is the constant monitoring and evaluation process of people to ensure that they are working to their potential. The application of this is detailed in Units 4 and 5.

Here there is a further link into motivation. For instance, the achievement of satisfactory profits as an objective may be difficult for some workers to interpret, so it is up to the supervisor to translate this into terms they can understand – in other words, setting clearly defined standards.

Task 2.40

We now have an overview of assessments. How would you suggest that the appraisal takes place? What sort of documents would you require to do this?

Feedback and assessment are very important so that both the supervisor and individual realize how effective the motivation and change of attitude have been. By carrying out an appraisal of work performance, clearly defined aims will be recognized. Standards will be specified and interpreted as targets for individuals and teams to work towards and the appraisal system should measure how effective this has been. Therefore, appraisal is designed to measure whether or not standards are being maintained. It also gives the basis for modifying the individual's behaviour if standards are not being maintained and so is used in the system of control.

Task 2.41

Produce a document called 'A performance appraisal form'. What information is relevant and why have you chosen to include the areas that are on the document?

There are three main ways in which documents like the one you have produced can be used by supervisors. They are as follows:

1 The open-ended report, which allows for free range and is relatively unstructured. The advantage of this style is that the supervisor can put his or her interpretation forward, but the disadvantage is that because there is no standard format it can ramble and not highlight specific areas of concern. This may mean that the opinion is not objective enough to be useful.

2 The closed grading or ranking system. This is used to classify the workforce into a range of performance grades or ranks. For example, the top 10 per cent of the workforce may be in the top grade, while the next 10 per cent will be in the second

grade and so on until all the workforce has been streamed or graded. This again may rely on a subjective view of the individual rather than an objective interpretation. This would give rise to problems as some workers may be in different gradings for different areas of their responsibilities. For example, someone may be good at organization but not as good at asking other staff to follow instructions. This would mean that they need to be in different bands for different aspects of their work.

3 Rating systems are probably the most popular, as they allow for more objectivity and less personal interpretation. In this system the supervisor rates the employee's work in specified areas. Hopefully this is the type of document you produced. Another example is shown in Figure 2.9. This would also give a standardized format to the assessment process and help to give everyone a similar set of criteria to follow and discuss, and it can be used in a range of situations. Many appraisal and review procedures are linked to promotion, pay and bonuses within the organization.

Disciplinary and grievance procedures

Under the employment legislation we have already reviewed there is a wide range of legal responsibilities to provide employees with fair and just conditions of employment and safeguards against unfair dismissal and discrimination. This procedure should ensure that any disciplinary action is not taken until the case has been thoroughly investigated and that employees are not dismissed for a breach of discipline, except in the case of gross misconduct (such as theft, etc.).

There should be a system through which employees are told if a complaint has been made against them and they should be given the opportunity to state their case before any decision is made. The employee should have the right to be accompanied by a 'friend' (either

PERFORMANCE APPRAISAL FORM

EMPLOYEE'S NAME ....

EMPLOYEE'S POSITION ....

DEPARTMENT/SECTION ....

SUPERVISOR/MANAGER'S NAME ....

TICK APPROPRIATE BOX	EXCELLENT	GOOD	SATISFACTORY	POOR	COMMENTS
TECHNICAL SKILLS					
INTERACTIVE SELLING SKILLS					
SOCIAL SKILLS					
EFFORT					
ENTHUSIASM					
INITIATIVE					
ABILITY TO GET ON WITH					
(a) CUSTOMERS					
(b) OTHER STAFF					
(c) MANAGEMENT/SUPERVISORS					

Figure 2.9 A performance appraisal form

a trade union representative or fellow employee) when stating his or her case. The procedure should also ensure that the employee knows the penalties that can be imposed and informed of the appeals mechanism.

The contents of a disciplinary code

Task 2.42

What actions do you think should be included in a disciplinary code? Make a list of the most important ones.

The contents of a disciplinary code should include reference to areas which cause genuine disruption to the smooth running of the firm. Hopefully your list includes some of the following areas:

- Persistent lateness
- Absenteeism
- Violation of health, safety and welfare regulations
- Theft
- Smoking in prohibited areas
- Drinking on duty
- Fighting or abusive behaviour

The seriousness of each of these will vary in terms of the number of times the action is committed and in relation to the situation in which it was committed, e.g. being drunk on duty might be viewed far more seriously if the welfare of other staff and guests was endangered. As a result of this, various penalties will be available depending on the circumstances.

Task 2.43

Draw up a fair disciplinary procedure. What stages should be covered and why? How many stages should there be?

---

1 The first stage is where all the information about the incident is collected. This will help in deciding whether disciplinary action is necessary. If it is necessary, then the procedure should be objective and treat the employee in a fair and reasonable manner.
2 Formal verbal warning. This will probably follow one or more informal verbal warnings, where there has been no improvement in behaviour. At this stage, a note will be made on the employee's personnel file that the verbal warning has been given. This will include details of the subject and the date.
3 First written warning. This will follow if there is no noticeable improvement after the formal verbal warning, or this may be issued if the offence is serious enough to warrant leaving out verbal warnings.

Task 2.44

Mr X is constantly late and his timekeeping is generally poor. Write a letter to him confirming this as being a written warning. What information is going to be important to include and what do you require back from the employee?

---

4 Final written warning. This is sent when there has been no improvement in behaviour since the written warning and it stipulates that any further occurrence will lead to suspension, dismissal or some other penalty. A copy should also be sent to the employee's representative or 'friend'.

Task 2.45

Write a letter to Miss Y as a final official warning about challenging the supervisor's authority and decisions. Again, think carefully about the information you would need to include to show that the company does have a 'case'.

---

5 Actual dismissal. This will follow a continuing serious situation that does not improve. First, the individual would be suspended on full pay pending the outcome of the hearing, but should be aware that it may lead to dismissal. If the employee is dismissed without notice, the individual should be informed and given the opportunity to reply. The employee should then be informed in writing within fourteen days of dismissal.

Task 2.46

Mrs Z has been found working for another company while on sick leave from your company. Write to Mrs Z telling her that she has been dismissed, after her hearing, and explaining why.

Appeals procedure

An appeals procedure should be drawn up and should be made available to employees. Employees who have been dismissed from their employment have the right to appeal to an industrial tribunal. However, some organizations have their own appeals procedure where dismissal is concerned.

Generally, appeals are best dealt with inside the organization, although sometimes an independent view may be the best means of resolving this situation, providing both parties agree to their decision.

Grievance procedure

The reason for having a grievance procedure is to maintain satisfactory working relationships between employees. Therefore, employees need to be aware of the procedure so that if the situation arises they can discuss problems regarding their terms and conditions of employment, their working conditions, methods of work and any other aspects of their employment. The procedure should have recognized stages, although it should be remembered that it is best to settle all grievances as near to the point of origin as possible. This indicates that the people trying to resolve the problem – either supervisors or middle management – must be trained to handle grievances.

Task 2.47

Put together a suitable grievance procedure for a large hotel. In this example the problem has arisen in the housekeeping department. Hopefully your procedure appears as follows – but again there are no hard-and-fast rules, simply suggestions to incorporate into the scheme.

- Stage 1 *The complaint or grievance should be discussed with the employee's immediate supervisor (e.g. housekeeper). If the employee is not satisfied with this, he or she may go to stage 2.*
- Stage 2 *The employee should inform his supervisor that he wishes to discuss his grievance with the house/food and beverage manager. If the employee is dissatisfied with this level of discussion, then he should inform the house/food and beverage manager that he wishes to discuss the issue with the general manager.*
- Stage 3 *The employee is able to present his grievance to the general manager, whose decision is final. Details concerning all grievance procedures should be recorded and the case notes passed on to the person dealing with the next stage. Employees should be encouraged to go on to the next stage and to use the procedure without any fears of retribution.*

Industrial tribunals

The function of these is to provide an informal and speedy method for employees to enforce their rights against employers for breach of some Acts including:

- Health and Safety at Work Act 1974
- Sex Discrimination Act 1975
- Race Relations Act 1976
- Employment legislation

For most situations, the tribunal will be made up of a chairperson and two other members. The chairperson must have been a barrister, advocate or solicitor for at least seven years. The other two members are appointed by the Secretary of State for Employment from lists proposed by the Confederation of British Industry, (CBI – an employers' organization) and the Trades Union Congress (TUC – an employees' organization). There can be appeals against the tribunal's decision (on a point of law).

Sources of information and advice

At a national level in industry, the employers are represented by the CBI and the employees by the TUC. We are now going to look at the role of trade associations and their responsibilities, the professional bodies and finally trade unions.

Trade association

This can best be described as a voluntary body of independent organizations formed to protect and advance the interest of their members. Trade associations are both nationally and locally based. National organizations (e.g. British Hotels and Restaurants Association) have local branches acting independently. They are non-profit making.

As well as protective roles, trade associations have developed a range of services available to their members (e.g. product and service information). They also negotiate with other official bodies such as Tourist Boards, on classification of membership, etc.

Other trade associations are more specialist and are consequently smaller in membership. A complete listing of trade associations and addresses is found in the *HCIMA Reference Book*.

Task 2.48

Find out other examples of trade associations for the hospitality and catering industry.

Publications

While not linked to trade associations there are trade publications that often take up issues on behalf of the industry and provide a voice for their readership, whichever association they belong to. The most well known of these is the *Caterer & Hotelkeeper*, which is published weekly and has a wide readership in the industry and associated trades.

Professional bodies

A professional body is an organization of individuals who are engaged in a particular occupation, and who have gained qualifications or experience in that occupation. The professional body will lay down standards by which members have to qualify for membership and these standards will be based on knowledge, expertise and competence to carry out the occupation. It will also set up a code of conduct for its members to abide by in order to retain their membership.

Trade associations membership is related to the business, being the qualification for membership, while a professional body represents an individual who will carry membership from one position to another.

Some professional bodies require academic qualifications to a certain level, either from a recognized examining body or through their own qualifications, others may require experience in order to gain entry. In most professional bodies there are differing levels of membership, ranging from student or associate to a fellowship and it is possible to progress from one level to another, subject to certain requirements. The principal association for the hospitality and catering industry is the HCIMA – the Hotel Catering and Institutional Management Association. While the Association is best known for its educational work, it provides a wealth of information about all aspects of the industry through a handbook which is updated annually. The Association also provides publications, advisory services, meetings, conferences and lectures to both industry and its members.

Task 2.49

Find out more information, particularly about the levels of membership in the HCIMA which is based in London but has regional representatives.

Trade unions

Traditionally trades union involvement in the hospitality and catering industry has been on a very small scale in comparison with other industries. This may be due to a number of factors. The industry is large and diverse and people are constantly gaining employment with new establishments or changing responsibilities within existing ones. This can mean keeping track of union members and could present considerable problems. The system of negotiating individual contracts also contributes to high levels of staff turnover in catering establishments, particularly when there is a change of management. This again is going to contribute to low trades union involvement.

A further problem is that there is no specific union representing the industry and so this again will affect union membership. Generally, unions recruit wherever the need for a trade union representation is felt, regardless of industry or craft. The Transport and General Workers Union (TGWU) and the General and Municipal Workers Union (GMWU) have both made efforts to provide representation for catering workers.

Legal advice

There may be some situations that require legal advice. If you are not in a trades union, so therefore not eligible for their assistance, there are sources of advice still open to people. The

Citizens Advice Bureaux is a voluntary organization that will give advice on situations regarding rights and obligations as well as financial information. This is a very useful source of facts. Another publisher that was not mentioned earlier is Croner Publications. Within this very useful source there is information about current legislation and codes of practice that are in operation. A subscription scheme operates and information is updated on a regular basis.

Conclusions

In this section we have looked at work standards and conditions. We have reviewed the legal position, in terms of both the employer and employee and their rights and responsibilities.

We have described the workplace procedures and the personnel function, which has highlighted the diversity of the work there. Finally, we have given an overview of the other sources of information such as the Citizens Advice Bureaux and legal publications such as Croner.

Hopefully these three sections on human resources have given an insight into the exciting, challenging and extremely important area of people as the most important resource in any industry.

▪ Assignment 2.3 ▪

You have been asked by your company to formulate an induction package for new employees. In the light of the information we have covered, complete a report for your manager showing the areas that you feel are important for inclusion in an induction scheme and justify your reasons. Remember, to a manager time is money, so time away from the job is expensive to the company. This implies that there may be opposition to your scheme, particularly from more traditional managers. How would you convince them to adopt your scheme?

Further reading

Anderson, C and Blakemore, D., *Modern Food Service*, Butterworth-Heinemann. 1991

Betts, P. W., *Supervisory Studies*, 5th edition, Pitman, 1989

Cracknell, H. L. and Nobis, G., *Mastering Food Service*, Macmillan, 1989

Croner's Catering, Croner Publications

Evans, Desmond W., *People, Communication and Organizations*, 2nd edition, Pitman 1990

Gale, Ken, *Behavioural and Supervisory Studies*, Gale Odgers Publications, 1985

Gale, Ken and Odgers, Peter, *Hotel and Catering Supervision*, Macdonald and Evans, 1984

Kinton and Ceserani, *The Theory of Catering*, 6th edition, Edward Arnold, 1989

Lockwood, Andrew and Jones, Peter, *People and the Hotel and Catering Industry*, Cassell, 1984

Plannett, Alan, *Principles of Hotel and Catering Law*, Holt, 1984

PROVIDING CUSTOMER SERVICE IN HOSPITALITY AND CATERING

This unit is concerned with 'providing customer service'. 'Easy', we might say, but is it? How many times have we had poor or inconsistent service? How do some businesses get it right while others fall by the wayside? The hospitality and catering industry is about what people want. People stay in hotels, visit attractions, go to restaurants or leisure complexes because they want to. Sometimes they need to be cared for in hospital or in a long- or short-stay residential home. The service they get depends on people like us.

Good customer service can increase income through repeat business, often by word of mouth. Therefore customer service is the key to the success of any business, and any business requires customers. If customers are not happy with the service we offer they will vote with their feet and go elsewhere. This unit helps us to understand why it is essential that we have good-quality customer service skills and covers:

- Types of customers
- The importance and purpose of customer service
- Customer needs and expectations
- Formulating customer service strategies
- The implications of customer care on costs and resources
- Statutory hygiene, health, safety and security associated with customer service

▪ CUSTOMERS ▪

We are all customers in some way, so are our friends and relatives, our neighbours, our employers and our lecturers. So too are the people in residential homes, the sick in hospital and the disabled, the rich and the poor. In other words, customers can come from every walk of life, be of any nationality or religion. All sorts of people will use the hospitality and catering industry every day. They even have a variety of names. You may hear them being referred to as guests, clients, consumers or, as in this unit, as customers.

No customer is unimportant, every customer has needs and expectations to be fulfilled. Some of these needs and expectations are shared by other customers, or even by all customers (such as the need for courtesy); some needs and expectations are different for different groups of people.

External and internal customers

We all think of the customer as being someone who comes into an outlet to use facilities or amenities or purchase products. If you buy a can of cola and a sandwich from the school/college refectory or go into a fast-food outlet with your friends at weekends for a burger and chips you are one of those people who are so important to the hospitality and catering industry – a *customer*.

When purchasing your cola from the school or college you are known to be an *external* customer. If purchasing your burger from a fast-food outlet on the high street you are also referred to as an external customer. Let us examine in more detail the different customer types.

External customers usually pay for the facilities, amenities and products they use. They could be staying in an hotel, visiting a restaurant, attending a conference or using a leisure facility. If they are disappointed they will not come again, and will not recommend our establishment to other people. Remember: we cannot exist without our customers: they are our best form of advertising. Without customers we have no jobs.

Some customers are already *in situ*, they may be patients in hospital or those needing short- or long-stay care. Within the outlet there are our colleagues who are also customers, they may work in another area of the outlet or even come from head office. This category includes all employees and suppliers of materials and services and are known as *internal customers*. They have less opportunity to choose whether or not to come again, but a disgruntled employee can cause a lot of ill feeling and difficulty, by being awkward, unhelpful and working without much interest in the job. An unhappy employee spreads doom and gloom and unhappiness to others in the workforce. Together the morale of the team drops, making colleagues inefficient and ready to leave.

Age groups of customers

Differing types of outlets will attract particular age groups. Teenagers and young adults go to clubs, as well as school, college and fast-food outlets and cafés. Pubs are visited by the young and the elderly. Business people, in the age group 30 to 55 are more likely to use hotels on a daily basis. The elderly will use residential homes, while all age groups are likely to frequent hospitals and restaurants. Families will make use of resort hotels and holiday camps.

Task 3.1

While you are surveying your local 'take-away' note the age group of the people who use it. Produce a table or graph showing the number in each age group.

Cultural background of customers

Restaurants selling Indian and Asian food supply the needs of those nationalities. It is not the aim of this section to cover all dietary needs but it is useful to be aware of the client groups who visit your outlet and have a basic knowledge of their cultural background and dietary requirements. Islam religion requires similar restrictions to Jewish people in that Muslims also do not eat pork. Their meat is prepared by a method known as Ha-lal, while those of the Hindu religion do not eat beef and are usually vegetarians. Those who do eat meat tend to eat goat meat, chicken or fish. Arabs are also mainly vegetarians and any meat they eat is generally lamb. Their method of preparing meat is known as Jhatka. Britain has a sizeable immigrant population, and yet the everyday establishments are only just beginning to cater for their needs. Some of the London hotels now incorporate ethnic restaurants as part of their policy in place of the traditional restaurants to which we have become accustomed.

As well as dietary needs we should also take account of the importance of recognizing the differing customs associated with religion and culture. For example, some cultures do not permit women to circulate or eat in public places. When observing Ramadan Muslim customers will observe a fast from sunrise to sunset and may require food outside normal service times. Sometimes the room may need the furniture rearranged to satisfy religious observance so that these customers may pray facing Mecca.

Many of our customers may speak a foreign language and it is therefore considered an asset for staff to have key phrases and knowledge of at least one other language. This enables you to communicate with the customers and make them feel welcome. General information about the outlet, instructions relating to fire and safety and menus are also printed in several languages as well as English to help the customer.

Customers with special needs

Some customers have needs which others do not have, because they are in some way different from the majority of people. They are described as customers with 'special needs'. These differences may be very minor, and require only slight adjustments to methods of service or menus, as for example, for a diabetic. Other differences may be substantial and require special access arrangements and diets, modified furniture or complete privacy and so on.

Physical disabilities are the special needs which often spring to mind, and some of these are expensive to accommodate. However, different sectors of the industry are beginning to realize the importance of customers with physical disabilities, and of their spending

power, and are beginning to make special arrangements for their needs and comfort. To this effect many outlets, when refurbishing, are modifying their accommodation and new projects are incorporating specially designed accommodation. The Forte travel lodges now have bedrooms designed for people with special needs and many other outlets provide facilities and amenities which allow access for these people (for example, widths of doorways to allow for wheelchairs, the height of reception desks which allows the customer to be seen).

Task 3.2

Imagine you are a person in a wheelchair. What special amenities or needs would you have if you were staying in a hotel for a week? Together with others in your group, investigate other outlets in your locality, and find out if they provide access to the facilities and amenities to satisfy the needs you have identified.

It is necessary that we are aware of the need to be sensitive to those who have sensory impairment. Difficulties can arise with notices and steps. All facilities in an outlet should be clearly labelled, signposted, coloured, well lit and placed at appropriate levels to be recognized. Many large buildings now have speaking lifts. Customers may have needs associated with health. For example, a customer with a heart complaint may not wish to have to climb too many stairs, another who requires dialysis treatment will have differing needs, but both may wish to stay in a hotel or both could be patients in a hospital. Whatever the need of the customer, it is important to recognize that they have a need, to be sensitive to the need, and to offer support without becoming intrusive.

Task 3.3

Select an outlet of your choice. What kind of help would you think the following customers might need?

- *Partially sighted person*
- *Deaf person*
- *Person with a broken leg*
- *Confused elderly customer*
- *Person suffering from tennis elbow or a frozen shoulder*

Task 3.4

Compare your list with those of others in your group. Arrange as a group to visit a nearby hotel, guest house or restaurant (not a take-away).

Using your list of items which you compiled in the previous task, identify how many of those needs would be met by the outlet you have chosen.

often referred to as very important people (VIPs) or commercially important people (CIPs):

1 *VIPs* Could be a celebrity, member of a royal family, foreign diplomat, president of another country, prime minister, etc.
2 *CIPs* Internal customers, e.g. a supplier or senior manger from the organization, chairperson, managing director of a large company

The attention bestowed on VIPs and CIPs is not to assume that they are in any way better than our other customers and the quality of service we offer but generally they pay a higher price for the additional service they receive.

Task 3.5

Why do you think management give extra attention to VIPs and CIPs ? Can you think of any VIP or CIP who may have visited your school, college or place of employment? What special attention or needs were provided for and why?

Special requirements

Special requests and requirements desired by the customer can also be seen to be a special need. Usually these requirements would be arranged in advance and sent on an internal memorandum to the various facilities within the outlet. For very important customers the head office of the organization may become involved. These needs might include security arrangements, personal acknowledgement by the management or complete privacy away from the media. A foreign diplomat may require confidentiality as to the itinerary and whereabouts, Royalty may require strict security measures to be enforced. These customers are

Task 3.6

Discuss with some of your group and make a list of ten VIPs or CIPs and how you would correctly address them:

- *If they decide to visit your school or college*
- *If you needed to write them a letter*

You could try role playing how you would verbally address them if responding to a question.

Individuals or groups

Individual customers are generally fairly easy to accommodate. Their needs do not put any strain on the resources of the outlet and are often well satisfied with the services they receive. In larger outlets it is not always possible to remember every customer, especially if there is likely to be greater movement of staff. It is custom and practice for there to be a customer history card and, if nothing else, it impresses the customer when special requests, favourite rooms, or tables are reserved. It is these small considerations which make our customers feel special and valued. History records may be kept manually or on computer and contain information about the customers' preferences and requirements so that their needs may be met next time they visit your outlet.

Business customers are usually travelling at their companies' expense and out of necessity rather than pleasure. Time will be important, therefore quick, efficient service is required.

to arrange than a group of twenty-four who all want adjacent single rooms or to be seated together on one table overlooking the sea. Groups and tours bring substantial income to many hospitality and catering outlets, and therefore should be considered as a special group as regards their requirements. Special arrangements are generally made to receive these customers on arrival. They may have an itinerary which needs to be kept to. Many hotels offer favourable terms to larger groups and even advertise special facilities and entertainment programmes to encourage their custom. Customer history records are also kept as often these groups will return, especially if they have enjoyed their visit.

Customers may be *regular, occasional* or *chance*. If you wish them to return all must be treated with respect and courtesy. *Remember*: a friendly smile can make all the difference.

Task 3.7

A businessperson arrives at your hotel late. The restaurant is closed. The customer wishes to check out speedily for an early start to the day. What services might this person request?

Women travellers often require additional services such as a hair dryer or an iron in their room. Seating locations within a restaurant are often planned with the single woman in mind. The attitude of staff towards women travellers is also important so that they are not humiliated in front of other guests. Groups of customers are more difficult to accommodate due to the numbers involved. A single customer requiring a room or a table overlooking the sea is easier

The hospitality and catering industry provides a service to its customers and as such, every customer is special and will require some slightly different service and have a different perceived need. It helps therefore to have a broad understanding of different types of customers and their groups. This is known as *market segmentation* and assists in providing a suitable service, facilities and amenities. Some outlets take a conscious decision to attract different markets to make use of their facilities.

Market segmentation

This is a classification or categorization of customers, by age, sex, occupation and culture which assists us in giving the best possible service and provision of facilities and amenities according to their needs. Your outlet will have a preferred house style and procedures guidance often referred to as the procedures manual. In this manual you will probably find all the help you will need to guide you in your contact with the different types of customers.

Task 3.8

List the likely needs of a business customer wishing to check into a hotel. Compare these needs with those of a patient about to be registered into a hospital. Design the procedures for receiving a visitor to the reception of your school or college in keeping with college style.

Purpose of customer service

Customer service is central for our organizations' survival. Whether we deliver is not an option in the hospitality and catering industry. It is a customer service industry and comes down to you providing a service on behalf of your organization or outlet. You are the face and voice and exhibit the personality which signifies what your outlet stands for.

You are expected to give a total service so positive that the customer cannot wait to come back and to:

- Create customer satisfaction
- Identify customer perceptions and requirements
- Maintain their well-being

In order to do this it is necessary to understand customer needs and expectations.

The whole purpose of customer service is to maintain and increase for your organization the market share through greater customer satisfaction. This means having more satisfied customers who will buy more of your products or use more of your services repeatedly.

Customer needs

The needs of customers can be diverse depending on the type of customer. For the most part the customers will require:

1 Advice – e.g. directions, security procedures, fire drill procedures, meal times
2 Information – of local amenities, the facilities of the outlet
3 Physical help – with baggage, if they have a special need, car parking
4 Assistance – response for service such as:
Valeting
Room service
Food and drink
Shower facilities
Sundry items

A typical hotel feeback sheet is shown in Figure 3.1.

Task 3.9

A customer arrives at a hotel without a toothbrush and enquires at Reception as to where a toothbrush may be purchased. The receptionist, in offering 'added value', not only has a supply in Reception but is able to supply a variety of soft and

OUR PRODUCT

HOW WELL DID WE MEET YOUR EXPECTATIONS?

(Please tick as appropriate.)

	Excellent	Good	Fair	Poor
AT RECEPTION	☐	☐	☐	☐
Welcome received	☐	☐	☐	☐
Check-in speed	☐	☐	☐	☐
Check-out speed	☐	☐	☐	☐
IN YOUR BEDROOM				
Cleanliness	☐	☐	☐	☐
Overall comfort	☐	☐	☐	☐
General maintenance	☐	☐	☐	☐
Ambience and decor	☐	☐	☐	☐
THE TELEPHONE SERVICE				
Staff telephone manner	☐	☐	☐	☐
Speed of response	☐	☐	☐	☐
RESTAURANT				
BREAKFAST				
Quality of food	☐	☐	☐	☐
Presentation of food	☐	☐	☐	☐
Speed of service	☐	☐	☐	☐
Friendliness of staff	☐	☐	☐	☐
LUNCH/DINNER				
Quality of food	☐	☐	☐	☐
Presentation of food	☐	☐	☐	☐
Speed of service	☐	☐	☐	☐
Variety of food offered	☐	☐	☐	☐
Friendliness of staff	☐	☐	☐	☐
LOUNGE/BAR				
Quality of food/beverage	☐	☐	☐	☐
Presentation of food/beverage	☐	☐	☐	☐
Speed of service	☐	☐	☐	☐
Friendliness of staff	☐	☐	☐	☐

VALUE FOR MONEY

How would you rate Forte Posthouse in terms of value for money?

	Excellent	Good	Fair	Poor
For accommodation	☐	☐	☐	☐
In the restaurant	☐	☐	☐	☐
In the bar	☐	☐	☐	☐
Overall	☐	☐	☐	☐

OUR PEOPLE

HOW WELL DID WE MEET YOUR EXPECTATIONS?
(Please tick as appropriate.)

HOW WOULD YOU RATE OUR STAFF:

	Excellent	Good	Fair	Poor
Friendly	☐	☐	☐	☐
Helpful & Efficient	☐	☐	☐	☐
Reliable	☐	☐	☐	☐
Meeting your needs	☐	☐	☐	☐
Ability to solve problems	☐	☐	☐	☐

AND FINALLY . . .

Was this your first stay at this hotel?
　　　　　　　　　　　　Yes ☐　　No ☐

Would you be happy to return　Yes ☐　　No ☐
to this hotel in the future?

As a result of the facilities here　Yes ☐　　No ☐

As a result of the cleanliness/　Yes ☐　　No ☐
housekeeping standards

As a result of the hospitality　Yes ☐　　No ☐
given

What other hotels have you stayed at in this area?

_____

Additional Comments _____

_____

_____

ARE THERE ANY OF OUR STAFF WHO DESERVE A SPECIAL MENTION?

_____

Figure 3.1 An expectations feedback sheet

firm bristles in a number of colours, together with a choice of toothpaste. To which of the customer needs – advice, information, physical help or assistance – is the receptionist responding?

Customer expectations

Each person or client group will have different expectations of a hospitality and catering outlet. Customers' expectations arise from many different sources.

- Advertising
- Your outlet's reputation
- Previous experience of your organization or outlet with your product or service
- What competitors offer – can they expect the same from your outlet?

As an example, a customer wanting afternoon tea in a high-class restaurant would expect a linen tablecloth, a pot of tea with hot water, a cup and saucer, and served at the table. The customer does not need such style of service but expects it. The customer would be appalled if served with a polystyrene cup and plastic stirrer. On the other hand, a visitor to a Wimpy bar would be surprised if served with a china cup and saucer and silver teaspoon.

Other establishments and situations encourage certain expectations, e.g. hotels with grading systems. Some people go to places just because they know what to expect, and they are upset if things are different. A patient in a private hospital expects a single room with television and telephone and private bath and toilet, with meals and drinks delivered to the room.

Good-quality service exceeds the expectations of customers. You need to *identify* with the service or product you are offering and give the customer a sense of belonging and being cared for.

Customers' expectations have risen over the last decade, with greater leisure, disposable income, increased travel, and, in general, greater

knowledge of what the hotel and catering industry can now offer. They have become more sophisticated, educated and demanding. This requires you to be:

- Competent
- Work quickly
- Have a do-it-now attitude

Customers are not willing to wait around until you can find the time, they will find somewhere else to go.

Most frequent reasons for customers not returning to a hotel

Room not clean
Poor maintenance and repair
Not feeling safe or secure
Poor temperature control
Too noisy
Uncomfortable bedroom
High room rates
Unfriendly, discourteous staff
Slow service

Task 3.10

Think of the last time you went to a café or fast-food outlet. Was the server competent at their job? Did you receive prompt service? Were your expectations met? If not, what could have been done better to satisfy them?

A customer in a NHS hospital would expect to have a bed in a ward with one or more people, with shared toilet and bath facilities, and a television in a lounge down the corridor. If a customer gets less than what was expected then this is a disappointment. Your skill, attitude and professionalism will make all the difference and this makes you important. Often you take on the role of:

1 Peacemaker – resolving customer complaints
2 Negotiator – ensuring that the customer feels satisfied

3 Detective – investigating the customer's needs and wants

4 Psychologist – listening and befriending the customer to establish needs

Expectations and requirements of hospitality services

Secretarial services
Soap and towels
Wake-up call facilities
Direct-dial telephone
Personal care items, shoe cleaning, toiletries, hair dryer
Room service
Swimming pool, health and exercise centre
Free morning newspaper
Cocktail lounge bar
Speedy checkout service
Car park
Complimentary breakfast
Fresh fruit, flowers in room
Study, work area in room
Dry cleaning, valet service.
Television with remote control

To give an example, a restaurant is almost full and a customer requires a table for four for lunch. You inform the customer that a table will be available in 30 minutes and the customer agrees to wait, the expectations being that a table will be ready in 30 minutes. You actually offer a table in 20 minutes. The customer's expectations have been more than exceeded and met. They are not only well satisfied but are also likely to be impressed with your service.

To help, here is an example. A man and wife arrive at the hotel for the night. The receptionist enquires as to the type of room. The man replies that he requires a smoking room, while his wife requests a non-smoking room in a quiet location of the hotel.

The receptionist offers a two-roomed suite which has a non-smoking bedroom overlooking the main road. Through *negotiation* and offering the suite at the same price as a standard bedroom both agree to take the suite, and, to an extent both needs are met.

Delivering customer service

Customer service should begin with senior management making a conscious effort and statement which they are prepared to support. They need to ensure every member of staff, including trainees, feel that they can contribute to customer service and are prepared to put *customers first*. In order to be successful every member of staff must want and believe it to happen, understand how to achieve customer satisfaction, and provide the 'added value' and exceptional service. Later in this unit we will look at how this can be achieved.

Task 3.12

Give two examples of when you have put others before yourself.

Task 3.11

In a group try to think of some examples of how, when offering customer service, you could take on one of the roles of peace maker, negotiator, detective, psychologist to meet customer expectations.

Customers may be *regular, occasional* or *chance.* You and other members of the staff will form a relationship with them. This may be *directly:*

- Face to face – as part of your work on a reception desk, in a restaurant or serving in a fast-food outlet such as McDonald's
- By telephone – receiving an enquiry for a room or restaurant booking, or dealing with a complaint

or *indirectly:*

- By offering a service which the customer receives but does not interact and come into direct contact with some members of staff. This could be a meal prepared in a hospital kitchen for a patient in a ward, or for a request for new light bulbs to be fitted in a guest's room by the maintenance department of an hotel.

Customer perceptions

This means that everything you do should be seen from the customer's point of view. It is how the customer perceives you that determines whether the level of service you provide is acceptable.

What makes your operation better than others is the 'value added' by you and the staff of your outlet. One well-trained member of staff in customer care is worth more than five or six performing at a low level of service in front of customers.

Levels of service

- Rude – which is unacceptable
- Indifferent – often referred to as impersonal
- Value added – considered to be the most favourable level of service

Customers' requirements

The customers want you to:

1 Pay attention and listen
2 Show respect
3 Show concern
4 Take responsibility for problems
5 Find solutions to problems
6 Be accurate with information
7 Attend to the basics
8 Remember that its their time and money and know that without them we have no job
9 Give prompt service

Remember: It takes, on average, five times more effort to attract a new customer than it does to retain an existing one.

Customer requirements within the hospitality and catering industry

The customer has many points of contact to form impressions, e.g. in a hotel the Linkman, Reception, Concierge, Restaurant, Housekeeping, to name a few. The impressions which are generally favourable are:

- Attention to detail
- Caring, friendliness and courtesy
- Dealing efficiently with requests for information
- Physical help when required (e.g. with luggage)
- Ability to resolve problems quickly
- Taking ownership of problems
- Cleanliness

A customer's perceptions may be altered by the impressions they receive. For example, if they see a dirty kitchen, they might then consider how clean are the staff and whether the food is handled hygienically. They may then debate whether they wish to give you their custom. The seeds of doubt have been sown. Is the food fresh? Is it good enough to eat? Do they really wish to stay?

Importance of prioritization

It is expected that you can prioritize and 'do it now' when there are urgent requests made and respond effectively (e.g. emergencies, security alerts or accidents) and limit disruption to other customers within your outlet (e.g. telephone calls). This may sometimes mean that you have to reschedule other tasks, and it is important to do tasks in the right order. If this is not done efficiently the customers gain a negative impression. *Negative impressions* come when, for example:

1 You have no opportunity to explain to a customer on the phone, but you can to a customer waiting to be attended to at the Reception desk
2 Keeping a customer on hold on the telephone without explanation
3 There are long queues
4 Not having information at your fingertips
5 Items are out of stock – sold out
6 Promises are forgotten
7 Surroundings are dirty
8 Customers are ignored
9 There is a failure to offer physical help

If customer perceptions of you or your outlet are poor you are fighting a losing battle and customers will not wish to return: Create a positive perception and exceed customer expectations, always try to deal with customers' problems as if they are the most important tasks you have ever had, try to see the problem as if you were in their shoes.

You do not win the battle by being right and clever unless the customer feels better and the problem is resolved. Research suggests that one satisfied customer tells four or five other customers, whereas a dissatisfied customer will talk to ten or more, in fact anyone who will listen. This sort of information is not helpful in increasing sales.

The level of personal attention should be the same for all customers. You never know who your customers are. All deserve the same level of service. You cannot rely on their appearance and often VIPs travel under an assumed name for security reasons. Remember to meet their expectations and perceived needs. Serve them quickly on their terms.

Influences on customer behaviour

The impressions we give to our customers influence how our customers behave. Every point of contact we make with the customer we communicate. Unfortunately we may not be communicating the right impression.

Your outlet will only be as successful as you allow it to be. You need to:

● Have a positive attitude
● Enjoy working with people
● Tune into what the customer expects
● Have a need to please
● Get things right the first time
● Let the customer know you care
● Be responsible
● Value the customer

In order to do these things effectively we need to watch our body language, our tone of voice, and the words we use, especially if face to face or over the telephone. The impressions we portray will elicit either a favourable or a negative response from our customers. What we seek to do is to create a favourable impression that will last.

Poor impressions are given when our body language, tone of voice and the words we use are cold, unfriendly or impersonal and requests to assist are ignored. Good impressions are given when the customer has been served and valued and is given a warm reception. You try to understand and empathize with the customer, you smile and we do not forget to thank them for their custom. It costs nothing to be polite to our customers. *Empathize:* customers want you to support, understand and respond.

Body language

What people say to you or what you say to your customers is often very different from what you or they feel or think. The body language you use allows others to interpret your thoughts by your gestures. To customers it affects how you heard them and how you ultimately deal with them.

If you shrug your shoulders you imply that you do not understand. A thumbs-up sign could mean that you are OK, you want to hitch a lift, or a rude gesture if jerked sharply upwards. A neck scratch indicates that you are not in agreement with your customer. We should therefore be aware of our own non-verbal signals and the effects they could have on customers.

Eye contact

Eyes can give clues to a person's thoughts. You must have heard the sayings 'looked daggers' at, 'the evil eye', 'shifty eyes', 'gleam in the eye'. Can you think of others?

As a person's attitude and mood change from positive to negative thought so the pupils of the eyes will dilate or contract. The different ways you direct your gaze could have a powerful effect on face-to-face contact with a customer.

Tone of voice

When speaking to a customer the tone of voice relays a signal to the customer and evokes differing responses depending on your manner and the emphasis placed on the spoken word. It is how we say it, not what we say that matters (e.g. raising one's voice).

We should treat our last customer just as we would the first and be consistently friendly. It is not easy in the hotel and catering industry after long hours of duty not to feel tired and let it show by our tone of voice and manner. How often have you said?

'It's time I went home!'
'Not another one, it's time we closed!'
'Here they come again!'

Practise the way we say 'have a nice day', 'next'. It can be made more friendly and positive by adding 'please' after 'next' and by smiling.

Telephone skills

In communicating with customers and in order to offer a service it is often necessary to deal with customers on the telephone. When answering the phone, be polite, smile with your voice, introduce your organization and identify yourself. A phone call should be answered within three or four rings.

Standard expressions are used as they save time for you, the receptionist or the switchboard operator and, most important, line time. This costs money to both the customer and the outlet. How you answer the phone is important. Reasons for answering the phone are:

● To obtain custom by selling your product or service.
● To ensure income.
● To be efficient and offer a service.

The three cardinal points for good telephone manner are C. A. S.

● Courtesy
● Accuracy
● Speed

Remember these points and you will be on your way to success.

Every organization will have its own style and procedures for answering the phone – e.g. 'Good morning, Turncliffe Hotel, Amanda speaking, how may I help you?' This evokes a response from your customers, they are reassured that they have connected correctly and have a point of contact should they need to call again and would avoid the caller repeating themselves as you already have some background information.

Avoid, if possible, keeping the caller on hold. If this is necessary it is probably because you need to transfer them to someone else or seek information. Always ask if the caller minds holding and wait for a response. Never hold for more than 45 seconds without coming back to the caller. Remember: the customer cannot see what is happening. Impressions are formed from your tone of voice, the words you use, body language and the delay in response to their questions. You should always stay on the line and introduce the caller. Never transfer if the other member of your outlet is not available. This leaves the caller in limbo. Customers do not like being transferred, they feel that they are being passed off. Avoid the use of the word 'transfer; as it makes the customer feel powerless. If you need to transfer the customer bear in mind that a lost customer is one lost forever. If they are disconnected or passed off they may not call back. If you cannot help state what you *can* do, not what you cannot. Be positive (e.g. 'Let me connect you', 'I can help you by putting you in touch with') or take their name, telephone number and offer to call them back and give an indication of when. It is better for you to do the legwork.

Keep your promises, even if you have not obtained the information. Return the call. The customer will then have a level of satisfaction in knowing you have tried to help. An answerphone, while taking the pressure off you, leaves the caller feeling processed rather than being given personal service. It is better to take the transfer call. If you have been introduced by the receiver you are able to give positive feedback and improve the customer's satisfaction by mentioning the customer's name and recapping the query example – e.g. 'Hello Mr Jones, this is Amanda I understand you have a query.'

Active listening skills

Customers want to feel welcomed, important, and understood. They wish to command your respect, concern and understanding. In order for this to happen you need to listen to your customers.

Hearing what the customers say is not sufficient. Hearing is listening to sounds – for example, a fire alarm, a crying child. Active listening is trying to understand the meaning of the words used and the unspoken message behind what is said. The tone of voice, emotion and the context of the situation as well as evaluation of the facts contribute to active listening. In listening we try to understand and appreciate the customers. We respond by letting them know we are listening, by simple gestures such as nodding the head, smiling, verbal reinforcement, using words such as 'I understand', 'All right', 'I see'.

Ways of active listening

1 *Be prepared* Have paper or notepad and pen. Have the computer cleared and ready for the next contact. If answering the telephone let the customers know if you are taking notes. Show that you are listening. Respond with eye contact body language. If on the telephone use attentive words such as 'OK', 'I see', 'I understand'.
2 *Ask questions* These must evoke a response 'e.g. How may I help you?' Get the customer to talk to find out what they really want.
3 *Show understanding* Repeat the message in your own words (e.g. If I understand correctly Mr Smith you require . . .', 'Can I conclude that . . . ?' 'Am I right in thinking . . . ?' Only repeat the main points.
4 *Silent pauses* You invite the customer to correct you if you have misunderstood before proceeding.

Task 3.13

Form a group of three. Tape the conversations. Take it in turn to listen to these conversations and then repeat what you think you heard. Play the tape back to check if you heard correctly.

Social skills

- Try to establish a rapport with the customers
- Use the customer's name and correct title
- If it is a difficult name to spell or pronounce ask the customer to spell it out for you and then repeat it
- Avoid jargon that the customer does not understand and be ready to explain if they ask
- Use eye contact wherever possible
- Be confident and competent: customers like to know that you are in control, otherwise they will seek someone else to assist them
- If unsure offer to check with someone else; respond quickly.

Task 3.14

In groups role play a situation of dealing with the following customers either face *to* face *or on the telephone. Note the differing body language, eye contact and tone of voice used for the different situations.*

1 A customer complaining about an overcharged restaurant bill

2 A partially sighted customer enquiring how to find the cloakroom

3 A patient reporting to reception wishing to register into the hospital

4 A business representative complaining that the hotel room is not available

In all the above situations the speed and style of how you respond will affect the customer's behaviour. Sometimes a lack of an appropriate response will, as well as affecting the customer's behaviour, also lose us custom. Try this next task.

Task 3.15

A supplier arrives in a hurry at the Waterside Restaurant to deliver some goods, and notices that special evenings are arranged on Fridays. Full of enthusiasm, the supplier enquires if it would be possible to make a reservation. The restaurant manager points to the reception desk were a commis waiter is seated. The commis hands the customer a booking form and departs to the kitchen to take a morning break. The supplier, a potential customer, leaves without making a reservation. Discuss the reasons why you think the customer did not make a reservation.

In all the situations in the previous tasks the one common denominator is that the *customer comes first*. You should have been friendly, accommodating and pleased to receive the customer and shown empathy, providing the service with a smile. If the customer can affect you by having a positive attitude, then you can also have an INFLUENCE on the customer when your attitude is negative.

Customers' well-being

It is not difficult to deal with people who are pleasant, friendly and cooperative, but from time to time occasions will arise when intelligence, care, understanding and common sense will be needed to handle awkard situations caused by a customer's behaviour. It takes self-discipline to deal with such customers without putting yourself or your outlet in the wrong or at risk.

Often a customer may be overtired, showing impatience or displaying aggressive behaviour. The influence of drink may alter a customer's behaviour. Drunkenness and disorderly behaviour is an offence on licensed premises, and, if permitted, could lead to the licensee losing the licence. Similarly, the influence of drugs, or lack of them, can cause customers to behave differently. Customers are often taken ill and require medical care. Sometimes you may have to contact a customer to deliver bad news and you should inform the customer as early as possible and in person. Get to the point quickly by saying 'You are not going to like hearing this' or 'I have some sad news', and be prepared for a reaction to this news. If a customer displays unacceptable or odd behaviour, it is best to accompany him or her to a more private area, such as an office or lounge. This then removes from public view any scene which may occur, gives privacy to the customer and allows for further assistance to be called, or first aid to be administered, without the customer feeling embarrassed or suffering loss of face. Remember: the customer may have to face you, other members of staff or other customers again.

Good 'value added' service practices can have many benefits for the customer. If guests feel welcome and receive friendly service with a smile they will come back. Their perception is favourable and we have satisfied customers. This increases business, involves repeat sales of products and services, your reputation as an outlet increases, and encourages staff to set and keep high standards of working.

In addition to benefiting the outlet, customer service practice gives satisfaction to us to know that customers are happy and we have been able to brighten their lives.

Conclusions

In this section we have looked at why we need customer service and the benefits:

- Different types of customer and their needs
- How customer service is delivered
- Why we sometimes need to prioritize our dealing with customers
- Some of the influences which can affect customer behaviour

• EVALUATING THE OPERATION OF CUSTOMER SERVICE •

This section investigates quality, i.e.

1 The quality of service we give to our customers
2 How we evaluate the service we give
3 If the data we use are reliable and what we do with the information we evaluate in order to deliver better quality
4 How we encourage and identify training for staff in order to operate a customer service policy

Evaluation is a measurement of how we are performing against the agreed standards which should reflect customer needs. You need to know:

- The reasons we evaluate a customer service policy
- How to effectively collect data from different sources
- How to formulate an ongoing monitoring system against reliable and valid data
- How to make recommendations for improving customer service
- What training and development needs are available

Monitoring is the method used to measure and check that the quality and standards relating to customer service are being met. Data is the information gathered from a variety of sources.

The need for a customer service policy

There could be several reasons why an organization or outlet needs to have a customer service policy, for example.

- To maximize customers
- To increase profitability
- To increase customer loyalty
- To create a reputation for being customer orientated
- To have the edge over competitors

Each organization or outlet will have its own aims and method of appealing to its customers. They must be compatible with the rest of the business plan and will be turned into targets or goals like those listed above. Given criteria such as time, profit and standards will need to be established so the targets and goals can be monitored and measured.

Business plan

This is a set of objectives for how the organization or outlet will carry out its business. Before you can evaluate a customer care policy you need to have some standards to monitor against and you must be able to give answers to such questions as:

1 What level of service do we wish to provide for our customers?
2 How many complaints do we get?
3 What staffing levels do we require?
4 How much time do we need to spend on customer service?
5 Do we require training?
6 Do we manage time effectively and offer a timely service to our customers?
7 How is the outlet perceived in the marketplace?
8 Is business increasing or decreasing?

have spoken to together with your own ideas. Ideas and comments such as you have gathered are used to form the standard by which a customer service policy operates. However, there are generally constraints placed on the organization, the outlet and sometimes the customer.

Constraints and limitations in providing customer service

A constraint is something which limits what we can do. Within the hospitality and catering industry you will find constraints such as legislation, financial and company regulations. Customers may have religious, moral or social constraints and you may have personal ones. These constraints may either hinder you or prove to be useful in formulating a customer service policy. For example, a fast-food outlet might limit the customers choice from the given menu in order to offer a speedy service. A restaurant may decline to charge half-price to children over a certain age in order to be more profitable. It is not unusual therefore to find that while some constraints are beneficial they can also impose limits on the outlets' wish to provide what the customers want.

Task 3.16

Look at your own school, college or workplace refectory, and see if you can answer the questions above. You may need to ask your colleagues or request an appointment to speak to someone who works there.

Task 3.17

In a group make suggestions on the possible constraints which could be placed on customers in:

● *A hotel*
● *A hospital*
● *A public house*

What constraints could be placed on each of the above outlets to prevent them offering what the customer wants?

You have probably established by now some interesting viewpoints from the people you

Reasons for evaluating customer service

We need to know what our customers want, and there is a difference between what they tell us they want and what they seem to want. The one way to meet customer expectations and create customer satisfaction is to evaluate the operation of the customer care policy in place in the outlet. It is essential that every member of the team is aware that customers come first and that your wishes and those of the outlet take second place. The customer is the most important person in the outlet, for without them there would be no outlet, and no need for us.

Standards

These are a level of quality, or achievement at a level thought to be acceptable, an agreed target at which to aim. If there is more than one outlet then the policy for that outlet is probably based on the standards set by the organization so that consistency is upheld (e.g. McDonalds', Little Chef, Nuffield Hospitals). The branding of very large organizations such as Forte Crest hotels into travel lodges, Post Houses and Prestige categories may also place different standards within the same organization. Customers exercise their right of choice but would still anticipate, for example, the same degree of friendliness from staff even though all the services are not the same. Customers would therefore acknowledge that there are differences in what each brand offers and that these differences are often reflected in the tariff or price.

The reason for evaluating customer service policy is to extract information that you can use to provide customers with what they want. It may be *subjective*, in other words expressing the customers' feelings:

- I really wanted
- We are looking for
- I would like
- Could we have

or the reasons may be *objective*, giving facts and figures about the customer service:

- We have been kept waiting 10 minutes
- The food is cold
- The bookings are down by 10 per cent on last month's figures

Before you can evaluate how well your outlet is at providing customer service in practice it is necessary to have some standards.

Customer service standards

These are what your organization or outlet aims to do in order to actively pursue good-quality practices which will lead to customer satisfaction and the measures by which it judges if it is successful. In order that these standards can be carried out there will need to be guidelines provided for staff on how to do things. These guidelines are usually to be found in standard of performance manuals or operational specifications. Each facility within your outlet usually has a copy written for that facility's operations. They are often referred to, especially when new staff are being inducted into the job or for training purposes. These specifications affect customer service when they become visible or affect the customer (e.g. the noise from the kitchen, an unanswered telephone ringing), or if something fails to meet their expectation (e.g. being told that there is a sauna and finding that it is out of order). The specification or standard does not really affect the customer. It is the impact that it has upon the customer that is important.

The impact on the customer

Customers are only interested in how the quality of your service standards affect them. For example, they may not be concerned that they do not have a linen napkin but would notice if there was no napkin at all, or be too bothered whether the guest towels were coloured or white but would be upset if they had been used or indeed found none in the bathroom.

The Mount Charlotte Thistle Hotel Group provides specification and standards in a manual for all its outlets. It is referred to as the training and development pack and is designed to help managers and heads of facilities to train their staff in customer care standards. Each outlet customized it to meet its own operational needs.

Customer-care training in isolation will have little lasting effect unless the performance of staff is monitored, the necessary action taken when it is not up to standard, and all new staff trained in customer care as part of their basic job training. To improve and maintain standards of customer care it is necessary to review and take corrective action on:

1 *Quality of staff care* If you are cared for and provided with good conditions of work you are more likely to be happy and offer a good service to customers

2 *Quality of systems for identifying the level of customer satisfaction and customer needs* If the standard procedures are clearly defined and are owned by you, in other words you have contributed to the development of these procedures you are more likely to follow them. You should consider how well you are performing against the procedures of the outlet. These should have been produced from the points customers have made about what they find important.

3 *Matching of the product and service to customer needs* You need to be aware of why the products and services of the outlet are offered to customers. You must also be given feedback as to what customers say they want. It is important for you to learn to recognize, interpret and act upon clues and comments that customers give about the standards of your organization or outlet. In addition, you should know the action that you can take and the mechanism for reporting back and to whom.

Examples of specifications from a standards manual

The standards may be divided into three parts:

● The key point or primary consideration
● The standard
● The specific requirement for the outlet

Let us look at some examples:

Key point Uniform
Standard Free from stains and odours, well pressed and in a good state of repair (e.g. no missing buttons, dropped hem)
Specific requirement Bow tie and winged collar to be worn. Name badge to be worn when on duty
Key point Communicating with customers in the bar
Standard Do not stand so close to customers as to make them feel uncomfortable
Specific requirement Disabled customers. Do not assume physical disability. Do not 'talk down' or shout. Talk to the disabled person, not to the companion

Generally the specifications are placed under headings such as:

Appearance
Behaviour
Service to be offered to customers
Special situations

Task 3.18

Try to think of some standards which would apply in your school or college refectory or restaurant. Pick one of the standards and try to write some specifications similar in format to the ones mentioned above.

Once it has been decided what standards need to be in place in your outlet and appropriate training given it will then be possible to monitor whether the customer-care policy is working. Through evaluating the policy and its operation it is possible to determine when and where corrective action needs to take place. Prevention is better than cure, but in the event of a customer complaint, measures must be taken to rectify the situation and provide customer satisfaction as soon as is reasonably possible. The feedback you obtain and evaluate is necessary if you are to offer a good customer-service policy.

Task 3.19

In a small group brainstorm the ways you think you could find out what customers want.

Some of your suggestions might include:

Talking to customers
Listening to customers
Observing customers
Interviewing customers
Sending out a questionnaire
Looking at data and statistics
Receiving suggestions or complaints from customers
Talking to other staff and colleagues

Examples of this in operation might be:

- *A chef circulates among the tables in the restaurant and talks to customers*
- *The porter discusses a customer's stay while accompanying then to the taxi*
- *The reception staff look at the customer forecasts for bookings and compare them with the same time last year*
- *Housekeeping uses a questionnaire for reporting on the standard and cleanliness of the room and its facilities. This may be in written form or a tickbox format*

Observation by management can provide useful information about customer expectations and comments. For example, long queues at Reception at peak times can cause frustration, encouraging a customer to walk out without settling an account. Both verbal and non-verbal signs can be observed. Remember our discussion on body language in the previous section?

Whatever the system the outlet decides to use to evaluate customer service it must be within the budget set aside and must prove to be cost effective. In other words, the financial constraints could prevent some of your suggestions being implemented. Even more important, the whole operation must be led by management and supported by every member of the customer-care team.

Customer service data

Whenever you gather information, be it written or verbal, this is known as data. Data can be presented in various forms:

- Tables
- Graphs
- Text

The methods of collecting may be both formal and informal using some of the suggestions previously discussed. Some establishments also make use of the unrecognized visitor who will use the service and facilities that your outlet provides to test the quality of your provision. Boddington's Village Hotel group operate this system to test out their own customer service policy. Other outside agencies, before making recommendations to the public, will often visit an outlet as a mystery customer for the same reasons, revealing who they are only before leaving. Whatever data you have and no matter their source, they are of little value if not acted upon. Remember, data can come from:

1 Customers
2 Colleagues

3 Staff
4 Management
5 Mystery customers

Techniques of data collection

- Questionnaire
- Interview
- Observation

Data may be written, verbal or experienced. In any event they must be reliable and valid. Putting yourself in the place of the customer and thinking the way the customer would can often help you in deciding whether the course of action, the comment or the suggestion is appropriate. This way you can often avoid giving rise to customer dissatisfaction.

Reliability and validity

By monitoring, measuring, assessing and reviewing repeatedly over a period of time it is possible to ensure that the data we use are reliable and valid. This means that they are consistent and dependable and cover all the processes for getting things right and checking to see that tasks are performed correctly. Different methods of collecting evidence may prove to be valid but unreliable. For example, a banquet is held for a hundred customers and only two complain about the meal. The complaint is valid in the eyes of the customers but is not reliable evidence in that a major rethink of the menu is necessary before it can be used again for future banquets. In this case the two customers had every right to complain if the meal did not meet their expectations, apologies should be given and the offer of alternative food and a possible refund made. There should have certainly been an apology. In future, it would seem to be good practice to enquire if customers had any special dietary requirements.

Other variables such as the time of year, weather and world crises such as war, can alter the data being analysed. If custom is normally very busy but due, for example, to a bad fall of snow it is very likely many customers decide not to travel, which could result in large cancellations, it would therefore be wrong to assume that there is a problem with the outlet's reputation. However, by careful monitoring a pattern should emerge if there is a problem.

Other sources of error

- Leading questions which indicate the response
- Non-response from customers: perhaps they do not understand the questions or they could be in a hurry and have no time to respond
- Misuse or interpretation of the data
- Sampling errors brought about because the customers selected for the gathering of evidence having been incorrectly decided. For example, a random sample of customer types may be chosen for a questionnaire or a random number of all questionnaires may be selected for analysis. It is therefore important to have consistency in your sampling method and to decide for what reason the data are to be used.

Sampling methods

- Random
- Quota
- Stratified
- Opportunity

Sometimes the wrong questions are asked on a questionnaire, if badly phrased and worded they can be ambiguous and confusing. Unless the same questions are asked of every customer the answers are not likely to be reliable.

Variables

These are the components of the service which affect the expectations of the customer service, e.g. price, value for money, comfort, time, atmosphere, flavour and appearance of food, temperature and cleanliness.

Task 3.20

Read the following case study and try to identify which of the above variables affected the expectations of Mr and Mrs Smith.

On arrival at the Sunnyside Hotel Mr Smith struggles with the baggage while Mrs Smith joins the long queue at the Reception desk waiting to 'Check In'. While waiting, Mrs Smith notices that there is only one receptionist on duty and the hall porter is sitting behind the porters' desk reading a newspaper. Meanwhile Mr Smith finds his way to the lift. The receptionist is very pleasant and helpful and offers to make a booking for the Smiths in the restaurant for that evening.

Mr and Mrs Smith arrive at their room. They are late arrivals and, on entering, find that their room has not been serviced, the bed not having been made up. Mrs Smith phones Reception, but they are still very busy and do not answer the phone for some time, the housekeeper having long since departed for the day. The Duty Manager suggests that Mr and Mrs Smith visit the restaurant while their room is made ready. After all, they do have a table booked.

On entering the restaurant they are greeted by the Head waiter and are shown to their table. Some 40 minutes later a waiter appears with a menu. The soup is served promptly, but the main course is delayed and on arrival it is cold and lacks flavour. Mr Smith complains to the Head waiter who says that it is not the fault of the waiting staff and will report the complaint to the kitchen.

Mr and Mrs Smith decide to leave the restaurant and return to their room. Noticing a customer questionnaire, Mrs Smith fills it in. Without having unpacked they 'check out' of the hotel feeling very dissatisfied. Their expectations have not been met.

No doubt the customer-evaluation form would give rise to concern by management and these data would need to be analysed along with other questionnaires handed in on that day.

Task 3.21

What comments and feedback do you think that the Sunnyside Hotel will have received from Mrs Smith's questionnaire?

Methods of evaluation

Data need to be sorted and organized in such a way that they are easy to analyse and sort into categories or headings. This makes it easier to interpret them. Comments given directly by customers will have more value than those from indirect sources. Improvements and changes should be based on facts and customers wants, not on what we think customers want. Any evidence should be sufficient, current and authentic, i.e. valid. Basic statistics such as frequency counts, mean, mode and median are used together with measures of probability in evaluating and interpreting information.

Unreliable data

Inconsistencies will show up regularly in unreliable data. Subjective comments should be avoided. Correct analysis of data cannot be undertaken if the data have been tampered with in any way or are incomplete. Sometimes data are spoilt.

Indirect sources

Records can provide customer information, customer letters, complaints book, compliments, reservations and profit and loss accounts.

Secondary sources

Information collected from other outlets, gossip, the media and information for other purposes.

Possible ways to evaluate your outlet

Complaints from customers should be measured in both number and type. If there has never been a customer feedback system a 'settling-down period' needs to elapse before the data are analysed. Your repeat business should be monitored, and use of history cards is one way of doing this.

Use the mystery or silent shopper to buy your goods and services. They will be able to experience first-hand how well they are received and give very positive feedback. It is useful to establish how well you perform alongside your competitors. By using this method you can test telephone technique, product knowledge, complaints procedures, response time and the effectiveness of the personal touch such as use of names.

Make use of interviews and questionnaires or surveys. Past feedback can be used as comparisons as to how well the outlet is performing. Eventually you will reach your targets to meet the basic levels of achieving customer expectations and you will wish to excel. Once you start to aim for excellence you will begin to develop a customer service policy which will increase your market share of the business and your reputation.

Task 3.22

In a small group decide on an outlet of your choice. Discuss and prepare a checklist of the points you would observe and the questions you might ask if you were to be a mystery customer. Justify the contents of your checklist with the others in your group.

Operations of customer service

This should be seen as a total experience. You should put yourself in the customer's shoes and try to visualize how the customer would react. Some organizations actually allow their staff to experience being a customer so that they can appreciate what the customer needs and expects. The standards are set by the customer – they will decide whether they return to give you their custom again. In planning your operation you should ask yourself:

1. How well am I performing?
2. Which things are important for my customers?
3. Do I get the right things done first time?
4. How can I improve?
5. What am I doing wrong?
6. How can I help to make the service better?
7. What appropriate changes and improvements do I need to make?
8. Am I responsive enough to customers, do I respond within the agreed time?

It is not always possible to make changes alone, and for this reason a team approach is necessary, which is a very effective way of getting things done. Simply put, having a team approach means working together as a group with common expectations and goals. You are able to help and support one another and your successes will rub off on new team members. New team members will also have good ideas. It is also a good way of encouraging those members of staff who are identified as being in need of training to polish up their customer-care skills. Team meetings will allow you to:

- Share what you know
- Brainstorm ideas
- Make recommendations for improvements
- Discuss new customer service policies
- Ensure that everyone in the team operates to the same standard
- Identify training and staff development needs
- Identify areas that need improvement
- Set goals and targets
- Assist and support one another

As an individual it is important that you follow the procedures set by your outlet. There will be many practices which have been tried and tested and you will find these in the standards manual previously discussed. All the procedures should be made into regular routines, with various members of the team being allocated jobs to ensure that the procedures actually happen. If no one is asked to this then nothing happens. Sometimes checklists are used to ensure that the procedures are being followed. If all the guidelines are followed and you work with your team it is likely that you will be well on your way to providing a quality service.

Quality

The hospitality and catering industry, like every other, is becoming very keen on quality. De Vere hotels was one of the first to become quality orientated and to achieve Investors in People. This is a benchmark by which customers can judge standards and quality of the organization. In future those organizations that fall short of this benchmark may well find that customers will be attracted elsewhere and the organizations will go out of business. Quality is about identifying the defects in the policy, the products and services we sell and taking appropriate action to eliminate them. Remember that we identified earlier that prevention is better than cure?

Quality criteria

Cost

Customers look for value for money. The outlet needs to consider cost when deciding how best it can give the customer value for money.

Time

The time taken to provide a good service relates to cost both to the outlet and to the customer. Prompt attention is required by those paying

for a service. For example, a group of businesspeople wish to use your restaurant, they need to get back to work and are likely to require a more speedy service than pensioners on a reunion outing. How you use your time will also have a cost factor and determine how quickly you get things done. Quality is also determined by the benefits gained from standard procedures and an agreed conformity to operate to those standards.

Staff

In any outlet there needs to be available resources, for without adequate resources the quality of the service suffers. The main resource is that of *staff*, properly trained and well motivated to serve and exceed customer expectations. You need to be flexible, able to adapt to a variety of situations and have a positive attitude, be energetic and enthusiastic. In addition, you need to know your outlet inside out and keep up to date on the products and services you sell.

The hotel and catering industry operates all day long, every week of every year – it is a continuous operation. While you may be feeling tired at the end of your working day, some of our customers may be just arriving. To become a really shining light you need to maintain all these characteristics all day long, despite the aching feet, the stress and the pressures that come with the job. The present customer will not necessarily be aware of the problems created by the previous one.

Administration

Quality can be affected by the efficiency of the administration, replying to customer queries, confirmation of bookings, and the speed and manner when answering the telephone.

Materials

A customer will make judgements on the quality of materials used to deliver the service. The towels may be thin and worn, or the food trays broken. These items, while only small, can affect the quality of the service as a whole and spoil the customer's experience. Remember Mr and Mrs Smith's visit to the Sunnyside Hotel?

Feedback

Feedback is a very important variable of quality. Remember that we noted earlier that the customer will tell anyone who will listen if the customer service is lacking? If feedback is not given it is difficult to know how we are performing and meeting those standards the outlet has set for us. Not all feedback is bad, but if it is, then it is necessary to take corrective action.

Task 3.23

Refer to the case study on the Sunnyside Hotel. Assume that Mr and Mrs Smith filled out a questionnaire for the hotel before leaving. What corrective action should the hotel take?

Measurement of customer service

Whatever system is implemented it is important that there is some way of measuring it against agreed parameters. You might want to measure the number of complaints you receive from customers using the facilities each week. This may well show that certain areas are experiencing difficulties such as Reception, who may be understaffed at peak times. The restaurant might wish to calculate the average spend per customer. The kitchen may well look at what comes back on the customer's plate and wish to enquire why.

Task 3.24

Look at the whole customer cycle from initial contact to final departure and see if you can identify any measures which you could use to assess the quality of a customer-service policy.

In this section we have looked at the reasons we have a customer service policy, how we measure and evaluate it and the types of data that could be used. The validity and reliability of data has been reviewed, and finally we looked at the criteria for quality and what you need to do to achieve becoming a shining example.

Training and development needs

Today customers have an increased disposable income and are more aware that your competitors are also vying for their custom. Exceptional service is no longer an option, it is a fact. *It is therefore essential.*

Your competitors may be able to compete on products, services and prices but the service you provide is special to your outlet, and it is this service that ensures your repeat custom. In order to provide this excellent customer service it requires you, others in your outlet and management to provide the necessary induction and training on any new customer-care policy that is introduced. All new staff should be inducted and trained in the relevant procedures before commencement of duties. One silly mistake could ruin the reputation of the outlet. For example, the Beauchamp Hotel was very short of staff. A new member of staff had started work the day before and was given the job of using the switchboard. Unfortunately, the new recruit was requested to operate the early-morning shift on the following day, this time unsupervised. All the incoming calls kept being diverted to the wrong rooms, waking up the guests who were not at all pleased. The callers were also becoming angry at being disconnected.

Management need to give their support for the provision of resources for training. This could mean providing in-house training for staff, sending some staff to the training sessions held by the organization or, indeed, sending staff on courses run by the Hotel and Catering Training Board in your area. All staff, including you, whatever your status, will need to become involved in some way. All staff behind the scenes such as cleaners, linen room, office workers, etc. need to be involved and consulted. After all, they are all very much part of the outlet and contribute to the overall service we give our customers. Very often these staff can see a different dimension to what we are trying to achieve. They are external customers themselves and can be internal customers within our outlet.

Many outlets have incentives and awards for the best staff member deemed to be offering an excellent service to its customers.

Any organization or outlet wishing to offer excellent customer service will need to continually strive for excellence in everything it does. It will need to commit itself to time, resources and investment in the staff it employs and every member of staff will need to put every effort in ensuring that the policy is successful. Success will depend upon every member of the team including your becoming involved at every stage of the customer cycle. You will need to:

1 Attend and participate in training activities related to customer service
2 Liaise with management in carrying out any agreed procedures and standards
3 Seek advice on any issues you are not happy with or do not understand
4 Take ownership of the policy or project

Remember: you and your team are important. To the customer you are the representative of the outlet, its voice. As the person who will come into contact with the customer on a day-to-day basis you represent all that your outlet or organization stands for, both the good and the bad.

Task 3.25

Can you think of any customer-care award that could be given to any staff in your school, college or workplace? What would the award be for? It might well be given to a porter for going out of his way to help the staff or visitors or even you.

For those of you who wish to add to your qualifications the National Council for Vocational Qualifications (NCVQ) has developed an NVQ in Customer Service as a recognized qualification for those who wish to excel in this area.

▪ PROVISION OF CUSTOMER SERVICE ▪

Following on from the previous sections where we defined customer-care service, identified our customers and evaluated their needs and wants, you now need to know:

● How to provide the best possible service to your customers according to their requirements
● How to prioritize your customer needs
● The measures to be taken to deal with different customers' behaviour
● How to deal with dissatisfied customers and the remedial measures you might take.
● Finally, the customer service you can offer regarding the health, hygiene, safety and security of your customers

Customer services

Services are required by our customers to satisfy their requirements, and within the hospitality and catering industry it is generally accepted that this includes a personalized contribution by staff which distinguishes it from the products you may well sell. In order to do this you need to:

1 Be considerate
2 Impress your customers
3 Exceed their expectations

Services are required for our customers for many reasons:

- To provide a need, perhaps a business traveller requires clothes to be valeted
- Security of self or belongings
- Comfort such as the provision of an extra pillow
- Pleasure, services such as newspapers
- The loan of an umbrella for fear of getting wet or a patrolled car park service to avoid theft of a car
- Many customers will require a service out of habit. You need to know your regular customers so that you can provide for the service they require. History cards are a good way of keeping records of customers habits.
- The customer realizes you offer a service such as a courtesy bus to the airport and decides to make use of it

Services are different from products in that they are less tangible. They are usually offered to match customers' needs and are often tailored to individuals, therefore the customer's presence is an essential element. The services you give to your customers may be offered in a slightly different way from that of your colleagues. It is therefore not always easy to establish the standards and even more difficult to ensure that the standards have been met.

Unlike a product which you may purchase, find faulty and thus return, if the service is found to be lacking your customer is very unlikely to return. This means that the quality of the services you offer depends very much on how you and your colleagues behave while providing the services on behalf of your outlet.

Requirements of good customer service

You need to:

1 *Be accessible* For example, the reception desk needs to be located near the entrance so that on entering the building customers can easily locate Reception staff.
2 *Communicate* There is a need to keep your customers *informed*. In a previous section we looked at methods of communicating. However, there is a need to *explain* to customers how to access facilities (e.g. operate the minibar or air conditioning). There may need to be an explanation for an increase in charges or the reason why the restaurant is out of use. Communication is a two-way process: it is also important to *listen* to what customers are saying.
3 *Be competent* You must have the necessary skills and knowledge your outlet, standards and procedures and the tasks you are responsible for in order to carry out the job to the customer's satisfaction.
4 *Be courteous* This includes being polite, even when the guest is difficult, inconsiderate or even rude and offensive. It includes being friendly without appearing overfamiliar. Be calm and positive.
5 *Have credibility* This means being trustworthy, dependable, reliable and putting the customer first. Any suspicion that the customer is being exploited (for example, overcharging) will be counter-productive and the customer will become dissatisfied.
6 *Be reliable* You need to be consistent and dependable and work according to your outlet's standards, to be punctual and prompt. An example might be to deliver an early-morning call on time.
7 *Be responsive* Service should be available as and when the customer requires it and not

when you wish to provide it. This includes being prompt in answering the telephone or providing a drink requested from the bar, It is *not* acceptable to continue a conversation with colleagues and keep a customer waiting. Some matters may be urgent and need immediate attention.

8 *Understand* You should make every effort to appreciate the differing requirements of your customers. Customers need to be treated and received as if they were the first.

Dealing with the challenging customer

Some customers are going to get upset, complain or be downright awkward and challenging. The situation is not helped if you are also challenging or discourteous. Once a dissatisfied customer, it is more than likely that the customer will find fault and complain throughout the duration of the visit to your outlet. It is therefore important for you to acquire the skills through practice to know how to deal with such situations.

Society is made up of all kinds of customers and they have the right to be challenging but not offensive. From time to time you will be faced with a customer who is not completely satisfied.

Remedial action

The policy of the organization or outlet should always be adhered to, particularly in relation to refunds, exchanges, discounts or hospitality.

Task 3.26

You are approached by customers. Decide to which of the following you would give a refund, exchange, discount or hospitality, and explain why.

1 *A telephone call is charged to the final bill which, you are informed, has not been made*
2 *A customer complains that the wine glass is dirty*
3 *The manager has invited the customer to have a drink on the house*
4 *A customer wishes to claim a special offer on weekend breaks*

The following are guidelines on how to keep the customer satisfied. However, the policy of the organization or outlet should always be adhered to and procedures acknowledged:

● Take the lead, the customer is giving you the opportunity to get it right for them. The complaints and concerns and even good feedback are very valuable information and can only serve to improve your service and products
● Always remain calm
● Apologize, but do not keep saying sorry
● Listen attentively to the customer. Let the customer vent his or her feelings
● Do not interrupt them. The customer may begin all over again
● Deal with the emotions first. Acknowledge how upset they are and make them feel valued
● Repeat. Let the customer know that you understand the nature of their concern

- Show concern and interest. This does not mean that you agree with the customer
- Do not make excuses
- Do not pass the blame
- Thank the customer from bringing the issue to your attention
- Take the necessary action by solving the problem immediately, or inform your line manager or supervisor

Why, then, do our customers get upset? It really has to do with the perceptions, how a customer feels at the time and what they expect. For example, a family book a weekend break at your hotel because it has a leisure club with an indoor swimming pool. They check with the hotel before making the booking that they can have use of it as guests of the hotel. The family arrive expecting to be able to use the pool at all times as no restrictions appear in the brochure. After the family have checked into their room they visit the leisure facility and are informed by the receptionist that the pool is only open for children up to 4 p.m. because, being a leisure club, it has times when only adults and members may use it. The family were very angry. In other words, the customers did not get what was promised. Expectations were not fulfilled.

Other reasons why customers get upset are:

1 If you are rude to a customer
2 If you are indifferent to a customer, having the 'I can't do' excuse or 'It's not my job to do that'
3 No one listened to the customer. This is a waste of feedback that can help you to improve your service

How to handle a customer complaint

- Listen to the customer
- Give your apologies, assure the customer that you are sorry and want to help
- Show sympathy and understanding
- Never disagree or agree
- Accept the blame, do not make excuses
- Advise the customer on how you will help

- Take the customer away from public view
- Refer to your supervisor or line manager if you cannot deal with the problem
- Record any awkward situations by logging them in the diary or handover book and make sure that others in your team are updated in case the problem arises again

How to deal with an enquiry

- Acknowledge the customer's presence promptly
- Greet the customer with a friendly smile, be courteous but not too casual or familiar
- Apologize for any delay which may have occurred, show concern
- Listen to the customer, do not interrupt
- Identify the customer's needs
- Give the information required or
- Refer the customer to the appropriate section or person
- Never refuse to help, always give an alternative suggestion

Customer referrals

On occasions it is not always possible for you to assist the customer and there is a need for you to pass them on to someone else. This is known as a referral. In order to do this you need to know who the staff are in your outlet and in some cases the organization of which you are a member. In addition, you must know the roles and responsibilities of these staff. Many outlets have an organizational chart. The in-house directory may also give you this information, and, failing this. Personnel could inform you. It is obviously much preferred if you become aware of the product knowledge of your outlet and try to get to know the staff with whom you work.

If there is a need to refer a customer you should explain why and give as much direction on how to find the new person as possible. It is a good idea to escort them if you can, or to ask them to be seated while you locate the new contact.

Hygiene, health, safety and security requirements

Every member of your outlet must be aware of the need to care for our customers and offer a service which conforms to statutory and regulated legislation. Every facility within your outlet will have appropriate legislation and codes of practice to follow and these are mentioned in each unit of this book.

We need to care not only for our customers, both internal and external, but also for their belongings. You need to know which legislation applies to you (e.g. laws on hygiene, health and safety at work). In addition, it is necessary to be aware of the laws relating to the premises in which you work and offer a service to the customer. Therefore you need to know that all customer services offered by you are consistent with hygiene, health, safety and security requirements.

Hygiene

It is important that a high standard of hygiene is maintained in all hospitality and catering service areas of the outlet. It is equally important that staff also maintain a high standard of personal hygiene. The relevant units of this book cover this in detail but it is important to note that, as well as contravening legislation, outlets and staff who do not have the highest of hygiene standards are not likely to attract customers to return and give you their custom.

Procedures in the event of a fire or security alert

Every customer, whether a conference delegate, a resident or a short-stay customer, should be made aware of the evacuation procedures in the event of a fire or security alert. In such cases the alarm should be raised immediately. Firefighting equipment should be used in accordance with the procedure. You should

follow the correct evacuation procedure laid down by your organization or outlet in a calm and orderly manner and on no account should you allow a customer to re-enter a building until the all-clear has been given. You should indicate to the customer how to get to the assembly point if necessary.

Suspicious items or packages

In offering a customer-care service you may be requested to look after packages or items belonging to a customer. It is necessary to be on constant alert and any suspicious item, package or luggage should reported in accordance with the procedures of your outlet and remain untouched. Sometimes items are forgotten or left unattended, but if it appears they have been left for no apparent reason then safety procedures need to be adopted.

Accidents

In any area where people meet there is likely to be at some point in time an accident or emergency that will require your attention. Minor accidents may be a spillage on a customer's clothes in a restaurant or a cut finger. More serious accidents could require medical attention. It could be a customer having a possible heart attack or one in need of medication. In the event of a death the management should call for a doctor who will in turn inform the police. After initial enquiries the body should be discreetly removed from the area. You may well need to care for the relatives or friends of the customer. This situation calls for a lot of tact and discretion, without fuss. Details such as the bill should tend to be forgotten or dealt with at a later date.

If you are not a first aider then you should know whom to contact immediately. You should also know the appropriate action to take to ensure the safety of injured and uninjured customers and be able to reassure them that assistance is on its way. As far as possible you should try to make any injured person comfortable without running the risk of making the injury worse. Any accident should be reported or documented in accordance with the procedures of your outlet.

It is important when carrying out your duties that you ensure that you work in a safe environment. It is also important that if you spot any potential hazards they are reported through the appropriate channel and that you take immediate preventative action to safeguard your customers. Notices and warning signs should be displayed to alert your customers to the dangers. Otherwise you could be deemed to be negligent if an accident occurs.

Security

Every outlet exists to provide a service to its customers. You have a responsibility for the security of your customers and their belongings. If customers feel insecure or under threat they will not give you their custom. When there are airline disasters, or unrest in particular countries, it affects the hospitality and catering industry. The Lockerbie air crash in 1988 deterred many American customers from visiting the UK and reduced trade for some time.

There are four aspects to security:

1 Loss of possessions
2 Personal damage
3 Damage to the building and its furnishings
4 Fraudulent damage

Unfortunately, not all customers are honest. Some may leave without paying their bill or they may help themselves to others' belongings. This is deemed to be theft. If, however, a person enters a building without permission, such as breaking into a guest's room, this is classed as burglary. You should assist your outlet in being alert at all times and know the correct procedures to follow in the event of a breach of security.

Section 1 of the Theft Act defines theft as dishonestly appropriating property belonging to another with the intention of depriving them of it. A person is guilty of burglary if entering a building as a trespasser intent on committing such an offence. Deception, that is, dishonestly obtaining services, is also an offence. Personal security is also important, especially when dealing with important customers. Bomb threats and other forms of terrorism cannot be taken lightly. Usually your outlet would be expected to liaise closely with the local police for advice when high-risk customers are visiting your outlet. Unfortunately, the hospitality and catering industry has many outlets which are vulnerable to undesirables masquerading as *bonafide* customers.

Telephone threats are a cause for concern and while many turn out to be hoaxes, they should not be ignored. You should be aware of the procedures to follow so that important information is not lost. It could save lives.

Confidentiality is important when dealing with customers. Some require complete privacy and may not wish to be disturbed. You may be given information in confidence that the customer does not wish you to repeat.

Customers' property can often be a security problem. They may carry around money and valuables which makes them obvious targets for muggers, thieves and confidence tricksters. Sometimes the customers themselves lose their belongings and suspicion could then be levelled at you and your colleagues.

How to avoid breaches of security

● Constant alertness and reporting of any suspicious activities
● Having a black list of unwanted customers or those who are not creditworthy. Often banks and finance companies will issue these
● Having a security person at the entrance to the building and regular patrols of the area ensure that anything suspicious is noticed. It

is often good practice to limit the number of unlocked entrances and exits, providing there is no breach of fire regulations

- Anyone looking suspicious should be politely questioned
- Burglar alarms and pressure pads will alert you to an approaching intruder
- Keys and other unlocking devices should be carefully monitored. You should not hand over security keys to anyone without being signed for nor should they be left lying around
- The use of safety deposit boxes or strong rooms are recommended. If a customer declines to make use of these facilities he or she is deemed to have accepted the responsibility

---

Task 3.27

A customer books into your hotel for the night and decides not to use the safety deposit box. While taking clothes from a suitcase the jewellery wallet falls to the floor. The customer picks it up, puts it on the dressing table and leaves the room for a while. On returning, the customer finds some jewellery missing and reports this to the management, indicating that it has been stolen. You are very concerned and decide to investigate.

- *What would you say to the customer?*
- *Who else would you speak to?*
- *What action might you take?*
- *If the missing jewellery is found by the Accommodation staff the next day after the customer has left, what action would you take?*

In this section you have looked at the provision of customer service. It is hoped that you now have the knowledge to be able to put customer service into practice. The following are some questions to test your knowledge. All the answers are to be found in the text. To complete customer service there is a unit assignment which will provide evidence for your portfolio.

Test your knowledge

1 Identify three points for good customer service
2 How would you deal with a complaint?
3 A customer has had too much alcohol and is drunk. How would you deal with this customer?
4 Identify four different types of customer
5 What do you understand by the term 'special needs'?
6 How might you deal with a customer who is in a wheelchair and who wishes to use your restaurant?
7 Why do we evaluate customer service programmes?
8 How might you monitor the effectiveness of your customer-care programme?
9 What customer service would you expect to find in order to satisfy safety in a swimming pool?
10 In prioritizing customer needs which of the following would you do first: answer the telephone or respond to a customer waiting to be served?
11 What is meant by logging a complaint?

▪ Assignment ▪

You are to carry out in groups the following tasks:

- Form a group and discuss the case study below
- Decide how you would evaluate the customer-service policy of the Tunnicliffe Hotel
- How would you use this information to plan an induction package for the Tunnicliffe Hotel?

- Decide the content, the format and the time scale in order to complete the training package
- Keep notes from your discussion and keep your own individual action plans
- Produce an induction package on customer service

Elements 3.1, 3.2, 3.3
Investigate customer service
Evaluate customer service
Provide customer service

Core
Communication
Working with others
Problem-solving information technology

Performance criteria
Element 3.1 PCs 1, 2, 3, 4, 5, 6
Element 3.2 PCs 1, 3, 4, 5, 6
Element 3.3 PCs 2, 3, 4, 5, 6

The aim of this assignment is to allow you to apply your knowledge and understanding of customer service and produce a customer service handbook for induction and training at the Tunnicliffe Hotel.

Case study

Mount Charlotte Thistle Hotels' training package requires staff to put the customer first. Using this theme read the following case study and carry out the tasks.

Quality service in hospitality and catering outlets means offering a consistent service, value for money and that little extra that dazzles the customer and exceeds expectations. The establishment of quality standards oversees all aspects of provision, from the condition of the outlet and its decor to its facilities and everyday routines such as cleaning.

Staff are the driving force of a quality approach to putting customers first. Their manner, attitude, motivation enthusiasm and reliability and competence are all key factors in ensuring quality customer service.

This approach relies on careful recruitment, training and the support of management and all staff. The hospitality and catering industry requires staff who have the right frame of mind, who are flexible and who can grow with the job and become competent.

Unfortunately, the Tunnicliffe Hotel has not realized that to put the customer first is important. With the present economic climate there is competition from other hotels in the area and the customer is becoming more discerning.

Problems seem to arise at the Reception desk. Quite a lot of chatter between the staff results in customers having to wait to be seen to. The switchboard is rather outdated and the new staff are not able to operate it effectively. Customers are cut off or diverted to the wrong extensions.

The ambience of the restaurant is welcoming, it is well furnished but the attitude and manner of the restaurant manager leaves a lot to be desired. There is no flexibility as to where you sit or indeed the choice of menu. You either take it or leave it. The restaurant staff are inexperienced, in fact one or two are students working for extra money and do not regard the job as anything more. The chef is trying hard to make the kitchen profitable and refuses to throw anything away. Cheese left from the evening restaurant, regardless of its condition, is served again the following lunchtime, looking very dry and unappetising.

The bar staff are very pleasant and keen to help, but the prices are very high and customers tend not to drink in the area. It has been known for guests to go to the local off-licence and bring their own drink into their rooms. Not that the porters would notice, as it is custom and practice for them to sit watching the television in the lounge unless they are bleeped by Reception.

The Accommodation staff work hard behind the scenes, but often they are delayed from servicing a room because the laundry has not arrived. The rooms are kept in excellent condition and the standard of cleanliness is exceptional. The Accommodation staff take a pride in their work, and they are well received by the regular customers. Unfortunately, the rooms never seem to be fully occupied and the staff are fearful that they may be made redundant. No customers, no jobs. Management is also very worried that the occupancy rates are low. The income generated from rooms compensates for the expenditure in the rest of the hotel. Management visit the hotel across the high street and act as mystery customers. Very impressed with the quality and standard of service, they return to the Tunnicliffe Hotel and call a meeting of the staff.

A complete evaluation of the situation at the Tunnicliffe Hotel takes place. You need to consider how you would evaluate this evidence and provide feedback to your team.

All staff, including those not normally in contact with customers, are to be inducted with a customer-service programme incorporating all aspects of quality provision and putting customers first in order to meet their expectations.

You must make provision for special needs, different cultural groups and different types of customer. There needs to be a procedure for dealing with challenging customers and complaints. In addition, the legal requirements must be made known to staff and explained. There needs to be a section on the levels of assistance from management down, as well as the importance of dress, manner and accountability. Monitoring by a cost-effective means needs to be introduced to ensure customer satisfaction and a feedback strategy planned for both the customers and staff.

Further reading

Abbott, P. and Lewry, S., *Front Office: Procedures, Social Skills and Management*, Butterworth-Heinemann, 1991.

Hotel Catering and Training Board, *A Question of Service*.

Mount Charlotte Thistle Hotels, *Training Manual*.

Customer Care Management, Butterworth-Heinemann,

FOOD PREPARATION AND COOKING

The food preparation and cooking requirements of the hospitality and catering industry are considered in this unit, which gives you an understanding of the skills and methods you will require if working in such an environment. The outlets in the industry offer a wide range of food and drink to meet a variety of customer needs and expectations. The required knowledge outlined in this unit should be combined with practice and it is very relevant to the work experience you should gain from a practical environment,. You should also apply this knowledge to the planning, implementation and evaluation of food preparation and cooking. The unit covers:

- The skills required for preparation of and cooking food
- The methods of food preparation and cooking
- Key requirements
- The need to understand and apply hygiene and safety measures
- Tasks required to plan and implement a successful food-preparation and cooking operation
- The monitoring and evaluation of a food-preparation and cooking operation and recommendations for improvement

▪ HYGIENE, HEALTH AND SAFETY ▪

In this section you will be finding out about the importance of hygiene, and health and safety to people who work in the hospitality and catering industry. We shall be considering how you will be affected by the legislation which regulates hygiene, and health and safety practices. When you have completed this section, you should be aware of how employers and employees are able to maintain a hygienic and safe working environment.

Legislation

Laws are passed by government to control how people may act in various circumstances. Legislation is often designed to protect people from the harmful practices of others. If breaking the law is a criminal act, then offenders are punished by fines and/or terms of imprisonment. Anyone who is injured or suffers ill health may also sue for damages and be awarded considerable sums of money in compensation. In 1974 the Health and Safety at Work etc. Act (HASAWA 1974) was designed with the intention of preventing accidents and generally making the workplace safer for employees and other people using it.

During the late 1980s it had become clear that the incidence of food poisoning was still increasing. Stricter measures were required to try to reduce the risk of food poisoning and make our food safer to eat. The existing law also needed updating to take into account changes in technology, which have led to new methods of food preservation such as cook-chill foods and a much longer food production chain.

Definition

- ***Food production chain** is growing, processing and selling our food. Much more of our food is now prepared ready to eat.*

(General) Regulations 1970 still govern the practices you will find in the workplace.

Food hygiene

Food hygiene means that food handlers must keep themselves and their workwear clean. We need to protect food from contamination by micro-organisms; store food at the correct temperature, to prevent multiplication of bacteria; and cook food thoroughly to kill harmful bacteria.

Food poisoning

Food poisoning is an illness caused by eating contaminated food. The most common kind of contamination is due to certain types of bacteria. The main symptoms of food poisoning are vomiting, diarrhoea, nausea and stomach pains.

Food-poisoning bacteria

There are several types of food-poisoning bacteria. Those that are most commonly found in our food and their sources are:

Bacteria	Sources
Salmonella	Human and animal intestines
Clostridium perfringens	Human and animal intestines
Staphylococcus aureus	Human skin, hair, mouth, nose and throat; cuts; septic infections
Bacillus cereus	Soil

Since these bacteria are found in our environment, they readily contaminate our food. We must assume that raw food is contaminated with food-poisoning bacteria but food may also become infected with bacteria after cooking. The types of foods likely to be contaminated are:

Bacteria	Food
Salmonella	Meat, especially pork and poultry; Eggs; Shellfish
Clostridium perfringens	Meat
Staphylococcus aureaus	Cooked meats such as ham, tongue, poultry; Desserts (e.g. custards, trifles, creams)
Bacillus cereus	Rice

Growth and multiplication of food poisoning bacteria

Bacteria grow and multiply rapidly provided they have suitable conditions. These are food, moisture, warmth and time. High-risk foods are those that encourage bacterial growth. The main groups are:

- Meat and poultry
- Cooked meat, gravy, soup and stock
- Shellfish and seafood
- Milk, cream and eggs
- Cooked rice.

A food handler is best able to control the temperature at which food is kept and the time for which it is held at that temperature. The Food Hygiene (Amendment) Regulations 1990 and 1991 set out the time/temperature tolerances for various foods, as we will see later. The Food Safety Act 1990 (FSA, 1990) has meant that the hospitality and catering industry has had much stricter controls on the handling of food. Some of the older laws still apply (for example, the Dangerous Machinery Order 1964). In the following sections you will find out how current legislation affects how you go about working in the kitchen.

The Food Hygiene (General) Regulations 1970 as amended by the Food Hygiene (Amendment) Regulations 1990 and 1991

These Regulations are concerned with your personal responsibilities to ensure that food is prepared and handled in a hygienic way. They also cover how your employer must maintain equipment and food rooms to ensure a hygienic working environment.

We shall now find out how these regulations affect what you must do. In order to comply with the law.

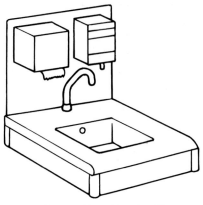

Figure 4.1 A cantilevered hand basin with paper and soap dispensers

1 You must keep all of your body clean, especially those parts that are likely to come into contact with food. This means that as well as bathing/showering several times a week and washing your hair regularly, you must be very particular about the cleanliness of your hands, fingernails and arms

2 You should wash your hands: when you go into the kitchen, before touching food, after handling raw food, between touching raw and cooked food, after handling waste food, after eating or smoking, after coughing, sneezing or blowing your nose, after touching your face, ears or hair, after using the lavatory, after cleaning up.

3 Your employer must provide you with a wash-hand basin, only to be used for hand washing, which has plenty of hot water: also soap, preferably liquid soap from a dispenser; a plastic nail brush with nylon bristles; paper towels or a hot air dryer to dry your hands (Figures 4.1 and 4.2).

4 Your protective clothing must also be kept clean, to prevent cross-contamination. Outdoor clothing can bring bacteria into the kitchen, so you must never take it into the

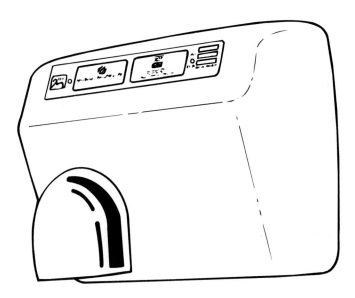

Figure 4.2 A hot-air dryer

Figure 4.3 Immaculate chefs

kitchen or travel to work in your 'whites'. You should have a clean set of chef's whites for each shift. If you get really dirty while you are in the kitchen (for example, blood on your apron while handling raw meat) then you must change your apron as soon as you have finished this job. You may be provided with disposable, plastic aprons to protect yourself while you are doing particularly dirty jobs (see Figure 4.3).

5   One of the dangers is that people spread a food-poisoning bacterium, called *Staphylococcus*. To reduce the risk of contaminating food with this particular micro-organism you should cover your hair while handling food. You must never smoke or spit in food rooms and should avoid touching your hair, nose, mouth, face or ears, all of which may be contaminated by *Staphylococcus*. Cuts and sores are also often contaminated with these bacteria, so they need covering with a blue, waterproof dressing to keep food free from infection.

Definition

● **Staphylococcus aureus:** *a type of food poisoning bacterium found on skin and hair, in the nose, mouth and throat, and in septic infections.*

The long hot summer and the vanilla slice

One very hot summer there was an outbreak of food poisoning, due to people eating infected vanilla slices. These were made by a bakery and consisted of a thick layer of cornflour custard between puff pastry, with icing on top.

The vanilla slices were made, as usual, during the night. The custard mix was stirred by the baker by hand. They were kept in the bakery until it was time to load them into vans for delivery to the shops. The next day there were reports of people being taken ill, within as little as 15 minutes after eating the vanilla slices. Some were enjoying them for lunch in the park, while making the most of the heat wave.

When the outbreak was investigated it was discovered that the baker had a cut on his hand. He had infected the custard with *Staphylococci*. Due to the hot weather, the night-time temperature had remained exceptionally warm. This allowed the *Staphylococci* to multiply rapidly, resulting in millions of bacteria in every gram of custard. The large amount of toxin they produced caused people to become ill very rapidly after eating the vanilla slices.

This is a good example of how a chain of events can set off a food-poisoning outbreak. The baker always stirred the custard by hand. The vanilla slices were never refrigerated. However, the hot weather gave just the right temperature for the bacteria to grow in the custard.

If that chain had been broken by making it a practice to refrigerate the slices the outbreak would have been prevented and a lot of people would not have had to suffer.

6 If you are suffering from certain infections, then report this to your supervisor, who will not let you work with food:

Vomiting and diarrhoea
Septic cuts or sores
Boils or whitlows
Discharges from your eyes, ears or nose.

7 You need to take care that you dispose of waste food and refuse immediately. It should be put down the waste-disposal unit or into the bin provided (see Figure 4.4). These bins must be emptied as soon as they are full.

8 Food should always be stored at the correct temperature. The golden rule is to keep it hot

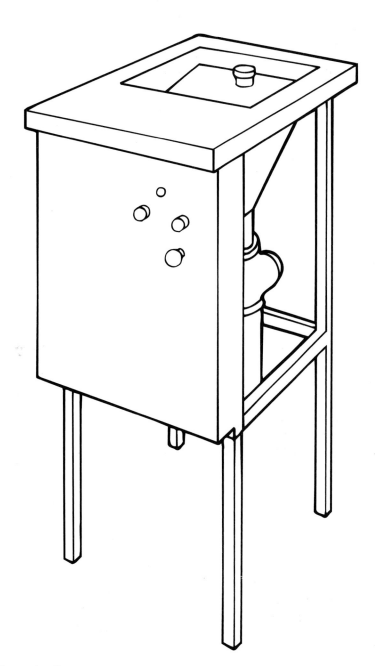

Figure 4.4 A waste-disposal unit

or keep it cold. Always cool food rapidly. Food must not be kept between 5°C–8°C and 63°C (see Figure 4.5).

9 The law on temperature controls for food has recently been changed. This is because bacteria called *Listeria* are able to grow in chilled food, if the temperature is not low enough. *Listeria* causes very serious symptoms, especially in young children or the elderly.

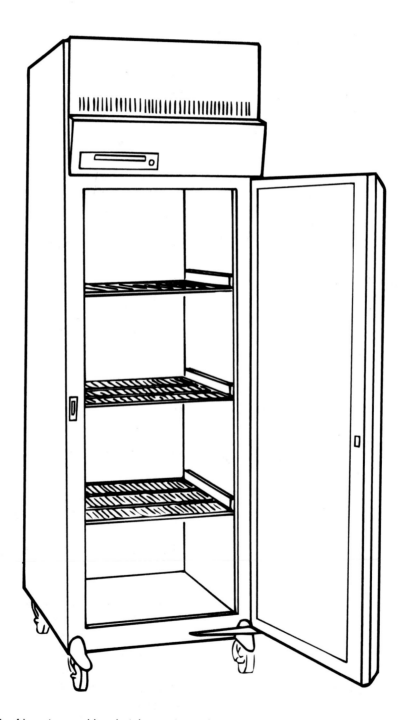

Figure 4.5 A typical refrigerator used in a hotel or restaurant

Definition

● **Listeria:** a type of food-poisoning bacteria found in the environment, which grows well at chill temperatures of 4°C

Task 4.1

Prepare a short induction booklet for trainees in the hospitality and catering industry, explaining in brief and simple terms what they need to do to comply with the Food Hygiene (General) Regulations 1970.

Task 4.2

Carry out a hygiene inspection in your college or school kitchen. Use the following checklist to find out if they are observing the Food Hygiene (General) Regulations 1970. An Environmental Health Officer would use a similar list when making an inspection.

Facilities	Comments

Wash-hand basins:
Suitable and sufficient?
Conveniently accessible?
Hot and cold water?
Soap?
Nail brush?
Drying facilities?
Clean and in good working order (plug?)
Used only for personal washing?
Sinks:
Suitable and sufficient?

Hot and cold water?
Clean and in good working order?

Facilities	Comments

Drainage and water supply:
Look for drain defects,
access for cleaning
Mains water?
Turn on tap to check pressure.
If flow rate is slow, tap may be
fed from storage tank
Lighting:
Suitable and sufficient?
Sanitary conveniences:
Cleanliness
Lighting
Ventilation
Position with respect to
food room
Now wash your hands notice?

Construction of premises

Item of structure	Material/ method of construction	Condition/ state of repair	Easy to clean/ maintain/ pest-proof
Ceiling			
Walls			
Floors			
Doors			
Windows			

The Food Hygiene (Amendment) Regulations 1990 and 1991

The amendment regulations make changes to the temperatures at which you are able to store food, replacing those given in the Food Hygiene (General) Regulations 1970. Food must be kept at chill temperatures (8°C or 5°C, depending on the food) or kept hot above 63°C. Table 4.1 shows you which foods must be temperature controlled at either 8°C or 5°C. In some work situations it may not be practical to meet these temperature controls. Table 4.2 shows you when you may allow temperatures to vary.

Table 4.1 Temperature controls for foods

Food	Temperature
Whole, ripened soft cheese Cooked products containing hard and soft cheese, to be reheated before eating Cooked products to be eaten reheated (meat pies, fish pies, pizzas, ready meals)	8°C
Portions of ripened soft cheese (Brie, Danish Blue, Stilton, Camembert, Roquefort, Dolcelatte) Cooked products containing hard and soft cheese, to be eaten without reheating Cooked products containing meat, fish, eggs, hard and soft cheese, cereals, pulses, vegetables Cooked products to be eaten without reheating (cold meat, vegetable salads, Scotch eggs, pork pies, quiches, sandwich fillings)	5°C

How to comply with the Food Hygiene (Amendment) Regulations 1990 and 1991

There are four main ways in which you can comply with these regulations:

1 Ensuring food is always at the correct temperature
2 Knowing the time/temperature tolerances
3 Checking and recording food temperatures
4 Checking the temperatures of food deliveries.

Task 4.3

Look at the chilled foods section in your local supermarket. Check the temperature indicators on the refrigerators/chillers. Note down how the foods are arranged and the storage temperatures used. Are the

Table 4.2 Exemptions to temperature controls (time/temperature tolerances)

Situation	Temperature	Time
Accepting a local delivery	All food may be up to 8°C	Put into chill store immediately
Defrosting refrigerators and breakdown of equipment when food is being prepared	8°C may rise to 10°C or 5°C may rise to 7°C	2 hours maximum
Serving 'hot' food	Below 63°C	2 hours before sale maximum
Serving 'cold' food	Above 8°C or 5°C	4 hours before sale maximum
Displaying food on sweet trolley, cheese board, self-service display, counter display	Outside controlled temperature	4 hours maximum
Sandwiches containing ripened soft cheese, smoked or cured fish, smoked or cured meat, meat, fish, eggs, hard cheese, vegetables	5°C 8°C	If not for sale within 24 hours If for sale within 24 hours
Sandwiches containing only hard cheese	Not covered	
Cold sandwiches to be sold within 4 hours of completion of preparation	Not covered	

temperature controls being followed? In what circumstances may time/temperature tolerances be relaxed?

Write a notice to be put on a display refrigerator for sandwiches, advising customers how to handle the sandwiches they have bought in order to minimize the risk of food poisoning.

Food Safety Act 1990

The Food Safety Act 1990 is a comprehensive law relating to food safety and consumer protection. It affects everyone who works in the food industry, including hospitality and catering. If your job involves:

- Production
- Processing
- Storage
- Distribution
- Preparation
- Sale

of food then FSA 1990 affects you. The act aims to:

1 Ensure that all food is safe to eat
2 Prevent food from being misleadingly presented
3 Strengthen the powers of Environmental Health Officers
4 Increase penalties
5 Alter defences
6 Change individual responsibilities
7 Enable further legislation
8 Keep pace with technological change

How to comply with FSA 1990

We should not:

- Sell food which does not comply with food safety requirements
- Make food harmful to health
- Sell food which is not of the nature, substance or quality demanded
- Describe food falsely or misleadingly.

How do we comply with food safety requirements?

1 By making sure that food is fit to eat (for example, it is not bad or poisonous or has a dead mouse in it
2 By checking that food is not contaminated with chemicals or pieces of metal. Food factories check their products for metal before they leave the factory. Pork pies are passed through a metal detector, which sounds an alarm if the pie has a metal object, like a screw, in it. Waterproof dressings also have a metal strip in them so that they can be detected if they fall off into food. On some occasions, imported beef has been found to contain horse meat. Horse meat may be heavily contaminated with *Salmonella*, as well as not being beef.

Definition

- ***Salmonella:*** *food poisoning bacteria found in animal intestines.*

How do we make food harmful to health? By doing something to it, such as choosing a heat treatment which will not make the food safe to eat.

Definition

- ***Heat treatment:*** *heating food to a temperature which makes it safe to eat.*

How do we sell food that is not of the nature, substance or quality the purchaser requires? By selling pilchards for sardines, cola instead of diet cola, or a casserole without enough meat in it.

How do we describe food falsely? By saying things about food or showing photographs of food which are untrue.

Who enforces the FSA 1990? Environmental Health Officers deal with:

● Hygiene
● Microbiological contamination of food
● Food unfit to be eaten by humans (including chemical contamination)

Trading Standards Officers are concerned with:

● Labelling of food
● Most cases of chemical contamination.

How do these officers enforce the Act? They may:

1 Enter food premises to investigate suspected offences
2 Inspect food
3 Take food samples for analysis
4 Seize suspect food
5 Condemn food

What powers do these officers have? They may issue:

1 Improvement Notices, which set a time limit in which we must correct faults to do with food hygiene
2 Prohibition notices, which close all or part of a food business that puts the health of the public at risk
3 Emergency Prohibition Notices, which close down immedietely food businesses that are an imminent risk to health

What is the due diligence defence? This defence is the main one which may be used if you are prosecuted for an offence under FSA 1990. To use this defence you need to be able to persuade a court that you took all reasonable precautions to avoid committing the offence.

How can you take due diligence to prevent offences? A food business must make sure that it has an effective control system for producing safe food. We need to check our suppliers for food hygiene and quality control procedures,

and train our operatives in food hygiene procedures. Supervisors are responsible for making the control system work. Managers must review the system, making changes if necessary.

Some of the procedures for food handling and hygiene, which are required to show due diligence, are given in Table 4.3.

Under FSA 1990 the Food Hygiene (General) Regulations 1970 have been amended, as we saw in a previous section, and the Food Labelling Regulations have been amended to

Table 4.3

Food handling and hygiene	What to do
Personal hygiene	Medical screening of food handlers Reporting of illnesses Providing hand washing routines Following the Food Hygiene (General) Regulations 1970
Product protection	Protecting food from contamination at all times by: Immediate reception of food Checks on deliveries for pests and any kind of damage Checks on temperatures of deliveries Rejection of goods not up to standard Clean protective clothing Clean utensils, storage containers and equipment Clean-as-you-go systems Separation of raw and cooked food Logging refrigerator and freezer temperatures Controlling pests
Cross-contamination	Prevent by: Correct food handling Correct food storage
Temperature of food	Using the correct temperatures for food production and food storage maintaining all equipment used in the temperature control of food.

introduce 'use by' dates. Two new regulations have been suggested:

1 Food businesses should be registered with their local authority, to enable the law to work better
2 Food handlers should receive training in food hygiene. The type of training will depend on the duties of the food handler. Operatives will need basic training in how to practise food hygiene. Supervisors and managers will receive more advanced training in food hygiene procedures.

The Food Premises (Registration) Regulations 1990 and 1991

The proprietors of food businesses must register with their local authority, using a special form. The purpose of these regulations is to provide information to food authorities about food businesses in their area so that they can enforce the law more effectively.

Task 4.4

There are many useful booklets about food safety. Obtain a list of food legislation material from:

Ministry of Agriculture, Fisheries and Food
Consumer Protection Division
Nobel House
17 Smith Square
London SW1P 3JR

Booklets on food safety and food labelling are available free of charge from:

Food Sense
London SE99 7TT

Cook–chill guidelines

Cook–chill systems provide a flexible way of preparing and serving meals. They are used in:

● Hospital catering
● Other types of institutional catering
● Commercial catering

Cook–chill food is safe and satisfactory, provided these guidelines are followed and that the highest standards of general and personal hygiene are maintained. The Food Hygiene (General) Regulations 1970 as amended by the Food Hygiene (Amendment) Regulations 1990 and 1991 must be complied with.

Cook–chill systems prepare and cook food, which is rapidly chilled, before being placed in chill storage for a maximum of five days, before reheating and service. To operate a cook–chill unit we should follow the guidelines concerning all aspects of our system (see Table 4.4).

Purchasing
Purchase foods to a good-quality specification

Preparation and storage
Store foods at the appropriate temperature
Prepare uncooked food in separate areas
Provide separate surfaces for raw meat, poultry and fish
Keep raw food preparation staff in that area
Identify and dedicate machines and utensils, especially knives, for raw or cooked food

Cooking and preparation for chilling
Cook food thoroughly to the centre and check the temperature with a probe thermometer
Prepare cooked food for chilling under strict hygiene conditions, handling it as little as possible. Hands must be washed frequently
Portion food within 30 minutes of it being cooked
Place cooked food portions in stainless steel, aluminium or porcelain trays, not more than 50 mm deep. Disposable containers may also be used
Clean and disinfect all equipment used

Chilling

Chill food within 30 minutes after cooking has finished

Chill food to between 0°C and +3°C within 90 minutes

Buy a chiller which will chill a 50 mm layer of food from 70°C to +3°C in 90 minutes, when it is fully loaded, which has a temperature indicator

Storage of chilled food

Dedicate a refrigerated store to cook–chill foods only

Refrigerate the food between 0°C and +3°C

Use a recorder to log the refrigerator temperature

Have a temperature-control alarm to indicate when the air temperature in the store is too high

Label each food container with the date of production and date of expiry

Table 4.4 Temperature and time controls for cook–chill food

Process	Temperature	Time
Cooking	70°C core temperature	Maintain for 2 minutes
Portioning	+10°C	Within 30 minutes after cooking
Chilling	From 70°C to +3°C	Within 90 minutes
Storage	0°C to +3°C	5 days
	If over +5°C but under +10°C	Use within 12 hours
	If over +10°C	Destroy
Distribution to outlets	0°C to +3°C	Same day
Distribution to reheating points	0°C to +3°C	Same day
Reheating	70°C	Maintain for 2 minutes
Service	63°C	Within 15 minutes of minimum reheating

Control food stocks so that they are used in rotation and not kept for more than 5 days. This includes the day of production and the day of eating

Destroy any food which is over the expiry date

Regeneration and service

Reheat food where it is to be eaten

Reheat food within 30 minutes of it being taken from chill storage

Reheat food thoroughly, using the standard times and temperatures required by the recipe

Serve food immediately it is reheated, no longer than 15 minutes after reheating

Keep the reheated food above 63°C;

Serve cold food within 30 minutes of taking it out of chill storage

Destroy any food that is not eaten

Follow a strict system of quality assurance

Cook–freeze guidelines

Cook–freeze is also a flexible and satisfactory way of preparing and serving meals. The food is cooked, rapidly frozen and stored in frozen storage, before reheating.

The same guidelines as for cook–chill systems apply for

- Purchasing food
- Storing and preparing food
- Cooking and preparing food for chilling.

Freezing

Freeze food within 30 minutes of it being cooked;

Freeze food to a core temperature of −5°C within 90 minutes of putting it in the freezer

Never refreeze food that has fully or partly thawed.

Storage of frozen food

Pre-cooked frozen food should be stored at −18°C

The storage time varies with the food, but up to 8 weeks is suitable for most foods.

Distribution to outlets

Food should not thaw during distribution

Refrigerated vehicles should be used to transport frozen food
Frozen food should be put straight into a freezer at −18°C on delivery.

Reheating and service
If food has to be thawed before it is reheated, then it should be thawed separately from other foods
After thawing, hold the food at + 3°C, in chill storage, until it is reheated
The rest of the procedure follows the cook–chill guidelines.

Definition

● **Temperature zoning:** *storing food at the correct chill temperature.*
● **Work zoning:** *keeping raw food preparation staff to raw food.*

Safety

Health and Safety at Work etc. Act 1974

The Health and Safety at Work etc. Act 1974 (HASAWA 1974) makes everyone at work legally responsible for health and safety. The Act sets out a framework of standards and protection. Its aim is to prevent sickness and injury to employees, customers and other people using business premises. In the hospitality and catering industry it applies to all types of establishments, however large or small they are. HASAWA, 1974 is supplemented by other legislation, which provides more detailed information.

How does the HASAWA 1974 affect us? When we are at work we have a legal duty to look after the health and safety of:

1 Ourselves
2 Our colleagues
3 Any one else affected by our work

Who is protected by the Act? Everyone at work and anyone affected by the work is protected, including:

1 Guests
2 Customers
3 Visitors
4 Delivery people
5 General public

What do employers have to do? They have to maintain a safe working environment for their employees and people affected by their work. Employers can do this by providing safe:

1 Equipment
2 Working methods
3 Storage
4 Workplaces

Our employers must also ensure health and safety through correct training and adequate supervision. They have to write a safety policy, making sure that all employees know about it. A safety policy should make us aware of the hazards which we may experience while we are at work and the actions needed to reduce the risks. We should all realize that kitchens are high-risk areas.

Who enforces the law? In most of the hospitality and catering industry Environmental Health Officers (EHOs) enforce the HASAWA 1974. If EHOs carry out an inspection and find that the law is not being observed then they may:

1 Give advice
2 Issue an improvement notice
3 Issue a prohibition notice
4 Prosecute
5 Seize or destroy items
6 Make items harmless

We should always listen to advice from EHOs. It will enable us to prevent health and safety problems or rectify things that are wrong. EHOs issue Improvement Notices when they want us to put right a breach of the law in a given time.

If there is a serious risk of personal injury then the EHO will issue a Prohibition Notice. This stops a dangerous activity until it has been made safe.

Who may EHOs prosecute? Since everyone has a responsibility for health and safety, we are all liable to be prosecuted if we break the law:

● Companies
● Employers
● Employees

As an offence under HASAWA 1974 is a criminal offence, we may be heavily fined or imprisoned, or both.

Dangerous equipment

This order supplements HASAWA 1974. Some of the equipment used in catering premises is classified as dangerous under the Prescribed Dangerous Machines Order 1964. We cannot use a dangerous machine unless we have been:

1 Trained how to use the machine
2 Warned of its dangers
3 Told what precautions to take.

When employees are using dangerous machines, they must be directly supervised by an experienced, trained person. All dangerous machines should have a warning sign on or near them, for example:

NOTICE TO EMPLOYEES

This slicing machine is DANGEROUS and must not be used or cleaned without permission. NEVER TRY TO OPERATE IT WHILE ANY GUARD IS REMOVED

USE	You may not use it unless you have been thoroughly trained or are being trained under supervision
CLEANING	You may not clean it unless you are at least 18 years of age and have been thoroughly trained or are being trained under supervision
Before cleaning:	disconnect electricity by means of plug and socket or by the isolating switch
	NEVER rely on the switch on the machine, remove the guards: to remove the blade use the safety carrier insert locking bar into hole next to centre mounting hole
After cleaning:	remove locking bar replace guards before reconnecting electricity

---

Power-driven dangerous machines are:

● Worm-type mincing machines
● Rotary knife bowl-type chopping machines
● Food mixing machines with attachments for mincing, slicing, cutting, chipping, crumbling

Power-driven or manual dangerous machines are:

● Circular knife slicing machines
● Potato chipping machines.

Task 4.5

Find out which of these dangerous machines you have in your college or school.

Our protection from dangerous machines

If we are at risk from moving parts of a machine, then we cannot clean it if we are under 18 years old. Guards must be fitted to protect us from the dangerous parts of all machines. We are given this protection by the Offices, Shops and Railway Premises Act 1963.

Donna and the dangerous machine

When Donna had completed her college course she obtained a job working as a chef. She decided to pay a visit to her old college to say how she was getting along. Her left hand was well wrapped up in a bandage. What had she done? She had been cleaning a large mixer, had leaned against the side of the machine, pressed against the switch and the beater had crushed her hand against the bowl.

It does not take long to forget all those health and safety sessions taken as part of a college course and receive a painful injury.

How to work safely in the kitchen

We all need to put into practice safe working methods if we are to avoid accidents and injury in the kitchen.

Equipment

- Listen carefully to all instructions about how to handle and use equipment; follow them exactly
- Never handle electrical equipment or switches with wet hands
- Report faults such as worn cables, faulty equipment or loose screws to your supervisor
- Follow instructions for lighting ovens exactly

How to light a gas oven

Be sure gas appliances are switched off before lighting them.

If the gas jets are switched on, but not lit, open the oven door and wait 5 minutes for the gas to escape.

Switch on the gas supply, the pilot light will ignite the gas jets.

Check the oven is lit.

If jets do not light immediately, switch off the gas supply.

Always keep your face and body as far away from gas jets as possible.

Knives

- Use the correct knife for the job
- Keep knives sharp and clean
- Keep knife handles free from grease
- Carry knives with the point downwards
- Place flat on the board or work surface
- Wipe clean with the cutting edge away from the hands
- Never leave knives in a sink of water.

Work methods

- Always wear the required protective clothing
- Work in a clean and tidy way
- Work quietly so that you can hear emergency instructions
- Never run in the kitchen
- Mop up spills immediately
- Close doors and drawers after use
- Never leave pots, pans, baking trays, mixing bowls on the floor
- Use steamer doors as a shield, while opening them slowly
- Never place pans of boiling liquids on high shelves or on tops of conventional ovens

- Use step ladders to reach high shelves
- Use safety goggles when using caustic cleaners like oven cleaner
- Lift correctly.

Figure 4.6 How to lift correctly

Control of Substances Hazardous to Health Regulations 1988 (COSHH 1988)

The COSHH Regulations aim to reduce the health risk to employees who use such substances and to prevent serious accidents happening. Cleaning chemicals carrying warning signs are covered by COSHH (see Figures 4.7–4.9). The dangers may be from cleaning chemicals coming into contact with our skin, swallowing then or inhaling their vapour. Employers must substitute less harmful substances where possible, provide safety equipment and keep cleaning processes separate, if this is practical.

Figure 4.7 A COSHH sign for corrosive materials

Figure 4.8 A COSHH sign for irritant materials

Handling cleaning chemicals safely

Cleaning chemicals are usually bought in bulk. These stocks should be kept in a locked store, which is used only for this purpose and is away from the kitchen. You will find instructions on the container label telling you how to use the chemical. These must always be followed. If necessary, the label will carry a hazard warning sign.

When chemicals are transferred to spray bottles for use this bottle should have a label stating the type of chemical, giving instructions for use and carrying any hazard warning sign required. If chemicals are to be used in the kitchen, they should be stored in a special area set aside for them. They must not come near food-preparation or service areas, otherwise food may become contaminated.

Employers are required to train their staff on the safe handling and use of chemicals (COSHH 1988). The important points to remember are:

1 Use cleaning chemicals *only* for the job they are intended to do
2 Read the instructions on the label
3 Use them at the correct strength
4 Handle containers with care in case of drips
5 Replace lids immediately
6 Wipe up spills at once
7 Do not leave chemical containers on the floor
8 Do not transfer chemicals to unlabelled bottles
9 Never mix cleaning chemicals
10 Wash spills off the skin with plenty of cold water

CATERING CAPERS PLC

COSHH ASSESSMENT   AREA:_____   SITE:_____

SUBSTANCES/MAIN COMPONENTS		STOCK CODE:

TASK/EXPOSURE POINTS	HAZARD	EH 40 EXP LIMIT:

FREQUENCY/DURATION OF EXPOSURE		NO. OF PEOPLE EXPOSED:

CONTROL MEASURES	W. I. REFERENCES:	

MONITORING REQUIRED: YES/NO   RISK: LOW   MEDIUM   HIGH

ACTION REQUIRED		RESPONSIBILITY	BY

SIGNATURE:	DATE FOR NEXT ASSESSMENT:

Figure 4.9 A typical COSHH assessment form

11 Immerse your eyes in a bowl of cold water if chemicals splash into them

12 If you swallow caustic cleaners never make yourself sick, you need hospital treatment

13 Wear long rubber gloves, goggles and protective clothing when using hazardous chemicals

Cleaning routines

Cleaning is carried out to remove waste food, grease and dirt. It reduces the risk of contamination with bacteria. Working surfaces and equipment must be cleaned, also floors, walls, windows, ceilings and light fittings.

A planned cleaning programme ensures that cleaning is done thoroughly and regularly. The programme gives detailed information about:

● What has to be cleaned
● Who has to do the cleaning tasks
● How frequently cleaning should be done
● What cleaning materials to use
● What cleaning equipment to use
● How to carry out the cleaning task
● What special safety measures are required
● Who will check the work

Fire safety

● Never wedge open fire doors (Figure 4.10)
● Make sure you have read the fire instructions (Figure 4.11)
● Make sure you know your exit route
● Know where the fire extinguishers are
● Only use a fire extinguisher if you have been trained and can do so safely

If you find a fire

● Raise the alarm by breaking a glass call-point
● Evacuate the room and close the door
● Leave by the nearest exit route
● Go to the assembly point

If you hear the fire alarm

● Shut down the equipment you are using
● Close doors and windows

Figure 4.10 A fire door notice

● Make sure the customers leave
● Evacuate the building by the nearest safe exit
● Do not stop to collect personal belongings
● Do not use or let anyone else use the lift
● Go to the assembly point
● Inform the fire officer if you think anyone is trapped or missing

Fire extinguishers

Colour	Type	Use
Red	Water	Most fires except those involving flammable liquids or live electrical apparatus
Cream	Foam	Most fires involving flammable liquids, e.g. fats and oils
Blue	Powder	Fires involving flammable liquids or electrical apparatus
Blanket		Suitable for burning clothing and small fires involving burning liquids

Fire action
Any person discovering a fire
  1. Sound the alarm.
  2. ████████ to call fire brigade.
  3. Attack the fire if possible using the
     appliances provided.
On hearing the fire alarm
  4. Leave building by ██████ route.
  5. Close all doors behind you.
  6. Report to assembly point.
  █████████

Do not take risks.
Do not return to the building for any
reason until authorised to do so.

Do not use lifts.

Figure 4.11 Fire instructions

Figure 4.12 A fire extinguisher

Task 4.6

Check the fire extinguishers in your college/school kitchen and restaurant. Where are they situated? What types are found in (1) the kitchen and (2) the restaurant.

How to prevent fire in the kitchen and restaurant

● Do not leave frying unattended
● Do not overfill pans
● Do not dry towels over stoves
● Do not wear loose clothing (for example sleeves)
● Clean ventilation equipment regularly
● Inspect flambe units regularly

The Fire Precautions Act 1971

All hotels and boarding houses are covered by this Act, unless they are very small. This means that they should provide sleeping accommodation for no more than six people. This includes guests and staff, sleeping on the first floor only.

The Act also covers places of public entertainment and facilities such as residential care homes.

People in charge of hotels and boarding houses must take adequate measures to deal with fire. They must provide:

1 Adequate means of escape (e.g. escape routes and fire escapes)
2 Fire precautions (e.g. fire-resistant doors, fire-fighting equipment, fire warning system, fire instruction and drills, advice to guests on proper fire procedure.

Premises covered by this Act must prove that they are complying with the law by obtaining a fire certificate from the local fire authority.

Fire Precautions (Factories, Offices, Shops and Railway Premises) Order 1989

Under this Order, small premises need not obtain a fire certificate. Small premises are where not more than 20 people work at any one time. However, they are not exempt from the Fire Precautions Act 1971.

Accidents

● Report all accidents to your supervisor
● Fill in an accident report form if you are a supervisor (Figure 4.13)

If a person is injured

● Attend to the injured person
● Call a first aider/doctor/ambulance
● Remove the danger, if you can do so without injuring yourself
● Inform your supervisor

Why do accidents happen? Accidents are caused by:

ACCIDENT REPORT FORM

Name of injured person: _____

Occupation of injured person: _____

Date of Accident: _____   Time of Accident: _____

Date of Report: _____   Time of Report: _____

Name of Supervisor: _____

Describe the injury: _____

_____

_____

_____

THE ACCIDENT

Place of accident: _____

Describe how the accident happened: _____

_____

_____

Witness statement: _____

_____

_____

Supervisor's recommendations: _____

_____

Supervisor's signature: _____   Date: _____

Figure 4.13 A typical accident report form

1 Being in too much of a hurry. This means we take chances, which inevitably lead to mishaps
2 Being distracted from our work. Our minds must always be on our work, to keep the risk of accidents down. If we do not concentrate on the job in hand or if we are distracted by someone else, then this could prove fatal

Cutting/mixing machines (Figure 4.14)

Accidents are easily caused if we misuse machines. When we are using them we must practise the following safety precautions:

1 Only one person should operate a machine. If two people are involved, a

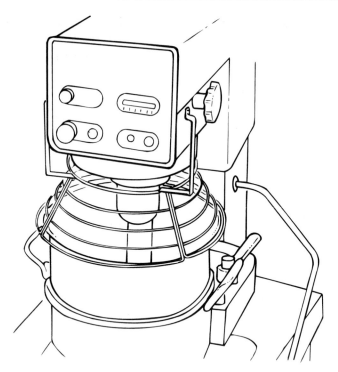

Figure 4.14 A mixing machine

misunderstanding could occur, resulting in the machine being switched on when the other person does not expect it.

2 We should assemble attachments correctly, making sure we use the correct equipment for forcing food through mincers or food processors.

3 Before we use cutting/mixing machines we must be sure the guard is in place. The guard must not be tampered with. Never push fingers, hands or knives past the guard. Wait until blades, whisks or hooks have stopped turning before putting hands or scrapers into mixing bowls. It is so easy to crush a hand or lose a finger.

4 Before we clean machines or remove guards we must switch off at the machine switch and wall switch or unplug the machine. This prevents it being accidentally switched back on. When we have removed slicing/cutting blades, we should not leave them unattended. Someone may put their hands on them by accident.

Floors

We may easily slip on wet or greasy floors. We should clean up our own spills immediately. Floors should be kept clean and clear. Pots, pans, baking trays or mixing bowls should never be left on the floor for someone to trip over.

Burns and scalds

Burns and scalds are very painful and are common in kitchens. The following precautions will help to prevent them:

- Keep sleeves of chefs' jackets rolled down
- Wear a long apron
- Use a thick, dry oven cloth

When carrying:

- Hold trays containing hot liquid with one hand on the side of the tray and the other hand on the end

- Never place containers of hot liquids on shelves above eye-level
- Do not let pan handles project over the edge of the stove
- Carry large pans with the forearm along the full length of the handle. Use your other hand to balance the pan where the handle joins the pan
- Move fritures only when the oil is cool

When frying:

- Place food in the pan away from the person when you are shallow or deep frying
- Drain and dry wet food before placing in hot oil
- Use a spider to take food out of the basket
- Turn off the heat at once if the oil in a friture bubbles over
- Cover oil fires with a fire blanket or a damp tea cloth

When straining:

- Keep your face well back, when passing hot liquids through conical strainers

When steaming:

- Stand behind the door to avoid escaping steam when opening steaming ovens. Open them slowly

possible hazards and always put into practice our safety training. During the preparation of the restaurant for service we should check that:

1 Tables do not tip or wobble, as hot food may spill onto customers
2 Flex runs round the edges of the room to prevent people from tripping over trailing flex
3 Coat stands are secure, to prevent them from falling onto customers
4 Fire exits are not blocked
5 Furniture and equipment is not put in places where people may fall over it

We should also report hazards to our supervisor:

- Broken equipment or fittings which may cause injury
- Frayed carpet which may cause people to trip
- Loose electrical fittings

When we are serving food and drink we should be safety conscious by:

1 Mopping up food or drink spills immediately
2 Avoiding stacking plates, as they fall over easily
3 Holding glasses by the stem or handle
4 Carrying glasses without stacking them inside each other, as they break more easily

---

Task 4.7

Prepare a checklist which you could use to make sure that people who work in the kitchen are using safe working methods.

Task 4.8

Prepare a checklist which you could use to make sure that people who work in the restaurant are using safe working methods.

How to work safely in the restaurant

When we are working in the restaurant we have responsibility for the health and safety of our customers. We must be constantly aware of

Describing Food

When we prepare menus we must be careful that we comply with the food labelling and advertising rules, which are set out in the Food

Labelling Regulations 1984. We must present food to our customers so that they are not misled as to the nature, substance or quality of the food. In the section on FSA 1990 we saw that this Act also makes it a criminal offence to describe or present food falsely.

If a menu describes a pie as a minced beef pie, then the meat must be 100 per cent beef. If there is another type of meat in the pie, even if only a small proportion, then the food is not of the nature or substance required. Food cannot be different from what is described or of a different composition. We are entitled to expect minced beef to be minced beef and nothing else.

Drinks are also covered by these regulations. If a menu offers diet cola and we serve ordinary cola then we are committing an offence. The drink is not of the quality expected by the customer, since it contains more calories than the diet drink.

The regulations also prevent us making some types of claims about food or giving misleading descriptions, when we are writing menus. Raspberry ice-cream must get its flavour mainly from raspberries. If a food flavour has been used to give the raspberry taste, then it must be described as raspberry-flavour ice-cream. If we are using canned or frozen peas which have been dried first then we cannot use the words 'fresh', 'garden' or 'green' to describe them. We must also say if a food has been processed, (for example, smoked mackerel). With some foods, there is such a variety that the name is not enough. Pâté is an example. We must say what sort of pâté we are serving (for example, Brussels pâté).

We must also remember that pictures must not mislead. Some menus have pictures of food on them. We cannot use pictures of raspberries if the food gets its taste from artificial flavourings.

Some well-known foods have been allowed to keep their names because we are not likely to be misled. Two of these are cream crackers and Swiss rolls.

Task 4.9

If you bought some toffees which said 'butter flavour' on the toffee paper, what would this information mean to you?

Task 4.10

Read the following children's menu:

Hamburger
or
Cod fish fingers
***
Chips
***
Baked beans
or
Green peas
******
Strawberry ice cream
or
Sponge pudding with chocolate custard

What information would you need to check that this menu complies with the Food Labelling Regulations?

▪ THE FACTORS THAT CONTRIBUTE TO FOOD PREPARATION AND COOKING ▪

This section investigates the various food production systems that are presently in use, and discusses the associated technical and cookery skills required of personnel using them. Staffing levels and labour costs are also addressed and the relationship of how technology has changed the labour requirements of the industry. Hygiene, health and safety issues are also analysed and how legislation can determine food production practices. At the end of this section you should know:

1 Cookery methods and food production systems in present use
2 How the methods and systems are matched to the requirements of different outlets in the hospitality and catering industry
3 The correct description of skills associated with different systems
4 An estimation of staff resources associated with different production systems
5 The legal aspects related to hygiene, health and safety as they affect food preparation and cooking processes

Cooking systems

There are two prime systems of cooking;

- Cook and serve systems
- Cook, store and serve systems

What are the differences?

Cook and serve systems

These are any system where the food is served immediately after it has been cooked. It is often served from the production area from where it was produced via a counter service or sometimes plated (as with hospitals using a conveyor belt plated system known as the 'Ganymede' system).

Where 'central' kitchens are used the food may be prepared in bulk and distributed to the smaller units in the local areas such as schools. This method will involve the use of heated containers and an effective transport system which is vital if the food is to reach the customer in good condition.

In the greater part, traditional cooking methods are used in a cook serve system but as cook and serve may be used in restaurants they may well be a system of part preparation and 'finishing' nearer the service times of the respective restaurant. Cook and serve systems are used in:

- Bistros/bars
- Cafes
- College refectories
- Fast-food restaurants
- Individual restaurants
- NHS and private hospitals
- Non-chain hotels
- Small industrial restaurants for service to staff and workers
- Some transport systems, ferries, railcar restaurants
- Tenant pubs

Task 4.11

With your knowledge so far, establish a list of problems associated with cook serve systems for the food preparation staff and suggest how they may be overcome.

Cook, store and serve systems

This production method is based around two methods:

- Cook–chill production
- Cook–freeze production

The emphasis with these types of operations is on the production of food for service at a future time. These storage conditions are dependent on:

1 How much later they are to be served
2 Volume of food required for service
3 The amount of storage space available
4 The system being used.

Let us now look at these systems in more detail.

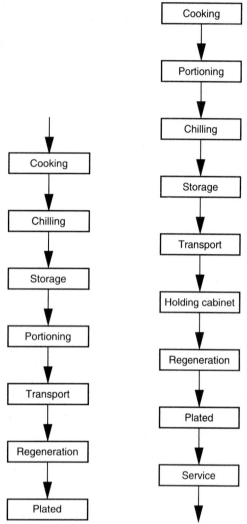

Figure 4.15 Regeneration with a plated meal system

Figure 4.16 Regeneration with stainless steel containers

Basic principles of the cook–chill process

The basic principles to be followed in the preparation of precooked food by a cook–chill operation are:

1 All food should be cooked completely to ensure the ruin of the vegetative stages of any pathogenic micro-organisms.
2 The chilling process should be begin as soon as possible after the cooking and portioning process – definitely within 30 minutes of completion.
3 The food should be chilled to 3°C (37°F) within the next 90 minutes. Most pathogenic organisms will not grow below 7°C (45°F). A temperature below 3°C is needed to reduce the growth of spoilage organisms and to ensure the correct storage life. However, care must be taken as growth does continue under such conditions and therefore storage life cannot be longer than 5 days.
4 The food should be stored at a temperature between 0°C and 3°C.
5 The chilled food should be distributed under such controlled conditions that any rise in temperature of the food during distribution is kept to a minimum.
6 For both safety and palatability the regeneration of food should follow immediately upon removal of food from chilled conditions and the temperature should be raised to a level of at least 70°C (158°F).
7 The food should be consumed as soon as possible and not more than 2 hours after regeneration. Regenerated food that is not consumed should be discarded.
8 The temperature of 10°C (50°F) should be regarded as the critical safety limit for chilled food. If the temperature should rise above this, it should be discarded and deemed unfit for consumption.

Advantages of cook–chill

Rapid chilling and chilled storage techniques simplify handling to such an extent that fluctuation in daily workloads can be practically

Cook–chill

Definition

Cook–chill is a catering system based on normal preparation and cooking of food followed by fast chilling. The food is then stored in controlled low-temperature conditions above freezing point 0–3°C (32–37°F) and subsequent reheating immediately before consumption. The chilled food is regenerated either at finishing kitchens or at the place of consumption (Figure 4.15 and 4.16).

removed. This is simply achieved by using the chill store as a buffer. Cook–chill offers the caterer the following benefits:

1 Divorce of production from service and consumption, allowing better usage of equipment and labour with higher efficiency.
2 All meals are prepared in advance of requirements and production can be scheduled to gain the best use of equipment, space and staff.
3 Reduced energy consumption, optimizing equipment use and staff are the benefits of the operation. Cook–chill utilizes one third of the energy of cook–freeze. This means reduced energy costs for both chilling and storage.
4 Chilled food suffers only minimal storage effects during the specified short preservation period, but, unlike frozen food which requires chemical additives and method changes in production, its life is strictly limited. Nutritional value can be potentially better than food produced conventionally and stored hot for long periods of time before service.
5 Many dishes such as delicate sauces, cold dishes, omelettes, egg dishes and hors d'oeuvres can be handled more simply than through freezing and cold storage techniques.
6 High food quality levels based on bulk-buying advantages and the opportunity to implement quality control over the suppliers.
7 Lower food costs based on bulk buying through centralized purchasing and supply to one production unit.
8 Less daily meal wastage because of additional flexibility in stock control.
9 Reduced labour costs. Cook–chill requires improved use of both skilled and unskilled staff. By concentrating activities of food into central units, these can be designed to operate to the maximum benefit to the caterer
10 Improved staff working conditions due to reduction in peak-time meal tension in service areas. Staff are more able to concentrate on presentation techniques during service.
11 Skilled staff are required for end cooking.
12 Appropriate savings can be made in space, food wastes and general preparation and service costs.

Are there any other forms of chilling processes ? The answer is yes. . . . The cook–chill process has been modified and amended over the years to suit specific types of operation which may involve issues such as:

- Limited skills of staff
- Limited kitchen space
- Poor portion control
- High wastage in cooking of food.

The 'sous-vide' system involving the process of cook–chill has evolved in order to allow chefs the opportunity to create elegant, artistic dishes while at the same time benefiting from the storage obtained via the chilling process. It also allows for 'centralized production' of the food, thus allowing the operation to concentrate its highly skilled chefs in one area, creating and harmonizing the cooking process. Then chilling and later distributing the food throughout the units or restaurants therefore help to expand the menu where limited skills are to be found. It also allows the training process to concentrate on the presentation and service of the food.

How does 'sous-vide' work?

This system comprises three processes:

1 Vacuum packing
2 Cooking en papillote – cooked in a bag, sealing in the juices
3 Rapid chilling

'Sous-vide' allows for few compromises. Chefs who opt for this system must learn to vacuum process and cook food of every type and texture.

Cooking advantages of the 'sous-vide system'

1 It seals in flavour, juices and nutrients
2 It extends shelf life
3 It is safe and hygienic
4 It economizes on ingredients
5 It reduces weight loss
6 It makes pre-cooking a possibility for à la minute (small food cooked to order) menus
7 It facilitates portion control

Benefits for the caterer

● Reduced dehydration and dip loss

Definition

● **Dip loss:** *food coated in breadcrumbs.*

Weight loss can be considerably reduced when meat is vacuum packed, and as this also cuts out the need to trim, financial benefits are significant. So great are they in fact, that the majority of large retail butchers now use vacuum packaging as a cost-effective way of maintaining the value of their stock. This benefit is equally available to the caterer.

● *Increased storage life.* To quote shelf life extension is always a dangerous practice, as many aspects are beyond the control of vacuum packaging. Poor food quality, cross-contamination prior to packing, food that has not been packed immediately after delivery and even the temperature in the refrigerator are examples. However, use-by times can be extended on chilled items (5°C max.) as follows; fresh meat 14 days, cheese 14 days, fruit and vegetables 7 days, fish 7 days.
● *Increased hygiene and reduced cross-contamination.* Vacuum pouches provide excellent barriers and will ensure food is protected in a hygienic condition, unaffected by any cross-contamination after packing.
● *Improved workflow.* In any restaurant, there will inevitably be periods of time which are

quiet. To spend that time vacuum packaging is not only an excellent use of your staff but also helps to relieve the workload when you or your staff are busy. Vacuum packaging will make optimum use of all available time by helping to even out the workload.

● *Prepackaging.* Variation in portion control can quickly provide dissatisfied customers if too small or will be uneconomical if too large. By pre-portioning and packaging without the pressure of time, accurate weights and a reduction of waste should be obtained. The food can be kept chilled until wanted. It can benefit planning of busy periods and overcome labour shortages at the weekend.
● *Wastage.* Despite the growth in eating out, more restaurants close each year than in any other business sector. One of the main reasons is wastage. Vacuum packaging in advance can help to keep this to a minimum by ensuring that unused portions are in peak condition for several days until required.
● *Satellite kitchens* These can readily be supplied with vacuum packed portions, eliminating the need for preparation in several areas. Preparation in a central area is the best use of space and can provide a fast service to the customer.
● *Bulk buying.* To buy in large quantities is usually cheaper and the use of vacuum packaging following delivery ensures that the food is kept in good condition for several days.
● *Freezer burn* Many foods like meat and fish are affected by burn or dehydration in the freezer. The protective qualities of a vacuum pouch ensures that this problem is eliminated.
● *Keeping the kitchen clean.* Many chefs have observed that with a vacuum packaging unit, fewer pots and pans are used, thus being labour saving in this area.

Problems

There are, however, certain problems which need to be recognized when vacuum packaging. Although many chefs will use packaging for soups and sauces, the shelf life of cooked foods should be kept to a minimum under chilled conditions and freezing is the more secure answer.

As a rule, cooked meats and cooked fish should not be packed unless 'sous-vide' techniques are used. It is vital that stock is used in correct date order and that old portions are not left at the bottom of the pile. To overcome this, all packs must be labelled not only with the contents and weight but also with the date of packaging and the 'use-by date'.

In the event of any pack becoming blown or leaking, the contents should be immediately opened, examined and repacked only if satisfactory. Vacuum packaging does not turn bad food into good! Strict hygiene, the immediate packaging of foodstuffs and accurate chill conditions are a vital part of the process. In staffing terms, the results should produce either greater output with the same staff or the same output but with reduced staff. Vacuum packaging is not difficult and the machine can be operated by unskilled staff, after being instructed on the procedure.

The Capkold system

This system involves the use of cook–chill and is best used for bulk production as it uses 'kettle cooking'. It is particularly suitable for the production of soups, sauces, casseroles and gravies. It is possible to prepare other food items, however.

Definition

- **Kettle cooking:** *large stainless steel boilers are used for cooking the food in quantity.*

Once the food is cooked, the item is transferred to cryuvac pouches at 83°C (pasteurization temperature) and is placed in a cold water bath which is agitated. The process reduces the temperature down to 2°C within one hour. This fast chilling process allows for an extended shelf life while the food is stored chilled.

Cook–freeze

This is a system of preparing and cooking high-quality food in economic quantities, retaining it in a state of 'suspended freshness' by rapid freezing and freezer storage, and serving it when and where required from finishing kitchens requiring low capital investment and minimal staffing.

Why cook–freeze?

Shortage of skilled catering staff and a high turnover of the staff employed suggest the following conclusions:

1 Skilled staff must be more fully utilized
2 Catering operations must be devised which may be operated with a greater proportion of unskilled staff
3 Benefits and conditions of employment must be improved to stabilize the movement of staff

Kitchen surveys have shown that 40 per cent of the time in a kitchen is spent on preparation, 26 per cent on cleaning and only 15 per cent on cooking. The remainder is spent on administration.

The scope of cook–freeze

Cook–freeze is generally arranged in one of the following three arrangements:

1 As a complete new installation planned as a self-contained 'food production unit' with separate food lines for individual meal items i.e. meat, fish, vegetables, sweet and pastry to give medium- or large-scale output as in factory-type operations.
2 As a smaller-scale operation formed from entirely new equipment (or regrouping of

existing equipment) to give a positive flowline, but generally conceived as a central location of cooking equipment as in the conventional catering kitchen. This will allow a rotation of bulk cooking individual menu items.

3 The retention of existing kitchen arrangements and the addition of only a scaling, portioning, wrapping, blast freezing and low-temperature storage facilities. These may be added as a unit supplied as a 'package deal'.

While standard catering equipment may be used in preparation and cooking areas, heavier-duty cooking models may be developed to meet the needs of a sustained 'full working day' production programme. This equipment will be somewhat akin to the normal larger factory units.

Conveyor systems may be applied to the cooking units. They will definitely be needed in the portioning areas prior to sealing for blast freezing.

Tunnel-type blast freezers will be used in larger units. Good supervision of stock control both for incoming stores and in the low-temperature storage distribution area will need the techniques of a food production engineer rather than a catering officer!

Balance of meals

Although a cook–freeze installation may be required solely for frozen food production, serving conventional kitchen operations in other places, it will often itself be part of a centralized kitchen complex in which the preparation and distribution of cold sweets, salads, soups, etc. must be accommodated. In some cases it may be preferable to allow such items to be prepared in the finishing kitchens to prevent unnecessary handling costs of distribution. Generally, only a large operation will justify preparation in the finishing kitchen, otherwise obvious economies will be lost.

Food service in the immediate area of the cook–freeze

Kitchen

Where frozen food is produced to supply a service on the same premises it is still necessary to route, cook, freeze, store and issue as if the product is to be distributed further afield. Particular attention must be paid to the hygiene requirements of 'clean catering', where the duties of staff and equipment can overlap the two functions of production and service. Positive work patterns must be laid down to separate these functions.

What is the object of freezing food?

The purpose of freezing food is to prolong its storage life. Under normal conditions food deteriorates rapidly through the action of micro-organisms and also enzymatic and chemical reactions. Reduction in the storage temperature inhibits the multiplication of bacteria and other micro organisms (yeasts, moulds, etc.) and slows down the chemical and enzymatic reactions. At normal refrigeration temperatures reactions are still taking place, but at a much slower rate, and at frozen food storage temperatures ($-20°C$ approx.) nearly all reactions cease.

Why freeze down to the region of $-20°C$?

At temperatures below freezing point most microbiological activity ceases, but to ensure that all enzymatic and chemical reactions have stopped it is necessary to take the temperature down to $-20°C$ or below. Failure to do so would result in chemical reactions to continue, producing 'off' flavours and reducing the natural flavour of the food.

What is blast freezing and what are the alternatives?

Blast freezing is the application of conventional refrigeration techniques to the problem of reducing food temperatures to as low as $-20°C$. The blast freezer consists of a compartment into which the food is placed, a compressor motor powering an ordinary compression refrigeration cycle and a heavy-duty fan which blasts the cold air around the freezing compartment. The power of the refrigeration compression would be geared to the capacity of the freezing compartment and the overall design of the blast freezing unit.

Alternative methods of deep freezing food

1 Liquid nitrogen freezing – which is a very fast, effective method whereby the food is sprayed with liquid nitrogen. But it is costly in terms of liquid nitrogen
2 Plate freezing – in which the food is placed on refrigerated metal plates probably in its appropriate carton. Initial costs are high and the plates need special design
3 Liquid brine freezing – used mainly in the broiler/poultry industry
4 Freon-12 freezing – currently being developed for food freezing

Freezing time

Quick freezing time is essential to ensure that small ice crystals are formed. Large ice crystals are undesirable as they rupture the cell structure of the food resulting in poor texture and moisture loss when reconstituted.

Nutritional value and palatability of food

The nutritional value and palatability of food will always suffer if it is cooked badly. For example, cabbage will lose nearly all its vitamin C content if it is overcooked or stored at 'eat-ready' storage temperatures for a long time. Cooked food, also kept in storage, for example in bain-maries, will lose its appeal and nutritional value if kept too long. Freezing food will not affect the vitamin content or palatability of food if it is done properly.

Definition

- **Palatability:** *the taste, texture and flavour that is acceptable to the customer.*

Finishing kitchens

These are a vital element in the process of cook–freeze. This is where the frozen food is re-cooked and made presentable for the customer. The main essentials of the finishing kitchen are a low-temperature cold store and a forced-air convection oven for reconstituting the frozen food. The forced-air convection oven is the exact opposite of the blast freezer in that it circulates hot air over the frozen food packs. Ancillary equipment will also be needed in the finishing kitchen to provide a complete meal service:

- Boiling rings for reheating frozen vegetables,
- Water boilers for beverages
- Small deep-fat fryers for cooking chipped potatoes
- A servery counter for entrees, salads and sweets

Now we have looked in depth at cook–chill and cook–freeze processes it would be interesting to make a comparison of the two:

1 Both systems have a number of similarities in their basic design.
2 Both approaches are based on the central preparation of food and the use of refrigeration to link preparation with service.
3 The main difference is the 'life' of the food once it has undergone refrigeration, obviously longer for frozen food.
4 The cost is about three times that for cook–freeze than for cook–chill.
5 Frozen food has a longer 'safe' life and hence can be held in stock for widely varying times, thus enabling the caterer to account for varying service demands and fluctuations in demand on labour, i.e. weekends and holidays.
6 Cook–chill has a 'safe' life of only between 2 and 5 days and therefore accurate short-time forecasting of demand is essential.
Each system scores against the other on certain counts. Analysis of the catering service required will determine where the best technique of benefits will be obtained (Table 4.5).

Table 4.5 Comparison of cook–freeze and cook–chill

Characteristics	Cook–freeze	Cook–chill
Increased labour productivity	*	***
Improved working conditions	*	***
Take advantage of the seasonal prices	***	**
Microbiological control and hygiene	***	**
Reduction of service kitchen floor areas	**	***
Reduced energy requirements	*	***
Ensured quality control	*	***
Range of dishes handled	*	***
Optimize capital investment	*	***
Improved portion control	**	**
Food service wastage control	**	**
Stock control capability	***	***
	21	32

Skills in the cooking process

In the previous section we looked at the processes in the production of food using either cook–serve or cook–store and serve systems. It was interesting to note that both systems are based on traditional cooking methods so we can expect to find the traditional range of culinary skills associated with them, or can we?

In order to investigate let us look at the range of skills associated with the cooking process but, at the same time, at the different level of people skills, e.g.

- Craft
- Supervisory
- Managerial.

Look at Table 4.6. This is based on the process of cook–chill production for a unit preparing 1500 meals a day. It is assumed that good-quality of menu(s) are in operation, offering craft personnel a challenge of both variety and composition of dishes. The table is not exhaustive but it does indicate the differences of skills, knowledge and attainment

Table 4.6 Cook–chill processes

Craft skills (associated)	Supervisory skills (associated)	Managerial skills (associated)
Knife skills – cutlery, filleting, chopping, etc.	Craft skills plus quality control of purchased items	Design and layout of unit
Butchery and larder skills	Ensuring targets are met on:	Ensuring good work flow process
Cooking skills – grilling, roasting, frying, sauces and garnishes	Production Monitoring portion control Monitoring chilling process Monitoring hygienic practice	Menu planning Purchasing specifications Recipe specifications
Weighing and measuring of food items	Staff training	Monitoring products produced or quality
Hygenic skills	Preparing written reports to management	Marketing of products
Presentational skills	Ordering of produce	Ensuring safe storage
Use of equipment safely and correctly	Maintenance of equipment	Ensuring life cycle of product
	Liaison with suppliers	Comparison of products produced
	Liaison with customers	Research and development of products
	Recipe development	

required by individuals operating within such a system.

The principle applies whether it be an industrial unit catering for its own workforce, a central production unit catering for its fleet of hotels or a commercial food producer catering for the convenience food market. There will be certain differences in issues such as portion control, presentation of food and in particular, marketing and packaging of the food produced. Otherwise these are generally the same.

Service of the food

Table 4.6 focuses on the cooking process, which, we have established, is generally the same no matter what type of operation. However, where the food is to be served *will* make the difference. The cook–chill process can and does alter for service of food in such areas as:

1 Hotels
2 Restaurants
3 School meals
4 Industrial catering settings
5 Airline catering
6 British Rail catering
7 Hospitals
8 Retail market for domestic consumption.

Where it is to be used can affect:

- The portion size
- The type, quality and variety of products used
- Presentation of the product
- Marketing used to sell the product

These, in turn, influence the skills required in the production and, more importantly, in the service of the food. Let us look at two contrasting examples:

Hotels

The cook–chill process is principally used to ensure that a wider range of products on the menu as well as uniformity in portion size, texture, flavour of the food. It also reduces staff at the 'finishing end' of the process, i.e. chefs and waiters. However, it does allow for the presentational skills of the finishing chef and the service skill of the waiter, hence, a shift to

Table 4.7

Food	Waxed or rigid plastic containers	Foil containers	Foil sheeting	Polythene bags or sheeting
Fresh meat			•	•
Fresh poultry and game			•	•
Cooked meats and fish dishes	•	•	•	•
Fresh vegetables	•			•
Fresh vegetables (bline pack)	•			
Fresh fruit (unsweetened or dry sugar pack)	•			•
Fresh fruit (syrup pack)	•			
Butter, margarine and fats		•	•	•
Cheese			•	•
Milk and cream	•			
Eggs	•	•		
Soups and sauces	•	•	•	•
Bread, cakes and biscuits			•	•
Pastry and pies		•	•	•
Desserts	•	•	•	•
Ice cream	•		•	

the customer skills required i.e. selling – then presentation and service of food.

Airlines

The cook–chill process here is in reverse as the service provision is via the steward or stewardess who has little time to concentrate on the service of food on to the plate, but has to cater for a range of food requirements. This problem is alleviated by controlling the cooking, presentation and service (via tray, packaging or plate) on the ground. Meticulous detail is given to the presentation of the food as it is known that the service of the food will be very quick while in the air.

These examples show that usage will determine the skills required, whether they be in the kitchen or restaurant or a combination of both. Table 4.7 indicates the most commonly used packaging materials for various types of food.

Task 4.12

Prepare a skill matrix (similar to Table 4.7 for the process of cook–freeze production. Assume that the operation is for an industrial company catering for its workforce which include directors, office workers and shopfloor technicians.

▪ PLANNING AND IMPLEMENTING A FOOD-PREPARATION AND COOKING SYSTEM ▪

In this section we shall look at the various cooking systems used for a variety of establishments and the resourcing, responsibilities and planning required by staff. We shall also consider issues which affect how

successfully the establishment operates and the implications of health and safety and hygiene in practice. At the end of this section you should understand:

- The cooking systems appropriate to a selection of establishments
- The planning and delivery of tasks within a range of establishments
- The success factors in using the various cooking systems
- The processes for monitoring quality within an operation
- The implications of hygiene, health and safety legislation

Planning cooking systems

In order to simplify how we can investigate suitable cooking systems for an establishment, look at Table 4.8. This is restricted to showing how an appropriate system is matched with a type of establishment. Note, however, that sometimes a combination of systems is used to complete the service. For example, in large chain restaurants and hotels there may be a central kitchen to produce the dishes which are then finished at the appropriate restaurant kitchen or hotel kitchen. This is known as *centralized production* and involves either a cook–chill or cook–freeze system.

Table 4.8 is not exhaustive, but gives an indication of the principal systems used in the more common outlets. Cooking systems should not be confused, however, with the service systems, which are used to convey the food to the customer and can include;

- Ashtrays in cafeterias, fast-food and buffet outlets
- Cartons in take-aways

Both the above involve 'customer service' which is linked to the type of cooking system used to minimize the time in serving food to the customer but as well as maximizing the number of customers who can be served.

Table 4.8

Type of establishment	Typical cooking system	Notes
Independent restaurant	*Cook and hold* Dishes will be prepared, cooked and held on hot plates or a bain-marie during the service. *Cooked to order* Dishes partly prepared, refrigerated and completed when the customer orders the dish.	Menu will either be table d'hôte or à la carte dishes for 'cook and hold' will suit the set menus, à la carte dishes will be cooked to order, but may be partly prepared to speed up the cooking time. The range of products will be a matter of fresh and convenience products.
Independent hotel	Again 'cook and hold' and 'cooked to order' there may be an element of 'cook and freeze' to suit function catering if the hotel offers this facility and has the appropriate freezer space.	Table d'hôte or à la carte, lunch and dinner usually offered and breakfast for residents' functions may include weddings, parties and small conferences.
Fast-food chain restaurant	*Collect to order* Product will usually be prepared in central kitchens but not cooked – dispatched via refrigerated transport to appropriate outlets and finished via traditional cooking methods, e.g. grilled, char grilled.	Products will be invariably mix of fresh and frozen produce with a high-volume turnover accounted for.
Chain hotel	May involve 'cook and hold', 'collect to order', 'cook and freeze' and 'cook and freeze'. This combination depends on the hotel group's preference. The two systems 'cook and hold' and 'cook to order' may well be operated via 'cook and chill' or 'cook and freeze' to underpin this food is transported from a central kitchen via refrigeration and is then used within table d'hôte or à la carte menus at the hotel kitchen.	Some hotel groups will devise cooking systems based on 'cook and chill' or 'cook and freeze' specifically for banquet and conference facilities. A typical system based on this principle is 'gastronomy') Cooking systems used in chain and group hotels depend a great deal on a mix of fresh and convenience produce to underpin the wide range of menus to cater for functions.
Chain restaurant	Mostly 'cook to order' but can involve an element of 'cook and hold' – for example, vegetables, chips and sauces.	A high degree of frozen produce tends to be used in chain restaurants because it minimizes distribution problems – fresh produce would require delivery, two, three or more times a week and would then require more space in the storage area. Menus tend to be standardized to produce uniform presentation and portion control within each unit.
Public houses	'cook and hold' as a percentage of the operation – frozen produce 'cook to hold'	Cooking systems will also depend on whether the public house is brewery owned or tenanted. Breweries have vast resources invested in central kitchens to produce frozen products. Tenanted pubs will be restricted and will operate via a more traditional system but will buy frozen products to increase the menu range and reduce space required for preparation of fresh produce.

Table 4.8 (Continued)

Type of establishment	Typical cooking system	Notes
Industrial catering unit	'Cook and hold' – small element of 'cook to order', for example, stir fry dishes or omelettes. Operation in large units sustained by 'cook and freeze' or 'cook and chill' systems. Smaller units may operate the same but will be supplied via a central kitchen for the products which will then be regenerated at the unit.	Industrial settings are often supported by a vending service to cater for the 24-hour service required – the vending service may well be used for on-site products which are chilled or frozen which are then reheated by microwave oven. This system is very useful where the main restaurant is too far for employees to travel and can be used in smaller dining areas throughout the industrial site.
Hospitals	Mostly 'cook and hold' (held via heated trolleys to wards) but small percentage of 'cook to order' in staff and public outlets.	Hospital systems may well involve 'cook and freeze' and occasionally 'cook and chill' to prepare the food but the distribution via trolleys involves holding the food at the required temperature hence 'cook and hold'. Some hospitals involve a distribution systems called 'gastronomy' prior to putting the food into trolleys.
		The formation of hospital trusts have seen hospitals involving themselves in more commercial ventures to include outside catering, In-house shops such as bakeries and hot and cold food via restaurants in food courts or shopping centres in the public areas of the hospital.
Retail shopping units	'Cook to order' mostly used but supported by frozen products and speciality dried and tinned produce.	The retail sector is varied and can involve one unit such as a shop, restaurant or cafeteria or the multi-unit combination found in large shopping malls, such as Meadowhall in Sheffield. There we find national chains such as McDonald's, Pizza Hut and others as well as ethnic restaurants including Chinese, Italian or Mexican. We also find more unusual products such as Donut sellers, all of which are reliant on passing trade, hence 'cook to order'.

Task 4.13

Investigate which type of cookery system is most commonly used by Airtours for its passengers and compare that with the system used by British Rail. What major differences are there for the operators and how is this allowed for by the caterers?

Planning resources and requirements

We looked at the types of cooking systems used in a selection of outlets and now we must identify the problems associated with operating these systems. When choosing a type of system it is not merely a question of installing equipment and buying in food products to be cooked by chefs and cooks. You need to adopt a strategy to ensure that your time and money are put to good use. Remember, it is not your money on occasions, but your company's and they will expect maximum benefit for minimal layout on costs. The following functions need to be considered when planning:

1 Money available for setting up the operation
2 Available space for the preparation and cooking areas
3 Numbers to be catered for
4 Type of customer being catered for
5 Number of outlets/restaurants to be supplied
6 Availability of staff expertise and skills
7 Availability of suppliers for commodities
8 Fuel supply:
   Gas
   Electricity
   Propane
   Mixed fuel supply

These factors should be part of any strategy for choosing a catering system.

Stages in the catering process

The stages shown in Figure 4.17 are integral to any catering operation, which, whatever its size, is made up of various sections linked together like a chain, and any weakness in that chain can create problems.

Obviously, the planning requirements will vary according to the scale of the operation envisaged and the solutions can range from simple groupings of equipment for small units to large complex equipment where large numbers of people or units require provision. In order to be cost effective planning is required right down to the smallest detail.

Figure 4.18 is a useful model in explaining the food flow between storage and preparation in a large kitchen complex. Resources for a kitchen of this nature will depend on the:

1 Numbers catered for
2 The menu
3 Range of provision:
   Breakfast
   Lunch
   Dinner
4 Staff skills

The single largest determinant in the resources for a kitchen is the menu itself. From the menu we can decide on the:

Type of products
Fresh
Frozen
Tinned
Dried

The type of equipment
Cooking ranges
Reheating ranges

Storage requirements
Chilling areas
Freezing areas
Dry goods areas

Preparation areas
Larder
Pastry
Vegetables
Fish

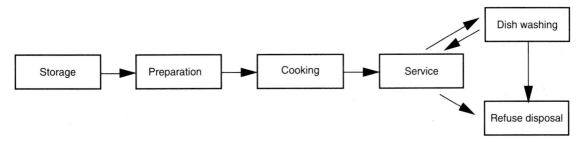

Figure 4.17 Stages in the catering process

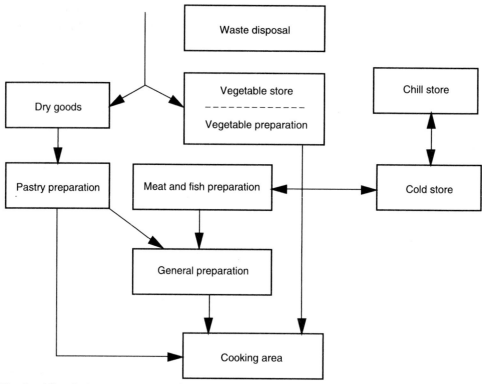

Figure 4.18 The food flow between storage and preparation

The lack of staff skills can be compensated by the products the caterer uses. For example, the range of soups can be increased by using tinned or dried soup mixes. This can be repeated to apply to the menu such as frozen fish, frozen vegetables, ready-prepared desserts or sauce mixes.

Principles of cooking

The traditional idea of classifying menus as either à la carte or table d'hôte is becoming less satisfactory for describing the range of menus that are now common. For example, many fast-food menus use the à la carte principle – that is, you make a choice from the menu and pay for each item – but we cannot really call these à la carte menus. In the same way, although some school meals and staff restaurants use the table d'hôte idea – that is, you pay for a set meal and choose one dish from each course – they are not really accepted as traditional table d'hôte menus. A fixed menu

with a limited choice is becoming popular with caterers for a number of reasons:

- It can be prepared by less-skilled staff once production methods have been learned
- It requires fewer food items to be held in stock
- It will reduce food wastage, as not so much food will have to be prepared in advance
- It will help to maintain the required standard of food production – the chef will find it easier to supervise a smaller number of dishes

This type of menu can be changed as required – daily, weekly, or after longer periods. A traditional table d'hôte menu used in many hotels and restaurants is a fixed menu with a fixed price. The customer selects one dish from each course.

The traditional kitchens of the late nineteenth century used to be very labour intensive, with many chefs who were highly skilled preparing only fresh produce. They would also prepare exotic dishes for people who had the time and money to enjoy them.

Modern era technology has reduced tedious tasks in the kitchen by vegetable peelers, potato chippers, vegetable shredders and, of course, the multi-purpose food processor. These innovations have been complemented by developments in the food areas such as dried mixes, tinned and frozen products, chilling and freezing of food items. All in all, this has given a sphere of choice to the caterer.

How has choice increased?

You may well ask yourself, what is the single biggest cost to any catering operation? Answer – labour! The cost of staff wages has to be borne in mind in any establishment. The caterer or restaurateur has to make a choice, whether to set a standard based on totally fresh ingredients, with a weekly menu choice or to compromise and use a percentage of fresh food and convenience products or totally convenience products. Either way, it can make a difference to his or her labour costs as it is time

that you are paying for and if you can produce more foods in less time versus cost of the product you are well on your way to profits or maximizing a subsidized operation such as an industrial unit.

Let us look at an example to prove our point. We will take a chicken casserole and compare two methods, one using only fresh produce, the other a mix of fresh and frozen (Table 4.9). These dishes have advantages and disadvantages but it is the overall outcome that matters. For example:

The fresh dish

Advantages	*Disadvantages*
More enhanced flavour using fresh produce	Waste products after preparation: not all chicken is used for the sole dish
More marketable as a fresh dish	Four chicken breasts left which will need storage for further use
	More time in preparation

The convenience dish

Advantages	*Disadvantages*
Less time in preparation	Higher initial costs
Less skill required by staff	Less control on quality of products
Less wastage	

Table 4.9 Chicken casserole

4 portions	4 portions
Ingredients (fresh)	Ingredients (convenience)
2 chickens (2½ lbs) (to obtain 4 portions, leg and thigh)	4 chicken portions
	2 lb pack frozen mixed vegetables
8 oz carrot, onion, leek and celery	Pinch mixed herbs
Pinch mixed herbs	3 pt water
2 pt chicken stock (Bones from chicken consommé)	2 chicken stock cubes
	2 oz mushrooms for garnish
8 oz mixed vegetables	Teaspoon of chopped parsley
Butter, water (3 pt)	
2 oz mushrooms for garnish	
Teaspoon of chopped parsley	
Approximate cost £7.00	Approximate cost £5.20
Preparation time 30 mins	Preparation time 10 mins
Cooking time 1½ hours	Cooking time 1 hour

Overall, the convenience dish from a cost point of view is better as it requires less labour cost and there is less wastage. The fresh dish, however, may taste better but takes longer to prepare and requires more skill from the chef, which in turn costs the caterer more. The bottom line is how the customer receives it. If the convenience product is acceptable then the caterer can sell more in less time, which in turn will compensate overall for the higher initial cost. It can also allow more time and training for the presentation of the food, rather than the preparation which the customer does not see, and the price charged may even be the same.

The last factor is often used in the concept of the central production kitchen (CPU) where larger caterers will put all their best chefs into one or two kitchens to prepare the full menu range used in their outlets. By using a cook–freeze or cook–chill system, they will distribute to the rest of the outlets, thus ensuring the highest quality and highest skills in the preparation of the dishes but also leaving time to be spent on the *presentation* at the finishing kitchen (such as a hotel) for the customer. This form of catering also saves space as less is required for storing chilled or frozen products as compared with fresh commodities.

Up to now we have looked at the various cookery systems to include:

- Cook–serve
- Cook–hold
- Cook–chill
- Cook–freeze

Cook–chill and cook–freeze were comprehensively treated earlier in this unit. Let us look now at the concept of cook–serve, as it involves a combination of processes the foremost being *batch cooking.*

Batch cooking

Batch cooking has resolved some of the associated problems with cook–serve and cook–hold systems. It is a technique by means of which freshly cooked food is supplied in limited quantities throughout a service period. This method is very useful in situations where freshly cooked items are needed over an extended service. The alternative is to cook all the menu items in advance of service and store them in hot cabinets or bains-marie until required.

Many food items deteriorate in colour, flavour, and texture if kept hot for long periods. This is especially true of green vegetables. There is also a considerable loss of vitamin C. Batch cooking

means that the quality of the product will be as good for your last customer as for your first.

Batch cooking involves cooking smaller quantities – often on specially designed equipment – immediately before they are served. This goes on during the whole of the service period, which in the case of some operations is for quite a long time. You will find it helpful if you have a good idea of the likely demand for certain items at peak periods, and this can often be the case in particular situations such as industrial canteens and cafeterias.

Not all menu items are suitable for batch cooking – particularly those that take a long time to cook, such as stewed or braised meats or steamed savoury puddings. Items that are especially suitable are those that deteriorate fairly quickly after cooking – green vegetables; grilled, shallow-fried and deep-fried foods; and hot egg dishes. The technique can also be used for frozen items. These should be regenerated in small quantities to meet the expected demand.

You must make sure that the batch-cooked products are used in the correct sequence. Care must be taken that the last items of one batch are completely used up before you start serving the first of the next batch. Some companies issue guidelines telling staff how long certain cooked food items can be left on display before they must be replaced by a freshly cooked batch.

Keeping records to help to forecast demand. Batch cooking is a good example of how the expected demand can be based on previous sales with some degree of accuracy.
The work of the kitchen staff in preparing the raw commodities for cooking is not affected by batch cooking.

Batch cooking should not be confused with the style of production used for à la carte service, where the demand for certain dishes is very unpredictable.

Planning your work

Working in the kitchen, you need to use your time and energy in the most effective manner. You will need to plan every activity in advance, making the most of the limited time available to you. In food preparation you will automatically be able to plan effectively, but while training you will need a more methodical approach towards planning.

Process

An analysis of the menu should provide you with information you need to work out what is required from you. You need to consult your chef or manager if you have any problems. Before undertaking any task, ask yourself the following questions:

What needs to be done?
Why is it required?
Where is it to be carried out?
When is action required?
How am I going to do it?

In order to use time effectively, you will need information about the tasks you are to perform. Some information will be obtained directly from your immediate supervisor, but some may have to be confirmed through checking. Information may be categorized under the following headings:

1 Name or menu description of food items
2 Preparation prior to cooking of food item
3 Size of the portion and amounts required for the menu
4 Weight and measure of ingredients to be used
5 Cooking methods and processes required within the exercise
6 Oven temperatures and cooking times of the food items
7 Style of service (e.g. Silver, Plate)
8 Time required by the customer.

When considering time planning, you will also need to take the following factors into account:

1 Arrange items requiring preparation so that the sequence of work requires the least movement within the work area
2 Work methodically to a set pattern
3 Maintain separate containers for all trimmings
4 Keep your working area clean at all times, cleaning and washing as you go, do not allow a build-up of items
5 When preparing large quantities of food organize the food so that lifting and moving items is reduced, especially heavy ones
6 Have all equipment ready to hand and clean
7 Arrange all food in containers, in a tidy fashion. This will help to keep your work area clear and reduce the risks of food hygiene problems
8 Conserve fuel. When not required, gas or electricity should be turned down or off.

You will become a more efficient food handler by taking time to plan, developing skills and knowledge in the process.

Why plan?

- To be more efficient in production
- To maximize production and quality
- To meet production targets and customer needs

How?

- Knowledge of tasks required
- Knowledge of techniques necessary for completing the task
- Knowledge of the equipment to be used
- Production of a method of work

What needs to be identified?

- Jobs, tasks and menus
- Recipes or chef's directives
- Preparation times for food items

What do you need to be aware of?

The complete range of foods. This means being aware of any necessity to prepare one item in order to produce another.

What needs to be organized?

- You and your colleagues to ensure success
- Materials and equipment
- Your working area

Knowing when advance preparation should stop without spoiling the finished product is really the crux of preparation and planning.

Drawing up a preparation plan

At this stage you can begin to allocate the time needed for each stage of preparation and handling. Many factors influence a time plan:

1 Using the correct tools for the task. Always use appliances designed for a specific purpose. Remember the rule: use the correct tools for the job
2 Cooking methods. Always follow technically correct procedures
3 Efficient use of equipment and resources. You will need to plan when to use equipment in order to avoid conflict or overutilization of specialized machinery
4 Protection of quality. Time planning prevents a crisis from arising because too many items demand attention at the same time
5 Protection of quantity. Make sure you measure ingredients accurately.

- *Why should equipment and materials be assembled before starting preparation?* In order to ensure that all items are available so work can progress without interruption and with less chance of error in the process.
- *On what factors should work plans be based?* Proper planning and sequencing to achieve maximum quality with minimum expense and swiftly without unnecessary effort and time.
- *How can work be done swiftly and easily?* By having supplies and equipment arranged for a smooth work flow, so that each movement can be made in the easiest way with the fewest steps in the process.

Planning of cooking systems maximizes the output to the customer and reduces costs. But in any catering operation it is not just the chefs who are involved in the overall delivery. It is the responsibility of the catering supervisor to check that all activities are sequenced to ensure smooth and effective operation. Figure 4.19 indicates how a day in an industrial unit is

Service		Breakfast				Lunch				
Time	7 a.m	8 a.m.	9 a.m.	10 a.m.	11 a.m	12 noon	1 p.m.	2 p.m.	3 p.m	4 p.m.
Catering manager		Job allocation–bookwork				Supervision				Admin.
Asst. manager		Bookwork				Supervisor and assistant				Cash-up bookwork
Head chef		Main meal preparation				Kitchen back-up				Clean down
Second chef		Main meal preparation				Kitchen back-up				
Grill/veg. chef	Breakfast prep.	Cooked breakfast to order grill bar prep..		Veg/salad prep.	Pre-service briefing	Call order grill bar			Staff lunch	
Cashier/vending		Fill, clean and replenish vending machines				Cas/salad replenish				
Food service assistant		Sandwich prep. and counter prep.				Counter				
Food service assistant		Sandwich prep. and counter prep.				Counter				
Kitchen porter		Lay tables–wash-up				Wash-up				

Figure 4.19 Staff roles and responsibilities in an industrial unit

made up of discrete activities and staff roles and responsibilities within it.

A question of success?

In order to ascertain any degree of success in a catering operation we have to consider some key questions:

1 *Will it be worth the effort?* Benefits of increased productivity, better morale, easier recruitment are difficult if not impossible to quantify. There is no doubt, however, that they can accrue from a well-planned, efficient catering operation. Many companies regard catering as having such importance that they have made it an integral part of their policy.

2 *Will the customers use the establishment?* If the food quality, choice and price are right, the service is efficient and cheerful and the surroundings are attractive and comfortable, there is every likelihood of success. But do not fall into the trap of regarding your staff as a 'captive' market. Standards must be maintained and catering management must be constantly on the lookout for subtle changes in demand if the catering operation is to continue to flourish.

3 *Have we chosen the right menu?* It is not easy to predict what people want to eat, but what you can do is to make an objective appraisal of the menus in other successful operations and get staff to answer a questionnaire. When operational, attention to customer reaction will help to ensure that 'menu fatigue' is avoided. The important thing to remember is that each item on the menu must earn its keep.

4 *Can we keep cost down?* A systematic approach will ensure that the two highest cost ingredients in the operation – food and labour – will be answerable to constant checks. Good staff supervision will produce and maintain a high level of quality and productivity.

5 *How much space can we afford?* With the use of new catering systems, which require less on-site preparation, and modern, compact and often multi-purpose equipment, space requirements are considerably less than those needed for traditional kitchen operations using traditional equipment and methods. Also, the latest, more efficient service equipment will increase the rate of flow through the dining area and further reduce the overall space requirement.

6 *Can we ensure the right equipment?* An experienced planning team should be employed to ensure that the correct equipment is selected from the impressive range now available. This team should check that the equipment is matched to the exact requirements of the menu, output and quality desired in order to obtain maximum equipment utilization.

7 *Can we keep fuel costs down?* The right equipment for the job will help here. Wherever possible, select equipment specifically designed for efficient energy use. But remember that staff must be thoroughly trained in the correct use of all equipment. Automatic controls can sometimes be fitted to ensure maximum efficiency.

8 *How can we ensure safety?* Good planning should include consultations with the local fire authority and Environmental Health Officers on the requirements of Health and Safety issues.

Monitoring issues

Monitoring of preparation and cooking processes

Catering operators need to be sure that the products they are producing are in line with their expectations and, above all, are meeting their customers' requirements whether in a hotel, restaurant, fast-food chain, hospital or industrial unit. Apart from internal information there will be external reasons for ensuring that the storage, preparation, cooking and serving of food is monitored, the principal one being food hygiene regulations. What other factors would the catering operator be concerned with? As a starting point, look at the following list.

Quality of the product in terms of:
Portion size
Taste
Texture
Colour
Temperature
General appearance
Cost
Wastage

Life-span of the product
Is it suitable for chilling?
Is it suitable for freezing?

Cooking
Does the product involve a lot of preparation and complex cooking?
Does the product reheat?
Is there any loss of flavour, texture, colour or taste?
Is the product suitable for reheating in a microwave oven, conventional oven, high-pressure steamer?
How long does it take to reheat to the correct temperature?
What are the labour costs?

Presentation
What does the product look like on the plate?
Is it attractive and inviting to the customer?
Does it require enhancement via garnish?

Quality
Is it value for money?
Is there a better alternative (is it cheaper)?

Hygiene
Are respective guidelines being met such as;

● Food Hygiene Regulations 1970 (and amendments)?
● Food Safety Act 1970?
● Cook–chill guidelines (DHSS)?

Failure to comply with these could see the total operation closed down.

Monitoring within the operation involves all the above questions. However, it would be impossible to monitor all of the issues at one time, so the process involves sampling, except where temperature is concerned but we will discuss that later. Let us select an example of the monitoring process to give us an understanding of what is involved.

Food products

Portion control may be monitored by conducting what is known as a 'yield test'. That is, how many products, (for example, scones) can we obtain from one recipe (see note on standard recipes below)? If there are six scones to a pound of recipe mix then it would be right to assume that if we were catering for 24 persons we would need 4 lb of scone mix.

At this point the scones would be cooked and other factors may be brought into the monitoring process such as length of cooking time, oven temperature and position in the oven. Once the scones have been cooked the yield test would continue with issues such as size of the cooked scone. Has it shrunk? Is it an appealing colour? And, of course, its taste and texture would be checked for customer satisfaction.

All these points would be logged against the cost to produce the scone in the form of cost of ingredients, fuel consumption in the oven, labour cost to produce and any packaging costs to achieve the projected costs versus selling price. You may think this a tedious task for just 24 scones. However, where an operation is producing 24,000 scones, yield is extremely important and any improvement in the production process can make great savings for the establishment.

Earlier we noted that temperature related to storage of food products is not a sampling process, it is a constant one and is a legal requirement when storing or transporting cooked or uncooked food items. It is important to stress this point in the monitoring process. How temperature is checked varies, and can be done via temperature gauges in the freezer, chiller or refrigerator or by using a temperature probe for inserting into the product to check its temperature while in storage.

The use of gauges is often linked to a circular graph which plots the time and temperature of the refrigerator whether it be a chiller or a freezer. This automatic monitoring can be plotted against a full 24-hour cycle and any major variances in temperature can be identified as well as their length. There are strict guidelines for temperature variances (see later in this section).

In conclusion, the monitoring process is a very effective way of ensuring quality in the cooking system and can bring about more cost-effective practices. These in turn will maximize the cost of labour, ensure a quality product and, above all, keep the customer happy.

Standard recipes

While it is quite common for a chef to vary a recipe when using it, the business needs to know that its costs, profits, cash forecasts, etc. will be maintained. This is why standard recipes should be prepared and used on all occasions whenever they are available. Whatever chef prepares the dish, the quality and cost should then remain the same. A standard recipe should always state:

1 The name and quantity of all ingredients
2 The method of production and service instructions
3 The expected yield from that quantity of ingredients.

The standard recipe card may also give details of the equipment to be used – the size of baking tins, for example. Thus the chefs in an establishment that uses a menu that repeats itself fairly regularly will work to the instructions laid down by the standard recipe card. The management can then be sure that they should achieve their target profits, as the

food used by the chefs will be as detailed on the costing sheet and its value will have been included in the selling-price calculation together with the appropriate mark-up to cover all other costs and profit.

Task 4.14

With the support of your tutor and supervisor in the kitchen, conduct a quality test on the production of vegetable lasagne (four portions). Include in your list all the criteria listed in the above cooking issues and also link it to the presentation issues. Present your finding in the form of a report.

▪ EVALUATING THE OPERATION OF FOOD PREPARATION AND COOKING ▪

In this section we look at the planning that is required in the preparation of food. The kitchen is a very busy area and requires much coordination of activities in order to ensure that all tasks are carried out. The chef or supervisor needs to know a lot about staff in order to plan and execute activities, the main points being:

● Skills of his staff
● Ability to coordinate activities
● Ability to follow instructions correctly
● Ability to interpret information from standard recipes or text

With all these factors and, of course, the pressure of time the final point the chef has to consider is the staff's ability to *work under pressure*. Let us look at this more closely.

The importance of skills

This may sound obvious but the chef needs to know this in order to plan the type and range of menus for the hotel or restaurant and/or refectory, industrial restaurant or hospital ward. If the menu is to be balanced then the skill range of the staff needs to be addressed.

Look at the following menu:

Crème Portuguese
(Cream of tomato soup with boiled rice)
Fillet of Sole Bonne Femme
(Poached fillet of sole with cream, white wine, shallots and mushrooms)
Poulet of Sauté Maryland
(Shallow-fried chicken in breadcrumbs, served with sweetcorn pancake, banana fritter, bacon rolls and tomato)
Croquet potatoes, peas and carrots
Soufflé au Citrus
(Hot lemon soufflé)

Let us assume that the chef wants all the menu items to be prepared fresh with no packets, tins or frozen food items being used. Let us look at the menu again in Table 4.10.

As you can see from our one menu, there are many tasks and specific skills required of the chefs and cooks who prepare the dishes. What you have just looked at are a few and the table is by no means comprehensive, nor is it a 'method of work' for each dish. But it does serve to show the complexity and range of skills required by staff in a typical kitchen using fresh produce.

How does it affect the chef's choices?

Where the chef knows who can and who cannot perform certain skills he can mix his staff or change their roles to ensure that he can deliver the course of action. He may choose to use a convenience product (say, frozen chicken

Table 4.10

	Skills tasks
Soup	Knowledge of preparing vegetables and stock Knowledge and skills of Cincassé of (removing skin, seeds and finely chopping tomatoes) Skill of vegetable cuts Preparation of bouquet garni (an envelope using a bay leaf filled with mixed herbs and peppercorns) used for flavour Knowledge of using a roux (mix of fish and flour, cooked to requered stage in order to thicken the soup) Preparing boiled rice to al dente (cooked leaving a little 'bite' in the rice – not too soft)
Fish	Knowledge and skill of filleting and skinning of fish Cuts of vegetables and freshly slicing and chopping vegetables Preparing a roux (see above) Preparing fish stock Making a cream sauce Preparing 'fleurons' (half-moon or crescent-shaped pieces of puff pastry which are baked and used as garnish) Knowledge of poaching fresh fish
Chicken	Preparation of 'rough plucked' poultry (larder work involving removing the innards of chicken) Cutting of chicken into joints Using purée (mixture of flour, egg white and breadcrumbs for cooking the chicken) Preparing frying batter for the banana and sweetcorn pancake Shallow frying of the chicken joints in correct sequence Preparation of the complete dish – garnishing
Vegetables	Preparing potatoes for a croquette mix using a purée (see above) for cooking the potato, shaping of croquette mix into cylinders and deep-frying at the correct temperature Assuming the peas are fresh: Removing peas from the pod Cooking for correct amount of time to ensure a maximum colour and flavour)
Soufflé	Knowledge and skill of: Separating egg white from yolks Preparation of a 'buerre munié' (a mixture of butter and flour for thickening) Zesting and removal of juice from lemon Whisking egg whites Buttering of soufflé in a bain-marié

pieces for the chicken dish) or change the menu to reflect the skills of his staff, either way, in knowing the skills of his staff it does give him a choice. Trial and error is not a good practice to involve yourself in a busy kitchen.

Task 4.15

Look at the menu item below and prepare a skill matrix of the tasks required to produce it. You may use a recipe book to check against if you wish.

'Curried chicken pieces with accompaniments'

Staff notes in the preparation of food

So far we have looked at the skills which may be required of staff and how the choice of menus can affect this. However, there must be some sort of organization and coordination of the team who works under the chef (this is dealt with in Unit 1). However, for the purposes of supporting our work in this section it will not harm to look at certain aspects again.

The Larder Chef

Everyone in the kitchen team needs to know their place and role within the organization. This needs to be confirmed by the chef in giving out the duties and responsibilities for each of his staff. In order to clarify this let us look at one role, the Larder Chef, and use it to explain our point (the same principle will then apply to all staff).

The Larder Chef operates within a public system (see Glossary) and is in charge of this very important area of the kitchen which involves:

- Preparing all butcher's meat for cooking
- Preparing all cold sauces for use within the kitchen such as mayonnaise, vinaigrette, etc.
- Preparing all cold soups on the menu
- Preparation of cheese for use as a course on the menu or for cooking (grating and slicing)

The Larder Chef may be seen as the 'foreman' of the team in the larder and he is responsible to the Chef de Cuisine (head chef) or his deputy the Sous Chef (second or relief chef). The Larder Chef will be responsible for ensuring that:

1 Only good-quality products are used
2 Portion ratios are achieved (amount expected from a range of food)
3 Hygiene, health and safety regulations are adhered to
4 Training of staff within the larder is undertaken
5 Coordination with other areas of the kitchen is obtained
6 Food requirements for the menu of the day are on time
7 Food requirements for future days are organized and commodities are ordered

As you can see, it is a demanding role and where a partial system is in use any hold-up in the larder can affect the other departments. For example, if the rib of beef has not been butchered and trimmed on time then the Roast Chef cannot cook it, causing delay and, even worse, cancellation of the dish from the menu. As we have said, the Larder Chef is one of a team and communication within the team is essential and that is the responsibility of the chef.

Weekly or daily team meetings are required in order to brief staff in the case of the Chef de Portions (the foreman) who in turn relay the duties to their team members. In short duties are explained and confirmed.

Task 4.16

With the aid of a textbook, look at the role of the Pastry Chef. List the roles and responsibilities of this foreman and compare it to our example of the Larder Chef. Are there any major differences?

Resources, equipment and staff in the preparation of food

Continuing with our planning of the preparation of food we now need to turn our thought to how resources, equipment and staff can affect our operation. Earlier we looked at a sample menu and listed the skills required by staff to prepare it. There are, however, other factors which the chef has to consider, i.e.:

● The amount of staff he has
● The menu or menus being offered
● The equipment in the kitchen for preparing the food
● The equipment the restaurant has to serve the food

All these factors will determine the type and quality of the menu which will be available.

Staffing ratios

The number of chefs employed in relation to the number of menus to be served is known as the 'staffing ratio'. This will be affected by the following:

1 Kitchen efficiency
2 Overheads (costs)
3 Type and complexity of the menus
4 Staff capabilities
5 Kitchen equipment
6 Preparation and service time available
7 Expectations of customers

Occasionally part-time staff are employed to increase the staffing to cover peak times such as the service periods of breakfast, lunch and dinner. Functions and banquets will also see a need for part-time staff.

Equipment and resources

As staff are known as a human resource so the equipment is called a physical resource. It has a major part to play in the planning of the preparation of food. Factors that need to be considered include:

● Type of refrigeration at your disposal, whether chillers or freezers
● Available storage space for
  Packet goods
  Frozen goods
  Fresh goods
● Cooking equipment available
● Solid-top space
● Open-top space
● Grills
● Fryers
● Steaming
● Small equipment available
● Service items
● Flatware
● Earthenware
● Heating equipment
  Hot plates
  Bain-marie
  Combination oven

The single largest factor, of course, is the menu itself, because from the menu we derive:

1 The type of dishes
2 The preparation equipment
3 Storage space and type required
4 Above all, the associated skills required of staff

There is a lot of information the chef or supervisor needs to consider, whether that be in a cook–chill, cook–freeze, cook–serve or traditional kitchen. It is important to remember that a lot of the planning is done very early, when the kitchen is being designed, particularly when something new is added to the menu or the chef is asked to prepare for a function which is slightly unusual or very important. You must, however, always plan for the unexpected such as:

- Staff are off ill
- Suppliers let you down
- Additional functions have been booked
- Additional numbers for a function

All these instances do happen and it is always a good idea to have options available to you such as having in stock:

- Convenience products
- Frozen menu items
- Special diet food

These items will help you to react to any emergency and, at the same time, keep the customers happy (as well as staff).

The unexpected can come in the form of:

- Power failure
- Cooking equipment breaks down
- Dishes are spoilt or burnt

It does happen! Once again, having extra items in stock can give you valuable time to choose an alternative approach (e.g. using the microwave or steamer if the oven packs up or if a menu item has been spoilt you can go to the freezer).

The only way you can be sure if your plan has worked is by carrying it out very often in college and schools. Students engage in practical cooking sessions linked to their restaurant, customers, staff dining room or on work experience. In the next few pages we shall look at some example material you might like to use in the role of chef or supervisor within your course. The material will link and cover the purpose of evaluation.

Recipe and method of work sheet

Event   Date   Chef de Cuisine

Menu dish – crumbled breast of chicken with asparagus

Preparation of chicken breasts (supremes)

Supreme – the wing and half the breast of a chicken with the trimmed wing bone attached, i.e. the white meat of one chicken yields two supremes.

Use chicken weighing $1\frac{1}{4}$-$1\frac{1}{2}$ kg ($2\frac{1}{2}$–3 lb)
Cut off both legs from the chicken

Remove the skin from the breasts

Remove the wishbone

Scrape the wing bone bare adjoining the breasts

Cut off the winglets near the joints leaving $1\frac{1}{4}$–2 cm ($\frac{1}{2}$–$\frac{3}{4}$ in.) of bare bone attached to the breasts.

Cut the breasts close to the breastbone and follow the bone down to the wing joint

Cut through the joint

Lay the chicken on its side and pull the supremes off assisting with the knife

Lift the fillets from the supremes and remove the sinew from each

Make an incision lengthways, along the thick side of the supremes, open and place the fillets inside

Close, lightly flatten with a bat moistened with water and trim if necessary

Chef de Cuisine

Checklist

1 Menu agreed with tutor
2 Alteration to menu (if used)
3 Numbers being catered for
4 Special diets (if any)
5 Food order substantiated to store keeper
6 All commodities can be obtained
7 Menu given to food service staff
8 Explanation of dishes given to food service staff
9 Duties and roles to kitchen staff
10 Explanation of food preparation requirements to kitchen staff
11 Advanced preparation required
12 Special equipment required
13 Service arrangements discussed

The checklist is seen as one way of ensuring that the major points for your exercise are entered. It is not meant to be prescriptive and you may build on it with other points if you so wish. It does, however, go some way towards providing evidence of your own contribution to the exercise (see Table 4.11).

The next example is stationery you may wish to use for staffing of the exercise. It includes details such as:

- Names of staff
- Their section
- Dishes to be prepared
- References
- Service particulars
- Notes for staff

Table 4.11 Event – French evening, date 14 March, Chef de Cuisine John Smith

Section	Staff	Dishes to be prepared	Comments	Service arrangements
First courses and starters	Mary Sawyer Richard Dunn	French onion soup Snails in garlic butter		Earthenware soup bowl Soup topped with cheese
Fish	Alison Moyer	Poached fillet of sole in white wine sauce with shallots and mushrooms		Plated, served with puff pastry. Fleuron and mushroom
Meat	Claudine Ambler Thomas Hardy	Shallow fried chicken breast with asparagus tips. Roast loin of lamb with orange and ginger sauce	As recipe sheet issued	Loin of lamb to be sliced and plated Chicken in bread crumbs served from flat
Vegetables and potatoes	Peter Hardey Bridget Maddock	Boullangère potatoes Mixed peas and carrots	As recipe sheet issued	The croquettes in the portion
Desserts	Christine Parry Paul Chatton	Poached pears in red wine Lemon soufflé pudding Bread rolls		Pear served in individual glass cups Fresh custard sauce with soufflé pudding

Notes
Advanced preparation required:
Larder work for chicken breasts
Larder work for loin of lamb
Poached pears to be prepared and soaked in red wine

Recipe and method – four portions

Crumbed breast of chicken with four portions Asparagus

	4 supremes of chicken	
25 g	seasoned flour	1 oz
	1 egg	
50 g	bread crumbs	2 oz
	For frying	
50 g	oil	20 oz
50 g	butter	2 oz
200 g	asparagus pureé	½ lb
	For finishing	
50 g	butter	2 oz
60 ml	juslié	⅛ pt

Pané the chicken supremes.

Shake off all surplus crumbs.

Neaten and mark on one side with a palette knife.

Heat the oil and butter in a sauté pan.

Gently fry the supremes to a golden brown on both sides (68 min).

Dress the supremes on a silver flat and keep warm.

Mask the supremes with the remaining 50 g (2 oz) butter cooked to the nutbrown stage.

Surround the supremes with a cordon of juslié.

Garnish each supreme with a neat bundle of asparagus points (previously cooked, refreshed and reheated with a little butter).

Place a cutlet frill on to each wing bone and serve.

Recipe and method sheet

The recipe and method sheet would be used to support where a dish is taken from a nqn-standard text which our colleges do not have, or an amendment to a dish has taken place to suit skills of staff or service arrangements. Note that the number of portions indicated is for four. Obviously this recipe would be increased to cater for the number required.

Production log

The production log will assist you in planning the duties of your staff and should help the staff in reaching targets within the timescale available (Table 4.12). You will note that as one section is cleaned down it assists another who is not yet at the service point. This team approach is imperative when you have only a small number of staff. Teamwork also helps in that a greater number of tasks may be carried out with a shared workload so that too much work is not placed on any one individual. The chef can adapt this principle particularly when a section is behind schedule. If the team are used to helping each other then they can expect the same when they are experiencing difficulties.

We continue with our example material, which can be applied to suit our 'French evening' example or for a central production exercise with volume production of food using cook–chill or cook–freeze. The principles of the example are exactly the same. Let us look at a checklist for evaluating an exercise – in this case our 'French evening'.

Evaluation checklist

1 Do not personalize an evaluation, remain objective
2 Present an evaluation in report format
3 Include the positive aspects, do not concentrate on negative aspects only
4 Establish criteria to evaluate against
5 Make recommendations for future use
6 Link the evaluation to customer feedback
7 Present your findings as soon as possible after the event (but allow a little time to mull over your findings)
8 Give a debriefing to your colleagues when complete

Table 4.12 Production log Event – French evening, date 14 March, Chef de Cuisine

Section	4.30–5.30 p.m.	5.30–6.30 p.m.	6.30–7.00 p.m.	7.00–7.30 p.m.	7.00–8.00 p.m.	8.00–8.30 p.m.	8.30–9.00 p.m.
First course		Prepare soup Correct seasoning Snails – fill shells, Prepare services dishes	Correct soup, finish croquettes, warm snails Warm soup bowls Warm soup bowls (hotplate)	Service of first courses	Cream		
Fish	Filleting and skinning of fish – make fish stock	Prepare poaching dishes Butter, season and fold plaice fillets Prepare shallots and mushrooms	Prepare white wine sauce Keep half of it to poach fish	Prepare and cook Cook off fish Correct if sauce with cooking liquor	Service of fish course	Clean down	Assist main course
Main	Check prepared supremes Check prepared loins of lamb Cook loins	Prepare, trim and cook asparagus tips Prepare the chicken breasts	Prepare orange and ginger sauce Seal off chicken breasts	Remove lamb allow to cool Check sauce Prepare plates and flatware for service	Slice plaice and lamb Cool off chicken	Service of main course	Clean down
Vegetables	Remove flatware trolleys and all service requirements for all courses	Prepare potatoes and onion layer in dishes	Prepare carrots and peas Cut carrots, blanch and refresh	Cook boulangère potatoes Arrange service dishes	Finish carrots and peas Check potatoes	Service of vegetables	Clean down
Desserts	Prepare dough for bread rolls	Prepare ingredients for lemon soufflé Pinch butter and shape bread rolls – egg wash	Cool off bread rolls Prepare egg custard put in bain-marie	Grease and sugar soufflé dishes Prepare soufflé mix – fill soufflé dishes	Prepare bread baskets Fill coupes with poached pears and garnish	Cook off soufflé, keep warm	Service of desserts

Evaluation criteria

The menu

Balance, colour and texture of dishes

Suitability for the event

Demands on equipment for preparation and service

Food ordering

Quality of produce obtained

Were all commodities ordered?

Shortages – what were they?

Additions required – what were they?

Preparation of food items

Was the *mise en place* conducted well?

Did staff collect ingredients in correct quantities?

Were commodities stored correctly when not in use?

Was there a logical approach to tasks?

Did the tasks sequence against production log?

Cooking of food items

Was food cooked in correct order?

Were there any items over- or under-cooked?

Was there any wastage of food items?

Was food corrected for serving, prior to service?

Presentation of food

Was food presented in correct manner?

Was colour taken into account when garnishing?

Plated items – were plates cleaned before service?

Were garnishes delicate and not 'chunky'?

Did food look appealing?

Staff

Did staff respond to duties given?

Did staff work in an orderly fashion?

Did staff clean as they worked?

Were trimmings put into correct waste areas?

Were good skills displayed in preparation and cooking of food?

Did staff work well as a team?

Did staff work well as individuals?

Were recipes and methods followed correctly?

Did staff taste the food prior to service?

Cleaning down

Was the kitchen left in a clean and orderly fashion?

Were items requiring refrigeration put away?

Were utensils checked before putting away?

Was specialist equipment checked prior to storage?

Food costing

Were financial targets achieved?

Was there an overspend?

Were portion ratios adhered to?

Were foods returned to stores recorded?

Customer care

Did the customers enjoy their meal?

What were the strengths of the menu?

What were the weaknesses of the menu?

Was it value for money?

Was food hot (when it should not have been)?

Was food cold (when it should have been warm)?

What did customers think of the taste and textures of the food on the menu?

Were there any delays in the service of the food?

Finally there should be an evaluation of your own contribution within the exercise. Again do not be too critical but do be objective. Factors you should consider are:

Planning

Was there sufficient planning?

Was there attention to detail?

Was there good communication between you and colleagues, prior to the event?

Were written instructions prepared as guidelines for colleagues?

Was the food order prepared correctly?

Was the food order submitted on time?

Did you prepare a production log?

Were you in the kitchen before your colleagues arrived?

Execution

Did you give clear and concise instructions to your staff?

Were you in authority and did you show good leadership?

Were you calm at all times?

If anything unexpected occurred did you handle it well?

Was there effective communication between you and the head waiter or restaurant manager?

Was guidance required and did you feel confident in demonstrating skills?

Evaluation

Have you conducted an evaluation?

Is it in report style?

Is it objective?

Does it personalize any issues?

Have you given an overall conclusion as to your impression of how the event went?

Have you thanked your team for their effort?

The previous pages were intended to help you cope with the role of supervisor in a production setting. Not everything has been included but, in general, most has. If you use it for guidance then you will be able to address the areas of 'planning and evaluating' within the Food Preparation and Cooking unit. Good luck!

Assignment activity

Scenario

As a catering manager within an industrial catering unit, you have been asked to investigate a suitable food-preparation and cooking system to replace the existing outdated system in present use. You have been asked within your findings to provide a comparison of two different systems in order to provide a choice of design, labour and production costs.

On completion of your investigations you are required to prepare a report on your findings of which you should include factors relating to:

1 Appropriateness of systems
2 Resources required for each system
3 Health and safety implications for each system

Your budget amounts to £250 to install the new system and it is expected that projected costs be included as part of your report.

Present scenario

Unit operates with 15 staff

Units caters of 600 meals per day, made up of:

● Breakfast
● Lunch
● Supper for nightshift

There is a small vending service for hot drinks only.

There are two dining areas, one for the workforce seating 500, one for office staff catering for 100.

Assessment coverage

Investigate a range of food preparation and cooking methods/systems

Performance criteria

● Methods/systems in current use are described
● Methods/systems are matched to the requirements of different outlets in the hospitality and catering industry
● Skills required at different levels for the methods/systems are correctly described
● Staff resources are realistically estimated in relation to methods/systems
● Legal aspects relating to hygiene, health and safety as they affect food preparation and cooking are identified and described

Core skills

Communication:
Elements 3.1, 3.2, 3.4

Information technology:
Elements 3.2, 3.3

Application of numbers:
Element 3.1

Assessment activity 1: Plan and organize cooking methods/systems

Scenario

As an employee in a catering design and planning consultancy, your company have given you an exercise to provide a guidance portfolio for prospective clients. As part of this portfolio they have asked you to supply general information on cooking systems such as cook–serve, cook–store–serve and have asked you to provide a detailed plan of one of them as an example The plan is required to show:

- Detailed plan of an outlet catering for 300 meals per day
- Details of suggested equipment to suit the system chosen
- How the system can be sequenced to provide maximum benefit to staff and management
- The effect on skills required by new and existing staff which may be incorporated into the operation
- Health and safety requirements which apply in the system and design chosen

The plan is to be suggested with the written guidance in the form of a manual. You are asked to supply a key to your plan linked to an appropriate scale for the drawing.

Assessment coverage

Investigate a range of food preparation and cooking methods/systems

Performance criteria

- Methods/systems in current use are described
- Methods/systems are matched to the requirements of different outlets in the hospitality and catering industry
- Skills required at different levels for the methods/systems are correctly described
- Staff resources are realistically estimated in relation to methods/systems
- Legal aspects relating to hygiene, health and safety as they affect food preparation and cooking are identified and described

Core skills
Communication:
Elements 3.1, 3.2, 3.4

Information technology:
Elements 3.2, 3.3

Application of numbers:
Element 3.1

Assessment activity 2: Implement a plan for preparing and cooking food

In the role of catering supervisor choose one of the three activities listed:

1 Central production unit (cook–store–serve)
2 Theme event (food production)
3 Counter service (food preparation)

From your chosen event, prepare a proposal for consideration by your instructor in outline form for menu, cost and organization required.

Subject to approval by your instructor:

Stage 1
Implement your chosen event taking into account the following considerations,

- You are required to submit the relevant food order for the event
- Provide details of roles and responsibilities of staff for the event
- Provide recipes and portion ratios for dishes chosen
- Detail hygiene, food safety and storage requirements that will be required (particularly if cook–store–serve system is chosen)
- Prepare a production log for the event

Stage 2
Conduct an evaluation of your event and present in report format information related to criteria you felt most important. Your evaluation should be presented within one week of conclusion of your event.

Assessment coverage

Implement a plan for preparing and cooking food

Stage 1

Performance criteria

- Staff allocation, taking account of skills required and skill levels, is carried out
- Staff roles are explained and confirmed
- Staff roles and timing of operation are logged according to appropriate monitoring
- Processes
- Plan is carried out in accordance with resource and staff allocation
- Own contribution to system is carried out and recorded
- Practices relating to hygiene, health and safety are observed, carried out and monitored
- Unexpected factors are handled appropriately

Core skills

Communication:
Elements 3.1, 3.2, 3.4

Information technology:
Element 3.4

Application of numbers:
Elements 3.1, 3.2

Evaluate the operation of food preparation and cooking methods/systems

Stage 2

Performance criteria

- Evaluation is relevant and covers all factors in the operation
- Appropriate sources are used to gather sufficient information to evaluate against monitoring criteria
- Opportunities for, and obstacles to, improving the operation are identified and explained
- Unanticipated factors affecting the operation are identified and explained
- Own contribution to the operation is evaluated

Core skills

Communication:
Elements 3.1, 3.2, 3.4

Information technology:
Element 3.4

Application of numbers:
Elements 3.1, 3.2

Test your knowledge

1 What are the *main* aims of the following laws?
   Food Safety Act 1990
   Food Hygiene (Amendment) Regulations 1990 and 1991
   Food Hygiene (General) Regulations 1970
   Food Labelling Regulations 1984
   Health and Safety at Work etc. Act 1974
   Dangerous Machines Order 1964
   Control of Substances Hazardous to Health Regulations 1988
2 What are the correct chill storage temperatures for:
   Steak and kidney pies, which are to be served hot?
   Pork pies?
   A whole Brie cheese?
   Cheesecake to be served as a cold dessert?
3 At 10.00 am a hospital kitchen is preparing sandwiches, which are to be sold during the lunchtime service, between 12.00 noon and 2.00 p.m. The sandwich preparation area is in a cooler part of the kitchen, away from the main cooking equipment. Are the regulations being observed? Explain your answer.
4 How may food handlers ensure that they may use the due diligence defence? Make a list of ten important procedures.
5 What are your responsibilities, when you are at work, under HASAWA 1974?
6 How can our employers ensure our health and safety in the workplace?
7 Why would you find the following notice near a machine?

```
┌─────────────────────────────────┐
│            WARNING              │
│   This machine must not be      │
│  operated by untrained staff or │
│   persons under the age of 18   │
└─────────────────────────────────┘
```

Assessment brief 4.1

Assignment title: What do we mean by the
hospitality industry?

Name:

Portfolio reference number: Date:

Task

For the sector of the industry you have been
allocated:

1 Find out:
   The size of the main outlets
   The number of employees
   The services and products provided
2 Provide a description of your sector

Vocational coverage	Evidence produced	Achieved	Not achieved
Unit:1 Element: 1.1 Performance criteria: PC1			

Core skill coverage	Evidence produced	Achieved	Not achieved
Unit: Communication Element: 3.3 Performance criteria: PC1 PC2 PC3			

Assessor signature   Candidate signature

Assessment brief 4.2

Assignment title: Cook–chill operations

Name:

Portfolio reference number: Date:

Task

Write a report discussing the way a cook–chill
system works, taking into account the
following:

- Equipment necessary to implement the process;
- Cost effectiveness in relation to other types of catering systems;
- Types of establishments which benefit from cook–chill systems;
- Temperatures and storage times involved;
- Advantages and disadvantages of the system;
- The operation of cleaning schedules;
- Recommended procedures which are used to make the food safe

Vocational coverage	Evidence produced	Achieved	Not achieved
Unit: 4 Element: 4.1 Performance criteria: PC1 PC2 PC3 PC4 PC5			

Core skill coverage	Evidence produced	Achieved	Not achieved
Unit: Communication Element: 3.2 Performance criteria: PC1 PC2 PC3 PC4			

Assessor signature   Candidate signature

Sources of information

Croner's Catering covers legislations of
importance to the hospitality and catering
industry and is regularly updated

Food Sense, London SE99 7TT Tel: 081 694 8862

HMSO Publications Centre (mail, fax and
telephone orders) PO Box 276, London
SW8 5DT

Telephone orders   071-873 9090
General enquiries   071-873 0011
Fax orders   071-873 8200

Ministry of Agriculture, Fisheries and Food,
Consumer Protection Division, Nobel House,
17 Smith Square, London SW1P 3JR

Ministry of Agriculture, Fisheries and Food, The Food Safety Directorate, Room 303a Ergon House, c/o Nobel House, 17 Smith Square, London SW1P 3HX Tel: 071-238 6550

The Institution of Environmental Health Offices, Chadwick House, Rushworth Street, London SE1 0QT Tel: 071-928 6006

Further reading

Croner's Catering, Croner Publications, Kingston-upon-Thames (1993)

Department of Health, *Clean Food*, HMSO, London (1992)

Department of Health Guidelines for the Catering Industry on the Food Hygiene (Amendment) Regulations 1990 and 1991, HMSO, London (1992)

Department of Health *Chilled and Frozen Guidelines on Cook–Chill and Cook–Freeze Catering Systems*, HMSO, London (1993)

HM Government, *The Food Safety Act 1990 and You*, 1991

Fire Safety Management in Hotels and Boarding Houses, HMSO, London (1991)

The Institution of Environmental Health Officers, *The Food Hygiene Handbook*, Highfield Publications, Wakefield (1987)

Ministry of Agriculture, Fisheries and Food, *Understanding Food Labels* (1991)

Core skills which you should experience

	Working with others	*Improve own learning and performance*	*Problem solving*
Level 1	1 Work to given collective goals and responsibilities. 2 Use given working methods in fulfilling own responsibilities.	3 Agree short-term targets. 4 Follow given activities to learn and to improve performance.	5 Select standard solutions to fully-describe problems.
Level 2	1 Work to given collective goals and provide feedback to help with the allocation of responsibilities. 2 Use given working methods in fulfilling own responsibilities, and provide feedback to others on own progress.	3 Contribute to identifying strengths and learning needs, and agree short-term targets. 4 Make use of feedback in following given activities to learn to improve performance.	5 Use established procedures to clarify routine problems. 6 Select standard solutions to routine problems.

Core skills which you should experience (continued)

	Working with others	*Improve own learning and performance*	*Problem solving*
Level 3	1 Work to given collective goals and contribute to the process of allocating individuals' responsibilities. 2 Agree working methods and use them, and provide feedback to others on own progress.	3 Identify strengths and learning needs, and agree short-term targets. 4 Seek and make use of feedbacks, follow given activities to learn and to improve performance.	5 Select procedures to clarify problems with a range of possible solutions. 6 Identify alternative solutions and select solutions to problems.
Level 4	1 Contribute to determining collective goals and to the process of allocating individuals' responsibilities. 2 Agree working methods and use them, and contribute to the process of maintaining standards of work.	3 Identify strengths and learning needs, and propose and agree short-term targets. 4 Seek and make use of feedback, select and follow activities to learn and to improve performance.	5 Extend specialist knowledge in order to clarify complex problems with a range of possible solutions. 6 Identify alternative solutions and select solutions to complex problems.
Level 5	1 Lead the process of determining collective goals and allocating individuals' responsibilities. 2 Agree working methods and use them, monitor overall progress of own and others' work.	3 Identify strengths and learning needs, and propose and agree long-term targets. 4 Seek and make use of feedback, select and follow a wide range of activities to learn and to improve performance.	5 Extend specialist knowledge in order to clarify complex problems with a range of possible solutions which include unknown/unpredictable features 6 Identify alternative solutions and select solutions to complex problems which include unpredictable features

FOOD AND DRINK SERVICES

This unit enables us to obtain a better understanding of the requirements of the hospitality and catering industry with regards to food and drink services. The outlets of the industry offering food and drink are many and varied, providing a wide variety of different styles of service to meet our customers' requirements. The unit enables you to obtain the underpinning knowledge required in order for you to provide a food and drink service, when working in a practical environment either in your own school or college or within the industry. The knowledge to be gained is directly applicable to the work and work methods of food and drink services. The unit enables you to gain knowledge and experience in planning and evaluating a food and drink service in which you will have gained some practical experience. It includes:

- Investigating the types of food and drink prepared and served in differing outlets
- The skills required and training needs
- The factors which contribute to a food and drink service operation
- Customer requirements
- The different types of service
- The requirements necessary to offer a food and drink service
- The planning, implementing and monitoring of a food and drink service

▪ THE VARIOUS SYSTEMS USED IN FOOD AND DRINK SERVICES ▪

Styles of service

Table 5.1 lists the types of outlets available within catering operations and matches it with styles of service used. This will help you later in establishing skills associated with them. Why are different forms of service required? Table 5.1 lists outlets and matches the types of service normally associated with them but we need to understand why these forms of service are required.

Hotels

It would appear that hotels use the widest range of food service systems. The reason for this is

that they offer more than the service of a meal. Depending on the type and size of the hotel, the facilities on offer could include:

- Function rooms
- Different styles of dining area, (bistro, coffee bar, formal restaurant, brasserie, public bar)
- Banqueting suite
- Leisure complex
- Conference area
- Private hotel suites

Because the facilities are greater the service systems offered need to reflect this. For example, function rooms may be used for weddings, parties, charity dinners, etc. which may require Plated, Full Silver, Buffet or, in some circumstances, Family styles of service dependent on numbers, whereas the 'formal' restaurant will seat fewer people but will offer a full Silver or even Guéridon style of service.

Table 5.1

Outlet	Service system
Hotels	Family, Modified Silver, Full Silver, Buffet, Guéridon, Room Service, Banquet
Restaurants	Family, Plated, Modified Silver, Full Silver, Guéridon, Banquet
Cafés	Plated, Family, Modified Silver
Public houses	Plated, Buffet, Family, Modified Silver
Fast-food/take-aways	Counter
Institutional (hospital, school, etc.)	Counter, Plated Buffet
Industrial	Counter, Plated Automatic Vending, Modified Silver
Transport sector	
Air	Plated
Train	Counter, Modified Silver
Ship/ferries	Counter, Buffet, Full Silver

The price the customer is prepared to pay often dictates the style and quality of the service as well as the category of hotel itself. The tourist boards and road agencies use a crown or star system and the AA and RAC a star system. There are minimum requirements for awarding a crown to a hotel and these are as shown in Table 5.2.

Task 5.1

Define the expectations of a customer staying in a 4-crown hotel. What style of service could the customer expect? What facilities could the customer expect? What tariff would the customer expect to pay for overnight accommodation? Examine how many 4-crown hotels there are in your area.

Restaurants

Next to hotels, restaurants have a wide variety of service systems and in many ways have the same reasons for offering them. Restaurants, however, are involved in only one aspect and that is the provision of a meal. This does not mean that they do not perform functions such as weddings or other forms of celebration such as parties, but they would not normally have associated facilities such as entertainment, disco or cabaret. Some public house restaurants, however, offer a function room adjacent for such entertainment.

The style of service adopted will be dependent on the type of restaurant. These can be categorized as:

● *Ethnic* such as Chinese or Indian
● *French* offering classical dishes
● *Bistro* less formal with a mixture of classical and modern presentations
● *Brassiere* combination of wine bar and bistro
● *Speciality* kebab houses, tavernas and trattorias or pizzerias
● *Steak house* Beefeater, Porterhouse and Harvester restaurants
● *Traditional English* Langan's Brasserie, Simpson's-in-the-Strand, Harry Ramsden's in Yorkshire
● *Fast food* McDonald's, Wimpy, Burger King (known as hamburger restaurants)

Let us now look at the service styles associated with those restaurants we list in Table 5.1.

Ethnic

Most ethnic restaurants offer a combination of modified Silver or Family style of service. This is because the dishes are often individual and have extensive accompaniments such as boiled or fried rice, curry trays offering diced apple, chutneys, coconut, etc. There is a very sociable element in eating in ethnic restaurants. They involve the use of 'turntables' on the dining table in order to circulate the dishes to your eating partners or a 'hot plate' for keeping the

Table 5.2 Crown criteria

Type	Bedrooms	Bathrooms	WCs	General
1 crown	1 A lock to be fitted that will ensure privacy for guests and security for their property 2 Guests to be provided with the keys being kept by management 3 Minimum bed sizes (except children's beds): single beds 6'3" × 3' (190 cm × 90 cm); Double 6'3" × 4'6" (190 cm × 137 cm) 4 Nylon bed linen not acceptable 5 Fresh soap for each new letting 6 Washbasin, with hot and cold running water available at all reasonable times, either in the bedroom or in a private bathroom 7 A light controlled from the bed 8 Mirror, with light, above or adjacent to washbasin 9 A 13 amp socket or suitable adaptor 10 Electric razor point adaptor available 11 One chair or equivalent per guest (minimum of two in family room) 12 Heating without extra charge 13 Resident guests permitted access to their bedrooms at all times	1 At least one bathroom equipped with a bath or shower for every 10 resident guests (other than guests in bedrooms with private bath or shower) 2 At least one bathroom to be for the sole use of guests	1 At least one WC for every 8 resident guests other than in bedrooms with private WC 2 Where there is only one WC it must not be in a bathroom and must be for the sole use of resident guests	1 Reception facility or bell to call for attention 2 Lounge area(s) with adequate number of easy chairs 3 Resident guests allowed access to lounge areas at all reasonable times 4 Use of a telephone 5 Tourist information available
2 crown	1 Double beds to have bedside lights or a single bedhead light. Single beds to have a bedside or bedhead light (twin beds may share a bedside light), in addition to a light controlled from the door 2 Double beds to have access from both sides 3 Electric razor point (near a mirror)			1 Dining/breakfast room separate from lounge (unless meals served only in bedrooms) 2 Early morning tea/coffee, served in bedrooms on request (unless beverage making facilities in bedrooms) 3 Hot beverages available on request in evening (unless beverage making facilities in bedrooms or nearby) 4 Early morning call, on request (or alarm clocks in bedrooms) 5 Colour TV in lounge (if no TV in bedrooms and signal available) 6 Assistance with luggage on request

Type	Bedrooms	Bathrooms	WCs	General
3 crown	1 At least 33% of bedrooms to have a private bath or shower and WC en-suite 2 One easy chair (plus one other chair if twin or double room) 3 Full length mirror 4 Luggage stand 5 Fixed heating, having automatic and individual control			1 Proprietor and/or staff available throughout the day 2 A lounge area, separate from a bar or TV lounge 3 Automatically controlled fixed heating in public areas 4 Shoe-cleaning facilities 5 Iron and ironing board available on request 6 Hair dryer available on request 7 Pay telephone
4 crown	1 At least 25% of bedrooms to have a private bath or shower and WC en-suite 2 One easy chair per adult guest (minimum of 2 per family room) 3 Radio and colour TV, if signal available 4 Telephone capable of making external calls			1 Access available to the establishment at all times 2 Passenger lift in establishments with four or more floors, including ground floor 3 Writing tables, if comparable facilities not available in bedrooms 4 Lounge service until 2400 hours 5 Toiletries, message taking, newspapers, etc. available on request
5 crown	1 All bedrooms to have private bath, fixed shower attachment and WC en-suite 2 Direct-dial telephone 3 Writing table, or equivalent, with appropriate seat 4 Trouser press (or valet service) 5 One or more suites available			1 Room service 2 All-night lounge 3 Hour return service for laundry (except at weekends) 4 Night porter

individual dishes hot while you are eating. In certain restaurants they will use a heated 'iron plate' set into a wooden tray. This is another form of 'hot plate' but has a dramatic 'sizzling' effect at the table. All this helps to create an exciting atmosphere where the differing cooking smells help in stimulating appetites.

French

The French restaurant is an expensive dining experience. This may be the case in England but is far from being so in its native country, where the service is less formal. French restaurants in the UK take two forms, one like the original in France with a less formal atmosphere similar to a 'bistro' and the other is situated in a town or city high street with extensive furbishment and very high prices. In the latter establishment we would find a combination of full Silver service and Guéridon service to complement the range of classical dishes and wines, whereas the less formal French restaurant would embrace a Family style service with a high proportion of dishes Plated. In both types of restaurant, however, we would find a wide range of French wines which is often the hallmark of quality restaurants.

Speciality restaurants

Here we find a real mix of service styles, from the Italian pizzeria with its traditional Plated service to the Greek taverna combining a range of Plated and Family service and the kebab house offering true skill and 'display' techniques with the 'Shaslik' sword or, more commonly, skewered dishes of lamb or fish. Either way, the service offered is in line with the traditional culture of the respective country but sometimes amended to suit more localized tastes. The success of the speciality restaurant is very often due to the personality of the 'patron' and his or her staff apart from the quality and authenticity of the dishes.

Steakhouse

One of the most successful types of restaurant in the UK is more often than not associated with a brewery such as Whitbread, John Smith or Burton. This attachment is historic due to the traditional inns and coaching houses owned by the brewery in the early days of travel in the UK.

The steakhouse offers a range of traditional dishes such as beef steaks, grills and fish dishes in a pub setting. These days, however, they have adopted a more Family approach, offering dishes suitable for children with marketing tests such as catering for children's parties.

Whitbread's Beefeater offers the very popular 'Mr Men' choice of meals for children with games, party hats and badges to accompany them. This Family approach is often limited to specific times of the day such as the 'tea-time' meal or 'Early Bird' dinner with cheaper prices to encourage the customer to take them.

The style of service is mainly Plated but sometimes can include Modified Silver. The chain steakhouse restaurants are actively changing their image of limited dining by widening the choice of dishes to include pastry and vegetarian options as well as chicken, turkey and ethnic dishes such as Samosas and onion bhajees, thus bringing them into a wider band of restaurants offering accommodation as well such as the Travel Inn operation of Whitbread.

Traditional English

Some caterers would argue that this type of restaurant is a myth with all the various styles of restaurants available today, with some including traditional dishes such as roast beef or steak and kidney pudding. There are, however, some restaurants specifically catering for the English requirement such as Langan's Brasserie. Here we find traditional English dishes served in a traditional manner but in an environment which is more similar to the expensive French restaurant. The wines, too, are a mixture of English and European.

The service we find in establishments such as Langan's Brasserie is Full Silver and this is reflected in the patronage that this type of restaurant has. It is frequented by international as well as British film stars, writers, actors and Members of Parliament. It proves the point that good English cuisine can hold its own provided it has fresh produce, cooked well and served correctly.

Fast-food and take-away restaurants

These are definitely the biggest growth industry in the UK. With more people having less time to prepare their meals in the home they have turned to the convenience product and the fast-food and take-away market.

Operators such as McDonald's, Burger King and Wimpy have expanded their businesses throughout the UK and provide a quick and effective product which suits both young and old. Their marketing strategies are based on high-profile aggressive campaigns via television, media and billboards. They cater for children in a way that makes it difficult for parents to avoid taking them to their units, and include play areas, games, T-shirts, toys and packaging which attracts the child's eye. Campaigns such as McDonald's using characters like 'Ronald McDonald' are highly effective in catching the children's market which in turn captures the adult one too!

Geography also plays all-important part. Units are always situated in high street shopping areas, shopping precincts and retail leisure parks, ensuring a high volume of business.

To cater for this high-volume turnover counter service is often used with several queuing points to cut down on congestion. With 'high-tech' equipment they can cater for hundreds of customers who frequent them. Because of the intense marketing of the fast-food giants, the customers always know what to expect of the product and inevitably get it.

Some fast-food operators now offer a drive-through area for customers in transit. These units are invariably on retail parks adjacent to major road networks, thus again ensuring a high volume of business.

The nature of the fast-food market has made it highly competitive and the giants of the industry have made life hard for the traditional fast-food outlet such as the fish and chip shop. These have reacted by increasing their product range, opening more frequently and updating their premises.

Novel approaches have also been adopted to consider the effects of the big operators. These include door-to-door service via businesses such as 'Dial-a-pizza' and Chinese or Indian take-away brought to customers' homes. This service has caught on and is a very convenient way to obtain a meal in the comfort of one's own home.

Task 5.2

List as many fast-food establishments you can think of that are in your area. Ask your friends which they use or have dined in, which is their favourite menu choice and accompanying drink and score each question. Use a sample of 20 people to obtain your results. Try to use the same age group as yourself. Once completed, prepare a league table of your results, e.g.:

- *Top establishment*
- *Top meal*
- *Top drink*

Skills in food and drink systems

In the previous section we discussed the styles of service used in various operations. Now we must look at the skills required of personnel working with them before we commence (see Table 5.3).

Table 5.3

Service style	Associated skills
Counter	Good social skills Good personal dress Ability to work under pressure Ability to conduct cash transactions correctly Good organizational skills
Full Silver service	Good social skills Good personal dress Skill in handling equipment Thorough knowledge of menu products Good organizational skills Good presentational skills Ability to work within a team
Guéridon service	Good social skills Good personal dress High degree of skill in preparing a range of food Items Thorough knowledge of menu products Good organizational skills Good presentational skills Ability to work under pressure and in close proximity to customers
Family service	Good social skills Good personal dress Good dexterity in using equipment Good organizational skills Ability to work under pressure Good clearing skills
Banquet service	Good social skills Good personal dress Highly dextrous in use of equipment Ability to work under pressure Good organizational skills Good presentational skills Good clearing skills Ability to work as a team member
Plate service	Good social skills Good personal dress Dextrous in carrying plates Good clearing skills
Home delivery	Thorough knowledge of area Good social skills Ability to conduct cash transactions correctly

Task 5.3

Write down all the social skills you feel would be required of a hotel receptionist. Keep your notes handy and refer to them once this section has been worked through.

Having now established the prime skills associated with each of the styles of service, let us now look back at Task 5.3. This member of staff was chosen because the receptionist is invariably the first point of contact for a visiting guest and in many ways it is the same for the person waiting on at the table or counter for a customer. He or she is the link and representative of the establishment. For a receptionist we would expect good social skills, good personal dress, good organizational ability and an ability to work under pressure. These are common with all our skills for service. The specific skills differ, however, as with the receptionist the specific skills could be sales and marketing techniques, computing skills, local knowledge of area, etc.

In conclusion, we can define the associated skills with service systems as 'general' and 'specific'. These skills will vary and will depend on the type and style of service being offered.

Task 5.4

What are the general and specific skills associated with cocktail bar staff?

In this section we will look at the benefits and constraints associated with the styles of service we described in the previous section. The catering operator needs to establish them in order to check the viability of offering them and the implications on business. The best way of doing this is by using three headings:

1 Style of service
2 Benefits in operating it
3 Constraints on operating it

These are listed in Table 5.4.

Task 5.5

Using the section on benefits and constraints complete the following table against the style of service. On completion, suggest which one maximizes its business potential.

Key
CE – Cost effective
FS – Flexible service
LSR – Low skill requirement
HSR – High skill requirement
HPR – High physical resource required
LPR – Low physical resource required

	CE	FS	LSR	HSR	HPR	LPR
Counter service						
Full silver service						
Banquet service						
Guéridon service						
Plate service						
Take away						

Skills and training needs

In the previous sections we have looked at styles of service, types of service and the benefits and constraints of each of them. In order for any establishment to maintain quality of service and products for the customer it must continually monitor its performance of staff and, where deficiencies exist, react to them whether in the form of a physical resource such as a new piece of equipment or the training of staff in the correct use of it. Staff training is a vital component of any operation. Without it systems and processes may break down, which may eventually result in loss of custom.

In order for training to be undertaken it is necessary to conduct an audit of the skills required within the establishment and those that your staff possess, those that they do not have and those that need updating. As examples, we have chosen the area of Silver service and Guéridon service, as these two styles embrace the majority of skills the service practitioner may be expected to possess. We consider the skills under the following headings:

● Manipulative
● Communication
● Preventional
● Motivational
● Organizational

Manipulative skills

● Use of spoon and fork for service (dexterity)
● Carving and filleting techniques
● Use of chafing pan and flare lamp
● Clearing techniques

Communication skills

1 *Social skills* Ability to converse with the customer
2 *Product knowledge* Ability to advise and indicate to the customer what is happening in the cooking process

Table 5.4

Style of service	Benefits	Constraints
Counter	Very cost effective Low skill requirement, very controllable Close proximity to production	Queuing required High-cost equipment Not flexible High associated costs Rates, marketing, etc. high street locations
Full Silver	Customer experiences full and attentive service Opportunities for selling exist Ability to cater for different clients Ability to cater for different functions	More service equipment required More staff required Labour costs higher Portering control may fluctuate Customer turnover lower Time consuming for staff
Guéridon service	Opportunity to display Customer-specific (small numbers) Relaxed dining experience for customer	Higher labour cost Low turnover of customers Menu costs high Inflexible form of service Time consuming for customers
Family service	Less time consuming than full silver service Opportunity for customer to participate Sociable form of dining Suits families with children	High volume of service Equipment required Careful portion control from kitchen Limits menu variety, time consuming Lots of space required Seasonality of business Less labour intensive
Banquet service	High volume of business can be catered for Set menus can be used	High labour requirement Equipment requirements are high
Plate service	Very controllable for operator Portion control maintained Easy to serve Low skill requirement Presentation of food is uniform	Heavy emphasis on kitchen skills rather than service Can be boring for staff who serve the food Time consuming for kitchen staff Needs close proximity to service point
Home delivery	Totally convenient for customer No space for service required Staffing costs reduced Emphasis on production equipment	Transport of food is dependent on special and geographical knowledge of staff Subject to bogus orders from pranksters Limited menu range can be offered Presentation is dependent on packaging available

3 *Protocol and etiquette* Correct procedure to follow
4 *Handling compliments and complaints* Correct channels to use

Ability to anticipate accidents
Ability to recognize dangerous practices in the use of equipment

Preventional skills
Knowledge of hygienic practices in the preparation and service of food
Knowledge of safe practice in the use of equipment

Motivational skills
Ability to recognize and reinforce good practices
Ability to give praise and encouragement to colleagues

Appreciate the concept of a job well done
Appreciate the role of a professional
Recognize and appreciate pride in the job
Set personal high standards
Appreciate the concept of team work

Organizational skills
Ability to watch and anticipate customers'
needs
Ability to prepare dishes in correct sequence
Ability to gather correct equipment in advance
Ability to coordinate team members' role
Ability to coordinate team members' timing in
the support role
Ability to work harmoniously with kitchen
personnel on timing of service to customer

Now we have audited the skills against the
headings we can look at the training required.
However, we may prefer to recruit rather than
to train. In either case we have the information
to prepare either a job specification for
matching against selection of staff or a training
specification for updating them.

Let us look at our Silver service and Guéridon
skills audit. From this the following has been
established. Staff require experience and/or
training in:

1 Technical skills
2 Customer care
3 Health and safety (licensing laws in some
   cases)
4 Behavioural skills
5 Supervisory skills

Having established the areas to address an
effective schedule of training can be conducted
in-house if the expertise exists, or by buying in
practitioners or by sending staff on courses to
colleges of education or head office training
schools. Training is an investment, it underpins
the establishment's most vital resource – *Staff*.

Task 5.6

*Using the headings chosen
for the Silver and Guéridon
service, conduct a skills audit
for counter service staff.
Suggest, on completion, the
training needs associated
with the skills established.*

▪ THE FACTORS THAT CONTRIBUTE TO FOOD PREPARATION AND COOKING ▪

In this section we shall be looking at the factors
which contribute to the success of food and
drink services, the relevance of each of the
factors and their importance to the overall
performance of an establishment, as well as the
hygiene and legal requirements that affect a
restaurant or dining operation. In order for you
to provide evidence for a portfolio in this
section you will need to know:

● The expectations of customers dining out
● The important factors in a successful dining
  operation
● The types of food and drink services required
  at special events such as functions, parties
  and business lunches

Customers' expectations

First, we must look at the needs and
expectations of customers. Some of the
information can be gained by asking customers
for their requirements, e.g. a wedding breakfast.
The restaurateur or hotel manager would ask
the clients:

1 What type of menu they would like
2 What would they be prepared to pay
3 The wedding card design

4 The room lay-out
5 The number of guests
6 Any special diets

By gaining this type of information the caterer can fulfil the requirements specific to the customers' wishes.

This situation is based on the customer going to the hotel or restaurant, but in many cases the caterer has to prepare for business over which he or she has no control. In order to cater for this they have to base their operations on customers' expectations and try to meet them. Further information on customer service is given in Unit 3.

Task 5.7

Tick off all the items below you would expect to find at a McDonald's restaurant.

Bright decor
Expensive crockery
Sweet trolley
Toys and gifts
Bar area
Breakfast menu
Waitress service
Reserved tables
Kiddies' play area
Food fact sheets
Kiddies' meals

Now tick areas in which you would expect to find a McDonald's unit

Shopping precinct
High street
Arcade
Village square
Museum
Theme park
Retail leisure park
Housing estate.

In answering the above task you have gone some way in establishing what in general would be most peoples' expectations of a visit to McDonald's. However, our industry is made up of many different types of meal providers such as French, Greek, Indian and Italian restaurants, etc. There are also different types of service such as formal and informal as well as dining situations from luxurious to basic. These factors all contribute to the style and appeal of the customer.

In establishing customers' expectations it is essential to find out why they are dining in the first place. This will be for one of many reasons, and some examples include:

● A celebration
● To give a friend or relation a treat
● To meet socially with friends
● Been invited out for a meal
● Business meeting

The most common reason is a social occasion. However, the type of occasion may increase the customers' expectations, such as a wedding anniversary, birthday or engagement. When people are dining out and not everything goes to plan, such as the wine ordered or a menu choice was not available or the service was slow, people generally will look on this with understanding, provided there are genuine reasons. However, when the occasion is very special, such as those indicated earlier, it is extremely important to ensure that everything *does* go to plan as the customer will be less likely to sympathize if it is an occasion which cannot be repeated.

A similar situation may exist with a business luncheon to clinch a deal or sell a new product to guests while the main purpose of the meeting is to talk business. This is not helped if the dining area is noisy or in a smoking area where a guest does not smoke or, worse still, if the meal is poor and service off-hand. These points may make the guest feel frustrated or angry and may have an effect on the meeting itself. Attention to detail and giving guests what they want is an important factor in successful catering.

Task 5.8

Imagine that you are in the West End of London and you are outside a restaurant called Maxim's. The exterior of the restaurant is designed in black marble with mahogany doors with brass handles and a brass menu display case. The restaurant sign has 'Maxim's' in brass lettering and the restaurant curtains appear to be velvet with tie-backs. What would your expectations be under the following headings?

- *Type of menu*
- *Type of service*
- *Type of wine list*
- *Decor and layout of restaurant*
- *Prices on menu*

Compare your thoughts with those of a colleague.

So far in this section we have described the expectations of customers and how we might cater for them. There are, however, other factors which will have a bearing on why a customer may choose a particular restaurant against another. Let us look at some of these.

Restaurants

Location

Many people like to dine close to home to avoid too much travel. They may even wish to walk in order to leave the car at home so that they can have a drink. The location may be the reverse (e.g. that there is plenty of parking space available for a function).

Atmosphere and service

This is a high priority for a lot of customers and will differ greatly. It is very important that the atmosphere and service matches the type of menu and the type of customers being catered

for. For example, in a bistro you would expect an intimate atmosphere, a variety of dishes, good wine choices and low-volume background music or even an acoustic guitar. You would not anticipate loud disco style music, hamburgers and milkshakes, nor would you expect self-service. Atmosphere and service can depend on the time of day such as dinner or lunch. At lunch people would expect it to be busier with, of course, a different style of menu being offered, but provided all the foods are in harmony then it will be recognized by the customers and they will be at ease with it.

Prices

These will always be a major consideration in choosing a restaurant and will depend on how much disposable income the customer has. Highly paid customers will probably pay more and dine out more frequently. It will also depend on whether customers see value for money and convenience (for example, the cost of preparing a meal at home). The highly paid customer may choose to eat out more often to avoid cooking at home and will be prepared to pay more for the convenience. Other customers with less disposable income may not be able to afford high prices or may not be prepared to pay the prices being asked. Therefore they will look for a restaurant based on price rather than on the menu being offered.

Having discussed the menu factors affecting choice of establishment it is a good idea to see how all the factors come together as discussed in the section on atmosphere and service. It is not sufficient for one factor to be acceptable, with the rest out of context and not in harmony with the others. Let us now consider how the factors are dependent on each other.

Menu

The type of food and drink that people choose to consume away from home depends on a number of factors which are of particular concern to them. These include:

1 The choice of food and drink available; whether the menu is limited or extensive; whether the operation revolves around one particular product (for example, steak houses and pizzerias); or whether there is a varied choice (for example, coffee shops and wine bars)

2 The quality of the product offered (for example, fresh or convenience foods, chateau-bottled or a blended non-chateau-bottled wine)

3 The quantity of product offered – the portion sizes. For example, does the restaurant offer children's meals or smaller portions for children?

4 The consistent standard of the product: customers returning to the restaurant and repeating their order of an item would expect the product to be the same as they had previously eaten or drunk

5 The range of tastes, textures, aromas and colours offered by a food dish or the taste, colour and aroma of a drink

6 That the food and drink are served at the correct temperatures (for example, the iced coffee is sufficiently chilled, or hot food is hot when it reaches the customer)

7 That the presentation of the food and drink enhances the product offered. This is particularly important at all levels of catering, from cafeteria to haute-cuisine service, where the visual presentation of the meal is very much part of the total experience

8 That the price and perceived value for money are both in line with customers' pre-meal anticipations

9 That the quality of the total meal experience matches or even enhances the expectations of the guests

Variety in menu choice

The type of menu offered by an establishment and the variety of menu choice should also enhance the total meal experience. At the lower level of the market the choice of menu items in a restaurant is usually fairly limited for a number of reasons. First, if a customer is paying £6–7 for a three-course meal the range of menu items that can be made available within the cost limits of such an operation is obviously more limited than in operations where the customer's average spending power is higher. Second, the amount of time taken to consume meals at this level of the market may vary between half an hour and one hour, but will rarely exceed this. Proportionately, little of this time is spent studying the menu choice. Third, it may be suggested that customers frequenting this lower level of the market may be uncomfortable if presented with a very large menu selection and may therefore prefer a more limited but still varied menu choice.

In high-class restaurants, where the average spending power is more than £40 per head, the menu selection is much greater. In these establishments which encourage a luxury meal experience, the minimum amount of time customers usually spend on a meal is one and a half hours, and may often be three hours, depending on the size of the group and the occasion.

The proportion of the time that may be devoted to reading the menu and selecting from the menu items is correspondingly greater. Customers frequenting these types of establishment would also expect to be offered not only a large menu selection but also a number of chef's and house specialities and wines.

Type of service

Broadly speaking, the higher the cost of the meal to the customer, the more service the customer expects to receive. In a food court where customers are spending approximately £3–5 for a two-course meal the degree of service received is comparatively low: customers collect and purchase their own food from particular food units, carry it to a table, and may clear their dishes from the table at the end of their meal. As the cost of the meal to customers increases so will the amount of service they receive. At the higher end of the catering market, where customers may be paying over £40 per head for a meal, full waiter Silver service is most likely to be provided.

The actual service of the food and beverages to the customer may be described as the 'direct' service. Part of the restaurant's total service, however, is also composed of 'indirect' services. These include the provision of cloakroom facilities (somewhere for the customer to leave coats and bags safely) and the availability of a telephone for customer use (this is particularly important in restaurants with a large business lunch trade).

Value for money

The concept of value for money will vary from one sector of the market to another and, indeed, from one customer to another. In the majority of cases, however, customers will frequent a restaurant not only because of its food and service but also because they feel that the prices they are paying represent value for money.

At the popular end of the market, inclusive (or packaged) price meals are often offered. For example, in the summer, many of the steak house operations sell rump steak and strawberries at an inclusive and competitive price, so that a prospective client is aware in advance what the main cost of the meal will be. This will help to alleviate any concern the customer may have about the total cost of the meal.

At the top end of the market, menu items are often charged for separately because at this level the total cost of the meal is not such an important factor to the customer as are perhaps the other aspects of the operation, such as the standard and range of food and beverages, the level of service offered, and the degree of comfort, decor and atmosphere. However, there has been some emphasis in recent years on the set-price menu in quality and luxury restaurants, particularly for lunch, to attract business account meals where an idea of the

cost can be ascertained beforehand. Today, some establishments include a service charge in the price of their meals, others show it separately, while some operations do not include a service charge but leave it to the customer's discretion.

Interior design and decoration

The overall interior design of a restaurant is one of the first physical aspects of a catering operation with which a customer will come into contact. This first impression of the restaurant is very important. Potential customers passing by may like the look of the establishment and decide to come and eat there. Customers who have actually planned to eat in the restaurant and like what they see when they enter will feel pleased with their choice of restaurant.

The interior design of a restaurant is composed of many different aspects: the size and shape of the room; the furniture and fittings; the colour scheme; lighting; air conditioning; etc. As with the aspects of a restaurant previously described, there is a need for a sense of totality in a restaurant's interior design. The colour scheme of the restaurant should blend and balance and be enhanced by lighting arrangements; tables and chairs ergonomically and aesthetically designed so that they not only satisfy their functional purpose but also look attractive.

The interior design of a restaurant contributes greatly to the creation of its image. A self-service cafeteria in an industrial situation, for example, may consist of a very large dining area, tables and chairs of a standard design and shape, the colour scheme of the restaurant having few variations and lighting arrangements being purely functional. For this type of catering operation a consistently steady seat turnover is required, and this is encouraged by designing the interior of the restaurant so that it does not invite diners to linger over their meal. In addition, a separate coffee lounge or area may be provided where customers may go afterwards and thus vacate their seats for the next diners.

In a luxury restaurant, however, seat turnover is not so critical. In fact, customers may be encouraged to stay in the restaurant to increase their average spend. In these types of establishment the interior design of the restaurant is made to be very comfortable: the lighting in the restaurant is quite subdued; the colour scheme has warmth and depth; there may be several particular points of interest in the restaurant. such as pictures, murals and large floral displays to hold the customer's interest; tables are farther apart, and may be separated from one another in booths or by partitions; and the chairs are so designed that customers may sit in them for several hours without feeling uncomfortable.

The interior design of a catering establishment needs to be carefully considered at the initial planning stage and, if necessary, professional advice sought in order to avoid costly corrective measures later.

Atmosphere and mood

The atmosphere or mood of a restaurant is a difficult aspect of an operation to define, but it is often described as a 'feel' inside a restaurant. Not all restaurants have an obvious type of atmosphere, others try to create one. For example, luxury high-class restaurants often have a very formal atmosphere which is created by the dress and attitude of the staff and the decor. Others such as steak houses, wine bars and pizza and pasta restaurants try to create a relaxed informal atmosphere, and one that is very sociable to be a part of and seen in.

The atmosphere of a restaurant is affected by many different aspects of the operation. These include:

- The decor
- The interior design of the restaurant
- The table and seating arrangements
- The service accompaniments
- The dress and attitude of the staff
- The tempo of service
- The dress and sex of the other customers
- Whether music is played
- The sound levels in the restaurant
- The temperature, bars and cloakrooms
- The overall cleanliness of the environment
- The professionalism of the staff

Again, the harmony between the product itself, the service and the overall environment is important. If one of these aspects is out of sync with the others, disharmony may result in the customer's image of the restaurant, and he or she will invariably leave feeling unsettled.

Let us now recap on what we have discussed:

1 Customer expectations in dining out
2 The importance of meeting customers' expectations
3 The factors which assist in meeting customers' needs and expectations
4 The importance of harmonizing factors which contribute to a successful catering operation
5 Matching factors with different types of establishment and evaluation of them

As you can see, there is a lot of information for the customer to consider when planning and delivering their service and many more factors which are controlled by the individuals themselves. Management has to make some kind of sense this and use it in designing the operation.

While we have spent a good deal of time on 'eating out' and in restaurants in particular, it is important to remember that the factors discussed in part affect operations such as:

- Guest houses
- Cafés
- Staff restaurants in factories and office blocks
- Hospitals (both staff and patients)
- Institutions such as prisons
- Armed forces

and many more.

However, not all factors will play a part but nevertheless they should be considered equal to this in the range of customer to be catered for. We have assumed UK citizens (here), but there are many others within this range that are just not catered for by the ethnic restaurant. There are a few ethnic restaurants in, for example, hospitals but the caterer has to provide for many religious as well as cultural clients, not to mention medically specific diets such as low protein, sulphur- and fat-free, etc.

Our needs and expectations are wide ranging and your further study will bear this out. A successful food and drink operation depends on identifying the market and where or establishment lies in it as well as the kind of customer and what their needs are.

Task 5.9

Identify the needs and expectations of customers/ patients in the following areas:

- *Children in a ward of a general hospital*
- *Business executives staying in a guest house on a half-board basis (bed, breakfast and evening meal)*

▪ PLANNING AND IMPLEMENTATION OF A FOOD AND DRINK SERVICE ▪

In this section we shall look at the objectives of successfully carrying out a food and drink service situation, the factors which contribute to a successful operation, dealing with staff, and the suppliers and equipment required to underpin such an event.

What are the objectives of a successful food and drink operation?

1 To ensure customer satisfaction
2 To provide a quality service to the customer
3 To meet financial objectives
4 To enhance the reputation of the establishment

How can we ensure that we meet these objectives? By:

- Planning of events
- Training staff
- Ensuring consistency of service
- Monitoring of events
- Evaluating events

These provisions will allow for amendment and customers' reactions, it is important not to be complacent where customers are concerned. Any establishment should listen to the customers' views, as they are the ones paying for the service and they can give information via comments or criticism on how they found their 'meal experience'. This in turn can then be used to change the menus or wines being offered, type of service, prices being charged and other factors such as design of restaurant and supporting services such as cloakrooms and toilets. Not all these issues may be relevant but they are typical examples and are fundamental in offering customer satisfaction. Let us now look at our objectives more closely.

Customer satisfaction

How can we do our utmost to ensure this? Very often it is attention to detail that counts. There is a saying in the food and beverage business, 'Watch and anticipate your customer's needs'. This means, for example, that if your customer's wine glass or water glass is approaching empty – fill it up again, if the butter dish is empty get a fresh one. If the customer is near to finishing a course – advise the waiter that your table will need the main course very shortly. This ensures minimum delay but 'not rushing the customer': this is the difference. It is this attention to detail that goes a long way to ensure customer satisfaction.

What else can we do?

Food service staff are expected to provide more than good service. When customers visit an establishment they can expect to find a warm welcome with a smile, to be greeted with their names (if known) and dealt with courteously at all times. A sense of humour also is important but just as important is monitoring how much conversation is suitable – too much can be viewed as intrusion. A good waiter will know when to say nothing and when to give advice. These points are known as 'social skills' and are extremely important in ensuring customer satisfaction. Social skills are part of the communication process and are a sign of the professionalism of food and drink staff.

The communication process starts at the enquiry stage when the customer makes the booking, whether in person or by telephone. How the customer is handled at this stage will give a first impression of the establishment and it is the first opportunity to enhance the image of the restaurant for the customer.

Further stages in the communication process are during the meal itself, with light conversation while the meal is being served, but, as we said earlier, too much is to be avoided. But where service involves the use of the guéridon (trolley) the customer may show an interest in the processes and a good waiter will explain what is happening but not to the neglect of his or her other customers.

After the meal when the customers settle the bill the waiter should enquire as to whether they enjoyed their meal and if there were any points of dissatisfaction not raised at the time of the meal. Assuming all is well, the waiter should thank the customers and escort them to the cloakroom for their coats, bags, umbrellas, etc., bid them goodbye and say that they would like to see them again at some future time.

Handling complaints

From time to time customers may have cause for complaint. The communication process at this time is an imperative. How the customer's complaint is handled will determine how quickly it can be resolved, and the following action is suggested in dealing with a customer complaint.

1 Listen attentively to the complaint
2 Apologize and, if appropriate, take immediate action
3 If you feel that you cannot handle the complaint refer it to your *line manager, head waiter* or *restaurant manager*
4 Do not ignore a complaint
5 Do not argue with the customer
6 Remain calm at all times

Note – a small problem may get out of control if not dealt with quickly and efficiently

Our second objective is to provide quality service for our customer. How can we ensure this in the first place? The answer is, with planning and preparation before the service takes place. As we said earlier, attention to detail is the hallmark of good service. The style of service will determine the preparation required but generally will involve:

● The menu being offered – table d'hôte, à la carte, buffet (hot or cold), curried or fork
● Equipment required – cutlery, glassware, crockery, flatware, linen
● Staffing required – number of staff in relation to numbers being served and the type of service (whether Silver, Platter, Family or Guéridon)
● The venue – the restaurant, function room and, if outside, marquee
● The location – how near or how far from the service point is the venue
● Sundries – wines, minerals or beers to be served whether from dispenser bar or purchased by the case outside the function
● Non-alcoholic drinks – coffee, tea, chocolate
● Cigarettes, cigars, chocolates, etc.
● Any special customer requirements – flowers, bouquets, etc. for tables and guests

Now that we have established the general criteria to be addressed – let us now look at how this can be applied to ensure our 'quality service' for the customer.

Ensuring quality service

The menu

As we can see, the menu is the single factor which determines most of the planning arrangements. The *type of function* and its *venue* in conjunction with the menu will give us the rest.

Style of service

The style of service chosen is important as it will determine the staff numbers required and the type of equipment you will need and will probably dictate the amount of time it will take to serve the meal for the guests. The style of service will also determine the type and skill of the staff you will need to employ, whether permanently or on a casual basis such as a function. Look at Table 5.5, which lists the salient points for a selection of service styles. You may need this when conducting your own food and drink service exercise.

Formal functions

For formal functions it is normal practice for the banquet head waiter to organize his or her staff so that at a given signal the top table service staff can commence to serve/clear, immediately followed by all the service staff. It should be remembered, therefore, that the top table service staff always commence to serve/clear first.

Less formal functions

These are an alternative to the formal service in which the staff double up with regard to the service of the main course. This means that two members of staff act as a team, with one serving the main meat dish and the other the

potato and vegetable dishes, followed by the sauce if served apart.

It should be noted here that the current trend seems to be for the starter and sweet course to be Plate served, while the fish and main course are Silver served. Coffee may be offered by the full Silver service method by serving black coffee and placing the sugar and cream on the tables for guests to help themselves.

Example of an order of service for a formal function

1 Dinner announced by the toastmaster
2 Grace
3 Guests seated. Chairs pulled out by waiters. Serviettes across laps
4 If first course is not already on the table, proceed to hot plate to collect first course
5 Line up top table first
6 Serve first course – top table waiter to commence service first
7 All waiters (food) to leave room after each course is served
8 Take in fish-course plates
9 Clear first course and lay fish plates
10 Take out dirties and collect fish-course
11 Serve fish course. Leave room taking dirty silver
12 Take in meat plates
13 Clear fish course and lay meat plates
14 Take out dirties and collect potato and other vegetable dishes
15 Deposit on sideboard or side table on a hot plate
16 Return to hot plate and collect main meat dish
17 Present on each table and serve
18 Serve accompanying potatoes and vegetables
19 Leave room taking dirty silver
20 Continue until end of the meal

Function organization

Seating

Of the total number of people attending a function it must be determined how many will be seated on the top table, and how

Table 5.5

Type of service	Situation found	Benefits	Constraints
Silver service – dishes are presented on flats, then served by the waiter using a spoon and fork	Good-quality hotels and restaurants	Presentation, the customer controls the portions	Service more labour intensive and therefore more costly
Silver/Plate service – main items are Plated, the rest is Silver served	Department stores, medium-class restaurants	Quicker service, faster turnover of customer	Can be slower in the kitchen, fewer service skills
French service – food is offered for customers to help themselves	Small functions, French restaurants	Presentation of food, personal service	Portion control varies
Guéridon service – dishes are prepared, cooked or flamed at the table	Top-class restaurants	Customers are given a personal service and staff display their skills	Expensive due to labour costs
Nouvelle cuisine – dishes decorated and arranged on a plate	High-class hotels and restaurants	Gives excellent visual presentation of the food	Labour intensive in the kitchen, can be expensive
Plate service – the meal is presented on a plate	Set-price restaurants, cafés, guest houses, grill rooms	Fast turnover of customer, saves on labour, maintains food presentation and portions	More kitchen work
Family service – dishes placed on the table for customers to help themselves	Banqueting suites, pubs and guest houses	Faster service, the customer controls the portions	Poor portion control, the customer can feel neglected if waiter is rushed
Counter cafeteria service – customer queues and selects meal from a counter or servery	Pubs, industrial canteens, schools, motorway service stations	Speed of service, reduced labour costs	Quality control
Fast food – customer is served quickly	Take-away, burger restaurants	Fast turnover	Quality control
Carvery – main course is collected by the customer from a carving point	Restaurants, pubs, motels	Looks appealing, choice	Portion control, quality of food kept hot

many on the sprigs, round or oblong tables, making up the full table plan. All tables, with the exception of the top, should be numbered. The table numbers themselves should be on stands of such a height that they may all be seen from the entrance of the banqueting room. These stands are sometimes removed after the guests are seated and before the service commences.

As far as possible, when making the table plan, you should try to avoid seating guests with their backs to the top table. Normally there are three copies of the seating plan. These go to:

1 The *organizer* – so that he or she may check all necessary arrangements
2 The *guests* – this seating plan should be placed in a prominent position in the

entrance of the banqueting suite so that all guests may see where they have been seated, who else is sitting at their table, and the position of their table in the room

3 The *banqueting manager* – for reference purposes

Tabling

The type of table plan put into operation for a particular function depends upon a number of factors:

- Organizer's wishes
- Nature of the function
- Size and shape of room where the function is to be held
- Number of covers for the function

For the smaller functions a U- or T-shaped table may be used, or where the luncheon or dinner party is more formal there may be a top table and separate tables, round or rectangular for the various parties of guests.

Before the table plans can be shown to the organizer when a function is being booked consideration must be given to spacing, i.e. widths of covers, gangways, size of chairs. This is to allow a reasonably comfortable seating space for each guest and, at the same time, give the waiter sufficient room for the service of the meal. The gangway space must be such that two waiters may pass one another during the service without any accidents.

Spacing

1 It is generally recognized that the minimum space between sprigs should be 2 metres (6 ft). This is made up of two chair widths: from the edge of the table to the back of the chair (4.6 cm or 18 in.) plus a gangway of 1 metre (3 ft), allowing each waiter passing space: total of 2 metres (6 ft)
2 Table widths are approximately 75 cm (2 ft 6 in.)
3 The length along the table per cover should be 50–60 cm (20–24 in.)

4 Round tables would be 1.0, 1.5 or 2 m (3, 5 or 6 ft) in diameter with the appropriate extensions
5 Suggested area allowance for sit-down functions per person is approximately 1.0–1.4 m² (12–15 ft²); for buffets the allowance is 0.9–1.0 m² (10–12 ft²)

In the next section we shall look at the planning required in a 'quality service' in a variety of situations such as a wedding function and, in particular, outdoor catering which involves detailed planning to ensure a smooth working operation. We shall also consider the supporting requirements which are a vital part of providing a service such as licensing regulations and health and safety issues.

Quality service in function catering

Types of function

There are three main types of function:

1 *Formal meals*
  Luncheons
  Dinners
  Wedding breakfasts
2 *Buffet receptions*
  Wedding receptions
  Cocktail parties
  Buffet teas
  Dances
  Anniversary parties
  Conferences
1 *Public relations*
  Press party to launch a new product
  Fashion shows
  Seminars
  Exhibitions

A further breakdown of the types of function may be as follows:

- Social
- Institutional dinners
- Luncheons (e.g. Rotarians)
- Receptions
- Cocktail parties

There are also conferences:

- Political conferences
- Trade union conferences
- Training conferences
- National and international sales conferences

Function staff and responsibilities

In large first-class establishments there is generally a small number of permanent staff solely dealing with functions. This includes the banqueting/conference manager, one or two assistant banqueting managers, one or two banqueting head waiters, bar staff, and a secretary to the banqueting manager. In smaller establishments where there are fewer functions and the necessary administrative and organizational work is undertaken by the manager, assistant manager and head waiter.

Banqueting/conference manager

The banqueting/conference manager is responsible for all the administration: meeting prospective clients, discussing arrangements with them concerning menus, table plans, costs, wines, bands, and so on. He or she must communicate to all the departments concerned.

Banqueting head waiter

The banqueting head waiter is in charge of the banqueting suites plus the organization required to prepare them for various forms of functions. He or she may also be responsible for the engaging of staff, on a casual basis, to cover the various duties at a function.

Bar staff

If they are members of the permanent banqueting staff, the bar staff are responsible for the allocation of bar stock for various functions, the setting up of bars, the organization of the bar staff, control of stock and cash during service and for stocktaking when a function is completed.

Banqueting head wine waiter

The banqueting head wine waiter may work in conjunction with the bar staff or, if there are no permanent bar staff, may take over the latters' duties together with organizing the banqueting wine waiters and allotting them.

Permanent waiting staff

The permanent waiting staff are usually experienced staff who can turn their hand to any jobs concerning banqueting and who generally do most of the preparation before the function. Their job during service is mainly wine waiting, but they may also help to clear after service is completed.

Casual staff

Care is taken as to the type of casual staff employed. They normally report approximately one hour before a function commences and are then allocated stations and are given brief directions on the procedure for the service of a particular function. A waiter at a banquet is generally expected to serve between ten and twelve covers on a station.

Apart from the top table no precedence is given to rank or sex at banquets. The waiters should all be numbered once the stations are allocated, so that the waiter with a station furthest from the service entrance will be nearer the head of the queue at the hot plate. The waiters on the top table are always at the head of the queue and enter the room first with each successive course. No waiter commences service on his or her station until those on the top table have commenced their service.

A banqueting wine waiter will serve approximately twenty-five covers, but this depends on the type of function, the amount of wines on offer, and whether any wine is inclusive in the price of the menu or if cash drinks are being served. The wine waiters will normally aid the food waiters with the service of vegetables and sauces for the main course. When cash drinks are served the wine waiters are normally given a float with which they may pay the cashier or bar staff as drinks are ordered and collected from the bar. The responsibility then rests with the wine waiter to collect the cash for any drinks served. This should be done immediately the liqueurs are served and before the toasts commence. The wine waiters may also be required to serve aperitifs at a reception before the meal and, if so, to do the necessary preparation to ensure that the reception area is ready.

Service methods in function catering

Generally it is recognized that at functions the service method may take any of the following forms:

- Silver
- Family
- Plate
- Assisted-service
- Self-service

The type of service method chosen is usually determined by:

- Host's wishes
- Time factor
- Skills of the service staff available
- Equipment available
- Type of function

Outdoor catering

The day-to-day business of an outdoor catering firm should continue throughout the year to ensure that the equipment provided for a particular function and staff is used to the full. As in function catering, the organization must be planned to the last detail and an initial survey should be exact and thorough. The following points should be included in the initial survey:

1 Type of function
2 Date
3 Site and distance from depot

4 Local transport
5 Local shops for buying food and drink items and availability
6 Staff recruitment
7 Lay-out of site
8 Number of people expected to attend
9 Availability of water, gas, electricity, drainage, refrigeration
10 Time allowance for setting up and dismantling
11 Type of licence if required
12 Photographers for function if required
13 Changing room and toilets for customers and staff
14 Insurance against weather/fire or any other event
15 First aid
16 Cost of overheads on a particular site such as room hire
17 Type of service – find the one most suited to each particular catering
18 Washing-up facilities
19 Containers supplied for litter

Each outdoor catering operation is different and varies to some extent in the main points that have to be noted during the initial survey. From the basic list shown above one appreciates the organization needed beforehand and some of the problems that may arise at the outset of or during an operation.

As the majority of staff employed at outdoor catering functions are taken on as casuals there are certain formalities that have to be observed from an administrative viewpoint. This is essential to ensure that all the legal aspects of employment are covered and that the staff are aware of their responsibilities both to the employer and to the customers.

Prior to an event each employee should receive the following:

- Casual worker registration form
- Acceptance of offer of employment – to be signed and dated by employees

It is important that the organization of outdoor catering events must be very thorough as it is often virtually impossible to rectify mistakes. Any items forgotten or not packed on the transport have to be gone without, which may result in a poor service and a loss of future business.

Licensing laws

Licensed premises must, in order to sell alcoholic liquor, obtain what is called a *justices' licence*. Licences are granted from 5 April each year. The Annual Licensing Meeting is held in the first fortnight of February, called the *Brewster Session*. In addition, there must be held at least four (but no more than eight) licensing sessions at regular intervals throughout the year. These are called Transfer Sessions. Licences are granted for the premises in whole or in part. Any alteration proposed must be agreed by the justices. The premises must be fit, i.e. meet the requirements of the local authority, police and the fire authority. Furthermore, *good order* must be maintained, i.e.:

- No drunkenness
- No violence
- No riotous conduct
- No prostitutes
- No gaming (justices may authorize certain games)

Full on-licence

The full on-licence allows the licensee to sell all types of alcoholic liquor for consumption on and off the premises. An on-licence may be limited by the licensing justices as to the type of alcohol that may be sold (e.g. beer only).

Restaurant licence

This can be granted for premises which are structurally built or adapted and are used in a *bona fide* way or are intended to be used for the habitual provision of the main midday and/or main evening meal. The licence will authorize the sale or supply of alcohol on the premises to people who take table meals there, but such liquor must be a support to the meal. In other words, customers must not frequent these establishments merely to drink.

For this purpose, the meal must be a *table meal*. This means that it must be eaten by a person seated at a table or a counter. Another aspect is that drinks other than alcohol must be available to the diners should they require them.

Residential licence

This may be granted for premises used, or intended to be used, for the purpose of habitually providing (for reward) board and lodging, including breakfast and at least one of the other customary main meals. This could apply to a boarding house if it provided bed, breakfast and either lunch or an evening meal. Many private hotels easily fulfil this qualification.

A residential licence will authorize the sale or supply of alcoholic beverages on the premises to people residing there or to their private friends who are genuinely entertained by such guests at their own expense. Under this licence the drinks can be sold or supplied at any time because there are no licensing hours.

Combined licence

This is granted for premises which fulfil the conditions required for both a restaurant licence and a residential licence (for example, a private hotel with a public dining room attached). Residents can drink in their own bar while the public can visit the premises for a meal in the dining room. When granting a combined licence the magistrates may impose a condition that the drinks are not supplied to the public in the dining room outside the normal permitted hours.

Occasional licence

This licence is granted by magistrates to holders of on-, restaurant or combined licences. It enables these licence holders to sell alcoholic beverages at another place or specified times (e.g. for outdoor catering).

Occasional permission

This is a licence available from licensing justices for eligible organizations to sell alcohol. It is similar to an occasional licence but may be applied for by non-licence holders (e.g. a football club or for a specific activity).

Permitted hours

The Licensing Act 1988 made changes in the licensing system in England and Wales mainly relating to permitted hours, i.e. hours during which licensed premises may be open. The changes also cleared up a substantial number of anomalies in the regulations and moved the operation of public houses towards a less controlled market environment. Historically, restrictions of permitted hours were introduced from 1872 onwards, although control of licences themselves had been on the Statute Book since 1495. Since 1872 there has been eighteen different items of legislation related to the licensing system, most of which were consolidated in the Licensing Act 1964 (England and Wales) and the Licensing (Scotland) Act 1976.

Permitted hours are currently:

Weekdays	11 a.m. to 11 p.m. (off-licences 8–11 p.m.)
On- and off-licences	Any hours
Sundays	Between 2 p.m. and 7 p.m.

Within these hours, licensees can choose when and for how long they close their premises.

Exceptions to permitted hours

- The first 20 minutes after the end of permitted hours for consumption only
- The first 30 minutes after the end of permitted hours for those taking table meals. Again this is for consumption only
- Residents and their guests (as long as only the resident purchases the alcoholic beverages)

Note: permitted hours in Scotland are broadly similar to those above.

Extensions to permitted hours

Special Order of Exemption

This is an extension of the normal permitted hours of on-licensed premises for any special occasion, e.g. wedding, buffet dance, dinners, carnivals and so on. Normally 'special occasions' do not continue for more than a few days, and the term does not cover such occasions as market days held on one day every week of the year. The duration of the extension is determined by the licensing authority and can only be determined by references to the Order itself.

General Order of Exemption

This allows a licence to be exempted from the normal permitted hours during a certain day or for a certain time. Such a notice must be displayed outside the premises for all to see. The effect of a General Order of Exemption is to extend the licensing hours to whatever time the licensing authority sees fit, either on one particular day, or several days, or generally throughout the week. The General Order of Exemption therefore is for the benefit of people who, for example, might attend a local market at times during which licensed premises would normally be closed, or for those following a particular trade which results in their working, and hence requiring refreshments, when licensed premises would normally be closed. The licensing authority is not bound to grant a

General Order of Exemption and need only do so at its discretion, and may at any time revoke or vary any Order.

Supper Hour Certificate

This is a grant by the licensing justices, once they are satisfied that the premises are suitable, of an additional hour to the permitted hours in a licensed restaurant for the sale and consumption of alcoholic liquor with a table meal. This certificate also allows any other bars and dispensing bars to remain open for the additional hour after the end of the permitted hours. The half-hour drinking-up time in the licensed restaurant would still be allowed after the additional hour.

The effect, therefore, of a Supper Hour Certificate extends the normal permitted hours in the evening. Such extensions only apply to those parts of the premises set aside for the service of table meals. A Supper Hour Certificate may be withdrawn if the premises at any time cease to qualify within the laid-down conditions, but otherwise it continues in force without need for renewal.

Special Hours Certificate

Where this certificate is in force the permitted hours in such licensed premises will be extended until:

● West End of London – 3.00 a.m. with consumption until 3.30 a.m.
● Elsewhere – 2.00 a.m. with consumption until 2.30 a.m.

This certificate will only apply if the following conditions are fulfilled:

1 The establishment itself is licensed
2 A music and dancing licence has been obtained
3 All, or any part, of the premises are structurally adapted and intended to be used for the purpose of providing 'live' music and dancing and substantial refreshment, to both of which the sale of liquor is ancillary

This certificate, if granted, will only apply to that part of the premises which qualifies as above. The premises must be such that they always provide, on a regular basis, the facilities indicated above. Therefore a Special Hours Certificate will not be granted for one isolated special occasion, or for any area in which a music and dancing licence is not required. In the latter case the licensee must make do with an Extended Hour Certificate. A Special Hours Certificate may be removed at any time if it appears that:

● The premises no longer possess a music and dancing licence
● The certificate has not been used
● The certificate is being used for the wrong purposes
● The premises have been conducted in a disorderly or unlawful manner

It is perhaps as well to note here that it is possible for different parts of the same licensed premises to be licensed in different ways. It is therefore possible to have a normal public bar closing at 11.00 p.m., a licensed restaurant remaining open for the sale of liquor with meals until 12.00 midnight and a separate ballroom operation under a Special Hours Certificate until 2.00 a.m.

Extended Hours Certificate

This extension is for the benefit of premises which qualify for a Supper Hour Certificate and which also provide regular musical or other entertainment (live), together with the table meal. Here the sale of liquor is ancillary to both the table meal and the entertainment. The refreshment and entertainment must be provided in a part of the premises normally set aside for the purpose. This certificate extends the permitted hours up to 1.00 a.m. The service of drink must cease when either the entertainment or service of table meals cease. The service of drink must end in any case at 1.00 a.m. There is a *drinking-up time* of 30 minutes allowed after the service of drink has ceased.

If granted, the Extended Hours Certificate may be limited to certain evenings in the week. The licensing justices have complete discretion as to whether or not they grant this certificate, and it may be revoked at any time if it appears that the premises no longer qualify or that the use of such a certificate has led to noisy and disorderly conduct.

It should be noted that the usual half-hour drinking-up time allowed at the end of each period of permitted hours, during which drinks were purchased with table meals, is allowed at the end of any of the following if they are in force:

1 General Order of Exemption
2 Special Order of Exemption
3 Supper Hour Certificate
4 Special Hour Certificate
5 Extended Hours Certificate

Music and dancing licences

These are not liquor licences. Generally, licences are required for public music and dancing, but the law varies according to the particular place. These licences are granted by local councils but are not required for:

- Radio
- Television
- Recorded music
- Not more than two live performances

▪ THE PLANNING AND DELIVERY OF FOOD AND DRINK SERVICES ▪

In this section we shall evaluate food and drink services and establish the criteria and sources of evidence of doing so. We shall discuss the analysis of information obtained through evaluation and indicate the strengths and weaknesses within the service situation that may occur. The formulation of an action plan will also be discussed.

Criteria

In any evaluation exercise it is important to establish the criteria to be used. In this instance it is the evaluation of a food and drink service situation. Let us look at the possible areas for inclusion: for purposes of generality we shall not state a specific situation. If we are to construct an evaluation, we are going to consider the following issues:

1 *Food*
  Menu
  Dishes
  Variety
  Quality
  Portion sizes
  Temperature
  Value for money
  Speed and efficiency of the service
  How well the food was cooked
2 *Drink*
  Range of wines, beers, minerals, soft drinks, cocktails and beverages on offer
  Prices
  Service
  Value for money
3 *Staff*
  Social skills, greeting on entering and leaving
  Technical skills
  Quality of service
  Communication skills – friendly, attentive, courteous, informative
4 *Environment*
  The restaurant
  Seating
  Table layout
  Decor
  Lighting
  Background music
  Facilities such as cloakroom and toilets
5 *Atmosphere*
  Intimate
  Formal
  Informal
  Noisy
  Too quiet
  Too dark
  Too bright
  Congested

Many of these issues relate to the 'delivery' of the exercise and not to the 'planning'. However, it is in analysis of the delivery that the necessary remedial action will be in planning any preparation to put things right (if actions are necessary).

The evaluation process is often twofold:

● Customer orientated
● Establishment

If you refer to our list of issues, on closer inspection we could divide the required information into areas of interest from the customer's point of view and from that of the establishment.

Customer orientation

Food issues (the customer's concerns) will be based on the menu, variety of dishes and, above all, value for money. Customers will not be concerned with the supplier, purchasing specification and the equipment's performance in cooking it. This comparison would apply for all the other areas of concern such as drinks, facilities and pricing. There would, however, be commonalties as to staffing in the service of the food, i.e. the establishment will be just as concerned with the quality, speed and efficiency of the service as the customer.

The following are a series of questions which might be raised in an evaluation exercise. These would deal with strengths and weaknesses in the operation. Reference may also be made to Unit 3, page 100.

Evaluation criteria

● Why is that member of staff not smiling or being courteous to customers? If a waiter is not smiling his or her feet might be hurting; no amount of telling him or her to smile will change this. Their shoes might be the problem.

● We all say 'please' and 'thank you'. In catering the use of 'sir', 'madam', 'please', 'excuse me' and 'thank you' is expected. If it is not being done are the staff in the wrong job? If they are in the right job, then what is the problem?
● What are the problems of each department in working with other departments?
● How does each department's problems affect the others?
● What are the difficulties that a guest could experience? For example, lack of information or direction signs
● Is the emphasis in the work areas put on the customer?
● What problems can be solved by physical changes? For example, staff congregating round a central sideboard will face inwards and not outwards to observe customers
● Are foreseen problems minimized? For example, large parties organized in advance
● Are staff informed of set procedures for foreseen problems?
● Are complaints used as an opportunity to show care for guests?
● Are there set procedures for dealing with complaints?

The way in which the evaluation exercise is conducted will depend on the time available and the expertise of staff or whether the exercise is conducted via hired agencies or consultants. The evaluation exercise would normally involve:

1 Observation
2 Interview
3 Questionnaire

and would require gathering information from:

1 Customers
2 Management
3 Staff

The following checklist and criteria could be used by students undertaking a 'themed event' in their college training restaurant and may be handed to colleges in the final production area.

Themed event – checklist for preparation

Dealing with complaints

Do not argue with the customer, always apologize and make an effort to remedy the situation.

If the complaint is about food

1 Remove the plate immediately
2 Offer the menu, inviting an alternative choice
3 Hope that the new dish is now satisfactory and to the guest's taste

If the complaint is about service

1 Explain to the customer what has gone wrong, but do not blame anyone
2 Reassure him or her that you are doing everything within your power to overcome the problem

Chef for the day

1 Check your appearance in the mirror before you enter the restaurant – look your best
2 Smile when you speak, and always look at the person
3 Offer a greeting before you ask the questions, e.g. 'Good afternoon, I'm chef for the day. Did you enjoy your meal?'

If the answer is 'Yes, thank you', reply by saying 'Good, I'm very pleased, thank you', and move to the next table. If the answer is 'No', immediately say 'I am sorry, why not? Try to discover the reason for the dissatisfaction, but do not be drawn into an argument. Say tactfully 'Thank you for drawing attention to it. I will check that next time the dish is on the menu', or 'Yes, I agree, the duck was very small, and had very little meat. I shall not offer it again until later in the season'. You don't have to tell a lie but you do have to sound convincing. The customer has to believe you.

Special categories of customers

- Children   Form of address, size of portion
- Business executives   May want unobtrusive table where they can talk undisturbed
- Vegetarians   Tend to be a bit faddy
- Foreigners   A phrase book might be useful!
- Disabled   A corner table? For your convenience as much as theirs

Reception – telephone technique

Any phone conversation of this nature has three components:

1 Greeting
2 Message, or substance, which is the reason for making the call
3 Farewell

But the receptionist should obtain the following information:

1 Name of person making the booking
2 Date and time of service
3 Number of covers required
4 Phone number of person making booking
5 Any special requirements, e.g. vegetarian, birthday, children

Formulating an action plan

Once an evaluation exercise has been carried out there are probably issues and shortcomings to be addressed. These could involve changes to:

- Physical resources – such as decor of the restaurant, seating arrangements, bar areas, etc.
- Human resources – staff, their number, their quality and, above all, their training.

The points which arise from an evaluation take time and cannot be addressed overnight. They require:

- Careful thinking
- Careful planning
- Provisioning
- Phasing

In doing this an objective approach can be carried out. Your plan may require the support of management and they will require clear and concise information on:

1 What needs to be done
2 When it needs to be done
3 Who is going to do it and (very often)
4 How much it is going to cost!

One of the most common outcomes of any evaluation exercise is training. Most companies will identify a shortcoming or deficiency in their training methods which usually results in lack of knowledge of a process, policy or working method. This further results in complaints by customers for many reasons such as:

- Poor service
- Incorrect billing
- Poor social skills, etc.

Training is usually high on the agenda of any action plan and the clarity and purpose of the training programme will have distinct advantages such as:

- Standards of performance required are identified
- Improved ability of staff
- Availability of a means of measuring ability
- More efficient working
- Clearer responsibilities

The role of the supervisor in training is to:

1 Ensure that staff are competent to carry out the duties required of them
2 Check that legal and company requirements are met
3 Develop and train staff as required
4 Develop existing staff to train others
5 Identify training needs of staff now and in the future

A training need is present when there is a gap between:

- The knowledge, skills and attitudes displayed by people in their jobs
- The knowledge, skills and attitudes needed for them to achieve the results the job requires both now and in the future

In our own establishment or departments we probably think we know what the 'gap' is – we see the evidence every day. However, it is worth trying to find the specific answers to questions such as the following:

Staffing
Who have we got on our staff?
Where do they fit in?
How long do they stay and why?
Where do they come from?
How do we choose them?
How many people do we take on and how often?

Agreed job descriptions
What do our staff do in theory and in practice?
Do they know clearly what they have to do?

Standards and performance
What results and standards do we expect from our staff?
Are they aware of these?
How well do they meet our requirements?
What stands in the way if requirements are not being met?

Present training
How do our staff learn their jobs now and from whom?
How well do they learn?
How quickly do they learn?

Key problems
Are there any special difficulties:
In the skills people have to learn?
In the circumstances under which they work?
In organizing training?

Resources
What training facilities exist within or outside the establishment which can be used or developed?

Future needs

Any change brings a training need with it, so we must ask questions that will show us what future training is needed, for instance:

Normal staff changes and development
What is the age structure of our staff?
What posts are we likely to have to fill due to:
  Retirement?
  Normal replacements?
  Transfers?
Is anyone earmarked for promotion?
What potential for promotion is there?
What have we in mind for our craft or other trainees?

Knowledge and qualities required of a food service handler
Location of table
The menu and drinks list (presentation and cleanliness)
Speed and efficiency of service
Quality of food and drink
Courteousness of staff
Obtrusiveness/attentiveness of staff
Method in which complaints are handled
Method of presenting bill/recovery payment
Departure attentiveness

The supervisor is responsible for minimizing potential customer problems. He or she should be as much concerned with the physical aspects of the service as with the way in which the service is operated and the interaction between customers and staff. In food and beverage service operations interaction also takes place with people outside the service areas (for example, kitchen staff, dispense bar staff, still room staff). It is important that the provision of food and beverages within an establishment is seen as a team effort between all departments, with each department understanding the needs of the others in order to meet the customers' demands.

As mentioned earlier, training is a high priority but there will be other issues to address in the action plan and will involve such issues as:

- Meeting financial targets
- Health and safety requirements
- Customer perceptions of the establishment
- Enhancing the reputation of the establishment

The above action plan is based on short-term results and many establishments will form a plan to cover one, two or even three years. It depends on the job to be carried out and the extent of the work involved. An action plan will form the basis of the tasks to be considered and the appropriate timescales. It brings an 'order' to the strategy and all good managers will have one.

Meeting financial targets

Demand and change of customers

All caterers are now more likely to respond to market demands, regardless of whether they are concerned with making a profit or not. As the industry has grown and become more competitive its customers have become more critical. In order to be successful the caterer needs not only to cook and present food well but must also offer consistent quality at a reasonable price. This may be achieved through increased efficiency and cost reduction. Striving for greater efficiency leads to pressure for change.

Within the catering industry there are four main elements of change:

1 *Food* The search for low-cost/high-profit alternatives and the response to developing trends, such as healthy eating and organic produce

2 *Menu* Responding to customer needs. With the exception of formal dinners the menu should be short, cheerful, based around a theme and offer good value for money.

3 *Catering system* A reflection of the demands of the menu, products offered and type of raw material purchased

4 *Technology* Developments in food processing and equipment place greater emphasis on the need to re-examine menus

A questioning approach should be adopted:

- Who are your customers?
- What do they eat?
- How much do they spend?
- Is lunch different from dinner? How? Why?
- Nutritional considerations
- Meeting local tastes
- Responding to wider social issues
- Attracting custom and promoting business

Social issues in custom

A catering operation is influenced by its environment, consequently the menu-planner must be alert to current social issues. For example, caterers have been aware of the needs of ethnic customers and vegetarians for some time. With the growth of the 'green' movement in society, healthy eating will have a greater influence on the planning of menus. Caterers may not only have to provide dishes free of (or less dependent on) meat but should also be conscious of the amount and type of fat present in food, whether or not their raw materials have been produced organically, as well as being able to identify a variety of flavours and colourings.

Developments in food legislation are not only doing more to protect the consumer but are also raising public awareness of possible dangers. Customers generally are becoming increasingly aware of healthy eating and food hygiene or, more precisely, the results of poor hygiene leading to the risk of food poisoning.

All this must be done in such a way as to generate a reasonable profit. In the welfare sector, caterers will have to compete on an increasingly commercial basis. The menu-maker will have to respond to demands for value for money.

Cost pricing of menus

These factors include:

1 Style and quality of the menu
2 Whether à la carte, table d'hôte or a blend of both
3 Menu range related to number, variety and standard of dishes
4 Preparation and cooking of each dish in terms of recipes, portions, quantities and service style
5 Speciality items to be featured (for advance planning of appropriate equipment)
6 Extent of processed and convenience foods usage (i.e. kind and quantities of foods to be produced and served determined so that requirements, in terms of processes and equipment, can be efficiently planned)
7 Style/method of service

The various kitchen sections (or parties) receiving advance copies of the menus will plan their work according to its requirements – from their point of view, as much as from the customer's.

The aim must always be for consistent, achievable quality, not just of the food but also of the total meal experience. The caterer will seek to understand why people choose to eat away from home and what influences their meal preference. Once identified, the factors that contribute to the enjoyment of the meal can and should be promoted through the menu.

To do its job, a menu should have visual appeal. Attention to style, design, typography and printing is obviously a matter for the relevant experts, but this does not mean that practical people in catering should not seek to be closely involved in all possibilities of business promotion through an effective menu.

It is not uncommon for food and beverage managers to seek ideas, price comparisons and lay-out tips from the menu examples of their competitors. But simply to find out what the other caterer is charging or what size and style they have chosen for actual menu cards or display material are only the beginnings of menu consciousness.

Awareness of menu development nationally and internationally, at all levels, means intelligent appraisal of as many relevant menu examples as can be obtained, including monitoring the trade press. Some features which the chef and others should think about include:

- *House specialities*   These should be rigidly specified and uniform in size and quality through the use of standardized recipes
- *Fresh local produce*   Be sure that the case for featuring local foods has been properly considered and that the product served is genuinely local in origin
- *Promoting desserts*   Consider having a separate menu for puddings and sweets. Customers might choose to miss the starter in order to reserve appetite for the sweet. Starters will appear more tempting if they do not have to compete with the sweet course
- *Novelty*   Tune the menu to modern trends. Search for something new. Balance innovations with old favourites
- *Family business*   Do not ignore the young as they are often an effective way of reaching the parents. Junior portions and special dishes are appropriate in many operations

Monitoring of events

Through the process of monitoring we can ascertain whether the service we are providing is good or bad or whether a few adjustments have to be made to establish a good service for our customers. The monitoring process, however, needs to be looked at and judgements have to be made on what we are actually monitoring. Is it

1 The service at the table to our customers?
2 The menu and variety of dishes?
3 The facilities offered to our customers?
4 The environment such as decor, lighting, cloakrooms and toilets, etc?
5 The staff and their performance?

Some further selective monitoring may also be undertaken such as marketing of the establishment. How did the customers hear of your restaurant? Advert, word of mouth, recommendation?

The monitoring process as a good tool for 'fine tuning' all the above example and the process usually involves one or several of the above areas. Monitoring may be conducted by:

1 Observation of the process
2 Asking questions in the presence of customers
3 Feedback from staff
4 Use of questionnaires

The monitoring process needs to conducted over a period of time to be effective and needs to cover the full framework of the operation, such as breakfast, lunch and dinner and across the full week for several weeks. It is possible, however, that an establishment does 'spot checks' on its service and wishes to monitor just one part, looking at the service on one day or even one service such as lunch or dinner. But results are and should be viewed in this context.

On conclusion of the monitoring process it will be necessary to establish the outcomes in some form of logical plan for future reference. This would be known as an action plan and will be covered in more detail later in this book. The monitoring process, however, will give the establishment information to work on. It may include aspects on issues such as:

- The menu – its choice, variety and, above all, its price
- The style of service – formal or informal, attentive or neglectful
- Atmosphere – intimate, noisy, disturbing, too hot, too cold
- Quality of the food – portion size, value for money, preparation, how well covered, etc.

However, the establishment then has to look at the results and react effectively. This could involve reviewing:

1 Menu compilation
2 Supplies of commodities
3 Portion sizes
4 Menu prices
5 Staff training
6 Design and lay-out of restaurant

The action plan would be formed around these issues with a suitable timescale to phase in new arrangements.

Internal monitoring

Other forms of the monitoring process could be used internally and these are usually based on working practices of staff and are often conducted by the head waiter or restaurant manager. They are used as a form of 'appraisal' of their staff and will look at how well or badly they are performing and what action needs to be taken to assist improvement such as further training in the restaurant or by attending courses at a training centre or college of further education. It could also involve changing working practices to make the service quicker and more efficient by removing or reducing repetitive tasks and movement within the working area, or streamlining the ordering sequence in the kitchen etc. All this is done to maximize the following;

- Improve the service to the customer
- Reduce costs
- Provide increased facilities

Task 5.10

To find out more about different catering businesses and how they promote their products, visit as many different types of cafés and restaurants as you can in your town or city. Make copies of the following survey and complete a new one for each establishment you visit.

Name of establishment

Item and price	£	p	Contents of meal
Cup of coffee			
Cup of tea			
Main course (1)			
Main course (2)			
Main course (3)			
Dessert (1)			
Dessert (2)			

Presentation of food
Is the food hygienically presented?

What measures are taken by the restaurant to ensure that its food looks fresh and attractive?

Standard of cleanliness
1 = very clean
5 = very dirty

Tables	1	2	3	4
Counter tops	1	2	3	4
Appearance of staff	1	2	3	4
General (walls, floors)	1	2	3	4

Type of service

| Waitress | |
| Self-service | |

Tick the words which best describe the service:

Efficient	Offhand	Terrible
Friendly	Unfriendly	Polite
Quick	Ill-mannered	Slow

Are there any other words you would use to describe the service?

Environment

(a) Are the staff in uniform?
    If yes, what is the colour?

(b) Is the menu design
    appealing?

(c) Is the seating comfortable?

(d) Is the temperature:
    Too hot?
    Too cold?
    Just right?

(e) Can you get to the table
    easily?
    Does the layout of the
    tables and chairs make it
    easy for the elderly,
    disabled or people with
    children to cope?

(f) Are toilets provided?
    Yes/No. If so, are the toilets
    well maintained and clean?
    Yes/No. Would you go back
    to this restaurant or café
    again?
    If yes, why?
    If no, why not?

In a group, decide which of the cafés and restaurants you visited presented its products in the most appealing way. Look up the correct address of the café or restaurant in your telephone directory or the Yellow Pages. Write a letter to the manager of the restaurant or café explaining why you carried out the survey and why you chose their restaurant as the most appealing. Invite the manager to comment on your findings.

Assembly of evidence: a log book of assessment activities

In the following pages you will find assessment activities which may be undertaken in support of evidence for this unit. The log book contains:

1 Introductory notes
2 Action plan sheet
3 Evaluation sheet
4 Core skills sheet
5 Performance criteria for the unit
6 Assessment activities

About this work log

In order to obtain more than a pass grade for this unit you must show that you are capable of planning your approach to the assessment, gather the appropriate information and use it properly, and finally, show that you are able to learn from your experience. In other words, that you can:

● Plan
● Gather information
● Evaluate
● This work log is divided into four parts:

Part 1 This gives detailed information about what you need to do in order to obtain a Merit or Distinction grade for each of the above.

Part 2 This is for you to write down how you intend to tackle the assessment, along with dates and deadlines for particular tasks to be completed.

Part 3 This is for you to record the activities which you undertake in order to complete the assessment. You should also record any difficulties that you encounter and any changes that you have made to your original plan.

Part 4 This is where you evaluate your approach to the assessment. Was it successful? What did you learn from the experience? How would you change things so that next time you could do better?

GNVQ Assessment and Accreditation Profiles

Unit title
Food and Drink Service Systems (Advanced)
Assessment title
Investigation of Food and Drink Service Systems
Assessment details
You are the Operations Manager of a new private hospital which is due to open in six months' time.

It is your job to advise and eventually select the food and drink service system for three areas. They are:

● Provision of food to patients in their rooms
● Provision of food to the visitors
● Provision of food to the staff

Select a system for each area that is suitable and give your reasons for each choice.

Accurately identify each chosen system.

To help yourself with recruitment at a later date you are asked to describe the skills required by staff for each system.

Present your findings in typewritten form and in a report

Element 4.1
Investigate methods of providing food and drink services

Core
3.1 – 1, 2, 3, 4,
3.2 – 1, 2, 3, 4
3.4 – 1, 2, 3

Performance criteria

● Food and drink service systems are matched to the requirements of different outlets in the hospitality and catering industry
● Skills required for the different food and drink service systems are described
● Benefits and constraints of different services are analysed
● The complexity of skills and appropriate training needs for each are identified
● Good practices for hygiene, health and safety are identified and explained

Assessment details
You are the food and beverage manager of a small but busy hotel and restaurant in your local area. Your business comes from regular business lunches in the week to wedding breakfasts and Sunday lunches at weekends. All are equally as important, of course, but the customers' needs and expectations are very different.

● You are to put together a training package to assist you in making your staff aware of these important differences and services which may be given to these three groups of customers.
● Include within your package any legal aspects which could affect the event. Explain the implications they may have.
● Produce your findings in a simple to understand form that your staff will find easy to follow, such as a matrix.
● Make comparisons of the three events, again a matrix may be used.

Produce your findings in typed form and present in an appropriate manner.

Element 4.2
Identify and evaluate the factors that contribute to successful food and drink services

Core
3.1 – 1, 2, 3, 4
3.2 – 1, 2, 3, 4
3.4 – 1, 2, 3

Performance criteria
● The expectations and needs of different customers are explained
● Factors contributing to successful food and drink services are described
● The relative importance of each factor in relation to different outlets within different sectors is explained and evaluated
● Implications of hygiene, health and safety standards and additional legal aspects affecting events and services are identified and explained

Assessment details
With a colleague you are to plan and implement the running of a lunch-time event within the restaurant. The event is up to you and your colleague to decide.

You must, however, cover the following points:

1 First, decide upon your objectives, i.e. your purpose or target.
2 Compile a suitable menu staying within the given budget.
3 Complete a food order form three weeks in advance fully costed out.
4 Marketing of the event is important, so to make it a success, 50 posters will need to be produced in plenty of time.
5 Produce plans that give clear instructions on the systems you require
6 Service of your food and drink, both production and service.
7 Devise an equipment list for the restaurant and ensure that all items are listed. See example.
8 Allocate roles and responsibilities to your group.
9 Make sure that your plans fall within any legal requirements, e.g. price display, trades description. Also consider hygiene and health and safety standards and how you are going to maintain them before, during and after service.

Record all stages of planning and implementing your event and include it in your assignment. Your work should be typed and presented in an appropriate manner.

Element 4.3
Planning a Food and Drink Event

Core
2.1 – 1, 2, 3, 4
2.2 – 1, 2, 3, 4
2.4 – 1, 2

Performance criteria
● Objectives of a successful food and drink service are determined
● Requirements to meet the objectives of a successful food and drink service are identified and incorporated within a plan
● Procedures, equipment, supplies and staffing needed for the service are realistically estimated and incorporated within the plan
● Roles and staff are allocated appropriately
● The plan is implemented to meet objectives and hygiene, health and safety standards

Assessment details
Following your event you are required to produce a *formal report*, looking at evaluating the planning and delivery of the food and drink event. The report must be typed and bound in an appropriate manner. You should consider the following areas:

● Identifying sources of evaluation and methods of obtaining evaluation, e.g. customers, colleagues, interviews, questionnaires.
● Look at your plan, its strength and weaknesses and examine them closely
● Perhaps improvements could have been made in respect of customers' needs/expectations, organization and motivation skills. Discuss these points and any others you feel are relevant.
● Give your recommendations for improvements for next time.

If you feel you did a perfect job then say so but think carefully. There is always room for improvement.

Element 4.4
Evaluation of an Event

Core
3.1 – 1, 2, 3, 4
3.2 – 1, 2, 3, 4
3.4 – 1, 3

Performance criteria
- Evaluation criteria and sources of evaluation evidence are identified
- Evaluation evidence is analysed according to the criteria
- Strengths and weaknesses of the plan are analysed
- Strengths and weaknesses of the delivery are analysed
- Appropriate measures for improvements are described and feedback is given through an action plan

Certified core skills

	Communication	Application of number	Information technology
Level 1	1 Take part in discussions with known individuals on routine matters 2 Prepare written materials in preset formats 3 Use images to illustrate points made in writing and in discussions with known individuals on routine matters 4 Read and respond to written material and images in preset formats	5 Gather and process data using group 1 mathematical techniques 6 Represent and tackle problems using group 1 mathematical techniques 7 Interpret and present mathematical data using group 1 mathematical techniques	8 Input data into specified locations 9 Edit and organize information within individual applications 10 Present information in preset formats 11 Use operating routines which maximize efficiency
Level 2	1 Take part in discussions with a range of people on routine matters 2 Prepare written material on routine matters 3 Use images to illustrate points made in writing and in discussions with a range of people on routine matters. 4 Read and respond to written material and images on routine matters	5 Gather and process data using group 1 and 2 mathematical techniques 6 Represent and tackle problems using group 1 and 2 mathematical techniques 7 Interpret and present mathematical data using group 1 and 2 mathematical techniques	8 Set up, use and input data into storage systems 9 Edit and organize and integrate information from different sources 10 Select and use formats for presenting information 11 Select and use operating routines which maximize efficiency

Certified core skills (continued)

	Communication	Application of number	Information technology
Level 3	1 Take part in discussions with a range of people on a range 2 Prepare written material on a range of matters 3 Use images to illustrate points made in writing and in discussions with a range of people on a range of matters 4 Read and respond to written materials and images on a range of matters	5 Gather and process data using group 1, 2 and 3 mathematical techniques 6 Represent and tackle problems using group 1, 2 and 3 mathematical techniques 7 Interpret and present mathematical data using group, 2 and 3 mathematical techniques	8 Set system options and set up, use and input data into storage systems 9 Edit, organize and integrate complex information from different sources 10 Select and use formats for presenting complex information from different sources 11 Select and use applications when they are an effective way of working with information
Level 4	1 Take part in and evaluate the effectiveness of, discussions with a number of people on a number of matters 2 Prepare, and evaluate the effectiveness of own written material on a range of matters 3 Use and evaluate the effectiveness of own use of images to illustrate points made in writing and in discussions with a range of people on a range of matters 4 Read and respond to written material and images, recognizing the factors which influence own interpretation	5 Gather and process data using group 1, 2, 3 and 4 mathematical techniques 6 Represent and tackle problems using group 1, 2, 3 and 4 mathematical techniques 7 Interpret and present mathematical data using group 1, 2, 3 and 4 mathematical techniques	8 Set up system options, use storage systems and prepare and input data 9 Set up and use automated routines to edit, organize and integrate complex information from different sources 10 Set up and use automated routines to format and present complex information from different sources 11 Evaluate and select applications for use by self

Certified core skills (continued)

	Communication	Application of number	Information technology
Level 5	1 Lead and evaluate the effectiveness of discussions with a range of people on a range of matters 2 Prepare and evaluate the effectiveness of own and others' written material on a range of matters 3 Use and evaluate the effectiveness of own and others' use of images to illustrate points made in writing and discussions with a range of people on a range of matters 4 Read and respond to written material and images recognizing the factors which influence own and others' interpretations	5 Gather and process data using group 1, 2, 3, 4, and 5 mathematical techniques 6 Represent and tackle problems using group 1, 2, 3, 4 and 5 mathematical techniques 7 Interpret and present mathematical data using group 1, 2, 3, 4 and 5 mathematical techniques	8 Set up system options, use storage systems, and validate, prepare and input data 9 Investigate and resolve problems in editing, organizing and integrating complex information from different sources 10 Investigate and resolve problems in formatting and presenting complex information from different sources 11 Evaluate and select applications for use by self and others

Core skills which you should experience

	Working with others	Improve own learning and performance	Problem solving
Level 1	Work to given collective goals and responsibilities Use given working methods in fulfilling own responsibilities	Agree short-term targets Follow given activities to learn and to improve performance	Select standard solutions to describe problems fully

Core skills which you should experience (continued)

	Working with others	*Improve own learning and performance*	*Problem solving*
Level 2	Work to given collective goals and provide feedback to help with the allocation of responsibilities Use given working methods in fulfilling own responsibilities, and provide feedback to others on own progress	Contribute to identifying strengths and learning needs, and agree short-term targets Make use of feedback in following given activities to learn to improve performance	Use established procedures to clarify routine problems Select standard solutions to routine problems
Level 3	Work to given collective goals and contribute to the process of allocating individuals' responsibilities Agree working methods and use them, and provide feedback to others on own progress	Identify strengths and learning needs, and agree short-term targets Seek and make use of feedbacks, follow given activities to learn and to improve performance	Select procedures to clarify problems with a range of possible solutions Identify alternative solutions and select solutions to problems
Level 4	Contribute to determining collective goals and to the process of allocating individuals' responsibilities Agree working methods and use them, and contribute to the process of maintaining standards of work	Identify strengths and learning needs, and propose and agree short-term targets Seek and make use of feedback, select and follow activities to learn and to improve performance	Extend specialist knowledge in order to clarify complex problems with a range of possible solutions Identify alternative solutions and select solutions to complex problems
Level 5	Lead the process of determining collective goals and allocating individuals' responsibilities Agree working methods and use them, monitor overall progress of own and others' work	Identify strengths and learning needs, and propose and agree long-term targets Seek and make use of feedbacks, select and follow a wide range of activities to learn and to improve performance	Extend specialist knowledge in order to clarify complex problems with a range of possible solutions which include unknown/unpredictable features Identify alternative solutions and select solutions to complex problems which include unknown/unpredictable features

PURCHASING, COSTING AND FINANCE

The hospitality and catering industry, whether commercial or catering services, needs to be economically viable. This unit explains the need to operate on a sound financial basis and takes you step by step through the various financial information you require, giving detailed explanations and reasons for measuring financial performance. The unit puts into context purchasing, costing and finance enabling you to identify more clearly its importance and relevance to hospitality and catering. It covers:

- The types of information
- The reasons and ways of measuring performance and the data used
- Sources of supply and methods of purchasing the operation of purchasing, and methods used to control the process
- The calculation of costs and selling price of goods and services

▪ MEASURING FINANCIAL PERFORMANCE ▪

Introduction

In this section we look at the data which are available in order to measure the performance of an organization. We will identify those who use financial information, the sorts of information they require and the different ways of presenting information. We will also examine why we need to measure the performance of the organization, and will learn some of the different ways in which performance can be measured.

Users of financial information

It is impossible to name *all* the possible users of financial information and the types of financial information they require. Those who use financial information need it in order to make decisions. Information which does not fulfil this purpose is of no use.

Even if no action is taken, there may still be a decision being made. For example, your take-home pay from your part-time job is notified to you on your wage slip (Figure 6.1). This is financial information. You may not take any action as a result of this information, but you may use it to decide that you have been paid correctly. You may even take action later – to work extra hours to boost your pay, for example.

Those responsible for running an organization, i.e. the management team, use financial information all the time to enable them to run it properly. Some information is needed very frequently – hourly, daily or weekly; other information is needed less frequently – perhaps once a year (annually). The management team is responsible for providing information to other users. To assist them, there will be other employees responsible for information at a lower level. This information will then be passed 'upwards', added to other information, perhaps summarized, and then provided to those who require it.

ACE HOTELS LTD

Wage Slip   **Week No. 41**

Employee No. 613   **Dept 4**

Basic pay	£100.00
Overtime	£15.00
Gross wages	£115.00
Less Tax	£35.00
National Insurance	£8.00
Net pay	£72.00

Figure 6.1 A wage slip

There are four main users of information, outside the management team:

- The owners of the organization
- The managers of the organization
- Those who provide finance or lend money to the organization
- The tax authorities and government departments

Let us look at each of these in turn, and the types of financial information which they might need.

Owners (also called *investors*)

These put money into (invest in) the organization, in the same way as you might put money into a Building Society. They usually want a *return* on their investment.

Definition

- *A **return** on an investment is the amount of money which the investment makes for the investors*

This means that they want the organization to make a profit, which they might be able to have paid to them. They will want to compare this return with the amount invested. If an owner invests £1000 for a year, and only gets a £1 return, this is poor. He or she might get £50 from a building society for the same amount invested. Most owners need to know the return on their investment on an annual basis – things change so often from day to day that it is not realistic to check too frequently on this information. Many organizations only calculate their profits annually, or perhaps quarterly, so the information is not available any more often than this.

There are different kinds of owners in different kinds of organization. In small businesses, such as cafés and restaurants, there might be only one owner, and this is called a 'sole proprietor'. In slightly larger organizations there might be a few owners, called a 'partnership'. In bigger organizations there might be hundreds or thousands of owners, each owning one or more 'shares' in the organization. These are 'limited companies', and the majority of our well-known hotel and restaurant chains are of this type.

> **Point of interest**
> Anita Roddick, who is now managing director of The Body Shop, started off as a sole proprietor. As the business grew, she joined forces with other investors, and formed a public limited company, where she is only one shareholder among many. No doubt she owns a lot of the shares, and receives a good salary for her work, but the organization became too big for her to fund on her own. As managing director of a limited company, she expects to earn more than she did as a sole proprietor, of course!

Some organizations are owned by the government or by trusts and charities, such as hospitals, prisons, schools and colleges.

Task 6.1

Make a list of hospitality organizations near your home, school or college. Find out whether they are owned by sole proprietors, partnerships, limited companies or government bodies. Try to find at least one of each type. You can probably guess at the ownership of some of them, or you can find out the ownership by examining their stationery.

Managers of hospitality and catering organizations

The managers of organizations look after the running of the organization on behalf of the owners. Sometimes the managers *are* the owners, especially in small, family-run businesses. Managers are usually involved in the *daily* running of the business. They need up-to-date information on what is happening in the business, so that they can take action to correct any mistakes or to improve the situation.

Different types of information are prepared at different intervals. The bank balance, for example, needs to be controlled at all times, so information on the up-to-date bank balance would be available daily. Reports on employee absence are usually prepared weekly or monthly – often enough for managers to realize if employees are taking too much time off and to find out why, but not so often that they are upsetting employees. The profit of a facility might be calculated quarterly or monthly, at most. Calculating profit is a difficult and time-consuming job, so to do this more often would be expensive. Most facilities experience 'ups and downs' in the level of business during a month, so to calculate profit more often might produce a misleading picture of a particularly poor week or an extremely good

weekend. Monthly is the most popular frequency for most financial information to be prepared in larger organizations; quarterly or less is common in small ones.

Different managers will require different information. Generally, more senior managers will need the sorts of information which are produced annually rather than weekly; they will need information which is summarized, rather than detailed (such as total food costs rather than the costs of individual commodities); they will not need figures to be precise – £25,000 will do, rather than £25,045. Junior managers will need more frequent information, with greater detail and accuracy, as they are dealing with activities on a daily basis, often involving smaller values.

Providers of finance

These are people who lend money to the organization. They include banks, building societies, finance companies, and also people who sell goods or services to the organization who are not paid at once. The amounts owed to these providers are called *liabilities*.

Definition

- **Liabilities** *are amounts owed by the organization to people who have provided it with money, goods or services.*

Some providers are 'long term', i.e. they are repaid over a long period of time, perhaps many years. Some providers are 'short term' or 'current', which means that they are paid fairly quickly, perhaps within a few weeks.

Providers are interested in knowing that the organization has enough cash or money in the bank to pay them back when they are due to be paid. In other words, they are interested in knowing what *assets* the organization has.

Definition

● **Assets** are things which an organization owns.

Like liabilities, assets can also be divided into two types. *Current assets* consist of things which the organization owns that could easily be turned into cash, without damaging or altering the nature of the organization. Current assets include cash and bank balances, stock of food, etc. *Fixed assets* consist of things which the organization intends to keep for a long time, and which, if sold, would damage or alter the nature of the organization. Fixed assets include land and buildings, equipment and machinery, furniture and fittings, etc.

Task 6.2

Think of four different situations where an organization might need to borrow money. Include at least one long- and one short-term borrowing.

The tax authorities

There are two main authorities requiring financial information of an organization. These are the Inland Revenue and the Customs and Excise. The Inland Revenue (often known as 'the tax people') want to know how much profit has been made, so as to charge the correct amount of *income tax* or *corporation tax*. This is done on an *annual* basis, so organizations need to produce *annual accounts*.

Definition

● **Annual accounts** are the sets of information which organizations produce covering a complete year.

Annual accounts come in different forms for different organizations, but most would include a statement showing turnover, *profit* and tax owing, a statement showing assets and liabilities, and information which can be used to calculate the return on investment. Some of these statements will be discussed later.

Definition

● **Profit** is the money which an organization makes from selling its goods and services, after deducting the costs of providing those goods and services.

The Customs and Excise want to know how much has been bought and sold so as to collect the correct amount of *Value Added Tax*. This is usually done on a quarterly basis.

Both of these authorities are government departments and the information they require is *statutory*. If something is statutory it means that we have no choice – we must do or give whatever the law says, and we could go to prison if we do not.

Definition

● **Income tax, corporation tax** and **Value Added Tax** are all taxes set by the government. You need not learn any more about income tax or corporation tax, but you will learn later how to calculate Value Added Tax.
● **Statutory** means 'by law', or forced upon us by the government.

Value Added Tax (VAT) is charged on goods and services sold by many organizations. The current rate is 17.5 per cent. It must be added to the selling price, and handed over to the government (Customs and Excise). The business cannot keep it, so it does not add to the profits of the business. However, the business can also *reclaim* from the government any VAT it has to pay on things it buys, so VAT does not add to its costs either. You must understand that the VAT has to be separated out from the selling price or cost price in order to determine the correct value to the business.

For example, if a bar *sells* drinks for £20, it must add VAT of £3.50 to the bill, and sell them for £23.50. It sends £3.50 to the Customs and Excise office, so it keeps only £20.00. If the bar *buys* drinks for £20, it has to pay out £23.50 because VAT will have to be added. But it can claim the VAT on things it buys *back* from the Customs and Excise, so £3.50 is refunded.

Turnover is another important piece of financial information in which all users are interested. It is the starting point for many calculations and later we will see how it is used to calculate many other figures.

Definition

● **Turnover** *is the income which an organization has earned from its sales before any costs or expenses are deducted.*

Reasons for measuring financial performance

We need to keep control of the activities of the organization in order to ensure that it meets the requirements of its users (for example, that it makes enough profit, it has enough cash, it settles its VAT on time, etc.). In order to keep control we need to measure the performance of the organization.

We also need to keep control on a regular basis. It is no use, for example, if we look at the cash position only once a year – we could run out of cash part-way through, or even on the first day! We must monitor what is happening throughout the year, at least monthly, and possibly daily. If we do that, we can take remedial action to correct the problem, such as asking the bank for a loan.

Some things cannot be measured as frequently as others because the information is simply not available. For example, we can compare our organization with others only when those others produce their information – which might be once a year. Some things do not need to be measured as frequently as others. For example, reading the electricity meter every day would be very misleading – some days are colder than others, so we need to take an *average* reading over several weeks to check on our potential heating bill.

There are four main reasons for measuring financial performance:

1 *Statutory* reasons (those required by law)
2 *Maintaining finance* (ensuring that sufficient funds or cash are available when required)
3 Comparing with *targets* (what we are aiming for)
4 Improving performance

Definition

● **Maintaining** *finance means making sure that there is sufficient cash or money in the bank to pay for the things that the organization needs.*
● **Targets** *are things to aim for. An organization might have a target to sell as much as it did last year, or 10 per cent more, or more than another organization does.*

Some of the reasons overlap each other. Comparison with targets, for example, is also needed to ensure that performance is improved

– you need to know what level of performance you are aiming for (this is your target). We can look at each of these reasons in turn.

Statutory reasons

We have already mentioned that the tax authorities need to know the profit in order to charge the correct amount of tax and to collect VAT. These are statutory reasons for the provision of information, which means that they are required by law. Another statutory reason is to inform the public about what organizations are doing. This includes giving information about:

● What assets they have
● What liabilities they have
● What they spend their money on
● How much their senior managers and directors are paid
● How many employees they have

Statutory information is needed especially from organizations such as hospitals, prisons, schools and colleges, because the public provides the money to run these.

In fact, all organizations are required by law to produce 'annual accounts'. Organizations are also required by law to produce certain statistics, if requested by the government. Some of these are looked at later. It is obvious that most organizations need to keep proper records and control of their activities if they are to fulfil these obligations.

Task 6.3

Obtain a set of accounts from a limited company (if you write to the head office of a large hotel or restaurant chain, they will probably send you a copy). List the various types of information given by the accounts.

Maintaining finance

We have already looked at some of the information which providers of finance need. They need to know that the organization can pay any interest due and can repay the debt when the time comes. So some are interested in the present or near-future position, whereas some are interested in the likely position in a few years' time.

Long-term lenders will also need to know if there are other long-term lenders due to be paid at the same time. If the organization does not make enough profit it may not have enough cash. Lenders may need to look at the other things which the organization has that could be sold if necessary to pay them back, e.g. land and buildings, and other *assets*.

Your parents and friends are the same. If they lend you money, they want to know that they will get it back. They don't often ask you to pay interest, but they might if you borrow it for a long time! They might also be reluctant to lend you money if they know that you already owe Grandma money too!

The organization must be able to keep track of its balance at the bank, and must be able to produce statements, from time to time, of its receipts and payments to enable management to see where the money comes from and goes to. In order to do this, a system of accurate recording of monies in and out of the organization is required.

Comparing with targets

The users of information, as mentioned earlier, will all have their own targets which they expect the organization to meet. The financial information produced will need to be compared with these targets in order to determine whether or not the organization is operating to their satisfaction. These targets are sometimes based on previous results – often, some improvement on the previous year is expected or hoped for. Or they may be based on the results obtained by other organizations in the same area of business. Or they may simply be based on the user's own personal expectations.

> Your own target might be to save £500 for a holiday.

Financial information should be produced at regular intervals, so that comparisons are made early enough for action to be taken. If a profit of £100,000 for the year is the target, and after six months only £30,000 has been made, there is still time to examine the reasons for this shortfall, and to try to improve performance for the second half of the year.

Targets are often long term, such as a restaurant owner having a target to open a second restaurant. Some targets might be very difficult to achieve, but they should be *capable of being achieved*. A target which is impossible can be very demotivating.

Improving performance

It is possible that this is the most important reason for monitoring financial performance – in order to improve it. Most organizations wish to improve – they want to expand their business, sell more, improve quality, increase turnover (sales), reduce expenses, have more cash, increase profits, and so on. And all for as little outlay (investment) as possible. There may even be occasions when performance cannot be improved, but monitoring is still needed to ensure that the situation does not get worse.

All these improvements, or reductions in inefficiency, involve very careful monitoring of the organization's performance in all the areas mentioned above.

Task 6.4

Look at your school, college or place of work, if you have a job. What areas can you find where performance could be improved? Can you suggest ways of making these improvements?

Types of financial statement and other data needed to measure financial performance

You have seen how different users have different needs for information, and that the same information can be used for several purposes. Some information may be provided 'on request', when it is asked for. This is fine for information which is required by only one or two users and is infrequently requested. But there are some items of information which are required frequently, even regularly, especially those required for statutory reasons. Therefore, most organizations produce certain items of information automatically and forward it to particular users as it is produced.

Presentation of information

Some information must be presented in a certain way, especially if it is required by statute (i.e. by law). Other information may be presented in any way which suits the organization or the users of the information, but even so, it is best to keep to 'standard' or well-used lay-outs for basic information, as the users are often accustomed to receiving information in a predefined form. Some information can be presented in charts or diagrams, which make it easier to understand.

Types of financial statement

The type of statement depends entirely on the information it is intended to provide. It needs to be sufficiently detailed to enable the user to determine the information he or she requires, but not so detailed that it provides unnecessary information or confuses the reader.

Some statements are designed for particular purposes and are therefore unique. The majority, however, are common to many organizations and their users. Some of these are considered next.

Before we discuss them, however, you should understand that statements can be prepared with *actual* or with *budgeted* figures.

Definition

- *Actual* figures are those which have already been achieved.
- *Budgeted* figures are those which are, or were, expected to be achieved.

Many of the statements contain *both* actual and budgeted figures to enable comparison between the two to be made.

A budget is a form of target. However, a budget should consist of results which you can expect to achieve or which are likely to occur. A target could be something to aim for which might be greater than the budget. For example, you might aim to open a new restaurant, but the opportunity might not arise for many years. This would be your target. To help in achieving your target, you might budget to increase profits by a small amount each year until you have raised enough to open the new restaurant.

You should also understand that some statements cover a period of time – for example a month or a year. Most organizations have a *financial year*.

Definition

- A *financial year* is a 12-month period which an organization uses to total up its figures. The financial year might run from any date, it does not have to be from 1st January but it must be for a complete 12-month period.

In addition to showing the figures for a month, some statements show the figures for the 'year to date', i.e. the total since the beginning of the financial year. So a statement for the month of July might also show the total for the seven months from 1 January to 31 July – i.e. the year to date.

The statements which an organization might prepare are as follows:

- Cost statements
- Operating statements
- Profit and loss accounts
- Balance sheets
- Cash flow statements

We will look at each of these in turn.

Cost statements

Any statement which shows the costs of doing something is a cost statement. A cost statement does not include *income* or *profit* – only costs.

Definition

- *Income* is the money earned or taken in by the organization.
- *Profit* is the amount of income left over after the running costs have been deducted from the income.

Some activities which need cost statements do not provide any income or profit in any case. For example, the Housekeeping *operation* in a hotel keeps the rooms clean and ready for occupation, and incurs costs in doing so, but it does not receive any income.

Definition

- *An **operation** is an activity or group of activities carried out in an outlet or facility. Some operations consist of entire departments, such as the Laundry department, which is resposible for the laundry operations.*

A cost statement might concern the cost of an operation, or the cost of a dish or menu, or the cost of a function or activity. Each area which incurs costs is called a *cost centre* or *cost heading*.

Definition

- *A **cost centre** is any part of an organization to which costs can be charged.*

A cost centre might also be an entire department, operation, a dish or menu, etc. Or it might be a piece of equipment, for which costs are incurred such as its purchase, insurance, repairs and maintenance, A cost statement might cover a period in time, say a month or a year; or it might be a 'one-off' – a

wedding, perhaps. It should show what the cost is made up of, and how the total is arrived at. Examples of cost statements are:

- Standard recipes
- Labour (wages) costs for a department for a week
- Maintenance costs for kitchen equipment for the year
- Costs of the Housekeeping department for a week
- Kitchen production costs for a week

Figure 6.2 is an example of a wages cost statement.

Task 6.5

Ask your supervisor at work if you can look at a cost statement for the week. What information does it contain? If you are at school or in college, perhaps you could look at the cost of running the canteen or refectory. (If you cannot obtain a real cost statement, ask your parents if they can work out a cost statement for running the house for a week – you will probably be surprised at how many different costs are involved, and how high some of them are!)

Departmental Wages Cost Statement				Restaurant
Month: December 1994				
Staff category	Basic wages	Overtime	Pension	Total
	£	£	£	£
Manager	1,500.00	–	60.00	1,560.00
Assistant Manager	1,000.00	–	40.00	1,040.00
Waitresses (6)	3,000.00	1,000.00	120.00	4,120.00
Total	5,500.00	1,000.00	220.00	6,720.00

Figure 6.2 A departmental wages cost statement

Operating statement

Some departments, activities or sections of an organization earn *revenue*.

Definition

● **Revenue** is the money earned. Other words for revenue are 'income' and 'turnover'.

An operating statement is prepared for 'revenue-earning' operations or departments, i.e. those which earn income for the organization. The operating statement shows the income earned, the costs of running the department and the profit which the department has made.

Some operations have no income – the Laundry department in a hotel, for example – and therefore have no profit. In a hospital or a prison there is no income from sales (although there is income from the government), but they may still produce an operating statement to suit their own needs.

The costs of some departments are spread among others. The cost of the Laundry department might be spread between accommodation (rooms) and restaurant, because both of these need to use the services of the Laundry department for clean linen.

Task 6.6

How many departments in a large hotel can you think of which earn revenue?
How many can you think of which do not earn revenue?

The operating statement often shows the actual figures and the budgeted figures as well for comparison and 'year-to-date' figures. An example of a simple operating statement for a restaurant, for the month of July, might be as follows.

ACE Hotels Ltd: Restaurant Operating Statement for July

	Actual		Budget	
	£	%	£	%
Sales	10,000	100	11,000	100
Food and drink costs	4,000	40	4,500	40.9
Gross profit	6,000	60	6,500	59.1
Wages	2,500	25	2,400	21.8
Net margin	3,500	35	4,100	37.3
Restaurant expenses	1,500	15	1,600	14.6
Net operating profit	2,000	20	2,500	22.7

An operating statement shows only those costs which are connected with that department or activity. General costs (such as bank charges, administration, telephone) would not appear on it, unless they could be identified with that department or activity. These general costs are sometimes called 'undistributed costs', and we will look at these later.

Only items which have been used up or consumed during the period are included on the operating statement. For example, food and drink costing £6000 may have been bought, but £2000 is still unused at the end of the period. Therefore, only £4000-worth of food and drink is shown as an expense on the operating statement.

The operating statement can show profit at different 'levels' if this is considered useful. We will look at those levels now.

Remember that the examples given here are of a restaurant, so we refer to 'food and drink', 'kitchen wages', etc., but if we were dealing with another type of outlet the costs might have different descriptions.

Gross profit

In a restaurant, for example, the most significant cost is usually food. Many restaurants find it useful to calculate the profit after deducting the cost of food and drink. This is known as the *gross profit*.

Definition

- **Gross profit** *equals the selling price less the cost of the food and drink.*

The Restaurant Operating Statement of Ace Hotels Ltd., shows that the actual gross profit for July is £6000:

Sales	£10,000
less food and drink costs	£ 4,000
Gross profit	£ 6,000

This can be seen more easily in a pie chart (Figure 6.3), where it is obvious at a glance that the gross profit is considerably greater than the cost of food and drink. But don't forget that other costs have still to be deducted before the net operating profit is calculated.

Constructing a pie chart

To construct a pie chart, we need to know that a complete circle has 360°.

Then we can follow these steps:

- Draw a circle of any reasonable size.
- Find the total 'size' of the pie – in the case of Ace Hotels Ltd, the total sales is £10,000 so this is the total of the pie.
- Find the 'size' of the parts of the pie, i.e.:
  Food and drinks costs £4000
  Gross profit £6000
- Divide the pie into slices, using the formula:

$$\frac{\text{Size of 'part'}}{\text{Total size of pie}} \times 360$$

So the slice of pie for food and drink costs is

$$\frac{4,000}{10,000} \times 360 = 144°$$

and the slice of pie for gross profit is

$$\frac{6,000}{10,000} \times 360 = 216°$$

A protractor is used to measure these angles. The total must equal 360°.

Computer technology could easily produce pie charts and other diagrams.

Gross operating profit or net margin

The cost of kitchen and restaurant wages is also a significant cost in the running of the restaurant, so another level of profit can be calculated, after deducting food, drink and wages – this is known as *gross operating profit*, and is also sometimes called *net margin*.

Definition

- **Gross operating profit** *equals the sales less the cost of food and drink and wages.*

The Restaurant Operating Statement for Ace Hotels Ltd., shows that the actual gross operating profit for July is £3500:

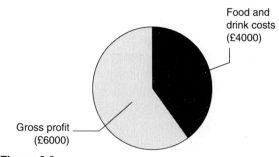

Food and drink costs (£4000)

Gross profit (£6000)

Figure 6.3

Sales		£10,000
less Food and drink costs	£ 4,000	
less Wages	£ 2,500	
		£ 6,500
Gross operating profit		£ 3,500

Another way of calculating gross operating profit is gross profit less wages. Both methods

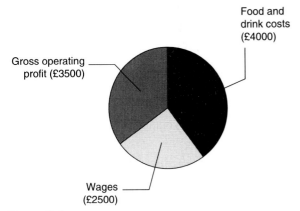

Gross operating profit (£3500)

Food and drink costs (£4000)

Wages (£2500)

Figure 6.4

should give the same answer. A pie chart showing food and drink costs, wages and gross operating profit would appear as in Figure 6.4.

Net operating profit

When other restaurant expenses have been deducted, such as laundry costs, heat and light, etc., the *net operating profit* is produced.

Definition

- **Net operating profit** is the sales less all other expenses of the departments for which we are preparing the operating statement.

The Restaurant Operating Statement for Ace Hotels Ltd shows that the actual net operating profit for July is £2000:

Sales		£10,000
less Food and drink costs	£ 4,000	
less Wages	£ 2,500	
less restaurant expenses	£ 1,500	
		£ 8,000
Net operating profit		£ 2,000

Another way of calculating net operating profit is gross operating profit less other expenses. Both methods should give the same answer.

Task 6.7

Draw a pie chart for the Restaurant Operating Statement for Ace Hotels Ltd to show the four 'slices' of food and drink costs, wages, other expenses and net operating profit.

The operating statement can also contain a 'percentage' column, which shows the value of each item as a percentage of sales income. To calculate an item as a percentage of another is as follows:

£4000 as a percentage of £10,000 is:

$$\frac{4000}{10,000} \times 100 = 40\%$$

Each of the percentages is the amount in pounds (from the first column), expressed as a percentage of sales, e.g.

Wages expressed as a percentage of sales is

$$\frac{\text{Wages}}{\text{Sales}} \times 100 = \frac{2,500}{10,000} \times 100 = 25\%$$

Some organizations show *all* their revenue-earning departments on the operating statement, so that they can be totalled and compared with each other. However, this can look quite complicated in larger organizations, especially if the statement also shows budgeted figures and percentages.

Summary of the 'levels of profit'

We can imagine the three levels of profit as a series of steps as in Figure 6.5.

Task 6.8

Draw up an operating statement for a student refectory for the month of May, and for the year to date, from the following information:

Sales	May	£18,000
	January–April	£60,000
Food costs	May	£ 8,100
	January–April	£27,780
Wages	May	£ 3,600
	January–April	£13,560
Other expenses	May	£ 2,700
	January–April	£ 9,780

Profit and loss account

We have just seen that an operating statement contains the income and expenses from a department or an activity, and is used to calculate the net operating profit for each one. When this has been done, the various operating statements are brought together in the profit and loss account. The profit and loss account shows the income for the whole organization, and all its expenses. It may keep separate sections for each of the main departments of the organization, such as rooms, restaurant, bar and other areas, or it may add them together.

Here is an example of a profit and loss account for Ace Hotels Ltd showing the three departments of Rooms, Restaurant and Bar separately as well as the totals:

ACE Hotels Ltd. Profit and Loss account for the month ending 31 July

	Rooms £	Restaurant £	Bar £	Total £
Sales	30,000	10,000	2,500	42,500
Cost of sales	–	4,000	1,200	5,200
Wages costs	6,000	2,500	800	9,300
Other expenses	1,000	1,500	200	2,700
Net operating profit	23,000	2,000	300	25,300

less undistributed expenses:	
Administration	8,000
Marketing	3,000
Rent, rates and Insurance	4,000
Finance charges	300
	15,300
Net profit	10,000

The top part of the profit and loss account contains the same information as in the operating statements we looked at in the previous section, except that it does not show gross profit or gross operating profit. This is just to make the statement easier to read. Now we are deducting the expenses which could not be spread among those departments – the *undistributed expenses* – to arrive at *net profit*.

Definition

● *Net profit* is the profit remaining *after* all other costs *have been deducted.*

Again, we could use a pie chart to show how the profit and loss account is made up (Figure 6.6). Note that the total of all the 'slices' equals the total sales – £42,500.

As with the operating statement, the profit and loss account can also show budgeted and year-to-date figures.

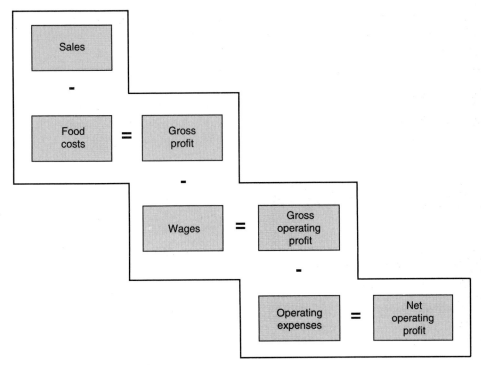

Figure 6.5 Levels of profit

Task 6.9

Draw up a profit and loss account for a restaurant, for the month of June, from the following information:

		£
Sales	-- meals	30,000
	– bar	5,000
Cost of sales	– meals	18,000
	– bar	2,500
Wages	– meals	3,000
	– bar	1,000
Other expenses	– meals	1,500
	– bar	500
Undistributed expenses:		
Advertising		1,200
Stationery		800
Rent and rates		3,500

Balance sheet

This is a statement which shows the *assets*, *liabilities* and *capital* of the organization at a point in time, and is used by those who need details of the security of their money, such as lenders.

Definition

● **Assets** are things owned by an organization.

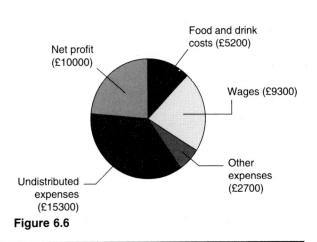

Figure 6.6

There are two main categories of assets:

1 *Fixed assets*. These are intended to be used for a long period of time. Examples include: land, buildings, equipment, furniture, furnishings.

2 *Current assets*. These are intended to be used for only a short period of time, or are expected to change frequently. They include stocks of food and liquor, stationery, bank balances.

Current assets also include amounts owing *to* the organization *by* other people. These are called *debtors* and they arise if customers buy goods or services 'on credit', which means that they do not pay for their goods or services at once; instead they pay later, perhaps at the end of the following month. The amount they still owe when the balance sheet is prepared is shown as a current asset because the organization owns money which is still held by these debtors.

Task 6.10

Look at your college, school or place of work. What assets can you find there? Which are fixed, *and which are* current *assets?*

Definition

● *Liabilities are amounts owed by the organization to people who have provided it with money, goods or services.*

There are two main categories of liabilities too:

1 *Current liabilities*. These are amounts which the organization expects to repay in a short period of time. A bank overdraft is usually a current liability.

Current liabilities also include amounts owing *by* the organization to other people. These are called *creditors* and they can arise if the organization buys goods or services 'on credit', which means that it does not pay for the goods or services at once; instead it pays later, perhaps at the end of the following month. The amount they are still owed when the balance sheet is prepared is shown as a current liability because the organization owes money to these creditors. (Do not confuse *creditors* with *debtors*, which are mentioned above under 'current assets'. Creditors are people who are owed money *by* the organization; debtors are people who owe money *to* the organization.)

2 *Long-term liabilities*. These are amounts that the organization has borrowed which do not require repayment in the immediate future. Examples include mortgages, loans, etc.

Definition

● *Capital is the money put into the organization by its owner or owners.*

In a limited company the capital is made up of 'shares' with owners investing in one or more shares each. Capital is increased by any profit made, which has been left in the organization, and it is decreased by any losses. Here is an example of a balance sheet:

ACE Hotels Ltd: Balance Sheet as at 31 July 199X

Fixed assets:	£	£	£	Author's comments
Land and Buildings		100,000		
Furniture and Equipment		60,000		
			160,000	(A) *Total of Fixed Assets*
Current assets:				
Stocks of food	2,000			
Debtors	1,500			
Bank and cas	12,000			
		15,500		(B) *Total of current assets*
less Current liabilities:				
Creditors		2,500		(C) *Total of current liabilities*
WORKING CAPITAL			13,000	(D) *Current assets less current liabilities*
			173,000	(E) *Fixed assets plus working capital*
less Long-term Liabilities:				
Loan			43,000	(F)
			130,000	(G) *All assets less all liabilities*
Financed by:				
Capital at start of year		120,000		
Net profit during year		10,000		
Capital at end of year		130,000		(H) *Equals total above*

Note that the two totals (G and H) of £130,000 are equal. If this does not happen, then a mistake has been made in preparing the balance sheet.

The balance sheet is based on the *accounting equation.*

Definition

- *The **accounting equation** states that:*
  Assets minus liabilities = owners' capital

In other words, the assets of the organization (what it owns) less its liabilities (what it owes) equals the value of the organization to the owners.

In the balance sheet above, the assets are those figures labelled A and B:

A (Fixed Assets)	= £160,000
B (Current Assets)	= £ 15,500
Total assets	= £175,500

and the liabilities are those figures labelled C and F:

C (Current Liabilities)	= £ 2,500
F (Long-term liabilities)	= £43,000
Total liabilities	= £45,500

Therefore, assets minus liabilities = £175,500 – £45,500 = £130,000 and we can compare this with the capital figure (H), which is also £130,000. So the above balance sheet proves the accounting equation.

You can compare this with your personal situation. Suppose you have a television worth £200, a personal stereo worth £50, and £20 in cash. These are your assets, and they total £270.

Suppose, however, that you bought the television on credit, and you still owe £40. This is a liability. Assets minus liabilities = £270 – £40 = £230.

If you were to sell your belongings for the above values, and repay your debts, you would be left with £230. This is your capital. Assets minus liabilities.

However, if you sold the stereo for more than £50 – say, you sold it for £60 – you would make a profit of £10. Your capital would be increased by the profit you had made, and you would then have £240.

Working capital is also shown on the above balance sheet.

Definition

● **Working capital** is current assets minus current liabilities, and it tells us how much 'ready money' the organization has.

The current assets can all be easily turned into cash without destroying the organization, and after paying off the current liabilities the working capital will be left over to run the organization.

In the above balance sheet, working capital is:

B (Current Assets) minus C (Current Liabilities)
= £15,500 – £2500
= £13,000

Alternative lay-outs for the balance sheet

The lay-out shown earlier is called 'vertical' because it works from the top to the bottom. It is the most popular lay-out used by organizations because it shows the working capital figure clearly. An alternative lay-out is the 'two-sided' one, shown below. It is often preferred by students as it seems easier to understand, but it is not often used in real life.

ACE Hotels Ltd: Balance Sheet as at 31 July 199x

Fixed assets	£	Owner's capital	£
Land and Buildings	100,000	Capital at start of year	120,000
Furniture and Equipment	60,000	Net profit during year	10,000
	160,000	Capital at end of year	130,000
Current assets			
Stocks of food	2,000	Long-term liabilities	
Debtors	1,500	Loan	43,000
Bank and cash	12,000	Current liabilities	
	15,500	Creditors	2,500
	175,500		175,500

It shows the same figures as the vertical lay-out, except for working capital, but it is organized into two 'sides', with assets on one side and liabilities and capital on the other. The totals of each side are equal. It still conforms to the accounting equation (assets – liabilities = capital), because this is the same as assets = capital + liabilities.

Task 6.11

Draw up a balance sheet from the following information as at 30 June:

Furniture	£25,000
Kitchen equipment	£ 8,000
Office equipment	£ 4,000
Bank balance	£ 7,200
Stocks of food	£ 800
Owing by customers	£ 500
Owing to suppliers	£ 1,400
Loan for kitchen equipment (repayable in 5 years)	£ 3,500
Capital at the start of the year	£37,600
Profit for the year	£ 3,000

Try both types of lay-out – the vertical and the two-sided one.

Cash flow statements

These are produced at least monthly for most organizations. Cash changes very rapidly, and often requires decisions to be made. There may be spare cash (a 'surplus') which needs to be invested temporarily; or there may be a cash shortage which requires borrowing to overcome it. A cash flow statement shows where the cash comes from and on what it is spent.

Below is an example of a cash flow statement for ACE Hotels Ltd. The statement covers a whole year, but is split into four 'quarters'. Thus, the March quarter will cover January, February and March, and so on. Some organizations might do this if their cash flow does not alter much from month to month, or if they just wanted a quick look at the cash flow situation.

ACE Hotels Ltd: Quarterly cash flow Statement for the year to 31 December 199X

	March £	June £	September £	December £
Opening balance	10,800	13,600	16,375	12,125
Receipts:				
Customers	13,000	15,000	10,000	13,700
Loans	10,000			
Other		175	50	
Total receipts	23,000	15,175	10,050	13,700
Balance available	33,800	28,775	26,425	25,825
Payments:				
Suppliers	6,500	6,400	6,000	6,100
Heat and light	1,500	1,200	1,350	1,300
Rent and rates	1,000	1,000	1,000	1,000
Insurances	400	400	400	400
Wages	2,500	2,600	2,750	2,650
Fixed assets	8,000		2,000	
Loan repayments		500	500	500
Interest	200	200	200	200
Bank charges	100	100	100	75
Other				
Total payments	20,200	12,400	14,300	12,225
Closing balance	13,600	16,375	12,125	13,600

A line graph could be used to show how the bank balance changes from quarter to quarter. To prepare a line graph, we plot the values up the side and the months or quarters along the bottom, and place a marker to show the balance at each date. We then join up the markers with straight lines (Figure 6.7).

Cash may come from various sources including:

- Normal sales
- Borrowed money
- Investment by the owners
- Sale of fixed assets such as equipment

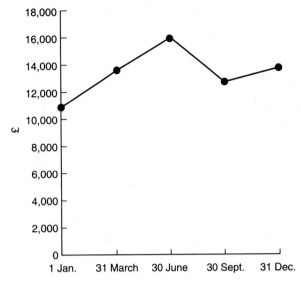

Figure 6.7 A line graph showing bank balances

It may be spent on:

- Supplies of materials (food, for example)
- Labour
- Various other operating expenses (such as heat and light, stationery, etc.)
- The purchase of fixed assets (such as equipment)
- Finance costs (such as bank interest)
- The repayment of loans

There may be an opening (starting) bank balance available.

The statement is usually organized so that:

Starting bank balance
plus
Monies received
less
Monies paid out
equals
Closing bank balance

This closing balance then becomes the starting balance of the next period.

Some transactions result in money coming in or going out immediately, others in money coming in or out at some other time, either earlier or later. For example, the above cash flow statement shows that in the March quarter, £10,000 was paid out for fixed assets. These may have been bought in the previous year (or the payment might have been a deposit in advance), but it is the moment of *payment* which determines when the item appears in the cash flow statement.

You have already seen how amounts still owing (debtors and creditors) are dealt with in the balance sheet. In the cash flow statement only the amounts which are paid are shown. Some may be paid in the same month as the goods are bought/sold, some may be paid later. You must take care to calculate the amount actually received or paid out correctly.

For example, sales to customers in the March quarter might have been £14,000, but if £1000 was not received until April then only £13,000 is shown on the cash flow statement as received in the March quarter.

Task 6.12

Prepare a cash flow statement for January, February and March, from the following information:

- *Bank balance at 1 January 1994 – £4500*
- *Sales – £20,000 each month, but in March, sales of £1000 are paid one month later in April*
- *Purchases – £10,000 each month, 90 per cent paid at once, 10 per cent paid in the following month*
- *Sale of a fixed asset for £6000 in February, received in March*
- *Wages – £2000 per month, paid in cash at once*
- *Rent – £6000 per annum, paid in twelve equal monthly instalments*
- *Heat and light paid – February £500*

- *A new oven is bought in March for £4000 with a loan from the bank of £3000, the remainder being paid in cash at once.*

Draw a line graph showing the changes in the balance.

Other data which might be required

In addition to the statements mentioned earlier, organizations might produce a variety of other types of data which, although not *financial* data, still help in the measuring of performance. These data might include items such as details of:

- Numbers of staff employed
- Numbers of rooms available and sold
- Numbers of covers or guests
- The charges made by the organization, sometimes called the *tariff*
- Types of costs incurred by the organization

Some of these data are confidential, and might only be available *within* the organization. However, the trends and information which it is used to calculate might be reported to the government or made public in some other way.

Ways of measuring financial performance

You know that the cost and financial statements are used to enable decisions to be made, so once they have been prepared, the information contained in them needs to be examined and analysed in various ways.

The aim of this examination and analysis is to measure and evaluate the performance of the organization. This can be done by *comparing* the results with other figures, to determine whether they are better, worse, or about the same. These measurements and comparisons are called *performance indicators* or *ratios*. It is important to realize that these comparisons are only a guide.

Without more detailed information, the user cannot know *why* the results are better, worse or the same. In fact, the use of the words 'better' 'worse' and 'the same' can be misleading – what is better to one person is not necessarily better to another.

Definition

- *A **performance** indicator is a calculation which helps to measure (indicate) how good or bad the performance of an organization has been. These indicators are sometimes called **ratios**.*

This section looks mainly at the types of performance indicator used in the hospitality and catering industry (some are used in other industries too), how to calculate them, and what they mean. It is not intended that you should be able to conduct a detailed analysis of accounting information, but you should understand what can be done with the information available.

Expression or presentation of performance indicators

Indicators may be expressed in different ways:

- As 'straight' figures, e.g. sales (turnover) this year was £40,000 and last year it was £20,000. This is acceptable where the figures are easy to compare and understand
- As percentages. This is useful where the figures are not so easy to compare and understand, perhaps because they are very large or they are not 'round' sums, e.g. sales were £40,000 and net profit was £10,000. Net profit as a percentage of sales is:

$$\frac{\text{Net profit}}{\text{Sales}} \times 100 = \frac{10,000}{40,000} \times 100 = 25\%$$

- As a value per unit, e.g. if sales were £40,000, and there were twenty employees, the sales per employee would be:

$$\frac{\text{Sales}}{\text{No. of employees}} = \text{£2000 per employee}$$

Task 6.13

Calculate the following:

1. *£27 as a percentage of £135*
2. *£246,000 as a percentage of £984,000*
3. *Sales per employee if sales are £14,000 and there are four employees*
4. *Selling price per cover (customer) if total sales are £57,000 and there are 3,800 covers*

Types of comparison

To be of use, each figure, percentage, value per unit or other calculation, should be compared with a target. There are many different types of target depending on what the user's requirements are. The four main types of target on which comparisons can be made are:

- Budgets
- Other targets, e.g. other industries
- Figures from previous periods
- Industry 'norms' or standards

These all assist the user to decide whether the current situation is as required, although, as said earlier, they do not give information as to *why* that situation exists.

Calculation and interpretation of performance indicators

There are many different performance indicators which can be of assistance in evaluating financial performance. Some of these are described below, together with the 'formula' for calculating each of them. The indicators (or 'ratios', as they are often called) are calculated from sets of financial information and other information provided by management. The sets of information provided will include:

- The profit and loss account
- Data regarding the number of employees
- Data regarding number of covers, sleepers, etc.
- Data regarding fixed and variable costs
- The balance sheet

Some of this information may be available only from within the organization. Information regarding the previous month or year is also often provided.

Let us look at the information and the performance indicators we can calculate from each of the above sets of information. The information in this section is all concerning another imaginary organization, Lewis Leisure Ltd. The first set of data we will look at is the *profit and loss account* shown in the box below.

We can use this account to calculate various performance indicators. It shows figures for both this year and last year for comparison with each other.

Turnover

Definition

- *Turnover* means income from sales. It is also called revenue.

This is used as a straight comparison with budgets and figures from previous periods, e.g. sales for this year are £563,000 compared with sales last year of £547,500. On its own, it does not convey much information, except that increases in sales are usually good. We could show the changes in sales in the three departments by means of a bar chart (Figure 6.8).

The change in turnover can be expressed as a percentage of the previous period, to see the extent to which it has increased or decreased. The calculation is:

Percentage change in turnover =

$$\frac{\text{Change}}{\text{Previous turnover}} \times 100$$

Lewis Leisure Ltd: Profit and loss account

	This year				Last year			
	Rooms £	Restaurant £	Bar £	Total £	Rooms £	Restaurant £	Bar £	Total £
Sales	400,000	125,000	38,000	563,000	380,000	130,000	37,500	547,500
Food and drinks costs	0	62,500	28,250	90,750	0	67,400	28,600	96,000
Labour costs	78,000	16,500	7,250	101,750	74,500	18,500	7,000	100,000
Expenses	16,000	7,000	1,000	24,600	15,500	5,600	1,400	22,500
Net operating profit	306,000	39,000	900	345,900	290,000	38,500	500	329,000
Undistributed expenses:								
Heat and light				92,000				95,000
Maintenance				15,000				18,000
Insurance				18,700				19,500
Phone, stationery, advertising				109,700				95,000
Administration				85,000				87,000
Net profit				25,500				14,500

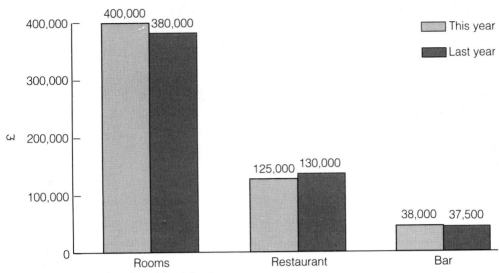

Figure 6.8 A bar chart comparing departmental sales

If the turnover can be broken down into the different departments of the organization this percentage becomes more useful, as there could be different increases and decreases in departments. For example, there might be an increase in the total turnover but a decrease in one department. The change in the total turnover is:

$$\frac{15,500}{547,500} \times 100 = 2.83 \text{ per cent increase}$$

Task 6.14

Using the profit and loss account for Lewis Leisure Ltd, calculate the percentage change in turnover for each department (rooms, restaurant and bar). Do they all change by roughly the same amount, or are some very different?

Gross profit margin

Gross profit is the difference between sales of food and drink and the cost of food and drink. It can be used as a straight comparison, as with turnover. But, as with turnover, it does not give much information on its own. An increase in gross profit might seem good, but if sales have increased, then gross profit is expected to do the same. What is better is a *larger* increase in gross profit than in turnover. More commonly, therefore, gross profit is expressed as a percentage of turnover (sales). The calculation is:

$$\text{Gross profit percentage} = \frac{\text{Gross profit}}{\text{Sales}} \times 100$$

This enables the user to see the change in gross profit in comparison to turnover. If the profit and loss account does not already show gross profit, then we need to work it out. For this year, gross profit is £472,250 (£563,000 – £90,750) and for last year it was £451,500 (£547,500 – £96,000).

The *total* gross profit percentage is:

(This year) $\dfrac{472,250}{563,000} \times 100 = 83.88$ per cent

(Last year) $\dfrac{451,500}{547,500} \times 100 = 82.47$ per cent

This shows that the gross profit percentage this year was higher than that of last year.

Task 6.15

Using the profit and loss account for Lewis Leisure Ltd, calculate the gross profit percentage for this year and for last year, for each department. Are the two years similar? Are there any major differences? What do you notice about the Rooms gross profit percentage? Which department generally has the lowest gross profit percentage?

Task 6.16

Using the profit and loss account for Lewis Leisure Ltd, calculate the gross profit mark-up percentage for this year and last year for the Restaurant and the Bar. Compare them to the gross profit margin percentages that you calculated in Task 6.15. Why are you not asked to calculate the mark-up percentage for Rooms?

Mark-up percentage

This ratio is similar to the gross profit margin ratio, except that it is based on the *cost of sales* figure rather than the sales figure. The calculation is:

Gross profit mark-up percentage =

$$\frac{\text{Gross profit}}{\text{Cost of sales}} \times 100$$

The total gross profit mark-up percentage is as follows:

$$(\text{This year}) = \frac{472,250}{90,050} \times 100 = 524 \text{ per cent}$$

$$(\text{Last year}) = \frac{451,500}{96,000} \times 100 = 470 \text{ per cent}$$

Notice that these percentages are very large in comparison to the gross profit *margin* percentages. That is because they are based on the *cost* and not the *selling price*, and the cost is, of course, a smaller figure. However, they still show the same basic information, i.e. that the gross profit mark-up this year is greater than it was last year.

Mark-up is used instead of the margin percentage where the cost of sales is small compared to the selling price. This is because mark-up shows up the differences more clearly.

Net profit percentage

As with gross profit, the net profit on its own is of little use. When compared to sales it becomes more informative. Net profit percentage is net profit expressed as a percentage of sales. The calculation is:

$$\text{Net profit percentage} = \frac{\text{Net profit}}{\text{Sales}} \times 100$$

$$(\text{This year}) \quad \frac{25,500}{563,000} \times 100 = 4.53 \text{ per cent}$$

$$(\text{Last year}) \quad \frac{14,500}{547,500} \times 100 = 2.65 \text{ per cent}$$

This shows that the net profit percentage this year was higher than last year.

Net profit can also be calculated at the *operating profit* level. At the *operating profit* level it can be calculated for each department, as with the gross profit percentage. The calculation is:

Net operating profit percentage =

$$\frac{\text{Net operating profit}}{\text{Sales}} \times 100$$

$$(\text{This year}) \quad \frac{345,900}{563,000} \times 100 = 61.44 \text{ per cent}$$

(Last year) $\dfrac{329,000}{547,500} \times 100 = 60.09$ per cent

Again, the percentage this year is higher than last year, though the increase is not as great as the increase in net profit percentage.

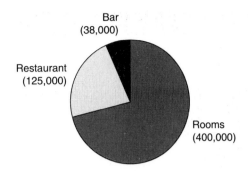

Figure 6.9 A pie chart showing departmental sales

Task 6.17

Using the profit and loss account for Lewis Leisure Ltd, calculate the net operating profit percentage for this year and last year for each department. Which department shows the highest net operating profit percentage? Why do you think this is?

Sales mix

In an organization with income from different sources, such as a hotel with income from rooms, restaurants, bar, functions, leisure facilities, etc., it is important to know what proportion of income comes from each source. The sales mix percentage gives each source as a percentage of the total. Its calculation is:

Sales mix percentage =

$$\dfrac{\text{Income from source}}{\text{Total income}} \times 100$$

For this year, the sales mix is:

$$\text{Rooms} = \dfrac{400,000}{563,000} \times 100 = 71 \text{ per cent}$$

$$\text{Restaurant} = \dfrac{125,000}{563,000} \times 100 = 22.2 \text{ per cent}$$

$$\text{Bar} = \dfrac{38,000}{563,000} \times 100 = 6.8 \text{ per cent}$$

Note that the percentages add up to 100. This information could also be shown as a pie chart (Figure 6.9).

Task 6.18

Using the profit and loss account for Lewis Leisure Ltd, calculate the sales mix for last year. How does it differ from this year? Do you think the difference matters? Why? You might be able to use the results you obtained from the previous task to help you answer this.

The second set of data we will look at is the *data regarding the number of employees* in Lewis Leisure Ltd:

Lewis Leisure Ltd: number of employees

	This year	Last year
Rooms	3	3
Restaurant	6	7
Bar	5	4

Using these data, in conjunction with the profit and loss account, we can calculate some 'employee efficiency ratios'. These are often compared to those of other organizations in the same industry to determine whether the employees are as efficient.

Turnover per employee

This is calculated as:

$$\text{Turnover per employee} = \frac{\text{Turnover}}{\text{No. of employees}}$$

It may be calculated on the *total* number of employees, or by department. For this year, the calculations are:

$$\text{Total} = \frac{563,000}{14}$$

= £40,214.29 turnover per employee

$$\text{Rooms} = \frac{400,000}{3}$$

= £133,333.33 turnover per employee

$$\text{Restaurant} = \frac{125,000}{6}$$

= £20,833.33 turnover per employee

$$\text{Bar} = \frac{38,000}{5}$$

= £7600 turnover per employee

The results show that the Rooms division has the greatest turnover per employee, while the Bar has the lowest. This is normally quite acceptable. The number of employees required to service rooms is quite small, and the amount of income per room is much higher than the amount taken at the bar for each guest.

Gross margin per employee

This is calculated in the same way as turnover per employee:

$$\text{Gross margin per employee} = \frac{\text{Gross margin}}{\text{No. of employees}}$$

Again, it may be calculated on the *total* gross margin or on individual departments. For this year, the calculations are:

$$\text{Total} = \frac{472,250}{14}$$

= £33,732.21 gross margin per employee

$$\text{Rooms} = \frac{£400,000}{3}$$

= £133,333.33 gross margin per employee

$$\text{Restaurant} = \frac{£62,500}{6}$$

= £12,500 gross margin per employee

$$\text{Bar} = \frac{£9750}{5}$$

= £1950 gross margin per employee

Task 6.19

Using the data regarding the number of employees in Lewis Leisure Ltd and the profit and loss account given earlier, calculate the turnover per employee for last year, for both total turnover and turnover per department. Is it different from this year? Can you think of any reasons for these differences?

Task 6.20

Using the data regarding the number of employees in Lewis Leisure Ltd and the profit and loss account given earlier, calculate the gross margin per employee for last year, in total and for each department. Are the results different from this year?

The third set of data we will look at is *data regarding number of covers etc.*

Definition

● *A **cover** is a guest served with food or beverages in a single period of opening.*

In a restaurant, a cover is a person eating a meal; there is only *one* cover, no matter how many courses the guest has. A table with four guests would be four covers, even if one person is paying the bill. A guest having meals at breakfast, lunch and dinner would be three covers in total.

In a bar, a cover is a single drink served, so one guest might have several drinks – therefore there would be several covers (this is because it is impossible to determine how many drinks one guest has had, without very elaborate record-keeping).

Lewis Leisure Ltd

	This year	*Last year*
Number of covers:		
Restaurant	4800	4850
Bar	2500	2600
Number of doubles		
let as doubles	2400	2700
Number of doubles		
let as singles	100	60
Number of singles let	500	450
Number of doubles available	3000	3000
Number of singles available	600	600
Rack room rate – double	£130	£130
Rack room rate – single	£ 90	£ 90

Definition

● ***Rack rate** is the normal charge for a room. It may be sold at less than that rate to certain customers.*

Point to note:
You may think that the examples so far are for a large organization, because the figures are quite high compared to those you are used to dealing with. In fact, the examples given are of a very *small* organization. In the table above, the number of doubles available is stated as being 3000 – but this is a statement for a whole year. If the hotel is open for 300 nights, that is only ten bedrooms available per night – this is really only as big as a boarding-house! The figures have been kept small deliberately, so that you will not get confused by very large amounts in your calculations. But remember that in the real world, some hotels have takings of several millions of pounds. As an example, the Greenalls Group plc, which includes the well-known De Vere Hotels, had a turnover in 1993 of nearly £600,000,000 – that's six hundred million pounds!

From the above set of data we can calculate the following ratios connected with the usage of the organization:

Occupancy ratios

These are concerned with how busy or full an organization is compared with its capacity. They use rooms, sleepers or income as a means of measurement.

Definition

● *A **sleeper** is a guest who stays the night. In a double room, there are normally two sleepers, but sometimes there may be fewer or more than two.*

There are four common occupancy ratios, all normally expressed as percentages. These are:

Room occupancy

Room occupancy =

$$\frac{\text{Number of rooms sold}}{\text{Number of rooms available}} \times 100$$

For this year in Lewis Leisure Ltd:

Rooms sold = 2400 + 100 + 500 = 3000
Rooms available = 3000 + 600 = 3600

$$\text{Room occupancy} = \frac{3000}{3600} \times 100$$

$$= 83.3 \text{ per cent}$$

This is quite high – most hotels rarely achieve 100 per cent occupancy for a single night, and many manage only around 60 per cent on average. De Vere Hotels were pleased to increase their occupancy from 60 per cent in 1992 to 67 per cent in 1993.

The British Hospitality Association published the following percentage Hotel Room Occupancy Rates for 1991:

London	60
England	51
Scotland	56
Wales	48

Sleeper occupancy

$$\text{Sleeper occupancy} = \frac{\text{Actual sleepers}}{\text{Possible sleepers}} \times 100$$

For this year:

Actual sleepers =
Double rooms
  let as doubles = 2400 × 2 = 4800 sleepers
Double rooms
  let as singles = 100 × 1 = 100 sleepers
Single rooms let = 500 × 1 = 500 sleepers
Total actual sleepers = 5400 sleepers

Possible sleepers =
Double rooms
  let as doubles = 3000 × 2 = 6000 sleepers
Single rooms = 600 sleepers
Total possible sleepers = 6600 sleepers

Thus sleeper
occupancy
$$= \frac{5400}{6600} \times 100$$

$$= 81.8 \text{ per cent}$$

This performance indicator can be a measure of the skill of the booking clerk in making the decision whether or not to let a double room for a single booking, or whether to refuse the single booking and risk the room staying empty. Previous booking statistics will help in making this decision.

Income occupancy

This shows the relationship between the income earned and the income which could have been earned if full occupation had existed at full rates. The calculation is:

Income occupancy =

$$\frac{\text{Actual income earned}}{\text{Possible total income}} \times 100$$

For this year:

Actual income = £400,000 (from the profit and loss account)
Possible income =
  doubles let as
    doubles = 3000 × £130 = £390,000
  singles = 600 × £90 = £54,000
  total possible income = £444,000

Thus income
occupancy
$$= \frac{400,000}{440,000} \times 100$$

$$= 90 \text{ per cent}$$

Double occupancy

This shows the proportion of double rooms actually let as double rooms. The calculation is:

Double occupancy =

$$\frac{\text{No. of doubles let as doubles}}{\text{Doubles available}} \times 100$$

For this year, the calculation is 2400/3000 × 100 = 80 per cent.

Task 6.21

Using the data regarding number of covers, sleepers, etc. for Lewis Leisure Ltd and the profit and loss account given earlier, calculate the occupancy ratios for last year, and compare them with those above for this year.

Average spend

This gives the average amount spent in the organization by each guest or customer. Its calculation is:

Average spend per customer =

$$\frac{\text{Total amount spent}}{\text{No. of customers}}$$

The calculation can be performed on the organization as a whole, or by taking each department separately. For this year, the calculations of average spend are:

Rooms = 400,000/5400 = £74.07 per sleeper
Restaurant = 125,000/4800 = £26.04 per cover
Bar = 38,000/2500 = £15.20 per customer

Task 6.22

From the data regarding the number of covers/sleepers, etc. for Lewis Leisure Ltd and the profit and loss account given earlier, calculate the average spend for each department for last year. Did any department have a greater average spend this year? Did any department have a lower average spend this year?

The fourth set of data we will look at is *data regarding fixed and variable costs*. This information would probably only be available to management. The information is used to calculate the *break-even point*.

Definition

- The **break-even point** is the point at which the organization sells just enough to break-even, i.e. it makes no profit, but it covers its costs.

The figures for Lewis Leisure Ltd for the restaurant are:

	This year	Last year
Selling price per cover	£26.04	£26.80
Food cost per cover	£13.02	£13.90
Variable wages cost per cover	£3.44	£3.81
Fixed costs in total	£33,250	£33,600

An organization's costs are of two types – fixed and variable.

Definition

- **Variable costs** are those which increase and decrease according to the level of activity.

An example of variable costs is food costs – the cost of two meals is twice the cost of one meal; the more meals produced, the greater the cost of food.

Definition

- **Fixed costs** are those which do not alter with the level of activity, at least not directly.

An example of a fixed cost is rent. The rent of the premises costs just the same whether one meal is produced or two, or even a hundred. That does not mean that rent never alters – we might need larger premises if we produce many more meals, and the rent might increase due to inflation. The point is, it does not alter according to the level of activity, so it is classed as a fixed cost.

Obviously, in a restaurant, every meal sold must cover its variable (food) cost, but it must also *contribute* towards the fixed costs. Its contribution is the difference between its selling price and its variable cost. This is the amount available to go towards the fixed costs, and eventually to make profits. If only one meal is sold, it needs to contribute a great deal to fixed costs, whereas if many meals are sold, each one makes a contribution.

Definition

- **Contribution** is the amount of money left over from the sale of a unit, after deducting variable costs. The contribution goes towards the fixed costs and to the profit, if there is still anything left over.

For example, if we sell a meal for £5, which cost £3 in variable costs such as food, there is £2 available to go towards fixed costs and profit.

The break-even point is the point at which there are enough meals sold to contribute to the whole of the fixed costs. The calculation of break-even point, therefore, is:

Number of meals to break-even =

$$\frac{\text{Fixed costs}}{\text{Contribution per meal}}$$

The break-even point for the restaurant for this year is calculated as follows:

Contribution per cover = selling price – variable cost

Variable cost = Food cost + variable wages cost
= £13.02 + £3.44
= £16.46

Contribution per cover = £26.04 – £16.46
= £9.58

$$\text{Break-even point} = \frac{33,250}{£9.58} = 3471 \text{ covers}$$

At this point, sales revenue would be 3471 covers × £26.04 = £90,384.84.

Task 6.23

Using the data given for Lewis Leisure Ltd, calculate the break-even point for the restaurant for last year. Which year do you think is better? What reasons can you think of for the change in break-even point?

A particular use of the break-even point is in deciding whether to accept bookings which are below the normal selling price. The break-even point is the point at which the fixed costs are all covered. Any sales made after that point need only cover the variable cost in order to be acceptable – and if they are sold at more than the variable cost, they will make extra profit.

In the example above, once 3471 covers have been obtained, any additional covers which bring in more that the variable cost of £16.46 this year must be acceptable because they will make a profit. Thus, if a booking is wanted for a number of meals at £17, this should be accepted unless we have other bookings at more than that amount.

The information could also be shown using a break-even chart. This is a graph which plots the sales revenue and the total costs for a range of levels of activity. The point at which the two lines of sales and cost meet is the break-even point.

Using the figures for Lewis Leisure Ltd we can calculate the following figures for this year:

No. of units sold	Nil	1000 £	2000 £	3000 £	4000 £
Selling price	Nil	26,040	52,080	78,120	104,160
Variable costs	Nil	16,460	32,920	49,380	65,840
Fixed costs	33,250	33,250	33,250	33,250	33,250
Total costs	33,250	49,710	66,170	82,630	99,090

The Sales and Total Costs lines can then be plotted on a graph, with the costs and selling

prices up the side and the number of units along the bottom. The point at which they cross is the break-even point. It should be at 3471 covers, or £90,384.84. If we also plot a line for fixed costs, we can see that this is a straight line across, because these costs are fixed for all levels of activity.

The chart would appear as in Figure 6.10.

Task 6.24

Using the data for Lewis Leisure Ltd for last year, plot the break-even point on a graph.

The final set of data we will look at is the *balance sheet*. The balance sheet for this year, with comparative figures for last year, is in the box on page 262.

The figures on the balance sheet can all be examined and compared to those of the previous year. For example, the premises figure this year is £18,000 higher than last year, which indicates that more premises have been purchased (or that they have increased in value). The bank balance has also increased, which would be expected if a profit has been made (but does not always happen).

Stock levels

The amount of stock on hand this year is almost double the amount last year. Keeping stocks costs money. They cost money to buy, and they cost money to store, insure, safeguard, etc. Organizations should aim to keep as little stock as possible, without running out. A regular check should be kept on the amounts held by having a set 'maximum stock level',

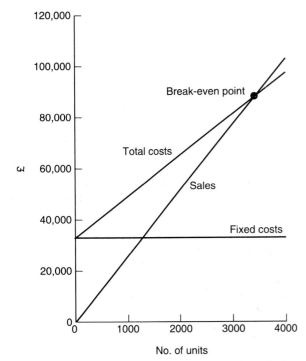

Figure 6.10 A break-even chart for Lewis Leisure Ltd

Lewis Leisure Ltd: Balance sheets as at 31 December

	199y			199x	
Fixed assets					
Premises		147,000		129,000	
Machinery		38,000		35,000	
Furniture		11,000		10,000	
			196,000		174,000
Current assets					
Stocks-food/drink	2,950			1,500	
Debtors	2,100			2,500	
Bank balance	13,600			10,800	
		18,650		14,800	
Less Current liabilities					
Creditors	1,550			1,200	
Working capital			17,100		13,600
			213,100		187,600
Less Long-term liabilities					
Loan			5,000		5,000
			208,100		182,600
Capital					
Opening Capital		182,600		168,100	
Profit for year		25,500			14,500
			208,100		182,600

and only reordering when the 'minimum stock level' is reached; the quantity to be reordered should also be carefully controlled.

The stock at the end of each accounting period, say a year, should be compared with that at the end of the previous period, and any significant change should be investigated and explained. It may be that there is a good reason for holding more stock – business might have increased, or you may be preparing for a large function.

Return on capital employed

'Return' is another word for net profit, which belongs to the owners. Capital employed is the amount of capital which the owners have invested in the business. The return on capital employed is the amount of profit earned in relation to the amount invested. Its calculation is:

Return on capital employed percentage =

$$\frac{\text{Net profit}}{\text{Owners' capital}} \times 100$$

Owners often compare this with other types of investment.

For this year, the return on capital employed is:

$$\frac{25,500}{182,600} \times 100 = 14 \text{ per cent}$$

This is a good rate of return when interest rates are generally low.

Task 6.25

Using the given balance sheet, calculate the return on capital employed for last year, and compare it with this year's return.

Conclusion

There can be no single impression given of the performance of an organization. As you can see from the various ratios and comparisons above, some areas of the business have improved, while some have become worse. Further information is needed in all cases to determine why the changes have taken place, and whether or not any action can be taken to prevent further deterioration or to improve the performance even more. The task of evaluating the performance of an organization is a highly specialized one, and in many cases even the experts get it wrong!

The aim is to provide users with as much information as possible and in the required format. Some users require full statements, others prefer summarized information, including ratios and percentages as we have just calculated. Internal management can use this information as a guideline, and to highlight areas where further investigation is required.

Test your knowledge

This section has looked at the need for monitoring and evaluating financial performance. See what you can remember.

1 Identify the main users of financial information. Describe the types of information each user is interested in.
2 Discuss the four main reasons for monitoring financial performance.
3 Give four examples of cost statements and briefly describe their contents
4 Describe the layout of an operating statement for a hotel. Describe the different levels of profit which the operating statement shows. As well as showing the monetary figures for the current period, what other information might be shown in an operating statement?
5 Describe the contents of a balance sheet. Identify the different categories of heading which appear on the balance sheet, and give examples of things which might be included under each heading. What is the accounting equation, and how is it shown on a properly laid-out balance sheet?
6 What is the purpose of a cash flow statement? What information does it contain? How would you deal with sales made on credit, on a cash flow statement?
7 Name as many performance indicators as you can, which can be calculated using the profit and loss account. Describe the method of calculation of each one, and what it is intended to 'indicate'.

▪ PURCHASING REQUIREMENTS, PROCEDURES AND CONTROLS ▪

In this section we will look at the systems of purchasing used in the hospitality and catering industry. Successful purchasing means buying the right products, with the right quality and price, at the right time. We will look at the different types of products which might be purchased, and the different sources from which they might be obtained. We will consider the responsibilities which individuals have for making sure that the system operates properly, using the correct procedures, and we will look at the various controls which should be incorporated into the system to ensure that everything runs smoothly and that mistakes are avoided wherever possible.

> **Point to note:**
> Later in this section you will be given some tasks to do involving the imaginary organization called ACE Hotels Ltd. Each task is to be completed before the next is attempted, and you will need to keep your work from each task in order to use it for the next.

The products to be purchased

The products to be purchased in a hospitality or catering organization are many and varied. You need only think of your own requirement for products to imagine how much more varied are those in an industry which is catering for large numbers of people.

You need food, clothing and shelter as your prime requirements, but also a whole host of other things to make life comfortable and rewarding – furniture, linen, kitchenware, equipment (cooker, refrigerator, washing machine, television, stereo), cars, petrol, drinks (non-alcoholic and alcoholic), stationery, and so on.

Deciding on the products to be purchased is only part of the problem – we also need to consider how far in advance we can buy them, and how we are going to store them. Some things require special storage conditions, to conform to hygiene and food safety legislation, or to prevent deterioration. This applies not just to food but also to other items such as stationery or electrical equipment, neither of which can be kept in a damp place. In addition, storing things costs money. There needs to be sufficient storage space, of the right kind, which might mean that space is taken away from other areas of the organization. Items need to be insured while they are being stored – another cost to consider. All these considerations are important when choosing a method of purchasing, depending on the type of product required.

The products to be purchased in the hospitality and catering industry can be put into four categories.

Food

This includes fresh, frozen, canned and dried goods as well as 'extras' such as spices, herbs and flavourings. Some foods will be left raw (e.g. salads and fruits), others will be used up in cooked or prepared dishes. Non-alcoholic beverages are often usually included as 'foods', unless they are specifically for use in a bar.

Liquor

This refers to alcoholic drinks and beverages used by bars, such as 'mixers'. Beers and lagers are sometimes purchased by the barrel and sold by the pint or half-pint. They are bought by the bottle and dispensed in small quantities. They are usually of high value and alcoholic strength, therefore extra care is taken over their storage and use. Bottled beers may be bought in returnable bottles, in crates, and these items must also be controlled to ensure that refunds are obtained when they are returned.

Equipment

An organization might have a variety of items classed as 'equipment'. These could include:

1 Kitchen equipment – ovens, refrigerators, freezers, knives, pans, crockery, dishwashers
2 Restaurant and bar equipment – tables, chairs, coffee machines, drinks dispensers, glassware, tableware, cutlery
3 Bedroom equipment – furniture, trouser presses, hair dryers, tea-makers
4 Office equipment – telephones, facsimiles, computers, typewriters
5 General equipment – vacuum cleaners and polishers, laundry equipment, conference equipment, audio equipment

and many, many more items

Consumables

This term refers to small items which are quickly used up in the running of the organization. Although these are regarded as running costs of the organization, there are often small stocks of these kept. Examples include:

- Restaurant and bar consumables – drinks mats, serviettes, straws, cocktail accessories, flowers, toothpicks
- Bedroom consumables – soaps, shampoos, beverages, biscuits, sewing kits
- Cleaning materials – polish, detergent, disinfectant
- Conference consumables – paper, pens, pencils, complimentary gifts

Task 6.26

Look at your own organization (school, college or wherever you have a part-time job), or visit an organization if you have the opportunity. Make a list of the different types of products which it might need to buy. Classify the products according to whether they are food, liquor, equipment *or* consumables. *Try to find at least three of each category.*

The different categories of product will have different considerations when it comes to choosing a supplier. For example, you would not expect to buy six industrial ovens from a cash and carry.

Sources of supply and methods of purchasing

There are many different places from which an organization can buy things. Each has advantages and disadvantages, and what suits one organization might not suit another. You only need to look around your own high street to see the wide range of shops, some of them selling the same kinds of items, and yet they all remain in business. You probably shop in some

of them, but not in others, and yet other people use the ones that you don't!

What makes these places different? Well, many things make them different from one another:

1 *Size* Some are large. Some are small. Some are medium-sized.
2 *Range of products* Some have a very wide range, making it easy for customers to buy a number of different items at once. Some are very specialized, selling only a small range of products.
3 *Type of customer* Some admit only businesspeople and tradespeople, others admit the general public, like us. Some places require you to have a membership card (like your local night-club or youth-club).
4 *Reputation* Some are well established and have a well-known reputation for good service and reliability. Others are newer or less well known.
5 *Price* Some deal in high-quality, individual goods, aimed at those who want expensive luxury. Some deal in everyday, medium-quality goods, aimed at the majority of the market.
6 *Quantity purchased* Some places sell only in bulk, to keep prices low.
7 *Payment terms* Some insist that you pay at once, others will allow periods of credit (time to pay). Some accept only certain methods of payment, such as cash or cheques, others will accept credit cards.
8 *Advice and expertise* Some places have experts who can advise customers on their purchases. Others leave it to the customer to make enquiries elsewhere before buying.
9 *Distance from the customer* Some places are a long way away, serving a wide area, but taking time and money to get there. There may also be a delay, and extra cost, in getting the goods delivered. Some places are close by, some even deliver to your door.
10 *Delivery arrangements* Some places deliver free of charge, others charge for delivery. Some do not offer a delivery service at all.

Task 6.27

Think of as many different places to buy things as you can. Draw up a table to show the different characteristics of each place. Try to include a variety of places so that you have a wide range of possibilities. To start you off, can you think of a large supplier, selling a wide range of products, which admits the general public? Is it nearby or far away? Can you think of any which do not admit the general public?

There are ten different characteristics given above. Can you think of any more?

There are several different methods of purchasing – buying things – even for the ordinary person like yourself. Let us look at some examples of things you might buy in different ways:

● You might have a regular order for milk to be delivered by the milkman every day
● If you want to build an extension to your house, you might invite several builders to quote a price for the job, and choose the cheapest
● You might buy meat for the freezer in bulk from your local butcher, and share it with your neighbours
● You might look for the cheapest petrol station when you need to fill up with petrol
● You buy your weekly food from a supermarket which stocks lots of different brands, and you pay for it at once and have to carry it all home yourself
● You travel several miles to buy a new car from a particular dealer
● You buy your daily newspaper from a local retailer

Did you imagine there were so many different methods of purchasing available to an ordinary person? The same applies to the hospitality and catering industry. The ones we are going to look at are:

1 Contract purchasing/purchasing by tender
2 Centralized purchasing
3 Purchasing by market list or quotation
4 Cash and carry purchasing
5 Wholesale purchasing
6 Retail purchasing

We will look at some of these purchasing methods now. It is important to realize that the organization can use several of these methods at one time, and even two methods for the same product – for example, contract purchasing can also be centralized.

Contract purchasing/purchasing by tender

Definition

● *A **contract** is an agreement to do something. Contract purchasing is where the organization contracts to purchase certain supplies from a particular supplier, either for a fixed amount of time or for a fixed quantity of goods.*

As a contract is legally binding, great care must be taken to choose the correct one. A contract for a fixed period of time is suitable for goods which do not vary much in price, otherwise the organization could lose out on price reductions during the period of the contract. A contract for a fixed quantity is suitable for goods which do not deteriorate, such as dry or tinned goods, and where quantities can be estimated well in advance.

Contract purchasing is usually used by larger organizations who are buying in large enough quantities to strike a good bargain with the supplier. The organization also needs to be able to judge well in advance what quantities it is going to need, otherwise it could over-order and be left with goods which it cannot use.

Purchasing by tender is very similar to contract purchasing, except that instead of the organization seeking out different suppliers, it invites the suppliers to contact them to offer prices for the goods it requires. A contract is then probably made with the supplier with the lowest price.

The advantages to an organization of contract purchasing are:

● Continuity of supply is ensured. The supplier agrees to supply for some time, and the organization can rely on that regular supply
● The price is known in advance, making planning much easier, and there are often discounts available for large quantities
● Time is saved. Once the contract is made, the organization need spend no more time searching for supplies
● Regular deliveries means that the organization does not need to hold high levels of stock. High stocks means loss of storage space and increased costs of keeping goods properly, as well as paying out for stocks long before they are used up and sold
● Payments can usually be spread over the time of the contract, perhaps at a fixed amount per month

The disadvantages of contract purchasing are:

● The choice of suppliers who offer this type of purchasing is limited. This in turn limits the choice of goods which can be bought this way
● Once the contract is made, the organization cannot take advantage of price reductions or special offers
● If the contract is for a fixed quantity, which turns out to be over-estimated, overstocking and deterioration could be a problem
● If the service given by the supplier proves to be unsatisfactory, it can be difficult to break the contract or to find alternative suppliers.

Task 6.28

Can you think of five types of goods which a restaurant might buy using contract purchasing?

Centralized purchasing

Definition

● ***Centralized purchasing*** *is a method of purchasing whereby goods are ordered from a single place (e.g. head office) and then distributed to other parts of the organization.*

This method is used by organizations who have several branches, departments or outlets, even perhaps spread across the country. The goods are ordered by a central buying department on behalf of all the branches. The goods may also be delivered to a central warehouse and then to the individual branches on request. Centralized purchasing could easily be combined with contract purchasing for the larger organizations.

The advantages of centralized purchasing are:

● The organization can buy in large quantities. Bulk-buying means that good discounts can be obtained
● Having a central store means that a wider range of goods is available to the branches, with less chance of running out of stock
● The central store can be more easily controlled and kept secure, thus reducing the chances of loss or theft
● Individual branches do not have to keep high stocks of goods, thus the overall stock held by the organization is much lower

- The quantities being purchased may give the organization the opportunity to insist on special treatment, on delivery for example, or to insist on a certain quality of goods
- All branches will be using the same types of goods, therefore quality and style will be consistent throughout the organization

A McDonald's cheeseburger is the same in *all* McDonald's restaurants throughout the country – you can rely on it!

- The person responsible for purchasing becomes an expert at dealing with a range of goods to be purchased

The disadvantages of centralized purchasing are:

- Individual branches have less control over the choice of supplier and type of goods supplied
- Loss of freedom of choice to individual branches may mean that branches with particular needs may be unable to meet those needs; similarly, branches with a special flair for a particular service may be unable to provide it
- Local price reductions or special promotions cannot be utilized
- There may be delivery problems unless there is an efficient system of distribution of goods from the central warehouse

Examples of large organizations which use centralized purchasing include Forte Hotels, Sutcliffe Catering, local and area health authorities. Forte have a separate company, Puritan Maid, whose business is the purchasing of goods for use by all Forte outlets. The benefits of centralized purchasing for such a large organization are tremendous. Sutcliffe Catering is a contract catering organization, supplying meals to a wide range of organizations. By purchasing centrally, it can pass on the benefit of its reduced costs and improved quality control to its customers.

Task 6.29

Look around your own town – can you see any organizations which are part of a large chain or group, and which might use centralized purchasing? Which goods might it buy using this method?

Purchasing by daily market list or quotation

Definition

- *Purchasing by **daily market list** or **quotation** involves obtaining the latest price each day from a number of suppliers, for the goods required.*

This method is used for items where the price changes daily or very frequently, such as fresh fruit and vegetables which are often bought from wholesale markets several times a week to ensure a continuous supply of fresh produce. Each day, several suppliers are telephoned to provide quotations for the goods required. In larger organizations, and nowadays in smaller ones too, the daily quotations will be sent automatically by facsimile (fax) machine, and orders placed in the same way.

The advantages of purchasing by market list or quotation are:

- The best price available can be chosen
- Suppliers compete with each other, thus prices are kept lower
- Daily purchasing means that supplies can be bought as they are required, and need not take up storage space unnecessarily
- Fresh produce is available at all times

The disadvantages of purchasing by market list or quotation are:

- It can be time consuming to obtain prices and make choices so frequently
- Small organizations who purchase in low quantities may not be able to obtain good prices or discounts
- There is a possibility that goods could be unavailable on a particular day, which could result in shortages for the organization

Cash and carry purchasing

Definition

- **Cash and carry purchasing** is a method of purchasing from depots or warehouses, whereby immediate payment is made for the goods, which must be transported away from the depot by the buyer.

Cash and carry depots often supply goods in bulk packs, sometimes called 'catering packs', or in multiple packs (e.g. 24 tins at once). The term 'cash' used to mean that only notes and coins were accepted as payment, but nowadays cheques and credit cards are accepted as well. However, they still insist that purchases are paid for at once by one of these methods.

Cash and carries are usually fairly local – most medium-sized towns have one. Some are very specialized, selling only sweets and tobacco, for example, or Chinese foods. Others are more general, selling a wider range of groceries and non-food items. Cash and carries are not usually very attractive places in which to shop. The goods are stacked on floors and shelves, holding large quantities which can be very heavy, customers have to serve themselves, the decor is very plain and there are rarely any additional facilities such as cafés or rest areas.

The advantages of cash and carry purchasing are:

- Prices are lower, due to bulk packaging and purchasing, customers serving themselves
- There are no minimum order levels, except for the bulk packs, so customers need not buy in very large quantities
- Although delivery is the customer's responsibility, most are fairly local so delivery costs are not too high
- Being local means that customers have access to fresh supplies regularly and overstocking can be avoided
- The range of products can be viewed before purchase

The disadvantages of cash and carry purchasing are:

- Poor surroundings
- There is no delivery service
- Credit is not available
- Some products may be out of stock at times of shortages, thus there is no guarantee of availability

Task 6.30

Make enquiries about cash and carries in your area – you may have to look at nearby larger towns or cities for some of the specialized ones. Find out if they admit members of the public and ask if they have any advertising leaflets they can send you to show the range of products available. Compare the prices they charge with those in your local supermarket – are they all cheaper? (Don't forget that most non-food goods bought from cash and carries need to have VAT added as well – your supermarket prices will already include VAT.)

Wholesale suppliers

Definition

● **Wholesaler suppliers** *are organizations which buy goods from the manufacturer and then sell them to retailers (who then sell them to us, the public).*

Many of the methods mentioned above are also wholesalers. However, there are some specialized wholesalers who deal in particular types of products only, and these can be considered separately from the other methods.

Common examples of specialist wholesalers include:

1 Wine shippers
2 Breweries
3 Sweets and tobaccos
4 Meat and meat products
5 Poultry and game

There are also several examples of catering wholesalers who provide a range of goods for the catering trade, including items such as tableware, linens, serviettes, glassware, etc.

The advantages of purchasing from specialist wholesalers are:

● They supply good-quality products, with consistent quality
● Specialist expert advice is available
● They supply a large range of products of that type

The disadvantages of purchasing from specialist wholesalers are:

● They stock only the 'specialist' products – customers must shop elsewhere for other items
● They often deal only with bulk purchases
● A delivery service might be unavailable (except for breweries)

In addition to the above, some breweries impose special terms which need careful consideration. For example, a brewery might be prepared to stock an entire cellar with its beers, and even with other drinks, and may not require payment immediately but as the cellar is restocked. In effect, the brewery owns the contents of the cellar. This can be very helpful to the organization who need not pay for the goods at once, but it often means that they are then 'tied' to that particular brewery. They have entered into a kind of contract with the brewery which might be difficult to amend.

Retail purchasing

Definition

● **Retail purchasing** *is purchasing from outlets which supply the public.*

As well as the above methods, some goods can be purchased at ordinary retail outlets such as supermarkets, off-licences, local markets, etc. This is useful for items which are needed at short notice, perhaps because the normal delivery has not arrived or because absolute freshness is required. The advantage is the ease of purchasing by this method, but the disadvantage is that the price may be higher than other methods.

Task 6.31

Your organization will require the following products on the first day of next month:

● *Fresh parsley for garnishing*
● *Fresh chicken portions*
● *Frozen beefburgers*
● *Disposable cleaning cloths*
● *Potatoes*

Suggest a suitable method of purchasing each of the products, for each of the following organizations:

- *The ACE Hotel Ltd, a 30-bedroomed hotel with a 60-cover restaurant, open to the public at lunchtimes and evenings*
- *A friend's mobile burger bar*
- *A city general hospital*
- *A 200-bed hotel, part of a national chain of hotels*

The stages in the purchasing process

The stages in the purchasing process are:

1 Initial requisition
2 Purchase specification
3 Quotation
4 Purchase order
5 Receipt of goods (and return of unwanted items)
6 Invoicing
7 Payment

This is quite a long list – you might ask if all these stages are necessary.

When you want to buy something, you just go out and buy it – it's as simple as that! Or is it?

Before you buy a new jacket, you go through several stages. First, you look in your wardrobe and you realize you need a new jacket – the old one is torn, faded or simply out of fashion. You are *requisitioning* a new one. Next, you think of the kind of jacket you would like. You look through some magazines, you see what your favourite stars are wearing, and you ask your friends what they think. You decide on a black, wool jacket, no hood, size medium, not too short, with two pockets and a zip-up front. You have just *specified* what you require. You set out to buy it. You look through some catalogues, but only one has what you want – some have hoods, others have buttons instead of a zip. You look round the shops – there are three which fit your needs, but the others are the wrong colour or size. You compare the prices of the three which suit – you are obtaining *quotations*. You choose the cheapest in this case, and ask the

assistant to bring you one. You are placing your *purchase order*. The assistant brings the jacket – *receipt of goods* – and gives you the *invoice*. You have brought your birthday money with you, so you pay at once.

You have just been through the *purchasing process*. Let us look at the process in more detail, and in respect of the hospitality and catering industry.

Requisition

Definition

- *A **purchase requisition** is a document used to request goods to be purchased.*

It is an internal document prepared by the person who needs the goods. It gives details of the goods required – quantity, quality, size, etc., although some of these details may already have been decided by the *purchase specification* (see below). The requisition is sent to the person responsible for purchasing such items. Figure 6.11 is an example of a requisition.

Task 6.32

Draw up a purchase requisition for each of the following:

- *Fresh chicken portions*
- *Disposable cleaning cloths*
- *Potatoes*

for the ACE Hotel, which is a 30-bedroomed hotel with restaurant seating 60, open to the public for lunches and evening meals. Choose any reasonable quantities, descriptions, etc. which you like. Explain briefly the purpose of a purchase requisition.

ACE HOTEL LTD		REQUISITION FOR GOODS	
DEPARTMENT _Kitchen_		REQUISITION NO. _406_	
REQUISITIONED BY _F. Turner_		DATE _13/9/94_	
Description of goods required	**Quantity**	**Required by (date)**	
Tinned plums, 400 gm tins	_50_	_18/9/94_	
ORDERED BY _P Green_		ORDER NO _1471_	

Figure 6.11 A requisition for goods

Purchase specification

Definition

● *A purchase specification is a document which exactly describes the goods that are required to be purchased.*

This document is prepared by the person responsible for ordering the goods, after discussion with the person who will be using them. There is no point in a purchasing officer ordering foods which a chef refuses to use in the cooking!

A purchase specification gives the details of the precise requirements of the organization for the

ACE HOTEL LTD	PURCHASE SPECIFICATION
14 Beach Road Weaverton BE1 4XX Tel: 0663 201499	REFERENCE NO _93_ DATE _13/9/94_
COMMODITY	_Victoria Plums (tinned)_
SIZE	_—_
WEIGHT	_400 gm tins_
QUALITY/DESCRIPTION	_Grade 1 – Unsweetened juice_
ORIGIN	_S. Africa_
COUNT	_14–16 per tin_
QUOTE REQUIRED	_Per tin_
DELIVERY DATE	_18/9/94_

Figure 6.12 A purchase specification

goods it wishes to purchase. It is then sent to selected suppliers, so that they know exactly what is required and can quote a price accordingly. The specification will include the following details:

1 Description of the goods, including:
   Size
   Weight
   Shape
   Colour
   Texture
   Quality
   Place of origin
2 Quantity required
   Per container (e.g. number of plums per tin)
   Per order
   Per month etc.
3 Delivery details
   Time
   Place
   Date
   Frequency
4 Packaging required, e.g. wrapped in foil, boxed, in pairs

Figure 6.12 is an example of a purchase specification for the goods on the requisition in Figure 6.11. Figure 6.13 is another example of a purchase specification, this time for fresh produce. The purchasing officer will keep a record of all the specifications issued to the various suppliers.

Task 6.33

Draw up a purchase specification for the fresh chicken portions required by ACE Hotel Ltd, which you requested in the Task 6.31. Ask your tutor for the address of possible suppliers to find out the sizes, weights, qualities, etc. available, or use your own ideas if this is not possible. Explain briefly the purpose of a purchase specification.

ACE HOTEL LTD 14 Beach Road Weaverton BE1 4XX Tel: 0663 201499	PURCHASE SPECIFICATION REFERENCE NO _____127_____ DATE ___27/8/94___
COMMODITY	Fresh chickens
SIZE	Medium
WEIGHT	1.8 kg – 2.0 kg
QUALITY/DESCRIPTION	Plump, no blemishes. Drawn, cleaned Giblets separate (max weight 10%)
ORIGIN	British
COUNT	10 per box
QUOTE REQUIRED	Per box
DELIVERY DATE	2 days after order

Figure 6.13 A purchase specification for fresh produce

Quotation

Definition

- *A **quotation** is a document issued by a supplier, giving details of the price and other terms for supplying the goods requested. Some quotations are made verbally.*

The suppliers contacted will issue quotations. These will state the price at which the suppliers are prepared to provide the goods as requested in the purchase specification and will include:

- Basic price as per the specification
- Discounts available, e.g. for bulk orders
- Delivery costs
- Payment terms, e.g. 30 days credit, cash with order
- Any other special terms or procedures

The purchasing officer will examine the quotations and perhaps compile a list of the goods requested and the quotations received. The quotations are then compared and the best one is chosen to supply the goods.

Often, it is the *cheapest* supplier who wins the order, assuming that the quality etc. is identical to all the other quotations received. Sometimes, though, other suppliers win the order for a variety of reasons. One good reason for accepting a quotation which is *not* the lowest is to give business to a supplier who we might need in the future, and to keep our name on that supplier's list for special offers etc. Or we might wish to try a new supplier, even though the quotation given is not the lowest. Or we might give the order to a supplier from whom we are ordering other goods, to keep down our paperwork.

Order

Definition

- *An **order** is a document requesting the goods from the chosen supplier.*

Once we have chosen our supplier, we can then place the order. The order might be for several goods at once, and should be in writing wherever possible, as once the supplier has accepted the order it is legally binding.

Official, pre-printed order forms should be used, and should be pre-numbered to prevent any from being lost, or to prevent staff from ordering goods for themselves. The forms should be in duplicate or triplicate as required – the top copy for the supplier, a copy for the purchasing officer and a copy for head office (if ordering is done locally) or for the branch (if ordering is done centrally). All orders should be signed by the purchasing officer.

Figure 6.14 is an example of an order for the plums we requisitioned earlier, assuming we choose a quotation from a supplier called Lorrimer Produce Ltd. We might also order other goods at the same time, which are included on the order.

Note that the 'description' includes the Purchase Specification Number so that there can be no mistake as to exactly what is required. The copy orders are filed away to await delivery of the goods.

Task 6.34

Draw up a purchase order from ACE Hotel Ltd, to Boothby and Harris, for the fresh chicken portions as per your specification issued earlier. Include also an order for eight turkeys, quoted at £7.00 each, and six whole chickens at £2.40 each.

Explain briefly the purpose of the purchase order, and how it should be used.

Receipt of goods

When the goods are received they must be checked to ensure that they are correct. This

ACE HOTEL LTD
14 Beach Road
Weaverton
BE1 4XX

Tel: 0663 201499

PURCHASE ORDER NO. 6347

TO: *Lorrimer Produce*

27 Market Street

Northtown

NE2 6JJ

Date _____ *14/9/94* _____

Quantity	Description	Unit size	Price quoted	Total value
			£	£
50	Tinned Plums	400 gm	0.70	35.00
50	Tinned Tomatoes	250 gm	0.20	10.00

Delivery date required:

_____ *18/9/94* _____ **Signed** _____ *P Green* _____ Purchasing Officer

Figure 6.14 A purchase order

checking involves several stages and sets of documentation. The supplier might include a *delivery note* with the goods.

Definition

- A **delivery note** is a document issued by the supplier and sent with the goods, giving a description of the goods included in the parcel.

The parcel should be checked to see that it contains the goods as stated on the delivery note. If there is no time to do this, the delivery note should be marked with the words 'goods unseen'. In either case, it should be signed by the person receiving the goods. Once the goods have been accepted, a goods received note is made out.

Definition

- A **goods received note** is a document raised by the purchaser to contain details of the goods received.

The delivery note can be used for this purpose, and many organizations do use it, but it is better if the organization uses its own documentation. Suppliers' delivery notes do not necessarily contain the information the organization requires, they are of varying sizes and types, and may contain confusing information. However, using delivery notes does save time in busy organizations, providing that the correct controls are included to provide security and accuracy. Computerized organizations may be able to recall the original order on the computer, and check it with the goods actually received, thereby doing away with the need for a goods received note at all.

The goods received note should be pre-numbered, to avoid losing any. If delivery notes are used, they should be numbered in sequence. A copy should be kept by the receiving department, and a copy should be passed to the purchasing officer to be compared with the original order. The purchasing officer clips the goods received note and original order together.

When the goods have been checked, and any damaged or incorrect items noted, the goods received note should be signed and entered in the *goods received book* in numerical sequence.

Definition

- A **goods received book** is a book which lists all the goods received notes issued.

Figure 6.15 is an example of a goods received note for the goods ordered from Lorrimer Produce Ltd earlier. Notice that there was a can of plums damaged, and two cans of tomatoes too many. These items are to be returned (see below).

Figure 6.16 is an example of a page in a goods received book. The damaged can of plums and the extra cans of tomatoes will be noted by the purchasing officer, who will do *two* things:

1 Request a credit note from Lorrimer Produce Ltd for the above items
2 Note on the original order that the credit note has been requested

This will ensure that the hotel does not pay for the incorrect items.

Task 6.35

Draw up a goods received note for the items you ordered from Boothby and Harris in Task 6.34. Assume that four of the chicken portions were of incorrect weight and you received one turkey too many. Explain briefly the purpose of a goods received note and how it should be used.

ACE HOTEL LTD

GOODS RECEIVED NOTE

Received from ___Lorrimer Produce___

___27 Market Street___

___Northtown___   **NUMBER 8003**

___NE2 6JJ___

DATE ___18/9/94___

Delivery Note Number _____

Received by ___T. Black___

Description of goods	Quantity	Comments
Tinned Plums	50	1 damaged – returned
Tinned Tomatoes	52	2 too many – returned

Order Number ___6347___

Checked with order ___P. Green___

Figure 6.15 A goods received note

ACE HOTEL LTD　　　　　　　　　**GOODS RECEIVED BOOK**

DATE _18/9/94_

GRN NO.	SUPPLIER	DELIVERY NOTE NO.	COMMENTS
8003	Lorrimer Produce	A361	1 can plums damaged 2 cans tomatoes surplus
8004	Smith & Jones	342	Stationery store
8005	Cauldwells	901364	—

Figure 6.16 A page from a goods received book

Returns

Goods may be returned for a variety of reasons, such as:

- They were damaged on arrival
- They were not as given in the purchase specification
- They were delivered without being ordered (or in excess of the quantity ordered)

As mentioned above, the purchasing officer will arrange for the goods to be returned, and will request a *credit note*.

Definition

- A **credit note** is a document issued by a supplier to a buyer, to reduce the amount charged for goods which were damaged, unsuitable, or for which a reduction in price has been agreed for some other reason.

Figure 6.17 is the credit note which would be received by ACE Hotel Ltd from Lorrimer Produce Ltd. Note that there is no VAT (Value Added Tax) on tinned produce.

Task 6.36

Draw up the credit note which would be received by ACE Hotel Ltd from Boothby and Harris for the goods delivered wrongly in Task 6.35. Explain briefly the purpose of a credit note.

Invoicing

Definition

- The **invoice** is the document which the supplier sends to the purchaser to request payment for the goods delivered.

LORRIMER PRODUCE LTD
27 Market Street
Northtown
NE2 6ZZ

Tel. 0663 204578

CREDIT NOTE

To: Ace Hotel Ltd
14 Beach Road
Weaverton
BE14XX

No. _8040_

Date _24/9/94_

Del. note no.	Description of goods	Quantity	Price each	Total value
			£	£
A361	Tinned Plums	1	0.70	0.70
A361	Tinned Tomatoes	2	0.20	0.40
		Total goods		1.10
		Plus VAT at 17.5%		—
		Total credit		1.10

Figure 6.17 A credit note

It might contain items which the organization may not want to pay for, such as goods returned or goods for which a lower price has been agreed. Therefore it needs careful checking to ensure that:

1 The goods have been received
2 Goods returned or reduced in price have been adjusted, or a credit note has been issued
3 The price charged is as stated in the original order
4 The quantities charged for are correct
5 Any agreed discounts have been given
6 The invoice has not already been paid

To check these items, the purchasing officer must compare the invoice with the goods received note (which has already been checked with the actual items received, and has details of any goods returned), and the original order. Someone should also check the calculations on the invoice, e.g. totals and VAT – but this might be done by the Accounts Department. The goods received note will be marked with the number of the invoice, so that if another invoice arrives for the same goods it can be queried or rejected. In some cases, the delivery note from the supplier also doubles as an invoice. This is obviously time saving, and perhaps paper saving, but it does mean that any errors on delivery will result in incorrect invoices. In addition, an invoice will be provided for every delivery, so an organization which has many deliveries from the same supplier will have a large number of invoices to deal with.

Figure 6.18 is the invoice which would be received from Lorrimer Produce Ltd for the goods ordered earlier. Remember that a separate credit note has been received for the incorrect goods, so the invoice will be for the total goods delivered. After checking by the purchasing officer, the invoice will be signed as 'approved' and passed to the accounts department for payment.

Task 6.37

Draw up the invoice which ACE Hotel Ltd would receive from Boothby and Harris. Remember that a credit note has already been received for the incorrect items, so the invoice will be for the full amount delivered. Describe briefly the purpose of an invoice and how it should be used.

LORRIMER PRODUCE LTD
27 Market Street
Northtown
NE2 6ZZ

Tel. 0663 204578

INVOICE

To: Ace Hotel Ltd
14 Beach Road
Weaverton
BE14XX

No. _____ P62841 _____

Date _____ 22/9/94 _____

Del. note no.	Description of goods	Quantity	Price each	Total value
			£	£
A361	Tinned Plums	50	0.70	35.00
A361	Tinned Tomatoes	52	0.20	10.40
	Total goods			45.40
	Plus VAT at 17.5%			—
	Total invoice			45.40

Figure 6.18 An invoice

Payment

Once the goods have been received and checked to ensure that they are acceptable, we are obliged to pay for them according to the terms agreed. Some suppliers insist on payment with order (e.g. cash and carries), so we might already have paid for these. If there were any faulty goods we will need to obtain a refund.

The majority of suppliers are prepared to wait a short while for payment. Their terms are often noted on the invoice. Some examples of payment terms are:

- Net – this means there is no reduction for prompt payment
- Net, 30 days – this means no reduction for prompt payment and payment is expected within 30 days
- 5 per cent within 10 days – this means that you can deduct 5 per cent discount if you pay within 10 days (or whatever time limit is stated)

Obviously, before any payment is made, we need to ensure that we deduct the total of any credit notes we have received for incorrect goods. The invoice should be approved for payment by the accounts department.

Responsibilities of the purchaser

It is the task of the purchaser to ensure that the best sources of supply for the products required are obtained in order to meet the objectives of the organization. Remember that different organizations will have different needs. A factory canteen will be more concerned with producing an inexpensive meal in reasonable surroundings for a reasonable price, while a high-class restaurant will be concerned with producing unusual and exotic dishes in luxurious surrounding, with price one of the lesser considerations.

The job of 'purchaser' is performed by different people in different organizations. Some will have several 'purchasers' for different types of product.

In a small organization the owner will probably perform all the purchasing functions, while in larger organizations a purchasing officer (with supporting staff) will be specially appointed to the job. In restaurants, the chef de cuisine might be responsible for the purchase of food, or the food and beverage manager in a hotel with banqueting facilities. In smaller hotels and restaurants, the general manager might be responsible for purchasing.

Whoever is responsible, it is important that they are aware of their duties, which are:

1 To identify the products required for purchase, with the help of the purchase requisition. To determine the quantity to be purchased
2 To assist in the preparation of the purchase specification, which in turn ensures that goods of the desired quality are purchased
3 To locate and select suitable suppliers to supply quotations
4 To examine quotations and choose the most appropriate in terms of cost, delivery and reliability
5 To ensure that the right goods are delivered on time, and in good condition
6 To organize returns and the receipt of credit notes
7 To issue goods to the departments requesting them
8 To maintain adequate records of goods in and out
9 To ensure that stocks are maintained at the right level, sufficient for each department's needs but without overstocking
10 To identify and investigate new products which might be more suitable in terms of quantity and/or price
11 To ensure that only those goods received correctly are paid for, and that the price and terms of payment are as agreed at the time of ordering, less any discounts offered

The purchaser must always stick to the procedures laid down for the purchasing function. Any change in those procedures should be made only after approval by senior management.

The job of the purchaser is a very important one, and in larger organizations it carries a high salary. It requires a good knowledge of the products of the organization and of the possible suppliers. Purchasing officers in some organizations become experts in dealing with certain products, to the benefit of the organization.

Task 6.38

Draw up a list of duties in respect of ordering and securing the delivery of the correct product for a purchasing officer in a factory canteen.

Controls in the purchasing system

The amount of money spent on goods purchased in any hospitality and catering organization is very considerable. In addition, the value of goods in stores, or moving around the organization (in kitchens, bars, housekeepers' trolleys, etc.) is very high.

You can see that it is important that proper control is kept on the goods purchased, otherwise a great deal of money could be lost, as well as causing possible disruption to the services offered by the organization.

The preceding sections have looked very thoroughly at the documents and records involved in the purchasing process at the various stages. It will be useful to list them all again as in Table 6.1 and to identify the areas where control is being exercised or where extra care should be taken. In addition to controls through documents and records, control is also possible by using physical checks or stock-counts.

You can see that some of the above controls are to do with *evidence*, i.e. making sure that the paperwork and the goods which exist are correct; some are to do with *authorization*, i.e. making sure that goods which are delivered and paid for were properly agreed as being needed, and are charged for correctly. Both these controls of evidence and authorization are very important.

Conclusion

The purchasing process is an important one in any organization, if only because of the amount of money involved in purchasing the four main types of product – food, liquor, equipment and consumables. You have seen how important it is to choose the correct method of purchasing for each type of product, because each method has its own characteristics. Some may be of advantage to the organization, but others may not, and mistakes can be very costly and difficult to correct.

You have also seen how the various *stages* in the purchasing process form part of a continuous system of control to ensure that the correct goods are requested, ordered, delivered and paid for at the correct price. Mistakes here can also be expensive ones. Goods can be mislaid or delivered incorrectly and in poor condition, and hence will be of no use to the organization. The control procedures included in the documents and records, together with proper authorization and physical check, ensure that mistakes are few and are quickly located and corrected.

It is the responsibility of the purchasing officer to ensure that these controls are in place and are kept to at all times. Although the purchasing officer might not personally carry out all of the tasks in the process, the position is one part of the purchasing 'team' and it is important that all members of the team play their part, and understand each others' roles in the organization. This then ensures the smooth running of the system to achieve the objectives of the organization.

Table 6.1

Stage	Points of control
Initial requisition	Purchaser accepts only those issued by approved members of staff
Purchase specification	Ensures that exact requirements are met in terms of quantity, quality (size, colour, weight, etc.), delivery and packaging Avoids incorrect ordering Avoids misunderstanding between organization and supplier Speeds up the obtaining of quotes as the purchase specification can be quickly withdrawn from the files and submitted to potential suppliers Speeds up checking of goods on arrival Encourages standardization throughout the organization
Quotation	Ensures that prices offered are in writing to avoid future misunderstanding Ensures that discounts, delivery terms, etc. are understood Enables purchasing officer to compare suppliers and choose the most appropriate
Purchase order	Pre-numbering ensures that none are mislaid Approval by a responsible employee ensures that goods cannot be ordered without authorisation On official forms, so that suppliers are confident that they are genuine Clearly states what is being ordered to avoid any misunderstanding Contract terms are made clear
Receipt of goods	Delivery note confirms the goods delivered, for checking Goods received note pre-numbered so none can be lost Physical checking of goods on arrival confirms that they are as the delivery note says, and compare with the original order Documents signed confirms correct receipt of goods Goods received book provides further confirmation
Returns	Damaged or unwanted goods, or non-deliveries, are noted on the goods received note and also in the goods received book, to ensure that full allowance is given against the price charged Credit note issued by supplier confirms that allowance is being given
Invoice	Provides written evidence of amount to be charged Checking with goods received note and original order ensures only being charged for goods as agreed. Confirms delivery and other charges, as stated by the contract terms Checking arithmetic on invoice and VAT calculations ensures accuracy Ensures that an invoice has not already been received by checking with goods received note
Payment	Ensures that invoice has correct discounts as agreed on quotation Ensures that credit notes are deducted from invoices before payment is made Payments authorized by both the purchasing officer and the accounts department ensures that no payments are made for goods which were not ordered and received correctly

Test your knowledge

This section has looked at the purchasing requirements, procedures and controls. See what you can remember:

1 What things would you consider before choosing a source of supply for a particular product? To give you a clue, one of the things you would look for is the range of products offered by the supplier.

2 List the main methods of purchasing for a hospitality and catering organization.

3 What are the advantages and disadvantages of each method of purchasing?

4 Name four types of product which a hospitality and catering organization might purchase.

5 List the stages in the purchasing process, with a brief description of the activities which take place and the documents used at each stage.
6 What information would you find on a purchase specification?
7 What are the duties of a purchaser?
8 What are the various types of control which should exist during the purchasing process, and where do they occur?

▪ CALCULATING THE COST AND PRICE OF GOODS OR SERVICES ▪

In this section we will look at the methods of establishing the cost of products and services, and of calculating selling prices. We will examine the different types of cost which occur, and how they can be classified or grouped together. We will also look at the ways in which costs behave – that is, how they change (or do not change) in response to changes in the activities of the organization.

We will also determine what is meant by a *unit* of goods or services – that is, a single item for which a cost or a selling price is to be calculated. We will see that some costs can be easily calculated and identifed with units, whereas others need to be shared among several units using various methods.

Throughout the section we will look at different ways of presenting cost information, so as to enable management to make decisions.

Types of costs

Costs can be classified in different ways. You can classify your own costs in various ways. For example, you can say that some costs are essential and some are non-essential. Some could be for permanent or long-lasting items, others for things which are quickly used up. Some costs are the same whatever happens – for example, your car tax and insurance have to be paid whether you drive much or not. Other costs vary according to your activities – the more driving you do, the more petrol you use. Costs can often be classified in several ways at once – your daily lunch is essential, quickly used up and its cost varies according to how much you eat.

Businesses also classify their costs in different ways, for different purposes. The way in which they are classified depends on the purpose of the classification – usually to help in making decisions.

The elements of cost

One way of classifying costs is to group them according to the three *elements of cost*, which are:

● Materials
● Labour
● Overheads

Definition

● *Materials* are goods which are sold or are made into saleable items.

In a hospitality and catering organization the main materials are food and drink. Items such as cleaning materials, materials used for maintenance and repairs, etc. (sometimes called *consumables*) are not normally classed as materials as they are not made into saleable items. Such items are normally classed as *overheads*. Some organizations, however, might class restaurant materials, such as serviettes, as materials, especially if they were bought for a particular function.

Definition

● *Labour* refers to the cost of employing the various types of staff employed by the organization.

Labour includes the cost of national insurance and pensions paid by employers, holiday benefits, overtime, staff meals, free accommodation, recreation facilities for staff, provision of uniforms, etc. The last three items are sometimes classed as *overheads* because they are difficult to identify with particular members of staff.

Definition

● **Overheads** are amounts spent on other items not classed as materials or labour.

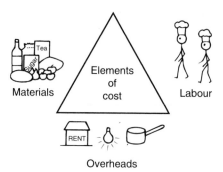

Figure 6.19 Elements of cost

It might include miscellaneous materials (e.g. cleaning materials) and labour costs such as recreation facilities, etc. provided for staff. Overheads will include items such as:

1 Heat and light, rent and rates, insurances
2 The cost of *service operations* such as laundry, maintenance, housekeeping, reception, personnel and training, administration departments
3 *Depreciation* of assets

Definition

● A **service operation** is an operation or department which performs services for other operations or departments.

Depreciation is a measure of the part of a fixed asset which has been used by the organization, and whose value has decreased due to wear and tear, or the passing of time.

Costs involved in buying fixed assets, such as equipment, furniture, etc., are not classed as costs in the way that the above items are, because they are not used up so quickly. Instead, they are kept for use in the future. However, they do decrease in value as time goes

by, and so a proportion of the original cost is included as an *overhead* cost. This proportion is called *depreciation*.

Overheads might be *general* throughout the outlet or facility, such as insurance; or *specific* to individual units, for example the cost of hiring special equipment for a function. Figure 6.19 shows the elements of cost.

Task 6.39

Classify the following items into the three elements of materials, labour and overheads. Assume that any materials which are not connected with making products are to be classed as overheads:

Meat and poultry	Lighting restaurant
Flour	Heating bedrooms
Flowers	Meals taken by kitchen
Chef's wages	staff
Dining-room staff	Depreciation of ovens
wages	Soaps for bedrooms
Restaurant manager's	Maintenance of ovens
salary	Bar staff wages
Cleaning materials	Beer mats
Restaurant bill pads	Cost of new furniture
Heating kitchens	

Direct and indirect costs

Another important classification is to group costs according to whether they are *direct costs* or *indirect costs*.

Definition

- **Direct costs** *are those that can be identified with a specific area of sales, e.g. to a particular dish, or to a particular function or operation.*

Very few costs can be classified as direct costs because it is so difficult to tie them down to specific items. In a hospitality and catering organization, direct costs usually consist only of food, drink and kitchen and bar wages – but not usually the wages of supervisors or managers. Occasionally, the cost of powering ovens is included, but this is difficult to determine. Therefore, direct costs usually consist only of direct materials and direct labour.

Definition

- **Indirect costs** *are costs which* cannot *be identified with a specific area of sales.*

Indirect costs usually includes the majority of costs other than direct materials and direct labour. It will therefore comprise indirect materials, indirect labour, and most overheads. Indirect costs are sometimes known as *shared costs* or *common costs*.

For example, an apple pie will have *direct materials* (apples, sugar, pastry) and *direct labour* (the wages cost of the person making the pie). These costs can be identified with that particular apple pie. But the dish in which it was baked will have been used for other pies; the electricity used to light the kitchen will also

light other working areas; the wages of the kitchen supervisor will cover the supervision of all the cooking and food preparation. These are all *indirect costs*. Indirect costs would also include costs which have nothing to do with the kitchen at all, such as personnel costs, marketing costs, etc.

Task 6.40

Put the items from Task 6.39 into the categories of direct materials, direct labour *and* indirect costs.

How costs change

Some costs change according to the level of activity of the organization. For example, if more meals are sold, then more are cooked and the cost of food will increase. Such costs are known as *variable costs*.

Definition

- **Variable costs** *are costs which change in proportion to the level of activity.*

Examples include food, drink and kitchen wages. In other words, it is *direct costs* which are *variable costs*.

Other costs do not change in this way, but only increase or decrease if the level of activity changes by a large amount. For example, the restaurant manager may be paid a fixed annual salary which remains the same whether there are fifty customers per night or sixty customers. Such costs are known as *fixed costs*.

Definition

- **Fixed costs** *are costs which do* not *change* in proportion to the level of activity.

The above definitions of variable and fixed costs need a little more explanation if you are to understand them more fully. The important words in both definitions are *'in proportion to the level of activity'*. If costs change *in proportion to the level of activity*, it means that if *one more item* is sold, the cost will increase. Let us look at an example to illustrate what is meant.

A restaurant produces 100 meals. The food costs £200, and the time taken to prepare them is 10 hours at a cost of £5 per hour for kitchen staff (that could be one person working for 10 hours, or two people working 5 hours each, or some other combination). These are the *direct* or *variable costs*, which amount to £250 for 100 meals, or £2.50 per meal. In addition, there are various other *fixed costs* including supervisors' wages, heating and lighting, rent and rates, insurance, etc., in total amounting to £300.

If *one more* meal is produced, the extra cost will be another £2.50. There will be no increase in the other costs because they do not increase *in proportion to the level of activity*. They will remain the same for the sake of an extra meal.

It is easy to see the relationship between fixed costs and variable costs with the aid of a graph. Using the information given above, we can first draw up Table 6.2 showing the costs for different numbers of meals. Remember, the *variable costs* are £2.50 per meal, and the *fixed costs* are £300. Note that there is a total cost of £300 even when there are zero meals produced – the fixed costs must still be paid, unless the organization closes down.

Table 6.2 Costs

No. of meals produced	0	10	20	50	100
	£	£	£	£	£
Variable cost – £1.50 each	0	25	50	125	250
Fixed cost	300	300	300	300	300
Total cost	300	325	350	425	550

We can draw a graph with the costs up the side and the number of meals along the bottom, and plot *two* lines on it (Figure 6.20):

1 A line showing fixed costs – this will be the same for all numbers of meals, so it will be a straight line across the graph
2 A line showing total costs – this will rise as the numbers of meals rises, but it will still be a straight line

---

Task 6.41

Draw a graph showing fixed and total costs, from the following data:

Variable costs – food £1.20 per meal
labour £0.80 per meal
Fixed costs   – £1000

Use any quantities you think are reasonable to draw your graph, from zero to 500 meals.

Neither of the above definitions of fixed costs and variable costs have anything to do with changes in costs which occur as a result of inflation, seasonal reductions, etc. *All* costs will change for these reasons, so in that respect no costs can be fixed.

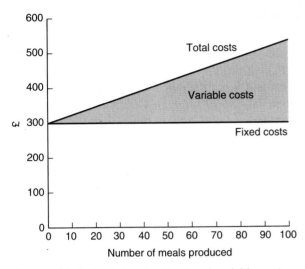

Figure 6.20 A chart showing fixed and variable costs

Some costs are *stepped costs*. This means that they do not alter as a result of *small* changes in the level of activity, but they do if there is a significant change. For example, heat and light might not alter at all if a few extra bedrooms are occupied for a night, but if there are enough extra rooms needed to open another floor then additional heating and lighting will be needed.

In fact, many costs incurred will be semi-fixed or stepped costs, and splitting them for costing purposes is a very difficult task – and one which will normally be performed by the accounting staff. Nevertheless, it is important that you understand the principles involved in the variation of costs.

Nor do fixed costs stay fixed for *all* levels of activity. If there are large increases or decreases in activity then fixed costs will alter. If the restaurant expands such that two managers are needed, or extra rent, rates and insurance are required, then fixed costs will change. The important point to note is that they do not change *in proportion to the level of activity*.

Some costs are *semi-fixed costs* (also called *semi-variable costs*). These *partly* change as a result in changes in activity, but part of them remains the same. An example of such costs is the telephone bill, where part of it is for the rental (which remains the same whatever the level of activity) and the rest is for calls (which will alter as the level of activity changes).

Another very important *semi-fixed cost* is the cost of labour. The majority of wages in a hospitality and catering organization do not go up and down as the level of activity changes. Most employees are paid a standard basic wage, which will not normally fall below that level even if business is a little slow for a few days, but if there is extra activity they will be paid overtime (which might be at a higher hourly rate), or additional staff will be brought in. So labour costs are often semi-fixed costs.

Table 6.3 illustrates how different types of cost can vary.

You can see from the table that the fixed

Table 6.3

Type of cost	Cost for 100 £	Cost for 120 £	Cost for 200 £
Direct materials	50.00	60.00	100.00
Direct labour	40.00	48.00	80.00
Fixed overheads	1000.00	1000.00	1200.00
Total cost	1090.00	1108.00	1380.00

overheads do not alter for 120 units, but for 200 units some expansion is needed, so they rise by £200. However, this rise is not *in proportion to the level of activity*, therefore it is not a variable cost. It is a stepped cost. On the other hand, the direct materials and direct labour vary exactly in proportion to the level of activity. The table does not show what would happen if only 95 units were produced, but it might be that direct labour stays at £40, because that is the minimum wage paid – remember, labour costs are often semi-fixed costs.

Task 6.42

Compile a table, similar to Table 6.3, to show how the following costs vary at different levels of activity:

Direct materials   £3.00 per unit
Direct labour   £1.00 per unit
Fixed costs   £1000 for up to 100 units, then £100 extra for every additional 50 units.

Use 50 units, 100 units, 150 units and 200 units in your table.

Time-based and usage-based costs

Some costs are dependent on the amount of time which they cover. For example, an annual rent charge for a machine will be the same whether the machine is used much or remains idle. The rent charged for a six-month period would be half that charged for a whole year – the charge is based on the amount of time covered. Many fixed costs are time-based. Indeed, many time-based costs are split into equal monthly or weekly amounts and paid for by regular instalments throughout the year. This would apply to costs such as salaries, insurance premiums, depreciation, etc. The longer the period of time which they cover, the higher the charge.

Other costs are dependent on the amount of use which is made of them, irrespective of the amount of time for which they are used. For example, an electricity bill depends on the amount of heat, light, power, etc. which has been used up during the charging period (although there is often also a fixed 'standing charge' which is time-based). Many variable or semi-variable costs are usage based. Examples include food and drink, laundry costs, hourly paid labour (particularly for overtime wages), etc. In practice, most costs are a mixture of fixed and variable, direct and indirect, time-based and usage-based.

The above sections have introduced you to the various ways in which costs can be classified. You will realize that it is not an easy task to divide costs into different 'sections'; sometimes even experienced accountants have difficulty. Some people say that accountancy is a form of art – different people can interpret figures such as costs and revenues differently. Perhaps you agree!

The costs which make up a 'unit' of goods or service

Before we can calculate the cost of the goods and services produced by an organization, we must first determine the *unit* upon which we are going to base the costs.

A *unit* of goods or service can be one of several things. Some examples are:

1 A *dish* (e.g. an apple pie, a beef casserole); a dish is also called a 'recipe', and is often divided into 'portions' (e.g. one piece of apple pie)
2 A *menu* (e.g. a lunchtime bar menu, a table d'hôte menu), consisting of several dishes
3 A *function* (e.g. a party, a conference), comprising a menu and the provision of other items such as a bar, music/entertainment, stationery, flowers, marketing costs, etc.
4 *Provision of accommodation* (e.g. a bedroom, a ballroom, a prison cell)
5 An *operation* or department in the organization (e.g. the kitchen, the laundry), which may produce goods or it may provide a service to other units
6 An *outlet* (e.g. a works canteen, a bar, or sometimes a whole facility such as a guest house)

It is beyond the scope of this qualification to produce costs and selling prices for a large facility, such as an entire hotel or group of hotels. Many of the techniques and theories you will learn are equally suitable for use in larger organizations, but they have additional components which are again beyond the requirements of this qualification.

Task 6.43

Make a list of the units of goods or service which you might find in a large hotel and classify them according to the categories given above. You can leave out the category of 'dish' as there are so many examples with which you are probably already familiar.

Now that we have looked at the various types of unit we can consider what a single unit of each type comprises. We need to do this before we can calculate the cost, and eventually the selling price, for a unit. We can see from the list above, and from the list you have made for Task 6.31, that units can be very different from one another. Some units consist of several units of the same kind together – for example, a menu consists of several dishes. Some units consist of several *different* kinds of units – for example, a function consists of dishes as well as other goods and services.

Weights and measures

Before we start to look at the different units, we need to know some basic rules regarding measurements of weight, length, volume, etc. Many of the quantities and other units of measurements used in the hospitality and catering industry are expressed in a mixture of imperial and metric units. You should practise converting from imperial to metric and vice versa with a variety of different units of measurement, e.g.

- Weight (pounds and ounces: kilos and grames)
- Liquid measures (pints, gallons: litres, centilitres)
- Length (yards, feet and inches: metres and centimetres)
- Area and volume (square/cubic yards, feet and inches: metres and centimetres)

Here are some useful weights and measures:

Imperial measurements	Metric measurements
12 inches = 1 foot	100 centimetres =
3 feet = 1 yard	1 metre
16 ounces =	1000 grams =
1 pound (lb)	1 kilogram
112 pounds =	
1 hundredweight (cwt)	
20 fluid ounces =	1000 millilitres =
1 pint	1 litre
4 gills = 1 pint	
8 pints = 1 gallon	

and here are some useful *approximate* conversions:

1 pint = 0.57 litres	1 litre = 1.76 pints
1 yard = 0.9 metres	1 metre = 1.1 yards
1 lb = 454 grams	1 kilogram =
	2.2 pounds

Note that the above are only *approximate* conversions. If you need more exact conversions, e.g. when measuring for a carpet, you will need to use a tape-measure or a more accurate conversion chart.

You will note that sometimes even more approximate conversions are used. For example, in many recipes, 1 lb is converted to 500 grams for ease of weighing using scales.

Task 6.44

Using the above conversion guidelines, find the metric or imperial equivalent for each of the following:

11 pints	16 fl. oz	2 kg
3 metres	250 grams	8 ounces
2.4 gallons	0.5 kg	3 lb 4 oz
7 ft 4 in.	2.2 cwt	1.4 litres

Now we will look at the units which exist in the hospitality and catering industry, and try to establish exactly what is included in each.

The costs which make up a dish

Definition

● A **dish** is a particular food or combination of foods in a recipe.

An example might be a steak and kidney pudding. In order to calculate a single unit of a dish, we need to know the ingredients of that dish. These should be predetermined and recorded on a *standard recipe* card.

Definition

● A **standard recipe** is a list of ingredients for a particular dish, showing the quantities required, the number of standard portions which the recipe produces and the method of preparation and cooking. It might also show the length of time taken to prepare the dish, although sometimes more than one dish is prepared at once.

The purpose of the standard recipe is to ensure that every time the dish is prepared it is of exactly the same quality and quantity as prepared previously, and takes the same amount of time and materials as before. It also assists in calculating the cost of the dish, as we shall see later.

Here is an example of a standard recipe:

Standard recipe No. 43

Steak and kidney pudding	Four portions
Ingredients	Quantity
Suetcrust pastry (Recipe 16)	250 g
Stewing steak	500 g
Lamb's kidneys	2
Flour	25 g
Salt	1 level tsp
Black pepper	Pinch
Hot pepper sauce	Dash
Onion	1 small
Beef stock (Recipe 104)	5 fl. oz

Method:

1 Add water to steamer and bring to boil
2 Grease 6-inch pudding basin
3 Roll out pastry into round, line basin with 3/4 of the pastry
4 Chop meats
5 Toss meats in seasoned flour
6 Chop onion
7 Mix meats, flour and onion, add to basin
8 Add stock to basin
9 Roll out 1/4 of the pastry to form lid and seal
10 Cover with greased foil and tie with string
11 Steam for 3–4 hours

The standard recipe can also have columns added to include the cost of the ingredients and hence the cost of the dish. We will look at this later.

Some of the ingredients in the standard recipe are taken from other standard recipes. These will be prepared and costed in the same way. They may be recipes for larger quantities than required by this dish, so we will need to calculate the proportion required. For example, Recipe 16 for suetcrust pastry might be a recipe for 500 g, thus this recipe only needs half of that quantity.

Many of the ingredients will have been purchased in bulk quantities, so again we will only require a proportion of the quantity purchased. For example, onions might be purchased in 5-kilo sacks, so we need to establish how much a single small onion weighs, and how many there are in a sack, in order to calculate the cost.

Some ingredients will be required in quantities which are too small to put an exact cost on them. In this case, we simply add a set amount, often just a few pence, to the total cost.

We will look at calculating the cost of the dish later but remember that the cost of ingredients and time taken is only part of the cost. There are indirect costs to be added as well, before calculating a selling price.

Some dishes are easy to calculate because there is no cooking, mixing or preparation involved in them. An example might be a piece of fresh fruit or, even more simple, something that is bought by the unit such as a grapefruit. However, indirect costs still need to be added when pricing the dish.

Beverage 'units'

These require separate consideration because beverages usually come in large containers, from which small amounts are dispensed at a time. For items such as tea, coffee and sugar, the use of single sachets makes it easy to determine a unit. If these items are bought in large tins, it is more difficult, but there are several different ways round the problem:

1 To 'test measure' a number of portions, say 100 spoons of coffee
2 To make up the beverages in large quantities, and then measure by individual cups
3 To ensure that all cups used are of the same size

4 To assume that all guests take a standard amount of milk and sugar

For alcoholic beverages, the calculation depends on how the beverages are packaged. Here are some useful standard measurements:

- *Spirits:* 1 measure = 1/6 gill (1 standard bottle = 32 measures)
- *Beers:* 1 firkin = 9 gallons (1 barrel = 4 firkins)
- *Wines* = 6 glasses per 75 cl bottle
- *Fortified wines* = 1/5 gill per measure

Some drinks, especially cocktails, can be difficult to measure because of the number of ingredients and the use of non-standard measures. In these cases, a standard recipe can be prepared in the same way as those for food.

Task 6.45

1 Calculate the number of cups of coffee which can be made from 500 g, if 50 g makes 30 cups.
2 Calculate the number of pints of beer left in a firkin if it is three-quarters full
3 Calculate the number of measures of gin used up from a bottle which has 1 gill remaining

The costs which make up a menu

Definition

- *A **menu** consists of several different dishes or portions of dishes.*

It might be a simple one-meal set menu, such as a single starter, main course and dessert, or it might be a full à la carte menu with a selection of dishes for all meals, including snacks. It could be a breakfast menu or a list of bar-snacks. Of course, it can also be a combination of various types of menu, to suit the occasion.

It is difficult to calculate the cost of a complete à la carte menu, because of the number of unknown factors involved, such as how many of each dish would be chosen by customers, but for set menus, table d'hôte menus and special functions, it is important to calculate the cost of each menu to enable a price to be set.

For these menus, a single price is calculated for the various dishes included in the meal. Thus it is important to calculate first the cost of a dish and then of a single portion of each dish, using the standard recipe card shown earlier.

In some cases, the menu might be for several people – such as a banquet (these are particularly common in foreign restaurants). The menu might then consist of a whole standard recipe for each dish, rather than individual portions. Some organizations offer several set menus at once, giving customers a choice of dishes, but still maintaining an overall price.

Again, do not forget that the cost of the direct materials and labour is only part of the cost. Indirect costs must be also added, as we shall see later.

The costs which make up a function

Definition

- *A **function** comprises a menu, or selection of menus, and other items as required for the occasion, such as music and entertainment, private bar, stationery, flowers, special marketing costs, etc. There may be additional wages costs as well as the normal wage costs of the organization's staff, such as overtime or casual labour. There might also be an extra cost for cleaning and preparing the function rooms.*

The food might be costed from the standard recipes, or if it is a large function, prepared and costed separately as an entire function. There may even be separate standard recipes for large quantities of dishes to be prepared at once.

Other items will also need careful calculation. Unless they are specified by the organizers of the function, you will need to decide yourself on the quantities required for items such as flowers, stationery, etc. You must not run short of anything, nor do you wish to be left with a surplus which cannot be used. As with all pricing, *indirect costs* must also be considered, before fixing a selling price, as we shall see later.

Task 6.46

From dishes of your own choice compile three different set menus, each consisting of a starter, a main course with suitable vegetables, and a sweet.

Task 6.47

Make a list of as many items you can think of which might be required for a wedding reception to be held in a large luxury hotel, apart from the food for the meal itself.

The costs which make up the provision of accommodation

Definition

● **Accommodation** is the provision of a room or rooms for a period of time.

Accommodation can be of different types in different organizations. In a hospital it is basically a bed; in a prison it is a small cell; in a hotel it is a bedroom; sometimes it might be a large 'function' room, or a suite of rooms for a conference.

In hotels and guest houses a bedroom might accommodate more than one person. Some of the types of bedroom accommodation commonly in use are:

● Single rooms
● Double and twin rooms
● Family rooms (for two adults and two children)
● Suites (sometimes with lounge/dining/study areas)
● Adjoining rooms (connected two or more bedrooms together)

In addition, extra beds can sometimes be added.

Some hotels allow guests to use rooms which are normally for more people, e.g. double and twin rooms might be let to a single guest, or a family room to a couple.

The accommodation might also include some meals. For example, you would expect to be offered your meals if you go into hospital. In private hospitals, the charge might include the room *and* the meals, or the meals might be priced separately. It is obviously important to know what is included and what is not.

In hotels, there are several possible combinations of accommodation and meals included in the price, as follows:

1 Room only
2 Room and breakfast (room and English or Continental breakfast)
3 Fully inclusive/en pension (room and all meals)
4 Half-board/demi-pension (room, breakfast and lunch *or* dinner)

In addition, some hotels quote prices for a single night, or for several nights, e.g. a long-weekend or a full week. The price per night for several nights is usually lower than for single nights.

It is difficult to cost accommodation, because the direct costs involved are quite small, although the indirect costs can be substantial. For example, the direct costs of a hotel bedroom might be nil while the indirect costs, such as heating, lighting, etc., can be very high indeed, but difficult to value. It is therefore extra-important that all indirect costs are properly costed themselves to ensure that accommodation is not under-priced.

Task 6.48

Make a list of the indirect costs of accommodation for a hotel bedroom. Which of these are costs incurred by other operations?

The costs which make up an operation

Definition

● An **operation** consists of an area of the organization where a single activity or group of related activities are carried out. A group of operations might form a department.

Operations can be divided into two types:

- *Revenue-earning operations* are those which earn money for the organization, by selling, or providing things for sale. An example is a restaurant.
- *Non-revenue-earning or service operations* are those which perform services for other operations. An example is a maintenance operation, which might do repairs in the restaurant or in the laundry

Task 6.49

From the list of operations which you might find in a large hotel, classify them according to whether they are revenue-earning *or* non-revenue earning, *and in each case state how you decided on your classification:*

Rooms/accommodation	Maintenance
Kitchen	Banqueting
Restaurant	Laundry
Portering	Gymnasium
Housekeeping	Reception
Bar	Administration

If the operation is involved with food and beverages, then it might incur *direct materials* as part of its costs. If it is a service operation, however, it might have only *labour* and *overhead* costs.

Definition

- A **service operation** is an operation which performs services for other operations.

It might be a revenue-earning operation or a non-revenue-earning operation. For example, the restaurant might provide food for a

conference, so in that case it is *servicing* the conference suite. The more common service operations, however, are the non-revenue-earning ones, such as Laundry.

The costs of service operations should be shared among the other operations wherever possible to ensure that they are taken into account when calculating prices.

There can be arguments in deciding which costs should be apportioned to which operations. For example, if the restaurant kitchen produces food which goes to a conference, there will be objections if the cost is left with the kitchen, and not allocated to the conference. There is no rule about what should be done – it is up to individual organizations to determine what is best for them.

Task 6.50

Identify the different costs which might be incurred by a Laundry operation in a hospital. Identify the different operations which might be 'serviced' by the Laundry operation.

The costs which make up an outlet

Definition

- An **outlet** is defined as a unit of management or an establishment found within each sector, usually on one site, for example a hotel, a public house, a restaurant, a hospital, normally comprising a number of operations.

In other words, it is an operation which provides the goods for sale to the customers. There might be several outlets in an organization – e.g. a large hotel might have two restaurants, a coffee-shop, a selection of bars, leisure areas, etc. A hospital might have outlets such as the kitchen producing the patients' meals, a visitors' café, and a staff dining room.

The cost of an outlet will include the direct costs and indirect costs associated with the outlet, plus a proportion of the costs of service operations wherever possible. In a works canteen, for example, the costs will probably be calculated by including the whole cost of the works kitchens and canteen, plus a proportion of other operations such as cleaning, maintenance, laundry, personnel and training and administration (to cover heating, lighting, insurance, etc.). We will look at how to calculate these costs in the next section. Figure 6.21 might help to summarize the various *units* of goods and services and how they fit into the overall organization:

Calculating costs

In the previous section we have looked at the different units for which costs might need to be calculated, and we described the types of cost which should be considered for each unit. Now we are going to look at ways of calculating those costs.

Calculating materials costs

Materials come into an organization via the purchasing process. This means that when they arrive, they have a cost already attached to them, which is the cost as stated on the invoice (assuming that it is correct).

Materials should be properly stored, to ensure their safety and quality, and records should be kept of movements in and out of the storage area. This applies to all types of materials,

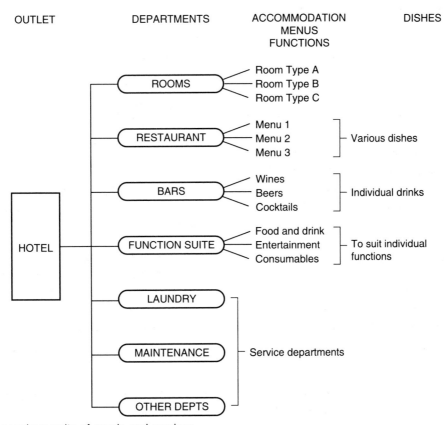

Figure 6.21 The various units of goods and services

Bin Card No. 345			Commodity: Potatoes	
Date	Reference	Receipts	Issues	Balance
1.1.95	Balance			45 kilos
12.1.95	Issues to kitchen		10 kilos	35 kilos
15.1.95	Issues to kitchen		20 kilos	15 kilos
27.1.95	Returned from kitchen	2 kilos		17 kilos
28.1.95	Purchases	15 kilos		32 kilos

Figure 6.22 A bin card

whether they are items of food, liquor or consumables. The materials are then passed out ('issued') to the operations of the organization who need them.

So at any one time there could be materials coming in, materials being held in stores, materials being held in operations throughout the organization, and materials being used up. It is obviously important to keep track of the whereabouts of materials, and to be able to put values on them.

The records kept by the storekeeper might contain only details of *quantities* received and issued. These are kept on cards called *bin cards*. Figure 6.22 is an example of a bin card for potatoes. Someone else might keep records of the *values* of stocks held in the stores or issued to operations and departments, and hence be responsible for calculating the value of materials used.

Definition

● A **bin card** is a document showing the quantities of goods received and issued, usually kept on the shelf or in the container with the goods in store.

There are many different methods of calculating this value. The task would be much more simple if every time an item was issued

from stock we knew exactly what we had paid for it. But storekeeping is not that easy, especially with large quantities, so we need to have some other method for determining the cost of the materials used. We are going to look at just two of those methods, but others are used in practice. The two we are going to describe are:

● FIFO – which stands for First In, First Out
● AVCO – which stands for Average Cost

The FIFO method is very easy to use, and for that reason it is very popular. The AVCO method is slightly more accurate, but a little more complex to use. The use of computers has, however, made this method more popular. The two methods are best explained by showing you a simple example.

Your organization keeps stocks of tinned tomato purée, and the movements during April are as follows:

1 April	Stock on hand	10 tins, cost £1 each
3 April	Issued to restaurant	8 tins
5 April	Purchased	12 tins, cost £1.20 each
10 April	Issued to restaurant	6 tins
15 April	Purchased	12 tins, cost £1.30 each
24 April	Issued to restaurant	6 tins
28 April	Issued to restaurant	6 tins

The FIFO method of stock valuation

The FIFO method assumes that the stocks which were purchased first are issued first (first in, first out). Figure 6.23 shows a stores record card using this method. The card starts off with a balance in stock of ten tins valued at £1 each. Purchases (receipts) are added to stock at whatever price paid for them, but issues are deducted from stock using the oldest price first.

With the issues on 3 April there is no problem – there are only £1 units in stock, so that is the value we use for the issues. There are then two tins at £1 each left. On 5 April, 12 tins at £1.20 are bought and added to the two tins at £1. On 10 April, six tins are issued. Using FIFO, we issue the earliest ones first, so we issue the two £1 tins, and four of the £1.20 tins. The £1 tins are all issued now, so we have eight tins left at £1.20 each. We continue adding purchases and deducting issues, using the oldest price first. Each time an issue is made, the balance column is ruled across and a new balance is shown. If we total up the issues for April we get a total of £29.60.

The AVCO method of stock valuation

The AVCO method is slightly more difficult. Each time a new purchase is made it is added to the previous balance, and a new total of Quantity and Total Value is found. A new Value Each is then calculated by dividing the Total Value by the total Quantity.

The stores record card for the above transactions using AVCO would be as shown in Figure 6.24.

Again, we started with ten £1 tins in stock. The issues on 3 April are £1 tins, because we have no others, so we have two £1 tins left over. On 5 April, however, when we purchase twelve tins at £1.20 each, we need to work out a new Average Value each. We need to add together the two £1 tins and the twelve £1.20 tins, as follows:

Present balance	2 at £1.00	= £2.00
Purchases	12 at £1.20	= £14.40
New total	14 tins	= £16.40

STORES RECORD CARD		RECEIVED		ISSUED		BALANCE		
DATE	REFERENCE	Qty	Cost	Qty	Value	Qty	Value each	Total value
			£		£		£	£
1 April	Balance in stock					10	1.00	10.00
3 April	Issued			8	8.00	2	1.00	2.00
5 April	Purchases	12	1.20			12	1.20	14.40
10 April	Issued	6 = 2 +4	2.00 4.80	8	1.20	9.60
15 April	Purchases	12	1.30			12	1.30	15.60
24 April	Issued			6	7.20	2	1.20	2.40
						12	1.30	15.60
April 28	Issued			6 = 2 +4	2.40 5.20	8	1.30	10.40

Figure 6.23 A stores record card using the FIFO method

STORES RECORD CARD		RECEIVED		ISSUED		BALANCE		
DATE	REFERENCE	Qty	Cost	Qty	Value	Qty	Value each	Total value
			£		£		£	£
1 April	Balance in stock					10	1.00	10.00
3 April	Issued			8	8.00	2	1.00	2.00
5 April	Purchases	12	1.20			12	1.20	14.40
	New average					14	1.17	16.40
10 April	Issued			6	7.02	8	1.17	9.38
15 April	Purchases	12	1.30			12	1.30	15.60
	New average					20	1.25	24.98
24 April	Issued			6	7.50	14	1.25	17.48
28 April	Issued			6	7.50	8	1.25	9.98

At the top of the card: AVCO — TINNED TOMATO PURÉE

Figure 6.24 A stores record card using the AVCO method

Therefore, the new average value each is £16.40 divided by 14 tins = £1.17. The issues on 10 April are then priced at this average of £1.17.

Using this method, in times of rising prices, the issues are valued at a slightly higher amount (£30.02), so increasing the costs of the organization, but the materials still remaining are valued at a slightly lower amount so that future costs will be reduced.

Task 6.51

Using the following information about the movements of tubs of margarine, prepare the stores record card using both the FIFO and the AVCO methods. Calculate the value of the materials issued in each case, and state which would provide the lowest cost to the restaurant.

1 May	Stock of margarine – 23 tubs at £1.40 each
4 May	Issued 12 tubs
7 May	Purchased 6 tubs at £1.50 each
18 May	Issued 10 tubs
19 May	Issued 3 tubs
23 May	Purchased 6 tubs at £1.60 each
24 May	Issued 5 tubs

Cellar records

Records of alcoholic beverages are kept by the cellar-keeper. These beverages are issued to the bar and restaurants for sale. Bar and restaurant records are often kept at *selling price*, so it is helpful if the cellar records also show the selling price of stocks to enable checks to be made. Because of the high value of alcoholic beverages, controls are more strict and checks on stocks are made more often. There are often separate records kept of cellar stocks received and issued, and a daily record of movements in and out.

Yield and wastage

Once we have calculated the value of the materials issued to the various areas of the organization, we need to calculate what can be produced from them. Some materials suffer loss due to shrinkage, wastage, etc. during use, and so the quantity which is issued may need to be increased in order to provide the quantity required.

Organizations will conduct 'test yields' to find out how much is normally lost during the preparation of these items, in order to establish a standard yield.

Definition

- The **yield** is the amount of usable material available from a particular product, after deducting losses due to wastage.
- **Wastage** is the amount of material lost during storage, preparation, cooking or serving, due to shrinkage, evaporation, boning, cutting, etc.

The following is an example of the loss which can occur during the preparation and cooking and serving of a turkey:

Original plucked and prepared weight of turkey	5.2 kg
including giblets	0.3 kg
Weight after cooking	4.3 kg
Weight when cooled	4.1 kg
Sliced weight	2.2 kg

You can see that the end weight of meat available (the yield) is only 2.2 kg, having lost 3.0 kg in the process of preparing, cooking and slicing. This loss is made up of:

Giblets	0.3 kg
Cooking and cooling	0.8 kg
Skin and bones	1.9 kg

In order to calculate the yield from a particular product or recipe we can use a *yield test card*.

Definition

- A **yield test card** is a document used to record the yield from one or more products when prepared and/or cooked under certain conditions.

It can be used to compare different methods of cooking, e.g. cooking in foil as opposed to 'open' cooking, or cooking meat on the bone as opposed to boned cuts. It can also be employed to compare yields from products from different suppliers. It is used to calculate the weight lost during preparation and cooking and cost of the usable product after preparation and cooking.

Figure 6.25 is an example of a yield test card for the above turkey.

The calculations on the yield test card are as follows:

- Percentage of original weight

$$= \frac{\text{Weight lost or remaining}}{\text{Original weight}} \times 100$$

so the percentage of weight lost in carving

$$= \frac{1.9}{5.2} \times 100 = 36.5 \text{ per cent}$$

- Cost per servable kilo

$$= \frac{\text{Total cost}}{\text{Servable weight}} = \frac{£6.24}{2.2 \text{ kg}} = £2.84$$

- Cost factor

$$= \frac{\text{Cost per servable kilo}}{\text{Original cost per kilo}} = \frac{£2.84}{£1.20} = £2.37$$

There are several other useful calculations which can come from the information regarding *yield* and *wastage*. Here are some of them:

Yield test card				
Item: Roast Turkey **Cost:** £6.24			**Purchase Specification No.** 123 **Cost per kilo:** £1.20	
	Weight	**% of original weight**	**Cost per servable kilo**	**Cost factor**
Raw weight	5.2 kilos	100.00		
Butchering loss	0.3 kilo	5.8		
Cooking loss	0.6 kilo	11.5		
Cooling loss	0.2 kilo	3.9		
Carving loss	1.9 kilos	36.5		
Servable weight	2.2 kilos	42.3	£2.84	£2.37

Figure 6.25 A yield test card

1 *The number of usable portions* depends on the required weight of a portion and the yield of usable meat. The number of portions is

$$\frac{\text{Usable meat}}{\text{Required weight per portion}}$$

If the required weight per portion is 0.14 kg, the number of portions is

$$\frac{2.2}{0.14} = 15.7 \text{ portions}$$

2 *Cost of usable food* – once we have calculated the yield, we can then calculate the cost of the usable food. This is calculated as:

$$\frac{\text{Cost of food as purchased}}{\text{Number of usable portions}} =$$

$$\frac{£6.24}{15.7} = 39.7\text{p per portion}$$

Another way of calculating the usable price would be to find the price per usable kilogram, and then use that to calculate individual portion sizes. For example, the price per usable kilogram would be:

$$\frac{\text{Price per kg as purchased}}{\text{Percentage yield}} =$$

$$\frac{£1.20}{42.3} \times 100 = £2.84 \text{ per usable kilogram}$$

Thus a portion at 0.14 kg = £2.84 × 0.14 = 39.7p per portion

3 *Weight of turkey for a given number of portions* – if the portion size is fixed at a certain weight, then the original weight of a turkey for any number of portions can be calculated as:

$$\frac{\text{Number of portions} \times \text{required weight of each}}{\text{Percentage yield}}$$

For example, if 20 portions at 0.14 kg are required, the starting weight of the turkey must be:

$$\frac{20 \times 0.14}{42.3} \times 100 = 6.62 \text{ kg}$$

or this could be calculated using the cost factor of 2.36:

Weight of turkey = number of portions $\times$ required weight of each portion $\times$ cost factor

$= 20 \times 0.14 \times 2.36$

$= 6.63$ kg

Task 6.52

The information regarding a leg of pork is as follows:

Original weight as purchased	*4.8 kg*
Price paid	*£2.40 per kg*
Weight lost in cooking	*15 per cent*
Weight lost in boning and slicing	*1.2 kg*

Calculate:

- *The percentage yield*
- *The cost per kg of usable meat*
- *The number of portions at 0.14 kg per portion*
- *The cost per portion at 0.14 kg per portion*
- *The cost per portion at 0.125 kg per portion*

Task 6.53

Compile a yield test card for the following:

Shoulder of pork, bought weight 4.2 kilos, costing £2.40 per kilo
Butchering loss, 8 per cent
Cooking loss, 18 per cent
Carving loss, 21 per cent

Calculating the materials cost of a standard recipe

Earlier we looked at standard recipes and their importance in ensuring that dishes are prepared in a consistent manner. Organizations will produce costings for their standard recipes using the latest information regarding the cost of materials. Calculations regarding the cost of materials issued will already have been prepared, using either FIFO or AVCO, and calculations of yield and wastage, and the kitchen will be presented with figures which are as up to date as possible. The cost of standard recipes should be reviewed regularly, especially where they contain ingredients which change frequently in price.

Using the standard recipe for steak and kidney pudding given earlier, we can now add costs. Let us say that the following costs have been passed to us:

Recipe 16	60p per 500 g
Recipe 104	12p per pint
Stewing steak	£3.50 per kg
Lamb's kidneys	£2.80 per kg, containing 24 kidneys
Flour	60p per kilo
Onions	20p per lb (4 small onions)

We can now complete the costing of the standard recipe, leaving the remaining columns for revisions of the cost.

Standard recipe no. 43

Steak and kidney pudding   *Four portions*

Ingredients	Quantity	Costs calculated at:			
		31.8.94			
Suetcrust pastry (Recipe 16)	250 gm	0.30			
Stewing steak	500 gm	1.75			
Lamb's kidneys	2	0.23			
Flour	25 gm	0.02			
Salt	1 level tsp				
Black pepper	Pinch	0.06			
Hot pepper sauce	Dash	(total)			
Onion	1 small	0.05			
Beef stock (Recipe 104)	5 fl. oz	0.03			
Total cost for four portions		2.44			
Cost per portion		0.61			

Method:

1 Add water to steamer and bring to boil
2 Grease 6-inch pudding basin
3 Roll out pastry into round, line basin with ¾ of the pastry
4 Chop meats
5 Toss meats in seasoned flour
6 Chop onion
7 Mix meats, flour and onion, add to basin
8 Add stock to basin
9 Roll out ¼ of the pastry to form lid and seal
10 Cover with greased foil and tie with string
11 Steam for 3–4 hours

Task 6.54

From the following information for a standard recipe, calculate the materials cost of the recipe and the cost per portion, assuming six portions per recipe:

Apple Pie

Cooking apples	500 g	costing 44p per lb
Shortcrust pastry	200 g	per recipe 27, costed at 40p per 250 g
Demerara sugar	125 g	costing 60p per kg
Cloves	Four	
Cinnamon	pinch	add 2p overall

Calculating the materials cost of a menu

A menu is a collection of dishes or portions of dishes. Many of them are taken from standard recipes, which are already costed. To cost the materials of the menu we need to take an average cost for all the dishes or portions it contains.

Example: Costing the materials for a table d'hôte menu

	Standard Recipe No	Cost per portion £
Starters		
Fruit juice	12	0.30
Tomato soup	14	0.40
Fish pâté	18	0.50
Main courses		
Beef casserole	101	0.90
Roast chicken	103	0.80
Vegetable lasagne	112	0.70
Vegetables		
Selection	117	0.35
Sweets		
Ice cream surprise	210	0.19
Apple pie	211	0.15
Plum tart	214	0.20

The total cost of the menu depends on the choices of the guests. We need to take an average for each of the dishes. To calculate an average, add up the cost of all the items and divide by the number of items, thus:

Starters	30p + 40p + 50p = £1.20 divided by 3 = 40p
Main courses	90p + 80p + 70p = £2.40 divided by 3 = 80p
Vegetables	35p
Sweets	20p + 15p + 19p = £0.54 divided by 3 = 18p
Total average cost per meal	£1.73

Of course, we might find that every guest chooses the most expensive items on the menu, in which case the average cost per meal will be higher.

Task 6.55

Using the following costings, calculate an average cost for a table d'hôte menu, consisting of a starter, main course with vegetables, and a sweet:

Starters:	Grilled grapefruit – recipe 10	15p
	Minestrone soup – recipe 16	12p
	Egg mayonnaise – recipe 17	18p
Main courses:	Grilled plaice – recipe 27	85p
	Lamb cutlets – recipe 29	75p
	Lasagne al forno – recipe 36	80p
Vegetables	Selection – recipe 52	50p
Sweets	Banana split – recipe 64	27p
	Crème caramel – recipe 67	24p
	Cherries jubilee – recipe 69	31p

Calculating labour costs for a dish

When the standard recipe is being prepared, the time taken to prepare the dish can also be calculated and noted on the card. The direct labour costs for the dish can then be found by multiplying the time taken by the hourly rate for the member of staff concerned. For example, if the pastry cook is paid £4 per hour, and a plum tart takes 15 minutes to prepare, the direct labour cost is £1. This cost can be added to the standard recipe and used in the calculation of complete menus.

Calculating labour costs for an operation or department

Many employees are paid a fixed wage, which is quoted in one of the following ways:

- An annual salary, usually paid monthly
- A weekly wage, paid weekly
- An hourly rate, paid weekly

The wage quoted might be for a certain minimum number of hours each week or day. Any hours worked above that minimum might be paid on top of the normal wage, perhaps at an increased *overtime* rate. For example, a Maintenance Operation has the following staff, paid at the following rates:

1 Chief Maintenance engineer, annual salary £15,600

2 Assistant engineers, weekly wages £200 each

3 Trainee assistant engineer, hourly rate £4

During week 23, the Assistant Engineers worked 10 hours overtime each, paid at £6 per hour, and the trainee worked 5 hours paid at time-and-a-half (i.e. one-and-a-half times the normal rate). Assume that there are 40 hours in a normal working week. The total wage bill for the week would be:

Chief engineer 15,600/52 weeks	£300.00
Assistant engineers	
– normal wages (£200 × 2)	£400.00
– overtime 20 hours at £6 per hour	£120.00
Trainee engineer	
– normal wages 40 hours at £4 per hour	£160.00
– overtime 5 hours at £6 per hour	£30.00
Total wages for week 23	£1010.00

In addition to these basic wage costs are the ancillary costs of employing people, such as employers' national insurance, pension contributions, cost of staff meals, training costs, personnel costs, etc. Some of these can be easily calculated by the wages operation, others must be calculated as part of other operations' costs, and then shared out between the operations, as we shall see below.

Task 6.56

Calculate the total wage bill for one week for the laundry operation:

Two supervisors at £10,400 per annum (year) each

Five assistant laundrymaids at £3.00 per hour each

Two part-time 'runners' at £2.50 per hour each, working for a total of 40 hours

During week 41, the laundrymaids work 6 hours overtime each at time-and-a-third, in addition to their normal hours of 35 per week.

Calculating overhead costs

Most overhead costs, apart from indirect materials and labour, are easy to calculate in that there are invoices or other forms of written evidence, often from outside the establishment, covering their cost. The exception to this is *depreciation*, which is the proportion of fixed assets that have been used up during the period.

Some overheads are *time-based*, that is, they are based on how much time has passed rather than how much they have been used. Examples include administration salaries, rent, rates, insurance, car tax, regular maintenance and usually depreciation. Loan charges might also be based on a period of time. Most of these are also fixed costs.

Other overheads are *usage-based*. They depend on the level of activity, but are not necessarily variable costs unless they vary *in proportion to the level of activity*. Examples include electricity, gas and heating oil – these all vary with the activity of the business, but not *in direct proportion*. Another example is the telephone bill – it alters, but it is not a truly variable cost. Other overheads might have little connection with the level of activity – for example, advertising might be higher when business is slack.

Calculating depreciation

Depreciation is a charge made for the use of fixed assets. The cost of fixed assets is not an overhead, but its decrease in value is. It is usually calculated in one of two ways:

1 *The straight-line method*   This simply takes the original cost and spreads it evenly over the expected life of the asset. If it is expected to *sell* the asset, the expected selling price is taken off so that only the *loss in value* is spread. The formula is:

Annual depreciation =

$$\frac{\text{Original cost less expected sale proceeds}}{\text{No of years' expected useful life}}$$

For example, if a car cost £1200 and expects to be sold in 5 years' time for £200, the annual depreciation is:

$$\frac{1200 - 200}{5 \text{ years}} = £200 \text{ per year}$$

and the asset's value goes down by that amount each year.

2 *The reducing-balance method*   This takes the original cost and reduces it by a fixed percentage per year. This is then taken off the original cost to give a new value. The new value is then reduced by the same fixed percentage next year, and so on. For example, if an oven cost £2000 and the fixed percentage depreciation is 40 per cent, the depreciation would be:

Year 1 – 40 per cent of £2000 = £800
(and the asset value goes down by this amount, so is now £1200)
Year 2 – 40 per cent of £1200 = £480
(and the asset value goes down by this amount, so is now £720)
Year 3 – 40 per cent of £720 = £288
(and the asset value goes down by this amount, so is now £432)
and so on

Task 6.57

A new oven costing £2400 is bought at the beginning of 1994. Calculate the depreciation to be charged to the kitchen during 1996 (year 3) by each of the following methods:

1 *The straight-line method, assuming the oven will last for 10 years and be scrapped*
2 *The reducing-balance method, using a rate of 25 per cent per annum*

Determining the cost of a unit of goods or service

Introducing 'allocated costs' and 'apportioned costs'

In order to calculate the total cost of a unit of goods or service we need to identify which costs which make up that unit and to calculate the value of those costs. Some costs are obviously part of the cost of a unit – an apple pie clearly contains the cost of an amount of apples and other ingredients. Such costs are called *allocated costs*.

Definition

● **Allocating** costs is to do with deciding to which unit *they belong. A cost can only be allocated to a unit if it is caused by that unit. If something else has caused it, or it would have happened anyway, then it cannot be allocated to that unit.*

Some costs can be allocated to cost centres, and then divided between the units within that cost centre. For example, flour can be allocated to the kitchen, and then reallocated to individual recipes such as apple pies.

We can only allocate costs where it is certain that they belong to a particular cost centre. If there is any uncertainty, then the costs should be allocated to a general heading for the time being. For example, the cost of food can be allocated to the kitchen, or perhaps even to a dish or a menu. Cleaning materials can be allocated to the Housekeeping department. Waitress wages can be allocated to the Restaurant.

Some costs are less obvious – usually the overheads costs, or the costs of service operations – and are more difficult to identify with the cost of a particular cost centre. These are collected together under general expense headings, such as rent, rates, heat and light,

insurance, etc. or according to the operation which uses the costs, such as the Laundry operation, and the totals are then shared out among the various cost centre and units of goods or service. These are called *apportioned costs*.

Definition

● **Apportioning costs** is concerned with sharing unallocated costs between two or more units of goods or service *or* cost centres, *in proportion to their estimated benefit from that cost.*

Therefore, costs which need to be *apportioned* are those which cannot be identified with or *allocated* to a particular unit.

Task 6.58

ACE Hotel Ltd has the following costs:

Monthly grocery bill
Cleaning materials
Wines and spirits
Nails and screws
Guest soaps
Liquid cleaner
Advertising a special function
Electricity bill
Wages of housekeeper
Beer mats for bar
Florist's monthly bill
Wages of chef
General manager's salary
Smoked salmon for function
Meat and fish

Allocate the above costs to the most appropriate unit, assuming that the units in your organization are Kitchen, Housekeeping, Restaurant, Bar, Maintenance, Functions and General administration. Use your judgement, and give an explanation of your choice in each case.

Allocating material costs

Materials are usually issued from stores to individuals or operations, and many stores' requisition forms have space for the destination of the materials to be entered. It is therefore straightforward to connect the materials with the unit concerned.

Food may be issued to the kitchen generally, in the first instance, and is then used by the kitchen in a variety of dishes, menus or even for a function. The costs for these can then be taken from the standard recipes. Where materials are purchased directly for a particular purpose it is also easy to identify them with the unit to which they belong. Wherever materials cannot be allocated to a unit, they must be collected together under a 'miscellaneous' heading, and are then treated as *indirect materials*.

Allocating labour costs

Direct labour costs are easily allocated to operations, where individuals work only in one operation. For example, the chef's salary is easily allocated to the kitchen. Where labour has been engaged for a specific function, this is also easy to allocate to that function. Where labour *can* be allocated to a particular operation it can be costed against individual products, dishes, menus, etc. using either an hourly rate or a rate per unit. For example, if a waitress serves 60 customers and is paid £30, the cost is 50p per cover.

Indirect labour costs could be more difficult, as they are often not broken down into individual persons. For example, training costs, recreation facilities, etc. often cannot be identified with individuals or even with operations, so they are allocated to a general heading such as 'Training costs'. Staff meals should be taken out of the cost of food and added to the cost of wages, as it is another way of paying staff for their services.

Allocating overhead costs

Overhead costs are the most difficult to allocate, unless they have been specifically incurred for a particular purpose, e.g. a function or an operation. Depreciation can be allocated according to the operation which uses the assets concerned. Other overheads are allocated to general headings for the time being, and then treated as *indirect expenses*.

The following is an example of materials, labour and overheads which could be allocated to a works canteen:

Direct materials
Food issued to the kitchens, less any left over in freezers and cupboards, after deducting the cost of staff meals
Direct labour
Wages of chefs and other kitchen staff involved in preparation and cooking
Direct expenses/overheads
Power costs for ovens (on a separate electricity meter)
Indirect materials
Serviettes, straws
Indirect labour
Supervisor's wages, waiters and waitresses, kitchen porters, serving staff, plus the cost of staff meals
Indirect expenses
Depreciation of ovens, fridges and freezers, crockery, etc.

Other costs, such as laundry, training, maintenance, administration, stationery, personnel, etc. are costs which are shared with other operations, so they cannot be allocated to the canteen. However, such costs might be shared among the units of the organization by *apportioning* them, as we shall see next.

Apportioning indirect costs

In the previous section we have seen that there are some costs which can be identified with individual units of goods or service and there are some which cannot. Those which can be identified in this way are said to be allocated to those units. The rest are grouped under various general expense headings and are then apportioned to units, using various methods, as we shall now see.

The purpose of apportioning is to calculate, *as nearly as possible,* the total cost of a unit of goods or service, whether it be a dish, a menu, a function, accommodation, an operation or an outlet. If these indirect costs are not apportioned correctly, then incorrect figures may be used. This could result in:

- Selling prices too high, so customers refuse to buy
- Selling prices too low, so losses are made
- Profits calculated too high, so decisions to decrease the price may result in losses
- Profits calculated too low, so decisions to increase the price may result in reduced business

We will now look at some of the common methods of apportioning indirect costs.

Apportioning indirect costs on the basis of selling price

Marketing costs are often apportioned on this basis, because their aim is to increase sales. Repairs and renewals are also sometimes apportioned in this way, because their costs increase as business increases.

Example:

A hotel has the following sales for July:

Rooms	£50,000
Restaurant	£20,000
Bar	£5000

The total costs of the marketing operation for July were £6000. To apportion the costs of the marketing operation on the basis of the sales of each operation, the formula is:

$$\frac{\text{Costs of marketing operation to be apportioned}}{\text{Total sales}} \times \text{sales of each operation}$$

So the apportioned marketing costs will be:

$$\text{Rooms} = \frac{6000}{75,000} \times 50,000 = £4000$$

$$\text{Restaurant} = \frac{6000}{75,000} \times 20,000 = £1600$$

$$\text{Bar} = \frac{6000}{75,000} \times 5000 = £400$$

Check that the total apportioned equals the total of the marketing operation's costs, i.e. £5000.

Task 6.59

The sales for your organization were as follows:

Rooms	£65,000
Restaurant	£15,000
Bar	£5000

The total cost of repairs and maintenance was £10,200. Apportion the costs of repairs and maintenance between the three revenue-earning operations on the basis of sales.

Apportioning indirect costs on the basis of floor area

This is suitable for expenses which vary according to the physical size of the department, such as cleaning, heating and lighting, insurances, etc. The method of calculating the apportionment between the departments is the same as previously, i.e.

$$\frac{\text{Cost to be apportioned}}{\text{Total floor areas}} \times \text{floor area of each department}$$

Task 6.60

A college has the following floor areas:

Classrooms
    8000 square feet
Teaching restaurant
    3000 square feet
Student refectory
    2000 square feet
Library
    1000 square feet

The heating and lighting bill for January was £6300. Apportion the heating and lighting bill between the four operations on the basis of floor area.

Apportioning indirect costs on the basis of direct labour cost

This is suitable for apportioning *indirect labour*, or costs connected with labour, such as personnel and training costs. These could also be apportioned on the basis of numbers of employees. The method of calculating the apportionment between operations is the same as previously, i.e.

$$\frac{\text{Cost of operation to be apportioned}}{\text{Total direct labour costs}}$$

$\times$ direct labour cost of each operation

Task 6.61

Direct labour costs for your organization are as follows:

Rooms	£15,000
Restaurant	£12,000
Bars	£4000
Leisure areas	£2500

The total cost of the training operation is £2520. Apportion the training operation cost on the basis of direct labour costs.

Other bases of apportionment of indirect costs

There are other bases which can be used to apportion indirect costs, such as:

1 Number of covers (used for reception costs, laundry)
2 Cost of equipment (used for maintenance and repairs, insurance)
3 Number of employees (used for personnel costs)

and other bases to suit particular circumstances. It is important to remember that these apportionments are to be used only as a guide to the overall cost of a unit, and are often only approximations. Some operations may end up with too heavy an apportionment of some costs, which can distort the impression given.

It is also important to remember that a business is a mixture of activities, and not all of the activities make healthy profits. In many hotels the restaurant is not profitable but the accommodation division is. As you cannot have a hotel without also offering food, then this situation may well be acceptable in order to attract customers to the hotel.

Task 6.62

Suggest a reasonable basis of apportionment for the following costs, given reasons for your choice:

- Printing and stationery
- Rent and rates
- Postage
- Cost of uniforms
- Cost of staff accommodation
- Staff recruitment costs

Calculating the total cost of goods and services

We have now looked at all the components which might go into a unit of goods or service. It might help to summarize them all:

- Direct materials (which are always variable)
- Direct labour (which is considered to be variable)
- Direct overheads (which are quite unusual)

  } all these are *allocated costs*

- Indirect materials (which are allocated from stores issues)
- Indirect labour (which is apportioned on the basis of direct labour)
- Indirect overheads (which is apportioned on a variety of bases, and of which there may be several)

For some purposes, all these items need to be included in the calculation of the cost, but for other purposes only some of them are included. We will now look at four different meanings of the word 'cost'.

Full cost

Definition

- *The **full cost** of a unit of goods or service is the total cost of all direct and indirect costs, including those apportioned from other cost areas.*

In other words, full cost contains all the above items. The procedure for calculating full cost is the same whether the unit of goods or service is a dish, a menu, a function, the provision of accommodation, an operation or an outlet:

1 Gather together all the *direct costs* of the unit
2 *Allocate* as many of the *indirect costs* as possible to the unit

3 *Apportion* the unallocated indirect costs to the unit, using the most suitable methods

The following is an example of the calculation of the total costs per person for a table d'hôte menu to serve 60 covers:

Direct materials – per standard recipes and averaged as shown earlier	£1.73
Direct labour – per standard recipes and averaged in the same way	£0.50
Direct overheads – e.g. menus, £6.00 for 60	£0.10
Indirect materials – e.g. flowers on tables	£0.05
Indirect labour – e.g. restaurant staff wages £30 for 60 covers	£0.50
Indirect overheads – cleaning, based on floor area, for one day	£0.05
– laundry, based on number of covers, for one day	£0.06
– advertising, based on sales, for one day	£0.03
Full cost of menu, per person	£3.02

Marginal cost

Definition

- *The **marginal cost** of a unit is the variable or direct cost allocated to that unit.*

Many organizations regard marginal cost as the correct cost to use in decision making, because the marginal costs are the only ones which alter if an extra unit is produced and sold. The other costs would all be incurred at the same rate, and therefore should be ignored.

Using the example above, the marginal cost of the menu would be £2.33 per person (this is found by adding together all the direct costs). If someone were to offer us £2.50 for a meal from that menu, we would still make a small profit, even though the full cost is £3.02. The reason is that the other costs would not alter because of an extra guest, and we would be losing the chance of 17p extra profit if we turned the guest away.

Replacement cost

Definition

● *The* **replacement cost** *is the cost of replacing the item with another in the same condition at the time the item is used up.*

It is not normally employed for accounting purposes, but it may be used to influence the selling price where prices have risen dramatically since the original purchase. It is sometimes used to determine the value of bar stocks, which are of high value.

Selling price used as cost

As with replacement cost, this is sometimes used as the cost of bar stocks. These are issued from the cellar to the various bars and restaurants, who then sell them at different prices. It is sometimes easier for control purposes to value them at their selling price because this is the value of which the bars and restaurants are aware.

Task 6.63

Describe four different meanings of the word 'cost' when calculating the cost of a unit. What are the differences between each meaning?

Calculating the selling price

Once the cost has been established, the selling price can be determined. Several factors influence the selling price chosen:

● The cost
● The profit required
● Any subsidies received, or losses permitted
● The market price
● The competition
● The addition of service charges
● Discounts offered
● Value Added Tax

Apart from some outlets such as works' canteens, selling prices are normally calculated so as to make a profit. This approach can cause several problems. For example, we have already seen that there can be different calculations of the cost – e.g. full cost, marginal cost, and replacement cost. We also know that it is possible for some operations in an organization to make losses in order to create profits for other operations – for example, a restaurant in a luxury hotel may make a loss but guests are prepared to pay high prices for accommodation which makes a handsome profit.

However, assuming that most organizations do not wish to price their products so as to make losses we can now look at the various factors which influence the selling price.

Cost

Most organizations would wish at least to cover their direct costs, so the lowest selling price likely is the direct cost of a unit of goods or service. Some will prefer to cover all their costs, so will use the full cost as a minimum selling price.

Cost plus

Definition

● **Cost plus** *pricing means taking the cost and adding a percentage to give selling price.*

If an organization wishes to make a profit, it must add something to its cost (whether that is full cost or some other cost), to determine its selling price. The amount to be added depends on three factors:

1 What cost is used as a starting point?
2 What other costs are to be 'covered' by the selling price?
3 What profit is required?

The amount added is often a percentage of the cost, and is carefully worked out using figures from previous periods, with adjustments where necessary.

Full cost plus

If *full cost* is the starting point, then only net profit needs to be added. This method can be used for function pricing, where most of the costs can be identified with the function.

Task 6.64

What is the selling price for a unit with a full cost of £16.00, if 25 per cent of cost is to be added?

Marginal cost plus

If *marginal cost* is the starting point, then an amount to cover indirect costs and net profit is required. This method can be used for pricing set menus and table d'hôte menus, where the cost of food and direct labour can be identified.

It is also useful in deciding whether or not to sell goods or services at below their normal selling price. If the selling price is high enough

to cover the marginal cost, then it is often better to sell for that amount than not to sell at all. This is especially true if the break-even point (i.e. the point at which all the fixed costs have been covered) has already been reached, as there will be no extra fixed costs involved in an extra sale.

Task 6.65

What is the selling price of a unit with a marginal cost of £12.00 if 33⅓ per cent of cost is to be added?

Direct materials cost plus

If *direct materials cost* is the starting point, then an amount to cover all other costs needs to be added. This amount is called the *gross profit mark-up*.

Definition

- **Gross profit mark-up** is the percentage of the direct materials cost which is added to that cost in order to determine the selling price.

For example, if wines are purchased costing £2.00 per bottle, and the gross profit mark-up is to be 150 per cent, then the amount to be added is:

$$\frac{\text{Cost price}}{100} \times \text{mark-up percentage} = \frac{2.00}{100} \times 150$$

$$= £3.00$$

and the selling price is therefore £2.00 plus £3.00 = £5.00 per bottle.

The £3.00 is not all profit, of course. Some of it will go towards the direct labour and the indirect costs as well. The mark-up therefore needs to be quite a high percentage.

- Total cost plus 10 per cent
- Marginal cost plus 25 per cent
- Gross profit mark-up 70 per cent

Task 6.66

What is the selling price of a unit with a direct materials cost of £8.00 and a gross profit mark-up of 60 per cent?

This method of setting a selling price by adding a large mark-up to the direct materials cost is extremely common in setting selling prices in the hospitality and catering industry. Because food prices change so quickly, and sometimes by large amounts, and because it is an industry where customers appear and disappear very quickly (often without warning), it is difficult to make calculations much in advance. Therefore quick methods of calculating selling prices based on the latest materials cost have been developed, and are often used.

It is a useful way of pricing à la carte menus, where some dishes are very expensive and others are cheaper. To prevent wide variations in profit, and to avoid guests choosing only the cheaper dishes, the profit mark-up is greater on cheaper dishes and less on more expensive ones, so that the prices are more even.

Task 6.67

A restaurant has a menu with the following cost:

Food cost   £10.00
Direct labour £4.00
Overheads   £2.00

Calculate three possible selling prices using:

Gross profit margin

Sometimes the required mark-up is not known, but the manager knows that a certain *gross profit margin* is to be obtained. This happens where the manager is trying to compete with other operations or other organizations who use this percentage.

Definition

- **Gross profit margin** is the percentage of the selling price which is added to the cost of the direct materials *in order to determine the selling price.*

If you think that definition sounds a little strange, you are right. How can you add a percentage of selling price to the cost when you do not know what the selling price is? The answer is, you cannot. But you can use it to find the selling price, by taking it away from 100 per cent, as follows:

$$\frac{\text{Cost of materials}}{100\% - \text{gross profit margin percentage}} \times 100$$

For example, if wines cost £2.00 per bottle, and a gross profit margin of 60 per cent is required, the selling price can be calculated as:

$$\frac{2.00}{40} \times 100 = £5.00 \text{ per bottle}$$

Note that this gives the same selling price, and hence the same gross profit, as the previous example using gross profit mark-up. Only the percentages quoted were different, because one was a percentage of cost price and the other a percentage of selling price.

Task 6.68

Calculate the selling price for the following units:

Food cost	Gross profit margin (%)
£13.50	30
£15.00	40
£20.00	25

Fixed cost plus

Accommodation has very low *variable costs*, so to use them as a starting point for calculating selling prices is very difficult. However, accommodation does have very high *fixed costs* and so this is a more reasonable starting point to use.

A percentage is added to the fixed costs to cover the variable costs and net profit, to arrive at the selling price. It is important to remember that few hotels have 100 per cent occupancy at all times, so the number of rooms available to cover the costs is not the same as the number of rooms in the hotel. *Average occupancy* needs to be considered as well.

Example

A hotel has 30 bedrooms with an average occupancy of 80 per cent. The hotel is open for 250 nights per year. Fixed costs are £120,000 per annum and the variable costs are £2 per room per night. The hotel wishes to make a net profit of £60,000 on accommodation for the year. The amount required, apart from the variable costs, is

£120,000 + £60,000 = £180,000

and the number of rooms able to provide this amount is

30 × 80% occupancy = 24 rooms × 250 nights
= 6000 rooms

The amount provided per room per night is therefore:

$$\frac{£180,000}{6000} = £30$$

Therefore the selling price per room needs to be £30 plus the variable costs of £2 per room per night = £32.00.

The advantage of this method of pricing is that if extra rooms above the average occupancy are let, then the whole of the income, apart from the small variable cost, will be profit. If special promotions are used, anything above £2 per night will increase the profits, so favourable rates can be quoted. The disadvantage is that if the average occupancy falls, then losses will be made, because there will be insufficient income to cover the fixed costs.

Task 6.69

Calculate a selling price for a hotel bedroom for one night, using fixed-cost-plus pricing, from the following information:

Net profit required	£20,000 per annum
Fixed costs of accommodation	£80,000 per annum
Variable costs of accommodation	£4 per room, per night
Number of bedrooms available	100
Average occupancy	60 per cent
Number of nights open	300 per annum

Subsidized cost

Some establishments, especially in industrial catering, do not make a profit. In these, the catering outlet is primarily to perform a service to the employees rather than be a profit-making concern. The selling price is therefore less than the total cost, and sometimes less than even the *direct cost.* This means that any loss is *subsidized* by the rest of the organization.

The selling price is set according to whatever subsidy is to be allowed. For example, if food costs are £1 per meal and other costs are £2 per meal, then a selling price of less than £3 will require a subsidy.

The selling price might be set on a 'cost plus' basis, to cover, say, the food costs and 40 per cent of the other costs, so the selling price would be:

Food cost	£1.00
40 per cent of £2.00	£0.80
	£1.80

Task 6.70

A factory canteen has annual food costs of £12,000 and other costs of £8000. Calculate the selling price per meal for 15,000 meals per annum, to cover food costs and 50 per cent of other costs.

Market rates

Even in very high-class organizations, there is a maximum price which can be charged for goods and services. The price cannot always be known with any degree of certainty, but customers will be discouraged if it is exceeded. Sometimes the maximum price can only be 'estimated', rather than calculated, but nevertheless it is there. Sometimes the maximum price is determined by the fact that customers complain, or by the fact that previous customers do not return.

If there are other organizations in the area or known by your potential customers you may need to consider what they are charging for similar goods and services. This is the market rate for those goods and services. You may be able to charge more than them, if you have a superior or different product, or it is presented in a different way. You may have other facilities to offer customers which warrants the extra price. You may have to charge less than them if you want to attract their customers to you.

Task 6.71

Visit a nearby large town and obtain the selling prices for similar meals at similar restaurants. Which do you think are affected by competition or market prices and why?

Write to a number of similar hotels (either in the same town or of the same size and type in different towns) and obtain prices for rooms. Which do you think are affected by competition or market prices and why?

Value Added Tax, service charges and discounts

Value Added Tax (VAT) is added to most goods and services offered for sale, and has been covered earlier. To remind you, the present rate of VAT is 17.5 per cent. The customer must pay the total, including the VAT, and the organization must pay the VAT portion to the government. However, businesses can also reclaim any VAT they pay to suppliers. Organizations such as schools, colleges, hospitals and prisons do not charge VAT but most hotels, restaurants, leisure centres, parks, etc. do.

Most hospitality and catering prices are quoted as including VAT, so if a customer requires a breakdown of the bill, this is done as follows:

$$\text{Amount of VAT} = \text{total bill} \times \frac{17.5}{117.5}$$

so the VAT included in a bill of £95.00 would be:

$$£95.00 \times \frac{17.5}{117.5} = £14.15$$

This formula is easy to remember – multiply the total bill by the rate of VAT and divide by 100 plus the rate of VAT. So as long as you know the current rate of VAT you can work out the VAT on any inclusive amount. If VAT dropped to 15 per cent, then you would multiply by 15 and divide by 115 to find the VAT.

Food and drink	£60.00
Service charge	£ 6.00
	£66.00
VAT at 17.5 per cent	£11.55
Total bill	£77.55

In the case of prices which already include VAT, the VAT does not need to be added on again. For example, if an inclusive price of £120.00 is charged, plus service charge of 10 per cent, the total bill is £132.00.

Task 6.72

Calculate the amount of VAT included in the following bills, assuming that VAT is included at the rate of 17.5 per cent.

- £87.50
- £105.75
- £118.50

Task 6.73

Calculate the total bill for the following situations:

- Food charges £50, plus service charge 15 per cent, plus VAT
- Food charges £90 including VAT, plus service charge 10 per cent

A *service charge* is an amount added to a bill in some hotels and restaurants. It is supposed to be the customer's contribution towards the staff who provided the service, and in some organizations it is passed on to such staff. In many cases, however, it is merely an extra charge and is retained as part of the profits of the organization. Some service charges are voluntary, being added to the bill as the customer wishes.

Service charges are subject to VAT, so they should be added to the bill before calculating the VAT. However, as most hotels and restaurants advertise their charges *including* VAT, the service charge is simply added at the end.

Example
The bill in a restaurant amounts to £60.00. Service charge of 10 per cent is to be added, plus VAT at 17.5 per cent. The total would be:

Discounts are reductions in the price to be charged. These are given to different customers for various reasons. In hotels, the standard charge for a room is called the *rack rate*. Charges of less than this amount are sometimes made to businesses and companies who send substantial numbers of guests to the hotel. This is called the *corporate rate*. Special charges also apply to groups of guests booking together, such as tour operators or groups who organize themselves. This rate is called the *tour rate* or *group rate*. Sometimes a reduction in price is given by deducting a percentage from the rack rate (e.g. 20 per cent).

Whatever the price charged, the VAT is calculated on the reduced rate. Thus, if the normal rate is £100 plus VAT, and a discount of 20 per cent is offered, the rate charged will be £80. The VAT is then calculated as 17.5 per cent of £80.

Task 6.74

Calculate the total bill if a discount of 25 per cent is given on a normal rate of £90, to which VAT of 17.5 per cent is to be added.

Preparing cost statements

We have looked at a variety of cost statements throughout this and previous sections. Cost statements are simply ways of presenting information so that it can be used to make decisions.

You should be able to prepare the statements that we have looked at, as well as understand them. Statements can be prepared in different ways, according to who is going to use them and what they are going to be used for. The ones described earlier are only *examples* of statements which you could use. You should not stick to a particular type of statement just because it appears in a textbook, or because it has been used before. You should be constantly thinking about what information you are trying to provide and whether it could be provided in a different, more understandable, way.

Statements might show either actual results or budgeted figures, or both. A budget is normally prepared in the same format as the actual statement. You would benefit from looking more closely at some of the statements in this book, and trying to think of ways in which they could be improved, or alternative methods of presenting them for different purposes.

Use of computers

Many of the calculations which you have learnt about in the preceding pages and the statements of cost and financial information are easily prepared using computers. Many

organizations have specially written programs to perform particular tasks, such as stock records, purchasing systems, etc. Other tasks can be performed using spreadsheets, which can be set up by the user to his or her specification. During your Information Technology studies you should have the opportunity to set up and use some of the programs and spreadsheet layouts. Take some of your Tasks along to the IT classes and see if you can perform them using the facilities available there. Keep your evidence for your portfolio.

However, although such computer programs greatly speed up the provision of information, and with improved accuracy, they can only do what they have been told to do, and very often they are not told correctly. It is up to *you*, as the user, to make sure that the system you are using is accurate and does what is required of it. In order to do that, you need to have enough knowledge to perform all the tasks manually, which the computer does automatically. Do not think that you do not need the calculation skills covered in this unit or the ability to prepare accurate statements manually. This knowledge is as vital today as it ever was, in spite of the increasing use of new technology.

Conclusion

Many of the decisions using cost data are to do with fixing a selling price, so it is obvious that the data must be very accurate otherwise we could set prices which may result in lower income for the organization or even cause money to be lost. In this section we have seen the different kinds of costs which organizations might have, and how those costs behave or vary with different circumstances. We have learnt how to identify and calculate a single unit of goods or service provided by the organization. We have learnt how to maintain records of costs of materials and labour, and how to allocate and apportion those costs to the units of goods or service. Selling prices were then calculated using different methods, and adjusting for service charges, discounts and

Value Added Tax. Finally, we have considered throughout the text how cost information might be prepared for the purposes for which it is needed.

Test your knowledge

See how much of this unit you can remember.

1 What do you understand by the terms 'direct costs' and 'indirect costs'? Give some examples of each.
2 What do you understand by the terms 'fixed cost' and 'variable cost'? What makes a cost variable? Do fixed costs ever change, and if so, why?
3 Can you name six different units of goods or service in a hospitality and catering organization?
4 Name two methods of calculation materials costs and briefly describe the differences between them.
5 How does the preparation and cooking of food affect the yield it produces?
   What sorts of calculations do you need to perform to work out how much food you get to eat after preparing and cooking it? How do you find the cost per portion if you have a set weight for each portion already decided?
6 What is the difference between costs which are *allocated* and those that are *apportioned*?
7 Name five ways in which costs could be apportioned to operations, and give an example of the type of cost which could be apportioned by each of the ways you have given.
8 What are the different ways in which selling prices can be determined?

▪ Assignment ▪

In view of the sheer size of this unit, we felt it too onerous on students to prepare a single assignment to cover the whole unit. At least one element of the unit stands alone, i.e. the Purchasing element, and the last element is so 'bitty' as to dictate a separate assignment. We also felt that students would have little opportunity to develop their grading theme skills with a single assignment.

The assignment we have devised is capable of being put together as a single assignment if tutors require; it has a common scenario, and a continuing role for the student to play. However, the three tasks are separate and have been written to facilitate three separate assignments.

Scenario

Funtime Incorporated is an organization which runs a theme park, established five years ago. Visitors were charged a daily admission fee, with reduced rates for 2- or 3-day passes. A survey showed that the 2- and 3-day passes were not popular because guests could not find suitable overnight accommodation nearby. To solve this problem, your organization built an accommodation complex adjoining the theme park, consisting of chalet-style self-catering accommodation. The complex also contains a restaurant offering a quality service and a fast-food/take-away facility. The accommodation complex is managed separately from the theme park. As a result of this addition, the 3-day passes now exceed all other admissions, and consideration is being given to extending the scheme to 5- to 7-day passes, following the addition of leisure facilities adjacent to the accommodation complex.

You are employed as assistant manager of the accommodation complex, and you are expected to assist in the operation and supervision of the chalets, restaurant and take-away facilities.

Your manager has expressed concern at the fall in net profit percentage this year, as compared with last year, and has asked you to investigate the reasons for this and to recommend suitable action if necessary.

Tasks

Task 1

Information given

You are given the following financial statements and related information for this year and last year:

- *Operating statements*
- *Profit and loss accounts*
- *Balance sheets*
- *Data regarding labour costs*
- *Data regarding number of covers and levels of activity*

You also have a summarized cash budget for this year, together with the actual cash flow statement.

Activity

You are asked to prepare a report discussing the statements and related data.

Your report should cover the following areas:

1. *A description of the purpose of each of the financial statements you have been given; include an outline of the contents of each statement, and identify the people or organizations who might be interested in the information it contains.*
2. *An examination of the information contained in the statements, and the related data you have been given; calculate suitable performance indications and discuss the implications of the results you obtain.*

Task 2

Information given

The Purchasing Officer, Mr Jones has recently been taken ill and you have appointed another member of staff, Mrs Walker, to be responsible for purchasing in his absence. During her first week in the new job the accounts department passed her some invoices from suppliers which they had just received, and asked her to approve them for payment. On investigating, she could find no evidence that these items had been received, and she could find no other documentation relating to them. She telephoned the suppliers, who said that they had been ordered verbally by Mr Jones, and were to be delivered to his home address, although they still had instructions to send invoices to Funtime Incorporated.

In addition, she discovers that orders for items which were genuinely required by Funtime Incorporated had been placed with suppliers chosen by Mr Jones, many of whom were owned by relatives of his. In some cases, the goods ordered were not exactly as required by the departments who wanted them, but Mr Jones had managed to convince these departments that the goods were the best available at the time.

To avoid any repetition of the above situation you recommend the immediate suspension of Mr Jones, pending further enquiries, and to appoint Mrs Walker in his place. Mrs Walker says that before she will accept the job permanently she will require:

- *A job description, detailing her responsibilities and those of others with whom she will be working*
- *A list of documents to be used in the purchasing system, together with a description of their contents; she asks that you pay particular attention to explaining how each one improves control in the system*
- *A catalogue of local suppliers of the various products required by the organization and the criteria for choosing particular suppliers. As examples, she asks you to advise on the criteria for choosing suppliers for the following:*

Fresh fruit and vegetables
Restaurant furniture
Frozen meat
House wines
Serviettes

Task 3

Information given

The accounts department has been responsible so far for determining the prices at which you sell the various goods and services in the accommodation complex. Your manager is not convinced that they fully understand the operation of the outlets, and he is surprised by the high cost which the accounts department calculate for some of the things you sell. Occasionally they are unable to provide you with a cost for some things, because they do not understand the contents of an individual 'unit' of goods or service.

Your manager has asked you to find out more about the methods of calculating the cost and selling price of your goods and services and to report back to him on your findings.

You have been to have a chat with one of the accounts assistants, who has explained to you what is meant by the terms 'direct costs' and 'indirect costs', and how costs vary with the level activity. You, in turn, have explained to her the different 'units' of goods and services which you provide, and what they consist of. You also talked about 'allocating costs' and 'apportioning costs' to units, and found that you learned a lot from each other. Finally, together you worked out the cost and selling price of a sample range of 'units', as follows:

- *A cheeseburger*
- *A breakfast menu*
- *A twin-bedded chalet*
- *A housekeeping department*

Activity

Prepare a report for your manager, covering the following areas:

1 *What you learnt about the types of costs, and variations in costs*
2 *How you identified various 'units' of goods and services provided by your facility*
3 *How you calculated the cost and selling price of the four units identified above*
4 *The results of your calculations in a proper format, together with supporting explanations where necessary*

ACCOMMODATION OPERATIONS

Accommodation Operations is central to the standards and quality of service in the types of accommodation available to customers. Throughout the hospitality and catering industry many different resources are required to provide accommodation services. This unit gives you the necessary underpinning knowledge to enable you to operate in a realistic environment using correct working practices. The unit covers:

● Types of accommodation to meet customer requirements
● Accommodation services
● Physical resources required to provide a service to customers
● The skills and work methods needed to operate while using safe working practices
● Storage of physical resources
● Evaluation of the contributions of staff in providing accommodation services, including roles of staff, organization of work and budgeting

---

▪ TYPES OF ACCOMMODATION ▪

The dictionary definition of the word 'accommodate' is 'to provide lodging or room for', and so, in its widest sense, it encompasses the whole of the hospitality and catering industry. This section focuses on the types of accommodation required for the various activities which take place within the industry and considers the customer needs in relation to the type of accommodation provided. The industry is very diverse and so the section concentrates in particular on those sectors of the industry which provide sleeping accommodation. It also looks at some of the standards related to the provision of accommodation within the various sectors.

Hotels, hospitals, hostels provide lodging in the rooms for sleeping as well as rooms for eating

and drinking. Restaurants of all types have a room in which people can eat the food they have purchased and public houses provide rooms in which customers can drink. A kitchen is a room for a chef to work in, a cellar is a room where wine is stored.

Task 7.1

Make a list of the different types of room you use during the course of one working day.

The prime purpose of any establishment which offers accommodation is to meet the needs of the customer. The management of any establishment can only start to do this when they can identify their customers, the reasons why they are spending time away from home and the type of facilities and services they expect.

There are a number of reasons why people choose or are obliged to leave their home. We leave our homes to go to work, to college, to go shopping or to visit friends. Sometimes we may go to a club or to a restaurant or out to watch or take part in some kind of sporting activity. In each instance we return to our homes to sleep.

Task 7.2

List the reasons why you have spent time away from your home but have returned to it to sleep.

We sometimes need to spend sufficient time away for us to have to find alternative sleeping accommodation. We may decide to visit friends in another part of the country or to go away on holiday. We may attend a conference or have to work away from home.

Task 7.3

Make a list of the reasons why you have spent one night or more away from your home – go back as far as you can remember. Extend your list by adding other reasons why people may choose or be required to spend time away from home.

Customer requirements

When we spend time away from home we are *customers* and, as such, we have a number of basic needs and expectations. If we are away for a number of hours we will probably need *food* and *drink*. We may also need to go to the *toilet* and to *wash* our hands.

Most of us have a number of choices where we can go to eat and drink away from home.

Task 7.4

Make a list of the places within walking distance of your home or college where you could go for food and drink.

If we go away for an overnight stay we will need somewhere to *sleep* as well as facilities for personal hygiene and for refreshment.

If we stay in a hotel as a customer we expect to be accommodated in a room of our own and, according to the price we are paying, we expect there to be a private bathroom for our sole use. We also expect to be offered a choice of rooms, for single, double or family occupancy.

If we have to go into a National Health Service hospital we are not likely to be surprised if we have to sleep in a ward, sharing it with a number of people whom we have probably not met before. We will expect to have to share the use of the bathroom facilities and will also expect these to be special arrangements if we are unable to get out of bed.

If we are at college or university and are accommodated in a hall of residence we expect to have a room of our own or perhaps to share with one other person. We do not expect the room to be very large, nor for it to have a private bathroom attached.

Task 7.5

State the type of accommodation for sleeping and for personal hygiene you would expect if you were a customer in

- *A boarding school*
- *A cross-channel ferry*
- *A guest house*
- *A holiday camp*
- *A private hospital*
- *A youth hostel*

Customer services

The basic function of accommodation operations is the servicing of customer accommodation. The cleanliness and good order of the accommodation provided for sleeping, eating and drinking are fundamental to meeting the customer's needs.

In *hotels*, however, the services extend beyond cleaning to include bedmaking and the provision of clean bed and bathroom linen on a regular basis. In luxury hotels this may be on a daily basis and may also include an evening 'turn-down' service.

Definition

Turn-down is a service offered in a few luxury hotels. It is done in the evening. Bedspreads are folded back and the bedding is turned back to make it easier for the guest to get into bed. Any night clothes may be laid out neatly on the bed. The bedroom and bathroom will be tidied and the curtains closed. Before leaving the Room Attendant may turn the bedside light on and leave a small box containing two or three complimentary chocolates on the pillow.

Other guest services which may be available in hotels are the service of drinks and meals in rooms or the provision of facilities for self catering such as a courtesy tray or a minibar.

Definition

*A **courtesy tray** provides all the equipment and commodities required to allow the customer to make their own hot beverages such as tea, coffee or hot chocolate. This will include a kettle, teapot, cups, saucers, sachets of tea, coffee, chocolate, sugar and milk. The customer may also be provided with biscuits.*

Definition

*A **mini-bar** is a small refrigerator containing miniature bottles of spirit and appropriate mixers (tonic, soda, ginger), quarter bottles of wine and small bottles of fruit juice. Some mini-bars also contain vacuum packs of cocktail nuts or potato crisps, The customers help themselves from the bar and this is checked by hotel staff. The customer is then charged for the items consumed.*

Facilities are offered for dealing with customers personal laundry and dry cleaning and for the provision of first aid items to guests.

Rooms may be equipped with a hair dryer, a trouser or skirt press and customers may request items such as bed board or an ironing board.

Definition

A bed board is a flat board which slides between the mattress and the bed base to make the bed firmer. It is requested by customers who have a back problem.

Customers with small children may require a cot or an additional single bed in their room and may be offered a baby-sitting service.

Valets were originally employed in hotels to look after gentlemen guests who were travelling without their own manservant. Traditionally the valet was always male but under equal opportunities legislation it is possible that this may now be a female job.

It is a service which, nowadays, is only found in the high priced establishments and involves pressing guest clothes, unpacking and packing guest luggage, minor repairs to guest clothing and dealing with guest laundry and dry cleaning.

In *hospitals* the beds are made with clean linen but on a less frequent basis. This is usually done by the medical staff and not the accommodation services staff especially if the patient is unable to get out of the bed.

Meals and drinks may be served by accommodation services staff but this is limited to the three main meals of breakfast, lunch and dinner with tea and coffee served at the appropriate times. With one or two exceptions hospitals do not provide a personal laundry service.

Students in *halls of residence* may be supplied with clean sheets on a weekly or fortnightly basis and are usually required to make their own beds. Some halls provide breakfast and an evening meal which is served in a dining room.

In others, students are expected to cater for themselves. Utility rooms are provided for students to make their own hot beverages or to do any cooking.

Definition

*A **utility room** is provided for approximately twelve students to share. There are facilities for storing milk and other perishables and appropriate facilities for cooking. There may also be limited facilities for students to do their own laundry and ironing. The utility room is often a place where students congregate while they eat and for socializing.*

In addition to accommodation for eating, drinking and sleeping and personal hygiene we will require *access* and *egress*, that is, means of getting into and getting out of the building. Some establishments provide entrances and exits which are separate for staff and for customers.

Once we are inside the building we will require ways of getting to the various rooms for eating, drinking, etc. This would be by using circulation areas, that is, corridors, stairs and lifts. There is a considerable amount of building and fire legislation which gives minimum standards as to the number of exits, corridors and stairs based on the maximum number of people who are likely to be using a building at any one time.

All customers will require ways of obtaining information either by means of a simple notice board or from a fully staffed enquiry desk. There will also need to be at least one method of communicating with the outside world by telephone, telex or fax.

Most customers wish to have some form of 'in-house' entertainment such as a television set. In some large hotels this includes satellite channels and in-house video programmes.

Task 7.6	Task 7.7

In groups of three or four contact the fire authority and the relevant local authority to find out what are the standards for the number of exits etc. in your area for hotels, restaurants and other catering and hospitality establishments. If you have difficulty, try the reference section of your local library.

Working in groups, contact the electricity, gas and water board or use the reference section of the library to find out the standards for the supply of these utilities.

We will also need some means of keeping warm. The majority of establishments within the hospitality and catering industry are centrally heated and fuelled by electricity, gas or oil. Some operations, especially those in old buildings, may feature an open coal or log fire to provide atmosphere and effect. Recommended temperature for bedrooms is 13–16°C and for hospital wards it is 19°C. For public spaces such as corridors, lounges the recommendation is 16°C.

Buildings must also provide adequate ventilation and have a specific number of air changes per hour if they are to be comfortable for customers and for staff. Recommendations are that restaurants have ten to fifteen changes, cloakrooms two and kitchens have twenty to sixty per hour. A number of modern buildings are air-conditioned which means that the air is clean, at an acceptable temperature and with a comfortable level of humidity.

Customers and staff will require a supply of hot and cold water. They will also need sanitation for personal washing, for laundry, for the preparation of food and for drainage. All buildings will need to provide systems of drainage for clearing away foul water, waste matter and other debris.

Maintenance

If you have ever been at home when the heating has gone wrong or the electricity has failed you will know how inconvenient that is. For problems like that to happen in a hospitality and catering establishment it is nothing short of a disaster. In a commercial establishment customers may be inconvenienced and may take their business elsewhere. In a caring establishment, such as a hospital, the repercussions may be even more serious.

- *Planned maintenance* – is a continuous programme of work which involves regular checking of major items and services, like the heating system
- *Preventative maintenance* – is done when something is wearing out and you know it is going to break down very soon
- *Corrective maintenance* – takes place when something has broken down and can be very disruptive in an establishment
- *Emergency maintenance* – must be carried out immediately. It is very costly and causes considerable disruption to customers. It is usually done if there are health and safety risks to your customers or a risk of further damage to yours or to adjoining property.

Task 7.8

Make a list of the tasks which should be included on a planned maintenance programme.

In order to maintain buildings such as hotels or hospitals to the level expected by the customer it may be necessary to have some specialist staff to do this.

Many large establishments employ their own engineers, plumbers, electricians, carpenters and painters and these are organized in a maintenance department under the management of the Works Manager or Chief Engineer. Smaller establishments may employ one or two general maintenance assistants and cal in specialist help when required.

Special customer needs

It is now a legal requirement that new buildings for hospitality and catering establishments must provide facilities for people who are disabled or who have other special needs. This includes people confined to a wheelchair, those who can only walk with difficulty, people who are blind, partially blind or who have hearing problems and those who are suffering from a temporary disability such as a broken leg.

The regulations also refer to people with special needs such as those who are elderly, travelling with young children or women in the late stages of pregnancy. It also includes people who have mental health problems or who have suffered some form of brain damage.

The building regulations which refer to providing suitable facilities for people with a disability or special need give minimum standards for access such as suitable car parking and the incorporation of ramps. Minimum standards for bedrooms refers to the width of the doorway, the provision of room numbers in Braille and an emergency call system. Bathrooms should have WCs, baths and basins at the appropriate height and with space to accommodate a wheelchair.

Task 7.9

Using the facilities of the library, find out some of the design criteria for providing accommodation which is accessible for people with disabilities or special needs. You will need to ask to look at the Building Regulations 1992, Access and Facilities for Disabled People.

Security

All customers will need to feel secure while they are in the building. In any establishment this involves the security of the building and grounds, security of the contents including cash and the security of the people who are using the building whether they are staff, residents or visitors.

Many large establishments such as hotels, hospitals and universities employ one or a team of security officers. They are responsible for advising management about security procedures and for ensuring that staff follow those procedures.

Control of keys

Most establishments will have a system of providing access to accommodation by both customers and staff. The most complex is the system used in hotels. This is based on a system made up of the following types of key:

1 *The grand master key* there are only one or two grand master keys in the system and these are carried by the Duty Manager and/or Security Officer. The key will lock and unlock any door on the system and has the additional facility that it will double lock any door in the system. This means that it can be opened only by a grand master key and not by any of the other types of key.
2 *The master key* is carried by Housekeepers and some others, e.g. Front Office Manager, Chief Engineer. It will open all doors in the system except those which are double locked.
3 *The sub master key* is carried by room Maids and floor Waiters and will open doors on one section of the building except those which have been double locked.
4 *The room key* is the individual key which will open only the appropriate room.

Many large hotels now use *electronic keys*. These are plastic cards linked to a computer system which have a unique lock combination and is changed with the arrival of each guest. For safety:

- If a key is lost the lock should be changed
- Keys should be secured to the holder either by a chain or a belt
- When not in use keys should be kept secure in a key cabinet
- Keys should be signed for when issued and signed back when returned
- Keys left in the key cupboard should be checked at regular times throughout the day

Bombs and bomb alerts

It is an unfortunate fact that, at times, hospitality and catering establishments have been targets for terrorist bombs whether actually placed in the establishment or sent through the post. If a telephone threat is received the receptionist is often the first person to be aware of any potential threat. It is important that every call received must be treated seriously.

Task 7.10

Each member of a group find out the procedures to be followed in a hospitality and catering establishment in the event of a bomb threat. Compare these with each other.

It is safe to assume that any device delivered through the post has been handled quite roughly and therefore it is possible for a trained person to remove it from the premises in some safety. Special care needs to be taken if the package is damaged, crushed, bent or distorted by handling or dropping.

In all cases suspect letter bombs are best left where they are found and no attempt must be made to open them. If in any doubt and there is just cause for suspicion then the police should be sent for.

There is a remote chance that radio transmissions may detonate a bomb and so they should be kept away from radio or 'bleep' equipment.

Fire precautions

We will need some means of defending us should there be other threats such as a fire. The law protects us in most public buildings. Under various Acts of Parliament it is unlawful for owners of buildings used by the public to continue with their business unless they possess a *Fire Certificate* issued by the local authority. This limits the number of people who can be on the premises at any one time. It also covers the provision of:

- Fire warning systems including notices for staff and guests
- Fire fighting equipment
- Escape routes

- Regular training for staff in fire fighting and evacuation procedures.

Should a fire start we would trust that there are detectors to locate smoke, flames or heat and that these are connected to an alarm system. We would also expect that the various areas within the establishment are equipped with the most appropriate fire fighting equipment.

Task 7.11

Compare the precautions taken in different buildings to prevent fire from breaking out and spreading. Find out the system(s) of fire detection in place. How are customers warned if a fire does break out?

Lost property

Customers need a system which deals with any property which they may lose while they are in the establishment. Lost property is generally delegated to the Accommodation Services Department. Found items should be wrapped and labelled with details showing

- Description of item
- Where found (room number)
- Who found it
- Date and time of finding

The items are then kept for a period until they are claimed by the rightful owner. If not claimed they are either handed back to the finder or sent to a charity.

Types of accommodation

There are several ways in which an establishment may be described and one

method is to indicate whether it offers sleeping accommodation. Establishments which do have sleeping facilities are known as *residential* and those that do not as *non-residential*. *Residential establishments* include all types of hotels, hospitals, hostels, university halls of residence, clubs. *Non-residential establishments* include all types of restaurant and bar, conference centres, leisure centres, *Hotels* are establishments which are selling accommodation, food and drink in order to make a profit. In the large majority of hotels it is the sale of the sleeping accommodation which makes the most profit.

Types of hotel room

1 *Single room*   A minimum of 5.60 m^2 with one bed designed for one person
2 *Twin room*   A minimum of 10.20 m^2 with two beds designed for two people
3 *Double room*   A minimum of 8.40 m^2 with one bed designed for two people
4 *Family room*   A minimum of 15.8 m^2 with one bed for two people and with two beds for children

Any of these rooms may be 'en suite'.

5 *En Suite*   A bedroom with a private bathroom forming a single unit. The bathroom must be a minimum of 3.52 m^2 (Figure 7.1).

Hotels can be classified in a number of different ways. One way is to consider the main type of customer.

International hotels are designed to meet the needs of the international traveller whether for business or for pleasure. These are to be found in most capital and other major cities in the world, many of them belonging to large companies who operate similar hotels in a number of different countries.

Customers may be away from home on business or on holiday. They expect and are prepared to pay for high-quality sleeping accommodation in large rooms. They may also expect to be able to stay in a suite of one or

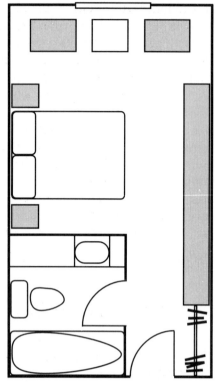

Figure 7.1 The layout of a hotel bedroom with an en suite bathroom

two bedrooms with a private sitting room and one or even two private bathrooms.

People who stay in an international hotel expect to have a choice of restaurant in which to eat and of bar in which to drink. They will also expect to be able to choose to be served food and drink in their room at any time of the day or night.

Task 7.12

Look in the catering press and identify hotels and hotel groups which are international. Try to obtain some brochures which will illustrate the type of accommodation which is offered. Evaluate the accommodation provision in these establishments.

Commercial hotels are designed to meet the needs of the business customer who requires sleeping accommodation for one or two nights and may also be looking for facilities for conferences and meetings. They are to be found in all towns and cities with commercial centres.

The customers of this type of hotel are likely to be travelling alone and will expect there to be a number of single and some twin rooms but there will not be as much demand for double or family rooms. Depending on the price level, customers will also expect the rooms to have a private bathroom en suite.

Larger commercial hotels may offer the customer a choice of restaurant and more than one bar. Customers may also expect a limited service of food and drink to their rooms. Customers in smaller hotels may not expect to find more than one bar or restaurant and will not expect to be served with meals in their rooms.

Task 7.13

Look in your nearest town or city and identify any hotels which could be classed as commercial. If possible, arrange to visit one or two and look at the accommodation which is provided.

Resort hotels are designed primarily for holidaymakers and tourists and are located in areas of special interest such as the coast, the Lake District or the mountains. This type of hotel will probably have a number of family rooms as well as some double, twin and single ones.

People on holiday will also require somewhere to eat their meals. The restaurant will provide accommodation for adults and will particularly cater for babies and young children. Customers staying in large hotels at resorts may expect there to be a choice of places for them to eat or drink.

Task 7.14

What particular facilities will a customer with a family require in a resort hotel which may not be available in other types of hotel?

A number of hotels in the larger resorts like Blackpool or Harrogate provide extensive conference facilities so that they can maintain their business outside the main holiday season.

Task 7.15

Do any of the hotels in your local area offer facilities for conferences? If so, what sort of conference accommodation is it?

Many older commercial and resort hotels were not built with en suite bathrooms but nowadays a large number of customers, having spent time on package tours in hotels abroad, are demanding private facilities. Hotel owners found that rooms without private bathrooms were becoming increasingly difficult to sell and many have taken steps to upgrade the accommodation by converting part of a bedroom into a bathroom.

Guest houses are small private hotels which provide the type of accommodation required in the area in which they are located. Those in towns and cities cater for the commercial and

business customer while guest houses in resort areas provide for tourists and travellers. A few guest houses have all bedrooms with en suite bathroom. More customers are demanding this facility and so guest house proprietors are gradually upgrading their accommodation.

Guest houses have the same eating and drinking facilities as hotel but these will be limited and may be available only to those guests who have booked sleeping accommodation. Customers staying in a guest house would not expect to be served with food and drink in their bedroom, although they would probably expect facilities for making a hot drink.

Task 7.16

Look in your local area and identify establishments which would be classified as guest houses. For which type of customer do they cater?

Motels are specifically designed for the motorist. They offer similar sleeping accommodation to that found in a commercial hotel and, in addition, have car parking facilities which are more extensive than in other types of hotel. Motels also offer similar facilities for the service of food and drink to that in commercial hotels.

Task 7.17

Using hotel guidebooks such as the ones produced by the AA, the RAC, Michelin or the English Tourist Board, find examples of the types of hotel described above. Are there any more types of hotel described?

Holiday camps were introduced just after the Second World War to give the less well-off the chance of a family holiday. Some originally used the barracks which had housed the wartime troops and consequently they were very basic. In recent years the operating companies have spent millions of pounds upgrading the accommodation and facilities and many have been renamed as *holiday centres*. Other holiday centres were built during the 1970s and 1980s as activity centres or theme parks.

Families are accommodated in chalet-style rooms which are equipped with self-catering facilities. The centres also offer the choice of a variety of styles of restaurant and bar as well as entertainment for the whole family.

Task 7.18

Visit a local travel agent and get copies of any brochures which advertise holiday centres. What are the facilities provided? How do they compare with each other?

Public houses are the original inns and many of them are very interesting old buildings. All pubs provide extensive facilities for drinking, mainly for customers in the locality. Within the last thirty years many have also developed a steady restaurant trade.

The majority of pubs do not offer sleeping accommodation, and those which do generally have less than ten bedrooms. They attract commercial and leisure customers who prefer the smaller establishment and a more personal service. Those which have a known historical connection attract a number of tourists, particularly from abroad.

Task 7.19

Find out if there are any public houses in your area which offer sleeping facilities. How many bedrooms are there? What kind of accommodation for eating and drinking do they offer? Do any of them have a connection with the past – e.g. Queen Elizabeth I slept there?

Hospitals

Most of the hospitals in the UK are operated within the NHS. Some hospitals are funded by the NHS but operate as trusts and there are also *private hospitals* operated by organizations such as BUPA. All hospitals provide facilities for people who require medical assistance or treatment. There are basically three types of customer, better known as patients:

1 *In-patients* require accommodation for one or more nights
2 *Day-patients* require accommodation for one or more days but spend the night in their own homes
3 *Out-patients* require accommodation for a short period while they receive treatment or see a specialist doctor.

In-patients in NHS hospitals are accommodated in wards each of which concentrates on one particular type of patient, e.g.

● *Coronary care unit* for patients recovering from a serious heart disease
● *Elderly-care unit* for patients who are elderly and receiving treatment for a variety of illnesses and conditions
● *Gynaecology* for female patients
● *Intensive care unit* for seriously ill or injured patients who require constant attention
● *Maternity* for female patients who are about to or have just given birth

- *Medical* for patients whose illness is being treated with medicines and drugs
- *Orthodontic* for patients with problems with their teeth
- *Orthopaedic* for patients requiring surgery on muscles or to correct deformed bones
- *Paediatric* for children
- *Psychiatric* for patients who are suffering from mental disorders
- *Renal unit* for patients who require regular treatment of their kidneys
- *Surgical* for patients whose illness or injury is being treated by surgery

Task 7.20

All in-patients are provided with a bed and with accommodation for personal hygiene. Using the list above identify any special accommodation problems which patients in each of these wards may have.

The wards in older hospitals or old parts of hospitals are arranged in what is known as the Nightingale pattern. These are long corridor-style wards with up to thirty beds arranged in two rows. The washing and toilet facilities are at one end with the clinical rooms, kitchen and office near the entrance (Figure 7.2).

Newer hospitals or hospital wings are built on the racetrack pattern. This has a number of four- or six-bedded units arranged around a central administrative area (Figure 7.3).

Day-patients are also accommodated in wards but the type of patient may change from day to day according to the treatment schedules.

Patients in wards are provided with meals brought to them from a central kitchen and drinks made for them on the ward by a domestic assistant.

Out-patients visit clinics which have a reception desk for them to check in, a waiting area and a number of private consulting rooms where they can see the doctor.

The Women's Royal Voluntary Service (WRVS) run shops and tea bars in many hospitals which are used by people visiting patients in hospital.

Other areas of a hospital which may be required by a patient include

- Accident and emergency
- X-ray
- Physiotherapy
- Pharmacy
- Radiography
- Operating theatres
- Mortuary

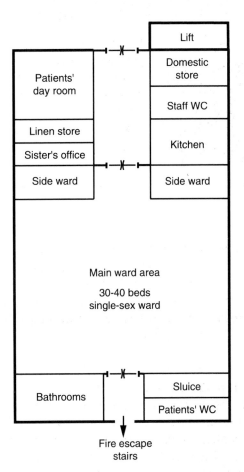

Figure 7.2 The typical Nightingale pattern of a hospital ward

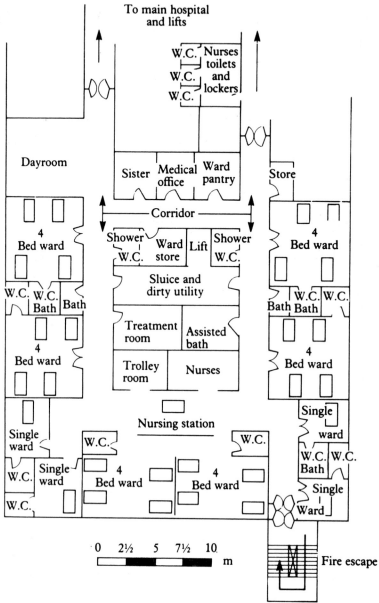

Figure 7.3 A typical race track hospital ward

Task 7.21

Explain the above areas. Visit your local hospital and identify other areas which a patient may need to use. What type of accommodation is provided for patients and visitors?

Hostels are provided by universities and some colleges for students who have to study away from home. These are known as halls of residence. Hostels are also provided by some employers, such as the police, hospitals and some hospitality and catering establishments, to accommodate staff who are working away from home.

University halls of residence may be on the same site as the classrooms and lecture theatres

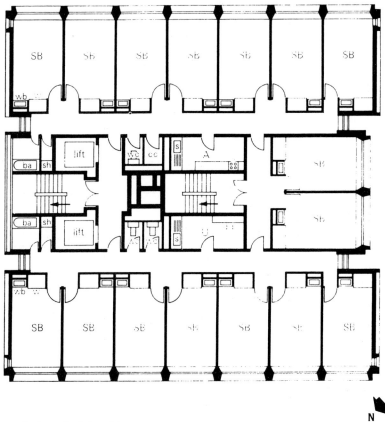

Figure 7.4 Layout of a typical students' residence

which means that students do not have to walk very far to get to their classes (Figure 7.4). These halls may not have dining facilities in the same building as the bedrooms. Dining rooms will be provided in one or more central areas and will serve all meals and refreshments throughout the day.

Alternatively, there may be some distance between the residential and the academic accommodation. The midday meal will be available in accommodation near to the classrooms. The halls of residence will have a dining room where students will be served with breakfast and an evening meal. Some halls of residence are now self-catering which means that the students are supplied with cooking facilities but they have to provide and cook their own meals.

Sleeping facilities are basic. Rooms are usually for single occupancy and provide a bed,

storage facilities and a wash-basin. Toilets, baths and showers are provided in separate cubicles for everyone to use. As students stay for a fairly long time they are also provided with a utility room where they can do their own washing and ironing or make themselves a hot drink.

A number of universities have decided to enter the tourist and conference market during the vacation periods in order to generate additional funds. In some of these the accommodation in the halls of residence has been upgraded to make it easier to let. Some rooms have had en suite bathrooms added and the dining and lounge areas are maintained at a level expected by a tourist or a conference delegate.

Universities are well equipped with bars and these are frequently operated under the management of the students' union.

Task 7.22

Arrange to visit a hall of residence at a nearby university. Note the standard and type of sleeping accommodation which are available for students. What facilities are there for eating and drinking? Is the university open during the vacation periods for customers other than students?

Clubs are designed for members and their guests only. Around the country the majority of clubs, e.g. cricket, golf or working men's clubs, concentrate on providing accommodation for eating and drinking. Others, most of them situated in London, have extensive sleeping facilities. A number of the clubs in London are designed for men only and began during the seventeenth and eighteenth centuries as a means of escape from women! Membership of many of these is still restricted to men only although they do provide a second dining room where women may be entertained to a meal.

Residential homes are provided for people who, for one reason or another cannot take care of themselves. The majority are for children or elderly people. Most of the children's homes and some of the elderly care homes are run by the local council and are not expected to make a profit. There are an increasing number of private elderly care homes and these are operated on a commercial basis.

Task 7.23

Make a list of the special requirements of customers who are accommodated in a residential home.

Leisure centres are quickly replacing the standard swimming pool provided by local authorities. A number of hotels have also had leisure facilities added. As well as a swimming pool, a leisure centre provides accommodation for some indoor sports such as table tennis and squash. There may also be a refreshment service area, some are licensed and others have extensive facilities which may be rented for birthday parties, wedding receptions and other types of function.

Task 7.24

List the accommodation required by a customer using a leisure centre.

Conference centres are used primarily for conferences but may also be used to hold exhibitions, meetings and other events such as sports competitions. Purpose-built centres are generally large with a number of business-support services such as a computer network, fax machines, audio-visual equipment and simultaneous interpretation of foreign languages.

Restaurants cater for a wide range customer from those with the very expensive elaborate menu to the short cheaper menu offered in the fast-food sector. All restaurants need to offer accommodation for the customer to eat the food they have purchased and the decor usually reflects the menu. The customer is provided with a dining area with seats and tables and, if the restaurant is licensed, a bar area. All restaurants are obliged to provide sanitary facilities for male and female customers.

Task 7.25

Look around your local area and see how many different types of restaurant you can identify. Does the outside and inside decor give some indication of the type of menu offered inside?

Industrial catering provides for employees in factories, shops and offices. Many establishments have more than one canteen or restaurant and some have as many as five. These provide a range of accommodation and services from the luxury directors' dining room to the self-service canteen. Customers in an industrial catering unit will require a dining area to eat their meal in comfort away from their place of work.

▪ Element assignment ▪

1 Visit a variety of establishments which offer accommodation for eating, drinking, sleeping, etc. Note the type or types of customer for which they are designed to cater. Make a note of the facilities offered to meet the diverse needs of the customers. Ask permission to take photographs or obtain a copy of the establishment's publicity brochures.
2 Working as a group, discuss the various establishments you have all visited. Make comparisons between the provision of accommodation for sleeping, personal hygiene, eating and drinking between the establishments.
3 Select at least three of the establishments. Write a report describing the accommodation provision showing how the needs of their customers are met. Include in your report a comparison of the type of accommodation offered for sleeping, personal hygiene, eating and drinking.

▪ PHYSICAL RESOURCES REQUIRED TO PROVIDE ACCOMMODATION SERVICES ▪

In the first section we identified that customers seeking accommodation away from home require facilities for eating, drinking, sleeping and personal hygiene. Customers have certain ideas as to the standard of accommodation and the level of services each will find acceptable in order to satisfy their needs and expectations. This section identifies the basic standards of accommodation and describes how establishments strive to achieve those that are appropriate.

The section looks at the physical resources used by establishments to provide the accommodation and services required by its customers. It identifies the wide range of goods required and the correct methods of storing these as well as the practical skills and working methods needed to provide accommodation services.

There are many different types of hospitality and catering establishment but the most complex are those which offer sleeping accommodation. This section, therefore concentrates on those establishments which have residential facilities but the products, methods and services also apply in establishments which do not provide sleeping accommodation.

The type of accommodation and establishment which the customer selects may depend on how this accommodation is presented.

● Is it clean?
● Is it attractive to the eye?
● Are the furniture and furnishings in good repair?

Task 7.26

When you visit different establishments make a note of your initial impression on entering. Is it clean and well maintained? Does it look attractive and welcoming? Use establishments such as shops, department stores, the cinema, the theatre, a restaurant, fast-food or otherwise, or, if you are old enough, a public house.

A large proportion of the work of providing accommodation services involves keeping the building clean to the standard expected by the customer. When we are customers we have more confidence in the cleanliness of the areas which we cannot see, like the kitchen, if care has been taken in the areas which we can see.

If something is described as 'clean' this usually means that it is free from dirt or contaminating matter such as dust, grease, stains or litter. We clean:

- To promote health and hygiene
- To improve the appearance of a surface
- To prolong the life of the fixtures and fittings

Types of cleaning

Routine cleaning is carried out on a regular basis, daily, nightly, weekly or bi-weekly. *Periodic cleaning* is carried out at specific times during the year. It may also be known as spring cleaning, special cleaning or deep cleaning. *Initial cleaning* is carried out in a new building before an area is used by the customer or in an existing one after a period of redecoration or refurbishing.

Cleaning methods

Methods used for controlling dust

Dust cannot be totally removed, it can only be controlled by the following methods.

High dusting

This is the control of dust from surfaces which are beyond arm's reach when the operator is standing on the floor. What happens is that the dust is dislodged from the surface and falls to a lower level where it is collected and disposed of. A *cornice brush* is used for high dusting ceilings and tops of walls and *feather flicks* are used to high dust walls.

Low dusting

This is the control of dust from surfaces which are within arm's reach when the operator is standing on the floor. *Dusters*, cotton check or flannelette, are suitable for low dusting or polishing wooden or metal surfaces.

Task 7.27

Make a list of all the surfaces in a room which are

- *Above arm's reach*
- *Within arm's reach*

Task 7.28

Using cleaning or catering industry magazines, identify other items of equipment which could be used to control dust from these surfaces.

Sweeping

Sweeping is the control of dust from a hard floor surface. *Brooms* are long-handled brushes used for sweeping floors. *Dust control mops* are a more efficient method of controlling dust on hard floor surfaces than sweeping with a broom. They consist of a wooden, metal or plastic frame attached to a long handle. A mop head is then stretched over the frame. There are basically three types of mop head:

1 *Impregnated mop heads* are made from loops of cotton stitched to a flat backing. The head is impregnated with a special mineral oil which helps the dust to stick to it.
2 *Static mop heads* are made from a synthetic fibre, such as nylon, which builds up a static charge as it is rubbed along the floor surface. The static charge holds the dust to the mop head.
3 *Disposable mop heads* are made from either non-woven paper or fibreglass which is lightly impregnated with a specially prepared oil.

Suction cleaning

This is the control of dust from all types of surface using an electrical suction cleaner and, possibly, a variety of attachments. There are basically two types of suction cleaner. The most common remove dust by sucking air into the machine and with it the dust. To prevent the dust being blown back out the machine is fitted with a filter. Some suction cleaners can be adapted to pick up water.

Task 7.29

The suction cleaners used to remove dust are colloquially known as 'Hoovers' but this is an incorrect term as many other manufacturers make them. Look in a variety of catering or cleaning industry magazines. How many different types of suction cleaners can you identify?

Upright cleaners are primarily designed for cleaning carpets. The dirt is dislodged by a beater bar and/or brush fitted to the head which rotates when the machine is switched on (Figure 7.5). *Cylinder cleaners* are suitable for light suction cleaning of surfaces such as hard floors, stairs, furniture and upholstery. *Back vacs* are cylinder cleaners which are designed to be carried on the back like a rucksack. They are particularly suitable for areas which are not easily accessible with any other type of suction cleaner (Figure 7.6). *Canister or tub cleaners* are

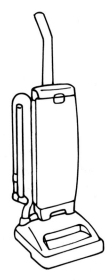

Figure 7.5 An upright suction cleaner

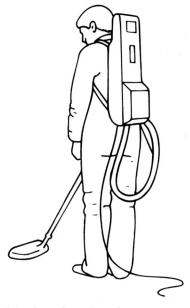

Figure 7.6 A back pack suction cleaner

Figure 7.7 A canister suction cleaner

2 *Disposables* paper or reprocessed cotton cloths for general cleaning designed to be discarded after use
3 *Sponge* synthetic cellular material which can hold a lot of water. Used instead of a dishcloth
4 *Wipes* non-woven cotton cloths for general cleaning available for a range of tasks, from wiping surfaces to cleaning cookers

Task 7.31

In some establishments, such as hospitals, cloths, sponges and wipes used for damp wiping are colour-coded, e.g. yellow for damp wiping kitchen surfaces. Why do you think they do this?

suitable for light suction cleaning from surfaces similar to cylinder cleaners. Because the air flow passing through the machine does not pass the motor, some machines may be adapted by the manufacturer to pick up dust or water (Figure 7.7).

Task 7.30

The range of tasks covered by each type of suction cleaner can be extended by using one of a selection of attachments. Identify the attachments available and the specific cleaning task for which each is designed.

Cleaning methods used to remove thin films of grease or stickiness to which dust may have adhered

Damp wiping uses a cloth dampened with water and either detergent or vinegar from surfaces within arm's reach. Equipment used for damp wiping includes:
1 *Dishcloth* cotton stockinette cloth used for washing or wiping dirt from the majority of surfaces

Damp/wet mopping uses a damp or wet mop and a bucket containing water and a detergent to remove greasy dirt from hard floor surfaces. Equipment used for damp and wet mopping includes:

1 *The socket or do-all mop* A round mop consisting of strands of cotton attached to a metal socket. The socket is fixed to a long wooden handle (Figure 7.8)

Figure 7.8 A round mop

Figure 7.9 A Kentucky mop

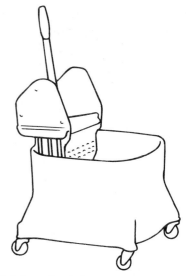

Figure 7.10 A lever bucket

2 *The Kentucky mop* A flat mop also made from cotton strands which is clipped to a specially designed quick-release fitting (Figure 7.9)

3 *The Foss mop* A dense cotton fringe attached to a weighted stock at the end of a long handle

4 *The sponge mop* A piece of synthetic sponge attached to a handle and fitted with a self-wringing device

Buckets

These are available in a variety of shapes and sizes but, in general, are designed for use with one of the types of wet mop described above. They are supplied in galvanized steel or reinforced plastic.

- *A strainer bucket* is designed to be used with the socket mop. The bucket incorporates a conical strainer for squeezing the water from the mop
- *A roller bucket* is designed to be used with a Kentucky mop. It has two rollers across the top and these are operated by a foot press to wring the water out of the mop
- *Lever buckets* are either single-, double- or triple-bucket systems either fitted with castors or mounted on a trolley (Figure 7.10).

They have one or more detachable presses which squeeze the water from the mop and are designed to be used with a Kentucky mop.

Glass cleaning

Equipment for removing greasy dirt from glass surfaces such as windows, mirrors, furniture and fittings includes:

- *Chamois leathers*, although originally these were the skins of the chamois, a type of wild antelope, they are now either split sheepskin or a synthetic alternative
- *Scrim*, a loose weave unbleached linen cloth which does not leave linters (short fibres) on the surface after cleaning

Cleaning of sanitary fittings

Equipment for sinks, wash basins, baths, toilets and urinals includes:

- *Bottle brush* – a small round brush for cleaning sink and wash-basin overflows
- *Toilet brush* – a stiff round or angled brush for cleaning inside a toilet bowl
- *Cloths and wipes* such as those used for removing grease and dirt

Methods used to clean and maintain hard floor surfaces using a rotary floor machine (Figure 7.11)

1 *Dry buffing* – using a tan or a white polyester pad to bring a shine to a hard floor
2 *Spray cleaning* – with a detergent solution in a hand spray and a red or blue polyester pad to clean and shine in one operation
3 *Spray polishing* – with a specially designed floor polish in a hand spray and a red or blue polyester pad to clean and shine in one operation. This method leaves a film of polish on the surface to achieve a deeper shine

Figure 7.11 A rotary floor machine

4 *Spin mopping* – with water and a detergent and a specially designed cotton bonnet to damp mop more quickly than with a mop and bucket
5 *Scrubbing* – with water and a detergent and either a green nylon pad or a scrubbing brush attachment to remove ingrained dirt and grease from a hard floor surface
6 *Stripping* – with water and an alkaline detergent and a coarse black polyester pad to remove old polish from a floor surface before putting down a new layer of polish

Methods used to remove greasy dirt from a carpet

1 *Bonnet buffing* – with carpet shampoo in a hand spray and a specially designed cotton bonnet to remove surface greasy dirt from a carpet
2 *Carpet skimming* – with carpet shampoo in a hand spray and a thin white polyester pad to remove surface greasy dirt from a carpet
3 *Carpet shampooing* – with carpet shampoo and a shampoo brush attached to a rotary floor machine
4 *Hot water extraction* – using a specially designed carpet cleaning machine with a low foam detergent and hot water

Trollies

Cleaning operatives usually have to carry around a variety of cleaning chemicals, equipment and supplies which are awkward to transport. Trollies are useful for

● Carrying cleaning chemicals and small equipment
● Holding rubbish
● Holding soiled linen
● Carrying supplies of clean linen
● Carrying guest supplies such as soap, toilet paper, stationery

If only a small amount of items are to be carried or a trolley would be difficult to manoeuvre and so create a nuisance, then a Housemaid's Box may be used. The transport of items can be made easier for the staff by:

● Reducing the number of items of cleaning equipment
● Standardizing cleaning chemicals, methods and guest supplies

Storage of equipment

Correct storage will help to keep equipment secure and in good condition and so lengthen the time it works efficiently. The size of the store will depend on the amount of equipment to be stored. There should be:

- Sufficient space for all equipment
- Shelves and cupboards for spare parts such as mop heads, floor machine pads and suction cleaner bags
- Hooks or clips for mops and brooms
- Adequate lighting
- A lockable door

Cleaning chemicals

These are chemicals, including water, which are used to remove or assist in the removal of soil from a surface.

Definition

- **pH** *is a method of expressing the acidity or alkalinity of a chemical in numerical terms, from 1 to 14. Substances which give a reading of below 7 are acid and those above 7 are alkaline. The nearer an acid is to 1 and the nearer to 14 an alkali is, the stronger they are. Those chemicals which show a reading of 7 are neutral, i.e. neither acid nor alkaline.*

It is important to know that:

1 Strong acids and alkalis are corrosive and will damage many surfaces
2 All alkalis, even mild ones, can cause skin irritation
3 Most protective seals and polishes will not bond to a surface which is alkaline
4 The colour dyes used in carpets and in furnishing fabrics may be destroyed by alkaline detergents

Task 7.32

Mix some solutions of common cleaning chemicals such as washing-up liquid, glass cleaner, toilet cleaner, toilet soap, washing soda and household bleach according to the manufacturer's instructions and, using Universal Indicator Paper, find out which are acid, which are alkali and which are neutral. Wear protective gloves as you will not know which chemicals may irritate your skin.

Water is a cheap and easily available cleaning chemical. It can be a very powerful cleaner when used under pressure and is very efficient at rinsing out dirt which has been dislodged by other cleaning chemicals. Used on its own, water has a number of disadvantages. Its molecular structure does not allow it to penetrate surfaces thoroughly, it does not quickly loosen dirt and it does not emulsify grease. If you have ever tried to wash greasy hands with water alone you will know what happens.

Task 7.33

Smear some grease onto a plate. Drop a small amount of water onto the greasy section. Notice how it stays almost spherical in shape. Add a small drop of washing-up liquid to the water. What happens?

It is necessary to use other chemicals which, when added to water, will break down surface tension, loosen and lift dirt and suspend soil in the water.

Soap is made from animal fats and vegetable oils mixed with caustic soda and is manufactured as tablets, liquid, powder or flakes. When used with water it will emulsify grease into tiny particles which are then washed away.

Soap is very effective in soft water but it does not lather easily in hard water. It forms a scum which resettles on the surface being cleaned, often proving very difficult to rinse away. For this reason, soap is rarely used in the hospitality and catering industry for cleaning surfaces but is widely used for personal washing.

Task 7.34

Find out the difference between hard and soft water.

Synthetic or *soapless detergents* are manufactured from a variety of chemicals many of which are a by-product of petroleum:

1 *Neutral detergents* have a pH of 7–7.5 and are used for washing up and general cleaning. They are available in powder form, primarily for laundrywork, but the majority for general cleaning are supplied as liquids and usually require further dilution before use.
2 *Alkaline detergents* have a pH of 9–12.5 and are used to remove grease and heavily embedded dirt. They are also used to strip old emulsion polish from a floor. These are available in liquid or powder form and usually require dilution before use. It is essential that the handler wears gloves when using this type of detergent.

3 *Gel cleaners* are fortified alkaline detergents. The gel sticks to the surface allowing the detergent to remain in contact for a longer period.
4 *Germicidal detergents* are a mixture of detergent and disinfectant and are designed for use in food hygiene areas and in places where urine, faeces or blood may be present. It is not advisable to try to mix these yourself as many types of disinfectant are rendered inactive by a detergent.
5 *Carpet and upholstery cleaners* are available for specific methods of cleaning and particular types of equipment designed for cleaning carpets and upholstery. Shampooing with a rotary floor machine needs a high-foam shampoo while a hot water extraction machine must be used with a low-foam cleaner.
6 *Solvent-based detergents* are made from white spirit and other additives with a detergent and are used to strip solvent-based polish from a floor.

Abrasive cleaners 'scratch' the dirt from a surface. They vary in texture, and very fine abrasives are used for cleaning metals such as silver while coarse abrasives may be used to lift the top surface from a floor. The most commonly used abrasive cleaners are designed for cleaning enamel or ceramic sanitary fittings such as wash-basins, baths and showers and are available as liquids, creams, pastes or powders. They should not be used on plastic or painted surfaces.

Glass cleaners are made from water, a solvent which can be mixed with water and a synthetic detergent or alkali. Some have also a fine abrasive added to improve the cleaning effect.

Acid cleaners are used for cleaning toilets and urinals and for removing stains in baths and wash-basins caused by dripping taps. Toilet cleansers are available in liquid or crystal form and remove the build-up of water-insoluble limescale which, if left, provides a breeding ground for bacteria. They are harmful to the skin and, if mixed with a hypochlorite (household) bleach, will produce a toxic chlorine gas.

Polishes are used on floors, furniture and metals primarily to protect but also to improve the appearance of the surfaces.

Floor polishes fall into two categories:

- *Solvent-based* waxes consist of a suspension of wax in a spirit solvent and are designed for use on wood, wood composition, cork and linoleum floors. Many of these floor surfaces are now pre-sealed by the manufacturer, in which case a solvent wax should not be used
- *Water-based* waxes are an emulsion of wax and water with a polymer resin. They incorporate harder waxes than solvent-based polishes and consequently provide a more durable finish. They have an added advantage that they can be used on a wide range of surfaces

Furniture polishes are a blend of wax, spirit solvent and silicone available as a solid wax, as a liquid or cream or as an aerosol spray. The silicone gives 'slip' to the polish making it easy to apply and buff to a shine. It does, however, make furniture polish with a high silicone content very dangerous if used to polish floors.

Metal polishes are manufactured from a fine abrasive powder and a solvent, an acid or an alkali, depending on the type of metal for which they are designed. They are available as an impregnated cloth, sponge or wadding or as a liquid.

Bleaches add oxygen or chlorine to the dirt to alter the chemical composition and make the dirt easier to remove:

- *Sodium perborate* is used in laundry detergents
- *Sodium hypochlorite* is also known as household bleach and is an effective and cheap bactericide. It has a short *shelf life* and is rendered inactive by organic material such as dirt and by detergent

Definition

- ***Shelf life*** *refers to the length of time a commodity can be stored before it deteriorates.*

- *Hydrogen peroxide* is used as a disinfecting agent but is not as effective as sodium hypochlorite. It does not, however, have such a pungent smell

Organic solvents are a group of chemicals which dissolve fats, oils, grease and a variety of other substances including plastic. They include methylated spirit, white spirit and acetone. Some are flammable and others are dangerous if inhaled.

Miscellaneous

There are a number of chemicals which do not fit neatly into the above categories. The most common is a carbon dioxide aerosol spray specifically designed for assisting in the removal of chewing gum. The carbon dioxide freezes the chewing gum making it easier to 'chip' off the surface.

Disinfectants cannot clean surfaces and should therefore be used only after cleaning has taken place. There are a number of different types of disinfectant available and for each of these to be fully effective it is essential that you follow the manufacturer's instructions.

The Control of Substances Hazardous to Health Regulations 1987 (COSHH)

These have been designed to try to eliminate accidents caused as a result of the misuse of substances such as those used for cleaning. They were introduced to protect people from most hazardous substances at work including:

- Substances labelled corrosive, irritant, harmful, toxic or very toxic

- Pesticides and other chemicals
- Products or by-products (dust, fumes, etc.)
- Micro-organisms (viruses, bacteria, etc.)
- Carcinogens (cancer causing agents)

Note: Certain substances such as asbestos and lead are covered by other regulations.

Task 7.35

As a requirement of the Control of Substances Hazardous to Health Regulations, chemicals used for cleaning must indicate if there is any hazard attached to their use. This is usually done using one of the following symbols:

| Dangerous for the environment | Highly flammable | Corrosive | Explosive | Oxidizing |

| Irritant | Harmful | Toxic | Very toxic | Extremely flammable |

Give examples of cleaning products which display each of the symbols.

COSHH Regulations require an employer to:

1 Assess the degree of hazard of substances used or made in the workplace
2 Take action to control or prevent the use of hazardous substances
3 Control the exposure of employees to those substances. Methods used range from eliminating the use of substances to providing satisfactory ventilation and supplying protective clothing or equipment
4 Make sure that measures for control are maintained

5 Check the air supply and atmosphere of the workplace and supervise employees using chemicals where appropriate
6 Inform, instruct and train employees on the risks created by exposure to substances and on the precautions to be taken when using hazardous substances .

Information on the hazards of substances which have been purchased is readily available from reputable suppliers.

Task 7.36

Select one or more cleaning chemicals and obtain, from the manufacturer or supplier, a copy of the hazard specification for that chemical. If each member of the group selects a different chemical you will be able to compare and evaluate the information given.

Under COSHH it is the *employer's* duty to:

- Make sure that any new chemicals or equipment are not introducing health risks
- Provide employees with information about any health risks and to supply protective equipment

and it is the *employee's* duty to

- Cooperate with any training which the employer arranges
- Practise safe work habits
- Report any hazard of which employees may be aware
- Wear any protective equipment provided

Customer supplies

Many of the establishments which provide accommodation services supply additional items to help to make the customer more comfortable. These can be separated into two main types:

1 *Guest supplies* which are placed in the room for guests to use while they are there and left for the convenience of subsequent guests. These include ashtrays, coat-hangers, 'do not disturb' cards, toilet paper, toothglasses.

2 *Guest giveaways* are placed in the room for guests to use while they are there and not intended for use by other guests. These include small sachets of bubble bath and shampoo, soap, shower caps.

Hotels offer the most comprehensive range of supplies and giveaways and the cost of these is included in the tariff charged to the customer. Some hotels provide equipment and items to allow customers to make their own hot beverages (courtesy tray) while others have a 'mini bar' which contains a selection of alcoholic and non alcoholic drinks. Other items which may be provided in hotels are hair dryers, trouser/skirt press, sewing kits, stationery and magazines.

Hospitals operated under the NHS do not charge the majority of patients and therefore the provisions are very limited. Private hospitals which charge the patient may include additional items.

Halls of residence try to keep the cost of providing accommodation to students as low as possible and provide only the essential supplies. Those halls which offer their accommodation to tourists and conference delegates during the vacations may provide additional items such as a courtesy tray, coat hangers and soap.

Task 7.37

Find out the range of supplies provided in a variety of establishments in your area.

Storage of cleaning chemicals and guest supplies

In a large establishment there may be a central store which will supply all departments with their requirements. In smaller ones the department manager may be responsible for ordering and storing all their own cleaning chemicals.

Any store must be kept locked and secured from unauthorized entry. Keys should only be issued to nominated members of staff. There needs to be sufficient space for all the chemicals and for a reserve stock as well as enough to allow staff to unpack, sort and take stock of supplies.

The store must be provided with suitable shelving. Each product type stocked should have its own designated space. To assist the staff, heavy items and liquids should be placed at the lower levels.

Most cleaning chemicals should be kept dry and stored in conditions which are free from damp. They also need to be kept cool as some chemicals are affected by heat while others may constitute a fire hazard. This does not mean they must be cold as, equally, chemicals may be destroyed if they are allowed to fall below freezing point.

Cleaning routines

Organizing cleaning routines is vital to the continued success of any establishment. Routines depend on *cleaning standards*. Customers have certain expectations from the various establishments. A guest in a hotel expects a level of cleanliness which is different from that expected by a student in a hall of residence.

Task 7.38

Think of the different areas of a hospital. Which areas would you expect to be extra clean as opposed to those which need to be generally clean?

Task 7.39

Think of areas within hotels, hospitals, hostels and other sectors of the industry which should be cleaned to each of these standards.

There are three basic standards of cleanliness referred to in cleaning operations:

1 *Normal or basic standard* This is the standard which we find in most colleges and schools. It is a level of cleanliness where all litter and obvious dirt is removed daily. University halls of residence, staff accommodation in hotels and hospitals are also cleaned to this standard.
2 *Clinical standard* This is where the level of cleanliness must be exceptionally high and the surfaces tested to see that harmful bacteria are not present. Operating theatres and areas of a hospital such as the burns unit need to be maintained to this standard.
3 *Prestige standard* This is where the level of cleanliness is high but emphasis is placed on the appearance of the surfaces rather than the level of bacteria. Hard floors, polished furniture, metal surfaces are kept shined, carpets, curtains and upholstered furniture are dust free. If necessary, areas will be cleaned more than once per day. It is a standard which many hotels aim for in the guest areas.

The level of dirt

The level of dirt depends on a number of factors.

- Where the building is situated
- How often an area is used. The entrance lobby of any building accumulates dirt more quickly than the top floor
- The age of the building. This will also have some bearing on the level of dirt. Older buildings often have many more corners, nooks and crannies where dirt can hide

General principles of cleaning

1 Open windows and remove litter and obstructions first
2 Start cleaning at the point which is furthest away from the exit and work towards the exit
3 Carry out dust-producing jobs (e.g. bed making) at an early stage
4 Avoid the spread of bacteria when cleaning sanitary areas work from the clean surfaces to dirty surfaces

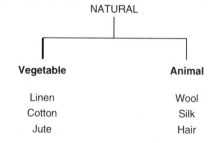

NATURAL		MAN-MADE	
Vegetable	**Animal**	**Regenerated**	**Synthetic**
Linen	Wool	Viscose rayon	Polyamide
Cotton	Silk		Polyester
Jute	Hair		Acrylic
			Polyurethane

Figure 7.12

5 Finish all wet work before dusting and polishing except for floors
6 Close windows before dusting
7 Dust from high to low – work from the top downwards
8 Use the method which is least likely to disturb the customer (e.g. do not vacuum early in the morning, damp dust in patient areas in a hospital)
9 Always work safely, use safety warning signs, do not stretch flex and leave a dry path when wet mopping
10 Always mop sweep before damp mopping or using a floor machine
11 Always clean the floor last

Task 7.40

In your group brainstorm and make a list of the cleaning tasks which need to be carried out in order to service a variety of rooms such as a hotel bedroom or your college restaurant. Using the principles listed above, place the tasks in the order in which they should be carried out.

Methods of organizing cleaning

- *Conventional or individual* – where one person completes all the tasks required in one room before moving on to the next
- *Block* – where one person completes one task in all rooms before moving to the next task.
- *Team* – where a group of three or four people work together each having their own task to complete in an area before the whole team moves on to the next area

Textiles

Bedding, carpets, furnishings such as curtains and cushions and uniforms are made from textiles. Textiles are made from either natural or artificial fibres (Figure 7.12).

Vegetable fibres are made from cellulose. They are:

- Absorbent
- Good conductors of heat
- Able to withstand high temperatures
- Strong
- Stronger wet than dry
- Not harmed by alkalis
- Damaged if they have contact with acids
- Attacked by a mould (mildew) if they are left in a damp state

Animal fibres are made from protein. They are:

- Elastic
- Resilient
- Soft
- Absorbent
- Poor conductors of heat
- Damaged by heat particularly sunlight
- Harmed by alkalis and chlorine bleaches

Regenerated fibres are manufactured by treating natural sources such as cotton linters or wood pulp. They are:

- Smooth
- Lustrous
- Not resilient
- Weak when wet

Synthetic fibres are polymers manufactured from a variety of sources including coal and petroleum by products. They are:

- Non-absorbent
- Very strong
- Hard wearing
- Frequently blended with natural fibres (e.g. polyester with cotton to produce a stronger fabric)
- Electrostatic

Task 7.41

Make a list of items used within the hospitality and catering industry which would be best manufactured from:
- *Vegetable fibres*
- *Animal fibres*
- *Synthetic fibres*

Fibres are spun into *yarns* which are then either knitted or woven into *fabrics*. Fabrics can be made from one single type of fibre or from a blend of mixed fibres.

Fabrics

The different combinations of the fibre content and the structure are what differentiates one fabric from another, e.g.

1 *Brocade*, a woven patterned fabric made from cotton and synthetic fibres and used for upholstery, curtains and bedspreads
2 *Candlewick*, a cotton or viscose fabric produced by inserting thick tufted yarn into a plain foundation cloth and used for bedspreads and bathmats
3 *Chintz*, a printed cotton fabric with a glazed finish used for curtains, loose covers and bedspreads
4 *Damask*, a woven figured fabric made from cotton or linen and used for tablecloths and napkins. Damask may be made for use as a furnishing fabric from cotton, linen, rayon, nylon or polyester
5 *Drill*, a heavy cotton fabric which is usually white and used to make kitchen and restaurant uniforms
6 *Folkweave*, a loosely woven cloth from thick cotton yarn in a primitive design used for curtains and bedspreads
7 *Gingham*, a checked cotton fabric used for tablecloths, curtains and some uniforms
8 *Huckaback*, a honeycomb weave linen or cotton fabric used for hand, face and roller towels
9 *Jersey*, a knitted fabric made from wool, cotton, nylon or polyester and used for loose covers and some uniforms
10 *Satin*, a smooth shiny woven fabric made from cotton or rayon and used for curtains, bedspreads and cushions
11 *Sheeting*, a woven fabric made from linen, cotton, polyamide or polyester and used for sheets and pillow slips
12 *Towelling*, a cotton fabric woven in a looped weave and used for towels and bathmats

13 *Velvet*, a woven fabric with a 'pile' made from cotton or rayon and used for upholstery, curtains and cushions

Task 7.42

Collect samples of these and other types of fabric which may be used within the hospitality and catering industry. Indicate their use(s).

Furnishings

These are made from textile fabrics and contribute to the interior design of a room by introducing colour, pattern and texture.

Curtains are used to give privacy either where windows are overlooked or around a bed in a hospital ward. They are also used to darken a room and to protect its contents from the effects of sunlight or from draughts. They can be hung around a shower to prevent the water splashing outside the area. Curtains may be used decoratively to divide a room or to hang along a wall to give the impression that there is a window behind.

Task 7.43

Pelmets, swags and valances are headings fitted over the top of curtains to add decoration or to hide the curtain hooks. Describe each of these.

Sheer curtains are made from net, a see-through fabric, and used for privacy during the daylight hours. They can also be used to mask an unsightly view.

Window blinds are used instead of or in addition to curtains.

Bedspreads are used as a decorative cover for bedding. There are two main types of bedspread: fitted and throwover (Figure 7.13).

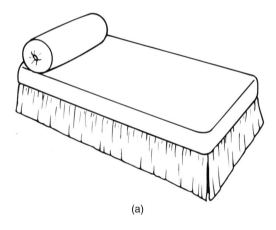

(a)

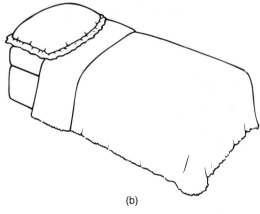

(b)

Figure 7.13 (a) Fitted bedspread; (b) throw-over bedspread

Loose covers are used to cover upholstered furniture either as protection over new furniture or to hide old and worn furniture. They may also be used as part of a change to the decor of a room.

Cushions are used to improve the comfort of chairs and to add a decorative touch to the room. They may be *fitted* to a particular chair or settee or they may be *scatter*, small square or round cushions used loosely around the chairs and settees.

Storage of linen and furnishings

Most establishments will require somewhere to store the linen which they use. In residential establishments this will be in a linen room which is fully staffed and in non-residential establishments a linen store which may be staffed only when items are being exchanged. The staff in the linen room are mainly responsible for

- Receiving and checking clean linen from the laundry
- Issuing clean linen to the various departments
- Receiving and sorting soiled linen from the departments
- Packing and sending soiled linen to the laundry

They may also be required to

- Mark all establishment-owned linen with tapes, ink, identity tags or embroidery to identify its ownership
- Repair torn items
- Renovate old items such as turning torn sheets into pillow slips or cot sheets
- Deal with uniforms worn by all members of staff, i.e. sending them for dry cleaning or laundering, repairing or altering to maintain a smart appearance
- Care for other textile items such as blankets, bedspreads, loose covers

The linen room should be placed to allow access for the receipt and despatch of linen to and from the laundry. It should also be easily accessible by staff from within the establishment.

The room should be warm so that the linen is properly aired before it is used. Items of linen are heavy – try lifting ten single sheets together – and it needs to be stored on strong shelves. The shelves need to be slatted to allow the free circulation of air. Linen which is not aired may be attacked by mildew, which is an unsightly mould caused by damp. In storage, linen should be kept free from dust, preferably covered by curtains or polythene sheeting.

Linen is a very valuable resource made up of large numbers of small, very portable items and to prevent loss or theft it needs to be kept secure. It should be stored in a secure room which is locked when not in use. Stocktaking must be done regularly to reduce the loss or damage of items. There also needs to be a strict system of issue and exchange within the establishment to control linen use.

Furniture

Furniture is used for seating, storage, support, working and relaxing. Basic items include beds, benches and chairs, cupboards, desks, shelves, tables and wardrobes.

There are many different styles of furniture designed to suit the wide variety of establishment requirements. Some are very plain and inexpensive while others are decorative and luxurious. There are basically four types of furniture:

1 *Built-in furniture* is incorporated into the building design such as a wardrobe
2 *Cantilevered furniture* is fixed to the wall and has no direct contact with the floor. Shelves are frequently cantilevered
3 *Fitted furniture* is constructed and fixed into the room. It can be moved but with some difficulty and disruption such as banquette seating in a restaurant

4 *Free-standing furniture* can be moved freely such as an upright chair

Beds are an important item of furniture in establishments providing residential accommodation. They are the most-used item of furniture in hospitals and hotels. In hotels and hostels they are often used to provide extra seating as well as for sleeping.

Task 7.45

Consider the specific requirements of beds which are to be used by customers in a university hall of residence and a hospital and in hotels.

A traditional bed consists of a base and a mattress, and these work together to provide support and comfort while we are asleep. Manufacturers produce a wide range of beds.

Task 7.46

How many different types of bed can you identify? Which of the three main types of establishment offering sleeping accommodation will use each type?

Hotel bedrooms, particularly those situated on the ground floor, may be required to be set up as meeting rooms during the day. Beds for this purpose are available which can be up-ended and hidden away in cupboards or a wall recess when not in use.

Task 7.47

Find out the size of:

- A standard single bed
- A standard double bed
- A king-sized bed

Chairs and other forms of seating are required in all areas of the hospitality and catering industry. *Tables* vary from the low coffee table to the long banqueting table.

Task 7.48

Identify the requirements of tables and seating to be used in:

- A hotel bedroom
- A silver service restaurant
- A banquet and function suite
- A hospital ward
- A study bedroom in a university
- A fast-food restaurant

Arrangement of furniture for functions

There are four basic patterns of furniture lay-out for functions:

1 *Classroom style*, where the chairs and tables are laid out in rows facing a main table at one end of the room
2 *Theatre style*, where the chairs are arranged in rows or in a semi-circular pattern facing a raised platform
3 *Banquet style*, with a top table and other round or long tables set for ten to twenty customers
4 *Dinner-dance style*, where tables and chairs are arranged around a dance floor

Storage furniture includes dressing tables, chests of drawers and wardrobes.

Task 7.49

Which customers will require the most and which the least storage?

Control of physical resources

The physical resources used within accommodation operations which must be controlled fall into the following categories:

- Cleaning equipment
- Cleaning chemicals
- Guest supplies
- Linen
- Uniforms
- Energy
- Contract services

Reasons for control of resources are:

- Increased cost effectiveness
- Maintenance of required standards
- Effective use of all resources
- Security and safety

Cost control

Costs can be affected by the prices the accommodation manager has to pay for equipment and linen, the amount of cleaning chemicals which are wasted and for breakages of crockery, glassware and equipment. You cannot expect the customers to be concerned about the costs of an establishment and so it must be the staff who keep a close watch on possible wastage:

1 Check for safety hazards that may cause an accident

2 Report any damage immediately. Quick action can save expensive long-term costs

3 Be careful with guests' property – if it is damaged by a member of staff the employer will have to compensate

4 Report missing items after a guest's departure

5 Check the level of heating and air conditioning in the guest rooms – make sure it is not left too high and switch it off if the room is unoccupied.

6 Ensure that the windows are closed when the heating is on

7 Keep a check on the frequency of changes of towel, soap and other guest supplies

8 Always report breakages

9 Use items for the correct purpose – don't use towels as cleaning cloths

10 Don't overload electrical sockets

Safe working practices

It is most important that establishments maintain a safe and a secure environment for staff and for customers. *Safety audits* (or *safety checks*) and *hazard spotting* are good methods of identifying health and safety problems. A safety audit is a thorough check, item by item, department by department, of equipment, installations, procedures, rules and working practices. It is an organized exercise. *Hazard spotting* is the ability to recognize and take action on dangerous or potentially dangerous places, systems or products which arise throughout the working period.

Task 7.50

Choose a hospitality and catering area such as a restaurant or a kitchen and carry out a safety audit and hazard-spotting exercise.

Some locations have more hazards than others. Kitchens may contain hot cookers, knives and slicers, stairs may be uneven, there may be no handrail or the lighting may be poor. Some products are more hazardous than others. Products such as toilets cleansers produce a toxic gas if mixed with sodium hypochlorite (household bleach) whereas substances for cleaning ovens are strong alkalis which are likely to damage the skin.

Task 7.51

Prepare a list of likely hazards within the various sectors of the hospitality and catering industry. Classify them into areas within establishments.

Under the Health and Safety at Work etc. Act 1974 (HASAWA) every employer is responsible for maintaining a safe working environment. HASAWA specifies six things which employers must do:

1 Provide safe equipment and safe ways of carrying out jobs

2 Make sure that the use, handling, storage and transport of everything is safe and without health risks

3 Provide information, instruction, training and supervision to ensure health and safety

4 Provide a safe workplace, including safe ways of entry and exit

5 Provide a safe working environment with adequate facilities

6 Write a safety policy

Task 7.52

Find out if your college, school or workplace has a copy of their safety policy for you to look at. What are the main points covered?

Case study

A cleaning supervisor was electrocuted when using badly maintained equipment. Mrs Mary Smith had hospital treatment for several days and had to take several weeks off work after she got an electric shock from a vacuum cleaner.

Her employers were fined a total of £5000 by the county magistrates after pleading guilty to eight offences under the Health and Safety at Work etc. Act. The court heard that the firm had not properly maintained five items of electrical equipment provided for use by the staff. It was also revealed that the firm has failed to provide health and safety training and information for its employees and had not produced a written health and safety statement. The company was fined £1000 for not having a written policy, £1000 for the unsafe vacuum cleaner and £500 for each other item of faulty equipment. They were also ordered to pay costs of £348 to the borough council.

Accident reporting

Accidents are unpleasant but are always likely to happen even in the best-organized establishments. In the event of an accident if you follow correct reporting procedures then

the information may be used to prevent similar accidents from occurring

All staff in the hospitality and catering industry should remember to record workplace accidents and dangerous occurrences, employee sickness and absences. The records help to analyse and prevent accidents and ill health in the future. There are also laws which require you to keep certain records and these may be used to provide essential evidence in the case of any legal action.

Task 7.53

Make a list of the different type of accidents which are likely to occur in the hospitality and catering industry.

It is important that procedures are developed for dealing with accidents. If you are present when an accident occurs you should

- Attend to the injured person
- Remove or isolate the danger if this is possible without injuring yourself
- Call a first aider, doctor or ambulance
- Inform a higher authority or a safety representative
- Make a careful mental note of the accident area and of anything that may have caused the accident
- Be prepared to make an accident report (Figure 7.14) or assist in the accident investigation. If you are a supervisor or a manager you may be the person who will have to carry out an investigation

If the accident is not serious and does not fall into the categories stated under RIDDOR (see below) then an Accident Book should be completed.

ACCIDENT BOOK

1 About the person who had the accident	2 About you, the person filling in this book	3 About the accident
▼ Give full name ▼ Give the home address ▼ Give the occupation	▼ Please sign the book and date it ▼ If you did not have the accident write your address and occupation	▼ When it happened ▼ Where it happened

Name		Your signature	Date	Date	Time
Address			/ /	/ /	
		Address		In what room or place did the accident happen?	
	Postcode		Postcode		
Occupation		Occupation			

Reporting of Injuries, Diseases and Dangerous Occurrences, RIDDOR 1985

For the Employer only

Please initial the box provided if the accident is reportable under RIDDOR

4 About the accident – what happened

▼ Say how the accident happened. Give the cause if you can.
▼ If any personal injury say what it is.

How did the accident happen?_____

Employer's initials

Figure 7.14 An accident report form

Task 7.54

Find out the information which must be recorded in an Accident Book.

Under the Reporting of Injuries, Diseases and Dangerous Occurrences Regulations 1985 (RIDDOR), the enforcing authority (usually the Environmental Health Department) must be notified where an accident at work involves an employee, a self-employed person, a trainee or a member of the public and if the accident results in:

1 Death
2 Major injuries or conditions including:
   A fracture of the skull, spine or pelvis
   A fracture of any bone in the arm or wrist but not a bone in the hand
   A fracture of any bone in the leg or ankle but not a bone in the foot
   An amputation of a hand or foot, finger, thumb or toe or any part of the joint or bone
 – The loss of sight of an eye or certain eye injuries
 – The injury or loss of consciousness from absorption of any substance by inhaling, swallowing or through the skin
 – Any illness requiring medical treatment where there is reason to believe that this

resulted from exposure to a pathogen or infected material
- The injury or loss of consciousness resulting from electric shock
- Any other injury resulting in the person being admitted into hospital for more than 24 hours

All of these are major injuries or conditions.

Dangerous occurrences must be reported, whether anyone is injured or not. These include the collapse of a lift or hoist, the explosion of a boiler, an explosion or fire resulting in work being suspended for more than 24 hours. Except where a person is a member of the public, notification must also be made in cases where the injured person is:

- Prevented from doing their normal work for more than 3 days as a result of an injury caused by an accident at work
- Dies within a year of a reportable injury that led to their death

An employer or company may be sued for damages in the civil courts where a person at work is killed, injured, suffers disease or mental or physical disability as a consequence of any work activity.

Fire precautions

There are almost 2000 fires per year in hospitality and catering establishments in the UK. Fire is a chemical reaction called *combustion*. To start and to maintain this reaction you need three ingredients

1 *Fuel*   something which will burn either solid, liquid or gas
2 *Oxygen*   the air contains approximately 20 per cent oxygen
3 *Heat*   once a fire has started it normally maintains its own heat

There are many causes of fire, most of them due to carelessness by both customers and staff. The majority are caused by:

- Careless smokers
- Electrical faults
- Open fires
- Stored chemicals
- Incorrect disposal of waste
- Cooking and heating equipment

Task 7.55

Working with a group of others make a list of the places where fires are likely to start. Try a brainstorming session to come up with ideas as to how fires may be prevented.

Pest control

A pest is anything which is destructive, noxious or troublesome. There are five categories of pests which are likely to be found in hospitality and catering establishments:

1 Pests which cause physical damage to the building such as woodworm, moths, carpet beetles, mice and rats
2 Pests which contaminate food and the environment such as cockroaches, flies, wasps, mice and rats
3 Pests which are comparatively harmless but disgusting to many people such as spiders, silver-fish, ants, earwigs
4 Pests which attack food such as flour beetles, bacon beetles
5 Parasites which directly attack human beings and feed on their blood such as bed bugs, head lice, fleas

Why do we need to control pests?

Pests cause harm to buildings, the environment and human beings. This is a good enough reason for us to try to eliminate them. Establishments, particularly those which serve food, are bound by law to protect the public and to keep the premises free from pests.

The hospitality and catering industry depends very much on its reputation and this can be ruined if pests are sighted or if guests can trace food poisoning back to an establishment. Loss of reputation results in loss of income and confidence in the organization of the establishment.

The physical damage to property and its contents by pests and fungi is considerable if it is not dealt with at an early stage. It is more economical to spend money on regular pest-control operations than larger sums on repairs and renewals.

Principles of good pest control

A supervisor or manager in the hospitality and catering industry should be able to identify pests or identify evidence of their presence.

Task 7.56

Identify ten common pests which may infest sectors of the hospitality and catering industry. Find out how you would recognize evidence of their presence in a building. What steps would you take to eliminate each pest?

Pest-control contractors can be employed to inspect premises and carry out any necessary treatment. Environmental Health Officers will offer free advice and may also run short training courses.

Contract hire

Contract hire is the leasing, renting or hiring of goods and/or services, from a company or contractor, for use in an establishment. You may be familiar with the idea of contract hire if you have ever rented a television or paid a window cleaner to clean your windows for you.

Goods and services which may be contracted by establishments within the hospitality and catering industry include:

Services and maintenance
Equipment servicing
Lift maintenance

Equipment hire
Cleaning equipment
Laundry equipment
Televisions
Furniture

Pest control
Regular service
Emergency cover

Security
Alarm systems
Night security

Laundry and linen services
Linen hire
Roller towels
Uniform hire

Specialist services
Carpet cleaning
Floral arrangement
Soft furnishing cleaning
Wall washing
Window cleaning
Sanibin services
Computer suite cleaning
Telephone cleaning and sterilization

Advantages of contract services

1 Contractors are specialists. They can train their staff thoroughly. They can use the correct equipment
2 Accommodation managers are relieved of the problems. Risk and hazard to direct labour

are reduced or removed (e.g. exterior window cleaning)

3 Extra work may be undertaken without increasing establishment staff levels
4 Emergency cleaning services may be provided at short notice
5 Reduction in the need for capital investment in specialized equipment
6 The contractor deals with staff problems

Disadvantages of contract services

1 Some contractors may not be specialist as the setting up of a firm is not governed by any regulation
2 Some elements of control are removed
3 Contract staff have divided loyalties
4 A contract may limit flexibility and may not cater for changing conditions
5 Minimal effort may be used to achieve maximum profit from the contractors point of view
6 Often the lowest tendered contract price is accepted sometimes with a deterioration in standards
7 Liaison with the client may be reduced

▪ STAFFING ACCOMMODATION SERVICES ▪

In order to satisfy customer expectations accommodation needs to be kept clean and properly maintained. Each establishment needs to be able to offer the type and standard of service which the customer expects. In the previous section we identified the physical resources required and here we look at the importance of staff in the provision of accommodation services.

Staff are our most expensive resource. Cleaning is one of the most expensive services. Approximately 90 per cent of the cost of any cleaning task is the cost of paying for the person to do it.

The money paid in wages and salaries represent the largest percentage of all expenditure. This is not just the amount of money paid directly to the person in the form of a wage or salary. It also includes meals, uniforms, transport, accommodation, statutory payments made by the employer such as social security contributions and the cost of recruiting and training new staff.

In this section we examine ways of organizing staff so that an efficient service can be provided in the most cost-effective way.

Administration

In a residential establishment the responsibility for the care of accommodation is usually delegated by the General Manager to an Accommodation Manager, although the actual job title may vary from one establishment to another.

1 An *Executive Housekeeper* is the accommodation manager in a large or medium-sized hotel and has greater managerial responsibility than a
2 *Head housekeeper* who manages accommodation in a small hotel or in a section of a large hotel
3 A *Domestic Services Manager* is responsible for the accommodation management in a large NHS hospital
4 A *Halls Manager* or *Accommodation Director* is in charge of all the accommodation on a university campus
5 A *Domestic Bursar* manages accommodation and sometimes the catering in one student hall of residence

(For the purposes of this section we will continue to use the general term Accommodation Services Manager.)

The Accommodation Services Manager is part of the management team of an establishment. In the establishment shown by the organization chart of a large hotel (Figure 7.15) the Accommodation Manager is known as the Head Housekeeper and will work closely with the

Front of House Manager and Works Superintendent to provide the customer with accommodation which is clean, attractive and in good repair.

In the organization chart for a hospital (Figure 7.16) the Domestic Services Manager is responsible to the Director of Hotel Services. The Hotel Services Manager is responsible for all the areas of the hospital which are not directly concerned with medicine. The Accommodation

Services Manager is supported by a team of accommodation services staff who have various responsibilities to help provide the customer with facilities and services required.

Accommodation Services Staff are *managerial*, *supervisory* or *operative*. Managerial staff are employed to control the activities of all the staff within their department in order to achieve the aims and objectives of that department.

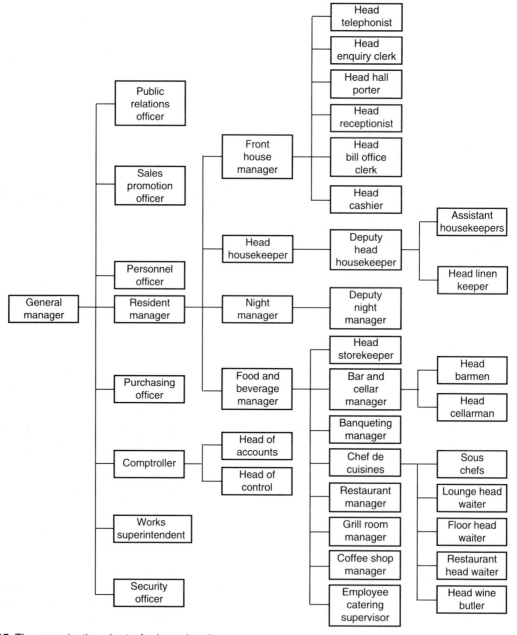

Figure 7.15 The organization chart of a large hotel

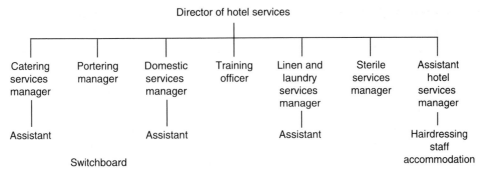

Director of hotel services

| Catering services manager | Portering manager | Domestic services manager | Training officer | Linen and laundry services manager | Sterile services manager | Assistant hotel services manager |

Assistant — Switchboard; Assistant; Assistant; Hairdressing staff accommodation

Figure 7.16 The organization chart for accommodation services in a large hospital

In many establishments this is far too large a job for one person and therefore some of the work is delegated to a number of supervisors. Supervisory staff are employed to oversee the day-to-day routine work of the department. The routine cleaning and servicing work is actually done by the operative staff.

Task 7.57

Look through the situations vacant sections of the catering press and identify the different job titles used to describe managerial, supervisory and operative positions within accommodation services departments.

To provide efficient and effective accommodation services it is essential that the resources used to provide those services are controlled. As we have already identified, the most expensive of our resources is staff. The services provided are:

- Cleaning and servicing of all types of room
- Linen and laundry facilities
- Maintaining the premises
- Supplying customers with personal services such as baby sitting
- Facilities for conferences

To provide any one of these services we need a member of staff. The resources should be controlled to:

- Increase the cost effectiveness of each service
- Maintain the standards required
- To make sure that staff are working effectively
- Ensure safety and security

In the previous section we identified the cleaning standards expected by customers using the hospitality and catering industry.

Task 7.58

Without turning back the pages see if you can remember what the three cleaning standards are.

The main difference between the three standards of cleaning is how often the cleaning tasks are done. Two establishments may use the same equipment, chemicals and methods. If, however, one of them cleans twice as often as the other then they should achieve a higher standard of cleanliness. It will also cost more in terms of staff time. There will also be an effect on the costs if one establishment offers more customer services than the other. Accommodation services need to be planned and organized so that they are carried out to the standard which the customers expect and in the most cost-effective way.

Planning and controlling the work relies on:

1 The ability of the Accommodation Services Manager to plan and organize the work effectively
2 The ability of the Supervisor to control and carry out the work efficiently
3 The ability of the Operative to carry out the work correctly

A planned cleaning programme consists of:

- Cleaning specifications
- Work schedules
- Job procedures

The first stage is to assess the scope of the work to be done. This will take into consideration the standard of service required, the availability of resources and the range of services provided by the organization.

A *cleaning specification* is a detailed description of the work to be carried out in a precise area. It should specify:

1 All the routine and periodic tasks which need to be done
2 The frequency of these tasks required to achieve the standard
3 Exactly which areas are included
4 Any special points which need to be considered

Identify any special points which would need to be considered (e.g. if you have chosen a dining room, the times the room is required for the service of meals).

The cleaning specification is used to prepare the next stage in the planning process.

A *work schedule* is an outline of the work to be carried out by either

- One or more members of staff or
- For a particular area

The work is listed in the order in which it should be carried out. The most common schedules are drawn up to show how routine work is to be organized to achieve the appropriate standard.

A work schedule should include:

- An indication of the times of meal and refreshment breaks
- Time for collecting and clearing away equipment

The work schedule may also contain details of the work which has to be carried out on a weekly basis stating the actual day when this is to be done. It may also show timings but should make allowances for unexpected events.

Task 7.59

In groups of two or three select a room such as a classroom, a dining room or a cloakroom. While you are in the room make a list of all the routine and periodic cleaning tasks which would be needed to keep the room clean. Decide which of the three standards you think is appropriate for this room. Identify the frequency with which these tasks should be carried out (e.g. daily, weekly, monthly, yearly).

Task 7.60

Take the cleaning specification which you completed earlier. Identify all the routine tasks which you think should be done every day. Place them in the order which you think these tasks should be carried out. Get together with other groups and work out a schedule for cleaning all the areas for which you have written a specification.

A *job procedure* is a description of the way a specific job is to be done by a particular person or people. Job procedures are frequently presented as *order of work cards*, which are pocket-sized cards giving details of the cleaning equipment, chemicals and method of work for either

● A specific task (e.g. cleaning a washbasin)
● A specific area (e.g. cleaning a bathroom)

When used in industry the operative is not given a choice of either equipment or chemicals. That choice will be made by the Accommodation Services Manager and everyone doing that task or tasks must follow the same method using the same type of equipment and the same chemicals.

Order of work cards are used extensively during training and in the weeks when an operative is new to the job. Experienced staff need them only when a new system of working or a new piece of equipment is introduced.

Task 7.61

Draw up a job procedure or an order of work card for a cleaning task such as cleaning a washbasin, damp mopping a vinyl floor or cleaning out a refrigerator.

Examples of standard times.

	Job No.	Basic Time (min)	Rest Allowance (%)	Contingency Allowance (%)	Standard Time (min)
Re-making a bed	1	1.8	22.0	10	2.38
Re-sheeting a bed	2	3.9	22.5	10	5.17
Cleaning a washbasin	3	1.2	13.0	10	1.48
Cleaning a bath	4	1.92	14.5	10	2.40
Cleaning a shower	5	1.0	13.0	10	1.23
Cleaning a W.C.	6	0.94	16.0	10	1.18
Dusting a dressing-table	7	0.43	11.0	10	0.52
Polishing a dressing-table	8	0.85	13.0	10	1.05
Emptying and cleaning wastepaper bin	9	0.72	11.0	10	0.87
Vacuum cleaning – hard floor per 10 m^2	10	1.8	13.5	10	2.22
Vacuum cleaning – carpet per 10 m^2	11	4.3	16.0	10	5.42
Mop sweeping – hard floor per 10 m^2	12	1.2	13.5	10	1.48
Damp mopping – per 10 m^2	13	2.4	16.0	10	3.02
Scrubbing – manual per 10 m^2	14	3.7	22.0	10	4.88
Scrubbing – machine per 10 m^2	15	2.3	13.0	10	2.83
Polishing – machine per 10 m^2	16	2.1	11.0	10	2.54
Cleaning glass – per m^2	17	0.65	13.5	10	0.8

These work measurement times are based on studies for specific equipment, cleaning agents and methods of work and made in an unobstructed area so can only be used as a guide. They do not include any allowance for getting ready, cleaning and putting away the equipment. The rest allowances vary with the job but an overall allowance of 10 per cent has been added for contingencies.

Figure 7.17 Standard times

Work measurement

Work measurement techniques are used to determine the time needed to complete the work. It is, along with method study, a part of the work study process. In industry managers use work measurement techniques to assist them in allocating work.

Method study is the systematic recording and critical examination of existing and proposed methods of work. It is done to develop and apply easier and more effective methods and for reducing costs. It is used in industry to determine *standard times* for carrying out a variety of operations (Figure 7.17).

In order to calculate the standard time the *basic time* is determined by method study. The basic time is the time required to do the job by an experienced worker using the agreed method of work, the correct equipment and chemicals and working to a predetermined standard, e.g.

It takes an experienced worker 1.8 minutes to make a bed or 3.9 minutes when putting clean sheets on.

This basic time was arrived at by watching (method study) a number of workers making beds. They would have been studied at various times of the day, at the beginning when they were fresh and at the end of the day when they were more tired. The resulting figure is an average of all the studies.

Once the basic time has been agreed, an *allowance* is added for *rest and relaxation*. This extra time allows workers to recover their energy and it also takes account of any environmental problems such as bad lighting, awkward work positioning, the need constantly to lift heavy loads or to climb up and down stairs.

The rest allowance also covers the time needed for coffee breaks, for changing in and out of uniform and for visits to the cloakroom. This would add 22 per cent to the bed-making times quoted above (22.5 per cent if resheeting the bed).

A *contingency allowance* may need to be built in for unforeseen interruptions or delays such as a room maid having to wait for people to vacate their rooms before being able to clean them. This allowance would add 10 per cent to the times given for bed making.

Basic time + rest allowance + contingency allowance = standard time

For remaking a bed:
 $1.8 + 0.396 + 0.18 = 2.376$

For resheeting a bed:
 $3.9 + 0.8775 + 0.39 = 5.1675$

Task 7.62

Using the standard times shown in Figure 7.17 calculate to the nearest whole minute the time it should take to clean a ladies' cloakroom daily. There are four WCs in separate cubicles, four washbasins, two mirrors each 1 metre high and 3 metres long, four wastepaper bins, and 50 square metres of vinyl tiled floor.

The work specification and work schedules provide detailed information for the Accommodation Manager and the Supervisors. Training and order of work cards ensure that each operative knows what has to be done, when and how to carry out each task and the time allowed to complete the work.

Inspection

To control and maintain standards *routine and periodic inspection of work* must also be carried out. Routine inspection of work is normally undertaken by the Supervisor and is done to make sure that the correct procedures and methods are used. This in turn will identify the person or people responsible and allow action to be taken to correct defective work. As a result complaints can be dealt with quickly and standards are maintained.

Inspection of a bedroom with en-suite bathroom

1 *Start at the door*   Check the general condition of the door and the lock.
2 *Move into the lobby*   Check that the walls and floor are clean and that the lighting is working.
3 *Move into the bedroom*   Inspect the cleanliness of the ceiling, walls and floor. Make sure that the telephone, luggage rack, pictures, furniture and mirrors are clean. Check that the room lighting and the bedside lights are working. Check that all guest supplies are present. While in the bedroom check the condition of the *windows* – shutters, sill/balcony, draught exclusion, ease of opening and closing, cleanliness of glass/frame. Check also the blinds and/or curtains. Are they clean and in working order?
4 Before leaving, check the *bathroom*   Inspect the sanitary appliances for cleanliness and make sure that they are working. Check the condition of taps and waste outlets. Check that the ventilation is working efficiently. Examine the walls and floor. Are they clean? Check that the guest supplies are correctly placed.

The Supervisor will need to check an operative's work at least twice during each work period. The first check should be at the beginning to see that it has started on time and the second when the work is finished to make sure that the standard is satisfactory.

Periodic inspection of work should be carried out by a higher-level supervisor or by manager at least once a month to establish that correct quality and time standards are being achieved. It is also done to make sure that supervisors are measuring work to the same standards and to assist in improving or maintaining morale and motivation of staff.

When checking work, memory alone should not be relied on. A *checklist* will provide a more thorough and systematic method of checking. A checklist is used to make sure that all the work is being carried out and that nothing has been overlooked. It can also be very useful when dealing with any complaints. It is difficult to deal with these from memory only (Figure 7.18).

Control of labour

As stated previously, the main costs arising from the servicing of a building are for labour. The control of labour is therefore very important and is the area where the greatest economy can be made. Work can be divided into two categories:

1 *Fixed work*, which is all the work that must be completed whether it is going to be used by one person or by a number of people using the building (e.g. public cloakrooms)
2 *Flexible work* relates directly to the level of activity. If a room is not used it may not be necessary to spend as much time to clean it as when the room is used (e.g. servicing of guest bedrooms in a hotel)

The cleaning specification will give the details of the tasks to be completed and the frequency of these tasks. The standard times will indicate how long the tasks should take. From these it is possible to estimate the time required to complete the work. It is also possible to decide from the cleaning specification whether the work is fixed or flexible.

Fixed work will have a fixed number of hours per week in which to complete all the routine tasks and a fixed number of hours per year to complete the periodic ones. Flexible work will have a period of time allocated to each task.

The Accommodation Services Manager will therefore have a number of hours in which to complete the work. They will then decide how and when the hours will be used taking account of the requirements of the establishment, e.g.:

● When the work needs to be done – early in the morning, in the evening, during the night

Quality control (hotel floor supervisors checklist).

Date .... Time .... Room number ....

	Yes	No		Yes	No
Door light			Plugs – electric		
Do not disturb			Shaving socket		
Fire notice			Shower fitting		
Door closer			Shower curtain		
Radio			W.C.		
Telephone			W.C. flush		
Telephone directories			Toilet rolls		
Headboards			Soap		
Gideon's bible			Glasses		
Ashtrays and matches			Sanibin		
Bedspread – clean			Washbasin		
Windows			Bath		
Net curtains			Plugs		
Heavy curtains			Towels		
Wardrobe			Towel rail		
Hangers (12)			Bath mat		
Chairs			Mirror		
Drawers and shelves			Tiles and bath panels		
Wastepaper bins			Light fittings		
Portable lights			Heating		
T.V.			Luggage rack		
Special promotions and guest supplies					

General – give your own opinion of the standard of the following:

	Good	Average	Poor		Good	Average	Poor
Carpet				Curtains			
Painted surfaces				Walls			
Wood surfaces				Lights			
Upholstery/covers				Literature			
General impression				Smell			

Please complete the maintenance docket for all defects.

Signed ....

Figure 7.18 Checklist

- The availability of labour – is it easier to get part-time rather than full-time staff. Is it easy to get staff at all?
- The cost to the labour budget

Full-time staff (over 35 hours per week) are preferable as they are likely to be the cheapest. The administration, recruitment and training costs are reduced as well as the cost of providing uniform and staff meals.

Task 7.63

Can you think of any reason why the employment of full-time staff may not be cost effective?

Part-time staff, although more expensive, are generally more flexible, more reliable and extend the labour supply.

Alternatives to the above arrangements include:

1 Offering existing staff overtime which, if bonus payments such as time and a half are offered, is more expensive but avoids possible redundancy situations. Paying overtime is a practice which is frowned on by a number of trade unions

---

Task 7.64

Why do you think the trade unions disapprove of overtime working?

---

2 Using temporary staff from an agency, which is expensive in the long term but can be useful in an emergency
3 Employing the services of an outside contractor

Task 7.65

At the Station Hotel the Accommodation Manager has been allocated 42 hours per week to clean and service the ground-floor public areas. An additional 48 hours have been allocated to clean the function rooms and a further 35 hours to clean the public corridors and stairs. The full-time staff work an 8-hour day and the part-time staff, a 4-hour day.

The ground-floor areas must be cleaned between 7.00 a.m. and 11.00 a.m. The function rooms need to be serviced between 7.00 a.m. and 9.00 a.m. and between 4.00 p.m. and 7.00 p.m. The public corridors and stairs must be cleaned between 11.00 a.m. and 4.00 p.m.

How many hours are available for use each day? How many staff if all full-time are required each day? How many staff if all part-time are required each day?

Generally, a mixture of full-time and part-time staff are employed in the majority of establishments. The calculations for flexible work are often based on the number of staff required to do the work which, on a day-to-day basis, makes these calculations less cumbersome.

Rotas or *rosters* are often used to show hours of duty and days off. They are frequently employed where staff are required to work shifts. Duty rotas are necessary to:

● Make sure that there are enough staff on duty to cover the work
● Make sure that there are not too many staff on duty for the work to be done
● Make sure that the staff work the correct number of hours
● Make sure that days off are as regular as possible, giving staff reasonable rest periods
● Plan days off for staff in a fair manner
● Help in preparation of wages reports
● Know who is on the premises in case of fire

Duty rotas should be drawn up well in advance so that all staff know when they will or will not be required to work. Before starting you will need to know

1 The coverage hours (those working hours when the department is operational)
2 The number of full- and part-time staff on the payroll
3 The number of hours worked per day or per week

4 Meal and coffee break allowances

5 Staff requests such as special days off or holiday periods. Periods of long-term illness may need to be taken into account and sometimes provision has to be made for last-minute sickness or absence

6 Special operational factors (e.g. spring cleaning or refurbishing projects)

When the workload is fixed and constant throughout the year the manager may operate one of the types of duty rota shown in Table 7.1.

On this rota the management will have full coverage from 7 a.m. to 7 p.m. The staff will work the same duties but each person will take a turn at a late shift – seven shifts in a seven-week period. The staff do not have the same days off each week but in rotation, as shown in Table 7.2.

When the workload is flexible the Accommodation Services Manager needs to calculate the requirements and compile the rotas on a week-by-week basis according to the various work levels. The first step when preparing a duty rota is to calculate the number of staff required to complete the work, assuming that 100 per cent of the work has to be done.

Example
A hotel has 320 twin-bedded rooms all with private bathroom en suite. The time allowed for each operative to service one room is 30 minutes. Each operative is required to work an 8-hour shift each day and for 5 days per week.

1 Calculate the total number of operative hours required per day when hotel occupancy is 100 per cent. *To do this* – Calculate the number of rooms which can be completed in one hour. Divide the total number of rooms by that number.

2 Calculate the number of operatives required per day when the hotel occupancy is 100 per

Table 7.1

Name	Mon	Tue	Wed	Thurs	Fri	Sat	Sun
Bashful	OFF	OFF	10.30–7.00	8.00–4.30	8.00–4.30	8.00–4.30	8.00–4.30
Doc	8.00–4.30	8.00–4.30	OFF	OFF	10.30–7.00	8.00–4.30	8.00–4.30
Dopey	8.00–4.30	8.00–4.30	8.00–4.30	8.00–4.30	OFF	OFF	10.30–7.00
Grumpy	8.00–4.30	8.00–4.30	8.00–4.30	8.00–4.30	8.00–4.30	OFF	OFF
Happy	10.30–7.00	8.00–4.30	8.00–4.30	OFF	OFF	10.30–7.00	8.00–4.30
Sleepy	8.00–4.30	OFF	OFF	10.30–7.00	8.00–4.30	8.00–4.30	8.00–4.30
Sneezy	OFF	10.30–7.00	8.00–4.30	8.00–4.30	8.00–4.30	8.00–4.30	OFF

Table 7.2

Bashful	Mon	Tue	Wed	Thurs	Fri	Sat	Sun
Week 1	OFF	OFF	10.30–7.00	8.00–4.30	8.00–4.30	8.00–4.30	8.00–4.30
Week 2	8.00–4.30	8.00–4.30	OFF	OFF	10.30–7.00	8.00–4.30	8.00–4.30
Week 3	8.00–4.30	8.00–4.30	8.00–4.30	8.00–4.30	OFF	OFF	10.30–7.00
Week 4	8.00–4.30	8.00–4.30	8.00–4.30	8.00–4.30	8.00–4.30	OFF	OFF
Week 5	10.30–7.00	8.00–4.30	8.00–4.30	OFF	OFF	10.30–7.00	8.00–4.30
Week 6	8.00–4.30	OFF	OFF	10.30–7.00	8.00–4.30	8.00–4.30	8.00–4.30
Week 7	OFF	10.30–7.00	8.00–4.30	8.00–4.30	8.00–4.30	8.00–4.30	OFF

cent. *To do this* – divide the total number of operative hours by the number of hours per shift.

This figure is the base number used to calculate staff requirements where the occupancy level fluctuates on a daily basis.

In establishments where the occupancy or the work level is stable and staff are required to work over a period of 7 days it is necessary to know how many staff to employ in total. On the assumption that the above hotel is such an establishment:

3 Calculate the total number of operatives required per week when the occupancy is 100 per cent. *To do this* – multiply the number of operatives required per day by the number of days there are in a week, i.e. seven. Divide the answer by the number of days each operative is required to work, i.e. five. In establishments where the occupancy level is not stable the calculation is similar.

4 Calculate the number of operatives required per day when the percentage occupancy is:

Monday	30	Friday	45
Tuesday	85	Saturday	42
Wednesday	94	Sunday	35
Thursday	89		

To do this – calculate the number of operatives required each day. Do not round up or down to the nearest whole number. Add these figures together and divide by the number of days each operative is required to work.

Task 7.66

The Majestic Hotel has 336 bedrooms all with private bathroom en suite. The standard time allowed for servicing each bedroom is 20 minutes. Calculate the number of room attendants required each day when the hotel is fully occupied.

This calculation needs to be done only once unless more rooms are built or some are closed down permanently as all other calculations are based on this figure.

In a hotel the Executive Housekeeper will receive an *occupancy forecast* from the Front Office giving some indication of the expected business. This may be on a written sheet or, as is more common in larger hotels, on a computer printout.

The following figures are based on actual bookings received and information from previous years' business:

Majestic Hotel

	Sun	Mon	Tues	Wed	Thurs	Fri	Sat
Date	8/4	9/4	10/4	11/4	12/4	13/4	14/4
No. of rooms	151	286	336	336	269	178	101
	45%	85%	100%	100%	80%	53%	30%

The occupancy forecast refers to the night of occupancy. From the accommodation services point of view these figures affect the work requirements of the morning after. Rooms occupied on Sunday night will require servicing on Monday morning, those occupied on a Monday night will require servicing on a Tuesday morning. and so on.

To calculate the number of room attendants required per day the Executive Housekeeper will always work from the number of room attendants required when the hotel has maximum occupancy. On Monday morning at the Majestic Hotel, the Housekeeper will therefore require sufficient staff to service 45 per cent of the rooms. Instead of repeating the calculation all that needs to be done is to work out 45 per cent of 14, which is 6.3.

Financial control

Financial control is important in both the public and the private sector of the industry. A *public organization* such as a hospital may not be required to make a profit but has to work within a strict budget and must provide the best service for the money.

A *commercial organization* such as a hotel exists in order to make a profit for the owner(s) whether these are single individuals, a group of shareholders or a financing company.

Task 7.67

Give further examples of profit-making and non-profit making organizations.

Budgets

A budget is a statement of the *anticipated expenditure* of an establishment or a department. In commercial establishments which are profit-centred organizations a budget is also a statement of *expected revenue or income*. A budget statement is for a fixed period of time, usually one year. The Accommodation Services Budget is part of the overall establishment budget and usually commences approximately six months prior to operation with the preparation of estimates.

There are three main types of budget:

1 *Labour costs* which is the money allocated to pay for staff wages. This is not just the amount of money paid directly to the person. It also includes statutory payments made by the employer such as Social Security contributions, meals, uniforms, transport, accommodation and the cost of recruiting and training new staff

2 *Operating costs* which are those items of day-to-day expenditure which will fluctuate according to the level of occupancy such as laundry, cleaning chemicals, guest supplies (soap, toilet paper, etc.)

3 *Capital expenditure* is for large items which last for more than a year such as carpets, curtains, bedding, furniture, cleaning equipment.

These are often listed in order of priority:

- First essential – required now
- Second essential – required within the next two years
- Third essential – required within the next five years

Costs can be affected by the prices the accommodation manager has to pay for supplies and the amount of cleaning chemicals which is wasted and for breakages of crockery, glassware and equipment.

Estimates

An estimate is the amount of money that the budget holder, usually the head of the department, feels is necessary for successful operation during the coming year. Estimates are prepared four to six months before the start of the financial year which may begin on 1st January or perhaps to coincide with the start of the tax year.

Task 7.68

What are the dates of the beginning and the end of the tax year?

There are two types of estimate.

1 *Revenue estimates* are for the money required to pay for the day-to-day running of the department such as cleaning, chemicals and laundry
2 *Capital estimates* are for the money required for items which need to be bought or replaced during the year such as carpets and furniture

Task 7.69

Identify other items which would be included in the calculation of the estimates. Indicate which would be for revenue and which for capital estimates.

The estimate depends on a certain amount of guesswork but will also take into consideration:

● An analysis of financial reports of the current year
● An analysis of financial report of the past three years
● A forecast of likely business for the year ahead
● Any proposed alteration in equipment, standard or type of work
● The monthly consumption figures

When the estimates are presented they must be supported by facts and figures. These are known as *quotes*. The exact requirements are given to manufacturers and suppliers who will give a quotation of their prices.

All the individual estimates are collated and checked by the accountant. The money is then allocated after discussion with the General Manager and the Senior Management. In many cases the money allocated is less than the amount estimated.

RECEPTION AND FRONT OFFICE OPERATIONS

Reception and Front Office is the nerve centre of the outlet. It has a central focus and is generally the first point of contact with the customer and often the last. This unit aims to give you an understanding of the purpose, procedure and requirements of Reception and Front Office to enable you to apply your knowledge and skill in a practical situation. The unit covers:

- The customer cycle and customer requirements
- The services, procedures and documentation required
- Reservation systems
- The need to maximize occupancy and revenue
- Communication skills
- Various systems in operation
- The benefits of new technology
- Legal requirements relating to Reception and Front Office procedures

---

▪ CUSTOMER REQUIREMENTS FOR RECEPTION AND FRONT OFFICE OPERATIONS ▪

Whenever you enter any business organization the chances are that your first point of contact will be in the Reception area or at the Front Office. In the hospitality industry this first contact point is critical as it sets the scene around which the customer will start to build an impression.

1 Was the receptionist cheerful and welcoming?
2 Was the hotel or restaurant expecting your arrival?
3 Did the Reception staff deal with your enquiry efficiently and politely?

4 Did you feel satisfied when you left the Reception/Front Office area?

We have all been customers and have experienced the positive and negative effects that good and poor Reception staff can create. Unfortunately the negative impressions tend to stick! The purpose of this section therefore is to examine carefully what customers require and expect when dealing with Front Office staff within a hospitality environment.

Every time a customer enters a hotel, leisure centre, restaurant, etc. they start the customer/ guest cycle. If we go to a new college and we are not sure where to go, the chances are that we will look for the Reception area. When they enter a new environment for the first time most people will seek help and assistance. This help and assistance is usually found at Reception.

It is important to realize that the Reception or Front Office is essential at all stages of the customer/guest cycle. It is here that records of all customers are kept, updated and maintained. The Front Office staff know whether a customer has paid or not; if the customer uses the facilities/services regularly; how much the customer usually spends. It is likely that the customer will contact Reception several times during their visit either for information or to request an additional service.

Goods and services in the hospitality industry

When considering the role of the Reception and Front Office operation in the customer/guest cycle we must clarify how this area can provide guest requirements relating to goods and services and the differences between the two.

Goods provided in the hospitality industry are things that you can touch and see and that provide satisfaction for the customers and guests. Examples of goods are: restaurant meals, pints of beer, 'Big Macs'.

A *service* is something which provides satisfaction and enjoyment for the customer, but service itself is not a physical thing. Service is not tangible and by its very nature is more difficult to measure than goods.

For example, Helen and Paul are employed as receptionists at the Majestic Hotel. However, Paul provides a better standard of customer service than Helen. How can we measure this?

The Reception desk or area is therefore the first point of contact for most people. It is where the customer meets someone who represents that business for the first time. The Reception or Front Office staff (so called because they deal directly with the public, face to face) are therefore the first stage in the guest cycle.

Every day customers using different sectors of the hospitality industry go through a series of stages or a process which takes them from their point of arrival to their point of departure. This process is called the customer/guest cycle (Figure 8.1).

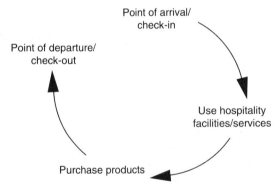

Figure 8.1 The customer/guest cycle

● *Which of these goods and services are provided by the Reception and Front Office staff?*

Customers/guests

In our analysis of the customer/guest cycle it is necessary to consider the variety of people who use the range of goods and services provided by the hospitality industry. Receptionists deal with many different people on a daily basis. Certainly the diversity of customers is as great as the population of the UK! However, there are several groups of which the Reception and Front Office staff need to be particularly aware:

1 *Tourists* Tourism has been a major growth industry in recent years and subsequently the number of tourist groups using the hospitality industry has increased during this period. Such customers make specific demands on the hotel's Front Office. Often tourists will travel as part of a named tour group. Therefore the arrival and departure procedures for such groups have to be planned in advance by the Front Office staff to ensure an efficient and speedy service for the guest. Tourists also require a great deal of local information – bus/train times, locations of main tourist attractions, etc. As well as providing this information the Front Office staff must also be able to deal with non-English-speaking tourists. Obviously, when dealing with these guests the receptionist needs to display particular skills of patience and tact.

Task 8.4

What other information would tourists expect from the Front Office?

2 *Corporate* Corporate guests are usually business guests. Such customers could be attending a company conference in the hotel, or there may be a series of local business meetings. Corporate guests make specific demands on the Front Office. Often they will require office services; secretarial facilities, photocopying, access to fax machines and word processors. Many corporate guests will incur large accounts during their stay (room service, direct-dial telephone charges) in addition to using other in-house services such as the health and leisure club. They may also require a valeting service to dry-clean and press a business suit, or to shine and polish a pair of shoes. At the end of the guest cycle it is important that the Front Office staff know who is settling the corporate customer's account – the company or the guest? It may be that 'extras' are settled by the guest but basic charges for accommodation and food are entered on a separate 'corporate account'.

Task 8.5

Consider other specific needs during the guest cycle that the corporate customer would expect the Front Office to provide.

3 *Special needs* Customers with special needs fall into two main categories; those with physical problems and those with mental disabilities. Different sectors of the industry provide different provisions for these customers. Throughout the guest cycle those customers with physical needs will rely on the industry to provide facilities which ease their mobility throughout the hospitality unit. The provision of ramps, lifts, wide corridors and doors are examples of careful planning with consideration for guests with physical disabilities. When dealing with

customers with mental disabilities special training is often required. Sometimes this is beyond the scope of the usual hospitality provision and specialist staff are required to accompany such guests. However, Reception and Front Office staff can provide such skills such as patience and empathy to meet the requirements of all special needs customers.

to be tactful, discreet and professional at all times. These qualities are very important in the 1990s as many VIPs now unfortunately attract a security risk wherever they visit. This is especially the case when the major political parties hold their annual conferences in major resort towns in the UK, using conference venues and local hotels as their base.

Task 8.6

What other assistance can the Reception and Front Office staff provide to meet the specific requirements of guests with special needs?

Task 8.7

Discuss other requirements that VIPs may expect the Reception and Front Office staff to provide or make available during their stay. What are the specific problems associated with accommodating VIP guests?

4 *VIPs* Very Important Persons (VIPs), obviously have special requirements and make specific demands on the Reception and Front Office staff. Such guests may include leading politicians, television and radio celebrities, pop stars and other well-known media people. Often such VIPs require privacy and are not keen to publicize their stay. In these cases the Reception and Front Office staff try to ensure that such guests enjoy as low a profile as possible. VIPs will often use many of the in-house services. They may well require all their meals to be served in their rooms/suite. They will tend to make use of the portering service and will expect the housekeeping service to be very attentive. VIPs may also request that they be allowed to use the health and leisure services outside normal opening hours. Such requests must be dealt with efficiently and politely by the Front Office staff and referred immediately to senior management for a decision. In order to avoid publicity it is very likely that the VIPs will request that the Reception staff handle all external phone calls and messages, only transferring approved callers to the VIP's room. Such people expect the Front Office staff

Customer/guest requirements

Now that we have identified the different types of people who will use the Reception and Front Office we must now consider their specific and varying requirements. The services provided by the Reception staff will differ depending upon the sector of the hospitality industry.

Hotels

This is probably the most complex sector providing a wide range of goods and services to meet specific guest requirements. Hotels provide three basic commodities:

● Food
● Drink
● Accommodation

However, hotels vary in terms of standards and prices. Luxury expensive hotels will provide a wide range of additional in-house services while smaller, less expensive, establishments will have more basic facilities. The Front Office staff in all hotels must be knowledgeable about the range of products provided and skilled in guest accounting and customer-care skills.

Restaurants/public houses

Although some restaurants and public houses provide accommodation, these sectors are mainly concerned with selling food and drink. The Reception staff therefore need to be able to handle restaurant bookings, and must also be familiar with guest accounting procedures.

In some establishments the Reception staff are also responsible for serving pre-lunch/dinner drinks to the guests before escorting them to their table in the restaurant. A knowledge of food and drink commodities is therefore essential.

Hospitals/residential homes

The customer requirements of Reception staff employed in hospitals and residential homes are very specific. Unlike the above sectors (restaurants, hotels) which are generally used as sources of enjoyment by guests, hospitals and residential homes are usually used by people because of need and/or necessity. The Reception staff should therefore have very proficient customer-care skills. They need particularly to be tactful and diplomatic at all times, as they will often deal with doctors and other care workers who will know very personal details relating to guests/patients.

In addition to taking bookings and liaising with senior staff, Reception will also be the first point of contact for visitors and enquiries from outside. Again, empathy and diplomacy are essential in order to protect and safeguard the guest/patient from unnecessary and/or unwanted intrusion during their convalescence.

Tourism/leisure

Receptionists within this sector of the hospitality industry usually provide a booking and information service. Within a leisure centre the receptionist will take payment for facilities,

make bookings and provide information on the range of activities provided.

In a tourist information office the reception staff will be able to take bookings or provide information on local hotels. They should also be up to date and knowledgeable on the locality, providing details of events and able to give directions to tourist attractions.

Task 8.8

- *What are the common qualities required of all reception and front office staff in the hospitality industry?*
- *Which of these qualities do you consider to be of greatest importance? Why?*

In-house services

The range of in-house services provided to meet customer needs and expectations is diverse and spans several sectors of the hospitality industry. Such services are included in our analysis of Reception and Front Office operations since many requests are often directed initially at the Front Office staff. Some of these services are provided in all sectors of the industry, others are specific to individual sectors.

Task 8.9

Consider what in-house services you would expect to be provided by a luxury, city-centre hotel. How would these differ from those in-house services available within a budget resort hotel?

Valeting

This is a very specialized in-house service provided by high-class establishments. A valet may act as a personal attendant to a guest looking after clothing, shoes, serving meals in the room. Valet parking is a system used in some hotels, restaurants, private clubs, etc., where the guests' cars are parked by a steward.

Room service

This is a service provided by hotels for guests who prefer to eat and drink in their room instead of using the public restaurants and lounges. VIPs will often use this service to avoid any unwanted publicity or attention that they may attract if they are seen in public areas. Often guests will use this service for snacks or drinks during the night when the bars and restaurants are closed. Even though it may be more expensive many guests find the prospect of room service breakfast far more preferable to the trauma of eating breakfast in public first thing in the morning.

Customer relations

In recent years the hospitality industry, along with others, has recognized the importance of projecting a positive impression to existing and future customers. As a result, many companies have spent a great deal of money in an attempt to improve the overall corporate image. Much of this money has been spent on staff training programmes intended to improve customer-care skills. This customer relations training has involved such diverse staff as hospital receptionists to night-club security staff! Much more detail relating to customer relations and staff training is included in unit 3.

Portering service

This service is still found in many large traditional hotels. Indeed, in several luxury hotels they still form a separate department coming under the supervision of the Head Hall Porter. The uniformed staff include doormen, liftmen, pages and porters. Of these the most common are porters, who carry guests' luggage to and from their rooms, set up meeting and conference rooms, and handle bulky items in the 'front of house' areas.

Task 8.10

Suggest reasons for the decline in numbers of 'uniformed' staff employed in recent years.

Accommodation service

This is a very specialized service and therefore, as you will be aware, there is a separate unit of study on the GNVQ (Advanced) programme: Accommodation Operations (see Unit 7). However, it is necessary to appreciate that both the Front Office and the Accommodation departments work closely together. The functions of both departments are dependent on the other. If the Accommodation department has not serviced any rooms then the Front Office cannot sell those rooms. However, if the Front Office does not sell any rooms then there is no work for the Accommodation department.

Needless to say, there is occasional friction between the two departments, especially when the pressure is on! However, for the most part both departments work and communicate well together. They maintain their separate identities, but also recognize their professional dependence on each other.

Office services

Many hotels and conference/leisure facilities now provide a full range of office services. These new services are designed to attract business clientele who otherwise would be unable to operate their business dealings except in their own office environments. Such services are viewed by the hospitality industry as a major selling feature in order to secure bookings and reservations from business customers.

Task 8.11

What do you consider to be the necessary range of office services that a hospitality establishment must offer in order to attract business customers?

Health and leisure services

Increasingly, many sectors of the hospitality industry are using the sales technique of providing health and leisure services in order to attract business. Hotels are offering such services as standard along with their other facilities. Such health and leisure services include swimming pools, saunas, fitness studios, solariums. Often specialist staff are also employed such as swimming and fitness instructors or beauty therapists. The Reception and Front Office staff are encouraged to sell these services whenever possible when dealing with guests at the front desk.

Task 8.12

On what occasions during the guest cycle will it be most appropriate for Reception staff to sell the range of in-house services offered by a hotel?

Reception and Front Office procedures

We have already considered the several stages of the guest cycle. It is therefore now necessary to investigate the procedures that must be carried out by the Front Office staff at each of these stages (Figure 8.2). Many of these procedures, as you may expect, are particular to the hotel sector. However, there are other procedures which are appropriate to several sectors of the hospitality industry.

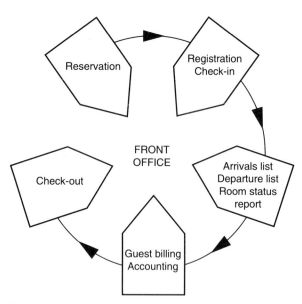

Figure 8.2 Front Office procedures

Reservation

There are a variety of ways in which a guest can make a reservation:

1 In person
2 Telephone
3 Letter
4 Fax
5 Computerized communication/electronic mail.

Other traditional methods may include using a telex.

Any reservation made before the event is known as an advance booking. We will consider the variety of advance booking systems used in the hospitality industry in the next section.

Task 8.13

The text has mentioned a number of different ways to make a reservation. Explain each of these in your notebook or folder. Which is the most popular?

Sometimes when recording a reservation for hotel accommodation some establishments will use a standard reservation form. This details the guest's specific requirements, and the information is then transferred to the appropriate booking system at a later stage. The layout of the form will vary from hotel to hotel, and an example is shown in Figure 8.3.

Reservation form

A/Date: _____ Stay Nt(s): _____ A/Time: _____

Room type: _____ No. persons: _____ Rate: _____

Name: _____ Phone no: _____

Address: _____
_____
_____
_____

Res. by: _____ Phone no: _____

Address: _____
_____
_____
_____

A/c instructions: _____

Special instructions: _____
_____
_____
_____

Guaranteed: ☐   Gtd to: _____ 6 pm: ☐

Clerk: _____ Today's date: _____

In person ☐   Phone ☐   Letter ☐   Telex ☐   Fax ☐   Computer ☐

T.B.C. ☐   By _____ Confirmed ☐   Wait list ☐

Figure 8.3 A typical reservation form

Task 8.14

- Investigate what is meant by a 'guaranteed' reservation
- What is the 'release time'?
- Why is it important to inform the guest of the 'release time'?

Registration/check-in

As we have previously mentioned, whenever a guest enters a hospitality establishment it is essential that he or she is greeted correctly so that a positive impression is created. However, when a guest enters a hotel and requests accommodation there are additional legal procedures that must be completed by the Reception staff. We will examine the exact legal requirements associated with guest registration later.

The purpose of guest registration is exactly as stated – to register everyone who uses sleeping accommodation in a hotel or guest house. There are two basic methods used for guest registration.

The first is the *registration book* (Figure 8.4). This is mainly used by guest houses and small hotels.

Larger hotels tend to use *registration cards* (Figure 8.5). These are easier to file and are more confidential than the registration book, which can be read by other guests. They can also be pre-printed prior to a guest's arrival and therefore the check-in procedure is speeded up.

Task 8.15

Design an alternative, more user-friendly registration card which is more welcoming than the example given in Figure 8.5.

Arrivals list

The purpose of the arrivals list is to inform other departments and the hotel management of the names and numbers of guests arriving on a specific date prior to those guests actually checking in. It is useful for the Housekeeping department to know how many rooms are likely to be used on a particular night. Similarly, the kitchen will find room occupancy information useful when planning the number of covers to cater for at dinner or breakfast. The layout of an arrivals list is shown in Figure 8.6.

Task 8.16

What other hotel departments will find the information contained on an arrivals list useful? Why?

Departure list

This is similar to the arrivals list. This information is produced in the front office and distributed to other departments who need to know guest departure information, i.e.

- Housekeeping
- Restaurant
- Bar
- Switchboard

Task 8.17

Why might the above departments find a departure list useful?

Date	Surname	Forenames	Address	Nationality	Room no.	Car reg no.	Passport no.	Place of issue	Next destination

Figure 8.4 A registration book

Registration card

Surname.. Arrival date..........................

Other names..

Nationality..

Home address..

....

....

Room no.. Car registration..................

For foreign visitors only:

Passport no... Issued at..........................

Next destination..

All visitors:

Signature..

Figure 8.5 A registration form

Date: .....31st....March..199.-......							
Name	No. of guests		Room		No. of nights	Arrival time	Remarks
	Adults	Children	Type	No			
ADAMS	2	—	TB	204	2	6·00	
JONES	2	1	TB	306	3	6·30	COT REQUIRED
LACY	1	—	S	110	1	7·00	REGULAR

Figure 8.6 An arrivals list

Room status report

At any time the hotel Reception staff must be able to identify the current status of each room. This means that they must know:

1 If a room is occupied, and for how long
2 If a room is unoccupied, whether it has been serviced by the Housekeeping department and is available for letting
3 If a room is out of order (OOO) for redecoration or repairs

Hotels use a variety of systems in order to keep track of this information. These can include:

- Bed sheets
- Room rack cards
- Whitney room status rack
- Computerized room status displays

Task 8.18

Investigate two of the above systems. Explain how they operate, with diagrams and illustration where appropriate.

Guest billing/accounting

This is a complex and detailed function of the Reception and Front Office procedures. Whenever we check into a hotel we immediately start to incur charges on our account:

- Restaurant
- Room service
- Bars
- Health and leisure services
- In-house movies
- Accommodation

Task 8.19

What other charges are guests likely to incur when staying in a luxury, city centre hotel?

Such charges are noted by the relevant department and this information is then sent to the Front Office. If the hotel has a computer network then these charges can be sent to the Front Office via the various points of sale (POS). Otherwise the charges must be recorded and carried manually to the front desk.

The purposes of any guest billing/accounting system are:

1 To maintain up-to-date records and accounts for each guest in residence
2 To provide a breakdown and analysis of all charges incurred per guest and per department (revenue-producing area)
3 To provide departments and management with up-to-date financial information

The guest billing/accounting process is achieved by using one of the following methods:

- Tabular ledger
- Electronic billing machines
- Computerized guest accounting systems

Task 8.20

- *Investigate fully each of the above methods of guest billing/accounting*
- *Consider the advantages and disadvantages of each system*
- *Which of these methods do you consider the most suitable for:*

Small bed and breakfast resort hotel (15 bedrooms)?

Luxury business hotel, city centre location (300 bedrooms)?

Explain the reasons for your choice.

We will further evaluate different types of guest billing/accounting systems later.

Check-out

This is the final stage in the customer/guest cycle. At this stage the guest should have settled the outstanding account, or agreed to whom the final invoice should be sent (as is the procedure with prearranged company accounts).The Front Office will notify other departments of the guest's departure, and then update the hotel's records.

It is also at this stage in the cycle, when the customer leaves the hotel, leisure centre, restaurant, that we are left to measure how far we have succeeded in satisfying the customers' requirements.

Task 8.21

How can a Reception and Front Office measure overall success in satisfying their customer requirements?

This section therefore has been concerned with the varying requirements which customers/guests expect Reception and Front Office to provide These requirements obviously vary depending upon the sector being used.

However, the basic principles of Reception and Front Office always apply.

We have considered as part of the guest cycle the different procedures and documentation used; the range of in-house services available; and the different types of customers/guests who daily use a Reception or Front Office in the hospitality industry.

Test your knowledge

1 Why are first impressions crucial when applied to Reception and Front Office operations?
2 What are the different sectors of the hospitality industry where Reception and Front Office operations are found?
3 List the range of customers/guests who use Reception and Front Office operations in the hospitality industry.
4 Why is the Reception/Front Office often referred to as the 'nerve centre' of the hospitality operation?
5 Explain what is meant by the guest cycle.
6 What are the full range of Reception and Front Office procedures from 'reservation' to 'check-out'?
7 Explain the different types of documentation used by a hotel's Front Office.
8 What is the purpose of guest billing/accounting?

▪ RESERVATION SYSTEMS FOR MAXIMIZING OCCUPANCY AND ROOMS REVENUE ▪

When we measure a hotel's overall success one clear performance indicator is its ability to sell rooms. Unlike the food and beverage areas, where commodities can be stored if they are not immediately sold, accommodation (hotel bedrooms, leisure areas, function rooms) are immediately perishable. For example, if I have a hotel with 50 rooms and I only sell 40 rooms tonight, the potential revenue on the remaining 10 rooms is lost for ever. We cannot store the product; it has already perished!

This means that the pressure is on Reception and Front Office staff to maximize occupancy and rooms revenue. In order for them to achieve this we need effective and efficient reservation systems.

The purpose of this section therefore is to investigate and analyse the different reservation systems currently available. In addition, we will consider how Reception and Front Office staff can improve room sales using a variety of techniques combined with positive selling skills.

Reservation systems

Whenever I make a reservation for accommodation in a hotel I am aware that there are several ways in which my reservation may be handled. The method used will largely depend upon the type and size of the hotel, and, to a lesser extent, its location (country-house hotel, city-centre business hotel).

Most hotels now use either manual or computerized systems occasionally a combination of the two is employed.

Task 8.22

What factors will a hotel take into account when deciding whether to use manual or computer reservation systems?

We will therefore consider the range of reservation systems employed, starting with the manual, most basic recording methods.

The traditional bookings diary

The diary, as the name indicates, is exactly that – a diary of reservation details (Figure 8.7). It is completed on a daily basis recording basic guest information. Once the date has passed, a new diary page is placed in the loose-leaf binder. Diary entries are made in the order that they are received for a particular day. Some of the reservation details are also recorded on a separate booking chart.

To us this now appears to be a very labour-intensive method for recording reservations. It is really only suitable for very small hotels and

Date of arrival	3rd March 199–				
Date booked	**Name**	**Stay**	**Room**	**Terms**	**Other details**
27.1.9–	Mr/s Carter	2N	24	B & B	Arriving late
3.2.9–	Mr Swann	1N	16	Room only	—
5.2.9–	Miss Price	3N	12	Inclusive	—

Figure 8.7 A traditional bookings diary

guest houses, where there are relatively few bookings and reservation details at any one time.

Task 8.23

Name several small hotels, guest houses in your locality where you think the traditional booking diary for recording reservation details may be appropriate.

The Whitney Advance Booking Rack

A more advanced manual system is the Whitney Advance Booking Rack.
The Whitney system uses standard size cards or Shannon slips (Figure 8.8(a)). These can be colour coded to indicate different types of reservations. (tours, VIPs).

D/arrival	Name	Room type	Rate	D/departure
How received		Who by		Date received
Agency (if any)				
Account instructions			Confirmation date	

(a)

(b)

Figure 8.8 (a) A Whitney slip: (b) a Whitney advance reservation rack

The slips containing the reservation details are then placed in light metal carriers. These carriers then fit into vertical racks and sets of racks are usually attached to the wall behind the front desk (Figure 8.8(b)). Only the top part of the slip can be seen by either the receptionist or the guest when the carrier is placed in the rack.

As you can see from Figure 8.8(b), these racks are usually hung side by side and can be lifted out as necessary. They are usually arranged in sequence so that the next 30 days' slips are placed in order and are easily retrievable by the Reception staff. Another section on the racks will be devoted to carriers containing slips for the following twelve months. There will probably be a further section for any booking beyond the 12-month period.

When the specific date arrives the necessary rack is taken out and the other racks moved forward. This system ensures that all the information is as current and as up-to-date as possible.

The Whitney system was used extensively in larger hotels until recent years. However, the increasing use of computerized reservation systems has now surpassed the Whitney Rack, although it is still used as a back-up in some hotels.

Task 8.24

List the main advantages of the Whitney Advance Booking Rack when compared with the traditional bookings diary.

Room availability records

So far, the systems we have examined have been concerned with reservation details. However, the next stage involves us checking as to whether there are rooms available for the specific reservation requests. The main types of room availability records currently used in the hospitality and catering industry are:

- The bedroom book
- The conventional chart
- The density chart

The bedroom book

The bedroom book is only really suitable for very small hotels (Figure 8.9). It can be used in conjunction with the booking diary which was explained earlier in this section. The bedroom book operates on the basis of one page per day of the year and can be loose-leaf or fastened. The book lists all the rooms down the left-hand side of the page with room types (S, single; T, twin; D, double). It also allows space for the guest's name and any particular details which are entered on each page for the duration of their stay.

Task 8.25

- *What are the main restrictions in using the bedroom book?*
- *Why is the bedroom book suitable only for small hotels?*

The conventional chart

Slightly larger or medium-sized hotels found the bedroom book very difficult to work with. It was time consuming, included repetitive guest details, and was too small to cope with the volume of reservation information recorded. Therefore the next development was the conventional chart. This chart is visually appealing, easy to understand and contains most of the information that a receptionist

Date: _3rd March 199–_		
Room	**Name**	**Particulars**
101 (S)	Collins	
102 (T)	Smith	
103 (T)		
104 (S)		
105 (T)	Martin	
106 (T)		

Date: _4th March 199–_		
Room	**Name**	**Particulars**
101 (S)	Collins	
102 (T)		
103 (T)	Porter	
104 (S)		
105 (T)	Martin	
106 (T)		

Figure 8.9 A bedroom book

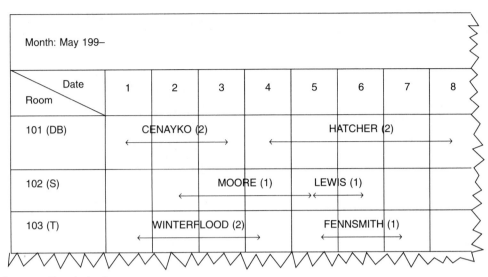

Month: May 199–

Date Room	1	2	3	4	5	6	7	8
101 (DB)		CENAYKO (2) ←———————→			HATCHER (2) ←———————→			
102 (S)			MOORE (1) ←———————→		LEWIS (1) →←———→			
103 (T)		WINTERFLOOD (2) ←———————→			FENNSMITH (1) ←———————→			

Figure 8.10 A conventional chart

needs to know immediately when charting further reservations (Figure 8.10).

It operates on the basis of an arrow system, with the arrow starting on the day of arrival and ending on the day of departure, e.g.

4th   5th   6th   7th   8th

←————Hatcher (2)————→

The arrow is usually placed midway through the column (12 noon) to clearly indicate arrival and departure days. The guest's name is printed above the arrow line with the number of guests in brackets. The left-hand column shows the room number and type. Additional guest information is recorded in the booking diary. The conventional chart is usually produced on a monthly basis so that all the reservations for a particular month are visible on one sheet.

Task 8.26

Despite its many positive features the conventional chart has several limitations. – Evaluate these possible limitations and list them in what you consider to be the ascending order of importance.

The density chart

The density chart reservation system is used mainly in medium-to-large hotels.
It was designed to overcome the main weaknesses associated with the conventional chart. You should have identified several of these weaknesses in Task 8.26.

However, the density chart can only be used effectively in hotels where there are standard rooms. This is because the principle of the density chart method is to block rooms of a particular type together. It is impossible therefore to differentiate between rooms of the same type. As a result, the Reception staff need only allocate rooms to guests when they arrive and are checking in.

The system is very simple to operate (Figure 8.11). For each day of the year a density chart sheet is produced showing the blocks of particular room types available. These blocks act as countdown indicators to the Front Office staff. When a reservation is received the receptionist indicates that a particular room type has been booked by putting a stroke through the highest remaining number available for that room type. In Figure 8.11 the Front Office staff can clearly identify that on 30 March 199– there are:

Density chart for 30ᵗʰ March 199–

Twins

96	95	94	93	92	91	90	89	88	87
86	85	84	83	82	81	80	79	78	77
76	75	74	73	72	71	70	69	68	67
66	65	64	63	62	61	60	59	58	57
56	55	54	53	52	51	50	49	48	47
46	45	44	43	42	41	40	39	38	37
36	35	34	33	32	31	30	29	28	27
26	25	24	23	22	21	20	19	18	17
16	15	14	13	12	11	10	9	8	7
6	5	4	3	2	1	–1	–2	–3	–4
–5	–6	–7	–8	–9	–10	–11	–12	–13	–14

Singles

48	47	46	45	44	43	42	41	40	39
38	37	36	35	34	33	32	31	30	29
28	27	26	25	24	23	22	21	20	19
18	17	16	15	14	13	12	11	10	9
8	7	6	5	4	3	2	1	–1	–2
–3	–4	–5	–6	–7	–8	–9	–10	–11	–12

Suites

16	15	14	13	12	11	10	9	8	7
6	5	4	3	2	1	–1	–2	–3	–4

Density chart for 31ˢᵗ March 199–

Twins

96	95	94	93	92	91	90	89	88	87
86	85	84	83	82	81	80	79	78	77
76	75	74	73	72	71	70	69	68	67
66	65	64	63	62	61	60	59	58	57
56	55	54	53	52	51	50	49	48	47
46	45	44	43	42	41	40	39	38	37
36	35	34	33	32	31	30	29	28	27
26	25	24	23	22	21	20	19	18	17
16	15	14	13	12	11	10	9	8	7
6	5	4	3	2	1	–1	–2	–3	–4
–5	–6	–7	–8	–9	–10	–11	–12	–13	–14

Singles

48	47	46	45	44	43	42	41	40	39
38	37	36	35	34	33	32	31	30	29
28	27	26	25	24	23	22	21	20	19
18	17	16	15	14	13	12	11	10	9
8	7	6	5	4	3	2	1	–1	–2
–3	–4	–5	–6	–7	–8	–9	–10	–11	–12

Suites

16	15	14	13	12	11	10	9	8	7
6	5	4	3	2	1	–1	–2	–3	–4

Figure 8.11 A two-night density chart

- 82 twin rooms still available
- 40 single rooms still available
- 14 suites still available

On the following night, 31 March 199–, we can see that there are:

- 85 twin rooms still available
- 41 single rooms still available
- 15 suites still available

The density chart system also allows receptionists to overbook. This is a particularly useful device as many hotels deliberately overbook in the knowledge that almost certainly there will be late cancellations. This technique enables hotels to achieve higher occupancy levels, thus maximizing rooms revenue.

In Figure 8.11 we can see that the hotel management allow up to a maximum of 14 twins, 12 singles, and four suites to be overbooked on any one night, hoping that there will be cancellations.

Task 8.27

- *List the main differences between the conventional chart and density chart reservation systems*
- *What are the main advantages and disadvantages of the density chart system?*
- *Which system provides the most satisfactory reservation procedures for a 50-bedroom budget hotel based in a large town? Explain the reasons for your choice.*

Computerized systems

As you may appreciate, many of the computer reservation systems have been created on the basis of previous manual systems. Most large hotels now handle all their reservations via a computer system. Computers can cope with greater volumes of information and can provide more up-to-date information regarding rooms availability than was possible with traditional systems.

When a receptionist wishes to make a reservation he or she accesses the advance reservations part of the Front Office program, and then calls up the availability display for the night(s) being requested. This process is similar to using a density chart as the computer will now display the number of rooms of each type available on a particular night (Figure 8.12).

If the reservation request is for several consecutive nights the receptionist simply scans forward to check the availability on those future dates. It is interesting to note that Front Office computer programs are now written with 'booking horizons' of up to five years ahead of the current date. When the receptionist is sure that there is availability for that particular reservation request he or she will enter the

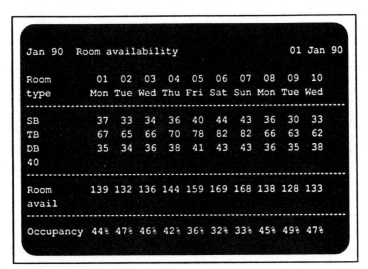

Figure 8.12 An advance reservations screen

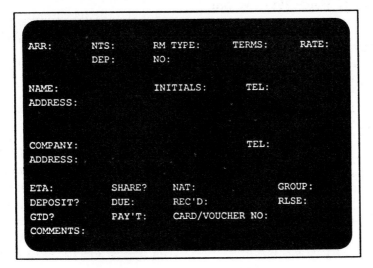

Figure 8.13 A bookings screen

booking onto the computer. The screen display for entering the booking is very similar in format and content to the reservation form which we considered earlier.

Once the details have been completed and confirmed with the guest, either face to face or on the telephone, the receptionist will then instruct the computer to accept the booking. The computer will automatically deduct the requested room from the overall total remaining rooms available (Figure 8.13). The screen display will then reset itself ready to accept another reservation.

This whole process is very quick, and once the receptionist is familiar with the system it is far less time consuming than handling reservations via a manual system.

Increasing room sales using improved selling techniques

We have now considered the range of reservation systems available. From the most basic to the latest computerized system, the purpose of any reservation process is to maximize occupancy and rooms revenue.

However, no matter how simple or advanced the reservation system, it will not achieve maximum operational effectiveness if the person using the system:

- Does not fully understand it
- Has poor product knowledge and selling skills

It is therefore necessary in our study of reservation systems to consider the role of those people using the systems – the receptionists.

Obviously any receptionist needs to understand the reservation system with which he or she is working. Unless the receptionist has 100 per cent appreciation of the operation and capabilities of the system, there is little hope that maximized occupancy and rooms revenue will be attained.

Training, retraining and updating are therefore essential features of any receptionist's job. As new systems are introduced and technology is improved the receptionist must accept that attendance at training sessions becomes an integral part of the day-to-day work role.

Task 8.28

- *Consider the advantages and disadvantages of using computerized reservation systems*
- *Are computerized reservation systems suitable for all types of hotels? Give reasons for your answer.*

Task 8.29

- *Compare the reservation systems employed at two hotels in your locality.*
- *How are they different?*
- *Which system do you consider is the most efficient? (If possible use two contrasting hotels for this task!)*

Task 8.30

- *What barriers might you have to overcome when encouraging receptionists to attend training sessions intended to introduce them to new or updated reservation systems?*

● *What particular problems might you encounter when the training is concerned with the transition from manual to computerized reservation systems?*

However, no matter how advanced the reservation system and well-trained the staff in its use, the system will still not help to maximize occupancy and rooms revenue if the receptionist has poor communication and selling skills.

Efficient reservation system + poor selling skills = poor occupancy and revenue.

We therefore need to investigate the several methods used to increase revenue, which will include improved communication and selling skills.

Methods of increasing revenue

The main objective of any Reception or Front Office operation is to sell space. In a hotel this function is particularly concerned with selling bed space, i.e. bedrooms! In fact it can be argued that in order for a Front Office to be successful the staff must attain the following two key aims:

1 Maximize occupancy
2 Maximize revenue

Now because of the nature of the hospitality industry it is not possible to achieve 100 per cent occupancy every night with every guest paying the full advertised room rate (known as the 'rack rate'). Front Office managers therefore have to achieve something of a balancing act as they try to sell rooms at the highest possible price without going beyond the point that potential guests are prepared to pay.

● Sell too high and guests will choose instead to stay with the cheaper competition
● Sell too low and the hotel is full of discounted business with reduced revenue

How to get more and better bookings

The Front Office is not simply an order-taking department that takes or rejects bookings, it is also a major selling department.

1 *Sell hospitality* Encourage the Reception staff to use positive body language, including smiling. This is dealt with in greater detail in Unit 3. It is essential that the staff create the right 'friendly' impression, using body language to convey interest in the person with whom they are dealing. Smiling, open gestures and eye contact convey enthusiasm and encouragement – you will create the right first impression!

2 *Offer Alternatives* If the hotel is full, offer the guest an alternative date. Most potential guests will not be prepared to change their travel plans. However, a significant percentage may be prepared to alter their arrangements if you can guarantee them a room. If the guest requests a single room and there are none left offer a twin or double for single occupancy. This will be more expensive, but many guests will agree to this rather than face the inconvenience of having to find alternative accommodation in another hotel.

3 *Use the guest's name* People like to feel wanted, that they belong. Therefore when you have found out the guest's name, use it! It sounds personal, as though you know them, and most people prefer being called Mr Moore/Mrs Hatcher rather than Sir/Madam. However, don't be over-familiar. Only use Christian names where it is appropriate to do so. You must be professional at all times, and over-familiarity can also lead to many other problems!

4 *Sell other hospitality facilities when the booking is made* Ask 'Do you need anything else?' 'Can I book you a table in the restaurant?' Such phrases are helpful to the guest and improve our standard of service – But, at the same time, the receptionist is selling!

5 *Encourage the guest to reserve accommodation for their next visit before they leave the hotel* Again, sometimes this is a successful selling

technique with regular guests. The right time to ask is when the guest is at the Front Office during check-out waiting for the bill. While the guest waits for the bill to be processed and printed he/she has absolutely nothing to do, so sell!

6 *Overbook* Most hotels deliberately operate an overbooking policy. From experience the hotel management can predict the possible number of guests who 'won't show'. This figure is usually expressed as a percentage. The Reception staff are therefore allowed to overbook by, say, 10 per cent on a given day. This figure may change depending on the day of the week, time of the year, etc. You should note that this is a controversial issue. Obviously there are problems if all the guests who have booked do arrive! However, usually this practice assists management to achieve higher occupancy and revenue figures.

Task 8.31

What other selling techniques can receptionists use to improve:

- *Accommodation sales?*
- *Overall sales in the hotel?*

The most important feature therefore of the Reception/Front Office is that it is a selling area. With properly trained staff great improvements can be made not only to accommodation sales but also to the overall sales of the hospitality unit. Reception staff should be encouraged to sell at every opportunity. The criteria for selling are simple:

1 Know your product
2 Believe in your product

If the Front Office/Reception staff apply these criteria selling becomes easier and improved sales inevitable!

In this section we have therefore investigated and analysed the range of Reception and Front Office reservation systems used in the hospitality industry. Currently there is an increasing and necessary use of computerized reservation systems in many hotels. However, it is important to remember that in the smaller establishments, which make up the majority of the UK hospitality industry, the traditional manual systems are still widely used. Certainly in the smallest guest house a manual reservation system will be far more adaptable and cost-effective than the latest computer technology!

However, no matter what reservation system is employed, it will be of little benefit if the reception staff cannot apply selling skills to maximize occupancy and rooms revenue. We have therefore considered the role of the Reception/Front Office as a major selling area within a hospitality unit. This analysis has included the variety of selling techniques that we can use to improve not only accommodation sales but also overall hospitality and catering sales.

Test your knowledge

1 What is an 'advance reservation'?
2 How does the traditional bookings diary operate?
3 List the different types of room availability records.
4 What is a bedroom book?
5 In which types of hotels would a conventional chart be used?
6 Why is a density chart not suitable in hotels with non-standard rooms?
7 List the benefits of a computerized reservation system?
8 What selling skills can the Reception/Front Office use to improve room sales?
9 How can the Reception/Front Office improve overall hospitality and catering sales?

• APPROPRIATE RECEPTION AND FRONT OFFICE INFORMATION SYSTEMS •

In this section it is necessary to apply much of the knowledge relating to Reception and Front Office operations that we have investigated in the previous sections. This will involve using and evaluating several Reception and Front Office information systems.

You may find that part of your GNVQ programme involves visiting various sectors of the hospitality and catering industry. Other students may experience periods of work placement during the GNVQ where they work alongside full- or part-time employees of a particular sector. If you visit or complete work placement within a Reception or Front Office you will find it very useful to complete this section of the workbook based on your experiences in industry.

As well as applying and evaluating Front Office information systems, this section will also introduce you to the different types of data and statistical information which are essential for any reception operation, particularly within the hotel sector of the industry.

Reception and Front Office information

By their very nature Reception and Front Office areas are dumping grounds for information and data. As we have already discovered most communications are directed via Reception. In fact, the Front Office is often referred to as the nerve centre for all information and communication activities.

These information and communication activities are not only produced internally within the organization, but, by the very nature of the hospitality and catering industry, they are also directed from/to external sources (Figure 8.14). For example, the receptionist

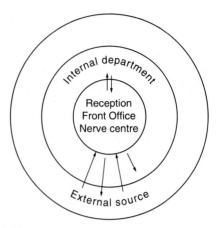

Figure 8.14

may deal with a reservation enquiry from outside:

External source → Reception

Alternatively, a company may query an invoice they have been sent from the hotel accountant. This call will be answered initially by Reception, so the communication chain will be

External source → Reception → Internal department

Information and communication are therefore obviously linked. All information is received via some method of communication. Indeed if you think about it, communication is what the Reception and Front Office activities are all about. All the equipment used by receptionists is concerned with storing, processing or communicating information.

Task 8.32

List as many devices as possible which are used in the Reception and Front Office area to store, process or communicate information.

Types of Front Office information

It is now appropriate to analyse the different types of information that the Front Office would expect to receive, handle and process on a typical day. As you already know, some of the information is handled by specific systems which we have considered in the previous sections. The following list indicates the range of information that is processed in the Reception/Front Office area:

- Customer requirements
- Reservation and registration details
- Customer/guest accounts
- Customer history data
- Forecasting and statistical data

Customer requirements

When customers make enquiries or reservations they sometimes state specific requirements which they expect the hospitality establishment to provide as a condition of their booking. The requirement may be something basic such as a specific room type in a hotel, or for tea/coffee to be served at a particular time to delegates at a conference venue. Other requirements that a guest may request when making a hotel booking may include:

1 Car parking space to be reserved
2 Room on the ground or lower floors
3 Fresh flowers/fruit in room on arrival
4 Non-feather duvet and pillows
5 Dinner to be booked in the hotel restaurant

Such information will be recorded on the guest's reservation form and transferred to the bookings diary as appropriate. Where a computer system is employed these requirements are added to the booking screen details.

Task 8.33

- *Consider other customer requirements which guests may request when making a hotel booking*
- *List those customer requirements which may be expected from customers making booking requests with reception desks in the following sectors:*
  Leisure centre
  Residential home
  Pub restaurant

Reservation information systems

We have already analysed the range of reservation systems employed in Reception and Front Office areas in the previous section. These include:

- The bedroom book
- The conventional chart
- The density chart
- Computerized systems

Evaluating suitable reservation systems

We are therefore now able to make comparisons between the efficiency and effectiveness of each particular reservation system. It is necessary to appreciate the limitations, advantages and disadvantages of each system. It is also important to assess the suitability of different reservation systems for different types of hotels.

Task 8.34

Paul Jackson has recently become the owner of the Fairway Hotel, a golf and country house hotel in the Lake District. There are forty rooms with a variety of room types. Due to the nature of the building it was not possible to standardize the rooms. Mr Jenkins wishes to install a new reservation system. He is not concerned whether a manual or computer system is adopted. Advise Mr Jackson as to which reservation system is likely to be the most suitable for this type of hotel. Explain the reasons for your choice, and indicate why you have rejected other available systems.

Computer/guest accounting systems

Earlier we identified the range of guest billing/accounting systems employed in Reception and Front Office operations. To remind you, there are three main types:

1 The tabular ledger
2 Electronic billing machines
3 Computerized guest accounting systems

You should have made notes in you folder or notebook on each of these systems.

As with reservation systems, the electronic billing machines and computerized guest accounting systems have been produced, and the appropriate software written, based on the principle of the traditional manual system, i.e. the tabular ledger. It is important therefore that you understand the process by which a guest account is produced using a tabular ledger.

Tabular ledger	Bill	Totals
Date	Date	
Room no. ———	Room no. ———	———
Name ———	Name ———	———
Sleepers ———	Sleepers ———	———
Rate	Rate	
B/fwd ———	B/fwd ———	———
Room ———	Room ———	———
Breakfast ———	Breakfast ———	———
Lunch ———	Lunch ———	———
Dinner ———	Dinner ———	———
Beverages ———	Beverages ———	———
Beers ———	Beers ———	———
Wines———	Wines———	———
Spirits etc. ———	Spirits etc. ———	———
Minerals ———	Minerals ———	———
Telephone ———	Telephone ———	———
Papers ———	Papers ———	———
Paid outs	Paid outs	
Totals		
Allowances ———	Allowances ———	———
Cash ———		
Ledger		
C/fwd ———	C/fwd ———	———

Figure 8.15 A vertical tabular ledger with bill superimposed

The tabular ledger

The main principle of the tabular ledger is that it provides a visual record of all charges incurred by guests during a 24-hour period (Figure 8.15). The Reception staff can see at a glance the charges that a particular guest has incurred, and the areas where these charges have been made. The 'tab' therefore produces the following information:

- A record of all charges, credits and outstanding balances
- A separate total for each guest's bill
- A separate total for each item/area of guest expenditure

An effective computer billing system should therefore produce and display such information with equal clarity.

Evaluating suitable guest accounting systems

The tabular ledger is still used in many smaller hotels where there are fewer rooms and guest turnover is relatively low. Although electronic billing machines were very popular until recently, these have now been replaced in the majority of larger establishments by computerized systems which can handle large numbers of guest accounts very quickly and efficiently.

Customer history data

The purpose of storing customer history data is to enable the hospitality establishment to provide a better service for regular customers/guests. People assume that if they regularly use a leisure club, short-stay residential home, hotel etc., the staff will remember their specific requirements. Of course, due to the volume of customers that staff deal with, this is not usually possible, except for those staff with very good memories! Therefore in order to assist us to provide this more personalized service many hospitality establishments use a system of recording details and requirements on a card index system.

In hotels some guests always like the same room or they prefer a certain table in the restaurant. Other guests always like fresh flowers in their room on arrival, or request particular newspapers. The guest history card therefore typically contains the following details:

- Date of previous stays
- Rooms used
- Total bills
- Any special likes or dislikes
- Other details

Task 8.35

Mr Jenkins at the Fairway Hotel is very pleased with the reservation system you suggested for his 40-bedroom country-house hotel. He now wishes to install a customer/guest accounting system for residents Suggest a suitable accounting system for this type of hotel. Explain the reasons for your choice, and why you rejected the alternative systems available.

Task 8.36

Design a guest history card for the Fairway Hotel. Complete the card as appropriate using the following guest information: 'Sir Paul Jordan always likes room 104 if available. If not, room 406. He always requests an early-morning call at 7.30 a.m. (including weekends), and reads The Independent. His most recent stays to date were 4–11 December (inc.) 1993, and 6–14 July (inc.) 1994. He always settles his account using Visa. His average account is £700–800.'

It is necessary to update such cards every time the guest uses the hotel. This can be time consuming for the Reception and Front Office staff, and therefore recording guest data is an expensive system to use. As a result, only luxury hotels which provide a very 'personalized' service tend to operate guest history records using a manual filing system.

However, in hotels with appropriate computerized systems the recording of customer history data is making something of a return. This is because it is easy to transfer guest reservation and registration details to other database files which are part of the complete Reception/Front Office system. Therefore even large, very transient hotels can improve their overall customer service due to technological advances in information systems.

Forecasting and statistical data

As part of its daily operation the Front Office will regularly produce information which assists management in assessing the overall performance of the accommodation product. In the same way as a food and beverage manager produces regular reports which comment upon trading levels, profitability, etc. in the restaurants and bars, the Front Office manager or head receptionist must produce Front Office/accommodation-based performance indicators. These performance indicators assist management for the following reasons. They:

1 Compare actual performance against projected performance. Are targets being achieved?
2 Enable forward planning – formulating the hotel's marketing and pricing policy
3 Identify sources of reservations – which companies are taking advantage of discounted rates?
4 Enable the compilation of operational reports and financial reports
5 Allow the business to identify how successful it is in terms of numbers of customers or the volume of transactions, as well as the volume of overall sales
6 Identify weaknesses in the selling skills of staff

It is necessary to be familiar with the following basic performance indicators.

Room occupancy (%)

This is calculated by:

$$\frac{\text{Actual number of rooms occupied}}{\text{Total number of rooms available}} \times 100$$

This will give a percentage figure of the total rooms occupied on a particular night/week, etc.

Sleeper occupancy (%)

This is calculated by:

$$\frac{\text{Actual number of sleepers in residence}}{\text{Total number of sleeper spaces available}} \times 100$$

This will give a percentage figure as to the number of people in residence against available bed space. You should remember that this figure will be different to the room occupancy (%) as it allows for two people in a twin room, three people in a triple, etc.

Double/twin occupancy (%)

This is calculated by:

$$\frac{\text{Actual number of twin/double rooms occupied}}{\text{Total number of twin/double rooms available}} \times 100$$

This gives you the percentage number of double and twin rooms occupied, excluding single rooms.

Average room rate

This is calculated by:

$$\frac{\text{Rooms revenue}}{\text{Number of rooms occupied}}$$

This figure will indicate the amount in pounds which each room earned on a particular night/week, etc. It is particularly useful in a hotel where a variety of different rates are available.

Average sleeper rate

This is calculated by:

$$\frac{\text{Rooms revenue}}{\text{Number of sleepers in residence}}$$

This figure will be different to the average room rate. It indicates the amount spent per guest on accommodation. It is useful to compare this figure with the average room rate.

You should now attempt the accommodation-based performance indicator exercise in the Resource Pack.

Task 8.37

Explain how Front Office statistical data (performance indicators) help in the effective management of a Reception/Front Office operation.

Front Office information systems which assist customer service

We have considered the range of Front Office information systems available, and evaluated these for ease of use and effectiveness. However,

due to advances in technology there have been developments in certain Front Office systems which now enable us to provide an improved customer service.

Computerized check-in

This is now very common in many medium/large hotels. It is an extension of the computerized reservation system. Instead of the previous check-in delay which occurred while the receptionist searched for the booking, the guest is now identified by surname or reservation number on a screen similar to that shown in Figure 8.16.

Guest details can be checked against the initial reservation and further information added. The whole process is very quick and hopefully reduces any queuing which may have previously occurred during busy check-in times.

Pre-printed registration cards

Included as part of the computerized check-in, many Front Office systems can now be programmed to pre-print registration cards prior to the guest's arrival. Obviously this has the advantage of making the check-in procedure even quicker. The guest has only to check the details on the registration card, and is usually required to sign it (although this is not a legal requirement).

Other advances in Front Office information systems

Other advances due to improved information systems include the 'automated check-in'. This allows the guest to check-in without any staff having to be present. Such a system, which is activated by swiping a credit card through a PDQ machine, already operates in Europe. It relies on the guest using a check-in machine which has a computer screen displaying a series of 'menu' alternatives. The guest chooses the

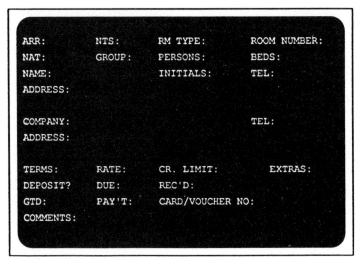

```
ARR:          NTS:        RM TYPE:        ROOM NUMBER:

NAT:          GROUP:      PERSONS:        BEDS:

NAME:                     INITIALS:       TEL:

ADDRESS:


COMPANY:                                  TEL:

ADDRESS:


TERMS:        RATE:       CR. LIMIT:      EXTRAS:

DEPOSIT?      DUE:        REC'D:

GTD:          PAY'T:      CARD/VOUCHER NO:

COMMENTS:
```

Figure 8.16 A check-in screen

appropriate menu options, i.e. room requirements, payment methods, etc. When all the information has been keyed in, the machine displays a personalized welcome and issues a computer-coded room key.

However, despite such a technological advance this system has not become particularly popular or well used. This is probably because the 'hospitality' element and personalized service associated with the check-in procedure is lost using such a 'hi-tech' process.

Task 8.38

List the positive and negative effects of the increased use of computerized information systems in a Reception/Front Office area. In which sectors will such technological advances be best/least suited?

Conclusion

This section has therefore been concerned with investigating the range of Front Office information systems. These have included

reservation systems, customer/guest accounting systems, customer history data, and statistical analysis using Front Office performance indicators. We have also considered how communication and information are handled by the Reception/Front Office and how information systems are compared in terms of effectiveness, efficiency and suitability for the varying types of Front Office operations.

Finally we considered the latest developments in Front Office information systems, and how such advances in technology are assisting the Reception staff to provide an improved level of customer service.

Test your knowledge

1 Why are Reception and Front Office areas 'dumping grounds' for information and data?
2 What is meant by:
  'External communications'?
  'Internal communications'?
3 List several specific requirements which a guest may expect a hospitality establishment to provide as a condition of the booking.
4 What are the main considerations for a hotel when investigating a new reservation system?
5 What features should be provided on an efficient/effective guest accounting system?

6 Why do we produce Front Office performance indicators? What do they measure?

7 Explain the latest developments in Front Office information systems which enable Reception staff to provide an improved level of customer service.

▪ THE IMPLICATIONS OF LEGAL REQUIREMENTS GOVERNING RECEPTION AND FRONT OFFICE OPERATIONS ▪

All business operations are governed by rules and regulations. Certainly the hospitality and catering industry is subject to a great deal of legislation and many legal requirements. Much of the legislation is applicable to all areas of hospitality and catering, and will have been investigated in other units on your GNVQ programme:

● Health and safety at work
● Fire precautions
● VAT
● Data protection
● Trade descriptions/sale of goods

However, there is additional specific legislation which applies to the Front Office area. This legislation has major implications on the operation of the hotel's Reception/Front Office. The purpose of this section therefore is to investigate this legislation, and the associated legal requirements which affect Reception and Front Office staff as they carry out their daily work activities.

The history of hotel legislation

Many of the laws which apply to hotels today developed from the seventeenth and eighteenth centuries. During this time travelling was a hazardous occupation, and travellers were just as likely to be robbed by the innkeeper as they were to be set upon by highwaymen. Many of the laws have evolved through custom and practice; to make sure that inns were a safe haven of rest, and that the innkeeper was responsible for the care and well-being of travellers.

Definition of a hotel

When is a hotel not a hotel? Yes, this may sound like some kind of joke, but actually the question is very serious and the answer affects how a hotel can operate. The answer also has implications on the manager's responsibilities and the duties which must be carried-out.

The Hotel Proprietors' Act 1956 defines a hotel ('inn') as: 'an establishment held out by the proprietor as offering food, drink and, if so required, sleeping accommodation, without special contract, to any traveller presenting himself who appears able and willing to pay a reasonable sum for the services and facilities provided and who is in a fit state to be received'.

Hotels in law

Guests stay in a wide range of accommodation – hotels, motels, guest houses, boarding houses, holiday camps. The Hotel Proprietors' act 1956 defines the responsibilities for 'inns'. But what is an 'inn'?

Most hotels offering accommodation, including the Savoy and Ritz in London, the Balmoral in Edinburgh and the many Forte Post Houses throughout the UK are 'inns'. However, many establishments which call themselves inns (The Welcome Inn in Blackpool) are not covered by this Act because they have no accommodation – they are usually public houses!

The situation becomes even more unclear when we consider establishments with the title 'private hotel'. These may or may not be inns. Generally, private hotels are those that choose their guests in some way or other. For example, some private hotels in town and city areas offer accommodation only to actors and actresses who are appearing at the local theatre with their touring stage show.

However, so that the picture does not become too confused it is convenient to refer to the hotels as defined in the 1956 Act as 'inns'. All other establishments, which are not 'inns', are referred to as 'private hotels'.

What was the original purpose of the inns that were opened near to the developing road network?

What types of 'guests' did they accommodate?

Inns versus private hotels

The distinction between inns and private hotels is of importance in three main ways:

1 In determining the duty to receive travellers
2 The responsibility for guests' property
3 The proprietor's rights in respect of unpaid bills

You should remember that the name given to an establishment does not provide a reliable guide as to whether it is an inn or a private hotel. It is up to the proprietor to decide whether he or she wishes to conduct the premises as an inn and to accept the duties and obligations arising out of it, or whether to be regarded as a private hotelier in the eyes of the law.

Inns	*Private hotels*
Duty to receive	
Must provide all respectable travellers with accommodation if available. Must also provide refreshment (food and drink).	Have a right to choose their guests and complete freedom to refuse them

Responsibility for guests' property

Loss of or damage to guests' property is, with certain exceptions, the liability of the innkeeper.	Not liable for guests' property unless the proprietor (or staff) can be proved negligent.

Unpaid bills

Have the right to detain a guest's property as security for an unpaid bill and a right of sale subject to certain conditions.	Have no right to detain guests' property as security for an unpaid bill.

List three establishments in your locality which you consider to be 'inns', and three which may be classified as 'private hotels'.

Legal duties of an innkeeper: care of guests' luggage

The law requires the innkeeper to undertake responsibility for the reception and safekeeping of all 'reasonable' items of luggage brought in by the guest. This liability extends from the midnight prior to the guest's arrival to the midnight following the departure.

Such items of luggage must be *reasonable* (i.e. average hand luggage).
The court will decide what is reasonable. However, the 1956 Act states that the innkeeper is no longer liable for:

● The safety of cars
● Property left in cars
● Horses or other types of animal

Task 8.41

For what traditional reason are horses specifically mentioned in this legislation?

Task 8.42

List other items of reasonable luggage for which the innkeeper could be legally responsible.

Extent of the innkeeper's liability

Under certain circumstances there is:

1 No liability
2 Full liability
3 Limited liability

No liability

Where the loss of or damage to the guest's property is caused by:

- An Act of God
- Action of the Queen's enemies (i.e. if war breaks out and the hotel is bombed)
- Total negligence on the part of the guest then the innkeeper incurs no liability whatsoever.

Full liability

The innkeeper is fully liable to the full extent of the loss or damage to the guest's property if:

- The loss or damage was caused solely by the negligence or wilful act of the innkeeper or his staff
- The goods had been entrusted to the innkeeper for safekeeping, or offered for safekeeping but refused by the management

Therefore if the reasonable item of property is accepted – hotel liable, but if the reasonable item of property is refused – hotel still liable!

Task 8.43

Suggest an example where the loss of the guest's property is entirely the fault of the innkeeper (or staff).

Limited liability

Where the loss or damage to the guest's property does not fit exactly into either of the above categories and, where the innkeeper has displayed a statutory notice concerning loss or damage to guest's property in a conspicuous part of the premises (i.e. near the main entrance or Reception area), then the innkeeper will be liable for a limited amount.

These limits are:

- £50 per article
- £100 maximum per guest regardless of the number of articles

If the statutory notice (see below) is not adequately displayed at or near the reception desk or main entrance then the innkeeper is liable for the full amount of the property.

Task 8.44

Suggest an example of limited liability where the loss or damage is a shared responsibility between the innkeeper and guest.

Other factors concerning the care of guests' luggage

Depositing valuables

When the guest leaves valuables with the innkeeper for safekeeping the guest must make it clear that he or she is doing so. Merely leaving them at the Reception/Front Office in a sealed packet without any word of explanation is not enough.

The property in question must be left with either the innkeeper in person or another member of the hotel staff who is an authorized agent of the Innkeeper (e.g. Receptionist, Front Office manager).

HOTEL PROPRIETORS ACT 1956

NOTICE
LOSS OR DAMAGE TO GUESTS' PROPERTY

Under the Hotel Proprietors Act, 1956, an hotel proprietor may in certain circumstances be liable to make good any loss of or damage to a guest's property even though it was not due to any fault of the proprietor or staff of the hotel.

This liability however:

(a) extends only to the property of guests who have engaged sleeping accommodation at the hotel;

(b) is limited to £50 for any one article and a total of £100 in the case of any one guest, except in the case of property which has been deposited, or offered for deposit, for safe custody;

(c) does not cover motor cars or other vehicles of any kind or other property left in them or horses or other live animals.

This notice does not constitute an admission either that the Act applies to this hotel or that liability thereunder attaches to the proprietor of this hotel in any particular case.

Disclaimer notices

The duty which the innkeeper owes to the guest in connection with their luggage cannot be evaded by means of a suitable exemption clause in the contract with the guest. Neither can an innkeeper contract out of his liability to guests who have engaged sleeping accommodation by exhibiting notices disclaiming responsibility (see below)

Non-resident guests

The hotelier in a 'hotel in law' is only liable for the *reasonable* luggage of guests who actually stay in accommodation provided by the hotel. The hotelier is not responsible for the luggage of guests who merely have a meal in the hotel.

The rights of an innkeeper

So far we have only mentioned the duties owed by an innkeeper to the traveller. However, the innkeeper ('hotel-in-law') has one very important right over the traveller which the proprietor of a private hotel or guest house does not possess. *This is the right of lien.*

The right of lien

Where an establishment falls within the definition of a 'hotel-in-law', the innkeeper has the right to detain guests' luggage if they do not pay the bill.

The right of lien is, of course, a type of blackmail because:

1 The very last thing an innkeeper wants to do is to take a guest to court to sue for an outstanding bill, because such action is both very time consuming and very expensive
2 Neither does the innkeeper want to sell the guest's luggage because it will have almost no monetary value.

Hopefully, therefore, the luggage is worth more to the guest than the outstanding bill! The right of lien exists in order to encourage the guest to pay the bill. Although the luggage may be worth little to the innkeeper, it should be worth more than the price of the hotel bill to the customer.

Items which the innkeeper can retain

The innkeeper can retain *reasonable* items of luggage e.g.:
clothes, watches, jewellery, radios, etc.

Task 8.45

List other reasonable items of luggage that the innkeeper can retain.

CUSTOMERS' PROPERTY

It is regretted that no liability can be accepted for the property of customers. The staff are without authority to accept any articles on any other terms.

Excluded items

The innkeeper has no right of lien over the clothes a guest is wearing, cars, property left in cars, the guest themselves, or any animals or pets.

Sale of lien goods

The Innkeeper Act 1878 gives the innkeeper the right of sale over lien goods if the guest has not settled the bill within six weeks of staying at the hotel. The innkeeper must sell the goods by public auction.

At least four weeks before the sale the innkeeper must advertise the sale by an advertisement in a local and a London newspaper. The advertisement must:

- State the Innkeeper's intention to sell the property
- List the items to be sold
- Give details of the date, place and time of the sale
- Give the name of the guest concerned

Task 8.46

Suggest a local and a national newspaper where it would be appropriate to advertise the sale of lien goods.

Proceeds of the sale

From the proceeds of the sale the innkeeper is entitled to deduct:

- The outstanding bill
- The cost of advertising

- The cost of organizing the sale and the auctioneer's commission

If there is any money left over it belongs to the guest. This must be paid to the guest 'on demand'. However, where the proceeds are not enough the innkeeper has the right to sue the guest in civil court for the outstanding debt.

Summary

The legal differences between 'inns' ('hotels-in-law') and private hotels are as follows:

1 Any other establishment other than a 'hotel-in-law' does not need to be open 24 hours a day, 7 days a week, 365 days a year providing food and drink when demanded
2 The innkeeper must generally receive and accommodate all travellers. The private hotelier is completely free to pick and choose
3 A 'hotel-in-law' incurs some liability for the loss or damage to the property of guests even though it may not have been the fault of the innkeeper or the staff (i.e. £50 per item up to a maximum of £100 per guest)
4 A private hotelier is never liable for any amount unless it can be proved that either the hotelier or authorized staff were negligent
5 Only 'hotels-in law' have the right of lien over the property of a guest who fails to pay the bill. A private hotelier has no such right. The only action available is to sue for the outstanding debt in court

Other legislation governing Reception/Front Office procedures

As indicated at the beginning of this section, there is a great deal of legislation which affects the Reception/Front Office staff. However, much of this is common to all areas of hospitality and catering, and you will be introduced to this legislation when completing other GNVQ units. The following areas of legislation are of specific interest to Reception/Front Office operations:

- Price display
- Law of contract (bookings/reservations)
- Guest registration

Price display

Since February 1978 hotels and guest houses have been required to comply with the Tourism (Sleeping Accommodation Price Display) Order 1977. This means that hotels and guest houses have had to display their room tariffs at the reception desk.

The aim of this Order is to ensure that tourists can have adequate information concerning room prices before taking up accommodation. The rate for each room type must be shown, together with the amount of any taxes and service charge. The main provisions of the Order are as follows:

1 The Order applies in England, Scotland and Wales to hotels, inns, guest houses and self-catering establishments. This extends where sleeping accommodation is offered to guests who have not booked in advance, and the establishment has at least four bedrooms or eight beds to let
2 Beds and bedrooms normally occupied by the same person for more than 21 nights are not included in the Order
3 The notice must be legible and prominently displayed in the reception area or, in the absence of a reception area, at the entrance
4 The display notice should include the following information:
 The price of the room for one person
 The price of the room for two persons
 The price of a bed in any other type of room
 If the prices include VAT, this must be shown
5 If the prices do not include VAT, this must be shown together with the amount of tax

6 If there is a service charge, it must be included in the price shown
7 If meals are included as part of the charge for the room, this must be stated
8 Where there is a range of room rates, both the lowest and the highest rates must be shown

Task 8.47

Produce a notice displaying the tariff for single, double and twin rooms at the County Hotel. Invent the prices but ensure that the notice complies with the Tourism (Sleeping Accommodation Price Display) Order 1977.

Law of contract

All bookings and reservations for accommodation which are handled by the Reception/Front Office are covered by the law of contract. This is quite a technical area of the law, but the following basic information is necessary for all Front Office staff.

Booking contracts

Bookings and reservations are covered by the law of contract.

The contract

The contract is made when there is a definite offer and acceptance of the offer within a *reasonable* time period.

Written/verbal contracts

There is no need for written confirmation of a contract in law. Naturally, a verbal contract is more difficult to prove, but is a contract nonetheless.

Postal contracts

It is generally understood that when a contract is made by post it comes into being as soon as the acceptance is posted. In order to avoid liability when making an offer of accommodation by letter it is better to add the following clause:

'This offer is subject to the accommodation being available at the time of receipt of the reply.'

A letter of offer from a hotel does not constitute a contract. Only when the offer is accepted by the guest does the contract come into being.

Offer

The first stage of any contract is the offer. A potential guest enquires whether or not accommodation is available on a certain night. The receptionist states that there is a room available at £40 per night – the offer has been made.

The acceptance

Next is the acceptance of the offer. The guest can accept the offer, reject it or make a counter-offer.

If the guest accepts the offer then the contract is formed. Remember, there is no need for written confirmation, but a verbal contract is more difficult to prove so it is normal practice to request confirmation in writing.

Cancellation

Cancellation of bookings is in the favour of the guest. If the guest wishes to cancel a booking, the cancellation takes effect from the moment the guest posts the letter of cancellation. However, should the hotel wish to cancel the reservation, the hotel's letter of cancellation does not take effect until it is received by the guest.

Task 8.48

Draw a flow chart which describes the process on the part of the guest/hotel for making and confirming a reservation.

Guest registration

All guests on arrival to a hotel who are intending using sleeping accommodation have a legal obligation to 'register'. This means that the guest has a requirement to disclose certain information during the 'check-in' process. Registration serves three main functions:

1 It satisfies legal requirements
2 It provides a record of actual arrivals
3 It confirms the guest's agreement to the terms and conditions of the booking

We have investigated the two basic methods used to record guest registration:

● Registration book
● Registration card

Task 8.49

Which registration method is most suitable for:

● *Small guest house?*
● *Large luxury hotel?*

What are the advantages and disadvantages of each method?

Legal requirements

All the legal requirements for registration are contained in the Immigration (Hotel Record) Order 1972 which applies to both 'inns' and private hotels. One of the main requirements of this Order requires the hotelier to differentiate between *aliens* and *non-aliens*. At first these sound like really strange terms! Non-aliens include:

1 British passport holders
2 Commonwealth citizens
3 Citizens of the Republic of Ireland (Eire)
4 Members of NATO armed forces serving in the UK
5 Foreign nationals serving with the UK's armed forces
6 Foreign diplomats, envoys and their staff (these people are exempted by the Diplomatic Privileges Act 1964)

Task 8.50

What is the difference between aliens *and* non-aliens *for registration purposes?*

Non-alien registration

A non-alien aged 16 or more who is resident for one night or more is required to disclose both full-name and nationality. It is interesting to note that this requirement does not apply to a person who is using a hotel bedroom for a short-period day-let (no overnight accommodation).

In law there is no requirement for a guest to provide an address, not even their real name! Obviously, a hotel would be rather wary of guests who provided fictitious names and addresses. For example:

Mickey Mouse
Alton Towers
Staffordshire

However, the use of a false name is common practice among celebrities and VIPs who wish to retain some anonymity.

It is not legally necessary for the guest to physically sign the register. Therefore a husband can register on behalf of his wife or vice versa. *However, each individual must be registered.* This also explains why a tour guide or conference organizer can register on behalf of a group of guests. Again, each guest must be separately registered.

Hotels, however, do normally request that the guest signs the registration document. This is to confirm the guest's acceptance of the hotel's terms and conditions. The signature is not a legal requirement of the registration process, although most guests are unaware of this.

Alien registration

Aliens are classified as any persons who do not fit the criteria for non-aliens (see above). When completing the registration process, aliens have to provide the following additional information as well as their name and nationality:

- Details of their passport number (or registration certificate) and its place of issue
- Their next destination
- The address of their next destination, if known

This information is required so that the police and other authorities can check, if necessary, on the movements of overseas visitors to the UK.

It is a legal requirement for both alien and non-alien registration that the information provided must be kept by the hotel for a minimum of 12 months. It can be requested at any time during this period by the police or a Home Office representative.

Task 8.51

For what reasons may the police or the Home Office wish to have access to a hotel's guest registration details.

Conclusion

This final section therefore has been concerned with investigating the implications of the legal requirements which govern Reception and Front Office procedures. As we have seen, this legislation is very diverse and covers many aspects of the day-to-day operation of a hotel's Front Office.

Specifically, we have investigated the legislation that affects the rights and responsibilities of both the provider (hotel) and the guest. We have examined the implications of the relevant legal requirements, and how this legislation affects the receptionist and the procedures employed.

Test your knowledge

1 Explain the history of hotel legislation.
2 What is the difference between a 'hotel-in-law' and a private hotel?
3 What duties must an innkeeper provide/satisfy?
4 What legal duties does an innkeeper have for the safety of guests' luggage?
5 What is the legal validity in an 'inn' of disclaimer notices concerning the care of guests' luggage?
6 What is the right of lien?
7 What rights have guests to be provided with the price of accommodation?
8 How does the law of contract affect hotel bookings/reservations for accommodation?
9 Who is an 'alien' when applied to hotel registration?
10 What information must all overnight guests provide when completing the registration process?

EXERCISE

The Tiga Manor Hotel is 'hotel-in-law' which displays the 'loss or damage to guests' property' notice near the Front Office area. Recently the following occurrences have been reported to the hotel management.

1 Susan Jenkins, the chambermaid for Room 16, forgot to lock the room when she had finished her duties. During the morning a portable radio went missing from the room.
2 Mrs Bowler left her room door open while she checked on her children who were staying in another room further down the corridor. Although she was only away for a couple of minutes her expensive wedding ring was stolen.
3 Robin Fowler, a businessman, wished to deposit his gold watch at Reception. The receptionist said that it was the hotel's policy not to accept items for safekeeping from guests who were in residence only for one night. During the night his room was burgled, and the gold watch was one of the items stolen.

Explain fully the hotel's liability under the Hotel Proprietors' Act 1956 (if applicable) in each of the above cases. What amount of compensation, if any, will be payable?

▪ ASSIGNMENT ▪

Rationale and aims

The main objectives of the Front Office assignment are:

1 To enable you to see how a Front Office works in practice
2 To compare what you have learnt about Front Office work since the beginning of this GNVQ unit with an actual system in use
3 To discover to what extent computerized and manual systems are employed

Core skills

This assignment can give you the opportunity to achieve the following core skills:

Communication: 3.1, 3.2, 3.3
IT: 3.2, 3.3, 3.4
                   (If allowed access to the Front Office computer).

Grading opportunities

The following GNVQ advanced grading opportunities can be attained via this assignment:

● Planning
● Information seeking
● Evaluation

Background and role

1 Choose a hotel to visit on your study day/during a vacation period. The hotel should have a minimum of 20 letting bedrooms. You will need to spend some time in the Front Office as an observer.

2 Approach the management of the hotel by letter now, asking to allow you to make this visit to their hotel. Explain in your letter who you are, why you wish to make the visit, and suggest a few dates. It may be necessary to approach more than one hotel to arrange a visit.

3 You are required to produce a mini-project based on your observations. This should include relevant charts and diagrams, and associated documentation to support your findings. You should also prepare to make a short presentation based on the results of your mini-project to the rest of your group.

Task

Your mini-project should include the following points:

Element 8.1 1 Description of the hotel; its size, location, type of clientele, tariff, pattern of business throughout the week, year, etc. In-house services available

Element 8.1 2 Particular methods, procedures and documentation used by the Front Office during the guest cycle. (Sample documentation can be included if available, with an explanation of how it is used.)

Elements 8.2 and 8.3 3 Front Office systems employed: Manual or computer Full explanation of the reservation and guest billing system Other office equipment; fax, switchboard, etc.

Include plan/diagram of the Front Office lay-out.

Element 8.2 4 Methods of increasing revenue/occupancy: Does the hotel offer bargain breaks, theme weekends, etc. in

order to increase occupancy during quieter periods?
What other selling techniques are used by the Front Office staff?

Element 8.4 **5** Legal aspects:
Does the Hotel Proprietors Act apply?
Is the right of lien used?
What other legal procedures are evident in the Front Office?

Grading opportunity
An evaluation of your visit:
How have you benefited?
What have you learnt?

Further reading

Abbott, P. and Lewry, S., *Front Office: Procedures, Social Skills and Management*, Butterworth-Heinemann, Oxford, 1991

THE WORK LOG

In order to obtain more than a pass grade you must show that you are capable of planning your approach to the assessment, gather the appropriate information and use it properly, and finally, show that you are able to learn from your experiences in other words, that you can:

Plan
Gather information
Evaluate

This work log is divided into four parts:

Part 1
This gives detailed information about what you need to do in order to obtain a Merit or Distinction grade for each of the above.

Part 2
This is for you to write down how you intend to tackle the assessment, along with dates and deadlines for particular tasks to be completed.

Part 3
This is for you to record the activities which you undertake in order to complete the assessment. You should also record any difficulties which you encounter and any changes which you have made to your original plan.

Part 4
This is where you evaluate your approach to the assessment. Was it successful? What did you learn from the experience? How would you change things so that next time you would do better?

Part 1: Grading themes and criteria for the Advanced GNVQ

Theme 1: Planning: the way the student lays down how they will approach and monitor the tasks/activities undertaken during a period of learning.

	Merit	Distinction
1 Drawing up plans of action	Student independently draws up plans of action for **a series of discrete tasks**. The plans prioritise the different tasks within the given time period.	Student independently draws up plans for **complex activities**. The plans prioritise the different tasks within the given time period.
2 Monitoring courses of action	Student independently identifies points at which monitoring is necessary and recognises where revisions to courses of action are necessary. Appropriate revisions to plans are made **with guidance from teacher/tutor.**	Student independently identifies points at which monitoring is necessary and recognises where revisions to courses of action are necessary. **Appropriate revisions to plans are made independently.**

Theme 2: Information-seeking and information-handling: the way the student identifies and uses information sources; and checks and establishes the validity of the information obtained from those sources.

	Merit	Distinction
3 Identifying and using sources to obtain relevant information	Student independently identifies, accesses and collects relevant information for a **series of discrete tasks**. Student identifies principal sources independently and additional sources are identified by **the teacher/tutor.**	Student independently identifies, accesses and collects relevant information for **complex activities. Student uses a range of sources, and justifies their selection.**
4 Establishing the validity of information	Student independently identifies information which requires checking for validity. Student checks validity of information using given methods.	Student independently identifies information which requires checking for validity. Student independently selects and **applies appropriate methods for checking validity.**

Part 1: Grading themes and criteria for the Advanced GNVQ – continued

Theme 3: Evaluation: the way the student retrospectively reviews; the activities undertaken; the decisions taken in the course of that work; alternative courses of action which they might have adopted; and examination of the implications of paticular courses of action.

	Merit	Distinction
5 Evaluating outcomes and alternatives	Student judges outcomes against criteria for success; identifies alternative criteria that can be applied in order to judge success of the activities.	Student judges outcomes against original criteria for success and identifies and **applies a range** of alternative criteria in order to judge success of the activities.
6 Justifying particular approaches to tasks/activities	Student justifies approach used: indicates that alternatives were identified and considered.	Student justifies approach used, basing justification on **a detailed consideration of relevant advantages and disadvantages. Alternatives and improvements are identified.**

Theme 4: Quality of outcomes: the way the student synthesises knowledge, skills and understanding; and demonstrates command of the 'language' of the GNVQ area.

	Merit	Distinction
7 Synthesis	Student's work demonstrates an effective synthesis of knowledge, skills and understanding in response to **discrete tasks.**	The student's work demonstrates and effective synthesis of knowledge, skills and understanding in response to **complex activities.**
8 Command of 'language'	Student's work demonstrates **an effective** command of the 'language' of the GNVQ area at Advanced level.	The student's work demonstrates **a fluent** command of the 'language' of the GNVQ area at Advanced level.

Part 2

Action	Target date

Briefly explain why you choose to approach the assessment this way

Part 3
What you actually did in order to complete the assessment

Date	Action

Part 4

Your evaluation of the way in which you approached the assessment and what you have learned from the experience

Which part/s of the assessment did you find the easiest/most difficult, and why?

	Part of assessment	*Why?*
Easiest		
Most difficult		

Looking back at the way in which you originally planned your approach to this assessment, and in the light of your grade and tutor's comments, how successful do you think your approach was?

How do you think you have gained from the experience of completing this assessment?

Certified core skills

	Communication	Application of number	Information technology
Level 1	1 Take part in discussions with known individuals on routine matters. 2 Prepare written materials in preset formats. 3 Use images to illustrate points made in writing and in discussions with known individuals on routine matters. 4 Read and respond to written material and images in preset formats.	5 Gather and process data using group 1 mathematical techniques. 6 Represent and tackle problems using group 1 mathematical techniques. 7 Interpret and present mathematical data using group 1 mathematical techniques.	8 Input data into specified locations. 9 Edit and organize information within individual applications. 10 Present information in preset formats. 11 Use operating routines which maximize efficiency.
Level 2	1 Take part in discussions with a range of people on routine matters 2 Prepare written material on routine matters. 3 Use images to illustrate points made in writing and in discussions with a range of people on routine matters. 4 Read and respond to written material and images on routine matters.	5 Gather and process data using groups 1 and 2 mathematical techniques. 6 Represent and tackle problems using groups 1 and 2 mathematical techniques. 7 Interpret and present mathematical data using groups 1 and 2 mathematical techniques.	8 Set up, use and input data into storage systems. 9 Edit and organize and integrate information from different sources. 10 Select and use formats for presenting information. 11 Select and use operating routines which maximize efficiency.
Level 3	1 Take part in discussions with a range of people on a range of matters. 2 Prepare written material on a range of matters. 3 Use images to illustrate points made in writing and in discussions with a range of people on a range of matters. 4 Read and respond to written materials and images on a range of matters.	5 Gather and process data using groups 1, 2 and 3 mathematical techniques. 6 Represent and tackle problems using groups 1, 2 and 3 mathematical techniques. 7 Interpret and present mathematical data using groups 1, 2 and 3 mathematical techniques.	8 Set system options and set up, use and input data into storage systems. 9 Edit, organize and integrate complex information from different sources. 10 Select and use formats for presenting complex information from different sources. 11 Select and use applications when they are an effective way of working with information.

Certified core skills (continued)

	Communication	Application of number	Information technology
Level 4	1 Take part in and evaluate the effectiveness of discussions with a range of people on a range of matters. 2 Prepare and evaluate the effectiveness of own written material on a range of matters. 3 Use and evaluate the effectiveness of own use of images to illustrate points made in writing and in discussions with a range of people on a range of matters. 4 Read and respond to written material and images recognizing the factors which influence own interpretation.	5 Gather and process data using groups 1,2,3 and 4 mathematical techniques. 6 Represent and tackle problems using groups 1, 2, 3 and 4 mathematical techniques. 7 Interpret and present mathematical data using groups 1,2,3 and 4 mathematical techniques.	8 Set up system options, use storage systems and prepare and input data. 9 Set up and use automated routines to edit, organize and integrate complex information from different sources. 10 Set up and use automated routines to format and present complex information from different sources. 11 Evaluate and select applications for use by self.
Level 5	1 Lead and evaluate the effectiveness of discussions with a range of people on a range of matters. 2 Prepare and evaluate the effectiveness of own and others' written material on a range of matters. 3 Use and evaluate the effectiveness of own and others' use of images to illustrate points made in writing and discussions with people on a range of matters. 4 Read and respond to written material and images recognizing the factors which influence own and others' interpretations.	5 Gather and process data using groups 1,2,3,4, and 5 mathematical techniques. 6 Represent and tackle problems using groups 1,2,3,4 and 5 mathematical techniques. 7 Interpret and present mathematical data using groups 1,2,3,4 and 5 mathematical techniques.	8 Set up system options, use storage systems and validate prepare and input data. 9 Investigate and resolve problems in editing, organizing and integrating complex information from different sources. 10 Investigate and resolve problems in formatting and presenting complex information from different sources. 11 Evaluate and select applications for use by self and others.

GLOSSARY

Accommodation is a *unit of goods* or *service* consisting of the provision of a room or rooms for a period of time.

The **accounting equation** states that: assets minus liabilities = owners' capital.

Actual figures are those which already exist.

à la carte is a style of service used in quality restaurants. The food is literally cooked to order and the items on the menu are individually priced.

Allocating costs is to do with deciding to which *unit* they belong. A cost can only be allocated if it is caused by that unit. If something else has caused it, or it would have happened anyway, then it cannot be allocated to that unit.

Annual accounts are the sets of information which organizations produce covering a complete year.

Apportioning costs is concerned with sharing unallocated costs between two or more units, in proportion to their estimated benefit from that cost.

Assets are things which an organization owns.

AVCO means Average Cost, and is a method of valuing stocks of goods.

The **average spend per customer** is the total amount spent by each customer, assuming that each customer spends the same amount:

$$= \frac{\text{Total amount spent}}{\text{No. of customers}}$$

A **balance sheet** is a statement which shows the *assets, liabilities* and *capital* of the organization at a point in time.

A **bed board** is a flat board which slides between the mattress and the bed base to make the bed firmer. It is requested by customers who have back problems.

A **bin card** is a document showing the quantities of goods received and issued, usually kept on the shelf or in the container with the goods in store.

Break-even means that enough sales must be generated to meet all the cost associated with those sales, e.g. the food, wages of those concerned, heating, lighting and other overheads, etc. No profit (or loss) is made or budgeted.

The **break-even point** is the point at which the organization sells just enough to break-even, i.e. it makes no profit, but covers its costs.

Budgeted figures are those which are, or were, expected to happen.

Capital is the money invested by owners. In a limited company it consists of shares issued. The amount of capital increases if a profit is made (and decreases if a loss is made). Sometimes referred to as *capital employed*.

Capital estimates are for the money required for items which need to be bought or replaced during the year such as carpets and furniture.

Capkold is the trade name for a method of cooking food. It keeps food longer than the usual period of other cook–chill systems.

Captive customers are those customers who have no choice of outlet.

Catering means meeting the basic needs of food, drink and accommodation.

Cash and carry purchasing is a method of purchasing from depots or warehouses, whereby immediate payment is made for the goods, which must be transported away from the depot by the buyer.

A **cash flow statement** shows where the cash comes from and on what it is spent.

Centralized production applied to food preparation, involves putting most of the staff and equipment and commodities into one kitchen, preparing the food (usually for a lot of people) and transporting it to smaller kitchens elsewhere for service to the customer.

Centralized purchasing is a method of purchasing whereby goods are ordered from a single place (e.g. head office) and then distributed to other parts of the organization.

A **conglomerate** is a group of unrelated firms which have merged together into one company. The original firms may have activities which complement each other, or they may be completely contrasting and unconnected.

Consumables are items which are quickly used up in the running of the organization, and which cannot be identified as direct materials.

Contract hire is the leasing, renting or hiring of goods and/or services, from a company or contractor, for use in an establishment.

Contract purchasing/purchasing by tender is a method of purchasing by making an agreement to buy either a fixed amount, or over a fixed amount of time, or both, from a particular supplier for a fixed price.

Contribution is the amount of money left over from the sale of a unit, after deducting its *variable costs*. The contribution goes towards the *fixed costs* and to the *profit*, if there is still anything left over.

Convection involves heat being applied to the surface of the food and allowed to penetrate slowly. Roasting is a good example of convected heat.

Corporate business is business with the senior management of companies.

A **correlation** is a relationship which exists between two or more things which causes each to change in response to changes in the others.

A **cost centre** is any part of an organization to which costs can be charged. See also **department, operation** and **unit of goods and services**.

A **cost heading** is a cost which needs to be identified separately, e.g. the cost of an oven; or it might be a group of costs which can be identified together, e.g. stationery might include the cost of several different items.

The **cost factor** is the amount by which the cost of a dish or item of food increases due to wastage.

Cost levels are the allowances given for the provision of food for one full week.

Cost plus pricing is a method of determining the selling price of a unit by adding a percentage to its cost.

A **courtesy tray** provides all the equipment and commodities required to allow customers to make their own hot beverages such as tea, coffee or chocolate. This will include a kettle, teapot, cups, saucers, sachets of tea, coffee, chocolate, sugar and milk. Customers may also be provided with biscuits.

A **cover** is a guest served with food or beverages in a single period of opening.

Coverage hours are those working hours when a department is operational.

A **credit note** is a document issued by a supplier to a buyer, to reduce the amount charged for goods which were damaged, unsuitable, or for which a reduction in price has been agreed for some other reason.

Cross-contamination is applied to food bacteria and occurs when foods are mixed in storage conditions which are unsafe or when food is prepared incorrectly, e.g. cutting meat and vegetables on the same cutting board.

Cryophillic are conditions where bacteria grow best at low temperatures – possibly below freezing point.

Current assets are items which the organization owns, such as stocks of food, stationery and money, etc. which are intended to be changed or replaced in a short period of time.

Current liabilities are amounts which the organization owes, which it expects to repay in a short period of time. A bank overdraft is usually a current liability.

Purchasing by **daily market list** or **quotation** involves obtaining the latest price each day from a number of suppliers for the goods required.

Dehydration is applied to processes where water is removed.

A **delivery note** is a document issued by the supplier and sent with the goods, giving a description of the goods included in the parcel.

Demographics is the study of population statistics.

A **department** is a **unit of goods or service** consisting of a single activity or group of related activities within the organization, to which costs can be charged. See also **cost centre** and **operation**.

Depreciation is a measure of the part of a fixed asset which has been used by the organization, and whose value has decreased due to wear and tear or the passing of time.

A **direct cost** is a cost which can be identified with a specific area of sales, e.g. to a particular dish, or to a particular function or department.

A **dish** is a **unit of goods** containing a particular food or combination of foods in a recipe.

Double occupancy is the number of double rooms let as doubles, expressed as a percentage of the number of double rooms available:

$$= \frac{\text{No. of doubles let as doubles}}{\text{Doubles available}} \times 100$$

Editorial features are articles of interest which are put into newspapers and magazines without cost to the subject of the article.

En papillote means 'cooked in the bag'. Applied to cook–chill or 'sous-vide' processes.

En suite refers to a bedroom with a private bathroom forming one unit.

FIFO means First In, First Out and is a method of valuing stocks of goods.

A **financial year** is a 12-month period which an organization uses to total up its figures. The financial year might run from any date, it does not have to be from 1 January, but it must be for a complete 12-month period.

Fixed assets are items which the organization owns, and which are intended to be used for a long period of time. Examples include: land buildings, equipment, furniture, furnishings.

Fixed costs are those which do not alter with the level of activity, at least not directly.

A **franchise** exists where an individual operator is granted a licence to operate an outlet using the larger organization's name and products.

Freezer burn refers to food that has been stored for some time in the freezer which may develop a dry, dark stain caused by drying out.

Freon-12 is a term applied to blast freezing. It involves very low temperatures ($-36°C$) and keeps food for a longer period than other forms of freezing (previously used in the industrial profession for storing eggs).

Frigophillic means that bacteria grow best at refrigeration temperatures.

Full cost is the total cost of all direct and indirect costs, including those apportioned from other cost areas.

A **function** is a **unit of goods or service** comprising a menu or selection of menus, and other items as required for the occasion, such as music and entertainment, private bar, stationery, flowers, etc.

A **goods received book** is a book which lists all the goods received notes issued.

A **goods received note** is a document raised by the purchaser to contain details of the goods received.

Gross operating profit is the sales, less the cost of food and drink and wages. See also **net margin**.

Gross profit equals the selling price less the cost of the food and drink.

Gross profit margin is the percentage of selling price which is added to the cost of direct materials in order to determine the selling price.

$$\text{Selling price} = \frac{\text{Cost of direct materials}}{\text{100\% minus gross profit margin percentage}} \times 100$$

Gross profit mark-up is the percentage of the direct materials cost which is added to that cost in order to determine the selling price.

Selling price =

$$\frac{\text{Cost of direct materials}}{\text{Mark-up percentage}} \times 100$$

Gross profit percentage is the gross profit expressed as a percentage of the selling price (sales):

$$= \frac{\text{Gross profit}}{\text{Sales}} \times 100$$

The **gross margin per employee** is the amount of gross margin (profit) per employee:

$$= \frac{\text{Gross margin}}{\text{No. of employees}}$$

Hazard spotting is the ability to recognize and take action on dangerous or potentially dangerous places, systems or products which arise throughout the working period.

Hospitality means providing the services which make the customer feel welcome – the ambience, the quality of staff service, warmth, the contribution to the 'comfort factor'.

Income is the money earned or taken in by the organization.

Income occupancy is the amount of actual income earned expressed as a percentage of the total possible income:

$$= \frac{\text{Actual income earned}}{\text{Possible total income}} \times 100$$

Income tax, corporation tax and **Value Added Tax** are all taxes set by the government.

An **indirect cost** is a cost which cannot be identified with a specific area of sales.

Indirect services – see **secondary services**.

Infrastructure means the basic services required to support a major development, e.g. road, rail and air links, etc.

The **Invoice** is the document which the supplier sends to the purchaser to request payment for the goods delivered.

Labour costs are the costs of employing various types of staff in an organization. The costs include National Insurance, pension contributions, training and recruitment costs, uniforms and staff meals.

Liabilities are amounts owed by the organization to people who have provided it with money, goods or services.

Limited liability means that there is a limit to the amount which an owner can be called upon to pay towards the debts of the organization.

Long-term liabilities are amounts which the organization has borrowed which do not require repayment in the immediate future. Examples include mortgages, loans, etc.

Maintaining finance means making sure that there is sufficient cash or money in the bank available to pay for the things which the organization needs.

Manipulative is usually applied to describing skills using the hands (e.g. the use of a spoon and fork by a waiter).

Margin means profit. See also **gross profit margin**.

Marginal cost is the variable or direct cost allocated to that unit.

A **market price** is the price at which similar goods and services are sold in similar organizations.

Mark-up – see **gross profit mark-up**.

Materials cost is the cost of the goods which are purchased in order to be made into saleable items.

Matrix is a table or chart describing points with supporting notes (e.g. skill matrix).

A **menu** is a **unit of goods** which consists of several **dishes** or portions of **dishes**.

Mesophyllic means having an ideal growth temperature, the best temperature being 37°C.

Method study is the systematic recording and critical examination of existing and proposed methods of work. It is done to develop and apply easier and more effective methods and for reducing costs.

A **mini bar** is a small refrigerator containing miniature bottles of spirit and appropriate mixers (tonic, soda, ginger), quarter-bottles of wine and small bottles of fruit juice. Some mini bars also contain vacuum packs of cocktail nuts or potato crisps. The customers help themselves from the mini bar and this is checked by hotel staff. They are then charged for the items consumed.

Net margin equals the sales less the cost of food and drink *and* wages. See also **gross operating profit**.

Net operating profit is the sales less *all* costs of departments or activities.

The **net operating profit percentage** is the net operating profit expressed as a percentage of the selling price (sales):

$$= \frac{\text{Net operating profit}}{\text{Sales}} \times 100$$

Net profit is the profit remaining after *all other costs* have been deducted.

The **net profit percentage** is the net profit expressed as a percentage of the selling price (sales):

$$= \frac{\text{Net profit}}{\text{Sales}} \times 100$$

Non-pathogenic means 'not harmful'. Applied to food bacteria.

A **non-revenue earning department** or **operation** is a department with no income from sales. It could perform a service for other departments.

The **number of meals to break even** is the number of meals which needs to be sold in order to pay for the fixed costs. At this point, no profit or loss will be made.

$$= \frac{\text{Fixed costs}}{\text{Contribution per meal}}$$

The same formula is used for number of sleepers, rooms, etc.

An **occupancy forecast** gives some indication of expected business. This may be on a written sheet or a computer printout.

An **operating statement** is a statement of the income, expenses and profit of a 'revenue-earning' department, operation or activity in an organization.

An **operation** is a single activity or a group of activities, to which costs can be charged. See also **cost centre**, **department** and **unit of goods or service**.

An **order** is a document requesting the goods from the chosen supplier.

An **outlet** is a group of departments or activities within an organization which provide goods or services for consumption by its guests.

Overheads cost is the cost of providing other items not classed as *materials* or *labour*.

Palatability is used to describe the taste and texture of food – how acceptable the food is to the customer.

Pathogenic means 'harmful'. Applied to food bacteria.

A **performance indicator** is a calculation which helps to show (indicate) how good or bad the performance of an organization has been.

pH is a method of expressing the acidity or alkalinity of a chemical in numerical terms, from 1 to 14. Substances which give a reading of below 7 are acid and those above 7 are alkaline. The nearer an acid is to 1 and the nearer to 14 an alkali is, the stronger they are. Those chemicals which show a reading of 7 are neutral, i.e. neither acid nor alkaline.

Profit is the amount of income left over after the costs have been deducted.

A **profit and loss account** shows the income for the whole organization, all its expenses and its **net profit**.

A **purchase specification** is a document which exactly describes the goods which are required to be purchased. It is prepared by the purchasing officer and sent to a selection of possible suppliers to find the most suitable to provide the goods.

A **quotation** is a document issued by a supplier, giving details of the price and other terms for supplying the goods requested.

Rack rate is the calculated price of a bedroom which includes direct and indirect costs and a standard profit margin.

Real disposable income is the personal income left after all main expenditures have been removed.

Regenerated applied to food preparation areas means reheating of food in special ovens so that the temperature required is achieved quickly.

Replacement cost is the cost of replacing an item with another in the same condition at the time the item is used up.

Retail purchasing is purchasing from outlets which supply the public.

A **requisition** is a document used to request goods. It is a document prepared by the person who needs the goods. It gives details of the goods required – quantity, quality, size, etc. It is sent within an organization to the purchasing officer.

A **return** on an investment is the amount of money which the investment makes for the investors.

The **return on capital employed percentage** is the amount of net profit earned by the organization, expressed as a percentage of the owner's capital invested:

$$= \frac{\text{Net profit}}{\text{Owners' capital}} \times 100$$

Revenue is the money earned. Another word for revenue is **turnover**.

A **revenue-earning department** or **operation** is one which has income from sales.

Revenue estimates are for the money required to pay for the day-to-day running of the department such as cleaning chemicals and laundry.

Room occupancy is the number of rooms sold expressed as a percentage of the total number of rooms available:

$$= \frac{\text{Number of rooms sold}}{\text{Number of rooms available}} \times 100$$

A **safety audit** is a thorough check, item by item, department by department, of equipment, installations, procedures, rules and working practices. It is an organized exercise.

Salaried staff are employees paid on a monthly basis, with litle or no payment for overtime. Overtime is infrequent and of small amounts, and is usually regarded as 'goodwill' towards the company.

The **sales mix percentage** is the proportion of total sales income made by each department or activity:

$$= \frac{\text{Income from source}}{\text{Total income}} \times 100$$

Satellite kitchen is a smaller kitchen some distance from the main or central kitchen.

Secondary services are ones which are not the main activity of the organization, but are provided to *support* the main activity. They are also called **indirect** services.

A **semi-fixed** or **semi-variable cost** is one which partly changes as a result of the level of activity and partly stays the same irrespective of the level of activity. An example is an employee's wage, which might be a basic weekly wage irrespective of the amount of work done but with overtime for specific increases in activity.

A **service department or operation** is one which provides services to other departments or activities – for example, laundry, maintenance, reception, administration.

Shelf life refers to the length of time a commodity can be stored before it deteriorates.

A **sleeper** is a guest who stays the night. In a double room there are normally two sleepers, but sometimes there may be fewer or more than two.

Sleeper occupancy is the number of actual sleepers expressed as a percentage of the total possible sleepers:

$$= \frac{\text{Actual sleepers}}{\text{Possible sleepers}} \times 100$$

Standardization means that wherever you go in the country (and some chains say this applies throughout the world) the product (e.g. a hamburger) will be exactly the same.

A **standard recipe** is a recipe for a dish which has been prepared and tested for suitability. It is then prepared in the same way every time to ensure consistent quality and cost.

Statutory means 'by law', or forced upon us by the government.

Stepped costs are costs which alter as a result of significant changes in the level of activity but which do not alter as a result of small changes.

Subsidized cost is a cost of providing goods and services which is greater than their selling price, the difference being borne by the organization or refunded from elsewhere. It is common in employee canteens, where the cost of a meal is greater than the amount it sells for.

Table d'hôte is a set menu with set prices (usually three courses). Literal meaning is 'Host's table'.

Targets are things to aim for. An organization might have a target to sell as much as it did last year, or 10 per cent more, or more than another organization does.

A **tender** is an offer to complete a certain task or provide goods and services within a certain time and for a fixed amount of money.

Thermophillic small organisms that like hot conditions in excess of 50°C (thermo means hot).

Turn-down is a service offered in a few luxury hotels. It is done in the evening. Bedspreads are folded back and the bedding is turned back to make it easier for the guest to get into bed. Any night clothes may be laid out neatly on the bed. The bedroom and bathroom will be tidied and the curtains closed. Before leaving, the room attendant may turn on the bedside light and leave a small box containing two or three complimentary chocolates on the pillow.

Turnover is the income which is earned from the sale of products and services. It is sometimes also called **revenue**.

The **turnover per employee** is the amount of sales income per employee:

$$= \frac{\text{Turnover}}{\text{No. of employees}}$$

Unallocated costs are costs which cannot be allocated to particular units, but may be able to be apportioned to units.

Undistributed expenses are costs which cannot be allocated or apportioned to individual departments or activities.

A **unit of goods or service** is a single item or activity or a group of items or activities for which a cost and/or a selling price can be calculated. See also **cost centre**, **department** and **operation**.

Unlimited liability means that there is no limit to the amount which the owner can be called upon to pay towards the debts of the organization.

A **utility room** is provided in a university hall of residence for 12–20 students to share. There are facilities for storing milk and other perishables and appropriate facilities for cooking. There may also be limited facilities for students to do their own laundry and ironing. The utility room is often a place where students congregate while they eat and for socializing.

Vacuum infusion is normally applied to coffee service as in 'cona coffee'. Hot water is sucked into the filter containing coffee granules. The sucking is achieved by a gush of air being drawn through the filter fibre similar to a siphon.

Vacuum packing is applied to cook–chill processes. Food is placed in plastic pouches and the air is removed in order to pressure the food while under refrigeration.

Variable costs are those which increase and decrease according to the level of activity.

Waged staff are employees paid on a weekly basis, with overtime, normally paid one week after the work has been done.

Wastage is the amount of material lost during storage, preparation, cooking and serving due to shrinkage, evaporation, boning, cutting, etc.

Wholesale suppliers are organizations which buy goods from the manufacturer and then sell them to retailers (who then sell them to us, the public).

Workflow is applied to staff movement within the kitchen or restaurant. The term is used to describe how staff go through tasks, the equipment they use, the distance they walk, etc. The intention is to reduce repetitive tasks and improve efficiency.

The **yield** is the amount of usable product from an item, after it has been prepared, cooked and served.

A **yield test card** is a document used to record the yield from one or more products when prepared and/or cooked under certain conditions.

INDEX

À la carte menus, 170, 416
Abrasive cleaners, 342
Accidents, 128–9, 152–5
  burns and scalds, 154–5
  floors, 154
  reporting, 353–5
Accommodation, 416
  bomb precautions, 326
  cleaning, see Cleaning
  contract hire, 356–7, 417
  customer requirements, 321–2
  customer supplies, 344–5
  financial control, 351–2, 367–9
    budgets, 368
    calculation of costs, 295
    estimates, 368–9
  furnishings, 348–50
    storage of, 349–50
  furniture, 350–1
    arrangement for functions,
      351
  key control, 325–6
  safety, 352–7
    accident reporting, 353–5
    fire precautions, 355
    pest control, 355
  staffing, 357–67
    control of labour, 363–7
    inspection of work, 362–3
    management, 357–61
    work measurement, 362
  textiles, 347–8
    fabrics, 348
  types, 327–35
    clubs, 334
    guest houses, 329
    holiday camps, 12, 330
    hospitals, 330–1
    hostels, 332
    hotels, see Hotels
    motels, 329
    public houses, 330
    residential homes, 334
    university halls of residence,
      332–3
Accounting equation, 247–8, 416
Acid cleaners, 342

Actual figures, 239, 416
Allocating costs, 305–6, 416
Annual accounts, 235, 416
Appointment, see Staff
Apportioning costs, 305, 306–8,
  416
Appraisals, staff, 92–3, 94
Assets, 235, 245–6, 416
Assistant cooks, 80–1
AVCO (Average Cost), 296, 297–8,
  416
Average room rate, 396
Average sleeper rate, 396
Average spend ratio, 259, 416

Bacteria causing food poisoning,
  134, see also Listeria;
  Salmonella; Staphylococcus
  aureus
Balance sheet, 245–7, 416
  alternative lay-outs, 248
  performance indicators, 262
Bars, 10–11
  turnover, 10–11
Batch cooking, 172
Bed board, 416
Bedroom book, 384
Beverage units, 291
Billing, 380–1
  tabular ledger, 394
Bin card, 296, 416
Bleaches, 343
Bomb precautions, 326
Bookings diary, 382–3
Break-even, 2, 259, 416
Buckets, 339
Budgeted figures, 241, 416
Budgets, 241, 368
Burns, 154–5

Capital, 248, 416
Capital estimates, 416
Capkold system, 161, 416
Captive customers, 17, 416
Caravan sites, 12

Career opportunities, 20–1
Carpet cleaning, 340
Cash and carry purchasing, 269,
  416
Cash flow statements, 248–50, 416
Catering, definition, 1, 416
Catering industry, see Hospitality
  and catering industry
Catering services industry, 2,
  13–17
  hospitals, 14–16
  outlets, see Outlets
Cellar records, 298
Centralized production, 417
Centralized purchasing, 267–8, 417
Checking in, see Registration of
  guests
Checking out, 381
Chef de cuisine, 80
Chef de partie, 80
Chef de rang, 81
Civil law, 31, 88
Classification of hotels, 5–6
  crown criteria, 194–5
Cleaning:
  buckets, 339
  carpets, 340
  chemicals, 341–3
    abrasive cleaners, 342
    acid cleaners, 342
    bleaches, 343
    detergents, 342
    floor polishes, 343
    furniture polishes, 343
    glass cleaners, 342
    metal polishes, 343
    organic solvents, 342
    soap, 342
  floors, 340
  glass cleaning, 339, 342
  methods
    damp wiping, 338–9
    dusting, 336
    mopping, 338–9
    suction cleaning, 337–8
    sweeping, 337
  routines, 346–7

Cleaning – *continued*
  safety, 148–50
    Control of Substances
      Hazardous to Health
      Regulations 1987, 148,
      343–4
  sanitary fittings, 339
  storage of equipment, 340–1
  trollies, 340
Clubs, 12, 334
Commercial and leisure hotels, 9,
  328–9
Commis chef, 80–1
Commis waiter, 81
Communication, 70–1
Competition effects on industry,
  30, 35
Complaints, dealing with, 127,
  208–9
Computers:
  booking systems, 387–8
  financial data preparation, 316
Conference centres, 334
Conglomerates, 23, 417
Consortia, 42
Consumables, 417
Contract, 266–7
  law of, 404–5
Contract catering, 13
Contract hire, 356–7, 417
Contract of employment, 33,
  88–90
Contract purchasing, 266–7, 417
Contribution, 260–1, 417
Control of Substances Hazardous
  to Health Regulations 1987,
  148, 343–4
Convection, 417
Conventional chart reservation
  system, 384–5
Cook-chill system, 158–61, 164
  advantages, 158–9
  Capkold system, 161, 416
  guidelines, 143–4
  principles, 158
  problems, 160–1
  'sous-vide' system, 159–60
  vacuum packaging, 159–61, 422
Cook-freeze system, 161–4
  finishing kitchens, 163
  freezing time, 163
  guidelines, 144–5
  methods, 163
  scope, 161–2
Cooking, *see* Food preparation
Corporate business, 52, 417
Corporation tax, 235
Correlation, 25, 417

Cost centre, 240, 417
Cost factor, 417
Cost heading, 417
Cost levels, 15, 417
Cost plus, 310–12, 417
Cost statements, 239–40
  preparation, 316
Costs:
  allocation, 305–6, 416
  apportionment, 305–6, 416
  depreciation, 284, 418
  direct costs, 285, 418
  fixed costs, 286–6, 418
  full cost, 309, 418
  indirect costs, 285, 419
  labour, 283–4, 306, 308, 419
  marginal cost, 309–10, 419
  materials, 283, 295–302, 419
    allocation, 306
    AVCO method, 296–8
    cellar records, 298
    FIFO method, 296–7
    yield and wastage, 299–301
  overheads, 284, 420
  replacement cost, 310, 421
  selling price as cost, 310
  semi-fixed costs, 421
  service operations, 284
  stepped costs, 422
  subsidized costs, 313–14, 422
  time-based costs, 288
  unallocated costs, 422
  unit-based costs, 288–9
    accommodation provision,
      293
    dish, 290–1
    functions, 292
    menu, 291–2, 302
    operations, 293–4
    outlet, 294–5
  usage-based costs, 288
  variable costs, 285, 422
Courtesy tray, 417
Cover, 257, 417
Coverage hours, 417
Credit note, 277, 278, 417
Creditors, 246
Criminal law, 31, 87
Cross-contamination, 417
Cultural influences on industry, 27
Current assets, 235, 246, 417
Current liabilities, 246, 417
Customer relations, 375
Customer service, *see* Service
Customers, 101–5
  age groups, 101
  corporate, 372
  cultural background, 101–2

  expectations, 107–8, 201–3
    external, 101
    internal, 101
    tourists, 372
    VIPs, 373
    well-being, 113–14
Customs and Excise, 235

Daily market list purchasing,
  268–9, 417
Dangerous equipment, 146–8,
  153–4
  legislation, 146
Data for customer service
  evaluation, 118–20
Data Protection Act 1984, 31
Data sources, 17
Debtors, 246
Dehydration, 418
Delivery note, 275, 418
Demographics, 27, 418
  effects on industry, 27–8, 37
Density chart, 385–6
Department, 418
Depreciation, 284, 418
  calculation, 307
Detergents, 342
Dip loss, 160
Direct costs, 285, 418
Direct materials cost plus, 310–12
Disciplinary procedures, *see* Staff
Disclaimer notices, 402
Discounts, 315
Dish, 290–1, 418
  costs calculation, 290–1, 305
Dismissal, 95–6
Disposable incomes, 24–5
Double occupancy, 259, 395, 418
Dusting, 336
Duty managers, 12

Economy, effects on industry,
  25–6, 34, 37–9
Editorial features, 49, 418
Educational establishments
  as catering services outlets, 16
Employment, 17–22
  management structure, 21–2
  numbers employed, 4–5
  opportunities, 20–1
  shifts, 18
  trends, 37
  women, 19–20
  see also Staff
En papillote, 418
En suite, 418

Enquiries, dealing with, 127
Environmental Health Officers, 142, 145
Equal Pay Act 1970, 90
Estimates, 368–9
Etrop Grange Hotel case study, 43–61
  current trends, 61
  employment patterns, 47–8
  history, 43–6
  internal influences, 46–7
  legislation influences, 53–4
  market targets, 52–3
  prospects, 61
  sales and marketing strategy, 49–50
  scope
    accommodation, 59
    conference facilities, 61
    dining facilities, 54–9
    reception, 59–61
  staff development, 48–9
  working conditions, 48
EU (General) Food Hygiene Directive, 32
European legislation, 34

Fabrics, 348
Facilities, 3
Fast-food outlets, 10–11
  service style, 197
FIFO (First In, First Out), 296–7, 418
Finance providers, 234
Financial information users:
  finance providers, 234
  managers, 234
  owners, 233
  tax authorities, 235–6
Financial performance measurement performance indicators
  reasons for, 236–8
  see also Performance indicators
Financial statements:
  balance sheet, 245–8, 416
  cash flow statements, 248–50, 416
  cost statements, 239–40
  gross profit, 242–3, 418
  net operating profit, 243–4, 420
  operating statement, 241, 420
  profit and loss account, 244–5, 420
Financial targets, 236
  comparison of financial information with, 237–8
  meeting, 221–3

Financial year, 239, 418
Fire precautions, 150–2, 355
  extinguishers, 150
Fire Precautions Acts, 32–3, 152
First floor, 32
First In, First Out (FIFO), 296–7
Fixed assets, 235, 246, 418
Fixed cost plus, 313
Fixed costs, 260, 286–8, 418
Floors
  cleaning, 340, 343
  safety precautions, 154
Food Hygiene Regulations, 32, 135–41
  compliance with, 140–1
Food Labelling Regulations 1984, 155–6
Food poisoning, 134
Food Premises (Registration) Regulations 1990 and 1991, 143
Food preparation:
  cooking systems, 167–8
    batch cooking, 172
    cook and serve, 157, 172
    cook-chill, see Cook-chill system
    cook-freeze, see Cook-freeze system
  food hygiene:
    food poisoning, 134
    legislation, 135–43
  evaluation, 185–6
  monitoring issues:
    food products, 176–7
    preparation processes, 175–6
    standard recipes, 177
  planning, 168–9, 173–5, 180–5
    equipment, 180–1
    production log, 183
    resources, 180–1
    stages, 169–70
Food production chain, 134
Food Safety Act 1990, 31, 91, 141–3
Food service, see Service
Franchise, 11, 418
Freezer burn, 418
Freezing of food, see Cook-freeze system
Freon 12, 418
Front office, see Reception office
Full cost, 309, 418
Full cost plus, 311
Full-time staff, 364
Functions, 209–13, 292, 418
  costs calculation, 292

  organization
    furniture arrangement, 351
    seating, 209–11
    spacing, 211
    tabling, 211
  service methods, 213
  staff responsibilities, 212–13
Furnishings, 348–50
  storage, 349–50
Furniture, 350–1
  arrangement for functions, 351
Furniture polishes, 343

General manager, 21
Glass cleaning, 339, 342
Goods received book, 276, 277, 418
Goods received note, 275, 276, 418
Grievance procedure, 96
Gross margin per employee, 256–7, 419
Gross operating profit, 242–3, 418
Gross profit, 242, 418
Gross profit margin, 312, 418
  as performance indicator, 253
Gross profit mark-up, 311–12, 419
Gross profit percentage, 419
Guest, 32
Guest giveaways, 345
Guest houses, 329
Guest supplies, 345

Halls of residence, 332, 333
Hazard spotting, 419
Head chef, 80
Head waiter, 81
Health and leisure services, 376
Health and Safety at Work Act 1974, 90, 145–6
Heat treatment, 141
Holiday accommodation, 29–30
Holiday camps, 12, 330
Hospitality and catering industry:
  catering services sector, 2
  commercial sector, 2
  employment, see Employment
  external influences, 23–35, 37–9, see also Etrop Grange Hotel case study
  competition, 30, 35
  crises, 35
  cultural influences, 27
  demographic trends, 27–8, 37
  disposable incomes, 24–5
  legislation, 30–4
  population, 26–7

Hospitality and catering industry –
    continued
    external influences – *continued*
        recession, 37–9
        socio-economic factors, 25–6,
            34
        tourism, 28–9, 35
    internal influences, 36–7
        control systems, 37
        facilities offered, 36–7
        labour market, 36
    organizational structure, 3
    outlets, *see* Outlets
    scale, 3–5
        numbers employed, 4–5
    sources of data, 17
Hospitals, 332–4
    as catering services outlets,
        14–16
        consumer types, 15–16
        tendering, 16
    customer requirements of
        reception, 374
Hostels, 332
Hotels:
    as commercial outlets, 5–9
    classification schemes, 5–6
        crown criteria, 194–5
    customer requirements of
        reception office, 373–4
    legislation, *see* Reception office
    market size, 6
    service styles, 165, 192–3
    turnover, 6–7
    types:
        commercial and leisure, 9,
            328–9
        guest houses, 329
        international, 8–9, 327
        residential, 9
        resort, 9, 328–9
        transient, 9
        see also Inns; Etrop Grange
            Hotel case study;
            Tunnicliffe Hotel case
            study
Housekeeping department
    functions, 82
Housekeeping service, 375
Hydrogen peroxide, 343
Hygiene:
    customer service role, 128
    food poisoning, 134
    legislation, 135–43

Immigration (Hotel Record) Order
    1972, 406–7

In-house services, 374–6
    customer relations, 375
    health and leisure services, 376
    housekeeping service, 375
    office services, 375–6
    portering service, 375
    room service, 375
    valeting, 375
Incentive schemes, 85
Income, 239, 419
Income occupancy, 419
Income tax, 235
Indirect costs, 285, 419
    apportioning of, 305–8
Indirect services, 2, 419
Individual characteristics, 64–71
    communication, 70–1
    motivation, 69–70
    perception, 67–9
Induction of new staff, 91–2
Industrial catering, 335
Industrial tribunals, 96
Information systems, 391–7
    customer history data, 394–5
    customer requirements, 392
    forecasting and statistics, 395–6
    guest billing, 393–5
        tabular ledger, 394
    reservation system evaluation,
        392
    reservations, 392
Infrastructure, 29, 419
Inland Revenue, 235
Inns:
    distinction between inns and
        hotels, 399, 403
    innkeeper's liability, 399–401
    innkeeper's rights, 402–3
        right of lien, 402–3
        see also Hotels
    Inspection of work, 362–3
International hotels, 8–9, 327
Invoicing, 277–9, 419

Kettle cooking, 161
Keys, control of, 325–6
Kitchen brigade, 79–81
    Chef de cuisine (head chef), 80
    Chef de partie, 80
    Commis chefs (assistant cooks),
        80–1
    Sous chef (second chef), 80
Kitchen safety, 146–8
Knives, safety precautions, 147

Labour costs, 283–4, 303, 419
Labour market, 36
Larder chef, 179

Legislation, 133
    food hygiene, 135–43
    influence on industry, 30–4
    reception office, 398–407
    safety at work, 145–62
    workplace, 87–91
Leisure centres, 334
Liabilities, 234, 246, 419
    innkeepers, 399–401
Licensing laws:
    combined licence, 214
    full on-licence, 214
    Licensing Acts, 33–4
    music and dancing licences, 217
    occasional licence, 215
    occasional permission, 215
    permitted hours, 215–17
        exceptions, 215
        extensions, 215–17
    residential licence, 214
    restaurant licence, 214
Limited liability, 40, 419
Listening skills, 112
Listeria, 138, 139
Long-term liabilities, 246, 419
Luggage:
    innkeeper's responsibilities,
        399–402
    innkeeper's rights, 402–3

Maintaining finance, 236, 237, 419
Maitre d'hotel, 81
Maître d'hôtel carée, 81
Management:
    accommodation services, 357–60
    structure, 21–2
    users of financial information,
        234
Margin, 419
Marginal cost, 309–10, 419
Marginal cost plus, 311
Mark-up percentage, 254
Market rates, 314, 419
Maslow's hierarchy of needs, 69
Materials, 283
Materials costs, 283, 295–302, 419
Measures, 289–90
Menus, 419
    à la carte, 170
    cost calculation, 291–2, 302–3
    table d'hôte, 170
Metal polishes, 343
Method study, 419
Mini bar, 420
Mopping, 338–9
Motels, 9, 329
Motivation, 69–70, 85–6
Multinational organizations, 41–2

Net margin, 242–3, 420
Net operating profit, 243–4, 420
Net profit, 240, 420
Net profit percentage, 254–5, 420
Number of meals to break even, 420

Occupancy forecast, 420
Occupancy ratios, 258–9
    double occupancy, 259, 395, 418
    income occupancy, 258, 419
    room occupancy, 7, 258, 395, 421
    sleeper occupancy, 258, 395, 421
Office services, 375
Operating statement, 241, 420
Operational managers, 12
Operations, 3, 240, 420
    costs calculation, 293–4, 303
Operatives, 22
Order, 274, 275, 420
Organic solvents, 342
Organizations, 3
    consortia, 42,
    multinational organizations, 41–2
    partnership, 40
    private companies, 41
    private sector, 40
    public companies, 41
    public sector, 40
    registered companies, 41
    sole trader, 40
Outdoor catering, 213–14
Outlets, 3, 420
    catering services industry, 13–17
        educational establishments, 16
        hospitals, 14–16
        prisons, 16–17
    commercial, 5–13
        caravan sites, 12
        clubs, 12
        contract catering, 13
        fast-food outlets, 10–11
        holiday sites, 12
        hotels, see Hotels
        public houses and bars, 11–12
        restaurants, see Restaurants
        take-away outlets, 10–11
    costs, 295–6
Overheads, 284, 420
    allocation, 305–6
    calculation, 304
Owners, 233

Palatability, 163, 420
Part-time staff, 365
Perception, 67–9

Performance assessment of staff, 92–3, 94
Performance indicators, 420
    average spend, 259, 416
    gross margin per employee, 256, 419
    gross profit margin, 253, 418
    mark-up percentage, 254
    net profit percentage, 254–5, 420
    occupancy ratios, 258–9
    return on capital employed, 262, 421
    sales mix, 255
    stock levels, 261–2
    turnover, 252–3, 422
    turnover per employee, 256, 422
Personnel, see Staff
Pest control, 355
pH, 420
Polishes, 343
Population influences on industry, 26–7
Portering service, 375
Prescribed Dangerous Machines Order 1964, 146
Principal statement, 33
Prisons, 16–17
Private companies, 41
Private sector organizations, 40
Professional bodies, 97
Profit, 235, 239, 420
Profit and loss account, 244–5, 420
    performance indicator calculation, 251
Proprietary clubs, 12
Public companies, 41
Public houses, 10–11, 330
    turnover, 10–11
Public sector organizations, 40
Public survey data, 17
Purchase requisition, 271
Purchase specification, 272–3, 420
Purchasing, 263–82
    controls, 281
    methods:
        cash and carry, 269, 416
        centralized purchasing, 267–8, 417
        contract purchasing, 266–7, 417
        daily market list, 268–9, 417
        purchasing by tender, 266, 417
        retail purchasing, 270, 421
        wholesale suppliers, 270, 423
    processes:
        invoicing, 277–9
        order, 274, 275, 420

payment, 280
    purchase specification, 272–3, 420
    quotation, 274, 420
    receipt of goods, 274–6
    requisition, 271, 421
    returns, 277
    products:
        consumables, 264–5
        equipment, 264
        food, 264
        liquor, 264
    responsibilities of purchaser, 280–1
    supply sources, 265–6

Quotations, 274, 420

Race Relations Act 1976, 90
Rack rate, 35, 54, 257, 421
Ratios, see Performance indicators
Real disposable income, 24, 421
Reception office, 82, 370–407
    customer requirements, 373–4
    information systems, see Information systems
    legislation, 398–407
        guest registration, 405
        law of contract, 404–5
        price display, 404
    maximizing revenue, 389–90
    maximizing room sales, 388–9
    procedures, 376–81
        arrivals list, 378
        checking in, see Registration of guests
        checking out of guests, 381
        departure list, 378
        guest billing, 380–1
        registration, see Registration of guests
        reservations, see Reservations
        room status report, 380
Recession:
    influence on industry, 37–9
Records, personnel, 92
Recruitment, see Staff
Registered clubs, 12
Registered companies, 41
Registration of guests, 378, 379, 396
    computerized systems, 396
    legislation, 405
Replacement cost, 310, 421
Requisition, 271, 421
Reservations, 376–7
    bedroom book, 384
    bookings diary, 382–3

Reservations – *continued*
  computerised systems, 387–8
  conventional chart, 385
  density chart, 384–5
  evaluation, 392
  room availability records, 383–4
  Whitney Advance Booking Rack,
    383
Residential homes, 334
  customer requirements of
    reception, 374
Residential hotels, 9
Resort hotels, 9, 328
Restaurants:
  as commercial outlets, 9–10, 334
  customer requirements of
    reception, 374
  factors influencing success:
    atmosphere, 203, 206
    decor, 205–6
    location, 203
    menu, 203–4
    prices, 203
    service, 203, 204–5
    value for money, 205
  service styles, 81, 192–9
    ethnic, 193–6
    fast-food, 197
    French, 196
    speciality, 196
    Steakhouse, 196
    take-away, 197
    traditional English, 196–7
Retail purchasing, 270–1, 421
Return of goods, 277
Return on capital employed, 262,
  421
Return on investment, 233, 421
Revenue, 7, 241, 421
Revenue estimates, 421
Right of lien, 402
Room availability records, 383–4
Room occupancy ratios, 7, 258,
  395, 421
Room service, 375
Room status report, 380

Safety at work
  dangerous equipment,146–8,
    153–4
  fire precautions, 150–2
  legislation, 90, 145–52
  safety audit, 421
  substances hazardous to health,
    148–50
Salaried staff, 19, 421
Sales mix, 255, 421

Salmonella, 141
Sanitary fittings, cleaning, 339
Satellite kitchen, 421
Scalds, 154–5
Second chef, 80
Secondary services, 2, 421
Security, 128, 129–30
Selling price:
  as cost, 310
  calculation, 310–15
    cost plus, 310–11
    direct materials cost plus,
      311–12
    discounts, 315
    fixed cost plus, 313
    full cost plus, 311
    gross profit margin, 312
    marginal cost plus, 311
    market rates, 314
    service charges, 314–15
    subsidized cost, 313–14
    VAT, 314–15
Semi-fixed costs, 421
Service
  customer satisfaction, 207–8
    complaints, 127, 208–9
  evaluation, 114–24, 218–26
    criteria, 218
    customer service policy,
      114–15
    data, 118–20
    internal monitoring, 224
    methods, 120–1
    monitoring of events, 223–4
    standards, 116–18
  in-house services, *see* In-house
    services
  operations, 121–2
  provision of, 108–14, 124–30,
    207–14
    accidents, 128–9
    challenging customers, 126
    complaints, 127, 208–9
    customer perceptions, 109
    customer referrals, 127
    customer requirements,
      109–10
    enquiries, 127
    function catering, 209–13
    hygiene, 128
    impressions given to customer,
      110
    listening skills, 112
    outdoor catering, 213–14
    safety, 128
    security, 128, 129–30
    social skills, 113
    telephone skills, 111–12

quality, 122–3
  skills, 197–8
  styles:
    airlines, 166
    functions, 209–13
    hotels, 165–6, 192–3
    outdoor catering, 213–14
    restaurants, 81, 193–7,
      203–7
Service charges, 315
Service operations, 284, 294
Sex Discrimination Act 1975, 90
Shareholder, 41
Shelf life, 343, 421
Shifts, 18
Sleeper, 257, 421
Sleeper occupancy, 258, 395, 421
Soap, 342
Social skills, 113
Socio-economic factors, influence
  on industry, 25–6, 34
Sole trader, 40
Sous chef, 80
'sous-vide' system, 159–60
Specification, purchase, 272–3, 420
Split shifts, 18
Staff
  appointment, 71–2
  appraisal, 92–3, 94
  disciplinary procedures, 93–6
    appeals procedure, 96
    disciplinary code, 94
    dismissal, 95–6
  grievance procedure, 96
  incentives, 85
  induction, 91–2
  industrial tribunals, 96
  information and advice
    legal advice, 98
    professional bodies, 97
    trade association, 97
    trade publications, 97
    trade unions, 98
  legislation, 87–91
  performance assessment, 92–3,
    94
  records, 92
  recruitment, 71–2
  staff satisfaction, 85–6
  training, *see* Training
Standardization, 10, 421
Standard recipe, 290, 422
  material costs, 301–2
Standards, customer service
  evaluation, 116–18
Staphylococcus aureus, 136
Station Head waiter, 81
Station waiter, 81

Statutory information, 235, 237
Statutory instruments, 31
Stepped costs, 422
Straight shifts, 18
Subsidized cost, 2, 313–14, 422
Substances hazardous to health:
   legislation, 148
   precautions, 148–50
Suction cleaning, 337–8
Supervisors, 22
Sweeping, 337

Table d'hôte menus, 170, 422
Take-away outlets, 10–11
   service style, 197
Targets, *see* Financial targets
Teams, 72–9
   attributes, 73
   development, 73
   roles of members, 74–8
   structure, 74
Telephone skills, 111–12
Temperature zoning, 145
Tender, 14, 422
Textiles, 347–8
   fabrics, 348
Themed event preparation, 219
Time-based costs, 288

Tourism:
   accommodation types, 29–30
   effects on industry, 28–30, 35
   reception functions, 374
   tourists, 372
Trade association, 97
Trade publications, 17, 97
Trade Union Reform and
   Employment Rights Act 1993,
   33, 88
Trade unions, 98
Trading Standards Officers, 142
Training, 82–5
   evaluation, 84–5
   implementation, 83–4
   planning, 83
Transient hotels, 9
Trollies for cleaning equipment,
   340
Tunnicliffe Hotel case study, 131–2
Turn-down, 422
Turnover, 7, 236, 422
   as performance indicator, 252–3
Turnover per employee, 256, 422

Unallocated costs, 422
Undistributed expenses, 422
Unincorporated associations, 40
Unit-based costs, *see* Costs

University halls of residence,
   332–3
Unlimited liability, 40, 422
Usage-based costs, 288
Utility room, 422

Vacuum cleaning, 337–8
Vacuum infusion, 422
Vacuum packaging, 159–61, 422
Valeting, 375
Value added tax, 235–6
   selling price calculation, 314–15
Variable costs, 259–60, 285, 422
VIPs, 373

Waged staff, 18, 422
Wastage, 299, 423
Weights and measures, 289–91
Whitney Advance Booking Rack,
   383
Wholesale suppliers, 270, 421
Work zoning, 145
Workflow, 423
Working capital, 248

Yield, 299, 423
Yield test card, 299–301, 423